IW
16/5/08

Butterworths New Law Guide
The Adoption and Children
Act 2002

D1494058

Butterworths New Law Guide
The Adoption and Children Act 2002

Editors

Professor Hugh Bevan
Emeritus Reader in Law, University of Hull

District Judge Stephen Gerlis

Martin Parry
Emeritus Reader in Law, University of Hull

Louise Potter MA (Oxon)
Barrister, Harcourt Chambers, London and Oxford

David Ryden LLB (Hons)
Manager of Social Services Legal Team, City of Bradford Metropolitan District Council; Director of Ryden Legal Publications Ltd

LexisNexis®
Butterworths

Members of the LexisNexis Group worldwide

United Kingdom	LexisNexis Butterworths, a Division of Reed Elsevier (UK) Ltd, Halsbury House, 35 Chancery Lane, London, WC2A 1EL, and RSH, 1–3 Baxter's Place, Leith Walk Edinburgh EH1 3AF
Argentina	LexisNexis Argentina, Buenos Aires
Australia	LexisNexis Butterworths, Chatswood, New South Wales
Austria	LexisNexis Verlag ARD Orac GmbH & Co KG, Vienna
Benelux	LexisNexis Benelux, Amsterdam
Canada	LexisNexis Canada, Markham, Ontario
Chile	LexisNexis Chile Ltda, Santiago
China	LexisNexis China, Beijing and Shanghai
France	LexisNexis SA, Paris
Germany	LexisNexis Deutschland GmbH, Munster
Hong Kong	LexisNexis Hong Kong, Hong Kong
India	LexisNexis India, New Delhi
Italy	Giuffrè Editore, Milan
Japan	LexisNexis Japan, Tokyo
Malaysia	Malayan Law Journal Sdn Bhd, Kuala Lumpur
Mexico	LexisNexis Mexico, Mexico
New Zealand	LexisNexis NZ Ltd, Wellington
Poland	Wydawnictwo Prawnicze LexisNexis Sp, Warsaw
Singapore	LexisNexis Singapore, Singapore
South Africa	LexisNexis Butterworths, Durban
USA	LexisNexis, Dayton, Ohio

A CIP Catalogue record for this book is available from the British Library.

ISBN 13: 9780406956545

Typeset by Letterpart Ltd, Reigate

Printed and bound in Great Britain by William Clowes Limited, Beccles, Suffolk

Visit LexisNexis Butterworths at www.lexisnexis.co.uk

Foreword

I am privileged to have been asked to commend, and delighted to be able to recommend, this immensely useful work to what I hope will be a large and appreciative readership.

The Adoption and Children Act 2002, with its associated secondary legislation and ministerial guidance, marks yet another important step in the never-ending endeavour to keep our family law in step with the needs of – in particular – children – in our constantly changing and ever more diverse society.

The distinguished and highly experienced team of family justice professionals and scholars who we have to thank for this important book are very conscious of the historical setting in which the Act is located. Not the least valuable part of what they give us is to be found in the Introduction, where they outline the historical background and illuminate those many and important respects in which the Act marks a break – a welcome break – with the past.

The core of the book, of course, comprises the meticulously annotated texts of the Act and its associated primary and secondary legislation. These do not merely provide the hard-pressed professional with a reliable and eminently practical guide through the legislative maze. Cross-referenced at every turn to the relevant ministerial guidance, the book also provides detailed illumination for practitioners of ministers' hopes and expectations for the new law.

Our authors are to be thanked and congratulated for the task they have undertaken. We are all beholden to them.

The Honourable Mr Justice Munby

20 November 2006

Preface

This book, which is intended for, and written by, family justice professionals and scholars, seeks to provide a detailed guide to the Adoption and Children Act 2002 and its associated Regulations. The Act was implemented incrementally, with the major, and final, implementation being on 30 December 2005. The guide is written in the light of that implementation and the amendments to the legislation that have already been made, together with early case law on the Act.

After an overview of the Act, its history and scope, each of its sections, as amended, is set out and analysed individually, with appropriate cross reference to other sections and related legislation. The analysis of the main sections begins with a general note in which the opportunity is taken to consider the nature and scope of the section together with consideration, as appropriate, of broader issues of policy and principle.

The reproduction and analysis of the Act is followed by similar reproduction and analysis of the new sections inserted into the Children Act 1989, the Adoption Agencies Regulations 2005, the Adoption Agencies (Wales) Regulations 2005, the Adoptions with a Foreign Element Regulations 2005, the Special Guardianship Regulations 2005, the Special Guardianship (Wales) Regulations 2005 and associated Guidance. Thereafter, for reference purposes, the Adoption (Intercountry Aspects) Act 1999, the Adoption (Designation of Overseas Adoptions) Order 1973 and the Family Procedure (Adoption) Rules 2005 are set out in the Appendix.

We express our thanks to the Honourable Mr Justice Munby for the Foreword and our families for their forbearance.

Our analysis seeks to state the law in England and Wales at 1 October 2006. The opportunity has been taken to identify forthcoming changes to primary and secondary legislation known at that date.

Hugh Bevan

Stephen Gerlis

Martin Parry

Louise Potter

David Ryden

Contributors

Professor Hugh Bevan

Professor Hugh Bevan, JP (formerly practised on the North eastern Circuit – mainly in family and chancery matters), LLM, Hon LLD, Barrister, Emeritus Professor of English Law, former Dean of Law and Pro-Vice Chancellor of the University of Hull, former Fellow of Wolfson College, Cambridge and now an Honorary Fellow. Professor Bevan, a founding editor of *Butterworths Family Law Service*, has also published a number of books for Butterworths: – with PRH Webb: *A Sourcebook of Family Law* (1964); *The Law Relating to Children* (1973); – with ML Parry: *The Children Act 1975* (1976); and *Child Law* (1989). He is also Chairman of the Committee of the Centre for Child and Family Law Reform, City University, London.

District Judge Gerlis

District Judge Gerlis was appointed as a full-time District Judge in 1988. He is also a Recorder in the County Court and was formerly a Crown Court Recorder. He was originally a solicitor and became secretary and President of the West London Law Society. He is closely involved with the appointments process for the judiciary.

He is author of *Domestic Proceedings in the Magistrates' Court* (Longmans); *County Court Practice Notes* (Cavendish); co-author of *The Civil Practitioner's Handbook* (Sweet & Maxwell), *Civil Procedure* (Cavendish); *Post-Woolf Briefing* (Hawksmere) and a contributor to the *Civil Court Service* (Jordans). He is also co-editor of the monthly *Busy Solicitors' Digest* which features on Lawtel and General Editor of *Civil Court Precedents* (Sweet & Maxwell). He has a regular column in the online Legal Section of *The Times*.

He is a frequent contributor to the Law Society's Gazette and Family Law and lectures widely on a range of subjects surrounding the work of the Civil and Family Courts.

Martin Parry

Martin Parry is an Emeritus Reader in Law at the University of Hull, where he taught, inter alia, Family Law for thirty years, and where he continues to lecture on Child Protection and Private International Family Law. He is a law graduate of Leicester University and was a solicitor in private practice before pursuing an academic career. He has published widely in the area of Family Law, including

Bevan and Parry, *Children Act 1975*; James, Wilson and Parry, *Social Work in Family Proceedings*; Parry, *The Law Relating to Cohabitation*; *The Children Act 1989: Conflict and Compromise* (editor) as well as numerous articles and book chapters. He was a founding editor, in 1983, of *Butterworths Family Law Service* and continues to have joint authorship of the *Children* volume. His appointments include membership of the Humber Family Justice Council.

Louise Potter

Louise Potter read Classics and English at New College, Oxford, before undertaking a law conversion course and the Bar Vocational Course. She then undertook pupillage and the first 5 years of practice at 1 Mitre Court Buildings, Temple, now 1 Hare Court. On moving chambers to 2 Harcourt Buildings, Temple, her practice expanded to take in more public law children work. From 1997 she has contributed to *Butterworths Family Law Service*, covering a broad range of topics, including adoption with a foreign element.

David Ryden

A solicitor for 19 years, David Ryden has spent the last 20 years working for Local Authorities, specialising in the field of child protection, adoption, care proceedings and community care. He is the manager of the Social Services Legal Team for Bradford Council, and has been an advisor to Adoption Panels. He is currently legal advisor to the Local Safeguarding Children Board, and is a member of the Leeds Family Justice Council and the Legal Group Advisory Committee of the British Association for Adoption and Fostering (BAAF). He is the author of Social Care Legal Newsletters, a monthly digest of the latest law and guidance concerning children, adoption, human rights, older people and disabled adults.

Contents

Contents

Interpretation

'Adopted person' (for ss 66–76 only)	Includes an adopted person within the meaning of the Adoption Act 1976, Pt 4 (s 66(3)).
'Adoption' (for ss 2–17, and 92–96 only)	The adoption of any person irrespective of habitual residence and under any law (ss 2(8) and 97).
'Adoption' (for ss 66–76 only)	Adoptions effected on or after 30 December 2005 which are adoptions in England or Wales (see s 46) or by order in Scotland, Northern Ireland, Isle of Man, Channel Islands, Convention adoptions, overseas adoptions, or one recognised in England and Wales and effected under the law of another country (s 66(1) and (2)).
'Adoption agency'	A local authority or registered adoption society (s 2(1)). For ss 92–96 this includes Scottish or Northern Irish agencies (s 97). For ss 125–131, it only means an English local authority or a registered adoption society with its principal office in England (s 130(1)).
'Adoption Order'	See s 46 for definition and effect.
'Adoption service'	Services maintained by local authorities under s 3(1) (s 2(1)).
'Adoption society'	Body whose functions consist of, or include, making arrangements for the adoption of children (s 2(5)).
'Adoption support agency'	An undertaking whose purpose (or one purpose) is the provision of adoption support services (with numerous exceptions) (s 8(1) and (2)).
'Adoption support services'	Counselling, advice and information, and services defined in the Regulations (s 2(6)).
'Adoptive mother, father' (or similar expressions)	Includes same-sex couples (s 68(3)).
'Adoptive relationship'	One existing due to a person's adoptive status (s 68(1)).

'Appropriate adoption agency' (for ss 56–65 only)

(a) If placed for adoption, either the adoption agency placing that person or (if different) the agency holding the information; (b) in other cases, the local authority to whom notice of intention to adopt was given (s 65(1)).

'Authorised to place for adoption' (for ss 18–65 only)

Authorisation under s 19 or by placement order (s 18(6)).

'Care Order'

See CA 1989, s 105(1) (and thereby, s 31(11) of the CA 1989), (Sch 6). It thus includes an interim care order.

'Child'

In the context of any adoption proceedings, whether or not concluded, includes a person reaching the age of 18 before those proceedings are concluded (s 49(5)). Otherwise, unless expressed as a description of a relationship, means a person under the age of 18 (s 144).

'Consent' (for ss 18–65 only)

In context of consent to placement for adoption or to an adoption order, is defined in s 52(5).

'Convention'

The Hague Convention (s 144).

'Convention adoption'

An adoption effected outside of the British Islands, in a Convention country, and certified as such (s 66(1)).

'Couple'

Married couple, two civil partners of each other, or two people (of any gender) living together as partners in an enduring family relationship (but see s 144(5) and (6) for certain qualifications) (s 144(4)).

'Court'

See s 144.

'Disposition' (for ss 66–76 only)

Includes the conferring of a power of appointment (including a discretionary power of appointment to transfer a beneficial interest in property without consideration), and any other disposition of an interest in, or right over, property (s 73(2)).

'Excepted payment'

See s 96.

'Guardian'

A guardian within meaning of the CA 1989, and including a special guardian (s 144).

'Local Authority'

A unitary authority, and any county council that is not such an authority (s 144). 'Unitary authority' is also defined in s 144.

'Local Authority foster parent'	See CA 1989, s 23(3) (Sch 6).
'1989 Act'	Children Act 1989 (s 2(5)).
'Notice of intention to adopt'	Notice to the appropriate Local Authority of intention to apply for an adoption order (s 44(2)).
'Organisation' (for ss 125–131 only)	Includes a public body and a private or voluntary organisation (s 131(1)).
'Overseas adoption'	Excludes Convention adoptions, and is one specified in an Order of the Secretary of State regarding adoption under the laws of any country or territory outside the British Islands (s 87(1)).
'Parent' (for ss 18–65 only)	In respect of giving or withdrawing consent to an adoption order or placement for adoption, means a parent having parental responsibility (with certain exceptions in s 52(9) and (10)) (s 52(2) and (6)).
'Parental responsibility'	See CA 1989, s 3 (Sch 6).
'Payment' (for ss 92–96 only)	Includes reward (s 97).
'Placed for adoption/placing child for adoption'	An adoption agency either placing a child for adoption with prospective adopter(s), or leaving a child with person(s) (with whom the child is already placed, under any Act) as prospective adopter(s) (s 18(5)). But this excludes existing carers who apply for adoption without approval by the agency (s 44(8)).
'Placed for adoption under section 19'	Placed for adoption under s 19, and still living there, even if consent has been withdrawn (s 19(4)).
'Placement order'	Court Order authorising a Local Authority to place a child for adoption with any prospective adopters of its choice (s 21(1)).
'Protected information' (for ss 56–65 only)	Where disclosure is restricted by s 57(1) or (2) (s 57(3)).
'Records' (for ss 77–82 only)	Includes certified copies of birth registry entries (s 82(1)).
'Register' (for ss 125–131 only)	The Adoption and Children Act Register (s 131(1)).

'Registered adoption society'	A voluntary organisation, operating as an adoption society, registered under the Care Standards Act 2000 (but only in respect of its facilities, and not if it is a condition of registration not to provide that facility) (s 2(2) and (3)).
'Registers of live births' (for ss 77–82 only)	The registers made under the Births and Deaths Registration Act 1953 (s 82(1)).
'Relationships'	Any relationships not qualified by the word 'adoptive' are to be interpreted as though that person had not been adopted (a 68(2)). For s 1 only, not confined to legal relationships (s 1(8)).
'Relative' (in s 1 only)	Includes the mother and father (s 1(8)).
'Relative' (in ss 80 and 98 only)	Regarding an adopted person, means a person who would be related (but for the adoption) by blood, half-blood, marriage or civil partnership (ss 81(2) and 98(7)).
'Relative' (for remainder of the Act)	Grandparent, brother, sister, uncle or aunt, by full blood, half-blood, marriage or civil partnership (s 144 and Sch 6).
'Scottish Adoption Agency'	See s 144(3).
'Section 56 information' (for ss 56–65 only)	See s 56(2).
'Special guardianship order'	See CA 1989, s 14A.
'Special guardianship support services'	Counselling, advice and information, and services defined in Regulations (CA 1989, s 14F(1)).
'Undertaking'	As defined in Care Standards Act 2000 (s 8(1)).
'Voluntary adoption agency' (for ss 9 and 10 only)	A voluntary organisation which is an adoption society (s 9(4)).

Table of Statutes

Paragraph references printed in **bold** type indicate where the section of an Act is set out in part or in full.

Table of Statutory Instruments and Practice Directions

Paragraph references printed in **bold** type indicate where the Statutory Instrument is set out in part or in full. References in the right-hand column are to division and paragraph numbers.

Table of Cases

References in the right-hand column are to paragraph numbers.

A

B

C

D

V

W

X

Z

Part A   Introduction

Introduction

[1]

By way of introduction to the Adoption and Children Act 2002 (hereafter ACA 2002) and prelude to the analysis of each of its sections, a brief overview follows of its scope, history and main provisions, with particular reference to placement for adoption, adoptions with a foreign element, special guardianship and the local authority perspective.

Scope of the Act

[2]

The ACA 2002 provides in Part 1 (ss 1–110) a comprehensive reform of the law relating to domestic and intercountry adoption in England and Wales, and in Part 2 (ss 111–122) significant amendments of other aspects of the law relating to children in the Children Act 1989. The nature and scope of Parts 1 and 2 are outlined further in the summary of the Act, see paras [6]–[16].

Part 3 (ss 123–150) has two chapters which make miscellaneous and final provision, in particular regarding restrictions on advertisements within the United Kingdom relating to adoption (ss 123–124), and to enable the establishment and maintenance of the Adoption and Children Act Register to suggest matches between children waiting to be adopted and suitable prospective adopters (ss 125–131).

The three Parts are supplemented by six Schedules relating to registration of adoptions (s 77(6) and Sch 1), disclosure of birth records by the Registrar General (s 79(6) and Sch 2), minor and consequential amendments of other legislation (s 139(1) and Sch 3), transitional and transitory provisions and savings (s 139(2) and Sch 4), repeal of legislation (s 139(3) and Sch 5), and a glossary of expressions used in the Act (s 147 and Sch 6).

The Act was implemented incrementally, the major and final implementation taking place on 30 December 2005.

Historical background

[3]

The major part of the ACA 2002 relates to adoption and is the product of a very lengthy consultation process which is best understood within its historical context.

The twentieth century

[4]

Adoption as a legal, rather than de facto, transfer of parenthood and parental responsibility by court order from the birth family to the adoptive family is a relatively recent concept in the legal history of England and Wales, having its origins in the Adoption of Children Act 1926 and the preceding Reports (Hopkinson, *Report of the Committee on Child Adoption*, Cmnd 1254 (1921); Tomlin, *Report of the Child Adoption Committee*, Cmnd 2401 (1925)), which sought to regulate the previous frequent practice, particularly following the First World War, of unregulated de facto adoptions.

The 1926 Act was extensively amended by legislation in the 1930s and 1940s, in the light of subsequent experience, and replaced in due course, following the Hurst Committee Report in 1954 (*Report of the Departmental Committee on the Adoption of Children*, Cmnd 9248) by the Adoption Act 1958, which repealed and consolidated all previous adoption legislation (which had earlier been consolidated in the Adoption Act 1950). Thereafter adoption orders reached a peak of approximately 25,000 in 1968, compared with approximately 3,000 a year, when first introduced forty years previously. Most adoptions during that period were in the private law context, often either third party childless couple 'closed' adoptions of illegitimate babies, or adoptions by the birth mother and step-father following divorce and remarriage.

Since the 1970s, there has been a steady decline in the number of adoption orders generally and a greater proportion being made in the public law context in respect of older children in local authority care, who could not be reunited with their birth families. The majority of adoptions are now of children who have been looked after by local authorities as a route out of state care (see *Adoption and Children Act 2002 Explanatory Notes* para 6).

Continuing dissatisfaction with adoption law and procedure following the significant social changes of the 1960s, resulted in further reform in the 1970s, in particular the establishment of a public law 'adoption service', freeing for adoption and introduction of custodianship by the Children Act 1975, following the Report of the *Departmental Committee on the Adoption of Children* in 1972 (Cmnd 5107, the 'Houghton Committee Report'), see Bevan and Parry, *The Children Act 1975* (1978). Greater attention was also being paid to the need for psychological, as opposed to biological, parenthood (see in particular Goldstein, Freud and Solnit, *Beyond the Best Interests of the Child* (1973)). The 1975 Act was immediately consolidated with the existing law in the 1958 Act into the Adoption Act 1976, which had a lengthy period of piecemeal implementation and was not fully in force until 1988. During that period, further changes in childcare practice had evolved, for example regarding contact and access to information, whilst adoption law continued to be based on the philosophies of the 1960s and 1970s.

Not surprisingly, the 1976 Act was itself amended by the Children Act 1989, Sch 10, in order to accommodate both the change of terminology and, to a degree, the change of philosophy consequential upon that Act, and to introduce certain ad hoc and significant changes which reflected some of the changes in childcare practice, for example a greater acceptance of 'open' adoption, and which anticipated a general review.

Hence, adoption law was not fundamentally reviewed and reformed in the 1980s, but was left until after the Children Act 1989 had introduced a fresh coordinated start for the rest of the private and public law relating to the upbringing of children. With the reforms introduced by the 1989 Act very much to the fore, the ensuing comprehensive and lengthy adoption review, which eventually culminated in the ACA 2002, lasted over a decade and was able to take into account the significant social changes in family forms and values which had impacted upon the parenting of, and responsibility to, children. That review was carried out initially by an Inter-Departmental Committee under the direction of the Department of Health which produced a series of Discussion Papers and Background Papers prior to a Report, *Review of Adoption Law, Report to Ministers of an Interdepartmental Working Group: a Consultative Document*, Department of Health and Welsh Office, in 1992. There followed a White Paper, *Adoption: The Future*, Cm 2288 in 1993, then further consultation before publication in 1996 of *Adoption – A Service for Children: Adoption Bill – A Consultative Document* by the Department of Health and Welsh Office.

The twenty-first century

[5]

A change of government in 1997 resulted in further initiatives in the *Prime Minister's Review of Adoption* (Performance and Innovation Unit, July 2000) and a further White Paper *Adoption: a new approach*, (Cm 5017) in December 2000 (Department of Health). In his Foreword to the latter, the Prime Minister identified a number of problems with the adoption process. 'Poor performance, widespread variations, unacceptable delays, agonisingly high hurdles for adopters to surmount – in far too many parts of the system, there is a lack of clarity, of consistency and of fairness. Most pressingly, children in an already vulnerable position are being badly let down'. This was particularly so regarding children languishing in the care system, some of whom suffered serious abuse in care as exemplified by the *Report of the Tribunal of Inquiry into the Abuse of Children in Care in the former County Council Areas of Gwynedd and Clwyd since 1974: Lost in Care*, HC 201 (The 'Waterhouse Report' TSO 2000).

The White Paper, *Adoption: a new approach* built on the *Prime Minister's Review* and 'set out the Government's plans to promote greater use of adoption, improve the performance of the adoption service, and put children at the centre of the adoption process' (*Adoption and Children Act 2002 Explanatory Notes* para 3). The subsequent Adoption and Children Bill based thereon fell when Parliament was prorogued in May 2001.

A revised version of the Bill was introduced in the next session of Parliament and, having been subject to a Special Standing Committee procedure, was enacted in November 2002 as the Adoption and Children Act 2002. Part 1 replaced the Adoption Act 1976 and consolidated some of the provisions in the Adoption (Intercountry Aspects) Act 1999. Part 2 makes a variety of amendments to both the private and public law provisions in the Children Act 1989 following from a variety of consultations and concerns. All of these reforms are outlined in the following summary of the Act's main provisions.

Summary of the Act

[6]

This summary of Parts 1 and 2 presents a broad guide to the nature and scope of the Act's main provisions so as to enable reference to be made to the appropriate commentary which follows each section of the Act. The main provisions of Part 3 were summarised at the outset of this introduction, see para [2].

Part 1: Adoption

[7]

Part 1 has 7 chapters which set out the framework of adoption law for England and Wales, including adoptions with a foreign element.

Chapter 1 (s 1) provides for the welfare of the child to be paramount whenever either a court or an adoption agency is coming to a decision relating to the adoption of a child (s 1(1)(2)). It thereby aligns adoption law with the paramountcy principle in the CA 1989, s 1(1). Delay is generally presumed to be prejudicial to the child's welfare (s 1(3)). Section 1(4) provides courts and adoption agencies with a checklist of some of the matters to which they must have regard in coming to a decision relating to an adoption, and agencies are under a duty in placing a child for adoption to give due consideration to the child's religious persuasion, racial origin and cultural and linguistic background (s 1(5)). Courts and agencies have a duty to consider their wide menu of powers in relation to the particular child (whether under the ACA 2002 or the CA 1989), see s 1(6).

Chapter 2 (ss 2–17) expands the duty on local authorities in England and Wales to maintain an adoption service, which includes making and participating in arrangements for the adoption of children and for the provision of adoption support services (s 3) and provides a qualified statutory right to request an assessment for adoption support services, including financial support (s 4). It also sets out a new regulatory structure for adoption support agencies, requiring them to register under the Care Standards Act 2000, Pt 2 (s 8), and enables the appropriate Minister to establish an independent review mechanism to consider qualifying determinations made by adoption agencies (s 12). The appropriate Minister is also given default powers to compel local authorities to comply with their duties under the Act (s 14). He may also arrange for the inspection of premises where certain children for whom adoption is intended are living (s 15).

Chapter 3 (ss 18–65) covers placement for adoption and adoption orders. Sections 18 to 29 introduce new measures for placement for adoption with consent and placement orders replacing the much criticised provisions in the Adoption Act 1976 for freeing orders as discussed below, see paras [9]–[13]. Chapter 3 also makes provision regarding: restrictions on the removal of children who are or may be placed for adoption by adoption agencies, to ensure that they are only removed by authorised people in an appropriate manner (ss 30–35); restrictions on removal of children where the child has not been placed by an adoption agency (ss 36–40); recovery orders in respect of a child who has been unlawfully removed or to prevent such removal, or to secure the return of a child unlawfully retained in breach of an order to return (s 41); preliminaries to adoption (ss 42–45); the making and effect of adoption orders (ss 46–51), including new provision for adoption orders to be made in favour of unmarried couples as well as married couples and single people (ss 49 and 144(4)); and parental consent to a child being placed for adoption or to the making of an adoption order, including new criteria for dispensing with such consent (s 52). It also makes new provision for disclosure of information prior to and following a person's adoption so as to ensure that the release of this sensitive information about adopted people and their birth relatives is protected and that its disclosure is subject to safeguards (ss 54, 56–65 and 98).

Chapter 4 (ss 66 to 76) covers the status of adopted children. It largely replicates, with minor amendments, the corresponding provisions in the Adoption Act 1976, Pt 4 (ss 38–46), and any reference in an enactment to an adopted person within the meaning of the ACA 2002, Ch 4 includes children adopted under Part 4 of the 1976 Act.

Chapter 5 (ss 77–82) makes continued provision for the Adopted Children Register (dealing with registration issues) together with the continuing duties of the Registrar General (ss 77–79 and Sch 1) and the Adoption Contact Register, which the Registrar General must also continue to maintain (ss 80 and 81). As under the previous law, the latter is in two parts designed to facilitate contact between adopted persons and their birth family where both have expressed a wish for contact. Neither register is open to public inspection.

Chapter 6 (ss 83–91) makes provision for the high standards applicable to domestic adoptions to apply to adoptions with an overseas element, both for children brought into the UK and for those sent out as discussed more fully below, see para [14]. Section 84 creates a new route to parental responsibility prior to overseas adoptions. These sections consolidate the law in relation to these adoptions.

Chapter 7 (ss 92–110) contains varied miscellaneous provisions, inter alia, largely restating the restrictions on making arrangements for adoption and penalties for breach (ss 92 and 93), and prohibition of certain payments in connection with the adoption (ss 95 and 96); introducing a new offence relating to the preparation of reports in connection with adoption (s 94); making provision for public access to and reporting of proceedings under the ACA 2002 (s 101); extending the powers of a CAFCASS officer, or Welsh family proceedings officer, to enable him to examine and take copies of an adoption agency's records relating to a proposed or actual adoption (ss 102–103); and avoiding delay by requiring a court in proceedings in which any question relating to an adoption order or placement order may arise to draw up a timetable and give directions so that it is adhered to (s 109).

Part 2: Amendments to the Children Act 1989

[8]

Part 2 makes a variety of amendments to the Children Act 1989 (the CA 1989) in both the private law and public law context. Particular consideration is given below to the local authority perspective, see para [16].

In response to the outcome of the Lord Chancellor's Consultation Paper *The procedures for the determination of paternity and on parental responsibility of unmarried fathers* (1998), s 111 amends CA 1989, s 4 as to provide for the automatic acquisition of parental responsibility by an unmarried father who jointly registers, or re-registers, with the mother their child's birth. Section 112 inserts s 4A into the CA 1989 so as to allow a more straightforward process than adoption for step-parents to acquire parental responsibility (but not parenthood), namely either by agreement of everyone with parental responsibility or by court order. Section 113 amends CA 1989, s 9 to allow a local authority foster parent to apply for a s 8 order if the child has lived with him for one year, rather than three years as previously. Section 114 amends s 12 so as to empower the court when making a residence order in favour of a person who is not a parent or guardian, to direct that the order continue until the child is 18, rather than 16 as would generally be the case.

Section 115, which must be read with Sch 3, paras 56–64, 68, and 70–72, introduces the new concept of special guardianship to the range of orders available in the CA 1989, so as to widen the range of options for providing permanence for children in cases where adoption is not appropriate. Section 115(1) inserts ss 14A–14G into CA 1989, the nature and scope of which are summarised more fully below, see para [15]. The new sections are supplemented by the Special Guardianship Regulations 2005, SI 2005/1109 and the Special Guardianship (Wales) Regulations 2005, SI 2005/1513. Sections 115(2)–(4) further amend the CA 1989 so as to apply the s 1 welfare checklist when the court is considering whether to make, vary or discharge a special guardianship order and to amend s 5 relating to the appointment of guardians to include special guardians.

Section 116 amends CA 1989, ss 17 and 22 to make clear that local authorities' powers to provide services for children in need includes power to provide accommodation and that children provided with such accommodation do not become 'looked after' children (s 116(1)(2)). Section 117 amends CA 1989, ss 24D and 26 by making further provision regarding inquiries carried out by local authorities into representations (including complaints) about the provision of services under Pt III of that Act. With the relevant regulations, it also extends the procedure to specified functions under CA 1989, Pts IV and V and under the ACA 2002. Section 118 amends CA 1989, s 26 to provide for a more intense focus in the review of care plans for looked after children and for the appointment of an independent reviewing officer in connection with the review of each case of such children. There are enhanced duties placed upon such officers in the context of human rights. Section 119 inserts s 26A in the CA 1989 to place a duty on local authorities to make provision for the arrangement of advocacy services for looked after children and young people leaving care who wish to make a complaint under the CA 1989. Section 120 amends the definition of 'harm' in the CA 1989 to make clear that harm includes any impairment of the child's health or development as a result of witnessing the ill-treatment of another person. Section 121 amends CA 1989, s 31 so that a care order may not be made until the court has considered a care plan with respect to the child. Section 121 also correspondingly inserts s 31A in the CA 1989 so as to require local authorities to prepare a care plan where an application is made on which a care order might be made. Section 122 amends CA 1989, s 41 to make an application for a placement order specified proceedings and to enable rules of court to make applications for s 8 orders specified proceedings (s 122(1)) and to amend CA 1989, s 93 to provide for the separate representation of children in relevant proceedings (s 122(2)).

Placement for adoption

[9]

The Act continues the policy that, save for exceptional circumstances (now permitted under s 92(3) and (4)), only an adoption agency can make arrangements and place a child for adoption; but it provides new measures authorising agency placements and abolishes the freeing for adoption process. That process enabled an adoption agency to apply for the surrender of the parents' rights and duties at an early stage in the process leading to the full adoption order. At a preliminary hearing, the parents would give their consent to their child's adoption or the court could dispense with it, on the permitted statutory grounds. The court could then declare the child free for adoption and, if it did, the parental rights and duties prospectively vested in the adoption agency until the adoption order was made. It did not take long after its implementation for the deficiencies in the process to be made apparent by research (see Lowe NV, Murch M, Borkowski M and Copner R, *Pathways to Adoption Project* (1991). Research undertaken in Scotland produced similar results; see Lambert L, Buist M, Triseliotis J and Hill M, *Freeing Children for Adoption* (1989)) and by critical scrutiny (see Lowe NV, 'Freeing for Adoption-the Experience of the 1980s' [1990] Journal of Social Welfare Law 220; White R, 'Freeing or placement: the dilemma for adoption agencies' (1989) 1 Journal of Child Law 41). Moreover, the case for freeing was weakened by an amendment which restricted the original right of any adoption agency to apply for dispensation with parental consent in respect of any children in their care, to local authority adoption agencies so applying in respect of children who were the subject of care orders (see Adoption Act 1976, s 18(2A), as inserted by the CA 1989, Sch 10, para 6(1)). Adverse criticism soon hardened. So much so that the *Review of Adoption Law* (1992) unequivocally recommended that freeing for adoption should be abolished. All the subsequent surveys of adoption confirmed that conclusion.

The main grounds of criticism of the freeing process were delay in the process leading to the freeing for adoption order, the unsatisfactory status of the child and the prejudicial effects on the birth parents. Some of the features of these grounds are now merely of historical interest, but others will, in the fullness of time, need to be tested against the new placement provisions.

(A) DELAY

[10]

(i) The procedural rules on a freeing application followed closely those on an application for an adoption order. Thus, the adoption agency had to compile a report covering all relevant matters relating to the interested parties. This process involved detailed investigation, particularly where the agency was applying for dispensation with parental consent to adoption, or where it was necessary to find out the intentions of an unmarried father with regard to seeking a parental responsibility order. Moreover, as the research projects demonstrated, the percentage of children with complicated backgrounds was much higher in freeing applications than in the usual 'straight' applications for adoption orders, and so they needed more detailed investigation, for example, of children with special educational needs or of those who had already been the subject of child-related proceedings (most often care proceedings) or those who had contact with both parents or who had already experienced two or more placements. Many of the children who will be placed for adoption under the new law will fall within the above and other special categories, especially where the adoption agency is a local authority and is applying for a placement order. It remains to be seen how far the Family Procedure (Adoption) Rules 2005 and the Adoption Agencies Regulations 2005 (and their Welsh equivalent) will facilitate and expedite detailed investigation and accord with the avoidance of delay principle.

(ii) In the case of local authority adoption agencies these problems associated with investigation were exacerbated by the inadequacy of specialisation and staffing of social workers to deal with adoption work, with consequent variation in the standards of practice maintained by those agencies. Will these deficiencies persist in operating the new law?

(iii) Nor were the courts exculpated. The research projects found several reasons for contribution to delay, namely, delays in the listing of hearings, often because of insistence on submission and filing of documents before listing; delays in the appointment of, and then completion of work by, reporting officers, shortage of guardians ad litem and delays in the submission of their reports; and frequent staff turnover in the courts. In so far as they still exist, shortage of guardians and court staff turnover are outside their province, but otherwise the comprehensive Family Procedure (Adoption) Rules 2005 (for example, the wide powers of the court to give directions) will, it is confidently predicted, minimise the risk of delay in the conduct of proceedings relating to placement for adoption.

(B) THE STATUS OF THE CHILD AND THE BIRTH PARENTS

[11]

A freeing order gave parental responsibility to the adoption agency and extinguished that of the birth parent (Adoption Act 1976, s 12(1) and (3) and s 18(5)). With its emphasis on parental responsibility, the CA 1989 highlighted the virtual denial of a legal relationship between child and birth parents under the freeing process. Since the effect of a freeing order was, as Butler-Sloss LJ (as she then was) put it in *Re C (minors) (adoption: residence order)* [1994] Fam 1 at 9, *sub nom Re C (minors) (parent: residence order)* [1993] 3 All ER 313 at 319, 'to deprive the natural parents of parental responsibility in the same way as after an adoption order', they ceased to be parents for the purposes of the CA 1989. This had a particular consequence with regard to parental contact with the child. Parents would require leave to apply for a s 8 contact order, and leave was only to be granted if there had been a fundamental change of circumstances since the making of the freeing for adoption order (see Thorpe J (as he then was) in *Re C (a minor) (adopted child: contact)* [1993] Fam 210, [1993] 3 All ER 259). That conclusion was expressed within the context of an adoption order, but it was widely accepted that it equally applied where a freeing order existed.). This effect on parental control is in sharp contrast with that under the new law. As will be seen in comments on ss 26 and 27 of the Act and the Adoption Agencies Regulations 2005 (and their Welsh equivalent), once the adoption agency has been authorised to place a child for adoption, contact arrangements can be made with parents and, indeed, other persons. If the parents or other persons cannot agree arrangements, they can apply for a contact order under s 26.

The practical effect of removing parental responsibility was to leave only marginal legal ties between birth parents and child. For example, a freeing for adoption order did not, until an adoption order was made, affect familial rights of succession and disposition of property on death. Moreover, the birth parents did have the limited right under the Adoption Act 1976, s 20, to apply for the revocation of the freeing order. It was limited because they could not apply for 12 months, and it was left to the court's discretion whether or not to revoke and, if it so chose, to do so on the condition that the local authority obtain a care order, which could thereby restrict the exercise of the parental responsibility (see CA 1989, s 33(3)(b) and (4)) that was restored to the parents by the revocation.

Where the freeing process did not apply, parents retained their parental responsibility until the adoption order was made, and that is now the position of all parents when children are placed for adoption. That said, the Act provides potential problems of its own for parents because in conferring parental responsibility on the adoption agency and on any prospective adopters, it will raise uncertainty over the extent to which the agency and the prospective adopters will have to consult the parents before exercising parental responsibility in respect of a particular matter. Moreover, the Act gives the agency power to restrict the parents' parental responsibility (see the comment on s 25).

(C) LOCAL AUTHORITY

[12]

Even if a local authority could not find adopters, and concluded that the freeing order no longer served any useful purpose, it could not apply for revocation and had to fall back on the use of the inherent jurisdiction to achieve that objective.

The new concept of placement

[13]

The basic principle is that an adoption agency is authorised to place a child for adoption only if it has parental consent to do so or, being a local authority agency, has obtained a placement order. The intention is to ensure that decisions about whether adoption is the right option for the child, whether the birth parents consent and, if not, whether parental consent should be dispensed with are taken earlier in the adoption process than at present, with court involvement where necessary. 'This is intended to provide greater certainty and stability for children by dealing as far as possible with consent to placement for adoption before they have been placed ......; to minimise the uncertainty for prospective adopters who under the current system possibly face a contested court hearing at the adoption order stage; and to reduce the extent to which birth families are faced with a 'fait accompli' at the final adoption hearing'. (*Adoption and Children Act 2002 Explanatory Notes* para 71).

The Family Procedure (Adoption) Rules 2005 and the Adoption Agencies Regulations 2005 (and their Welsh equivalent) provide safeguards for parents when deciding whether or not to consent to placement for adoption. These include counselling and advising the parents on what consent involves, and the requirements relating to the taking and witnessing of consents and reporting them to the court. Parents are further protected by the rule (see s 52(4)) that they can withdraw their consents at any time before an application for an adoption order is made.

The placement order is one of the features of the policy of the Act to align adoption law, so far as is appropriate, with the CA 1989. Unless there is a care order in force, the same threshold for compulsory intervention in family life applies where the child has suffered, or is at risk of, significant harm. Apart from the exceptional case of an orphaned child, there can be no placement order unless there is a care order, or the CA 1989, s 31(2) conditions exist (see s 21(2)).

As will be apparent, the placement provisions (ss 18–29), especially those relating to placement orders, leave much to implication and inference. The same general comment also extends to restrictions on removal from their present homes or other accommodation of children who are, or may be, placed for adoption (ss 30–41). The Act imposes a general prohibition on removal but allows certain persons limited rights to secure removal. In this regard, it draws a distinction between agency placements and non-agency cases where the child's home is with persons who have given notice of their intention to adopt him.

Adoption with a international element

[14]

The ACA 2002, ss 83–91, and their dependent regulations, make provision for the high standards applicable to domestic adoptions to apply also to adoptions with an overseas element, both for children brought into the UK and for those sent out. These sections need to be set in the context of the rest of the scheme of the Act, its dependent regulations, and other statutory provision. Appropriate reference is thus made within the commentary to the Adoption (Intercountry Aspects) Act 1999 (AIAA 1999), the Adoptions with a Foreign Element Regulations 2005 (AWAFE Regs 2005), the Adoption Agencies Regulations 2005 and the Family Procedure (Adoption) Rules 2005.

The first five years of the 21st century saw a comprehensive reform of the law and procedures relating to international adoption. From the early 1970s, a list of designated countries has existed. Adoptions that have taken place in those listed territories were automatically recognised as valid adoptions under English law, subject to certain criteria being satisfied. Adoptions that took place in other territories required adopters to apply for the child to be adopted again under English law. There was no statutory provision regulating assessment of adopters or for setting up formal intercountry communications and administration of these adoptions. Intercountry adoption was managed between the Department of Health and the courts, with immigration considerations providing a third element of the process. There was guidance as to good practice, which appeared to be followed in about three-quarters of cases. It became apparent that a more modern, coherent scheme was required to provide good quality arrangements for children.

The first major reform occurred when the United Kingdom ratified and acceded to the Convention on Protection of Children and Co-operation in respect of Intercountry Adoption, concluded at the Hague on 29th May 1993, ('the Hague Convention'), given statutory force by the AIAA 1999. The Hague Convention sets up a scheme of sending and receiving States, and makes provision for a scheme applicable to all signatory states of assessment, exchange of information and procedure for moving a child across an international boundary either after adoption in the child's home country or for adoption in the home country of adopters. Central Authorities in each of the signatory states are responsible for the co-ordination of adoptions. The Central Authority for England is the Department for Education and Skills, which has replaced the Department of Health as the government department with responsibility for international adoption. The AIAA 1999 also strengthened sanctions for those who breached good practice in relation to seeking and adopting children from abroad.

Before the AIAA 1999 came into force in January 2003, the Adoption of Children from Overseas Regulations 2001 were introduced, making it a requirement that prospective adopters of a child from overseas were formally assessed and approved. Those regulations were replaced by the Adoption (Bringing Children into the United Kingdom) Regulations 2003, which introduced a requirement that prospective adopters of a child from abroad must have a certificate of eligibility to adopt that showed their approval as suitable to adopt and that no immigration difficulties should apply. At the same time, the Intercountry Adoption (Hague Convention) Regulations 2003 were brought into force, providing regulation of Hague Convention adoptions.

The AIAA 1999 remains the statute that brought the Hague Convention into force. The ACA 2002 scheme, together with the regulations that form a crucial part of the new law, aim to create as unified a system as possible applying to all adoptions with an international element, whether from a Hague Convention country or not. The AWAFE Regs 2005 have many provisions which adapt the main statute specifically for cases with an international element. Policy considerations regarding the welfare of the child, including protection from trafficking, and international co-operation resonate throughout. The responsibilities of local authorities in terms of assessment and panel approval are contained within the Adoption Agencies Regulations 2005.

Of prime practical importance when dealing with adoptions with an international element is the issue of immigration. A detailed discussion of immigration considerations is outside the scope of this work; however, one point of general application can be made, and that is that early and expert consideration of immigration issues forms a vital part in the planning of any adoption with an international element.

Further reform of the law in this area is provided for in the Children and Adoption Act 2006, which is not yet in force. Sections 9–12 permit the suspension of adoptions from abroad (including from Hague Convention countries) where overseas practices in relation to adoption of children are contrary to public policy (this provision arising after complexities illustrated by *R (on the application of Charlton Thomson) v Secretary of State for Education and Skills* [2005] EWHC 1378 (Admin) [2005] 2 FCR 603). Section 13 permits fees to be charged by the Department of Education and Skills in relation to the administration of an intercountry adoption. Section 14 amends ACA 2002, s 83 to enhance the extent to which assessment and approval requirements must be met.

Special guardianship

[15]

Special guardianship is the revocable transfer of quasi-exclusive parental responsibility to a person other than a parent of the child, by court order. This new concept, which s 115(1) inserts into the CA 1989, has its origins in chapter five of the White Paper *Adoption: a new approach*. It was widely welcomed in public consultation (per Lord Hunt, HL Grand Committee, 2 July 2002, col CWH 162) and during the Adoption and Children Bill's passage through Parliament. Like adoption, it must be conferred by court order. Special guardianship is conferred by a private law order to provide a new option, primarily but not exclusively, to meet the needs of looked-after children for whom rehabilitation with the birth family is not considered to be an option. In many such cases, the irrevocable severance of all connection between the child and his birth family consequent upon adoption will not be in the child's best interests. As the White Paper acknowledged in para 4.8, the child may wish, for example, to retain links with his birth family. He may be a member of a minority ethnic family that has religious and cultural difficulties with adoption. The child's carers may not wish to uproot legally the child from his family by adoption or they may be members of his birth family, hence adoption would distort existing relationships. In the words of the Secretary of State for Health during the second reading of the Adoption and Children Bill, special guardianship orders 'give permanence to the child, by giving day to day responsibility for his or her care to the special guardian without severing all legal ties with the birth family. That new flexibility will give new opportunities to children who have been by-passed by the current adoption laws.' (HC 2R, 29 October 2001, col 656.) Special guardianship is, however, just one option for such children. There will remain some children for whom neither adoption nor special guardianship is appropriate and who continue to require a high level of professional support within a foster placement.

By introducing special guardianship as a legal status short of adoption, to provide an additional option designed to meet the needs of children being looked after, either by foster carers or relatives, the ACA 2002 parallels the introduction, by the Children Act 1975, of the short lived hybrid concept of custodianship, which was not implemented until 1984 and survived only until the CA 1989 came into force in October 1991. Just as custodianship could only be fully understood within the comparative context of the former concepts of custody and guardianship, so too special guardianship is a hybrid concept, whose nature and scope can only be fully understood within the context of the current concepts of guardianship and a residence order as explained in the commentary on s 115(1), see paras **[519]–[519.1]** or **[704]–[715.1]**. Guardianship remains confined to cases of transfer of parental responsibility on the death of a parent. The exclusive exercise of parental responsibility during parental lifetime is to be by way of special guardianship. They are to be seen as complementary concepts. In a case of parental death, appointment of a guardian rather than special guardian may better accord with the child's welfare. In view of its intended use in the public law context, special provision is also appropriate in respect of special guardianship (but neither guardianship nor a residence order) regarding the availability, in appropriate cases, of local authority support services, see the CA 1989, s 14F.

Like both guardianship and a residence order, special guardianship is closely allied to the concept of parental responsibility, but not parenthood (which is unaffected). The latter distinction makes special guardianship of notably less legal and practical significance than adoption in terms of parental autonomy. Adoption is legally-created parenthood and hence provides an enduring life-long relationship. A special guardianship order confers quasi-exclusive parental responsibility, see CA 1989, s 14C, which ends at the very latest when the child attains the age of 18 and is susceptible to earlier revocation in accordance with the CA 1989, s 14D. Special guardianship provides the child with a *feeling* of permanence, rather than providing legal permanence.

Special guardianship confers exclusive responsibility for decision-making regarding the day to day care and upbringing of the child, but subject to consent of all those with parental responsibility where the law so requires regarding parental decision-making on more than day-to-day matters. For example, the written consent of everyone with parental responsibility or leave of the court is required to either any change of the child's surname or his removal from the United Kingdom, see the CA 1989, s 14C. In contrast, a residence order is based upon the concurrent, rather than exclusive, exercise of parental responsibility. 'A special guardianship order cements the relationship between the special guardian and the child to a greater degree than a residence order, from which it is different in kind', per Robin Tolson QC in *A Local Authority v Y, Z* [2006] 2 FLR 41 at 20.

The special guardianship ss 14A–14G which the ACA 2002, s 115(1) inserts into the CA 1989, see paras **[519]–[519.1]** or **[704]–[715.1]**, are supplemented by ACA 2002, s 139(1) and Sch 3, paras 56–64, 68 and 70–72 which make minor and consequential amendments to the CA 1989, so as to accommodate special guardianship within the overall context of the law relating to children provided by the CA 1989. The new sections are also supplemented by the Special Guardianship Regulations 2005, SI 2005/1109 and the similar, but certainly not identical, Special Guardianship (Wales) Regulations 2005, SI 2005/1513. The Department for Education and Skills and Welsh Assembly Government have issued respectively *Special Guardianship Guidance* (DfES, 2005) and *Guidance to Support The Special Guardianship (Wales) Regulations 2005* (NAFW 2006), designed to support the introduction of special guardianship orders and provide detailed guidance on the interpretation of the different regulations. Both sets of regulations and Guidance are fully analysed at paras **[1101]**ff and **[1201]**ff.

Local authority perspective

[16]

From a local authority perspective, a number of significant changes are made to legislation in a wider context than adoption law, in particular the CA 1989, in response to either judicial decisions, or concerns that the existing legislation was insufficiently rigorous in certain areas.

The House of Lords decision in *Re S (Minors) (Care Order: Implementation of Care Plan); Re W (Minors) (Care Order: Adequacy of Care Plan)* [2002] UKHL 10, [2002] 1 FCR 577, although overturning the decision of the Court of Appeal in respect of the remedy, accepted the view of the Court of Appeal that there were inadequacies in the protection of the human rights of families within care proceedings, arising from the structure of the CA 1989 and associated regulations, particularly in relation to children. In consequence, the ACA 2002, s 118 amends the regulations governing the review of cases of looked after children, enhances the role and duties of the Independent Reviewing Officer (IRO), and places obligations upon that person to act, by pursuing matters within the organisation and, ultimately, to CAFCASS Legal, if there are serious concerns about failures in the planning process. In addition, the role of the IRO is also enhanced between reviews, and the allocated social worker for the case is also explicitly made responsible for notifying the IRO of any serious difficulties in implementing the review decisions.

The origins of the phrase 'care plan' lie in the Department of Health Guidance introduced in support of the implementation of the CA 1989, where it is the phrase used to describe the legislative requirements for local authorities to make the appropriate written 'arrangements' for all looked after children. That guidance set out the minimum requirements for the contents of such care plans. Subsequently, various attempts were made to increase the emphasis upon the detail and effectiveness of such plans, through Department of Health Circulars and judicial guidance. The introduction of lengthy packs of forms to complete for reviews for children within the local authority planning process did not meet with the approval of the judiciary, and guidance was given about a separate format for care plans within the context of care proceedings, which led to a two-tier system, with care plans for children who were the subject of care proceedings separate from the documents provided and maintained for the majority of looked after children who were not the subject of any legal proceedings.

It became apparent that greater safeguards were required to ensure the adequacy of care plans, although again, the focus has been upon care plans within care proceedings. The ACA 2002, s 121 inserts a new s 31A into the CA 1989, imposing a duty on local authorities to prepare a care plan for a child within the context of public law proceedings, within a time scale fixed by the court. Section 31 of the CA 1989 is also amended, to prohibit the court from making a final care order unless the court has considered such a plan.

Concerns about the efficacy of the complaints procedures concerning local authorities and looked after children led to amendments introduced by the ACA 2002, s 117, which amends the CA 1989, ss 24D and 26, so as to change the legal framework for complaints procedures, and also to bring within their scope a range of functions under the new Act and associated regulations governing adoption.

The Children Act 1989 Representations Procedure (England) Regulations 2006 came into force on 1 September 2006, replacing the Representations Procedure (England) Regulations 1991. The DfES has also produced guidance, under Section 7: *Getting the Best from Complaints: Social Care Complaints and Representations for Children and Young People and Others*. Originally, it had been proposed that the final stage of the complaints procedures should be completely independent of local authorities, but for England, this was ultimately not pursued, leaving the final Stage 3 of the complaints procedures still under the control of local authorities, albeit with a higher degree of independence. In Wales, however, complaints can now be pursued to independent panels, although the scope of the subject matter of complaints is more restrictive

Prior to the ACA 2002, the question of the support for the adoption of children was primarily seen within the context of financial support for the placement, and when cases were being considered by the adoption panel and, subsequently, by the agency decision-maker, the focus was normally upon the determination of whether the child qualified for the purposes of paying financial support to the prospective adopter, in anticipation of the prospective placement. Although financial support remains extremely important, Chapter 2 of Pt 1 to the ACA 2002, and associated regulations, mark a qualitative shift away from that narrow approach, and introduce a comprehensive concept of 'adoption support services', and assessments for the purposes of such services. The Adoption Agencies Regulations 2005, and the similar (but by no means identical) Welsh Regulations, which govern the functions of adoption panels and adoption agencies in England and Wales, should also be considered within this context, as well as the regulations referred to in the commentary, which define adoption support services and govern the process of assessment and review.

Greater emphasis has been placed upon the rights of those who wish to adopt, within the context of their entitlement to seek an independent review of a provisional decision not to approve them as adopters, and that legislation was introduced prior to December 2005.

One of the concerns arising from the previous experience of adopters and adoption workers was the variable quality, on occasions, of the information given to prospective adopters at the time of the placement of a child. Although the local authority was partially successful in its appeal against the judgment at first instance, the Court of Appeal decision in *A v Essex County Council* [2003] EWCA Civ 1848, [2004] 1 FCR 660 added weight to the view that, as a matter of law, there was an obligation to provide adequate information to prospective adopters. This has now found expression within the Adoption Agencies Regulations 2005 (and their Welsh equivalent), with the introduction of a detailed regulatory regime for providing information to adopters, and agreeing the plan for placement and future support.

Within the Adoption Agencies Regulations, which must be read with the respective Guidance on Adoption from the DfES and the Welsh Assembly, strict time limits are laid down for the procedural aspects of assessing prospective adopters, taking cases to an adoption panel, for the adoption agency to make decisions, and for the notification of decisions by the agency.

In conclusion

[17]–[100]

Each section of the Act, as amended, is now set out and analysed individually, with appropriate cross reference to other sections and related legislation, particularly the amendments made to the CA 1989. The analysis of the ACA 2002 and the new sections inserted into the Children Act 1989, are followed by a similar analysis of the Adoption Agencies Regulations 2005, SI 2005/389, the Adoption Agencies (Wales) Regulations 2005, SI 2005/1313 (W.95), the Adoptions with a Foreign Element Regulations 2005, SI 2005/392, the Special Guardianship Regulations 2005, SI 2005/1109 and the Special Guardianship (Wales) Regulations 2005, SI 2005/1513 (W.117). Thereafter for reference purposes, the Adoption (Intercountry Aspects) Act 1999, the Adoption (Designation of Overseas Adoptions) Order 1973, SI 1973/19 and the Family Procedure (Adoption) Rules 2005, SI 2005/2795 are set out in the Appendix.

Part B   Statutes

Adoption and Children Act 2002

2002 CHAPTER 38

An Act to restate and amend the law relating to adoption; to make further amendments of the law relating to children; to amend section 93 of the Local Government Act 2000; and for connected purposes.

[7th November 2002]

BE IT ENACTED by the Queen's most Excellent Majesty, by and with the advice and consent of the Lords Spiritual and Temporal, and Commons, in this present Parliament assembled, and by the authority of the same, as follows:—

[101]

Part 1
Adoption

Chapter 1
Introductory

1 Considerations applying to the exercise of powers

(1) This section applies whenever a court or adoption agency is coming to a decision relating to the adoption of a child.

(2) The paramount consideration of the court or adoption agency must be the child's welfare, throughout his life.

(3) The court or adoption agency must at all times bear in mind that, in general, any delay in coming to the decision is likely to prejudice the child's welfare.

(4) The court or adoption agency must have regard to the following matters (among others)—

(a) the child's ascertainable wishes and feelings regarding the decision (considered in the light of the child's age and understanding),

(b) the child's particular needs,

(c) the likely effect on the child (throughout his life) of having ceased to be a member of the original family and become an adopted person,

(d) the child's age, sex, background and any of the child's characteristics which the court or agency considers relevant,

(e) any harm (within the meaning of the Children Act 1989 (c 41)) which the child has suffered or is at risk of suffering,

(f) the relationship which the child has with relatives, and with any other person in relation to whom the court or agency considers the relationship to be relevant, including—

    (i) the likelihood of any such relationship continuing and the value to the child of its doing so,

    (ii) the ability and willingness of any of the child's relatives, or of any such person, to provide the child with a secure environment in which the child can develop, and otherwise to meet the child's needs,

    (iii) the wishes and feelings of any of the child's relatives, or of any such person, regarding the child.

(5) In placing the child for adoption, the adoption agency must give due consideration to the child's religious persuasion, racial origin and cultural and linguistic background.

(6) The court or adoption agency must always consider the whole range of powers available to it in the child's case (whether under this Act or the Children Act 1989);

and the court must not make any order under this Act unless it considers that making the order would be better for the child than not doing so.

(7) In this section, 'coming to a decision relating to the adoption of a child', in relation to a court, includes—

(a) coming to a decision in any proceedings where the orders that might be made by the court include an adoption order (or the revocation of such an order), a placement order (or the revocation of such an order) or an order under section 26 (or the revocation or variation of such an order),

(b) coming to a decision about granting leave in respect of any action (other than the initiation of proceedings in any court) which may be taken by an adoption agency or individual under this Act,

but does not include coming to a decision about granting leave in any other circumstances.

(8) For the purposes of this section—

(a) references to relationships are not confined to legal relationships,

(b) references to a relative, in relation to a child, include the child's mother and father.

NOTES

Initial Commencement

To be appointed

To be appointed: see s 148(1), (2).

Appointment

Appointment: 30 December 2005: see SI 2005/2213, art 2(a).

Extent

This section does not extend to Scotland: see s 149(2).

See Further

See further, the application of this section, with modifications, in relation to an external adoption order effected within the period of six months of the making of the adoption, and in respect of adoptions under the 1993 Hague Convention on Protection of Children and Co-operation in respect of Intercountry Adoption: the Adoptions with a Foreign Element Regulations 2005, SI 2005/392, regs 11(1)(a), 52, 55.

General

[102]

This introductory section to 'Part 1 Adoption' of the Adoption and Children Act 2002 (ACA 2002) lays down new general principles applicable whenever either a court or an adoption agency is coming to a decision relating to the adoption of a child (s 1(1)(7)). In so doing, it also provides guidance for all professionals and families involved in the adoption process upon the criteria applicable throughout the process, for example regarding placement for adoption, and the making of an adoption order. It draws upon the well-known welfare principles in the CA 1989, s 1, whilst reflecting the unique nature of the adoption of a child as the irrevocable transfer of parenthood and parental responsibility from the birth family to the adoptive family. The paramount consideration of the court or adoption agency must be the child's welfare throughout his life, and they must constantly remember that delay is generally prejudicial to the child's welfare (s 1(2), (3)). The adoption process must be child-centred. To that end, s 1(4) provides courts and adoption agencies with a checklist of some of the matters to which they must have regard in coming to a decision relating to an adoption, and agencies are under a duty in placing a child for adoption to give due consideration to the child's religious persuasion, racial origin and cultural and linguistic background (s 1(5)). Courts and agencies have a duty to consider their wide menu of powers in relation to the particular child, (whether under the ACA 2002 or CA 1989), see s 1(6). In that regard, they must remember that the ACA 2002 is both an Adoption Act and a Children Act, and significantly amends the Children Act 1989. Section 1(6) places courts under an additional duty not to make any order under the ACA 2002 unless doing so would be better for the child than not doing so.

Section 1(1), (7)—scope of s 1

[103]

Section 1(1) makes s 1 an overarching section which applies whenever a court or adoption agency is coming to a decision relating to the adoption of a child.

A 'court' means the High Court, a county court or a magistrates' court, subject to any provision made by CA 1989, Sch 11, Pt 1, see ACA 2002, s 144(1).

An 'adoption agency' means a local authority or registered adoption society in accordance with the definition in s 2.

'Child' generally means a person who has not attained the age of 18 years in accordance with s 144(1), but references in the ACA 2002 to a child in connection with any proceedings (whether or not concluded) for adoption include a person who has attained the age of 18 before the proceedings are concluded in accordance with s 49(5). An adoption order may be made if the proceedings are concluded before the person attains the age of 19 in accordance with s 47(9).

By virtue of s 1(7), 'coming to a decision relating to the adoption of a child' includes (but is not confined to), a court coming to a decision:

(a)   in any proceedings where the orders that the court might make include:

- an adoption order, or the revocation of an adoption order,

- a placement order, or the revocation of a placement order,

- a contact order under ACA 2002, s 26 or the revocation or variation of such an order,

(b)   about granting leave in respect of any action (other than the initiation of any court proceedings) which an adoption agency or individual may take under the Act,

but does not include coming to a decision about granting leave in any other circumstances.

Coming to a decision in any proceedings where the court might make an adoption order or a placement order includes, for example, coming to a decision whether or not to dispense with parental consent to a child being placed for adoption or to the making of an adoption order in accordance with s 52(1)(b). Moreover, s 1(7) is not exhaustive in identifying in relation to a court what constitutes coming to a decision relating to the adoption of a child.

Section 1(2)—the paramountcy principle

[104]

In making the child's welfare the court's or adoption agency's paramount consideration, s 1(2) implements the proposal in the White Paper, *Adoption: A New Approach,* para 4.14 to align the adoption legislation 'with the Children Act 1989, to make the needs of children paramount in making decisions about their future'. It brings the criteria for decision making in adoption proceedings into line with the criteria in CA 1989, s 1(1) applicable to decision making when a court determines any question with respect to the upbringing of a child, or the administration of a child's property or the application of any income arising from it. It also accords with the United Nations Convention on the Rights of the Child, art 21, which provides that 'States parties that recognise and/or permit the system of adoption shall ensure that the best interests of the child shall be the paramount consideration'.

The principle of paramountcy of the child's welfare applies not just to judicial decision making, as under CA 1989, s 1(1), but also decision making by adoption agencies. Moreover, in order to reflect the irrevocable and lifelong nature of such decisions, courts and adoption agencies must treat the child's welfare throughout his life as their paramount consideration. Under the former adoption law, most recently in the Adoption Act 1976, s 6, a court or adoption agency was required to 'have regard to all the circumstances, first consideration being given to the need to safeguard and promote the welfare of the child throughout his childhood', although that did not mean that benefits after the child reached majority were irrelevant, for example the continuing care that would be provided by foster parents for a severely mentally handicapped child after he reached the age of 18, see *Re D (a minor) (adoption order: injunction)* [1991] Fam 137. Such benefits are now clearly to be considered in the application of s 1(2). As would, for example, the benefit conferred if British citizenship were acquired as a result of the making of an adoption order shortly before the child attains majority.

The distinction between first consideration being given to the need to safeguard and promote the child's welfare, as required by the Adoption Act 1976, s 6, and the court or adoption agency having to regard the child's welfare as their paramount consideration, as required by s 1(2), is a fine one. Under the first consideration welfare test, courts and agencies had to take into account the interests of all parties concerned, namely the child, the birth family and the adopting family. Although the child's welfare, coming first, was the single most important consideration, it was not overriding. In the words of Lord Simon in *Re D (adoption: parent's consent)* [1977] AC 602 at 638: 'In adoption proceedings the welfare of the child is not the paramount consideration (ie, outweighing all others) ... but it is the first consideration (ie, outweighing any other) ... though the welfare of the child is not a consideration overriding all others, it is the first consideration outweighing any other'. The total severance of the legal relationship between the child and adoptive family was seen as requiring thorough consideration of the claims and interests of the birth parents as well as those of the child. The paramountcy principle in s 1(2) means that the overriding consideration for courts and adoption agencies is the welfare of the child, which outweighs any other consideration. Whenever they make a decision relating to the adoption of a child, it will have to accord with the paramountcy of the child's welfare, which connotes in the words of Lord MacDermott in *J v C* [1970] AC 688 at 710: 'a process whereby, when all the relevant facts, relationships, claims and wishes of parents, risks, choices and other circumstances are taken into account and weighed, the course to be followed will be that which is most in the interests of the child's welfare'.

In applying that principle, court and agencies must ask what is best for the particular child in the light of the range of options available. Any other factor or interest is only relevant in so far as it helps to answer that question. In so doing, they will be acting consistently with the European Convention on Human Rights, art 8 (right to private and family life), for as Lord Hobhouse stated in *Dawson v Wearmouth* [1999] 2 AC 308 at 329 '[t]here is nothing in the Convention which requires the courts of this country to act otherwise than in accordance with the interests of the child'. Although the European Convention on Human Rights does not accord the child's welfare paramount importance, the European Commission on Human Rights held in *Hendricks v Netherlands* (1982) 5 EHRR 223 that where there is a serious conflict between the interests of the child and one of his parents, which can only be resolved to the disadvantage of one of them, the interests of the child must prevail under art 8(2).

Section 1(3)—avoidance of delay principle

[105]

The White Paper *Adoption, A New Approach*, para 1.15, highlighted that for many children and adopters there was too much delay in the adoption process and that children suffered unnecessarily. Moreover, one of the problems surrounding the unmet needs of looked-after children under the former law, identified in para 2.8, was that 'decisions about how to proceed to provide a secure, stable and permanent placement, including adoption, are not addressed early enough, focused clearly enough or taken swiftly enough' and 'where plans for permanent placements, including adoption are made, they are not delivered quickly enough, from the point of view of the child's timescales', see also paras 5.14–5.19.

Section 1(3) establishes as a major general principle, that courts and adoption agencies must constantly bear in mind that, in general, any delay in coming to a decision is likely to prejudice the child's welfare. The principle is in line with art 6(1) of the European Convention on Human Rights which requires that cases be heard within a reasonable time. It also mirrors the principle in CA 1989, s 1(2), applicable to court decisions determining any question regarding the upbringing of a child. The principle is a general one aimed at the avoidance of prejudicial delay, not purposeful delay. Bearing in mind that an adoption order, unlike any Children Act 1989 order, is a legal transplant which irrevocably terminates the legal relationship between the child and his birth family, in favour of the adoptive family, it is vital for the child's welfare that properly considered and investigated decisions are reached by agencies and courts. Hence, the avoidance of delay principle is subject to the paramountcy principle in s 1(2). Moreover, it has been cogently argued that: 'Delay, in the sense of a measured consideration of the proportionate response to the child's needs, is therefore not only appropriate but mandated by human rights obligations' (Bainham, *Children – the Modern Law* (3rd edn), p 270).

There is a close relationship between s 1(3) and the duty upon courts by virtue of s 109, in proceedings in which a question may arise as to whether a placement order or an adoption order should be made, or any other question with respect to an order, to draw up a timetable with a view to determining the question without delay, and to give directions for ensuring that the timetable is observed. That duty is comparable with those in CA 1989, s 11(1) applicable to s 8 proceedings, s 14E(1) applicable to special guardianship proceedings and s 32(1) applicable to care and supervision proceedings. As part of the overriding objective of enabling the court to deal with cases justly, the Family Procedure (Adoption) Rules 2005 (SI 2005/2795), r 1, emphasises the need, so far as is practicable, to ensure that they are dealt with expeditiously. All professionals involved with an application should assist the court in meeting its duty of avoiding delay.

The avoidance of delay principle is reflected also in the *National Adoption Standards* (Department of Health, 2001) which 'include timescales within which decisions for most children should be reached and action taken, to ensure that children are not kept waiting for a family' (White Paper, para 4.6).

Section 1(4), (8)—the welfare checklist

[106]

Section 1(4) introduced into adoption law a statutory list of factors to which the court or adoption agency must have regard in deciding what accords with the child's welfare, rather than providing a definition of welfare itself. It requires that in discharging their duties to decide what is best for the child, the court or adoption agency must consider, among others, the matters listed in the so-called welfare checklist. They must do so when coming to any decision relating to the adoption of a child. In addition to the court and adoption agency, others should pay regard to the checklist, in particular practitioners involved in the adoption process, for example when preparing reports for the court, as well as the parties themselves. The checklist is not exhaustive and is modelled upon, but is a modified version of, CA 1989, s 1(3). The modifications reflect the unique nature of adoption as the irrevocable transfer of parenthood and parental responsibility from the birth family to the adoptive family, see in particular s 1(4)(c) and (f).

Section 1(4)(a)

[107]

The prominence given to the child's wishes and feelings by s 1(4)(a) reflects that the adoption process must be centred on the child and his voice heard effectively. As with the CA 1989, s 1(3)(a), the emphasis is upon the child's entitlement to be consulted about, rather than decide upon, the decision in question. The significance to be given to his wishes and feelings is a matter for the court or agency. The child's wishes are not determinative unless the court or agency considers that they accord with his welfare. Most notably, the consent of a competent child to the making of a placement order or adoption order is not required, as it is in some other countries, although in practice if the child is of an age and understanding to decide that he does not wish the order to be made, it will be highly unusual for it to be in his best interests, and the lack of consent may well be determinative of what is for his lifelong welfare. It is recognised that ascertaining the child's wishes and feelings must depend upon the child's age (see also s 1(4)(d)) and understanding, and the CA 1989 jurisprudence in that context will be relevant.

Section 1(4)(b)

[108]

Section 1(4)(b) reflects that the child's particular needs will be central to his welfare and they are to be given the widest possible interpretation. They include his physical, emotional and educational needs, but are not so limited as they are in the CA 1989, s 1(3)(b) and will include for example, health and social needs. Regard must be paid to the child's needs throughout his life as well as his current particular needs, in order to assist the court or agency to give the consideration to the child's welfare required by s 1(2).

Section 1(4)(c)

[109]

The likely effect upon the child of having ceased to be a member of his original family and become an adopted person in s 1(4)(c) highlights the unique and irrevocable nature of an adoption order and the legal transplant which it brings about.

The court or agency must have regard to what the child will lose as a result of termination of his membership of his birth family as well as what he will gain by becoming a member of the adoptive family and must balance the effect of the losses and gains throughout the child's life. There is a link between s 1(4)(c) and s 1(4)(f) in terms of the loss of relationships with his family. An adoption order will terminate the legal relationship of parent and child (and other original family members) and the associated exercise, during dependent childhood, of parental responsibility. Other potential associated losses include succession and inheritance rights, citizenship and domicile as well as intangible, but no less important, losses in terms of identifying with, and being wanted by, the birth family. Adoption is a very serious interference with the right to family life recognised by art 8 of the European Convention on Human Rights, that requires considerable justification in terms of being necessary and proportionate and in the child's best interests, as the European Court of Human Rights has recognised (see *Johansen v Norway* (1996) 23 EHRR 33). The need to consider the long-term effects of a permanent separation from a natural parent was acknowledged by that Court in *Gorgulu v Germany* [2004] 1 FCR 410. In terms of the gains by becoming an adopted person, an adoption order has, by virtue of s 67, the general effect of creating between the child and the adopter a legal relationship almost wholly the same as that between a parent and his natural, legitimate child. The order provides irrevocable legal permanence to that relationship. It should bring with it a sense of belonging and security for the child and removes the uncertainty associated with foster care and orders relating to residence and parental responsibility, in particular a CA 1989, s 8 residence order and, to a lesser extent, a s 14A special guardianship order introduced by the ACA 2002, s 115, see para **[519]**.

Section 1(4)(d)

[110]

The factors listed in s 1(4)(d) mirror those in CA 1989, s 1(3)(d) and emphasise the subjective nature of the adoption process regarding consideration of the child, and the need for the court or adoption agency to pay regard to his particular circumstances, characteristics and background, including, for example, any disability. There is a clear link with the requirement in s 1(4)(b) to consider the child's particular needs. The age of older children, as adopted children have tended to be in recent years, is relevant also in the context of their wishes and feelings in s 1(4)(a) and links to the birth family in s 1(4)(c) and (f). The particular child's religion, racial origin, cultural and linguistic background will be significant when the court or adoption agency is considering his background and characteristics and must be given due consideration under s 1(4)(d) in decision making relating to adoption, as well as specifically by the adoption agency under s 1(5) in placing the child for adoption.

Section 1(4)(e)

[111]

Under s 1(4)(e), evidence of any harm, or a risk of harm, to the child is likely to weigh heavily against the perpetrators, depending upon its significance, as it does under CA 1989, s 1(3)(e). 'Harm' has the same meaning as in that Act. It means ill-treatment (including sexual abuse, physical and non physical ill-treatment); or the impairment of (physical or mental) health, or (physical, intellectual, emotional, social or behavioural) development, including, for example, impairment suffered from seeing or hearing the ill-treatment of another, in accordance with CA 1989, s 31(9) as amended by the ACA 2002, s 120, see para **[543]**. The interpretation of s 31(9) applies to the ACA 2002, s 1(4)(e).

Section 1(4)(f) and s 1(8)

[112]

Section 1(4)(f), together with 1(4)(c), reflects the unique nature of adoption as the irrevocable transfer of parenthood and parental responsibility from the birth family to the adoptive family. Hence the need for the court or adoption agency in deciding what is in the child's best interests, to have regard to the child's relationships with his relatives and, moreover, anyone else, for example a carer, they consider relevant. The older the child and the more stable and enduring the relationship the more likely its continuance will accord with his best interests. Section 1(8)(a) puts beyond doubt that for the purposes of s 1, relationships are not confined to legal relationships, hence consideration must be given to the child's relationships with his wider social family as well as his birth family. In the latter context, s 1(8)(b) includes within 'relative' the child's mother and father, in addition to those listed in the Act's general meaning of relative, ie, a grandparent, brother, sister, uncle or aunt, whether of the full blood or half blood or by marriage or civil partnership (see s 144(1) as amended).

Section 1(4)(f) gives more emphasis to existing family relationships than does CA 1989, s 1(3), in view of the termination of those relationships that will largely follow from adoption, which is not the case in proceedings under the 1989 Act, being concerned, as they are, with entitlement to exercise certain aspects of parental responsibility. Hence, the wishes and feelings of the child's family regarding the child are included in the s 1(4)(f) factors, which they are not in the CA 1989, s 1(3) checklist.

In having regard to the child's existing relationships with his family, as widely defined, s 1(4)(f) requires consideration to be given to, inter alia, the likelihood of any such relationship continuing and the value to the child of its doing so; the ability and willingness of the wider family to meet the child's needs and provide him with a secure environment in which he can develop; and their wishes and feelings regarding the child. Hence, the court and adoption agency must have regard to whether the child's existing family are able to meet the child's right to a family life which is secure and will meet his developmental needs. Courts and adoption agencies will need to pay particular regard to existing sibling relationships, the value to the child of such relationship continuing, and how this can be achieved if the child's placement for adoption separates him from a sibling or siblings. How far is such separation an interference with the child's right to respect for family life within art 8 of the European Convention on Human Rights? What are the alternatives bearing in mind, as the court or agency must, the whole range of powers available to it in the child's case, whether under the ACA 2002 or the CA 1989, as required by the ACA 2002, s 1(6)? The termination of parenthood and parental responsibility is a serious interference with the right to family life that requires considerable justification. The proposed adoption must be necessary and proportionate in accordance with art 8(2), such that the child's best interests cannot be served by some alternative action which maintains the child's existing links with his family, see for example *Re B (a child)(adoption order)* [2001] EWCA Civ 347, [2001] 2 FCR 89.

Section 1(5)—due consideration of the child's background when agency places a child for adoption

[113]

The particular child's religious persuasion, racial origin, cultural and linguistic background will, as seen, be relevant considerations when the court or adoption agency is making *any* decision relating to adoption, as required by s 1(4)(d). These factors are given specific significance, in terms of 'due consideration', by s 1(5), when the agency is placing the child for adoption. They are modelled on the duty which CA 1989, s 22(5)(c) places on a local authority looking after (or proposing to look after) a child, before they make any decision, including placement, with respect to the child. Their significance is that much greater in adoption where placement decisions have potentially lifelong implications and particularly where international adoption is being considered if there is to be any change of religious, ethnic or cultural upbringing. The factors must be given due consideration, however, in the overall context of s 1 principles, including paramountcy of the child's welfare and avoidance of delay (see also *National Adoption Standards*, A.8 and 9).

There is a strong case, but not a rule, for ensuring that those with whom a child is placed are of the same, or similar, religious persuasion and ethnic origin as the child so as to meet the child's needs, regarding his cultural identity. Consideration must be paid, however to all the needs of the child. As the courts have made clear, prior to the ACA 2002, agencies are concerned with the welfare of the individual child, which is of course now paramount, and the child's best interest must not be obscured by the unquestioning application of any general social policy, see *Re N(a minor)(adoption)* [1990] FCR 241; *Re P(a minor)* [1990] 1 FLR 96; *Re JK (adoption: transracial placement)* [1990] FCR 87; *R v Lancashire County Council* [1992] 1 FCR 28. Government guidance, in response to the doctrinaire approach sometimes followed, also made clear that 'it is unacceptable for a child to be denied loving adoptive parents solely on the grounds that the child and adopters do not share the same racial or cultural background' (Local Authority Circular (98) 20 'Adoption – Achieving the Right Balance', para 14).

Adoption agencies should be particularly careful in placing the child for adoption that the prospective adopters appreciate the additional responsibilities and difficulties which absorption into a different cultural environment may create. Where, as in *Re C (adoption: religious observance)* [2002] 1 FLR 1119, a child's heritage is very mixed, it will rarely be possible for it all to be reflected in the placement. It may be in the child's best interests to be placed in a family where only one strand of the heritage is reflected, provided that the prospective adopters are sufficiently sensitive to help the child understand and take pride in all elements of his heritage.

Section 1(6)—range of powers available to the agency or court and no order unless better for the child

[114]

Section 1(6) contains two distinct but related principles which are similar to those in the CA 1989, s 1(3)(g) and 1(5). The first applies to the court or adoption agency, the second applies additionally to the court. Both impose a duty.

The first requires that the court and adoption agency *always* consider the whole range of powers available to it, and is modelled on the court's duty in the CA 1989, s 1(3)(g). Courts and agencies must not confine themselves to the range of powers (and orders) in the ACA 2002 and must also consider those in the CA 1989, in deciding which powers and orders (if any) are in the child's best interests. So the court will need to be mindful of the menu of orders available to it. For example, to make a residence order under the CA 1989, ss 8 and 10(1)(b) (coupled, if appropriate, with a restriction under s 91(14)), or a special guardianship order under s 14A(6)(b), see para **[705]**, if it is felt that maintaining relationships with the child's birth family (see s 1(4)(c) and (f)) would better secure the child's best interests than adoption, as for example in the pre-ACA 2002 case *Re M (a minor)(adoption or residence order)* [1998] 1 FCR 165. The paramount consideration must of course be the child's welfare throughout his life in accordance with ACA 2002, s 1(2). The case for an alternative to adoption better serving the child's interests may be particularly strong if the proposed adopter is a relative of the child, in view of the potential distortion of family relationships that such an adoption will produce. Step-parents have the option under the ACA 2002, s 112 amendment to the CA 1989 (see s 4A as amended by the Civil Partnership Act 2004, s 75 and para **[702]**) of entering a parental responsibility agreement or applying for a parental responsibility order.

Many children are adopted having been looked after by a local authority in accordance with the Children Act 1989, s 22. In chapter 5 of the White Paper, *Adoption A New Approach*, the Government set out the changes it proposed to make to achieve permanence for looked after children, including, at p 27, 'establishing a full range of options for permanent families' and identified either the child returning home to the birth parents, or where the birth parents are unable to look after the child, long term local authority foster care; informal care; residence orders; special guardianship and adoption. 'Under the Children Act 1989, the first duty of local social services authorities, where children cannot live with their birth parents, is to seek a home for them with their extended family. Finding a safe and caring new home for children with their wider family or friends allows them to keep important attachments and connections in their lives, and is therefore the preferred choice where it is possible and consistent with the child's welfare', para 5.4. It accords also with the right to respect for private and family life in art 8(1) of the European Convention on Human Rights. If the balance between adoption and an alternative is equal, the least interventionist approach should be followed so as to accord with art 8. As Bainham puts it, 'if another alternative will equally well serve the child's interests, adoption would be an unnecessary and disproportionate response and would violate both the Convention rights of the child and those of the parent' (*Children – the Modern Law* (3rd edn) p 294).

PART B – Statutes

Linked to the least interventionist approach when the court has regard to the whole range of powers and orders at its disposal, is the second principle in s 1(6), which is similar to that in CA 1989, s 1(5). It directs the court not to make any order under the ACA 2002, unless it considers that doing so would be better for the child than not doing so. It should be noted that if, after considering the whole range of powers available to it, the court is proposing not to make an order under the ACA 2002, but instead make one under the CA 1989, it must apply the corresponding principle in CA 1989, s 1(5).

The, what might be called 'no-order unless better for the child principle' in s 1(6) requires the court to be satisfied that the making of an ACA 2002 order will improve things for the child. Hence, the burden is on the applicant to establish that it is in the child's best interests, as required by s 1(2), that an order under the 2002 Act should be made. As the Court of Appeal held in *G (children)* [2005] EWCA Civ 1283, [2006] 1 FLR 771 in the context of the CA 1989, s 1(5), the principle raises no presumption, but merely demands that the court ask whether the making of an order would be better for the child than making no order? In asking itself that question, one difference from CA 1989 cases is that the court must have regard to the potentially lifelong effect of orders under the ACA 2002 in comparison to those under the 1989 Act. Applying both principles in s 1(6), as the court must, should enable it to determine whether making an order will be better for the child, and if so, then in light of the whole range of its powers, which order is the necessary and proportionate one which best accords with the child's welfare.

Section 1(7)

[115]

This subsection elaborates upon what is meant by a court coming to a decision relating to the adoption of a child and was considered in the context of the scope of s 1 (see s 1(1) and para [103]).

Section 1(8)

[116]

This subsection elaborates upon the meaning of references to 'relationships' and 'a relative, in relation to a child' for the purposes of s 1 and was considered in the context of s 1(4)(f) of the welfare checklist where the references appear (see para [112])

[117]

> ## Chapter 2
> ## The Adoption Service
>
> ### The Adoption Service
>
> #### 2 Basic definitions
>
> (1) The services maintained by local authorities under section 3(1) may be collectively referred to as 'the Adoption Service', and a local authority or registered adoption society may be referred to as an adoption agency.
>
> (2) In this Act, 'registered adoption society' means a voluntary organisation which is an adoption society registered under Part 2 of the Care Standards Act 2000 (c 14); but in relation to the provision of any facility of the Adoption Service, references to a registered adoption society or to an adoption agency do not include an adoption society which is not registered in respect of that facility.
>
> (3) A registered adoption society is to be treated as registered in respect of any facility of the Adoption Service unless it is a condition of its registration that it does not provide that facility.

(4) No application for registration under Part 2 of the Care Standards Act 2000 may be made in respect of an adoption society which is an unincorporated body.

(5) In this Act—

'the 1989 Act' means the Children Act 1989 (c 41),

'adoption society' means a body whose functions consist of or include making arrangements for the adoption of children,

'voluntary organisation' means a body other than a public or local authority the activities of which are not carried on for profit.

(6) In this Act, 'adoption support services' means—

(a) counselling, advice and information, and
(b) any other services prescribed by regulations,

in relation to adoption.

(7) The power to make regulations under subsection (6)(b) is to be exercised so as to secure that local authorities provide financial support.

(8) In this Chapter, references to adoption are to the adoption of persons, wherever they may be habitually resident, effected under the law of any country or territory, whether within or outside the British Islands.

NOTES

Initial Commencement

To be appointed

Sub-ss (1)–(5), (7), (8): to be appointed: see s 148(1), (2); sub-s (6): to be appointed: see s 148(6).

Appointment

Sub-ss (1)–(5): appointment: 7 December 2004: see SI 2004/3203, art 2(1)(a); sub-ss (6)–(8): appointment (in relation to England in so far as relating to Sch 4, para 3 hereto for the purposes of making regulations): 10 March 2003: see SI 2003/366, art 2(2)(b); sub-ss (6)–(8): appointment (in relation to England in so far as relating to Sch 4, para 3 hereto for remaining purposes): 6 October 2003: see SI 2003/366, art 2(6)(b); sub-s (6): appointment (in relation to Wales): 7 February 2004: see SI 2004/252, art 2(a); sub-ss (6)–(8): appointment (in relation to England for remaining purposes): 7 December 2004: see SI 2004/3203, art 2(1)(a); sub-ss (7), (8): appointment (in relation to Wales in so far as relating to Sch 4, para 3 hereto): 28 November 2003: see SI 2003/3079, art 2(1)(a); sub-ss (7), (8): appointment (in relation to Wales for remaining purposes): 7 December 2004: see SI 2004/3203, art 2(1)(a).

Extent

This section does not extend to Scotland: see s 149(2).

Subordinate Legislation

Adoption Support Services Regulations 2005, SI 2005/691 (made under sub-ss (6), (7)); Adoption Information and Intermediary Services (Pre-Commencement Adoptions) Regulations 2005, SI 2005/890 (made under sub-s (6)); Adoption Support Services (Local Authorities) (Wales) Regulations 2005, SI 2005/1512 (made under sub-ss (6)(b), (7)); Adoption Support Agencies (Wales) Regulations 2005, SI 2005/1514 (made under sub-s (6)(b)); Adoption Information and Intermediary Services (Pre-Commencement Adoptions) (Wales) Regulations 2005, SI 2005/2701 (made under sub-s (6)); Adoption Support Agencies (England) and Adoption Agencies (Miscellaneous Amendments) Regulations 2005, SI 2005/2720 (made under sub-s (6)(b)); Adoption Information and Intermediary Services (Pre-Commencement Adoptions) (Wales) (Amendment) Regulations 2005, SI 2005/3293 (made under sub-s (6)).

General

[118]

This Section should be read in conjunction with s 144 (general interpretation, etc) and s 147, together with Sch 6 (glossary), in providing definitions of words and phrases in the Act.

'Adoption', for the purposes of Chapter 2 only (ss 2–17), is widely defined as including the adoption of persons irrespective of their habitual residence and under the law of any country (s 2(8)).

An 'adoption agency' is either a local authority or a registered adoption society (s 2(1)).

'the Adoption Service' refers collectively to the services maintained by a local authority under the duties created by s 3(1): namely the services designed to meet the needs, in relation to adoption, of children who may be adopted and their parents and guardians, of those wishing to adopt, and of adopted persons and their adoptive parents, natural parents and guardians (s 2(1)). These services include arrangements for the adoption of children, and 'adoption support services' (see below) (s 3(2)).

An 'adoption society' is any body that wholly or partly makes arrangements for the adoption of children (s 2(5)).

'Adoption support services' are defined in s 2(6)(a) and (i) for England in the Adoption Support Services Regulations 2005 (SI 2005/691) (ASSR), as amended by the Adoption Support Agencies (England) and Adoption Agencies (Miscellaneous Amendments) Regulations 2005 (SI 2005/2720) (ASAEAAMAR), and (ii) for Wales in the Adoption Support Services (Local Authorities) (Wales) Regulations 2005 (SI 2005/1512) (ASSLAWR) and the Adoption Support Agencies (Wales) Regulations 2005 (SI 2005/1514) (ASAWR). The enabling power is s 2(6)(b). Other than financial support, they can include services provided in the context of the adoption of a child by a natural parent or his/her partner (ASSR, reg 3(2), and ASAEAAMAR, reg 3(1)(a)/ASAWR, reg 2 and ASSLAWR, regs 3, 4 and the definition of 'adoptive parent' in reg 2).

Adoption support services comprise:

- Assistance, (including, in England, mediation), regarding contact between an adoptive child and his/her natural family, 'related person', or former guardian (ASSR, reg 3(1)(c)/ASSLAWR, reg 3 and ASAWR, reg 2). A 'related person' means a 'relative' within the meaning of s 144(1) or a person who seems to the local authority to have a beneficial relationship with the child having regard to the matters in s 1(4)(f)(i)–(iii).

  In England, assistance can be given in cash (ASSR, reg 3(3)).

- Assistance to maintain the relationship of an adoptive child with the adoptive parent(s), including training of those parents to meet the child's special needs, and respite care, (in England, respite care can only be provided if such accommodation is provided either by or on behalf of a local authority under CA 1989, s 23 or by a voluntary organisation under CA 1989, s 59) (ASSR, reg 3(1)(e) and 3(4)/ASSLAWR, reg 3). In England, assistance can be given in cash (ASSR, reg 3(3)).

- In both England and Wales, assistance to adult adopted persons or their 'relatives' to facilitate contact between the adopted person and such relatives. 'Relatives' for this purpose means anyone *but for the adoption* who would be related by blood, half-blood, marriage or civil partnership (ASAEAAMAR, reg 3(1)(c)/ASAWR, reg 2(2)(e) and (f)).

- In Wales only, this assistance can be extended to helping them obtain information about the adoption. Part 3 of the ASAWR provides a procedure for such requests for help in Wales. The provision of these particular services is discretionary, even if the agency has commenced provision, and before deciding to provide such a service the agency must have regard to the welfare of the person requesting the service, any reg 13 veto (see below) and any information on the Adoption Contact Register (see the notes to ss 80, paras [386]–[390] and 81, para [392]) (ASAWR, reg 11). The agency must not help to find a person under the age of 18 unless there are exceptional circumstances, a person with parental responsibility for the child has given consent, and either the child is competent and has consented, or, if not, his/her wishes and feelings have been taken into account.

- In Wales, there is a veto on the provision of services under reg 2(2)(e) or (f) if the subject is either (i) the adopted person, or (ii) a relative of the adopted person and that relative has informed the agency in writing that he/she does not wish to be contacted by the agency at all, or only by named persons or in specified circumstances (ASAWR, reg 13). An agency must then not disclose 'identifying information' (ie capable on its own, or with other information held by the person making the request, of enabling that person to identify and trace the subject) without consent, and must take all reasonable steps to ensure that enough information is given to the subject to enable an informed choice to be made. If the subject has died or lacks capacity, the agency has a discretion to disclose identifying information about the subject, after taking account of the welfare of those who might be affected by disclosure. This may involve eliciting their views (ASAWR, reg 12). The agency, despite any veto, refusal of consent or inability to obtain consent, can disclose such non-identifying information as it considers appropriate (ASAWR, reg 14).

- If a person in Wales requests adoption support services under reg 2(2)(e) or (f), the agency must provide written information about counselling, to the person making the request and to the person considering whether to consent to the disclosure of information. The agency must then provide it upon request, either directly or through another registered provider, and must provide support to a person if he/she is considering whether to pay a fee for the counselling (ASAWR, reg 15).

- In England only, assistance to adoption agencies to prepare and train adoptive parents (ASAEAAMAR, reg 3(1)(b)).

- Assistance where an adoptive placement, or adoption arrangement following an adoption order, has disrupted or is in danger of disrupting. This can include mediation and arranging and running 'disruption meetings' (ASSR, reg 3(1)(f)/ ASSLAWR, reg 3 and ASAWR, reg 2). In England only, assistance can be given in cash (ASSR, reg 3(3)).

- Counselling, advice and information (s 2(6)(a)).

- Financial support payable under ASSR, regs 8–12 or ASSLAWR, regs 11–14 (ASSR, reg 3(1)(a)/ASSLAWR, reg 3) (see note to s 3, para **[123]**).

- Services to enable groups of adoptive children, adoptive parents and the natural parents (or, in England, former guardian) of the child to discuss matters relating to adoption (ASSR, reg 3(1)(b)/ASSLAWR, reg 3). In England only, assistance can be given in cash (ASSR, reg 3(3)).

- Therapeutic services for an adoptive child (ASSR, reg 3(1)(d)/ASAWR, reg 2). In England only, assistance can be given in cash (ASSR, reg 3(3)).

The '1989 Act' is the Children Act 1989 (s 2(5)).

A 'registered adoption agency' is (with minor exceptions) a voluntary organisation operating as an adoption society and registered under the Care Standards Act 2000, Pt 2 (s 2(2)). For any facility of an Adoption Service it is to be treated as registered unless prohibited by its terms of registration (s 2(3)).

A 'voluntary organisation' cannot be a local authority or public body, and is one where the activities are not carried on for profit (s 2(5)).

[119]

3 Maintenance of Adoption Service

(1) Each local authority must continue to maintain within their area a service designed to meet the needs, in relation to adoption, of—

(a) children who may be adopted, their parents and guardians,

(b)   persons wishing to adopt a child, and
(c)   adopted persons, their parents, natural parents and former guardians;

and for that purpose must provide the requisite facilities.

(2)   Those facilities must include making, and participating in, arrangements—

(a)   for the adoption of children, and
(b)   for the provision of adoption support services.

(3)   As part of the service, the arrangements made for the purposes of subsection (2)(b)—

(a)   must extend to the provision of adoption support services to persons who are within a description prescribed by regulations,
(b)   may extend to the provision of those services to other persons.

(4)   A local authority may provide any of the requisite facilities by securing their provision by—

(a)   registered adoption societies, or
(b)   other persons who are within a description prescribed by regulations of persons who may provide the facilities in question.

(5)   The facilities of the service must be provided in conjunction with the local authority's other social services and with registered adoption societies in their area, so that help may be given in a co-ordinated manner without duplication, omission or avoidable delay.
(6)   The social services referred to in subsection (5) are the functions of a local authority which are social services functions within the meaning of the Local Authority Social Services Act 1970 (c 42) (which include, in particular, those functions in so far as they relate to children).

NOTES

Initial Commencement

To be appointed
Sub-ss (1), (2), (5), (6): to be appointed: see s 148(1), (2); sub-ss (3), (4): to be appointed: see s 148(6).

Appointment
Sub-ss (1), (2), (5), (6): appointment: 30 December 2005: see SI 2005/2213, art 2(b); sub-ss (3), (4): appointment (in relation to England for the purpose of making regulations): 7 December 2004: see SI 2004/3203, art 2(1)(m)(i); sub-ss (3), (4): appointment (in relation to Wales): 6 June 2005: see SI 2005/1206, art 2; sub-ss (3), (4): appointment (in relation to England for remaining purposes): 30 December 2005: see SI 2005/2213, art 3(a).

Extent
This section does not extend to Scotland: see s 149(2).

Subordinate Legislation
Adoption Support Services Regulations 2005, SI 2005/691 (made under sub-ss (3), (4)); Adoption Support Services (Local Authorities) (Wales) Regulations 2005, SI 2005/1512 (made under sub-ss (3), (4)(b)); Local Authority (Adoption) (Miscellaneous Provisions) Regulations 2005, SI 2005/3390 (made under sub-s (4)(b)); Adoption and Children (Miscellaneous Amendments) Regulations 2005, SI 2005/3482 (made under sub-s (4)(b)).

General

[120]

This section creates a duty for a local authority to maintain an adoption service, including facilities. Those facilities must include adoption support services. See the note to s 2 (para [118]) for the scope of adoption support services. Section 3, with the relevant Regulations – summarised below – sets out the powers and duties in relation to adoption support services. There is a duty to extend such provision to defined persons, and a power in relation to others.

Adoption Guidance; Chapter 9 [2005] DfES/*Adoption Agencies (Wales) Regulations Guidance* [April 2006] National Assembly for Wales, and *Adoption Support Agencies: National Minimum Standards (England)* [2005] DfES/*Adoption Support Services (Local Authorities) (Wales) Regulations 2005 Guidance* [April 2006] National Assembly for Wales, set out important guidance and requirements in relation to such adoption support services and adoption services.

Section 3(1)

[121]

Each local authority must maintain an 'Adoption Service' (see s 2(1) for definition), to meet the needs, regarding adoption, of children who may be adopted and their parents and guardians, those who wish to adopt, and adopted persons and their adoptive parents, natural parents and former guardians. The local authority must, to that end, 'provide the requisite facilities'.

Section 3(2)

[122]

Those facilities must include making and participating in arrangements for children to be adopted, and the provision of 'adoption support services' (see note to s 2, para [118], for definition of 'adoption support services').

Section 3(3)

[123]

There is a duty to make arrangements to extend the provision of 'adoption support services' to those prescribed by Regulations, and a discretion to make arrangements to provide them to others. See the note to s 2, para [118], for the definition of 'adoption support services'.

In Wales, it is made explicit that the arrangements must be made available to the relevant groups of people, irrespective of whether a service is provided for a particular person (Adoption Support Services (Local Authorities) (Wales) Regulations 2005 (SI 2005/1512) (ASSLAWR), reg 4(8)).

The Adoption Support Services Regulations 2005 (SI 2005/691) (ASSR), reg 4 and the ASSLAWR, reg 4, define those to whom a duty to have arrangements in place is owed, as follows:

> Counselling, advice and information must be extended to children who might be adopted, and their parents and guardians; those wishing to adopt; adopted persons, their adoptive parents, natural parents and former guardians; the children of adoptive parents (for clarity, in England this is confirmed as meaning irrespective of whether they are adopted); the natural full- or half-siblings of adoptive children (ASSR, reg 4(2) and ASSLAWR, reg 4(2)); and (in England only) 'related persons' regarding adoptive children (see note to s 2, para [118], for wide definition of 'related persons') (ASSR, reg 4(2)).

In England, the duty to extend financial support is confined to an adoptive parent of an 'agency adoptive child' (defined by ASSR, reg 2 as either a child adopted after being placed by the agency, a child whom the agency has matched with a prospective adopter or placed for adoption, or a child whose adoptive parent was a local authority foster-parent (as defined in the CA 1989) where the authority does not oppose the adoption (ASSR, reg 4(3)).

In Wales, arrangements must be in place for financial support for adoptive parents of adoptive children, which specifically includes both agency and non-agency placements, other than adoptions by parents or step-parents (ASSLAWR, regs 4(3) and 2(1)).

In England, it is a pre-requisite for financial support that it is payable to the adoptive parent for the purpose of either supporting the placement of the child, or the 'continuation of adoption arrangements' after the child is adopted (ASSR, reg 8(1)).

In England, 'adoptive child' is a wider definition than 'adopted child'. It means either a child who has been adopted, a child in respect of whom the prospective adopter has given notice under s 44, or a child matched, or placed, with prospective adopters with a view to adoption (ASSR, reg 2(1)). A child is 'matched' if an adoption agency 'is considering placing the child for adoption with that person' (ASSR, reg 2(3)). In Wales, an 'adoptive child' means both agency and non-agency adoptive children, and for agency children means from the point of match by the agency, and for non-agency children from the point of s 44 notice being given and subsequently through to, and after, being adopted (provided this is not by a parent or step-parent) (ASSLAWR, reg 2(1)).

In both countries, for the purposes of financial support the definition is extended to the conclusion of relevant education and training even after the age of 18 (ASSR, reg 2(2)/ ASSLAWR, reg 2(3)).

An 'adoptive parent' is a person who has adopted a child, or has give notice of intention to adopt under s 44, or with whom an adoption agency has matched a child or placed the child for adoption (but in Wales excludes natural parents and step-parents)(ASSR, reg 2(1)/ ASSLAWR, reg 2(1)).

The circumstances in which financial support is payable to adoptive parents are as follows:

- In England, where it is necessary to ensure the adoptive parent can look after the child; where the child has special care needs requiring 'greater expenditure of resources', arising from disability, illness, emotional or behavioural difficulties, or the consequences of past abuse/neglect; where special arrangements are needed to facilitate the placement, linked to the child's age, ethnic origins, or desirability of being placed with a sibling (or other child with whom he/she has shared a home); recurring costs in relation to travel for contact; and a 'contribution', at the authority's discretion, towards the legal costs of the adopters, the costs of introductions, or accommodation/maintenance costs for the child (ASSR, reg 8). Payments can be as a lump sum, if necessary in instalments, or in periodic payments if expenditure is likely to recur (ASSR, reg 10). Periodic payments are contingent upon the adoptive parent agreeing to conditions concerning notification of changes in circumstances and the provision of an annual statement to the authority, while any financial support (lump sum or periodic) can be subject to other conditions that the authority may consider appropriate (ASSR, reg 12).

  Chapter 9, *Adoption Guidance* [2005] DfES, reminds English local authorities that they are not obliged to fund the legal costs of non-agency adoption applications, nor of ones that they oppose where the child was previously looked after. In this context, local authorities are advised to refer them for legal advice and consideration of Legal Services Commission (LSC) funding.

  That Guidance also requires English local authorities to 'have regard to' the fostering allowance that would have been paid if the child were fostered instead of being adopted, when considering what financial support to provide, with a general presumption that this 'core allowance', together with any additional amount paid because of that child's specific needs, will be the maximum that the authority could consider paying by way of adoption support. It is important to distinguish between fostering allowances and any fees containing a reward element that may be paid by individual authorities (see below in relation to existing foster-carers). See also the recently-published DfES Guidance: *The National Minimum Fostering Allowance and Fostering Payment Systems* [July 2006] concerning the recommended minimum fostering allowances for children who are looked after.

Financial support can be suspended or terminated for breach of conditions (ASSR, reg 12(3) and (4)) and comes to an end when the child either qualifies for income-support or job-seeker's allowance in his/her own right, reaches 18 (unless in full-time education or training), finishes such education/training, or ceases to live with the adoptive parent (ASSR, reg 11).

Such financial support cannot involve any element of remuneration, unless the adoptive parent has been a local authority foster-parent for the child, those fostering payments already included an element of remuneration, the decision to include an element of remuneration for the adoption is made prior to the child being adopted, and the authority considers that such payments are 'necessary to facilitate the adoption'. Even so, the remuneration element must cease after two years from the date of adoption, unless the authority considers that such payments must continue due to 'the exceptional needs of the child or any other exceptional circumstances' (ASSR, reg 9). *Adoption Guidance*, Ch 9 [2005] DfES, states that the 'purpose of the two-year transitional provision is to enable local authorities to maintain payments to foster parents who go on to adopt, at the same rate as they received when they were fostering the child. This is intended to give the family time to adjust to their new circumstances'.

- In Wales, in one or more of the following circumstances: where financial support is necessary to ensure that the adoptive parent (whether agency or non-agency) can look after the child; where the child has been adopted and financial support is needed to ensure he/she continues to look after the child; where the child has a 'strong and important relationship' with the adoptive parent prior to the adoption; to enable the child to live with a sibling or a child with whom he/she previously shared a home; where the child needs special care requiring greater expenditure than average (for a wide variety of reasons); and where special arrangements have to be made to facilitate the placement due to the child's age, gender or ethnic origin. Before any financial help can be given, the adoptive parents have to agree certain conditions concerning annual financial statements and notification of changes in circumstances (ASSLAWR, reg 11).

A Welsh Authority, before making a decision on financial support for the following purposes, must have regard to any adoption panel recommendations and a financial assessment of the adoptive parent(s) and child, and it must exclude any benefits that they could claim: legal costs in relation to the adoption (but see below); the cost of accommodating the child, including furniture, equipment, adaptations to the home, transport, clothing and toys; damage to the home arising from special behavioural difficulties; costs arising from any of the child's special needs; and travel costs if the child has contact (ASSLAWR, reg 12(2), (4) and (6)). However, if the child is looked after, the local authority supports the adoption and the application is opposed, the authority cannot means-test the financial support for the legal costs. Nor can the agency means-test for expenditure connected to the child's introductions (ASSLAWR, reg 12(2), (5) and (6)).

In Wales, the financial adoption support cannot include any element of reward, unless the adoptive parent was formerly a foster-carer for that child, fostering payments will cease, the agency has approved the match, and the decision to make periodic payments is made prior to the child being adopted. These payments can

PART B – Statutes

continue until two years after the adoption, or for longer in certain circumstances as long as those circumstances existed at the time of the original decision to pay financial support. Those circumstances are: in both agency and non-agency placements, where the financial help is 'necessary' to ensure that the child can be looked after; where the child will live with a sibling or another child with whom he/she previously lived; where the child requires greater than average expenditure due to special needs; or where special arrangements are needed, due to age, gender or ethnicity, to enable the child to be placed. Unlike in England, there is no requirement, for payment beyond a period of two years, of 'exceptional' needs of the child or circumstances (ASSLAWR, reg 13(8), (9) and (10)). The *Adoption Agencies (Wales) Regulations 2005 Guidance* [April 2006] Welsh Assembly (para 73) suggests that the two-year 'transitional' period is 'intended to give the family time to adjust to their new circumstances', and it is silent on cases where such a reward element may be paid for over two years.

The financial support in Wales can be a lump sum or in periodic payments, which may be with conditions, and the support must be reviewed at least annually. There is a power to vary, suspend or terminate this support, and to recover past payments in certain circumstances. Support must end when the child leave home, reaches the age of 18 (unless in full-time education or training), or starts work or claims income support or job-seeker's allowance (ASSLAWR, regs 13 and 17).

The duty to provide services to enable discussions to take place on adoption matters (see note to s 2, para [118]) is confined to agency adoptive children, an adoptive parent of such a child and the natural parents (or, in England, former guardians) of such children (ASSR, reg 4(4)/ASSLAWR, reg 4(4)).

The duty to provide assistance in relation to contact (see note to s 2, para [118]) is owed to agency adoptive children, an adoptive parent of such a child, the natural parents, former guardians, natural full- and half-siblings of the child (in England), and 'related persons' regarding the child of agency adoptive children (see note to s 2, para [118], for wide definition of 'related person', so the Welsh Regulations cover siblings in any event) (ASSR, reg 4(5)/ASSLAWR, reg 4(5)).

The duty to provide therapeutic services (see note to s 2, para [118]) is confined to agency adoptive children, adoptive children subject to s 83 restrictions (children being brought into the UK) and adoptive children in the context of Convention adoptions (ASSR, reg 4(6)/ASSLAWR, reg 4(6)). The duty to provide assistance intended to maintain a relationship between an adoptive child and adoptive parent, and assistance in the context of actual or imminent disruption, is owed to this same group of children, and also to the adoptive parents of such children and their own children (in England, this explicitly covers whether or not they are adopted) (ASSR, reg 4(7)/ASSLAWR, reg 4(7)).

The local authority can provide its own adoption services facilities, or arrange for either a registered adoption society (see note to s 2, para [118], for definition) or another prescribed person to provide them (sub-s (4)). This can be another local authority, Local Health Board, (in Wales, an NHS Trust), a Primary Care Trust, local education authority or a 'registered adoption support agency' (meaning a person registered under the Care Standards Act 2000, Pt 2) (ASSR, reg 5/ASSLAWR, reg 5).

Even where there is only a discretion to provide adoption support services, this means that the agency can choose to do so, for example, 'to prevent disruption' of the child's existing placement (*Adoption Guidance*, Ch 9 [2005] DfES).

Section 3(5) and (6)

[124]

The provision of adoption services must be coordinated with the other social services functions (especially those relating to children) of the local authority and any registered adoption societies in its area, so as to coordinate 'help' in a way avoiding duplication, omissions or delay. 'Social services functions' are widely defined in the Local Authority Social Services Act 1970 for this purpose.

[125]

4 Assessments etc for adoption support services

(1) A local authority must at the request of—

(a) any of the persons mentioned in paragraphs (a) to (c) of section 3(1), or

(b) any other person who falls within a description prescribed by regulations (subject to subsection (7)(a)),

carry out an assessment of that person's needs for adoption support services.

(2) A local authority may, at the request of any person, carry out an assessment of that person's needs for adoption support services.

(3) A local authority may request the help of the persons mentioned in paragraph (a) or (b) of section 3(4) in carrying out an assessment.

(4) Where, as a result of an assessment, a local authority decide that a person has needs for adoption support services, they must then decide whether to provide any such services to that person.

(5) If—

(a) a local authority decide to provide any adoption support services to a person, and

(b) the circumstances fall within a description prescribed by regulations,

the local authority must prepare a plan in accordance with which adoption support services are to be provided to the person and keep the plan under review.

(6) Regulations may make provision about assessments, preparing and reviewing plans, the provision of adoption support services in accordance with plans and reviewing the provision of adoption support services.

(7) The regulations may in particular make provision—

(a) as to the circumstances in which a person mentioned in paragraph (b) of subsection (1) is to have a right to request an assessment of his needs in accordance with that subsection,

(b) about the type of assessment which, or the way in which an assessment, is to be carried out,

(c) about the way in which a plan is to be prepared,

(d) about the way in which, and time at which, a plan or the provision of adoption support services is to be reviewed,

(e) about the considerations to which a local authority are to have regard in carrying out an assessment or review or preparing a plan,

(f) as to the circumstances in which a local authority may provide adoption support services subject to conditions,

(g) as to the consequences of conditions imposed by virtue of paragraph (f) not being met (including the recovery of any financial support provided by a local authority),

(h) as to the circumstances in which this section may apply to a local authority in respect of persons who are outside that local authority's area,

(i) as to the circumstances in which a local authority may recover from another local authority the expenses of providing adoption support services to any person.

(8) A local authority may carry out an assessment of the needs of any person under this section at the same time as an assessment of his needs is made under any other enactment.

(9) If at any time during the assessment of the needs of any person under this section, it appears to a local authority that—

(a)   there may be a need for the provision of services to that person by a Primary Care Trust (in Wales, a Health Authority or Local Health Board), or

(b)   there may be a need for the provision to him of any services which fall within the functions of a local education authority (within the meaning of the Education Act 1996 (c 56)),

the local authority must notify that Primary Care Trust, Health Authority, Local Health Board or local education authority.

(10)   Where it appears to a local authority that another local authority could, by taking any specified action, help in the exercise of any of their functions under this section, they may request the help of that other local authority, specifying the action in question.

(11)   A local authority whose help is so requested must comply with the request if it is consistent with the exercise of their functions.

NOTES

Initial Commencement

To be appointed
To be appointed: see s 148(6).

Appointment
Sub-s (1)(a): appointment (in relation to England): 30 December 2005: see SI 2005/2213, art 3(b); sub-s (1)(a): appointment (in relation to Wales): 30 December 2005: see SI 2005/3112, art 2(a); sub-ss (1)(b), (5): appointment (in relation to Wales for the purpose of making regulations): 7 February 2004: see SI 2004/252, art 2(c); sub-ss (1)(b), (5): appointment (in relation to England for the purpose of making regulations): 7 December 2004: see SI 2004/3203, art 2(1)(m)(i); sub-ss (1)(b), (5): appointment (in relation to England for remaining purposes): 30 December 2005: see SI 2005/2213, art 3(b); sub-ss (1)(b), (5): appointment (in relation to Wales, for remaining purposes): 30 December 2005: see SI 2005/3112, art 2(a); sub-ss (2)–(4): appointment (in relation to England): 30 December 2005: see SI 2005/2213, art 3(b); sub-ss (2)–(4): appointment (in relation to Wales): 30 December 2005: see SI 2005/3112, art 2(a); sub-ss (6), (7)(b)–(i): appointment (in relation to England in so far as relating to Sch 4, para 3 hereto for the purposes of making regulations): 10 March 2003: see SI 2003/366, art 2(2)(b); sub-ss (6), (7)(b)–(i): appointment (in relation to England in so far as relating to Sch 4, para 3 hereto for remaining purposes): 6 October 2003: see SI 2003/366, art 2(6)(b); sub-ss (6), (7): appointment (in relation to Wales): 7 February 2004: see SI 2004/252, art 2(b); sub-ss (6), (7)(b)–(i): appointment (in relation to England for remaining purposes): 7 December 2004: see SI 2004/3203, art 2(1)(b); sub-s (7)(a): appointment (in relation to England): 7 December 2004: see SI 2004/3203, art 2(1)(b); sub-ss (8)–(11): appointment (in relation to England): 30 December 2005: see SI 2005/2213, art 3(b); sub-ss (8)–(11): appointment (in relation to Wales): 30 December 2005: see SI 2005/3112, art 2(a).

Extent
This section does not extend to Scotland: see s 149(2).

Subordinate Legislation
Adoption Support Services Regulations 2005, SI 2005/691; Adoption Support Services (Local Authorities) (Wales) Regulations 2005, SI 2005/1512 (made under sub-ss (1)(b), (5)(b), (6), (7)).

General

[126]

This section, with the accompanying regulations (Adoption Support Services Regulations 2005 (SI 2005/691) and Adoption Support Services (Local Authorities) (Wales) Regulations 2005 (SI 2005/1512)), provides for assessments for adoption support services, plans for such services and the provision of adoption support services, including financial support, together with the variation and termination of support. See the note to s 2, para [118], for the definition of adoption support services and that to s 3, para [123], for those categories of persons to whom such services may or must be provided.

Section 4(1) and (2)

[127]

Local authorities have a duty, on request, to assess some persons for their needs for adoption support services; in relation to other persons, they have a discretion to do so.

The local authority must appoint an adoption support services adviser (at least one in Wales) (ASSR, reg 6/ASSLAWR, reg 6). His/her powers and duties are defined in those regulations, and are more extensive in England as far as they concern the adviser assisting other local authorities.

There is a duty to carry out such an assessment for children who may be adopted, their parents and guardians, those wishing to adopt a child, adopted persons and their parents, natural parents and former guardians, the child of an adoptive parent (in England, it is made explicit that this is whether or not they are adopted), a natural sibling (half- or full-blood) of an adoptive child, and (in England only) a 'related person' in relation to an adoptive child (see note to s 2, para [118], for wide definition of 'related person'). In Wales, a 'related person' only falls within this definition if the services relate to pre-existing contact arrangements between the related person and an adoptive child (s 4(1) and ASSR, reg 13/ASSLAWR, reg 7).

Section 4 obligations extend to certain persons outside of the local authority area: an agency adoptive child placed for adoption, a child who was adopted after being placed there by the authority, an adoptive parent of such a child, and a child of such an adoptive parent (in England, this explicitly states that this is whether or not that child was adopted) (ASSR, reg 7/ASSLAWR, reg 15). But these duties cease three years after the adoption order, save for financial support continuing after the adoption order if the decision to provide that financial support pre-dated the adoption (ASSR, reg 7/ASSLAWR, reg 15). The provision of that financial support remains the responsibility of the placing agency for as long as the family qualifies. In Wales, if the new authority has provided help (other than advice and information, for which it cannot charge) within the first three years at the request of the placing authority, it can recover its costs from the placing authority (ASSLAWR, reg 15(3) and (4)). In England, such costs can be recovered in those three years unless the recovering authority owes adoption support duties to the recipient of those services and he/she is the child, adoptive parent or adoptive parent's child (ASSR, regs 7 and 23).

After three years, the 'recovering/receiving authority will become responsible for contact arrangements', but the two authorities are encouraged to adopt a pragmatic approach (*Adoption Support Services* (*Local Authorities*) (*Wales*) *Regulations 2005 Guidance* [April 2006], National Assembly for Wales, paras 86 and 88). This applies to contact plans, such as letter-box contact, agreed prior to the adoption and also taking into account any changes over time.

The s 4 powers in relation to other persons is preserved for anyone outside the local authority area for whom it wishes to provide support services (ASSR, reg 7/ASSLAWR, reg 15(5)).

In making its decision regarding those to whom it owes this duty, if that person only requests a particular type of support service, or it appears to the local authority that the person's needs can be adequately met in the context of a particular type of support service, the local authority can choose to carry out its assessment only in that context (ASSR, reg 13(2)/ASSLAWR, reg 7(2)). Furthermore, in England, in complying with its duty to assess a person for adoption support services, it is made explicit that the authority is not obliged to assess him/her for a service that is not prescribed for that person by ASSR, reg 4 (ASSR, reg 13(3)).

PART B – Statutes

In Wales, if a local authority proposes to place a child for adoption in the area of another local authority, it must consult that authority in writing about the placement and the results of the assessment for adoption support services, and a period of 20 days must elapse before the proposed match can be placed before the adoption panel. Any response by that authority must be taken into account by the adoption panel (ASSLAWR, reg 7(4), (5) and (6)).

Section 4(3)

[128]

In carrying out its assessment, the local authority can request the help of a registered adoption society, another local authority, a registered adoption support agency, a Local Health Board, NHS Trust or Primary Care Trust, or a local education authority (s 3(4) and ASSR, reg 5/ASSLAWR, reg 8(4)).

Section 4(4)

[129]

At the conclusion of its assessment, if the local authority decides that a person needs adoption support services, it has a discretion whether to provide any services to that person, and must make a formal decision on this question.

Section 4(5)

[130]

If the decision is in the affirmative, (and, in England, extends to more than advice or information), and the services are to be provided on more than one occasion, the local authority must prepare an adoption support plan, nominate a person to monitor the provision of services under the plan, and keep the plan under review (ASSR, reg 16/ASSLAWR, reg 10). Before preparing the plan, if it appears that services may be needed from a Primary Care Trust, Local Health Board, NHS Trust or local education authority, that body must be consulted before the plan is prepared (ASSR, reg 16/ASSLAWR, reg 10).

Sections 4(6) and (7)

[131]

These sub-sections should be read in conjunction with the relevant regulations, as follows.

In carrying out the assessment, an English local authority must have regard to all of the following insofar as they are 'relevant' to the assessment: the needs of the person and how they might be met; the needs of the adoptive family (comprising the adoptive parents, the adoptive child, and any other child of the adoptive couple [whether or not adopted]) and how they might be met; the needs, including developmental needs, of the adoptive child and how they might be met; the adoptive parent's parenting capacity; wider family and environmental factors; if the child is (or was) placed or matched for adoption, the circumstances leading to that decision; and any previous assessment of that person's needs for adoption support (ASSR, reg 14(1)).

In Wales, an assessment must have regard to the following: the needs of the person being assessed and how they might be met (but where the request is from a person 'related' to the adoptive child, insofar as the needs of that related person are concerned this is limited to assistance with pre-existing contact arrangements); the needs of the adoptive child and adoptive family; if placed for adoption, the circumstances leading to that placement (not match, as in England); and any of the child's special needs relating to him/her having been looked after by a local authority, having been habitually resident outside the British Isles, or from being related to the adoptive parent (ASSLAWR, reg 8(1)). The assessment must be carried out by, or under the supervision of, a suitably qualified person (ASSLAWR, reg 8(2)). It is recommended that this is based on the *Framework for Assessment of Children in Need and their Families* [2001] National Assembly for Wales: see *Adoption Support Services (Local Authorities) (Wales) Regulations 2005 Guidance* [April 2006], para 42: National Assembly for Wales.

Where it considers it appropriate, the local authority must interview the person whose needs are being assessed during the assessment. If this is an adoptive child, this should include the adoptive parents. A written assessment report must be produced (ASSR, reg 14(3)/ASSLAWR, reg 8(5)). During the assessment, if it appears that the person may need services from a Primary Care Trust, NHS Trust, Local Health Board or local education authority, that body must be consulted (ASSR, reg 14(4)/ASSLAWR, reg 8(4)).

In England, if services are urgently required, they can be provided before any requirements for assessments, preparation of support service plans, or notices are complied with (ASSR, reg 21). Since, under the Regulations, there are procedures that must be followed prior to the provision of support services, it may be that in Wales emergency support has to be provided under other powers, such as those under CA 1989, s 17.

Before making a decision, the local authority must first notify the person of the proposed decision, giving written notice of the person's needs for adoption support services, the basis of any financial support determination, whether it is intended to provide adoption support, and if so, how, any conditions to be attached by the authority, and the time allowed for the person to make representations. In England, where a support plan is required (see below) a copy of the draft must be attached. The local authority must then make its decision under s 4(4) once the time limit has expired, and the person has made representations or has notified the authority of his/her satisfaction with the proposals/draft plan (ASSR, reg 17/ASSLAWR, reg 17).

Section 4(8)

[132]

For the avoidance of doubt, any assessment for adoption support services can be carried out at the same time as an assessment of needs under any other statute.

Section 4(9)

[133]

If at any time during the assessment it appears that there may be a need for one of the above-mentioned bodies to provide services to the person, the local authority must notify that body accordingly.

Section 4(10) and (11)

[134]

In carrying out its functions, a local authority can request help from another local authority for a specified purpose, and that authority must comply provided that this is consistent with the exercise of its functions. The authority providing help ('the recovering authority') can in most cases recover its expenses from the requesting authority, other than for advice or information under s 2(6)(a), but not where the recovering authority is an authority with s 4 obligations to a person outside its area (see note to sub-ss (1) and (2) above, para [127]).

Once a s 4(4) decision has been taken on whether or not to provide adoption support services to a person with assessed needs, written notice with reasons must be given, including details of the support plan (if applicable) and the identity of the person nominated to monitor the plan (ASSR, reg 18(1) and (2)/ASSLAWR, regs 10 and 13). If the services include financial support, detailed provision is made for the information to be provided in the notice (ASSR, reg 18(3)/ASSLAWR, reg 13).

In England, non-financial support must be reviewed in the event of a change in circumstances, at any relevant point in the implementation of the plan, and at least annually. In Wales, adoption support services must be reviewed if the authority becomes aware of a change of circumstances. The assessment procedures set out above (such as consultation, considerations, interviews, written reports, etc) apply equally to reviews. Any proposed revision (or, in England, termination) of support requires written notice, draft revised plan (if being revised), the scope for making representations, written decision and a revised plan (if being revised not terminated) (ASSR, reg 19/ASSLAWR, reg 16).

Periodic financial support must be reviewed at least annually, and must also be reviewed if there is a change in circumstances (in Wales, this means of the child or adoptive parent, including address), a breach of condition (this is only obligatory in England) or, in England, at any time considered appropriate during the implementation of the plan. As above, the requirements for consultation, considerations, interviews, written reports, etc, apply to such reviews, and similar provisions apply about written notice, representations, any draft revised plan, and written notice of final decision and any revised plan, save that the authority can suspend payments during the process, even prior to a final decision (ASSR, reg 20/ASSLAWR, regs 13 and 17).

For termination of support, see the note to s 3(3), para [123].

[135]

> **5 ...**
>
> ...
>
> **NOTES**
> **Amendment**
> Repealed by the Children Act 2004, s 64, Sch 5, Pt 1; date in force (in relation to England): 1 March 2005: see SI 2005/394, art 2(1)(l); date in force (in relation to Wales): 1 April 2006: see SI 2006/885, art 2(2)(h).

General

[136]

This section was repealed by the Children Act 2004, s 64 and Sch 5. The Children Act 2004, ss 17 and 24 and regulations made thereunder, create a statutory duty in England and Wales for local authorities to produce and maintain Children and Young People's Plans.

[137]

> **6 Arrangements on cancellation of registration**
>
> Where, by virtue of the cancellation of its registration under Part 2 of the Care Standards Act 2000 (c 14), a body has ceased to be a registered adoption society,

the appropriate Minister may direct the body to make such arrangements as to the transfer of its functions relating to children and other transitional matters as seem to him expedient.

NOTES

Initial Commencement

To be appointed

To be appointed: see s 148(6).

Appointment

Appointment (in relation to England): 30 December 2005: see SI 2005/2213, art 3(c); appointment (in relation to Wales): 30 December 2005: see SI 2005/3112, art 2(b).

Extent

This section does not extend to Scotland: see s 149(2).

General

[138]

Where a body ceases to be a registered adoption society, by having its registration cancelled under the provisions of the Care Standards Act 2000, the Minister has a wide discretion to make directions to that body about the transfer of its functions relating to children.

[139]

7   Inactive or defunct adoption societies etc

(1)   This section applies where it appears to the appropriate Minister that—

(a)   a body which is or has been a registered adoption society is inactive or defunct, or

(b)   a body which has ceased to be a registered adoption society by virtue of the cancellation of its registration under Part 2 of the Care Standards Act 2000 has not made such arrangements for the transfer of its functions relating to children as are specified in a direction given by him.

(2)   The appropriate Minister may, in relation to such functions of the society as relate to children, direct what appears to him to be the appropriate local authority to take any such action as might have been taken by the society or by the society jointly with the authority.

(3)   A local authority are entitled to take any action which—

(a)   apart from this subsection the authority would not be entitled to take, or would not be entitled to take without joining the society in the action, but

(b)   they are directed to take under subsection (2).

(4)   The appropriate Minister may charge the society for expenses necessarily incurred by him or on his behalf in securing the transfer of its functions relating to children.

(5)   Before giving a direction under subsection (2) the appropriate Minister must, if practicable, consult both the society and the authority.

NOTES

Initial Commencement

To be appointed

To be appointed: see s 148(6).

Appointment

Appointment (in relation to England): 30 December 2005: see SI 2005/2213, art 3(d); Appointment (in relation to Wales): 30 December 2005: see SI 2005/3112, art 2(b).

Extent

This section does not extend to Scotland: see s 149(2).

General

[140]

This section makes provision for where a former registered adoption society has not complied with directions about the transfer of its functions (see s 6), and for where a society is inactive or defunct.

Section 7(1), (2) and (5)

[141]

If a former registered adoption society has received directions from the Minister as a result of its registration being cancelled (see note to s 6, para [138]), but has not complied with those directions concerning the transfer of functions relating to children, or if a former or existing society seems to be inactive or defunct, the Minister may direct that a local authority takes any action concerning children that the society could have taken. If practicable, the Minister must first consult the adoption society and the local authority before making directions.

Section 7(3)

[142]

The local authority is then expressly authorised to act, notwithstanding previous limitations on its powers.

Section 7(4)

[143]

The Minister has the power to charge the adoption society for transfer costs.

[144]

8 Adoption support agencies

(1)   In this Act, 'adoption support agency' means an undertaking the purpose of which, or one of the purposes of which, is the provision of adoption support services; but an undertaking is not an adoption support agency—

(a)   merely because it provides information in connection with adoption other than for the purpose mentioned in section 98(1), or

(b)   if it is excepted by virtue of subsection (2).

'Undertaking' has the same meaning as in the Care Standards Act 2000 (c 14).

(2)   The following are excepted—

(a)   a registered adoption society, whether or not the society is registered in respect of the provision of adoption support services,

(b)   a local authority,

(c)   a local education authority (within the meaning of the Education Act 1996 (c 56)),

(d)   a Special Health Authority, Primary Care Trust (in Wales, a Health Authority or Local Health Board)[, NHS trust or NHS foundation trust],

(e)   the Registrar General,

(f)   any person, or description of persons, excepted by regulations.

(3)   In section 4 of the Care Standards Act 2000 (basic definitions)—

(a)   after subsection (7) there is inserted—

'(7A)   "Adoption support agency" has the meaning given by section 8 of the Adoption and Children Act 2002.',

(b)   in subsection (9)(a) (construction of references to descriptions of agencies), for 'or a voluntary adoption agency' there is substituted 'a voluntary adoption agency or an adoption support agency'.

NOTES

Initial Commencement

To be appointed

To be appointed: see s 148(6).

Appointment

Appointment (in relation to England for the purpose of making regulations): 7 December 2004: see SI 2004/3203, art 2(1)(m)(ii); appointment (in relation to England for remaining purposes): 30 December 2005: see SI 2005/2213, art 3(e); appointment (in relation to Wales): 30 December 2005: see SI 2005/3112, art 2(b).

Extent

This section does not extend to Scotland: see s 149(2).

Amendment

Sub-s (2): in para (d) words ', NHS trust or NHS foundation trust' in square brackets substituted by the Health and Social Care (Community Health and Standards) Act 2003, s 34, Sch 4, paras 125, 126: date in force: 1 April 2004: see SI 2004/759, art 2.

Subordinate Legislation

Adoption Support Agencies (England) and Adoption Agencies (Miscellaneous Amendments) Regulations 2005, SI 2005/2720 (made under sub-s (2)(f)).

PART B – Statutes

General

[145]

This section defines an adoption support agency, and makes consequential amendments to the Care Standards Act 2000.

Sections 8(1) and (2)

[146]

In the Act, in both England and Wales, the definition of an 'adoption support agency' excludes a registered adoption society (even if it provides adoption support services); local authorities; local education authorities; Special Health Authorities; Primary Care Trusts and NHS Trusts or Foundation Trusts; Welsh Health Authorities and Local Health Boards; and the Registrar General (s 8(2)). In England, the following are also excluded: a barrister or solicitor providing adoption support services during his/her practice; an undertaking facilitating groups of adoptive children, adoptive parents, natural parents or former guardians discussing adoption-related matters; and respite care providers, in relation to adoption, where a person is either registered under the Care Standards Act 2000 or the respite is provided by way of day-care or child-minding (s 8(2) and Adoption Support Agencies (England) and Adoption Agencies (Miscellaneous Amendments) Regulations 2005 (SI 2005/2720), reg 4).

Nor is a body an 'adoption support agency' merely because it provides information about adoption, unless that is for the purpose of helping those who have attained the age of 18 before 30 December 2005 to obtain information about their adoption (s 8(1) and s 98(1)).

Otherwise, an undertaking whose sole function, or one of whose functions, is the provision of adoption support services is an 'adoption support agency' for the purposes of the Act (s 8(1)). This includes self-employed individuals providing therapeutic or counselling services as adoption support. These individuals must be registered as adoption support agencies.

However, in September 2006, junior Minister Parmjit Dhanda announced the government's intention to amend the regulations, so that independent practitioners providing adoption support services on behalf of other organisations would not need to register as adoption support agencies. However, those who provided such services directly would still need to be registered (*Community Care* [28 September 2006]).

Section 8(3)

[147]

This subsection adds 'adoption support agency' to the definitions of those who are subject to registration, inspection, etc, under the Care Standards Act 2000 and associated regulations.

[148]

Regulations

9   General power to regulate adoption etc agencies

(1)   Regulations may make provision for any purpose relating to—

(a)   the exercise by local authorities or voluntary adoption agencies of their functions in relation to adoption, or

(b)   the exercise by adoption support agencies of their functions in relation to adoption.

(2)   The extent of the power to make regulations under this section is not limited by sections 10 to 12, 45, 54, 56 to 65 and 98 or by any other powers exercisable in respect of local authorities, voluntary adoption agencies or adoption support agencies.

(3)   Regulations may provide that a person who contravenes or fails to comply with any provision of regulations under this section is to be guilty of an offence and liable on summary conviction to a fine not exceeding level 5 on the standard scale.

(4)   In this section and section 10, 'voluntary adoption agency' means a voluntary organisation which is an adoption society.

NOTES

Initial Commencement

To be appointed
To be appointed: see s 148(6).

Appointment
Appointment (in relation to Wales): 7 February 2004: see SI 2004/252, art 2(b); appointment (in relation to England): 7 December 2004: see SI 2004/3203, art 2(1)(c).

Extent
This section does not extend to Scotland: see s 149(2).

Subordinate Legislation
Adoption Agencies Regulations 2005, SI 2005/389 (made under sub-s (1)(a)); Adoption Support Services Regulations 2005, SI 2005/691 (made under sub-s (1)(a)); Disclosure of Adoption Information (Post-Commencement Adoptions) Regulations 2005, SI 2005/888 (made under sub-s (3)); Adoption Information and Intermediary Services (Pre-Commencement Adoptions) Regulations 2005, SI 2005/890 (made under sub-ss (1), (3)); Adoption Agencies (Wales) Regulations 2005, SI 2005/1313 (made under sub-s (1)(a)); Adoption Support Services (Local Authorities) (Wales) Regulations 2005, SI 2005/1512 (made under sub-s (1)(a)); Adoption Support Agencies (Wales) Regulations 2005, SI 2005/1514 (made under sub-s (1)(b), (3)); Suitability of Adopters Regulations 2005, SI 2005/1712 (made under sub-s (1)); Independent Review of Determinations (Adoption) (Wales) Regulations 2005, SI 2005/1819 (made under sub-ss (1), (2), (4)); Access to Information (Post-Commencement Adoptions) (Wales) Regulations 2005, SI 2005/2689; Adoption Information and Intermediary Services (Pre-Commencement Adoptions) (Wales) Regulations 2005, SI 2005/2701; Adoption Support Agencies (England) and Adoption Agencies (Miscellaneous Amendments) Regulations 2005, SI 2005/2720 (made under sub-ss (1)(b), (3)); Local Authority (Non-agency Adoptions) (Wales) Regulations 2005, SI 2005/3113 (made under sub-s (1)); Local Authorities (Prescribed Fees) (Adoptions with a Foreign Element) (Wales) Regulations 2005, SI 2005/3114; Local Authority Adoption Service

---

(Wales) Regulations 2006, SI 2006/xxxx (made under sub-ss (1), (3)); Adoption Information and Intermediary Services (Pre-Commencement Adoptions) (Wales) (Amendment) Regulations 2005, SI 2005/3293; Independent Review of Determinations (Adoption) Regulations 2005, SI 2005/3332; Local Authority Adoption Service (England) (Amendment) Regulations 2005, SI 2005/3339 (made under sub-s (1)(a)); Voluntary Adoption Agencies (Amendment) Regulations 2005, SI 2005/3341 (made under sub-s (1)(a)); Local Authority (Adoption) (Miscellaneous Provisions) Regulations 2005, SI 2005/3390 (made under sub-s (1)(a)); Adoption and Children (Miscellaneous Amendments) Regulations 2005, SI 2005/3482 (made under sub-s (1)).

Note to Subordinate Legislation
The Local Authority Adoption Services (Wales) Regulations 2006 are expected to come into force on 31 December 2006 when they will revoke the 2005 regulations of the same name. References in this book are to the 2006 Regulations, but at the time of publication, the Welsh Assembly and English Parliament had not yet allocated a number for these Regulations.

General

[149]

This is a wide enabling power, taken together with s 10, to make regulations governing the adoption functions of local authorities, voluntary adoption agencies and adoption support agencies (s 9(1)), including the power to create summary criminal offences for breaches (s 9(3)). These powers are expressly unlimited by a number of other enabling provisions in the Act or by 'any other powers' in relation to those bodies (s 9(2)).

See the note to s 10 (paras [151]–[152] for the details of the relevant provisions.

Definitions: a 'voluntary adoption society' is a voluntary organisation acting as an adoption society (s 9(4)). For 'adoption society': see note to s 2(5).

[150]

10   Management etc of agencies

(1) In relation to local authorities, voluntary adoption agencies and adoption support agencies, regulations under section 9 may make provision as to—

(a)   the persons who are fit to work for them for the purposes of the functions mentioned in section 9(1),

(b)   the fitness of premises,

(c)   the management and control of their operations,

(d)   the number of persons, or persons of any particular type, working for the purposes of those functions,

(e)   the management and training of persons working for the purposes of those functions,

(f)   the keeping of information.

(2) Regulations made by virtue of subsection (1)(a) may, in particular, make provision for prohibiting persons from working in prescribed positions unless they are registered in, or in a particular part of, one of the registers maintained under section 56(1) of the Care Standards Act 2000 (c 14) (registration of social care workers).

(3) In relation to voluntary adoption agencies and adoption support agencies, regulations under section 9 may—

(a)   make provision as to the persons who are fit to manage an agency, including provision prohibiting persons from doing so unless they are registered in, or in a particular part of, one of the registers referred to in subsection (2),

(b)   impose requirements as to the financial position of an agency,

(c)   make provision requiring the appointment of a manager,

(d)   in the case of a voluntary adoption agency, make provision for securing the welfare of children placed by the agency, including provision as to the promotion and protection of their health,

(e)   in the case of an adoption support agency, make provision as to the persons who are fit to carry on the agency.

(4)   Regulations under section 9 may make provision as to the conduct of voluntary adoption agencies and adoption support agencies, and may in particular make provision—

(a)   as to the facilities and services to be provided by an agency,

(b)   as to the keeping of accounts,

(c)   as to the notification to the registration authority of events occurring in premises used for the purposes of an agency,

(d)   as to the giving of notice to the registration authority of periods during which the manager of an agency proposes to be absent, and specifying the information to be given in such a notice,

(e)   as to the making of adequate arrangements for the running of an agency during a period when its manager is absent,

(f)   as to the giving of notice to the registration authority of any intended change in the identity of the manager,

(g)   as to the giving of notice to the registration authority of changes in the ownership of an agency or the identity of its officers,

(h)   requiring the payment of a prescribed fee to the registration authority in respect of any notification required to be made by virtue of paragraph (g),

(i)   requiring arrangements to be made for dealing with complaints made by or on behalf of those seeking, or receiving, any of the services provided by an agency and requiring the agency or manager to take steps for publicising the arrangements.

NOTES

Initial Commencement

To be appointed
To be appointed: see s 148(6).

Appointment
Appointment (in relation to Wales): 7 February 2004: see SI 2004/252, art 2(b); appointment (in relation to England): 7 December 2004: see SI 2004/3203, art 2(1)(d).

Extent
This section does not extend to Scotland: see s 149(2).

Subordinate Legislation
Adoption Support Agencies (Wales) Regulations 2005, SI 2005/1514 (made under sub-ss (1), (3), (4)); Adoption Support Agencies (England) and Adoption Agencies (Miscellaneous Amendments) Regulations 2005, SI 2005/2720 (made under sub-ss (1), (3), (4)); Local Authority Adoption Service (Wales) Regulations 2006, SI 2006/xxxx.

Note to Subordinate Legislation
The Local Authority Adoption Services (Wales) Regulations 2006 are expected to come into force on 31 December 2006 when they will revoke the 2005 regulations of the same name. References in this book are to the 2006 Regulations, but at the time of publication, the Welsh Assembly and English Parliament had not yet allocated a number for these Regulations.

General

[151]

This section is an enabling power, taken together with s 9, for the control and regulation of local authorities, voluntary adoption agencies and adoption support agencies. See the list of regulations set out in note to s 9 (para [148]).

See also the *Adoption Support Agencies National Minimum Standards* (*England*) [2005] DfES, published under the provisions of the Care Standards Act 2000, s 23, and the *Adoption Support Services* (*Local Authorities*) (*Wales*) *Regulations 2005 Guidance* [April 2006] issued by the National Assembly for Wales.

Section 10(1), (2), (3) and (4)

[152]

Each local authority must appoint an officer to manage its adoption service, and notify the Commission for Social Care Inspection (CSCI) of the name and date of appointment or termination of appointment (Local Authority Adoption Service (England) Regulations 2003 (LAASER) (SI 2003/370), reg 5/Local Authority Adoption Service (Wales) Regulations 2006 (LAASWR) (SI 2006/xxxx), reg 9). He/she must be fit for that purpose, meaning of integrity and good character, being physically and mentally fit for the purpose, with the necessary qualifications, skills and experience (in Wales, he/she must be a social worker, and meet minimum criteria of experience and qualifications), and full information must be available, as prescribed, about identification, qualifications, employment history, criminal record certificate, and references. In England, but not Wales, qualifications and experience must include the field of adoption support services (LAASER, reg 6 and LAASER, Sch 3 (as amended by Local Authority Adoption Service (England) (Amendment) Regulations 2005 (LAASEAR) (SI 2005/3339)/LAASWR, reg 10 and LAASWR, Sch 3).

[The Local Authority Adoption Services (Wales) Regulations 2006 are expected to come into force on 31 December 2006 when they will revoke the 2005 regulations of the same name. References in this book are to the 2006 Regulations, but at the time of publication, the Welsh Assembly and English Parliament had not yet allocated a number for these Regulations.]

The manager must manage the adoption service with appropriate care, competence and skill, having regard to the local authority's statement of purpose, the need to safeguard and promote the welfare of children who may be, or have been, placed for adoption (in England, but not Wales, also for the welfare of those who are receiving adoption support services from the authority, and the number and needs of those persons who are receiving adoption support services from the authority). He/she must also undertake appropriate training (LAASER, reg 7 (as amended by LAASEAR)/LAASWR, reg 11).

If he/she commits any criminal offence, he/she must notify CSCI/the National Assembly in writing with the details (LAASER, reg 8/LAASWR, reg 12).

The local authority must identify an alternative person who is available to take over the manager's functions if he/she is continuously absent for 28 days or more (LAASER, reg 14/LAASWR, reg 18).

An organisation cannot run a voluntary adoption agency unless fit to do so, which requires CSCI/the National Assembly to be given notice of the details of the director, manager, secretary or other officer who will supervise the management of the agency, where that person is of integrity and good character, physically and mentally fit, and full information is available, similar to those details above for local authorities (Voluntary Adoption Agencies and Adoption Agencies (Miscellaneous Amendments) Regulations 2003 (VAAAA(MA)R) (SI 2003/367), reg 5). A manager and, where appropriate, a branch manager, must be appointed, who are also fit and of good character and with the necessary skills, experience and pre-requisites (VAAAA(MA)R, regs 6 and 7).

An adoption support agency must notify CSCI/the National Assembly if the registered provider who is in day-to-day control, or the registered manager, is to be absent for a continuous period of 28 days or more. This must be 28 days' notice (less if agreed with CSCI), except in an emergency, with specified details provided. Any return to duty must be notified within seven days (five in Wales) (Adoption Support Agencies (England) and Adoption Agencies (Miscellaneous Amendments) Regulations 2005 (SI 2005/2720), reg 26/ASAWR, reg 29).

Similar provisions apply to voluntary adoption agencies (VAAAA(MA)R, reg 21).

In England, an adoption support agency must not be carried on by a person unless, acting as an individual, that person is fit to do so, or acting in a partnership and all are fit to do so, or acting as an organisation and the 'responsible individual' (eg, director, secretary etc), as notified to CSCI, is fit to do so. In Wales, the restrictions are on organisations, and notification is to the National Assembly. 'Fitness' requires the person to be of integrity and good character, physically and mentally fit, and for there to be available proof of identity, criminal record certificate, written references, full employment history, documentary proof of qualifications, and a satisfactory written explanation of any gaps in employment history and (where practicable) verification of reasons for leaving previous positions working with children or vulnerable adults. Prohibitions apply in the context of bankruptcy, sequestration of estates, and composition or arrangements with creditors (ASAEAAMAR, reg 7 and Sch 2 and Adoption Support Agencies (Wales) Regulations 2005 (SI 2005/1514), reg 5 and Sch 2). The person or body carrying on the adoption support agency is called the 'registered provider'.

In England, if the registered provider of the adoption support agency is a partnership or organisation, is not a 'fit person' to manage it, or is not, or does not intend to be, in full day-to-day charge of that agency, it must appoint a manager (ASAEAAMAR, reg 8). In Wales, a manager must be appointed in all cases (ASAWR, reg 6). The same provisions apply as for local authorities appointing the manager of the adoption service (see above) (ASAEAAMAR, reg 9 and Sch 2/ASAWR, reg 7 and Sch 2).

The 'registered person', and any 'responsible individual' (in Wales, the registered manager), for an adoption support agency must carry on or manage the agency with adequate care, competence and skill, having regard to the support agency's size, statement of purpose and the number and needs of those receiving such support services. Adequate training must be undertaken to ensure the experience and skill to carry on or manage the agency (ASAEAAMAR, reg 10/ASAWR, reg 8). CSCI/the National Assembly must be notified immediately of the details of any criminal conviction of a registered person or responsible individual (ASAEAAMAR, reg 11/ASAWR, reg 9).

In Wales, each local authority, in operating the adoption service, once it considers that adoption is 'the preferred option for a child', or a child is relinquished by a parent, must provide a counselling service and advice for the natural parents, and as much information as the parents reasonably require insofar as the authority is in a position to give it (LAASWR, reg 6).

In Wales, each local authority must have a written strategy to recruit adequate numbers of adopters, a written policy and procedure for the process of preparation and approval, and it must provide the prospective adopters with written information about the adoption process, the arrangements for assessment and provision of adoption support services, and the local consortium arrangements (LAASWR, reg 7).

In Wales, each local authority must establish an adoption panel, as required by the Adoption Agencies (Wales) Regulations 2005 (SI 2005/1313), have a training strategy for panel members, and ensure that the panel is properly advised by a suitably qualified person when adoptions with a foreign element are being considered (LAASWR, reg 8).

Each local authority must maintain a Statement of Purpose for its adoption service, containing the aims and objectives of the adoption service, details of the manager, staff, organisational structure and quality control mechanisms of the service, the procedures for the recruitment, preparation, assessment, approval and support of prospective adopters, the procedures for assessments for adoption support services (in Wales, this must also include details of the arrangements and procedures for the provision of adoption support services, and details of the adoption support service advisor), a summary of the complaints procedure, and contact details for CSCI/the National Assembly (LAASER, reg 2 and Sch 1 (as amended by LAASEAR)/LAASWR, reg 3 and Sch 1). In England, the procedures must include how the adoption support agency will decide whether to provide an adoption support service to particular service users (National Minimum Standard 4: see general note above).

The registered person for each adoption support agency must maintain a Statement of Purpose containing the aims and objectives of the agency, details of the registered provider and any registered manager and/or responsible individual, any registration conditions for the provider and/or manager, the qualifications and experience of the provider and/or manager, the numbers, qualifications and experience of the staff, the structure of the agency, the services offered, the procedure for assessing the needs of those requesting adoption support services, the quality control system and complaints procedure, and the contact details for CSCI/the National Assembly (ASAEAAMAR, reg 5/ASAWR, reg 3). The document must be reviewed and amended as appropriate, and CSCI/the National Assembly notified of any changes within 28 days (ASAEAAMAR, reg 6/ASAWR, reg 4).

Each voluntary adoption agency must maintain a Statement of Purpose containing the aims and objectives of the agency, details of the registered provider, individual and manager(s), any registration conditions in force, the qualifications and experience of the manager(s), the numbers, qualification and experience of staff, the quality control system and complaints procedure, the contact details for CSCI/the National Assembly, and the procedures for recruiting, preparing, assessing, approving and supporting prospective adopters (VAAAA(MA)R, reg 3 and Sch 1). Copies for inspection must be available on request to employees, children who may be adopted and their parents and guardians, those wishing to adopt, adopted children and their adoptive parents, natural parents and former guardians, any local authority, and – if that agency is also able to provide adoption support services – those receiving such services from the agency (including a person acting for a child) or who are making enquiries about receiving such services for themselves or a child (VAAAA(MA)R, reg 3, as amended by Voluntary Adoption Agencies (Amendment) Regulations 2005 (SI 2005/3341), reg 2(4)).

Each local authority must have a Children's Guide to the adoption service, setting out a summary of the Statement of Purpose, a summary of its procedures when adoption is identified as the appropriate plan for a child, and, in England, a summary of its adoption support services, or, in Wales, information about the adoption support services advisor and a summary of the procedures for seeking an assessment for adoption support services. It must also contain a summary of the complaints procedure, details of how a child can access independent advocacy services so as to bring a complaint, and the contact details for CSCI/the National Assembly and the children's rights director/Children's Commissioner for Wales (LAASER, reg 3 and Sch 2 (as amended by LAASEAR)/LAASWR, reg 4 and Sch 2). A copy of this Guide must be provided to CSCI/the National Assembly, each prospective adopter once a child is placed, (in England, to each adult acting on behalf of a child in receipt of adoption support services), and, subject to age and sufficient under-standing, each child who has been, or may be, placed for adoption (or, in England, is receiving adoption support services) (LAASER, reg 3/LAASWR, reg 4).

The registered person for each adoption support agency must produce a Children's Guide to the adoption support service, in a form appropriate to the age, understanding and communication needs of the children to whom it provides adoption support services, setting out a summary of its Statement of Purpose, a summary of the complaints procedure and the contact details for CSCI/the National Assembly. A copy of this Guide must be provided to CSCI/the National Assembly, each adult acting on behalf of a child in receipt of adoption support services, and, subject to age and understanding, each such child (ASAEAAMAR, reg 5/ASAWR, reg 3). Such Guides must be reviewed, and revised as

PART B – Statutes

51

appropriate, any change must be notified to CSCI/the National Assembly within 28 days, and copies of the revised edition must be provided to adults and children as above (ASAEAAMAR, reg 6/ASAWR, reg 4).

Where a voluntary adoption agency can provide adoption support services to children, similar provisions apply (VAAAA(MA)R, reg 24C, as inserted by VAAAR, reg 2(4)).

The local authority must have a written policy intended to safeguard from abuse or neglect children who are placed for adoption or in receipt of adoption support services (in Wales, this includes children who may receive adoption support services), including the procedure to be followed in the event of an allegation of abuse or neglect (LAASER, reg 9 (as amended by LAASEAR)/LAASWR, reg 13).

In England, that policy must in particular provide for: allegations of abuse/neglect of children placed with prospective adopters in another area to be referred promptly to that local authority; written records of allegations and action taken; the measures to be taken if there are allegations of abuse or neglect of children placed with prospective adopters; and the arrangements for those working for the service, prospective adopters, children who have been placed for adoption by the authority and any person to whom it is providing adoption support services to have access to information enabling them to contact CSCI if they have concerns about 'child welfare and safety' (LAASER, reg 9 (as amended by LAASEAR)). In Wales, the Regulations do not prescribe the scope of these procedures, which are left to local discretion, except that they must be consistent with the procedures of the Local Safeguarding Children Board (LAASWR, reg 13).

An adoption support agency must implement a written policy intended to safeguard children who are receiving adoption support services from abuse or neglect, especially the procedure to be followed in the event of allegations of abuse or neglect. The latter procedure must provide for liaison and cooperation with any local authority conducting child protection enquiries, and written records of the allegations and action taken in response. It must also provide adequate information to enable staff, adults and children to contact the local authority and CSCI/the National Assembly (ASAEAAMAR, reg 12/ASAWR, reg 16). In England, these procedures must extend to 'allegations of historical abuse which may be made by service users during the course of service provision' (National Minimum Standard 2: see note at para [151] above).

Similar provisions apply to voluntary adoption agencies (VAAAA(MA)R, regs 10 and 24E, as amended by VAAAR, reg 2 (4)).

The registered person or local authority, as appropriate, must ensure that adoption support services for a person are appropriate having regard to the needs for such services identified in an assessment (ASAEAAMAR, reg 13 and LAASER, reg 9A, as inserted by LAASEAR/ASAWR, reg 17). The same applies to adoption support services provided by a voluntary adoption agency (VAAAA(MA)R, reg 24F, as inserted by VAAAR, reg 2(4)).

Appropriate records must be kept by the local authority or adoption support agency, as appropriate, where adoption support services are provided, including details of the request, assessment of needs and services provided (LAASER, reg 9B as inserted by LAASEAR; ASAEAAMAR, reg 14; ASAWR, reg 18). If the services are provided by an agency on behalf of a local authority, that fact must also be recorded. In Wales, such records must be kept for at least 75 years.

Each local authority must ensure there are adequate numbers of workers for the purposes of the adoption service with suitable qualifications, experience and competence, having regard to the size of the authority, its statement of purpose, the need to safeguard and promote the welfare of children who have been, or may be, placed for adoption, or are receiving adoption support services (in Wales, this includes those who may receive adoption support services), and (in England only) the number, and needs, of children who are receiving adoption support services (LAASER, reg 10 (as amended by LAASEAR)/LAASWR, reg 14).

Each adoption support agency must ensure there are adequate numbers of workers for the purposes of the agency with suitable qualifications, experience and competence, having regard to the size of the agency, its statement of purpose and (in England) the needs of those to whom it provides adoption support services (ASAEAAMAR, reg 18/ASAWR, reg 21). Counsellors in England, other than those providing birth records counselling, must hold suitable professional membership or accreditation as set out in National Minimum Standard 11: see general note above).

Each voluntary adoption agency must ensure there are adequate numbers of suitably qualified, experienced and competent workers for the purposes of the agency, having regard to the size of the agency, its statement of purpose, and the need to safeguard and promote the health and welfare of children placed for adoption by the agency, placed for adoption by another adoption agency but with prospective adopters approved by the voluntary agency, or receiving adoption support services from the agency (VAAA(MA)R, reg 13, as amended by VAAAR, reg 2(4)).

Local authorities are prohibited from employing staff in the adoption service, and from allowing those employed by third parties to work for the purpose of the adoption service, if their duties may bring them into regular contact with children who may be, or are, placed for adoption or in receipt of adoption support services, unless they are 'fit' for those purposes. This means being of integrity and good character, having the necessary skills, experience and qualifications, physically and mentally fit for the work, and full and satisfactory information is available as set out in Sch 3 to LAASER (as amended by LAASEAR)/Sch 3 to LAASWR (proof of identity, criminal record certificate, written references, verification of the reason for termination of previous employment with children or vulnerable adults, documentary proof of qualifications, (in England, this includes qualifications and experience in the context of adoption support), and a full employment history). Others who are employed by third parties and used in the adoption service must be appropriately supervised (LAASER, reg 11/LAASWR, reg 15). Similar provisions apply to adoption support agencies (ASAAEAAMAR, reg 19 and Sch 2), and to voluntary adoption agencies (VAAAA(MA)R, reg 14 and Sch 2).

Local authority permanent appointments must be subject to the satisfactory completion of a period of probation, and all employees must have a suitable job description, receive appropriate training, supervision and appraisal, and be enabled to gain further suitable qualifications (LAASER, reg 12/LAASWR, reg 16). Similar provisions apply to adoption support agencies (ASAEAAMAR, reg 20) and voluntary adoption agencies (VAAAA(MA)R, reg 15).

Records about the local authority staff must be maintained, containing information about their identity, qualifications, contractual terms, employment history, training, supervision, appraisals, complaints against them and their disciplinary record. In Wales, the records must also contain their Criminal Records Bureau checks, written references with confirmation of these having been checked by telephone, and a full employment history. These records must be retained for at least 15 years (LAASER, reg 15 and Sch 4/LAASWR, reg 19 and Sch 4). Similar provisions apply to adoption support agency staff, plus records about the form of employment and whether he/she works there as a volunteer (ASAE-AAMAR, reg 22 and Sch 3). Similar provisions apply to voluntary adoption agencies (VAAAA(MA)R, reg 17).

The local authority must have a staff disciplinary procedure that provides for suspension of staff if necessary in the interests of the safety or welfare of children who have been, or may be, placed for adoption, or who are receiving adoption support services from the authority (in Wales, this includes those children who may receive such support services), and makes it a ground for disciplinary proceedings for an employee to fail to report to an 'appropriate person' an incident of abuse (or suspected abuse) of a child who is either in receipt of adoption support services (or, in Wales, may receive such services) or is placed for adoption (or, in Wales, may be placed for adoption). An 'appropriate person' is the manager of the adoption service, a CSCI/National Assembly officer, the police or NSPCC, or – if the child is placed out of authority – an officer of the other local authority (LAASER, reg 13 (as amended by LAASEAR/LAASWR, reg 17)).

An adoption support agency must have a similar procedure, with suspension where necessary for the welfare of those to whom the agency provides adoption support services; an 'appropriate person' is the registered person for the agency, CSCI/the National Assembly, the police or NSPCC, or an officer of the local authority for the area of the child or the agency (ASAEAAMAR, reg 21/ASAWR, reg 24). In Wales, the failure to report an incident of abuse or suspected abuse of any child must be made a disciplinary offence.

A voluntary adoption agency must have a similar procedure, with suspension where necessary for the welfare of children placed for adoption by the agency; an 'appropriate person' is the registered provider, manager or branch manager, CSCI/the National Assembly, the police or NSPCC, an officer of the local authority for the area of the agency (or its branch), or an officer of the local authority for the area where the child is placed for adoption (VAAA(MA)R, reg 16).

Adoption services premises, voluntary adoption agency premises and adoption support agency premises must be suitable to meet the aims and objectives of their statements of purpose, with adequate security for the premises and records. In Wales, case records set up under the Adoption Agencies (Wales) Regulations 2005 (SI 2005/1313), regs 12 and 22 (on children and prospective adopters), must be retained for at least 100 years (LAASER, reg 16/LAASWR, reg 20; ASAEAAMAR, reg 23/ASAWR, reg 23; VAAAA(MA)R, reg 18).

The adoption service, voluntary adoption agency or adoption support agency must keep records of complaints regarding the service, including the investigation, outcome and any action taken, and such records must be retained for at least three years. CSCI/the National Assembly can require the production of a summary of any complaint made in the last 12 months, and of the action taken (LAASER, reg 17/LAASWR, reg 21; ASAEAAMAR, reg 17; VAAAA(MA)R, reg 12).

An adoption support agency must have a written complaints procedure open to those to whom it has provided a service or whom it has refused a service (in Wales, who have requested, and by inference have been refused a service), which is to be provided on request to any such person or an adult acting on behalf of such a child. The procedure must include contact details for CSCI/the National Assembly and details of any procedure for complaining to CSCI/the National Assembly. It must provide for an early informal resolution stage, and the subsequent exclusion from the process of any person who is the subject of the complaint. Any complaint must be fully investigated and the outcome, with any action taken, notified to the complainant within 28 days (20 days in Wales) if reasonably practicable. Children must be enabled to complain, and there must be no reprisals against any complainant (ASAEAAMAR, regs 16 and 17/ASAWR, regs 19 and 20).

A voluntary adoption agency must have a written complaints procedure for children who may be adopted, their parents or guardians, persons who wish to adopt, and adopted persons, their adoptive parents, natural parents and former guardians, with a copy to be made available to them on request. If empowered to provide adoption support services, the procedures must extend to those receiving such services, those who have received such services, and those refused such a service. The procedure must include contact details for CSCI/the National Assembly and details of any procedure for complaining to CSCI/the

National Assembly. It must provide for an early informal resolution stage, and the subsequent exclusion from the process of any person who is the subject of the complaint. Any complaint must be fully investigated and the outcome, with any action taken, notified to the complainant within 28 days if reasonably practicable (VAAAA(MA)R, regs 11,12 and 24H, as amended by VAAAR, reg 2(4)).

If the adoption support agency or voluntary adoption agency notifies the Secretary of State or the National Assembly about a person working for the agency, under the provisions of the Protection of Children Act 1999, s 2(1)(a), the registered person must also notify CSCI/the National Assembly (ASAEAAMAR, reg 24 and Sch 4, ASAWR, reg 27 and Sch 4, and VAAAA(MA)R, reg 19 and Sch 4).

If a child (or, in Wales, an adult) dies or suffers a serious injury 'in the course of' receiving adoption support services, that agency must notify CSCI/the National Assembly, the Primary Care Trust or Local Health Board for the child's/adult's area, and (for deaths of children only) the local authority for the area of the agency. In England, if the child lives in a different local authority area, that authority must be notified of child deaths and injuries, as must the Secretary of State in the case of child deaths. Notifications must be given orally immediately, and in writing within 14 days (in Wales, ten days) (ASAEAAMAR, reg 24 and Sch 4/ASAWR, reg 27 and Sch 4).

If a child placed for adoption by a voluntary adoption agency dies, the agency must notify CSCI/the National Assembly, the local authority and Primary Care Trust or Local Health Board for the child's area, and the Secretary of State if CSCI is the registration authority for the agency. If such a child suffers a serious accident or illness, that agency must notify the local authority and Primary Care Trust or Local Health Board. Serious complaints about prospective adopters approved by the agency must be reported to CSCI/the National Assembly, and also to the local authority for that area if a child has been placed there for adoption by that agency, and to the placing agency if not placed by the agency (and the local authority for the child's area, if that local authority is not the placing authority). The agency must report on the investigation and outcome of any child protection enquiry to CSCI/the National Assembly and the local authority for the child's area (VAAAA(MA)R, reg 19 and Sch 4). If the agency is empowered to provide adoption support services, and a child dies or suffers serious injury in the course of receiving such services, the agency must notify CSCI/the National Assembly (and the Secretary of State if he is the registration authority), the Primary Care Trust or Local Health Board, the local authority for the area of the voluntary adoption agency, and any other local authority for whom the agency is providing those support services (VAAAA(MA)R, regs 19 and 24K, as inserted by VAAAR, reg 2(4)).

The registered person of an adoption support agency must notify CSCI/the National Assembly in writing of a variety of changes regarding the registered person or provider, or any partnership, details of a variety of changes in an organisation, bankruptcy, liquidation and death of a registered person (if only one such person, the personal representatives are responsible) (ASAEAAMAR, reg 27/ASAWR, reg 30). Notification must be made to CSCI/the National Assembly forthwith by any receiver or manager of property of a company or partnership, or liquidator, of a company/partnership that is a registered provider of an adoption support agency, or by a trustee in bankruptcy of a person who is the registered provider of an adoption support agency. He/she must provide details of the reason for appointment, appoint a manager if there is no registered manager, and within 28 days set out details of his/her future intentions regarding the agency's operations (ASAE-AAMAR, reg 28/ASAWR, reg 31). Similar provisions apply to voluntary adoption agencies (VAAAA(MA)R, regs 22 and 23).

The registered provider of an adoption support agency must carry on the agency in a way likely to ensure its financial viability, keep adequate and up-to-date financial records, and produce any financial, accounting and insurance information requested by CSCI/the National Assembly (ASAEAAMAR, reg 25/ASAWR, reg 28).

ASAEAAMAR, reg 29/ASAWR, reg 32 make a variety of breaches of these Regulations criminal offences, liable on summary conviction to a maximum fine of level 5. In England, CSCI must first issue a Notice under reg 29(3) seeking specified action within a relevant timescale, and prosecution can follow only if the time limit has expired and the necessary action has not been taken (ASAEAAMAR, reg 29). There are no similar restrictions in Wales.

[153]

11 Fees

(1) Regulations under section 9 may prescribe—

(a) the fees which may be charged by adoption agencies in respect of the provision of services to persons providing facilities as part of the Adoption Service (including the Adoption Services in Scotland and Northern Ireland),

(b) the fees which may be paid by adoption agencies to persons providing or assisting in providing such facilities.

(2) Regulations under section 9 may prescribe the fees which may be charged by local authorities in respect of the provision of prescribed facilities of the Adoption Service where the following conditions are met.

(3) The conditions are that the facilities are provided in connection with—

(a) the adoption of a child brought into the United Kingdom for the purpose of adoption, or

(b) a Convention adoption, an overseas adoption or an adoption effected under the law of a country or territory outside the British Islands.

(4) Regulations under section 9 may prescribe the fees which may be charged by adoption agencies in respect of the provision of counselling, where the counselling is provided in connection with the disclosure of information in relation to a person's adoption.

NOTES

Initial Commencement
To be appointed
To be appointed: see s 148(6).

Appointment
Appointment (in relation to Wales): 7 February 2004: see SI 2004/252, art 2(b); appointment (in relation to England): 7 December 2004: see SI 2004/3203, art 2(1)(e).

Extent
This section does not extend to Scotland: see s 149(2).

Subordinate Legislation
Adoption Agencies Regulations 2005, SI 2005/389 (made under sub-s (1)(b)); Disclosure of Adoption Information (Post-Commencement Adoptions) Regulations 2005, SI 2005/888 (made under sub-s (4)); Adoption Agencies (Wales) Regulations 2005, SI 2005/1313 (made under sub-s (1)(b)); Local Authorities (Prescribed Fees) (Adoptions with a Foreign Element) (Wales) Regulations 2005, SI 2005/3114 (made under sub-ss (2), (3)); Local Authority (Adoption) (Miscellaneous Provisions) Regulations 2005, SI 2005/3390 (made under sub-s (2)).

General

[154]

This section enables the regulations made under the powers in s 9 to prescribe the fees that can be charged by local authorities, and charged and paid by adoption agencies.

Sections 11(1) and (4)

[155]

Adoption agencies can pay fees to those providing or assisting in providing facilities as part of the adoption service.

An adoption agency may charge fees for the provision of services to those who provide facilities as part of the adoption service, and for counselling if that is provided within the context of the disclosure of information about a person's adoption.

Section 11(2) and (3)

[156]

Local authorities can charge fees for the provision of prescribed facilities of their adoption service, where they are provided in connection with the adoption of a child brought into the UK for the purposes of adoption or in connection with a Convention adoption, an overseas adoption or an adoption effected under non-British law.

[157]

PART B – Statutes

12 Independent review of determinations

(1) Regulations under section 9 may establish a procedure under which any person in respect of whom a qualifying determination has been made by an adoption agency may apply to a panel constituted by the appropriate Minister for a review of that determination.

(2) The regulations must make provision as to the description of determinations which are qualifying determinations for the purposes of subsection (1).

(3) The regulations may include provision as to—

(a) the duties and powers of a panel (including the power to recover the costs of a review from the adoption agency by which the determination reviewed was made),

(b) the administration and procedures of a panel,

(c) the appointment of members of a panel (including the number, or any limit on the number, of members who may be appointed and any conditions for appointment),

(d) the payment of [fees to] members of a panel,

(e) the duties of adoption agencies in connection with reviews conducted under the regulations,

(f) the monitoring of any such reviews.

(4) The appropriate Minister may make an arrangement with an organisation under which functions in relation to the panel are performed by the organisation on his behalf.

(5) If the appropriate Minister makes such an arrangement with an organisation, the organisation is to perform its functions under the arrangement in accordance with any general or special directions given by the appropriate Minister.

(6) The arrangement may include provision for payments to be made to the organisation by the appropriate Minister.

(7) Where the appropriate Minister is the Assembly, subsections (4) and (6) also apply as if references to an organisation included references to the Secretary of State.

(8) In this section, 'organisation' includes a public body and a private or voluntary organisation.

NOTES

Initial Commencement

To be appointed

To be appointed: see s 148(6).

Appointment
Sub-ss (1)–(3): appointment (in relation to Wales): 7 February 2004: see SI 2004/252, art 2(b); sub-ss (1)–(3): appointment (in relation to England for the purpose of making regulations): 7 December 2004: see SI 2004/3203, art 2(1)(m)(iii); sub-ss (1)–(3): appointment (in relation to England for remaining purposes): 30 December 2005: see SI 2005/2213, art 3(f); sub-ss (4)–(8): appointment (in relation to England): 30 December 2005: see SI 2005/2213, art 3(f); sub-ss (4)–(8): appointment (in relation to Wales): 30 December 2005: see SI 2005/3112, art 2(c).

Extent
This section does not extend to Scotland: see s 149(2).

Amendment
Sub-s (3): in para (d) words 'fees to' in square brackets substituted by the Children Act 2004, s 57: date in force (in relation to England): 1 March 2005: see SI 2005/394, art 2(1)(i); date in force (in relation to Wales): 30 December 2005: see SI 2005/3363, art 2.

Subordinate Legislation
Disclosure of Adoption Information (Post-Commencement Adoptions) Regulations 2005, SI 2005/888 (made under sub-s (2)); Independent Review of Determinations (Adoption) (Wales) Regulations 2005, SI 2005/1819 (made under sub-ss (1)–(3)); Independent Review of Determinations (Adoption) Regulations 2005, SI 2005/3332.

General

[158]

An enabling power, permitting the creation of regulations to establish a procedure for persons challenging a 'qualifying determination' of an adoption agency by applying to an independent panel for a review of that decision.

Section 12(1), (2) and (3)

Qualifying determinations

[159]

The regulations must define those 'qualifying determinations', and may encompass a variety of issues ranging from the powers and duties of the panel, its administration, procedures, appointments, fees, the duties of adoption agencies in connection with such reviews, and the monitoring of these reviews.

The relevant regulations in England are the Independent Review of Determinations (Adoption) Regulations 2005 (SI 2005/3332) (IRDAR), and in Wales the Independent Review of Determinations (Adoption) (Wales) Regulations 2005 (SI 2005/1819) (IRDAWR).

See also the Adoption Agencies Regulations 2005 (SI 2005/389), reg 27/the Adoption Agencies (Wales) Regulations 2005 (SI 2005/1313), reg 29, for the link of this procedure to the adoption agency decision-making process when considering whether to approve prospective adopters.

Section 12(4), (5), (6) and (8)

[160]

In England, the Minister can arrange for an organisation to provide the panel on a paid basis, and that organisation must perform its functions under his/her direction.

Section 12(7)

[161]

In Wales, the appropriate Minister can make payments to the organisation for the same purpose.

The regulations

[162]

The regulations cover two forms of 'qualifying determination'. The first is a determination by an adoption agency that it does not propose to approve a prospective adopter as being suitable to adopt a child (IRDAR and IRDAWR, reg 3). This applies in England and Wales. The second is a qualifying determination under the Disclosure of Adoption Information (Post-Commencement Adoptions) Regulations 2005 (SI 2005/888), reg 15(1) (see note to s 61, paras [348]–[349]). This only applies in England. The Welsh regulations also include a decision that an approved prospective adopter has ceased to be suitable as a 'qualifying determination' (IRDAWR, reg 3(b)).

The Secretary of State and National Assembly for Wales maintain a central list of IRM panel members, including medical practitioners, social workers with adoption experience, and other suitable persons, including, if practicable, those with personal experience of adoption. On receipt of an application under IRDAR, reg 10 or IRDAWR, reg 11 (see below) a panel must be constituted to review the qualifying determination.

In England, there must be no more than ten people for a 'suitability to adopt' determination, with at least two social workers, one medical practitioner and four from the third group. The quorum is five. For a 'disclosure' determination, there must be three people on the panel, including at least two social workers. All three must be in attendance. Restrictions are placed on members who have prescribed links to the agency making the determination and on those who know the applicant in either a personal or professional capacity (IRDAR, regs 4 and 8)

In Wales, there must be no more than five people on a panel, including an adoptive parent and an adopted person aged 18 or over. The panel must be advised by a medical practitioner with adoption expertise, a social worker with at least five years' experience in adoption and family placement, and, at their discretion, a legal advisor. Restrictions are placed on members or advisors acting if they were employed (in a wide sense) by the adoption agency in the last two years. The National Assembly must appoint an experienced chair and a vice-chair, and must provide clerking facilities for the panel (IRDAWR, regs 4, 5, 6 and 9).

An application for a review is made in writing, with grounds, to the Secretary of State or National Assembly for Wales (IRDAR, reg 10/IRDAWR, reg 11). In Wales, the application must be made within 20 days of receiving notification of the qualifying determination (IRDAWR, reg 11). Upon receipt, the Secretary of State or National Assembly must send a copy to the adoption agency (in Wales, within five days of receipt: IRDAWR, reg 13) and constitute a panel (if in Wales, within 25 working days), notifying the applicant and the agency and (in England only) telling the applicant that he/she can provide further written submissions prior to the panel and make oral submissions at the panel (IRDAR, reg 11/ IRDAWR, regs 12 and 13). In Wales, the review must take place within three months of the qualifying determination.

In the case of a 'suitability to adopt' determination, the panel reviews it, and where there is available a full prospective adopter's report under the Adoption Agencies Regulations 2005, reg 25 or the Adoption Agencies (Wales) Regulations 2005, reg 26, the panel must make a recommendation as to whether the applicant is suitable to adopt a child.

PART B – Statutes

Where, in England, the agency prepared a brief prospective adopters' report (Adoption Agencies Regulations 2005, reg 25(7)) because, from the information received during the assessment (but before the assessment was completed), it believed the person was unlikely to be suitable, the panel can recommend either that the applicant is unsuitable, or that a full prospective adopter's report should be prepared (IRDAR, reg 5).

Where, in Wales, the agency follows the *Adoption Agencies (Wales) Regulations 2005 Guidance* [April 2006]: National Assembly for Wales, paras 53 and 54, and accepts a recommendation from the panel not to proceed with a full assessment due to initial contra-indicators, the Guidance states that that is a qualifying determination.

In the case of a 'disclosure' determination in England, the Panel reviews it, and recommends whether or not the agency should proceed with the original determination to disclose or not disclose information (IRDAR, reg 6).

In both cases the panel can obtain legal advice or ask the agency to obtain further information or provide further assistance to the panel, and (in England) it can seek legal or medical advice regarding a 'disclosure' determination (there is already a medical member of a 'suitability to adopt' panel) (IRDAR, regs 5 and 6/IRDAWR, reg 5). Fees can be paid, and records must be maintained (IRDAR, regs 7 and 9/IRDAWR, regs 8 and 10). The panel can make an order for the agency to pay reasonable costs (IRDAR, reg 13/ IRDAWR, reg 15).

The panel's recommendation can be a majority view, and that recommendation and the reasons for it must be recorded and a copy sent (in Wales, within 10 working days) to the applicant and the adoption agency, which then has the task of considering whether to accept the panel's recommendation (IRDAR, reg 12/IRDAWR, reg 14). See notes to the Adoption Agencies Regulations 2005, reg 27 (para [857]) and the Adoption Agencies (Wales) Regulations 2005, reg 28 (para [953]).

[163]

Supplemental

13 Information concerning adoption

(1) Each adoption agency must give to the appropriate Minister any statistical or other general information he requires about—

(a)   its performance of all or any of its functions relating to adoption,
(b)   the children and other persons in relation to whom it has exercised those functions.

(2) The following persons—

(a)   the [designated officer] for each magistrates' court,
(b)   the relevant officer of each county court,
(c)   the relevant officer of the High Court,

must give to the appropriate Minister any statistical or other general information he requires about the proceedings under this Act of the court in question.

(3) In subsection (2), 'relevant officer', in relation to a county court or the High Court, means the officer of that court who is designated to act for the purposes of that subsection by a direction given by the Lord Chancellor.

(4) The information required to be given to the appropriate Minister under this section must be given at the times, and in the form, directed by him.

(5) The appropriate Minister may publish from time to time abstracts of the information given to him under this section.

PART B – Statutes

NOTES

Initial Commencement

To be appointed

To be appointed: see s 148(6).

Appointment

Appointment (in relation to England): 30 December 2005: see SI 2005/2213, art 3(g); appointment (in relation to Wales): 30 December 2005: see SI 2005/3112, art 2(d).

Extent

This section does not extend to Scotland: see s 149(2).

Amendment

Sub-s (2): words 'designated officer' in square brackets substituted by the Courts Act 2003, s 109(1), Sch 8, para 411: date in force: 1 April 2005: see SI 2005/910, art 3(y); for transitional provisions see SI 2005/911, arts 2–5.

General

[164]

This section governs the provision of information to the Government, and publication of information by the Government.

Section 13(1)

[165]

Adoption agencies must provide the Minister with any general information or statistics required concerning their performance of any of their adoption functions or any of the persons in relation to whom it has exercised those functions.

Section 13(2) and (3)

[166]

The courts must provide the Minister with any general information or statistics required about proceedings under the Act.

The Minister can publish abstracts of the information that is provided.

[167]

14 Default power of appropriate Minister

(1) If the appropriate Minister is satisfied that any local authority have failed, without reasonable excuse, to comply with any of the duties imposed on them by virtue of this Act or of section 1 or 2(4) of the Adoption (Intercountry Aspects) Act 1999 (c 18), he may make an order declaring that authority to be in default in respect of that duty.

(2) An order under subsection (1) must give the appropriate Minister's reasons for making it.

(3) An order under subsection (1) may contain such directions as appear to the appropriate Minister to be necessary for the purpose of ensuring that, within the period specified in the order, the duty is complied with.

(4) Any such directions are enforceable, on the appropriate Minister's application, by a mandatory order.

NOTES

Initial Commencement

To be appointed

To be appointed: see s 148(6).

Appointment
Appointment (in relation to England): 30 December 2005: see SI 2005/2213, art 3(h); Appointment (in relation to Wales): 30 December 2005: see SI 2005/3112, art 2(d).

Extent
This section does not extend to Scotland: see s 149(2).

General

[168]

This section provides default powers for the Government to take action against local authorities within the context of the Act and also inter-country adoption.

This creates a default power for the Minister to act, if satisfied that a local authority has failed, without good reason, to comply with its duties under either this Act, or the Adoption (Inter-Country Aspects) Act 1999, s 1 (regulations concerning the Hague Convention), or s 2(4) (enforcement by local authorities of art 9(a)–(c) of the Hague Convention).

Reasons must be given for such an order, it can contain directions for ensuring compliance with the relevant duty within a suitable timescale, and such directions can be enforced in court by a mandatory order.

[169]

15 Inspection of premises etc

(1) The appropriate Minister may arrange for any premises in which—

(a) a child is living with a person with whom the child has been placed by an adoption agency, or

(b) a child in respect of whom a notice of intention to adopt has been given under section 44 is, or will be, living,

to be inspected from time to time.

(2) The appropriate Minister may require an adoption agency—

(a) to give him any information, or
(b) to allow him to inspect any records (in whatever form they are held),

relating to the discharge of any of its functions in relation to adoption which the appropriate Minister specifies.

(3) An inspection under this section must be conducted by a person authorised by the appropriate Minister.

(4) An officer of a local authority may only be so authorised with the consent of the authority.

(5) A person inspecting any premises under subsection (1) may—

(a) visit the child there,
(b) make any examination into the state of the premises and the treatment of the child there which he thinks fit.

(6) A person authorised to inspect any records under this section may at any reasonable time have access to, and inspect and check the operation of, any computer (and associated apparatus) which is being or has been used in connection with the records in question.

(7) A person authorised to inspect any premises or records under this section may—

(a) enter the premises for that purpose at any reasonable time,
(b) require any person to give him any reasonable assistance he may require.

(8)   A person exercising a power under this section must, if required to do so, produce a duly authenticated document showing his authority.

(9)   Any person who intentionally obstructs another in the exercise of a power under this section is guilty of an offence and liable on summary conviction to a fine not exceeding level 3 on the standard scale.

NOTES

Initial Commencement

To be appointed

To be appointed: see s 148(6).

Appointment

Appointment (in relation to England): 30 December 2005: see SI 2005/2213, art 3(i); appointment (in relation to Wales): 30 December 2005: see SI 2005/3112, art 2(d).

Extent

This section does not extend to Scotland: see s 149(2).

General

[170]

This section provides for the inspection of records and premises, and visits to children in such premises, by the appropriate Minister.

Section 15(1)

[171]

The Minister can arrange for the periodic inspection of any premises where a child has been placed by an adoption agency, or premises where a child is living, or will be living, and notice of intention to adopt has been given under s 44 (the latter procedure is for children who have not been placed for adoption by an adoption agency).

Section 15(2), (6) and (7)

[172]

The Minister can require an adoption agency to provide any information, or allow the inspection of its records, regarding any of its adoption functions. The inspector must be allowed access at reasonable times to the agency's computers and associated equipment. Premises can be entered at reasonable times for this purpose, and reasonable assistance is to be given by any person to the inspector.

The premises can be entered at any reasonable time, and the inspector must be given reasonable help by any person as required.

Section 15(3) and (4)

[173]

The Minister must authorise a person to be an inspector, although such authorisation of a local authority officer is subject to the consent of that local authority.

Section 15(5)

[174]

The inspector may visit the child at the premises, and make any examination of the condition of the premises or the child's treatment as he/she considers necessary.

Section 15(8)

[175]

A person exercising any power under this section must, if required to do so, produce authenticated identification.

Section 15(9)

[176]

It is a criminal offence intentionally to obstruct an inspector exercising a power under this section, with a maximum penalty of a level 3 fine on summary conviction.

[177]

16   Distribution of functions in relation to registered adoption societies

After section 36 of the Care Standards Act 2000 (c 14) there is inserted—

'36A   Voluntary adoption agencies: distribution of functions

(1)   This section applies to functions relating to voluntary adoption agencies conferred on the registration authority by or under this Part or under Chapter 2 of Part 1 of the Adoption and Children Act 2002.

(2)   Subject to the following provisions, functions to which this section applies are exercisable—

    (a)   where the principal office of an agency is in England, by the Commission,

    (b)   where the principal office of an agency is in Wales, by the Assembly.

(3)   So far as those functions relate to the imposition, variation or removal of conditions of registration, they may only be exercised after consultation with the Assembly or (as the case may be) the Commission.

(4)   But—

    (a)   where such a function as is mentioned in subsection (3) is exercisable by the Commission in relation to an agency which has a branch in Wales, it is exercisable only with the agreement of the Assembly,

    (b)   where such a function as is mentioned in subsection (3) is exercisable by the Assembly in relation to an agency which has a branch in England, it is exercisable only with the agreement of the Commission.

(5)   The functions conferred on the registration authority by sections 31 and 32 of this Act in respect of any premises of a voluntary adoption agency are exercisable—

    (a)   where the premises are in England, by the Commission

    (b)   where the premises are in Wales, by the Assembly.

(6)   In spite of subsections (2) to (5), regulations may provide for any function to which this section applies to be exercisable by the Commission instead of the Assembly, or by the Assembly instead of the Commission, or by one concurrently with the other, or by both jointly or by either with the agreement of or after consultation with the other.

(7)   In this section, "regulations" means regulations relating to England and Wales.'

NOTES

Initial Commencement

To be appointed

To be appointed: see s 148(6).

Appointment
Appointment (in relation to Wales): 1 February 2003: see SI 2003/181, art 2; appointment (in relation to England in so far as it inserts the Care Standards Act 2000, s 36A(1)–(4) so far as relating to functions conferred on registration authorities under Pt II of the said Act and the Adoption Act 1976): 25 February 2003: see SI 2003/366, art 2(1)(a); appointment (in relation to England in so far as it inserts the Care Standards Act 2000, s 36A(5)–(7) so far as relating to functions conferred on registration authorities under Pt II of the said Act and the Adoption Act 1976): 30 April 2003: see SI 2003/366, art 2(4)(a); appointment (in relation to England for remaining purposes): 30 December 2005: see SI 2005/2213, art 3(j).

Extent
This section does not extend to Scotland: see s 149(2).

General

[178]

This section creates a new Care Standards Act 2000, s 36A, governing the regulation and inspection of voluntary adoption agencies by the Commission for Social Care Inspection (CSCI).

[179]

17 ...

...

NOTES
Amendment
Repealed by the Inquiries Act 2005, s 48(1), 49(2), Sch 2, Pt 1, para 23, Sch 3; for transitional provisions and savings see s 44(5) thereof: date in force: 7 June 2005: see SI 2005/1432, art 2.

General

[180]

This section was repealed by the Inquiries Act 2005, ss 48, 49 and Sch 3.

[181]

Chapter 3
Placement for Adoption and Adoption Orders

Placement of children by adoption agency for adoption

18 Placement for adoption by agencies

(1) An adoption agency may—

(a) place a child for adoption with prospective adopters, or
(b) where it has placed a child with any persons (whether under this Part or not), leave the child with them as prospective adopters,

but, except in the case of a child who is less than six weeks old, may only do so under section 19 or a placement order.

(2) An adoption agency may only place a child for adoption with prospective adopters if the agency is satisfied that the child ought to be placed for adoption.
(3) A child who is placed or authorised to be placed for adoption with prospective adopters by a local authority is looked after by the authority.
(4) If an application for an adoption order has been made by any persons in respect of a child and has not been disposed of—

(a)   an adoption agency which placed the child with those persons may leave the child with them until the application is disposed of, but

(b)   apart from that, the child may not be placed for adoption with any prospective adopters.

'Adoption order' includes a Scottish or Northern Irish adoption order.

(5)   References in this Act (apart from this section) to an adoption agency placing a child for adoption—

(a)   are to its placing a child for adoption with prospective adopters, and

(b)   include, where it has placed a child with any persons (whether under this Act or not), leaving the child with them as prospective adopters;

and references in this Act (apart from this section) to a child who is placed for adoption by an adoption agency are to be interpreted accordingly.

(6)   References in this Chapter to an adoption agency being, or not being, authorised to place a child for adoption are to the agency being or (as the case may be) not being authorised to do so under section 19 or a placement order.

(7)   This section is subject to sections 30 to 35 (removal of children placed by adoption agencies).

NOTES

Initial Commencement

To be appointed

To be appointed: see s 148(1), (2).

Appointment

Appointment: 30 December 2005: see SI 2005/2213, art 2(c).

Extent

This section does not extend to Scotland: see s 149(2).

See Further

See further, the application of this section, with modifications, in relation to an external adoption order effected within the period of six months of the making of the adoption, and in respect of adoptions under the 1993 Hague Convention on Protection of Children and Co-operation in respect of Intercountry Adoption: the Adoptions with a Foreign Element Regulations 2005, SI 2005/392, regs 11(1)(b), 52, 55.

General

[182]

Apart from exceptional circumstances (permitted under s 92), only an adoption agency can make arrangements, and place a child, for adoption; but the Act makes profound and complex changes governing agency placements. The basic principle is that an adoption agency is authorised to place a child for adoption only if it has parental consent to do so or, being a local authority adoption agency, has obtained a placement order (see ss 18(1), 19(1) and 21(1)).

Section 18(1)

[183]

An exception to those rules is made in respect of a child who is less than six weeks old. What this exception means is that an agency may place such a child for adoption before authorised to do so under s 19 or under a placement order, if it obtains, in accordance with the Adoption Agencies Regulations 2005, reg 35(4), the written agreement of the parent or guardian to do so. This is most likely to be a single mother. When the child reaches the age of six weeks, the agency should then obtain her consent under s 19 to continued placement. It may well be that the agency has already identified prospective adopters, Until so authorised under s 19 the agency does not acquire parental responsibility (see s 25(1) and (2)), even though it has already placed the child for adoption. If the mother at the end of the six-week period changes her mind and refuses consent, the agency must return the child to her, unless it is a local authority and it decides that the circumstances enable and justify seeking a placement order.

Section 18(4) and (5))

[184]

For the purposes of the Act placement of a child for adoption covers not only the case of an agency handing over the child to prospective adopters for adoption but also that of an agency having initially placed a child with any persons (whether under the Act or not) and later leaving the child with them as prospective adopters, for example, where the initial placement was with local authority foster parents and the local authority later decides that they are suitable prospective adopters. The placement then becomes an adoption agency placement. Many of the children whom the Act seeks to assist will fall within this extended meaning. If the local authority decides that they are not suitable prospective adopters, there cannot be an agency placement. So, if they wish to pursue the possibility of adopting the child, they will have to give notice (under s 44) to the local authority of their intention to apply for adoption, but the child must have his home with them for at least one year preceding the application (see s 42(4)). Although the local authority decides that the foster parents are not suitable prospective adopters, it *may* leave the child with them until the application for an adoption order is disposed of, but it is not obliged to do so (see s 18(4)(a)). If it does remove the child, the adoption application can proceed since the court is already seised of the matter, but when it comes to hear the application the local authority's withdrawal of the child will be a significant factor in applying the paramountcy principle in s 1 of the Act.

Section 18(3)

Placement by local authority

[185]

A child who is placed or authorised to be placed for adoption with prospective adopters by a local authority is looked after by the local authority within the meaning of the CA 1989 (see s 18(3) and the Glossary in Sch 6 to this Act). Thus, a child is looked after not only where he has been placed with prospective adopters because the local authority has been authorised to place him, but also where so authorised it has not yet done so. This rule operates whether the local authority placed the child for adoption with parental consent or under a placement order. It should ensure that the local authority properly reviews and supervises the adoption placement and promotes and safeguards the child's welfare. It also means that the child will have access to the services that are available to children looked after under the 1989 Act, and this will continue to be available should the adoption placement break down and the local authority then places the child with foster parents or otherwise provides accommodation for him.

Should the child be placed for adoption?

[186]

An adoption agency may only place a child for adoption with prospective adopters if the agency is satisfied that the child ought to be placed for adoption. Since the agency 'is coming to a decision relating to the adoption of the child' (s 1(1)), its decision must be determined in accordance with the paramountcy of the child's welfare. In considering whether to recommend to its agency that a child should be placed for adoption and whether placement should be with particular prospective adopters, an adoption panel is expressly

PART B – Statutes

directed to have regard to the duties imposed by s 1 (see Adoption Agencies Regulations 2005, regs 18(2) and 32(2) respectively); Adoption Agencies (Wales) Regulations 2005, regs 18(2) and 33(2).

Where a local authority is seeking a placement under a placement order, the paramountcy principle is subject to the conditions and restrictions imposed by the Act (see s 22).

[187]

19 Placing children with parental consent

(1) Where an adoption agency is satisfied that each parent or guardian of a child has consented to the child—

(a) being placed for adoption with prospective adopters identified in the consent, or

(b) being placed for adoption with any prospective adopters who may be chosen by the agency,

and has not withdrawn the consent, the agency is authorised to place the child for adoption accordingly.

(2) Consent to a child being placed for adoption with prospective adopters identified in the consent may be combined with consent to the child subsequently being placed for adoption with any prospective adopters who may be chosen by the agency in circumstances where the child is removed from or returned by the identified prospective adopters.

(3) Subsection (1) does not apply where—

(a) an application has been made on which a care order might be made and the application has not been disposed of, or

(b) a care order or placement order has been made after the consent was given.

(4) References in this Act to a child placed for adoption under this section include a child who was placed under this section with prospective adopters and continues to be placed with them, whether or not consent to the placement has been withdrawn.

(5) This section is subject to section 52 (parental etc consent).

NOTES

Initial Commencement

To be appointed
To be appointed: see s 148(1), (2).

Appointment
Appointment: 30 December 2005: see SI 2005/2213, art 2(c).

Extent
This section does not extend to Scotland: see s 149(2).

General

[188]

For placement for adoption to be authorised with consent the consent of each parent or guardian must be given.

1 The parent

[189]

For this purpose and for giving consent to the making of an adoption order the term 'parent' means a parent having parental responsibility (see s 52(6)), as defined in the CA 1989 (see the Glossary in Sch 6 to this Act). The term covers the following:

(1)   a child's 'married parents', ie the mother and father who were married to each other at the time of their child's birth (CA 1989, s 2(1) and (3)); but, by virtue of the Family Law Reform Act 1987 (s 1), that description extends also to:

    (1)   parents of those children of void marriages who are treated as legitimate children (Legitimacy Act 1976, s 1);

    (2)   parents of legitimated children (as defined by the Legitimacy Act 1976, s 10);

    (3)   adoptive parents under the ACA 2002 (s 139(1) and Sch 3, para 51, amending the Family Law Reform Act 1987, s 1(3)(c)) or under the Adoption Act 1976 (since the status of adopted children and their adoptive parents under Pt 4 of that Act remains protected by the ACA 2002, Sch 5);

    (4)   parents of children otherwise treated in law as legitimate. This residual category of married parents covers:

        (i)   parents of a child who is legitimate according to the rules in the conflict of laws;

        (ii)   parents by virtue of a parental order under s 30 of the Human Fertilisation and Embryology Act 1990; and

        (iii)   parents by virtue of s 28(2) of that Act, namely, where the child is born of a married woman as the result of artificial insemination or embryo transfer and the sperm donor is not the husband but it is not proved that the husband did not consent to the insemination or transfer—the wife and the husband are the parents.

Where the mother and father are not married, the term 'parent' for the purposes of parental consent automatically applies to the mother (see CA 1989, s 2(2)(a)), but not to the father unless and until he acquires (and then as long as he retains) parental responsibility by way of registration as the child's father or a parental responsibility agreement with the mother or a parental responsibility order (see CA 1989, s 2(2)(b) and 4, as amended by this Act, s 111). He will also acquire parental responsibility by marrying the mother (see legitimation, above) or by appointment as the child's guardian.

An unmarried father includes a man who is not the natural father but is treated as the child's father by virtue of the Human Fertilisation and Embryology Act 1990, s 28(3) (joint licensed treatment for a woman and man, but he is not the sperm donor).

2   The guardian

[190]

For the purposes of adoption law 'guardian' has the same meaning as in the CA 1989, but now also includes a special guardian. Since special guardianship is intended as a legally secure placement for children for whom adoption is not appropriate, a subsequent placement for adoption thus requiring the consent of the special guardian is remote.

The Adoption and Children Act 2002 makes one significant difference to the meaning of guardian. The definition section in the Adoption Act 1976, s 72(1) made all definitions therein subject to the proviso, 'unless the context otherwise requires'. The proviso led to the judicial conclusion that a person appointed as guardian under a foreign law might qualify as a guardian for the purpose of English adoption proceedings; see *Re AMR (adoption procedure)* [1999] 3 FCR 734, [1999] 2 FLR 807; *Re N (adoption: foreign guardianship)* [2000] 2 FLR 431; but for the contrary conclusion see *Re D (a minor: adoption)* [1999] 3 FCR 418, sub nom *Re D (adoption: foreign guardianship)* [1999] 2 FLR 865. The exclusion of the proviso from s 144(1) of the new Act precludes recognition of a foreign guardian.

The CA 1989 (s 12(3)(b)) continues expressly to exclude any person who is not a parent or guardian but who has parental responsibility by virtue of a residence order from any right to consent or to refuse to consent to the making of an adoption order. The 1989 Act is not expressly amended by this Act to take account of the new placement for adoption with consent, but by the latter's reference in s 19(1) only to a parent or guardian it is implicit that the above exclusion also applies to placement. Also excluded are step-parents, even if they have acquired parental responsibility (under the CA 1989, s 4A, as inserted by s 112 of this Act); but they, like holders of residence orders, relatives and others without parental responsibility, including a father without it, do have the express safeguard conferred by s 1(4)(f) of this Act, namely, that the adoption agency when deciding whether or not to place the child for adoption and the court when deciding whether or not to make an adoption order must have regard to their relationship with the child, including their wishes and feelings on placement and the making of an order.

Choice of prospective adopters

[191]

Each parent may give consent for the child to be placed for adoption with prospective adopters who are identified in the consent or with any prospective adopters who may be chosen by the agency; or they may combine those consents so that, if the child is removed from or returned by the identified prospective adopters, the agency may then place the child with prospective adopters whom it chooses. If the parents do not like the agency's proposed subsequent placement, they can, as in all cases of parental consent placement for adoption, withdraw their consent before that placement is made (see s 19(1)).

Withdrawal of consent

[192]

A child who has been placed for adoption with prospective adopters with parental consent continues to be treated as placed for adoption whether or not consent is later withdrawn (s 19(4)). If consent is withdrawn before an application for an adoption order is made, the adoption agency must return the child to the parents or, if it is a local authority adoption agency and the requisite conditions obtain (under s 22), it may apply for a placement order and not return the child pending the determination of the application. If an application for an adoption order has already been made, any subsequent, purported withdrawal of consent is ineffective (see s 52(4)). The judicial process prevails. The parents may still seek to contest the adoption at the final hearing of the adoption application, but will only be able to do so if they obtain the leave of the court, which can only be granted if the court is satisfied that there has been a change of circumstances since the parental consent was given (see s 47(7)). If leave is granted, the court will then have to decide whether to uphold the parents' refusal to consent or dispense with it (under s 52(1)).

Section 19(5)

Subject to s 52

[193]

Section 19(5) expressly incorporates s 52, which contains several provisions regulating parental consent to placements for adoption. Equally, s 20(6) incorporates that section in relation to advance consent to the making of adoption orders.

Thus, all consents need to be given unconditionally and with full understanding of what is involved (s 52(5)). Although a parent cannot impose conditions about his child's religious upbringing, the Adoption Act 1976 (s 7) did expressly require an adoption agency when placing a child for adoption to have regard so far as practicable to any wishes of the parent on the subject. That duty is now imposed by the Adoption Agencies Regulations 2005, reg 14(1)(c)(ii) and the Adoption Agencies (Wales) Regulations 2005, reg 14(1)(c)(ii), which require the agency to ascertain the parents' 'wishes and feelings about the child's religious and cultural upbringing'. That duty is part of the agency's wider duty (under s 1(5)) when placing a child for adoption to give due consideration to his religious persuasion, racial origin and cultural and linguistic background.

The requirement that there must be 'full understanding' by the parent of what is involved in placing the child for adoption with consent and consenting to an adoption order presupposes that the parent is fully informed and advised on the adoption process and its consequences. There is a lesson to be found in the former law. In *Re A (a child) (adoption: consent)* [2001] 2 FCR 174, [2001] 2 FLR 455, CA, because of the special circumstances involving a 14-year-old mother who was a refugee from the Kosovo conflict and whose child was conceived as a result of rape, it was held unlikely that her consent was 'sufficiently informed, sufficiently mature, sufficiently stable or sufficiently maintained'. That was a case involving the former freeing for adoption proceedings where special care was needed to explain the complex relationship between the freeing order and the adoption order. There are several complex provisions in the new Act and its regulations, none more so than those relating to placement for adoption. The Adoption Agencies Regulations 2005 (reg 14) and the Adoption Agencies (Wales) Regulations 2005 (reg 14) seek to ensure full understanding. It is vital that they do, because an adoption order is rarely revocable.

Subsections (9) and (10) of s 52 deal with the situation where consent to placement under s 19 is given by 'a parent' having parental responsibility for the child and at a later time 'the other parent' acquires parental responsibility. The latter is treated as having at that time given consent to the placement in the same terms as 'the first parent' gave consent. Since the only circumstance in which this possibility can arise is where the first parent is the unmarried mother and the unmarried father later acquires parental responsibility, it is surprising that the subsections are not framed in terms of mother and father, not parents. The purpose of the rule is to prevent the placement otherwise lapsing immediately the father acquires parental responsibility.

Although the unmarried father is 'treated' as having given consent to the placement, this will not prevent him from withdrawing his consent and, if this is done before an application for an adoption order has been made, the placement under s 19 is no longer authorised. If done after such an application, the purported withdrawal is ineffective (under s 52(4)). If the mother has given advance consent under s 20 to the making of an adoption order, the court will have to decide whether or not to dispense with his consent to the making of that order, and it will only be able to grant him leave to oppose the adoption if there has been a change in circumstances since the time when he was 'treated' as having given his consent to the placement (see s 47(7)). This, for example, could be crucial if the mother were to die before the hearing of the adoption application and the father wanted to bring up the child by himself. Of course, it may well be that the father supports adoption and, if so, after acquiring parental responsibility he, too, can proceed to give advance consent to the making of an adoption order.

Procedure

[194]

1   Applicants for adoption who wish to keep their identity confidential are able to apply for a serial number to be assigned to them for the purpose of adoption proceedings (see Family Procedure (Adoption) Rules 2005, r 20). It is submitted that nevertheless the use of the word 'identified' in s 19(1) means that it will continue to be possible for parents to consent to placement for adoption with specific prospective adopters

who are unnamed but about whom sufficient characteristics and details are given to the parents, usually by way of a profile from the adoption agency.

2   The Family Procedure (Adoption) Rules 2005, r 28, prescribes Forms of Consent or forms to like effect to be used for consenting to placement for adoption (see Forms A100, A101 and A102) and the Form A103 for giving advance consent to the making of an adoption order. A reporting officer must witness the signature of the parent or guardian (see r 71). This will be an officer of CAFCASS or, where the child is ordinarily resident in Wales, a Welsh family proceedings officer.

[195]

20   Advance consent to adoption

(1)   A parent or guardian of a child who consents to the child being placed for adoption by an adoption agency under section 19 may, at the same or any subsequent time, consent to the making of a future adoption order.
(2)   Consent under this section—

(a)   where the parent or guardian has consented to the child being placed for adoption with prospective adopters identified in the consent, may be consent to adoption by them, or
(b)   may be consent to adoption by any prospective adopters who may be chosen by the agency.

(3)   A person may withdraw any consent given under this section.
(4)   A person who gives consent under this section may, at the same or any subsequent time, by notice given to the adoption agency—

(a)   state that he does not wish to be informed of any application for an adoption order, or
(b)   withdraw such a statement.

(5)   A notice under subsection (4) has effect from the time when it is received by the adoption agency but has no effect if the person concerned has withdrawn his consent.
(6)   This section is subject to section 52 (parental etc consent).

NOTES
Initial Commencement
To be appointed
To be appointed: see s 148(1), (2).

Appointment
Appointment: 30 December 2005: see SI 2005/2213, art 2(c).

Extent
This section does not extend to Scotland: see s 149(2).

General

[196]

Where the parent consents to adoption by any prospective adopters whom the agency may choose, he may do so without knowing the identity of the persons in whose favour the adoption order will be made (see s 52(5)). Although s 20 does not expressly so provide, it impliedly follows from its rules that, where the parent combines alternative consents to placements for adoption (under s 19(2)), he can combine them with alternative advance consents to adoption. A parent can withdraw his advance consent at any time before an application for an adoption order is made, but not thereafter (see s 52(4)).

Future non-involvement

[197]

The parent may give notice to the agency stating that he does not wish to be informed of any application for an adoption order. This relinquishment of the child and non-involvement in the adoption proceedings is in line with the former procedure (under the Adoption Act 1976, s 18(6)) in freeing for adoption that enabled a parent to make a declaration that he did not wish to be concerned in future questions concerning the child's adoption. A notable difference between the new provision and the former is that, whereas a statement can be withdrawn, a declaration, once recorded by the court, could not. On the other hand in *Re C (minors: adoption)* [1992] 1 FLR 115 at 130, Balcombe LJ opined that non-compliance with the rules governing a declaration did not invalidate a freeing order, and it seems that correspondingly an invalid notice of statement would not affect the placement for adoption.

Declarations were only made in a small minority of cases. Use of the new provision is unlikely to be greater. Indeed, the parent's retention of parental responsibility until an adoption order is made, unlike its loss when a freeing order was made, is likely to discourage use of the new provision.

Procedure

[198]

In its Report to the court, which is to hear the application for an adoption order, the adoption agency must include the names of those who have made statements under s 20(4)(a), the dates that the statements were made and the dates of any withdrawal of statements; see Family Procedure (Adoption) Rules 2005, r 29(3) and Practice Direction, Reports by the Adoption Agency or Local Authority, Annex A, Section B, Pt 3, para (c).

[199]

---

21 Placement orders

(1)   A placement order is an order made by the court authorising a local authority to place a child for adoption with any prospective adopters who may be chosen by the authority.

(2)   The court may not make a placement order in respect of a child unless—

(a)   the child is subject to a care order,

(b)   the court is satisfied that the conditions in section 31(2) of the 1989 Act (conditions for making a care order) are met, or

(c)   the child has no parent or guardian.

(3)   The court may only make a placement order if, in the case of each parent or guardian of the child, the court is satisfied—

(a)   that the parent or guardian has consented to the child being placed for adoption with any prospective adopters who may be chosen by the local authority and has not withdrawn the consent, or

(b)   that the parent's or guardian's consent should be dispensed with.

This subsection is subject to section 52 (parental etc consent).

(4)   A placement order continues in force until—

(a)   it is revoked under section 24,

(b)   an adoption order is made in respect of the child, or

(c)   the child marries[, forms a civil partnership] or attains the age of 18 years.

'Adoption order' includes a Scottish or Northern Irish adoption order.

NOTES

Initial Commencement

To be appointed
To be appointed: see s 148(1), (2).

Appointment
Appointment: 30 December 2005: see SI 2005/2213, art 2(c).

Extent
This section does not extend to Scotland: see s 149(2).

Amendment
Sub-s (4): in para (c) words ', forms a civil partnership' in square brackets inserted by the Civil Partnership Act 2004, s 79(1), (2); date in force: 30 December 2005: see SI 2005/3175, art 2(9).

See Further
See further, the application of this section, with modifications, in relation to an external adoption order effected within the period of six months of the making of the adoption, and in respect of adoptions under the 1993 Hague Convention on Protection of Children and Co-operation in respect of Intercountry Adoption: the Adoptions with a Foreign Element Regulations 2005, SI 2005/392, regs 11(1)(c), 52, 55.

General

[200]

The second route to adoption through an adoption agency is by way of a placement order, but it is available only to local authority adoption agencies. Following consultation with interested groups, the government agreed that it would be inappropriate for voluntary adoption agencies to be empowered by a court order to place a child compulsorily for adoption against parental wishes. Moreover, the placement order is closely associated with the care order of the CA 1989. The order authorises a local authority to place a child with any prospective adopters chosen by the authority – it may well be the child's present foster carers – and not with prospective adopters to be identified in the order. Consequently, if a placement turns out to be unsuccessful, the local authority may proceed to choose other prospective adopters without having to return to the court for a new order. This avoidance of delay in making further placement accords with the no-delay principle embodied in s 1(3) of the Act. Furthermore, the rule properly recognises the different functions of the court and the agency: the one to determine whether placement for adoption is in the best interests of the child; the other, with its skills and experience, to select and match the child with prospective adopters. The rule also leaves with the local authority flexibility over other future decisions.

Prerequisites to the making of a placement order

1 Section 21(2)

[201]

Apart from the exceptional case of an orphaned child, who may also satisfy one of the other two requirements, these requirements are another feature of the policy of aligning adoption law, so far as appropriate, with the CA 1989. Unless there is already a care order in force, the same threshold for compulsory intervention in family life applies where the child is at risk of significant harm. Unless the circumstances fall within s 22(1) of the new Act, a placement order cannot therefore be made in respect of a child who is being accommodated by the local authority at the parents' request under CA 1989, Pt III. He can only be placed for adoption by the local authority with parental consent in accordance with s 19.

2 Section 21(3)

[202]

It is likely that in many applications for placement orders dispensation with consent will be needed. Whether the child's welfare requires dispensation (under s 52(1)(b)) depends upon the circumstances. Particularly relevant will be the grounds on which a care order was made or the conditions in CA 1989, s 31(2) are met. In those cases where parents may be willing to consider consent to placement, much may depend upon whether or not the local authority already has prospective adopters in mind and, if it has, whether or not it has already engaged the parents in the prospective choice. The local authority must raise the issue of consent with the parents before it applies for the placement order, because the appropriate form for dealing with consent, namely Form A100, must be attached to the Form of Application in accordance with the Family Procedure (Adoption) Rules 2005, r 18.

Procedure

[203]

For the procedure regulating dispensing with consent see Family Procedure (Adoption) Rules 2005, r 27.

Duration of placement orders

[204]

The making of a special guardianship order does not automatically terminate a placement order. This is surprising, given that the purpose of special guardianship is to provide an alternative legally secure placement for children for whom adoption is not appropriate. The government justified this negative consequence on the ground that, when deciding whether or not to make a special guardianship order, the court needed to make a positive decision to revoke the placement order and that would be ensured by the local authority applying for revocation, if it agreed that a special guardianship order was appropriate. Without that application, the court hearing the special guardianship application would look only at CA 1989, s 1, which, unlike s 1 of the new Act, was not 'specifically tailored' to adoption and the issues surrounding it. The argument, it is submitted, underestimates the duty of the court under CA 1989, s 1, to take into account all relevant circumstances in applying the principle of the paramountcy of the child's welfare. The factors listed in the checklist (s 1(3)) are not exclusive. The court would therefore also be obliged to take into account all the relevant factors tailored in the checklist in s 1(4) of the new Act – the reference to s 1(4) could have been directed in the Children Act provisions governing special guardianship. Those factors would be presented to the court by the relevant local authority in its report (under the CA 1989, s 14A(8)), which would either support or oppose the special guardianship application. It would then be a matter for the court to decide whether to allow further attempts to be made for adoption placement and dismiss the special guardianship application or, if not, to revoke the placement order and make a special guardianship order. Regrettably, the new Act does not permit this possibility because the court has no power of its own motion to revoke a placement order.

Section 21(4)(c)

[205]

Note its amendment by the Civil Partnership Act 2004, s 79(2).

[206]

22 Applications for placement orders

(1) A local authority must apply to the court for a placement order in respect of a child if—

(a) the child is placed for adoption by them or is being provided with accommodation by them,

(b)   no adoption agency is authorised to place the child for adoption,

(c)   the child has no parent or guardian or the authority consider that the conditions in section 31(2) of the 1989 Act are met, and

(d)   the authority are satisfied that the child ought to be placed for adoption.

(2)   If—

(a)   an application has been made (and has not been disposed of) on which a care order might be made in respect of a child, or

(b)   a child is subject to a care order and the appropriate local authority are not authorised to place the child for adoption,

the appropriate local authority must apply to the court for a placement order if they are satisfied that the child ought to be placed for adoption.

(3)   If—

(a)   a child is subject to a care order, and

(b)   the appropriate local authority are authorised to place the child for adoption under section 19,

the authority may apply to the court for a placement order.

(4)   If a local authority—

(a)   are under a duty to apply to the court for a placement order in respect of a child, or

(b)   have applied for a placement order in respect of a child and the application has not been disposed of,

the child is looked after by the authority.

(5)   Subsections (1) to (3) do not apply in respect of a child—

(a)   if any persons have given notice of intention to adopt, unless the period of four months beginning with the giving of the notice has expired without them applying for an adoption order or their application for such an order has been withdrawn or refused, or

(b)   if an application for an adoption order has been made and has not been disposed of.

'Adoption order' includes a Scottish or Northern Irish adoption order.

(6)   Where—

(a)   an application for a placement order in respect of a child has been made and has not been disposed of, and

(b)   no interim care order is in force,

the court may give any directions it considers appropriate for the medical or psychiatric examination or other assessment of the child; but a child who is of sufficient understanding to make an informed decision may refuse to submit to the examination or other assessment.

(7)   The appropriate local authority—

(a)   in relation to a care order, is the local authority in whose care the child is placed by the order, and

(b)   in relation to an application on which a care order might be made, is the local authority which makes the application.

NOTES

Initial Commencement

To be appointed

To be appointed: see s 148(1), (2).

Appointment

Appointment: 30 December 2005: see SI 2005/2213, art 2(c).

Extent

This section does not extend to Scotland: see s 149(2).

See Further

See further, the application of this section, with modifications, in relation to an external adoption order effected within the period of six months of the making of the adoption, and in respect of

adoptions under the 1993 Hague Convention on Protection of Children and Co-operation in respect of Intercountry Adoption: the Adoptions with a Foreign Element Regulations 2005, SI 2005/392, regs 11(1)(d), 52, 55.

General

The duty to apply

(1)   Section 22(1)

[207]

The following is an illustration of the duty under s 22(1).

> The child is being provided with accommodation by the local authority. The parents consented to his being placed for adoption but have withdrawn their consent. The local authority still takes the view that the child ought to be placed for adoption. Meanwhile, it has come to the attention of the authority that there is evidence that he is likely to suffer significant harm if he returns to his parents. The authority must apply for a placement order.

(2)   Section 22(2)(a)

[208]

An adoption agency is no longer authorised under s 19 to place a child for adoption with parental consent once an application has been made on which a care order might be made and the application has not been disposed of (s 19(3)(a)). It may have come to the attention of the local authority while engaged with the parents in possible placement for adoption with their consent that there is evidence of abuse by them of their child that justifies an application for a care order followed up by an application for a placement order if the authority is satisfied that the child ought to be placed for adoption. The question of parental consent is then regulated by s 21(3). In cases of this kind the local authority will be involved in the dual capacity of an adoption agency and an applicant under CA 1989, s 31, but exceptionally the adoption agency initially involved could be a registered adoption society. Thus, in the above example the evidence of abuse might have emerged when the voluntary adoption agency was arranging placement for adoption and then informed the local authority of it.

(3)   Section 22(2)(b)

[209]

Where parental consent to place a child for adoption has already been given but a care order is subsequently made, the authorisation for the placement under s 19 no longer applies (s 19(3)(b)). If the local authority is still satisfied that the child ought to be placed for adoption, it must apply for a placement order, and here again the question of parental consent is regulated by s 21(3).

(4)   The child's welfare

[210]

In considering whether it has a duty to apply for a placement order, the local authority must come to a decision whether or not it is satisfied that the child ought to be placed for adoption. It must therefore apply the principle of the paramountcy of the child's welfare.

PART B – Statutes

Where an application for a care order is proceeding, the local authority may apply for a placement order application to be heard as part and parcel of the continuing trial of the care order application. It is then a matter for the discretion of the trial judge to allow concurrent adjudication, which may be challenged if it can be shown that to allow it would be unfair to a party to the proceedings. In a case of this kind it is entirely proper for the local authority, if it has proposed in its care plan the route of adoption for the child, to refer the child's case to its adoption panel before the final hearing of the care order application. If, in accordance with the Adoption Agencies Regulations 2005, reg 18(3) or the Adoption Agencies (Wales) Regulations 2005, reg 18(3), the panel recommends placement – and in so doing it may give advice about whether an application should be made for a placement order – and if, in accordance with its duty under reg 19 of both of those Regulations, to take account of the panel's recommendation in deciding whether the child should be placed for adoption, the local authority so decides, it may proceed to apply for a placement order. See *Re P-B (a child)* [2006] EWCA Civ 1016.

The discretion to apply

[211]

If the child is subject to a care order and the local authority is *then* authorised to place the child under s 19, it has a discretion to apply for a placement order. Since parental consent has been given, the consequent requirement in s 21(3)(a) is *ipso facto* satisfied. The discretion to apply does not impose an express condition that the local authority must be satisfied that the child ought to be placed for adoption, but the omission is academic. The court will have to be so satisfied and apply the paramountcy principle. So, the local authority will have to address its mind to the principle and the statutory checklist in presenting its application for an order.

Alternatively the local authority may decide to place the child with parental consent without the need for an order. There is nothing in s 19(3) to prevent this. It is likely that local authorities will prefer this alternative. But certain consequences flow from placement orders that do not extend to placements under s 19 (see ss 29 and 34), and these may need to be taken into account when deciding which alternative to pursue.

The child and the local authority

[212]

It has already been noted (see comment on s 18(3)) that a child who is placed for adoption by a local authority is looked after by the authority within the meaning of CA 1989, s 22. The rule is extended (by s 22(4) of the new Act) (a) to where a local authority is under a duty to apply for a placement order and (b) to where it has applied for a placement order and the application has not been disposed of. Where the application is made in respect of a child who is already the subject of a care order (s 22(2)(b)), he will already be looked after by the authority. The practical significance of s 22(4) is to extend protection to those children who fall within the scope of s 22(1) or (2)(a).

Procedure

[213]

(1) For the parties to proceedings for a placement order see Family Procedure (Adoption) Rules 2005, r 23; for the matters to be included in the application, Form A50; and for the persons to whom the court officer must send copies of the application form, r 24(1)(b)(ii) and the relevant accompanying Practice Direction. Note: if a party does not want the child's address to be disclosed to any other party, that information should not appear on Form A50 but on Form A65.

(2) For a summary of the steps to be taken from the issue of an application for a placement order to the final hearing see the President's Guidance (*Adoption: The New Law and Procedure*) [2006] 1 FLR 123 at paras 20–24.

(3) Where an application for a placement order is pending and no interim care order is in force, the court has the same power (under s 22(6)) to give directions for the child to undergo medical or psychiatric examination or assessment as a court has when making an interim care order under the CA 1989 (s 38(6)). The power is subject to the same right of the child to refuse to submit to examination or assessment if he is of sufficient understanding to make an informed decision.

The decision to make a placement order

[214]

In deciding whether or not to make a placement order, the court must apply the welfare test, with its checklist, in accordance with s 1 of the Act. It will have to consider its full range of powers under the Act and under the CA 1989, and must not make a placement order unless it considers that making that order would be better for the child than not doing so (s 1(6)). The circumstances may justify various possibilities. For example:

(1) The court makes a placement order.

(2) The court decides that it is best to return the child to his parents. If the application for a placement order is based on the local authority's undisposed of application on which a care order might be made (section 22(2)(a)), the court will refuse both orders. If the application for a placement order is in respect of a child who is subject to a care order, the court will refuse the former and discharge the latter on the application of the parents (in accordance with CA 1989, s 39(1)(a)).

(3) The court decides that it is best to hand over the child to wider members of the birth family, e g an uncle and aunt. The court may of its own motion grant them a residence order. In refusing a placement order it will also, depending upon which of the above alternatives applies, refuse a care order or discharge an existing care order. The court cannot of its own motion discharge a care order. In the above circumstances the most likely applicant for discharge will be the child. The uncle and aunt will not be eligible (under CA 1989, s 39) to apply as persons having parental responsibility, because the care order must be discharged before the court can make a residence order.

(4) The court refuses to make a placement order, but makes a care order or allows an existing care order to continue in force. This solution may be appropriate where the child is shown to be hostile to adoption.

(5) The court makes both a placement order and a care order. This could often be desirable in anticipation of failure of a suitable placement and revocation of the placement order; for example, because it is found that the child is not suited to adoption. It would mean that parental responsibility given to the local authority by virtue of the placement order (under s 25) would continue under the care order. But so long as a placement order is in force a care order, whether already existing when the placement order was made or was concurrently made, does not have effect (see s 29(1)). If there is no existing care order and the placement order is revoked, the local authority could then apply for a care order, preferably as part of the revocation proceedings so as to achieve the continuity of parental responsibility referred to above.

[215]

23   Varying placement orders

(1)   The court may vary a placement order so as to substitute another local authority for the local authority authorised by the order to place the child for adoption.

> (2)   The variation may only be made on the joint application of both authorities.
>
> **NOTES**
> **Initial Commencement**
> *To be appointed*
> To be appointed: see s 148(1), (2).
>
> **Appointment**
> Appointment: 30 December 2005: see SI 2005/2213, art 2(c).
>
> **Extent**
> This section does not extend to Scotland: see s 149(2).

General

[216]

Such is the purpose of the placement order that it does not lend itself to variation, but s 23 allows for one possibility. The exception recognises that there may be liaison policies among local authorities over adoption placement. A joint application would, for example, be appropriate where the prospective adopters move from one local authority area to another.

Procedure

[217]

For the respondents to proceedings see Family Procedure (Adoption) Rules 2005, r 23. The form of application is Form A51.

The child's welfare

[218]

Section 1 of the Act expressly provides that the principle of the paramountcy of the child's welfare extends to applications for placement orders and to applications for their revocation, but no mention is made of applications for their variation. Arguably, the paramountcy principle should also apply to those applications, because when a court is deciding whether or not to vary a placement order it is 'coming to a decision relating to the adoption of a child'. The guidance notes to Form A51 equivocally require the applicants to state 'why the transfer [of responsibility between local authorities] would be in the best interests of the child, and any administrative reasons which make the transfer desirable'. Certainly, local authority administrative convenience should not override the best interests of the child, but only promote them.

[219]

> ### 24   Revoking placement orders
>
> (1)   The court may revoke a placement order on the application of any person.
> (2)   But an application may not be made by a person other than the child or the local authority authorised by the order to place the child for adoption unless—
>
> (a)   the court has given leave to apply, and
> (b)   the child is not placed for adoption by the authority.
>
> (3)   The court cannot give leave under subsection (2)(a) unless satisfied that there has been a change in circumstances since the order was made.
> (4)   If the court determines, on an application for an adoption order, not to make the order, it may revoke any placement order in respect of the child.
> (5)   Where—

(a)   an application for the revocation of a placement order has been made and has not been disposed of, and

(b)   the child is not placed for adoption by the authority,

the child may not without the court's leave be placed for adoption under the order.

NOTES

Initial Commencement

To be appointed

To be appointed: see s 148(1), (2).

Appointment

Appointment: 30 December 2005: see SI 2005/2213, art 2(c).

Extent

This section does not extend to Scotland: see s 149(2).

See Further

See further, the application of this section, with modifications, in relation to an external adoption order effected within the period of six months of the making of the adoption, and in respect of adoptions under the 1993 Hague Convention on Protection of Children and Co-operation in respect of Intercountry Adoption: the Adoptions with a Foreign Element Regulations 2005, SI 2005/392, regs 11(1)(e), 52, 55.

General

The local authority

[220]

The local authority authorised by the placement order to place the child for adoption is entitled at any time to apply for revocation of the order. For example, it may apply where the placement breaks down and there is no alternative adoptive family available or where adoption may no longer be the best solution for the child, for example because he has shown by his conduct during the placement that he is hostile to adoption.

The child

[221]

The child (or a person acting on his behalf) is also entitled at any time to apply. This is in line with his counterpart seeking discharge of a care order (see CA 1989, s 39(1)(b)), but is in sharp contrast to his counterpart seeking a s 8 order under the 1989 Act who needs leave to apply and that may only be granted if he has sufficient understanding to make the proposed application (s 10(8)).

Any other person

[222]

Any other person may apply only with leave of the court and then only if the child is not placed for adoption by the local authority, which covers both the case where the child has not yet been placed and that where a placement has been made but withdrawn. The court cannot grant leave unless satisfied that there has been a change in circumstances since the placement order was made. Thus, the parents, for example, may seek to show that their circumstances now enable the child to be rehabilitated with them. However, the burden of proving a change in circumstances is likely to be a heavy one. In applying the principle of the paramountcy of the child's welfare when deciding to make a placement order, the court will have considered alternatives and taken into account the views of the parents and their capacity or lack of it to provide a stable and secure environment. Moreover, since leave can only be sought as long as the child is not placed for adoption and since the local authority is not likely to delay placement, the time scale militates against change in circumstances. It may be easier to prove a change during the period between a failed placement and the possible making of a further placement; for example, where the applicants for revocation are relatives who are now in a position to provide long-term care for the child. In those circumstances the court may decide to revoke the placement order and of its own motion make a joint residence order in favour of the relatives, which it is empowered to do since the revocation proceedings are family proceedings within the meaning of CA 1989, s 8(4)(d) (as amended by the new Act, Sch 3, para 55).

Procedure

[223]

For the respondents to proceedings for revocation see Family Procedure (Adoption) Rules 2005, r 23. Application for revocation is in Form A52. Application for leave to apply must be made using Form FP2.

Section 24(4)

[224]

If the court decides not to make an adoption order, it is free to revoke the placement order. On the one hand, it may consider that the child should still be placed for adoption and so decide that the placement order should continue. This might, for example, be appropriate where the reason for deciding not to make an adoption order is the unsuitability of the prospective adopters. On the other hand, if it is deciding to revoke the placement order, it will need to consider the alternatives available. It will not be in the best interests of the child to leave him in limbo. If there is already a care order in existence, its revived operation may be sufficient or, if the circumstances continue to warrant it, making a care order may be appropriate or a special guardianship order or a residence order in favour of concerned relatives.

Section 24(5)

[225]

Where the child is not placed for adoption and an application for revocation of the placement order has been made but not yet disposed of, the local authority may not meantime place the child for adoption unless the court grants leave. In deciding whether or not to grant leave, much will depend on the imminence or otherwise of the hearing of the revocation application. In this latter regard the duty of the court (under s 1(3)) to avoid delay is relevant.

[226]

---

25 Parental responsibility

(1) This section applies while—

(a)   a child is placed for adoption under section 19 or an adoption agency is authorised to place a child for adoption under that section, or

(b)   a placement order is in force in respect of a child.

(2) Parental responsibility for the child is given to the agency concerned.

(3) While the child is placed with prospective adopters, parental responsibility is given to them.

(4) The agency may determine that the parental responsibility of any parent or guardian, or of prospective adopters, is to be restricted to the extent specified in the determination.

General

[227]

The Act provides for the concurrence of parental responsibility with the parents, the adoption agency and the prospective adopters. The abandonment of the concept of freeing for adoption now means that in all cases the parents retain their parental responsibility until it is extinguished by the adoption order (see s 46(2)(a)). Once a child is placed under s 19 or an adoption agency is authorised to place a child under that section, or once a placement order is in force, the agency concerned acquires parental responsibility, and so long as the child remains placed with prospective adopters, they, too, have parental responsibility. The effect of the concurrence is that the agency and, through the agency, the prospective adopters, will have to consult with the parents about any important matters affecting the child's upbringing, for example, major medical treatment. Although an agency may restrict the parental responsibility of a parent (see below), there still is, it is submitted, a duty to consult on such matters. Any consequent dispute could lead to withdrawal of parental consent to placement where the placement is authorised under s 19, and any advance consent (under s 20) to the making of an adoption order would also be withdrawn. Where it is too late to withdraw consent because the application for an adoption order has been made (see s 52(4)) or where the placement is under a placement order, the parents could apply for a specific issue order or a prohibited steps order, as indeed they could instead of withdrawing s 19 consent.

Section 25(4)

Restricting parental responsibility

[228]

The adoption agency may restrict the parental responsibility of a parent or guardian or prospective adopters. When the agency has decided to place the child with particular adopters, it must send them an adoption placement plan (see Adoption Agencies Regulations 2005, reg 35(2) and Sch 5; Adoption Agencies (Wales) Regulations 2005, reg 37(2), (4) and (5)). This must include a statement about whether the parental responsibility of the prospective adopters for the child is to be restricted and, if so, the extent to which it is to be restricted.

The power to restrict is similar to that conferred on a local authority in relation to a parent where there is a care order in force (see CA 1989, s 33(3)(b)). The latter power may only be exercised where it is necessary to do so in order to safeguard or promote the child's welfare (see CA 1989, s 33(4)). There is no such express condition imposed under the new Act, but the necessary implication is that, since the adoption agency is coming to a decision relating to the adoption of the child, his welfare is the paramount consideration. Research (see Freeman and Hunt *Parental Responsibility Care Proceedings* (1998)) suggests that it is very difficult for parents to challenge the exercise of that power and to insist on participation in their child's upbringing. There is no reason to conclude that it will be otherwise in relation to the power under the new Act. One parental power that is unassailable is that of the unmarried mother to enter into a parental responsibility agreement with the father; see *Re X (parental responsibility agreement: children in care)* [2000] 2 All ER 66, [2000] 1 FCR 379, [2000] 1 FLR 517. If she does so after consenting under s 19 to placement of their child, the father is treated as having given consent to the placement at the same time as she did (see s 52(9) and (10)). Other powers that are unassailable are parental appointment of a testamentary guardian and parental consent needed to remove the child out of the United Kingdom. It is doubtful whether a parent could change a child's surname during the adoption process, but any attempt to do so could be met by the adoption agency's seeking a prohibited steps order.

Where a local authority allows a child who is the subject of a care order to live at home with his parents, they can do what is reasonable in the circumstances to safeguard and promote his welfare (see CA 1989, s 33(5)). There is no express provision in the new Act that prospective adopters can act similarly, but the conferment of parental responsibility in itself enables them to do so, subject to any restrictions imposed on it by the adoption agency.

Where there is an application for a special guardianship order, the local authority may well apply for revocation of its placement order. If it does not and a special guardianship order is made, the parental responsibility of the special guardian is subject to the local authority's power to restrict it under s 25(4) (see s 29(7)(a)). Given that special guardianship is aimed at providing a secure placement as an alternative to adoption, it is difficult to envisage circumstances where s 25(4) will be invoked.

Reviewing the parental responsibility of prospective adopters

[229]

The conferment of parental responsibility on the prospective adopters may encourage early full commitment to bringing up the child; but in practical terms the responsibility will be limited to day-to-day bringing up. The exercise of parental responsibility will be subject to regular review of, and visits to, the prospective adopters by the adoption agency; see the Adoption Agencies Regulations 2005, reg 36(2)–(4); Adoption Agencies (Wales) Regulations 2005, reg 37(2), (4) and (5). When carrying out a review the agency must consider the arrangements in relation to the exercise of parental responsibility and whether they should continue or be altered; see reg 36(6)(d) and reg 37(7)(d) respectively of those Regulations. If the agency considers that the prospective adopters are not properly exercising their responsibility in the best interests of the child, it may give them notice to return the child to the agency in accordance with s 35(2) of the Act.

[230]

26 Contact

(1)   On an adoption agency being authorised to place a child for adoption, or placing a child for adoption who is less than six weeks old, any provision for contact under the 1989 Act ceases to have effect [and any contact activity direction relating to contact with the child is discharged].

(2)   While an adoption agency is so authorised or a child is placed for adoption—

(a)   no application may be made for any provision for contact under that Act, but
(b)   the court may make an order under this section requiring the person with whom the child lives, or is to live, to allow the child to visit or stay with the person named in the order, or for the person named in the order and the child otherwise to have contact with each other.

(3)   An application for an order under this section may be made by—

(a)   the child or the agency,
(b)   any parent, guardian or relative,
(c)   any person in whose favour there was provision for contact under the 1989 Act which ceased to have effect by virtue of subsection (1),

(d)   if a residence order was in force immediately before the adoption agency was authorised to place the child for adoption or (as the case may be) placed the child for adoption at a time when he was less than six weeks old, the person in whose favour the order was made,

(e)   if a person had care of the child immediately before that time by virtue of an order made in the exercise of the High Court's inherent jurisdiction with respect to children, that person,

(f)   any person who has obtained the court's leave to make the application.

(4)   When making a placement order, the court may on its own initiative make an order under this section.

(5)   This section does not prevent an application for a contact order under section 8 of the 1989 Act being made where the application is to be heard together with an application for an adoption order in respect of the child.

(6)   In this section, ['contact activity direction' has the meaning given by section 11A of the 1989 Act and] 'provision for contact under the 1989 Act' means a contact order under section 8 of that Act or an order under section 34 of that Act (parental contact with children in care).

NOTES

Initial Commencement

To be appointed

To be appointed: see s 148(1), (2).

Appointment

Appointment: 30 December 2005: see SI 2005/2213, art 2(c).

Extent

This section does not extend to Scotland: see s 149(2).

Amendment

Sub-s (1): words 'and any contact activity direction relating to contact with the child is discharged' in square brackets inserted by the Children and Adoption Act 2006, s 15(1), Sch 2, paras 13, 14(1), (2); date in force: to be appointed: see the Children and Adoption Act 2006, s 17(2); sub-s (6): words '"contact activity direction" has the meaning given by section 11A of the 1989 Act and' in square brackets inserted by the Children and Adoption Act 2006, s 15(1), Sch 2, paras 13, 14(1), (3); date in force: to be appointed: see the Children and Adoption Act 2006, s 17(2).

General

[231]

Sections 26 and 27 make provision for enabling application to be made for a contact order in respect of a child whom an adoption agency has been authorised to place for adoption under s 19 or under a placement order or of a child placed for adoption less than six weeks' old ('a baby placement'), but the power to make a s 26 order must be seen against the background of contact arrangements under the Adoption Agencies Regulations 2005 and the Adoption Agencies (Wales) Regulations 2005.

Contact arrangements

[232]

When an adoption agency is so authorised to place for adoption or where there is a baby placement, any existing contact order under CA 1989, s 8 or any order under CA 1989, s 34 for contact with children in care ceases to have effect (s 26(1) and (6)). [When the Children and Adoption Act 2006 comes into force, this terminal effect will also extend to any contact activity direction as defined by the new CA 1989, s 11A, which the 2006 Act introduces.] The possibility of a contact order existing in the case of a baby placement is remote, but could occur, for example, where a baby is removed from the mother after birth under an emergency protection order, followed by an interim care order and a concurrent contact order in favour of the mother. This rule in s 26(1) recognises that the contact arrangements may no longer be appropriate, given the actual or prospective adoption placement.

Under the Adoption Agencies Regulations 2005, reg 46, once an adoption agency has decided that a child should be placed for adoption and is authorised to do so, it must consider what arrangements it should make for allowing any person contact with the child. In coming to a decision relating to these 'contact arrangements' it must:

(a)   take into account the wishes and feelings of the child's parent or guardian, including also, if the agency considers it appropriate, those of the child's unmarried father who does not have parental responsibility and whose identity is known to the agency;

(b)   take into account any advice given by the adoption panel to the agency about the proposed contact arrangements (under reg 18(3));

(c)   have regard to the principle that the child's welfare is paramount and to the checklist in section 1(4) of the Act. It is submitted that this obligation extends also to determining the appropriateness of the agency's taking into account the wishes and feelings of the unmarried father without parental responsibility. The agency should assess the reality of the relationship between father and child and decide the appropriateness in accordance with the child's best interests. This would be consistent with the father's right under Article 8 of the European Convention on Human Rights.

Under reg 46 the agency must notify the following persons of the contact arrangements:

(a)   the child, if the agency considers he is of sufficient age and understanding;

(b)   if their whereabouts are known to the agency, the parent or guardian and, where the agency considers it appropriate, the unmarried father who does not have parental responsibility;

(c)   any person in whose favour there was a provision for contact under the CA 1989 which ceased to have effect by virtue of s 26(1); and

(d)   any other person the agency considers relevant, for example interested relatives or former long-term foster parents of the child.

When the agency decides that the child should be placed with particular prospective adopters, it must review the contact arrangements already made in the light of the views of the prospective adopters and any advice given (under reg 32(3)(a)) by the adoption panel. If the agency proposes to make any changes to the contact arrangements which affect any of the above persons who must be notified of the arrangements, it must seek the views of the affected person and take them into account in deciding what arrangements it should make for allowing any person contact with the child while he is placed for adoption with the prospective adopters.

The agency must set out the contact arrangements in the placement plan and keep them under regular reviews, when it must consider the existing circumstances and whether they should continue or be altered (see regs 36(6)(c) and 46(7)).

There are no provisions in the Adoption Agencies (Wales) Regulations 2005 corresponding to reg 46, but it is submitted that the safeguards within the regulation should be considered as good practice in Wales; see para [989].

The making of a contact order

[233]

If the parents or others who formerly had contact under a CA 1989, s 8 order or a CA 1989, s 34 order cannot agree new contact arrangements with the adoption agency and with those with whom the child is living or to live, application can be made for a new contact order, not under the 1989 Act but under s 26. Moreover, when making a placement order, the court may on its own initiative make an order under s 26 (see sub-s (4)).

Applicants for contact orders are listed in s 26(3) and respondents in the Family Procedure (Adoption) Rules 2005, r 23. Designated applicants are entitled to apply; any other person requires leave. Application must be in Form A53; application for leave to apply must be made by using Form FP2.

A s 26 order is defined in the same terms as a s 8 contact order. It may provide for visiting or staying contact or indirect contact, usually by letter writing and telephone calls or sometimes by video recordings. In deciding whether or not to grant an order and, if so, to include appropriate conditions (as permitted by s 27(5)), the court must apply the paramountcy principle in s 1. In so doing, factors that are likely to be particularly relevant are the child's wishes and feelings, his particular needs (for example, transport arrange-ments for visiting contact where he is disabled) and the relationship which he has with the applicants for the s 26 order.

Duration of contact order

[234]

A s 26 order has effect while the adoption agency is authorised to place the child for adoption or the child is placed for adoption (s 27(1)(a)), but the court may vary or revoke the order on an application by the child, the agency or a person named in the order (s 27(1)(b)). That can be the person who has contact with the child or the person with whom the child lives and who is required to allow contact (see s 26(2)(b)). An application to vary or revoke must be in Form A54. The respondents to the proceedings are the parties to the proceedings leading to the contact order and any person named in that order (Family Procedure (Adoption) Rules 2005, r 23). The power to vary or revoke must be exercised in accordance with the paramountcy principle in s 1.

The adoption agency has a limited power to suspend contact (s 27(2)). It may refuse to allow it if (a) satisfied that it is necessary to do so in order to safeguard or promote the child's welfare and (b) the refusal is decided upon as a matter of urgency and does not last for more than seven days. The agency must communicate its decision, the date and the reason for it and the period of refusal to (a) the child if the agency considers he is of sufficient age and understanding, (b) the person in whose favour the s 26 order was made, and (c) if the child is placed for adoption, the prospective adopters (see s 27(3)(a) and the Adoption Agencies Regulations 2005, reg 47(1) and (3); the Adoption Agencies (Wales) Regulations 2005, reg 47(1), (4) and (5)). Alleged abuse of the child during contact visits, for example, may justify suspension, but the maximum period is very short and the agency may seek to expedite proceedings to revoke the s 26 order or to vary it by inserting conditions.

The terms of a s 26 order may be departed from by agreement between the adoption agency and any person for whose contact with the child the order provides, but:

(a)   subject to the child's agreement, where he is of sufficient age and understanding; and

(b)   where the child is placed for adoption, subject to consultation with the prospective adopter before the agreement is reached; and

(c)   subject to written confirmation of the terms of the agreement being given to (i) the child if the agency considers he is of sufficient age and understanding, (ii) the person in whose favour the s 26 order was made, and (iii) if the child is placed for adoption, the prospective adopters (see s 27(3)(b) and the Adoption Agencies Regulations 2005, reg 47(2) and (3); the Adoption Agencies (Wales) Regulations 2005, reg 47(2), (4) and (5)).

Contact and placement orders

[235]

Before a court makes a placement order it must consider the contact arrangements which the adoption agency has made or proposes to make and invite the parties to those proceedings to comment on the arrangements (s 27(4)); compare the similar duty imposed on a court before making an adoption order (s 46(6)).

As already noted, when making a placement order the court may of its own motion make a s 26 order (s 26(4)).

Section 26 does not prevent an application for a contact order under CA 1989, s 8 being made where the application is to be heard together with an application for an adoption order (s 26(5)). In relation to those concurrent applications, s 26 is likely to prove either of positive or of negative significance. The hand of an applicant for a later CA 1989, s 8 order is very likely to be strengthened if the contact under the s 26 order in his favour has proved beneficial to the child. A harmful result under the latter order will almost certainly be fatal for any later application. Indeed the harmful consequences may have led to revocation of the order. An applicant for a s 8 order who did not agree to the contact arrangements initially proposed by the adoption agency but did not seek a s 26 order may well be asked why he did not do so.

[236]

27 Contact: supplementary

(1)   An order under section 26—

(a)   has effect while the adoption agency is authorised to place the child for adoption or the child is placed for adoption, but

(b)   may be varied or revoked by the court on an application by the child, the agency or a person named in the order.

(2)   The agency may refuse to allow the contact that would otherwise be required by virtue of an order under that section if—

(a)   it is satisfied that it is necessary to do so in order to safeguard or promote the child's welfare, and

(b)   the refusal is decided upon as a matter of urgency and does not last for more than seven days.

(3)   Regulations may make provision as to—

(a)   the steps to be taken by an agency which has exercised its power under subsection (2),

(b)   the circumstances in which, and conditions subject to which, the terms of any order under section 26 may be departed from by agreement between the agency and any person for whose contact with the child the order provides,

(c)   notification by an agency of any variation or suspension of arrangements made (otherwise than under an order under that section) with a view to allowing any person contact with the child.

(4)   Before making a placement order the court must—

(a)   consider the arrangements which the adoption agency has made, or proposes to make, for allowing any person contact with the child, and

(b)   invite the parties to the proceedings to comment on those arrangements.

(5) An order under section 26 may provide for contact on any conditions the court considers appropriate.

NOTES

Initial Commencement

To be appointed
Sub-ss (1), (2), (4), (5): to be appointed: see s 148(1), (2); sub-s (3): to be appointed: see s 148(6).

Appointment
Sub-ss (1), (2), (4), (5): Appointment: 30 December 2005: see SI 2005/2213, art 2(c); sub-s (3): appointment (in relation to Wales): 7 February 2004: see SI 2004/252, art 2(b); sub-s (3): appointment (in relation to England): 7 December 2004: see SI 2004/3203, art 2(1)(f).

Extent
This section does not extend to Scotland: see s 149(2).

Subordinate Legislation
Adoption Agencies Regulations 2005, SI 2005/389 (made under sub-s (3)); Adoption Agencies (Wales) Regulations 2005, SI 2005/1313 (made under sub-s (3)).

General

[237]

The provisions of s 27 are so closely integrated with those of s 26 that comments on them have been included with those on s 26 (paras [231]–[235]).

[238]

28 Further consequences of placement

(1) Where a child is placed for adoption under section 19 or an adoption agency is authorised to place a child for adoption under that section—

(a) a parent or guardian of the child may not apply for a residence order unless an application for an adoption order has been made and the parent or guardian has obtained the court's leave under subsection (3) or (5) of section 47,

(b) if an application has been made for an adoption order, a guardian of the child may not apply for a special guardianship order unless he has obtained the court's leave under subsection (3) or (5) of that section.

(2) Where—

(a) a child is placed for adoption under section 19 or an adoption agency is authorised to place a child for adoption under that section, or

(b) a placement order is in force in respect of a child,

then (whether or not the child is in England and Wales) a person may not do either of the following things, unless the court gives leave or each parent or guardian of the child gives written consent.

(3) Those things are—

(a) causing the child to be known by a new surname, or
(b) removing the child from the United Kingdom.

(4) Subsection (3) does not prevent the removal of a child from the United Kingdom for a period of less than one month by a person who provides the child's home.

NOTES

Initial Commencement

To be appointed
To be appointed: see s 148(1), (2).

Appointment
Appointment: 30 December 2005: see SI 2005/2213, art 2(c).

Extent
This section does not extend to Scotland: see s 149(2).

See Further
See further, the application of this section, with modifications, in relation to bringing children into and out of the United Kingdom for the purposes of adoption or under an external adoption order effected within the period of six months of the making of the adoption, and in respect of adoptions under the 1993 Hague Convention on Protection of Children and Co-operation in respect of Intercountry Adoption: the Adoptions with a Foreign Element Regulations 2005, SI 2005/392, regs 6(a), 7, 11(1)(f), 52, 53, 55.

General

[239]

Sections 28 and 29 create several other consequences to flow from placement for adoption, especially where placement is under a placement order. Many of them restrict applications for other orders or affect orders that are in force.

(1)Where placement, or authorised placement, under s 19

Section 28(1) imposes two restrictions where a child is placed for adoption under s 19 or an adoption agency is authorised to place for adoption under that section:

(a)   A parent or guardian is not allowed to apply for a residence order for the obvious reason that such an application would be incompatible with the placement. The option open to the parent or guardian is to withdraw consent. But that option is no longer open to him once an application for an adoption order has been made (see s 52(4)). He can then oppose the making of the adoption, but only if the court grants leave (s 47(3) or (5)). If it does, the parent or guardian may then apply for a residence order (section 28(1)(a)), so that the competing claims of the prospective adopters and the parent or guardian can be heard together at the final hearing of the adoption application.

(b)   Similarly (under s 28(1)(b)), if there is placement or authorised placement under s 19 and an application for an adoption order has been made, a guardian of the child who thinks that special guardianship vested in him is better for the child than adoption by the prospective adopters can only apply for a special guardianship order if granted leave to oppose the adoption application.

(2)Where there is placement, or authorised placement, under s 19 or a placement order is in force

A person cannot cause the child to be known by a new surname or remove him from the United Kingdom unless with the leave of the court or with the written consent of each parent or guardian (s 28(2) and (3)). The restrictions apply whether or not the child is in England and Wales; for example, the child has not yet been placed for adoption and is temporarily living in Scotland. Leave or written consent is, it is submitted, highly unlikely. A possible example is of leave being granted to prospective adopters to change the surname of an orphan (who is the subject of a placement order) where their application for an adoption order is likely to be granted but meantime the child's registration in a different school is imminent. The restriction on removal does not apply where the removal is by 'a person who provides the child's home' and is for a period of less than one month (s 28(4)). The exception is primarily intended to allow prospective adopters to take the child on short foreign holidays, but it will also extend to the case where the authorised agency has not yet placed the child for adoption and those with whom he is living wish to take him on holiday.

There are similar restrictions on change of surname and removal where a special guardianship order is in force (CA 1989, s 14C(3) and (4)), but, where there is a placement order the restriction on removal imposed by the Act prevails over that regulating special guardianship (s 29(7)(b)). The important practical difference is that it is prospective adopters, not the special guardian, who can take the child abroad on holiday, but only for less than one month and not for less than three months as the special guardianship rule (CA 1989, s 14C(4)) allows.

Procedure

[240]

Applications for permission to change a child's surname or to remove him from the United Kingdom must respectively be by way of Form A55 and Form A56. Eligible applicants and respondents to proceedings are listed in the Family Procedure (Adoption) Rules 2005, r 23.

[241]

29 Further consequences of placement orders

(1) Where a placement order is made in respect of a child and either—

(a)   the child is subject to a care order, or

(b)   the court at the same time makes a care order in respect of the child,

the care order does not have effect at any time when the placement order is in force.

(2) On the making of a placement order in respect of a child, any order mentioned in section 8(1) of the 1989 Act, and any supervision order in respect of the child, ceases to have effect.

(3) Where a placement order is in force—

(a)   no prohibited steps order, residence order or specific issue order, and

(b)   no supervision order or child assessment order,

may be made in respect of the child.

(4) Subsection (3)(a) does not apply in respect of a residence order if—

(a)   an application for an adoption order has been made in respect of the child, and

(b)   the residence order is applied for by a parent or guardian who has obtained the court's leave under subsection (3) or (5) of section 47 or by any other person who has obtained the court's leave under this subsection.

(5) Where a placement order is in force, no special guardianship order may be made in respect of the child unless—

(a)   an application has been made for an adoption order, and

(b)   the person applying for the special guardianship order has obtained the court's leave under this subsection or, if he is a guardian of the child, has obtained the court's leave under section 47(5).

(6) Section 14A(7) of the 1989 Act applies in respect of an application for a special guardianship order for which leave has been given as mentioned in subsection (5)(b) with the omission of the words 'the beginning of the period of three months ending with'.

(7) Where a placement order is in force—

(a)   section 14C(1)(b) of the 1989 Act (special guardianship: parental responsibility) has effect subject to any determination under section 25(4) of this Act,

(b)   section 14C(3) and (4) of the 1989 Act (special guardianship: removal of child from UK etc) does not apply.

NOTES

Initial Commencement

To be appointed
To be appointed: see s 148(1), (2).

Appointment
Appointment: 30 December 2005: see SI 2005/2213, art 2(c).

Extent
This section does not extend to Scotland: see s 149(2).

> **See Further**
> See further, the application of this section, with modifications, in relation to an external adoption order effected within the period of six months of the making of the adoption, and in respect of adoptions under the 1993 Hague Convention on Protection of Children and Co-operation in respect of Intercountry Adoption: the Adoptions with a Foreign Element Regulations 2005, SI 2005/392, regs 11(1)(g), 52, 55.

General

[242]

Section 29 is concerned with imposing further consequences in relation to placement orders, but not all of its implications are readily apparent.

Section 29(1)

Suspending the operation of existing care orders

[243]

This suspensive rule has been questioned on the ground that the purpose of a placement order is simply to empower a local authority adoption agency to place a child for adoption, and this should be seen as an adjunct to an existing care order. The objection, it is submitted, is misconceived. Matters such as parental responsibility, restrictions on its exercise, restrictions on changing the child's surname or removing him from the United Kingdom and allowing contact between the child and his parents and others are covered by the Act itself and are deliberately substituted for corresponding provisions in the CA 1989. Admittedly, the local authority's obligation to implement and review its care plan will be in limbo while the placement order operates, but, when deciding whether or not to grant the local authority's application for that order, the court will, and certainly should, take account of the care plan. Indeed, the care plan may itself have contemplated an adoption placement.

Section 29(2)

Section 8 orders and supervision orders

[244]

The making of a placement order has the effect of discharging any CA 1989, s 8 order and any supervision order; (so far as concerns a s 8 contact order, the rule in s 29(2) is already covered by s 26(1)). Where a placement order is made in respect of a child who is already the subject of a care order, any s 8 order or supervision order will have ceased to have effect by virtue of the care order (see CA 1989, s 91(2) and (3)). Section 29(2) is therefore directed to cases of placement orders being made because the threshold conditions in CA 1989, s 31(2) have been satisfied or exceptionally in respect of orphaned children.

Thus, for example, a residence order granted to a mother where later abuse of her child justified a placement order will cease to have effect.

A necessary corollary to the rule that a placement order automatically discharges any s 8 order or supervision order is the bar to the making of any of those orders so long as the placement order is in force. The bar also extends to child assessment orders (s 29(3)). An exception is allowed in respect of residence orders (s 29(4)). If an application has been made for an adoption order and the parent or guardian obtains leave under s 47 to oppose the making of that order, he may apply for a residence order, as he may do where there has been a s 19 placement (see s 28(1)). But the exception under s 29 can also extend to other persons who are granted leave under that section. For example, the parents may have so abused the child that leave under s 47 is refused, but there are concerned relatives wishing to bring up the child. Leave may be given to them under s 29 to make a competing application for a residence order.

Section 29(5), (3)

Special guardianship orders

[245]

There is a similar exception to the rule that no special guardianship order may be made where a placement order is in force. If an application has been made for an adoption order and a guardian of the child obtains leave under s 47 to oppose the making of that order, he may apply for a special guardianship order. So, too, may any other person who obtains leave under s 29 to apply for it. Written notice of intention to apply must be given, but is not restricted by the general rule that notice must be given at least three months before the date of the application (see s 29(6) read with the CA 1989, s 14A(7)).

[246]

> ## Removal of children who are or may be placed by adoption agencies
>
> ### 30 General prohibitions on removal
>
> (1) Where—
>
> (a) a child is placed for adoption by an adoption agency under section 19, or
> (b) a child is placed for adoption by an adoption agency and either the child is less than six weeks old or the agency has at no time been authorised to place the child for adoption,
>
> a person (other than the agency) must not remove the child from the prospective adopters.
>
> (2) Where—
>
> (a) a child who is not for the time being placed for adoption is being provided with accommodation by a local authority, and
> (b) the authority have applied to the court for a placement order and the application has not been disposed of,
>
> only a person who has the court's leave (or the authority) may remove the child from the accommodation.
>
> (3) Where subsection (2) does not apply, but—
>
> (a) a child who is not for the time being placed for adoption is being provided with accommodation by an adoption agency, and
> (b) the agency is authorised to place the child for adoption under section 19 or would be so authorised if any consent to placement under that section had not been withdrawn,
>
> a person (other than the agency) must not remove the child from the accommodation.
>
> (4) This section is subject to sections 31 to 33 but those sections do not apply if the child is subject to a care order.
> (5) This group of sections (that is, this section and those sections) apply whether or not the child in question is in England and Wales.
> (6) This group of sections does not affect the exercise by any local authority or other person of any power conferred by any enactment, other than section 20(8) of the 1989 Act (removal of children from local authority accommodation).
> (7) This group of sections does not prevent the removal of a child who is arrested.

PART B – Statutes

> (8)   A person who removes a child in contravention of this section is guilty of an offence and liable on summary conviction to imprisonment for a term not exceeding three months, or a fine not exceeding level 5 on the standard scale, or both.
>
> **NOTES**
>
> **Initial Commencement**
>
> *To be appointed*
> To be appointed: see s 148(1), (2).
>
> **Appointment**
> Appointment: 30 December 2005: see SI 2005/2213, art 2(c).
>
> **Extent**
> This section does not extend to Scotland: see s 149(2).

General

[247]

The Act draws a clear distinction between restrictions on the removal from their present homes or other accommodation of children who are, or may be, placed for adoption by adoption agencies (ss 30–35) and restrictions in non-agency cases where the child's home is with persons who have given notice of their intention to adopt him, such as local authority foster parents, his parent's partner, his relatives or private foster parents (ss 36–40). All the restrictions have a common purpose, to prevent sudden removal of the child from a stable environment while adoption is, or may be, pending; but that purpose has to be measured against the extent of the right of the parent and other authorised persons to recover the child.

Section 30 imposes a general prohibition on removal; ss 31–33 provide for sets of circumstances in which parents or guardians are able to request and secure their child's return; s 34 prohibits removal where a placement order is in force; and s 35 provides for the return of the child in other cases. All these sections apply whether or not the child is in England and Wales (ss 30(5), 34(8) and 35(6)).

Scope of the prohibition

[248]

The prohibition operates in each of the following circumstances

(1)   Where child already placed for adoption

It is an offence for anyone other than the adoption agency itself to remove the child from the prospective adopters:

(a)   where he is placed for adoption by the agency with parental consent under s 19; or

(b)   where he is placed for adoption by the agency and either he is less than six weeks old (see section 18 and the Adoption Agencies Regulations 2005, reg 35(3) and (4); the Adoption Agencies (Wales) Regulations 2005, reg 36(7)) or the agency has at no time been authorised to place him for adoption. The combined effect of this alternative is that if a mother consents to the placement of her baby while under six weeks of age but at the end of that period the agency delays obtaining her s 19 consent to the placement, the prohibition on removal continues to operate (see comment on s 18(1)).

(2)   Where child is not placed for adoption but is accommodated by a local authority and there is an application for a placement order pending (s 30(2))

The restriction, breach of which is an offence, will in most cases apply where the child has not yet been placed for adoption, but the words 'is not for the time being placed' also allow for the case where there has been an earlier adoption placement. For example, the child was placed with s 19 parental consent which was withdrawn, but by the time the child was returned to the local authority by the prospective adopters the authority was alerted to the risk of abuse of the child if he was returned to the parents, the risk (for example, based on evidence of parental abuse of the child's siblings) justifying a placement order application in accordance with the threshold text in CA 1989, s 31(2).

The reason that the court's leave is required to remove the child pending the hearing of the application for a placement order is to minimise the disruption to the child, otherwise the child might be returned to the parents and removed again if a placement order is made. For that reason the granting of leave will be exceptional. A possible example is where a parent is terminally or dangerously ill, provided removal is in the child's best interests.

The local authority may be accommodating the child in one of its homes or with foster parents. Section 30(2) allows it to change the accommodation from one to another pending the hearing of the placement order application.

(3) Where child is not placed for adoption but is accommodated by an adoption agency and either s 19 parental consent has been given or has been withdrawn (s 30(3))

This subsection operates where sub-s (2) does not, but it applies to any adoption agency, whether a local authority or voluntary adoption agency. Only the agency may lawfully remove the child from the accommodation.

The restriction will continue to operate if parental consent is withdrawn before placement and will do so until the child is returned to the parent (in accordance with s 31(1) and (2)).

Again, the words 'is not for the time being placed' cover not only the case where there has not yet been a placement for adoption, but also where an earlier placement was brought to an end, for example, where the adoption agency withdrew the child from prospective adopters as being persons unsuitable to adopt.

[249]

---

31 Recovery by parent etc where child not placed or is a baby

(1) Subsection (2) applies where—

(a) a child who is not for the time being placed for adoption is being provided with accommodation by an adoption agency, and

(b) the agency would be authorised to place the child for adoption under section 19 if consent to placement under that section had not been withdrawn.

(2) If any parent or guardian of the child informs the agency that he wishes the child to be returned to him, the agency must return the child to him within the period of seven days beginning with the request unless an application is, or has been, made for a placement order and the application has not been disposed of.

(3) Subsection (4) applies where—

(a) a child is placed for adoption by an adoption agency and either the child is less than six weeks old or the agency has at no time been authorised to place the child for adoption, and

(b) any parent or guardian of the child informs the agency that he wishes the child to be returned to him,

unless an application is, or has been, made for a placement order and the application has not been disposed of.

> (4) The agency must give notice of the parent's or guardian's wish to the prospective adopters who must return the child to the agency within the period of seven days beginning with the day on which the notice is given.
>
> (5) A prospective adopter who fails to comply with subsection (4) is guilty of an offence and liable on summary conviction to imprisonment for a term not exceeding three months, or a fine not exceeding level 5 on the standard scale, or both.
>
> (6) As soon as a child is returned to an adoption agency under subsection (4), the agency must return the child to the parent or guardian in question.
>
> **NOTES**
>
> **Initial Commencement**
>
> *To be appointed*
>
> To be appointed: see s 148(1), (2).
>
> **Appointment**
>
> Appointment: 30 December 2005: see SI 2005/2213, art 2(c).
>
> **Extent**
>
> This section does not extend to Scotland: see s 149(2).

General

[250]

As the rules imposing a general prohibition on removal indicate, the complexity of the law regulating adoption agency placements persists in the regulation of removal from placements. The distinction between placement with s 19 parental consent and placement under a placement order remains the basis on which removal is permitted. Additionally, the right of a parent to recover his child from a placement has to be considered against the background of the rules that he has the right ay any time before an application for an adoption order is made to withdraw his consent to the placement (see s 52(4)), that withdrawal must be either in the prescribed form or by notice in writing (see ss 52(8) and 164(1) and for the prescribed form see Family Procedure (Adoption) Rules 2005, Form A106), that before the prospective adopters are able to apply for an adoption order the child must have has his home with them, or at least one of them, for a minimum of ten weeks (s 42(2)), and that only the adoption agency can remove the child from the prospective adopters and oversee the return of the child.

Sections 31–33 provide the scope and circumstances of recovery. All deal with cases where the parent informs the adoption agency that he wishes the child to be returned to him. The agency must then give notice in writing to the prospective adopters, if the child is with them, to return the child to the agency.

Recovery by parent where child not placed or is a baby

Section 31 covers two kinds of cases.

(a) The parent has consented to placement of the child for adoption, the child 'is not for the time being placed' and is being accommodated by the adoption agency. The parent withdraws his consent and informs the agency that he wishes the child to be returned to him. The parent can withdraw his consent either by written notice or by way of Form A106. On either alternative he must separately state that he wants the child returned. Usually he will do this along with the notice or Form A106, but withdrawal of consent does not necessarily imply a request for an immediate return. It may be that he wants a period to plan for the child's return.

Once the parent requests return, the agency must return the child within seven days from the request. Seven days is a sufficient period for the agency to arrange for the child to be removed from the foster parents or the agency's residential home where he is accommodated. The immediate duty to return the child does not apply if the adoption agency is a local authority and an application 'is, or has been, made' for a placement order and the application has not been disposed of. Thus, if the local authority considers that the significant harm threshold in the CA 1989, s 31(2), is met and that the child ought to be placed for adoption, it is under a duty to apply for a placement order and can make the application before the seven day period expires.

(b)   The child is placed for adoption by the adoption agency and either he is less than six weeks old or the agency has at no time been authorised to place him for adoption. The parent requests the child's return. Unless the application is, or has been, made for a placement order and is pending, the agency must give notice to the prospective adopters of the parental request, and they must return the child to the agency within seven days beginning with the day on which the notice is given. Failure to comply is an offence. As soon as the child is returned to the agency, it must return the child to the parent.

[251]

32   Recovery by parent etc where child placed and consent withdrawn

(1)   This section applies where—

(a)   a child is placed for adoption by an adoption agency under section 19, and
(b)   consent to placement under that section has been withdrawn,

unless an application is, or has been, made for a placement order and the application has not been disposed of.

(2)   If a parent or guardian of the child informs the agency that he wishes the child to be returned to him—

(a)   the agency must give notice of the parent's or guardian's wish to the prospective adopters, and
(b)   the prospective adopters must return the child to the agency within the period of 14 days beginning with the day on which the notice is given.

(3)   A prospective adopter who fails to comply with subsection (2)(b) is guilty of an offence and liable on summary conviction to imprisonment for a term not exceeding three months, or a fine not exceeding level 5 on the standard scale, or both.

(4)   As soon as a child is returned to an adoption agency under this section, the agency must return the child to the parent or guardian in question.

(5)   Where a notice under subsection (2) is given, but—

(a)   before the notice was given, an application for an adoption order (including a Scottish or Northern Irish adoption order), special guardianship order or residence order, or for leave to apply for a special guardianship order or residence order, was made in respect of the child, and
(b)   the application (and, in a case where leave is given on an application to apply for a special guardianship order or residence order, the application for the order) has not been disposed of,

the prospective adopters are not required by virtue of the notice to return the child to the agency unless the court so orders.

NOTES

Initial Commencement

To be appointed
To be appointed: see s 148(1), (2).

Appointment
Appointment: 30 December 2005: see SI 2005/2213, art 2(c).

Extent
This section does not extend to Scotland: see s 149(2).

See Further
See further, the application of this section, with modifications, in relation to an external adoption order effected within the period of six months of the making of the adoption, and in respect of

adoptions under the 1993 Hague Convention on Protection of Children and Co-operation in respect of Intercountry Adoption: the Adoptions with a Foreign Element Regulations 2005, SI 2005/392, regs 11(1)(h), 52, 55.

General

Recovery by parent where child placed and consent withdrawn

[252]

Where a child is placed for adoption by an adoption agency with parental consent, that consent is withdrawn and the parent informs the agency that he wishes the child to be returned, then, unless an application is, or has been, made for a placement order and is pending, the agency must give notice to the prospective adopters of the parental request and they must return the child to the agency within 14 days beginning with the day on which the notice is given. It is difficult to see why a longer period of 14 days is needed to enable the prospective adopters to return to the agency a child who has been placed for adoption with parental consent, when a period of seven days is considered adequate to enable them to do so if the child has been placed for adoption with them when less than six weeks old or the placement was unauthorised. What additional difficulties can arise in the one case but not in the other to justify the extension?

If, before the notice of removal is given to the prospective adopters, an application for an adoption order in England and Wales (or Scotland or Northern Ireland) or for a special guardianship order or a residence order or an application for leave to apply for a special guardianship order or a residence order in respect of the child has been made and the application for the other has not been disposed of, the prospective adopters do not have to return the child to the agency unless the court orders return. There are several points concerning this rule:

(i) Neither the Act nor the Family Procedure (Adoption) Rules 2005 require courts to ensure early expedition of the hearing of any of the above applications – the same comment applies to applications for placement orders – but they must be mindful that, in general, any delay in coming to a decision is likely to prejudice the child's welfare. Moreover, delay is prejudicial to the parent's possible right of recovery of his child.

(ii) With regard to an application for an adoption order, it is not easy to relate the present rule to the prohibition imposed by s 52(4) of the Act, that withdrawal of consent is ineffective if given after an application for such an order has been made. Prima facie the rule seems superfluous, but what it appears to do is to give the court a residual discretion to order the return of the child after the application for an adoption order has been made but before the hearing, a strange consequence.

(iii) Whichever of the above applications is made, it is difficult to envisage circumstances where the court will order the return of the child to the agency and then to the parent, but, if that order is made and later the application is successful, the child will have to be handed over to the successful applicant. Such to-ing and fro-ing is scarcely likely to be in the child's best interests.

Where s 19 parental consent is withdrawn and the adoption agency is a local authority, then on receipt of the Form or notice of withdrawal the authority must immediately review its decision to place the child for adoption and, if it decides to apply for a placement order, it must as soon as possible notify:

(a) the child's parent or guardian,

(b) his father, where the latter does not have parental responsibility, his identity is known and the local authority considers it appropriate to notify him, and

(c)   if the child is placed for adoption, the prospective adopters (see Adoption Agencies Regulations 2005, reg 38(1) and (2); Adoption Agencies (Wales) Regulations 2005, reg 39(1) and (2)).

The appropriateness of notifying the father without parental responsibility will depend upon his interest in his child, past, present and future.

Where parental consent is withdrawn and the adoption agency is a registered adoption society, it must immediately consider whether it is appropriate to inform the local authority in whose area the child is living. It would certainly be appropriate where the agency has evidence that might satisfy the threshold test under the CA 1989, s 31(2) and so justify an application for a placement order (see reg 38(3) and 39(3) respectively of the English and Welsh Regulations).

[253]

33   Recovery by parent etc where child placed and placement order refused

(1)   This section applies where—

(a)   a child is placed for adoption by a local authority under section 19,
(b)   the authority have applied for a placement order and the application has been refused, and
(c)   any parent or guardian of the child informs the authority that he wishes the child to be returned to him.

(2)   The prospective adopters must return the child to the authority on a date determined by the court.

(3)   A prospective adopter who fails to comply with subsection (2) is guilty of an offence and liable on summary conviction to imprisonment for a term not exceeding three months, or a fine not exceeding level 5 on the standard scale, or both.

(4)   As soon as a child is returned to the authority, they must return the child to the parent or guardian in question.

NOTES

Initial Commencement
To be appointed
To be appointed: see s 148(1), (2).

Appointment
Appointment: 30 December 2005: see SI 2005/2213, art 2(c).

Extent
This section does not extend to Scotland: see s 149(2).

General

[254]

This section applies where a child is placed for adoption by a local authority with s 19 parental consent, the authority applies for a placement order, its application is refused and a parent informs the authority that he wishes the child to be returned to him. The prospective adopters must return the child to the authority on a date fixed by the court hearing the application. Failure to comply is an offence. It is likely that the date will be within seven days and not more than 14 days. As soon as the child is returned to the local authority, it must return him to the parent.

Concluding comment on ss 30–33

[255]

Section 30 expressly provides that none of the provisions in that section and in ss 31–33 prevents the removal of a child who has been arrested or his removal as a result of a local authority or any other person exercising a power conferred by any enactment other than CA 1989, s 20(8) (see s 30(6) and (7)). Moreover, the parental rights of recovery under ss 31–33 are excluded if the child is subject to a care order (see s 30(4)). The exclusion of the removal provisions are primarily aimed at protecting the child protection powers of local authorities under the CA 1989. Thus, applied for example in relation to s 32, if the child has been placed for adoption by a local authority with s 19 parental consent which is withdrawn and if then no application for a placement order has been made within the 14–day period, the local authority will have to return the child to the parent, but not if he is the subject of a care order. With regard to CA 1989, s 20(8), that provision is overridden by ss 30–33, as s 31(1) and (2) illustrate. If a parent has consented to placement for adoption by a local authority adoption agency which, because it has not yet placed the child, is looking after him and if the parent withdraws his consent, he cannot call for the immediate return of the child or, indeed, turn up and remove the child from the prospective adopters, if the placement is known, but will have to allow the seven day period for the prospective adopters to return the child to the local authority in accordance with s 31.

[256]

34 Placement orders: prohibition on removal

(1) Where a placement order in respect of a child—

(a) is in force, or
(b) has been revoked, but the child has not been returned by the prospective adopters or remains in any accommodation provided by the local authority,

a person (other than the local authority) may not remove the child from the prospective adopters or from accommodation provided by the authority.

(2) A person who removes a child in contravention of subsection (1) is guilty of an offence.

(3) Where a court revoking a placement order in respect of a child determines that the child is not to remain with any former prospective adopters with whom the child is placed, they must return the child to the local authority within the period determined by the court for the purpose; and a person who fails to do so is guilty of an offence.

(4) Where a court revoking a placement order in respect of a child determines that the child is to be returned to a parent or guardian, the local authority must return the child to the parent or guardian as soon as the child is returned to the authority or, where the child is in accommodation provided by the authority, at once.

(5) A person guilty of an offence under this section is liable on summary conviction to imprisonment for a term not exceeding three months, or a fine not exceeding level 5 on the standard scale, or both.

(6) This section does not affect the exercise by any local authority or other person of a power conferred by any enactment, other than section 20(8) of the 1989 Act.

(7) This section does not prevent the removal of a child who is arrested.

(8) This section applies whether or not the child in question is in England and Wales.

NOTES

Initial Commencement

To be appointed
To be appointed: see s 148(1), (2).

Appointment
Appointment: 30 December 2005: see SI 2005/2213, art 2(c).

Extent
This section does not extend to Scotland: see s 149(2).

General

[257]

Sections 31 and 32 (see s 31(2) and (3) and s 32(1)) show that once an application is made for a placement order the right of the parent to recover his child is suspended until the determination of the application. Under s 33, if the application is refused, the child must be returned to the parent unless he is the subject of a care order. Section 34 is concerned with the position where a placement order is made or later revoked. Like s 30, it imposes a general prohibition on removal.

Scope of the prohibition

[258]

The section applies where (a) a placement order is in force, or (b) the order has been revoked but the child has not been returned by the prospective adopters or, as the case may be, remains in accommodation provided by the local authority. It is an offence for anyone other than the local authority to remove the child from the prospective adopters or from the authority's accommodation. When revoking the placement order the court may decide that the child is not to remain with the prospective adopters and fix a period within which they must return him to the local authority. The court may further decide that the child is to be returned to the parent. If it does, the local authority must so return the child as soon as he is returned to the authority by the prospective adopters. If the child is not placed with prospective adopters but is in local authority accommodation, the authority must return him to the parents 'at once'.

Like s 30, s 34 expressly provides that none of its provisions prevents the removal of a child who has been arrested or his removal by a local authority or any other person exercising a power conferred by any enactment, other than of the CA 1989, s 20(8); see s 33 above and the concluding comments there on ss 30–33.

[259]

> ### 35 Return of child in other cases
>
> (1) Where a child is placed for adoption by an adoption agency and the prospective adopters give notice to the agency of their wish to return the child, the agency must—
>
> (a) receive the child from the prospective adopters before the end of the period of seven days beginning with the giving of the notice, and
>
> (b) give notice to any parent or guardian of the child of the prospective adopters' wish to return the child.
>
> (2) Where a child is placed for adoption by an adoption agency, and the agency—
>
> (a) is of the opinion that the child should not remain with the prospective adopters, and
>
> (b) gives notice to them of its opinion,
>
> the prospective adopters must, not later than the end of the period of seven days beginning with the giving of the notice, return the child to the agency.
>
> (3) If the agency gives notice under subsection (2)(b), it must give notice to any parent or guardian of the child of the obligation to return the child to the agency.
>
> (4) A prospective adopter who fails to comply with subsection (2) is guilty of an offence and liable on summary conviction to imprisonment for a term not exceeding three months, or a fine not exceeding level 5 on the standard scale, or both.
>
> (5) Where—
>
> (a) an adoption agency gives notice under subsection (2) in respect of a child,
>
> (b) before the notice was given, an application for an adoption order (including a Scottish or Northern Irish adoption order), special guardianship order or

residence order, or for leave to apply for a special guardianship order or residence order, was made in respect of the child, and

(c) the application (and, in a case where leave is given on an application to apply for a special guardianship order or residence order, the application for the order) has not been disposed of,

prospective adopters are not required by virtue of the notice to return the child to the agency unless the court so orders.

(6) This section applies whether or not the child in question is in England and Wales.

NOTES

Initial Commencement
To be appointed
To be appointed: see s 148(1), (2).

Appointment
Appointment: 30 December 2005: see SI 2005/2213, art 2(c).

Extent
This section does not extend to Scotland: see s 149(2).

See Further
See further, the application of this section, with modifications, in relation to bringing children into and out of the United Kingdom for the purposes of adoption or under an external adoption order effected within the period of six months of the making of the adoption, and in respect of adoptions under the 1993 Hague Convention on Protection of Children and Co-operation in respect of Intercountry Adoption: the Adoptions with a Foreign Element Regulations 2005, SI 2005/392, regs 6(a), 8, 11(2), 52, 55.

General

[260]

Whereas ss 31–33 are concerned with circumstances where the parents want their child to be returned to them, s 35 is concerned with cases:

(a) where the prospective adopters no longer want to proceed with adoption; or

(b) where the adoption agency considers that the child should no longer remain with them.

In the one case the agency must receive the child within seven days from when the prospective adopters give the agency notice of their wish to return the child; in the other the prospective adopters must return the child to the agency within seven days from when the agency gives them notice to do so. In both kinds of cases the agency must tell the child's parents (or guardians) what is happening, so that they may consider their position. For example, the prospective adopters may have been identified in the s 19 parental consent without the alternative being given to the agency to choose other prospective adopters (see ss 19(1) and (2)); the parents could then decide whether or not to give further consent to placement.

Section 35(5)

[261]

This is in precisely the same terms as s 32(5), where the implications are examined.

Removal of children in non-agency cases

36 Restrictions on removal

(1)   At any time when a child's home is with any persons ('the people concerned') with whom the child is not placed by an adoption agency, but the people concerned—

(a)   have applied for an adoption order in respect of the child and the application has not been disposed of,

(b)   have given notice of intention to adopt, or

(c)   have applied for leave to apply for an adoption order under section 42(6) and the application has not been disposed of,

a person may remove the child only in accordance with the provisions of this group of sections (that is, this section and sections 37 to 40).

The reference to a child placed by an adoption agency includes a child placed by a Scottish or Northern Irish adoption agency.

(2)   For the purposes of this group of sections, a notice of intention to adopt is to be disregarded if—

(a)   the period of four months beginning with the giving of the notice has expired without the people concerned applying for an adoption order, or

(b)   the notice is a second or subsequent notice of intention to adopt and was given during the period of five months beginning with the giving of the preceding notice.

(3)   For the purposes of this group of sections, if the people concerned apply for leave to apply for an adoption order under section 42(6) and the leave is granted, the application for leave is not to be treated as disposed of until the period of three days beginning with the granting of the leave has expired.

(4)   This section does not prevent the removal of a child who is arrested.

(5)   Where a parent or guardian may remove a child from the people concerned in accordance with the provisions of this group of sections, the people concerned must at the request of the parent or guardian return the child to the parent or guardian at once.

(6)   A person who—

(a)   fails to comply with subsection (5), or

(b)   removes a child in contravention of this section,

is guilty of an offence and liable on summary conviction to imprisonment for a term not exceeding three months, or a fine not exceeding level 5 on the standard scale, or both.

(7)   This group of sections applies whether or not the child in question is in England and Wales.

NOTES

Initial Commencement

To be appointed

To be appointed: see s 148(1), (2).

Appointment

Appointment: 30 December 2005: see SI 2005/2213, art 2(c).

Extent

This section does not extend to Scotland: see s 149(2).

See Further

See further, the application and disapplication of this section, with modifications, in relation to bringing children into and out of the United Kingdom for the purposes of adoption, and in respect of adoptions under the 1993 Hague Convention on Protection of Children and Co-operation in respect of Intercountry Adoption: the Adoptions with a Foreign Element Regulations 2005, SI 2005/392, regs 6(b), 52, 54.

PART B – Statutes

General

[263]

Section 36 sets the limits for allowing the removal of children in non-agency cases.

Where a child has his home with persons with whom he has not been placed by an adoption agency, and they:

(a)   have applied for adoption, or

(b)   have given notice of intention to adopt (as required by section 44), or

(c)   have applied for leave to apply for an adoption order under section 42(6) because the child has not lived with them for the relevant period prescribed by section 42,

then the child may only be removed from them in accordance with ss 36–40, except that none of the restrictions prevents removal of a child who is arrested.

Section 36(2)

Notice of intention to adopt

[264]

Under s 44(3) a notice of intention to adopt can validly last as long as two years before an application for an adoption order is made, but to prevent restrictions on removal operating for so long s 36(2)(a) provides that the restrictions apply for four months from the giving of the notice. Equally, under s 36(2)(b) the restrictions cease to operate if a second or subsequent notice of intention to adopt is given within five months of the preceding notice. The purpose is to prevent repeated notices of intention being used to prevent removal of the child.

Section 36(3)

Application for leave to apply for an adoption order

[265]

If leave is granted, the application is treated as continuing for three days. The restrictions on removal therefore continue and the period allows the successful applicants to give notice of their intention to adopt.

Section 36(3)

Parent or guardian

[266]

Where a parent or guardian may remove the child, those with whom the child has his home must at the request of the parent or guardian return the child at once.

[267]

37 **Applicants for adoption**
If section 36(1)(a) applies, the following persons may remove the child—
(a)   a person who has the court's leave,
(b)   a local authority or other person in the exercise of a power conferred by any enactment, other than section 20(8) of the 1989 Act.

PART B – Statutes

NOTES

Initial Commencement

To be appointed

To be appointed: see s 148(1), (2).

Appointment

Appointment: 30 December 2005: see SI 2005/2213, art 2(c).

Extent

This section does not extend to Scotland: see s 149(2).

See Further

See further, the disapplication of this section, with modifications, in respect of adoptions under the 1993 Hague Convention on Protection of Children and Co-operation in respect of Intercountry Adoption: the Adoptions with a Foreign Element Regulations 2005, SI 2005/392, regs 52, 54(1).

General

[268]

Once an application for adoption has been made the child may only be removed with leave of the court or by a local authority or other person in exercise of a power conferred by any enactment. As with removal in adoption agency cases, the local authority's child protection powers under the CA 1989 are therefore not prejudiced, and, if the child is being accommodated by the authority under Pt III of that Act, the power under s 20(8) of a person with parental responsibility to remove the child at any time does not apply.

[269]

38   Local authority foster parents

(1)   This section applies if the child's home is with local authority foster parents.

(2)   If—

(a)   the child has had his home with the foster parents at all times during the period of five years ending with the removal and the foster parents have given notice of intention to adopt, or

(b)   an application has been made for leave under section 42(6) and has not been disposed of,

the following persons may remove the child.

(3)   They are—

(a)   a person who has the court's leave,

(b)   a local authority or other person in the exercise of a power conferred by any enactment, other than section 20(8) of the 1989 Act.

(4)   If subsection (2) does not apply but—

(a)   the child has had his home with the foster parents at all times during the period of one year ending with the removal, and

(b)   the foster parents have given notice of intention to adopt,

the following persons may remove the child.

(5)   They are—

(a)   a person with parental responsibility for the child who is exercising the power in section 20(8) of the 1989 Act,

(b)   a person who has the court's leave,

(c)   a local authority or other person in the exercise of a power conferred by any enactment, other than section 20(8) of the 1989 Act.

NOTES

Initial Commencement

To be appointed

To be appointed: see s 148(1), (2).

Appointment
Appointment: 30 December 2005: see SI 2005/2213, art 2(c).

Extent
This section does not extend to Scotland: see s 149(2).

See Further
See further, the disapplication of this section, with modifications, in respect of adoptions under the 1993 Hague Convention on Protection of Children and Co-operation in respect of Intercountry Adoption: the Adoptions with a Foreign Element Regulations 2005, SI 2005/392, regs 52, 54(1).

General

[270]

Whereas s 37 relates to cases where there is an application for an adoption order, ss 38–40 relate to those where there is a notice of intention to adopt or (in ss 38 and 40) an application for leave to apply for an adoption order. Subject to the differences noted in those sections, the same restrictions on removal apply as in cases falling within s 37. The only persons who may remove the child are (a) those who have the court's leave, or (b) a local authority or other person in the exercise of a power conferred by any enactment, other than CA 1989, s 20(8).

Section 38 is concerned with local authority foster parents with whom the child has his home. The above restrictions apply where the foster parents apply for leave for adoption and also where the foster parents give notice of intention to adopt and the child has lived with them for five years or more. But, where he has been with the foster parents for one year (but less than five), they give notice to adopt and the child is voluntarily accommodated under the CA 1989, the child may also be removed by any person with parental responsibility for the child exercising his power under CA 1989, s 20(8).

[271]

39 Partners of parents

(1) This section applies if a child's home is with a partner of a parent and the partner has given notice of intention to adopt.
(2) If the child's home has been with the partner for not less than three years (whether continuous or not) during the period of five years ending with the removal, the following persons may remove the child—

(a) a person who has the court's leave,
(b) a local authority or other person in the exercise of a power conferred by any enactment, other than section 20(8) of the 1989 Act.

(3) If subsection (2) does not apply, the following persons may remove the child—

(a) a parent or guardian,
(b) a person who has the court's leave,
(c) a local authority or other person in the exercise of a power conferred by any enactment, other than section 20(8) of the 1989 Act.

NOTES
Initial Commencement
To be appointed
To be appointed: see s 148(1), (2).

Appointment
Appointment: 30 December 2005: see SI 2005/2213, art 2(c).

Extent
This section does not extend to Scotland: see s 149(2).

See Further
See further, the application and disapplication of this section, with modifications, in relation to bringing children into and out of the United Kingdom for the purposes of adoption, and in respect

of adoptions under the 1993 Hague Convention on Protection of Children and Co-operation in respect of Intercountry Adoption: the Adoptions with a Foreign Element Regulations 2005, SI 2005/392, regs 6(b), 52, 54.

General

[272]

This section additionally allows a parent or guardian to remove the child, unless the child has lived with the partner of the parent for three out of the last five years. To allow removal by the parent where there has been this longer period is not likely to be in the child's best interests. It is up to the parent to try to persuade the court otherwise and seek leave to remove.

[273]

40   Other non-agency cases

(1)   In any case where sections 37 to 39 do not apply but—

(a)   the people concerned have given notice of intention to adopt, or
(b)   the people concerned have applied for leave under section 42(6) and the application has not been disposed of,

the following persons may remove the child.

(2)   They are—

(a)   a person who has the court's leave,
(b)   a local authority or other person in the exercise of a power conferred by any enactment, other than section 20(8) of the 1989 Act.

NOTES

Initial Commencement
To be appointed
To be appointed: see s 148(1), (2).

Appointment
Appointment: 30 December 2005: see SI 2005/2213, art 2(c).

Extent
This section does not extend to Scotland: see s 149(2).

See Further
See further, the disapplication of this section, with modifications, in respect of adoptions under the 1993 Hague Convention on Protection of Children and Co-operation in respect of Intercountry Adoption: the Adoptions with a Foreign Element Regulations 2005, SI 2005/392, regs 52, 54(1).

General

[274]

Where the child has his home with persons who are neither local authority foster parents nor the child's parent's partner and they give notice of intention to adopt or apply for leave to apply for an adoption order, the same restrictions on removal apply as they do, under s 37, where application has been made for an adoption order.

[275]

Breach of restrictions on removal

41   Recovery orders

(1)   This section applies where it appears to the court—

(a)   that a child has been removed in contravention of any of the preceding provisions of this Chapter or that there are reasonable grounds for believing that a person intends to remove a child in contravention of those provisions, or

(b)   that a person has failed to comply with section 31(4), 32(2), 33(2), 34(3) or 35(2).

(2)   The court may, on the application of any person, by an order—

(a)   direct any person who is in a position to do so to produce the child on request to any person mentioned in subsection (4),

(b)   authorise the removal of the child by any person mentioned in that subsection,

(c)   require any person who has information as to the child's whereabouts to disclose that information on request to any constable or officer of the court,

(d)   authorise a constable to enter any premises specified in the order and search for the child, using reasonable force if necessary.

(3)   Premises may only be specified under subsection (2)(d) if it appears to the court that there are reasonable grounds for believing the child to be on them.

(4)   The persons referred to in subsection (2) are—

(a)   any person named by the court,

(b)   any constable,

(c)   any person who, after the order is made under that subsection, is authorised to exercise any power under the order by an adoption agency which is authorised to place the child for adoption.

(5)   A person who intentionally obstructs a person exercising a power of removal conferred by the order is guilty of an offence and liable on summary conviction to a fine not exceeding level 3 on the standard scale.

(6)   A person must comply with a request to disclose information as required by the order even if the information sought might constitute evidence that he had committed an offence.

(7)   But in criminal proceedings in which the person is charged with an offence (other than one mentioned in subsection (8))—

(a)   no evidence relating to the information provided may be adduced, and

(b)   no question relating to the information may be asked,

by or on behalf of the prosecution, unless evidence relating to it is adduced, or a question relating to it is asked, in the proceedings by or on behalf of the person.

(8)   The offences excluded from subsection (7) are—

(a)   an offence under section 2 or 5 of the Perjury Act 1911 (c 6) (false statements made on oath otherwise than in judicial proceedings or made otherwise than on oath),

(b)   an offence under section 44(1) or (2) of the Criminal Law (Consolidation) (Scotland) Act 1995 (c 39) (false statements made on oath or otherwise than on oath).

(9)   An order under this section has effect in relation to Scotland as if it were an order made by the Court of Session which that court had jurisdiction to make.

NOTES

Initial Commencement

To be appointed

Sub-ss (1)–(4): to be appointed: see s 148(1), (2); sub-ss (5)–(9): to be appointed (in relation to England and Wales): see s 148(1), (2); sub-ss (5)–(9): to be appointed (in relation to Scotland): see s 148(5)(a).

Appointment

Sub-ss (1)–(4): appointment: 30 December 2005: see SI 2005/2213, art 2(c); sub-ss (5)–(9): appointment (in relation to England and Wales): 30 December 2005: see SI 2005/2213, art 2(c); sub-ss (5)–(9): appointment (in relation to Scotland): 30 December 2005: see SSI 2005/643, art 2(a).

Extent

Sub-ss (1)–(4) do not extend to Scotland: see s 149(2).

General

[276]

Section 41 provides for the recovery of children who have been removed in breach of the restrictions on removal imposed in both adoption agency cases and non-agency cases. It also applies where there is a failure of the prospective adopters in agency cases to return the child, as the case may be, to the agency or the local authority within seven or 14 days or on the date set by the court.

Evidence

[277]

A person who is required by the recovery order to disclose information must do so even if it might constitute evidence that he has committed an offence; but in any criminal proceedings in which he is charged with an offence (except any of those excluded by s 41(8)) the prosecution cannot adduce evidence relating to the information provided or ask any questions about it, unless it is raised by or on behalf of that person.

Procedure

[278]

For an application for a recovery order see Family Procedure (Adoption) Rules 2005, r 107 and Form A57.

[279]

Preliminaries to adoption

42 Child to live with adopters before application

(1) An application for an adoption order may not be made unless—

(a) if subsection (2) applies, the condition in that subsection is met,

(b) if that subsection does not apply, the condition in whichever is applicable of subsections (3) to (5) applies.

(2) If—

(a) the child was placed for adoption with the applicant or applicants by an adoption agency or in pursuance of an order of the High Court, or

(b) the applicant is a parent of the child,

the condition is that the child must have had his home with the applicant or, in the case of an application by a couple, with one or both of them at all times during the period of ten weeks preceding the application.

(3) If the applicant or one of the applicants is the partner of a parent of the child, the condition is that the child must have had his home with the applicant or, as the case may be, applicants at all times during the period of six months preceding the application.

(4) If the applicants are local authority foster parents, the condition is that the child must have had his home with the applicants at all times during the period of one year preceding the application.

(5) In any other case, the condition is that the child must have had his home with the applicant or, in the case of an application by a couple, with one or both of them for not less than three years (whether continuous or not) during the period of five years preceding the application.

(6) But subsections (4) and (5) do not prevent an application being made if the court gives leave to make it.

---

(7) An adoption order may not be made unless the court is satisfied that sufficient opportunities to see the child with the applicant or, in the case of an application by a couple, both of them together in the home environment have been given—

(a) where the child was placed for adoption with the applicant or applicants by an adoption agency, to that agency,

(b) in any other case, to the local authority within whose area the home is.

(8) In this section and sections 43 and 44(1)—

(a) references to an adoption agency include a Scottish or Northern Irish adoption agency,

(b) references to a child placed for adoption by an adoption agency are to be read accordingly.

NOTES

Initial Commencement

To be appointed
To be appointed: see s 148(1), (2).

Appointment
Appointment: 30 December 2005: see SI 2005/2213, art 2(c).

Extent
This section does not extend to Scotland: see s 149(2).

See Further
See further, the application of this section, with modifications, in relation to bringing children into and out of the United Kingdom for the purposes of adoption or under an external adoption order effected within the period of six months of the making of the adoption, and in respect of adoptions under the 1993 Hague Convention on Protection of Children and Co-operation in respect of Intercountry Adoption: the Adoptions with a Foreign Element Regulations 2005, SI 2005/392, regs 6(a), 9, 11(1)(i), 52, 55, 56.

General

[280]

This section makes provision for the period of time that a child must live with a prospective adopter before an adoption application may be made.

Before an adoption application can be made, the child must live with the applicant(s) for a minimum period of time preceding the application(s), which varies according to the circumstances. In addition, before the child can be adopted, a further condition must be satisfied regarding the child being seen, as set out in s 42(7).

Section 42(1)–(6)

The first condition: time living with applicant(s)

(A) PLACEMENT BY ADOPTION AGENCY

[281]

If the child was placed with the applicant(s) by an adoption agency (including a Scottish or Northern Irish adoption agency: see s 42(8)), placed there further to a High Court Order, or the applicant is the child's parent, the child must have lived with the applicant (or at least one of them, if a couple), for a continuous period of ten weeks preceding the application (s 42(2)). This period cannot be reduced by the court (s 42(6)).

Although the effect of s 18(5) is that a child is 'placed for adoption' by an adoption agency if the agency has placed the child with a person, under any enactment, and then left the child with him/her as a prospective adopter, s 44(8) excludes that person from being treated as having the child left with him/her as a prospective adopter if a local authority has placed the child with him/her other than for adoption and then he/she gives notice of intention to adopt under s 44. For example, a local authority foster-parent who is not matched with the child for adoption by the agency. Such applications will therefore be non-agency applications for the purposes of the Act (s 44(8)) unless and until 'converted' to an agency adoption by the foster parents being approved as adopters of the child by the agency, and the granting of a placement order or giving of s 19 parental consent to placement for adoption.

(B)   NON-ADOPTION AGENCY PLACEMENTS

[282]

If the applicant, or one of the applicants, is the partner of the child's parent, the child must have lived with the applicant(s) for a continuous period of six months preceding the application (s 42(3)). This period cannot be reduced by the court (s 42(6)).

If the applicants are local authority foster-parents (including independent sector foster-parents with whom the authority has placed a child) the child must have lived with them for a continuous period of one year preceding the application (s 42(4)). Under the Interpretation Act 1978, s 6, this will also apply to a sole foster-parent application. This period can be reduced if the court gives leave (s 42(6)). See commentary above for where a foster-parent has not been matched with the child by the adoption agency.

In all other cases, the child must have lived with the applicant, or at least one of them if a couple, for a period of at least three years in the period of five years preceding the application. Unlike the other pre-conditions above, this period of three years need not be continuous (s 42(5)). This period can be reduced if the court gives leave (s 42(6)).

Section 42(7)

The second condition: child to be seen with applicant(s)

[283]

Before an adoption order can be made, in all cases the court must be satisfied that enough opportunities have been given for the child to be seen with the applicant in the home, and with both of them together if the applicants are a couple. As this is expressed in the plural, this must as a minimum include at least two visits. If the child was placed there by an adoption agency, it is that agency's role to make these visits. In all other cases, it is the role of the local authority for the area where the child and applicant(s) live (s 42(7)). The latter will simply be a question of fact concerning the location of the home, and is not a question of ordinary residence.

The application of this section is modified in certain respects for some foreign adoptions: see the Adoptions with a Foreign Element Regulations 2005, regs 6, 9, 11, 52, 55 and 56.

[284]

43   Reports where child placed by agency

Where an application for an adoption order relates to a child placed for adoption by an adoption agency, the agency must—

(a)   submit to the court a report on the suitability of the applicants and on any other matters relevant to the operation of section 1, and

(b)   assist the court in any manner the court directs.

NOTES
Initial Commencement
To be appointed
To be appointed: see s 148(1), (2).

Appointment
Appointment: 30 December 2005: see SI 2005/2213, art 2(c).

Extent
This section does not extend to Scotland: see s 149(2).

See Further
See further, the application of this section, with modifications, in relation to an external adoption order effected within the period of six months of the making of the adoption, and in respect of adoptions under the 1993 Hague Convention on Protection of Children and Co-operation in respect of Intercountry Adoption: the Adoptions with a Foreign Element Regulations 2005, SI 2005/392, regs 11(1)(j), 52, 55.

General

[285]

Section 43 governs adoption applications where an adoption agency has placed the child for adoption. Section 44 governs adoption applications in all other cases. See s 42 for pre-conditions to applications and the making of adoption orders.

A notice of intention to adopt, under s 44, such as by a local authority foster-parent, does not convert a placement into one made by the adoption agency under s 18(1)(b) (see s 44(8)).

In cases where an adoption application is made in respect of a child placed by an adoption agency (including Scottish or Northern Irish adoption agency: see s 42(8)), the agency must prepare a Report on the suitability of the applicant and on matters 'relevant to the operation of Section 1' This is a very wide obligation, extending to the paramount nature of the child's welfare throughout his/her life, the presumption that delay is likely to be prejudicial, the welfare checklist in s 1(4), the child's religious persuasion, racial origin and cultural and linguistic background, the range of powers available to the Court, and the fact that the Court should not make an order unless that would be better than not doing so.

See Annex A to the Practice Direction: *Reports by the Adoption Agency or Local Authority, supplementing the Family Procedure (Adoption) Rules 2005* for the contents of this report. All matters in Annex A must be covered in the report, unless they do not apply, in which case the reason for their omission must be stated (Practice Direction, para 1.3).

In addition, the adoption agency must assist the court in any way that the court may direct.

For reports, see the Family Procedure (Adoption) Rules 2005, r 29 and Practice Direction: *Reports by the Adoption Agency or Local Authority*.

The application of this section is modified in certain respects for some foreign adoptions: see the Adoptions with a Foreign Element Regulations 2005, regs 11, 52, and 55.

[286]

44 Notice of intention to adopt

(1) This section applies where persons (referred to in this section as 'proposed adopters') wish to adopt a child who is not placed for adoption with them by an adoption agency.

(2)   An adoption order may not be made in respect of the child unless the proposed adopters have given notice to the appropriate local authority of their intention to apply for the adoption order (referred to in this Act as a 'notice of intention to adopt').

(3)   The notice must be given not more than two years, or less than three months, before the date on which the application for the adoption order is made.

(4)   Where—

(a)   if a person were seeking to apply for an adoption order, subsection (4) or (5) of section 42 would apply, but

(b)   the condition in the subsection in question is not met,

the person may not give notice of intention to adopt unless he has the court's leave to apply for an adoption order.

(5)   On receipt of a notice of intention to adopt, the local authority must arrange for the investigation of the matter and submit to the court a report of the investigation.

(6)   In particular, the investigation must, so far as practicable, include the suitability of the proposed adopters and any other matters relevant to the operation of section 1 in relation to the application.

(7)   If a local authority receive a notice of intention to adopt in respect of a child whom they know was (immediately before the notice was given) looked after by another local authority, they must, not more than seven days after the receipt of the notice, inform the other local authority in writing that they have received the notice.

(8)   Where—

(a)   a local authority have placed a child with any persons otherwise than as prospective adopters, and

(b)   the persons give notice of intention to adopt,

the authority are not to be treated as leaving the child with them as prospective adopters for the purposes of section 18(1)(b).

(9)   In this section, references to the appropriate local authority, in relation to any proposed adopters, are—

(a)   in prescribed cases, references to the prescribed local authority,

(b)   in any other case, references to the local authority for the area in which, at the time of giving the notice of intention to adopt, they have their home,

and 'prescribed' means prescribed by regulations.

NOTES

Initial Commencement

To be appointed

To be appointed: see s 148(1), (2).

Appointment

Appointment (for the purpose of making regulations): 7 December 2004: see SI 2004/3203, art 2(1)(m)(iv); appointment (for remaining purposes): 30 December 2005: see SI 2005/2213, art 2(c).

Extent

This section does not extend to Scotland: see s 149(2).

See Further

See further, the application of this section, with modifications, in relation to an external adoption order effected within the period of six months of the making of the adoption, and in respect of adoptions under the 1993 Hague Convention on Protection of Children and Co-operation in respect of Intercountry Adoption: the Adoptions with a Foreign Element Regulations 2005, SI 2005/392, regs 11(1)(k), 52, 55, 57.

Subordinate Legislation

Local Authority (Non-agency Adoptions) (Wales) Regulations 2005, SI 2005/3113 (made under sub-s (9)); Local Authority (Adoption) (Miscellaneous Provisions) Regulations 2005, SI 2005/3390 (made under sub-s (9)).

General

[287]

This section governs the procedure for adoption where the child was not placed for adoption by an adoption agency (including a Scottish or Northern Irish adoption agency: see s 42(8)). See s 43 for children placed by an adoption agency.

The application of this section is modified in certain respects for some foreign adoptions: see the Adoptions with a Foreign Element Regulations 2005, regs 11, 52, 55 and 57.

Section 44(2), (3), (5) and (6)

[288]

Prior to making an application to adopt a child, the proposed adopter(s) must give a 'notice of intention to adopt' to the appropriate local authority (see below for definition), at least three months before making the application, and no more than two years prior to doing so.

Upon receipt of the notice, the local authority must investigate all relevant matters, but in particular the suitability of the proposed adopter(s) and all relevant aspects of s 1. See note to s 43 (para [285]) for the breadth of this investigation. The local authority must then prepare a court report.

In Wales, the local authority must obtain an enhanced criminal record certificate under the Police Act 1997, s 115, in respect of the proposed adopter(s) and any members of that household aged 18 or over (Local Authority (Non-agency Adoptions) (Wales) Regulations 2005 (SI 2005/3113), reg 4. See the note to the repealed Adoption and Children Act 2002, s 135, for relevant case-law concerning the ECHR, art 8, and non-conviction information.

See Annex A to the Practice Direction: *Reports by the Adoption Agency or Local Authority*, supplementing the Family Procedure (Adoption) Rules 2005, for the contents of this report. All matters in Annex A must be covered in the report, unless they do not apply, in which case the reason for their omission must be stated (Practice Direction, para 1.3).

Section 44(4)

[289]

If leave of the court is required before an application can be made to adopt (see s 42 above), that leave must first be obtained before notice is given to the local authority.

Section 44(7)

[290]

If the local authority receives a notice in respect of a child whom they know was looked after by another local authority immediately before, it must give the other authority written notice to that effect within seven days.

Section 44(8)

[291]

A placement with foster-parents is not converted into a placement by the adoption agency, for the purposes of ss 18 and 43, by the service of a s 44 notice.

Section 44(9)

[292]

Unless otherwise prescribed by regulations, the appropriate local authority for notice is that for the area where the applicant has his/her home at the date of the notice. In Wales, in the case of a proposed adoption by one person who no longer lives in that country, or by a couple who lived together when they last lived in Wales, the prescribed authority is the one for the area where that person or couple last lived in Wales. If they did not share the last home each had in Wales, the couple must nominate the authority for the location of one of those homes (Local Authority (Non-agency) (Wales) Regulations 2005, regs 2 and 3).

[293]

---

45 Suitability of adopters

(1) Regulations under section 9 may make provision as to the matters to be taken into account by an adoption agency in determining, or making any report in respect of, the suitability of any persons to adopt a child.

(2) In particular, the regulations may make provision for the purpose of securing that, in determining the suitability of a couple to adopt a child, proper regard is had to the need for stability and permanence in their relationship.

NOTES

Initial Commencement

To be appointed
To be appointed: see s 148(1), (2).

Appointment
Appointment: 7 December 2004: see SI 2004/3203, art 2(1)(g).

Extent
This section does not extend to Scotland: see s 149(2).

Subordinate Legislation
Adoption Agencies (Wales) Regulations 2005, SI 2005/1313 (made under sub-ss (1), (2)); Suitability of Adopters Regulations 2005, SI 2005/1712 (made under sub-ss (1), (2)).

General

[294]

Regulations governing an adoption agency's powers concerning the suitability of a person to adopt can include the matters that can be taken into account by the agency, and in particular, if it concerns a couple, the stability and permanence of their relationship.

The Suitability of Adopters Regulations 2005 are referred to, where relevant, in the footnotes to the Adoption Agencies Regulations 2005 and the Adoptions with a Foreign Element Regulations 2005.

[295]

The making of adoption orders

46 Adoption orders

(1) An adoption order is an order made by the court on an application under section 50 or 51 giving parental responsibility for a child to the adopters or adopter.

(2) The making of an adoption order operates to extinguish—

(a) the parental responsibility which any person other than the adopters or adopter has for the adopted child immediately before the making of the order,

(b) any order under the 1989 Act or the Children (Northern Ireland) Order 1995 (SI 1995/755 (NI 2)),

---

(c)　any order under the Children (Scotland) Act 1995 (c 36) other than an excepted order, and

(d)　any duty arising by virtue of an agreement or an order of a court to make payments, so far as the payments are in respect of the adopted child's maintenance or upbringing for any period after the making of the adoption order.

'Excepted order' means an order under section 9, 11(1)(d) or 13 of the Children (Scotland) Act 1995 or an exclusion order within the meaning of section 76(1) of that Act.

(3)　An adoption order—

(a)　does not affect parental responsibility so far as it relates to any period before the making of the order, and

(b)　in the case of an order made on an application under section 51(2) by the partner of a parent of the adopted child, does not affect the parental responsibility of that parent or any duties of that parent within subsection (2)(d).

(4)　Subsection (2)(d) does not apply to a duty arising by virtue of an agreement—

(a)　which constitutes a trust, or

(b)　which expressly provides that the duty is not to be extinguished by the making of an adoption order.

(5)　An adoption order may be made even if the child to be adopted is already an adopted child.

(6)　Before making an adoption order, the court must consider whether there should be arrangements for allowing any person contact with the child; and for that purpose the court must consider any existing or proposed arrangements and obtain any views of the parties to the proceedings.

NOTES

Initial Commencement

To be appointed

To be appointed: see s 148(1), (2).

Appointment

Appointment: 30 December 2005: see SI 2005/2213, art 2(c).

Extent

This section does not extend to Scotland: see s 149(2).

General

[296]

Adoption orders have been updated by this Act by extending the range of people who can apply for them (see ss 49–51); setting minimum times for residence of a child with proposed adopters (see s 49); making the orders conditional on either a placement order having already been made (see ss 18–29) or on required consents (see s 52); by requiring questions of contact to be considered before any order is made (see s 46); and by extending the welfare checklist under the Children Act 1989 to any application for contact (see s 26).

Adoption orders are now supplemented in terms of 'permanent' orders for children by the new 'Special Guardianship Orders' (s 115) and 'Extended Residence Orders' (s 114).

The ACA 2002 for the first time recognises the status of a child of a step-parent/partner relationship. The status of an adopted person includes being treated in law as if born as a child of the adopter(s) and as the child of the relationship of the couple or one of the couple, where adopted by the partner of a parent: s 67.

The primary ground for the making of an adoption order is that such an order is justified in all the circumstances, the paramount consideration being given to the child's welfare through the child's life under ACA 2002, s 1. Note that by s 46(5) a child may be adopted more than once.

The Family Procedure (Adoption) Rules 2005 (SI 2005/2795), apply to proceedings in all three court tiers: High Court, county court and magistrates' court. Certain county courts are designated as adoption centres and applications for an adoption order to a county court must be commenced in such a centre.

The Family Procedure (Adoption) Rules 2005, Pt 5, apply to applications for adoption orders. The overriding objective in r 1 applies to adoption order applications (see below). The relevant form is Form A58. A report on the health of each applicant and of the child must be attached to the application, except where (a) the child was placed with the applicant(s) by an adoption agency or (b) the applicant or one of the applicants is a parent of the child or (c) the applicant is the partner of a parent of the child (r 30). Health reports must cover the matters set out in the Practice Direction *Reports by a Registered Medical Practitioner.* The respondents to the application are set out in r 23. Proceedings are started when the court officer issues the application at the request of the applicant (r 19).

The overriding objective

[297]

The Family Procedure (Adoption) Rules 2005, r 1, sets out the overriding objective, which it is the court's duty to achieve in respect of all proceedings under the ACA 2002. That objective is 'to enable the court to deal with cases justly, having regard to the welfare issues involved.' 'Dealing with a case justly' includes, so far as is practicable:

(i)   Ensuring that it is dealt with expeditiously and fairly;

(ii)   Dealing with the case in ways which are proportionate to the nature, importance and complexity of the issues;

(iii)   Ensuring that the parties are on an equal footing;

(iv)   Saving expense;

(v)   Allotting to it an appropriate share of the court's resources, whilst taking into account the need to allot resources to other cases.

The duty is on the court to further the overriding objective by actively managing cases. Active case management includes the exercise of powers as listed in r 4(2).

Section 46(2)

'extinguish'

[298]

Once a natural parent has lost parental responsibility under this provision, it appears that, post-adoption, any further application by that parent under the CA 1989, s 8, requires the leave of the court (CA 1989, ss 9 and 10). But note the court's power to consider contact before making the adoption order (ACA 2002, s 46(6)).

Section 46(2)(d)

'any duty arising'

[299]

No mention is made as to an adoption order extinguishing a statutory obligation to make payments to the child, such as under the Child Support Act 1991. However, by CSA 1991, s 26(2) the parent of a child who has subsequently been adopted is exempted from liability under the Act.

Section 46(6)

'contact with child'

[300]

The requirement to consider questions of contact before an adoption order is made was added the last minute to the ACA 2002. It mans that at the final adoption hearing the court may make a s 8 contact order. This supports the 'clean break' principle, giving control into the hands of the adoptive parents (see *Re V (A minor: Dispensing with Agreement)* [1987] 2 Fam 57; *Re C (A minor)(Adoption Order: Conditions)* [1989] AC 1 at 17; *Re D (A minor)(Adoption Order: Conditions)* [1992] 1 FCR 461). In considering such applications, the court will be mindful of ECHR, art 8, when considering whether the cutting off of all contact between the child and his natural family is a proportionate response and justified by the overriding necessity of the interests of the child. A useful guide as to how matters of adoption and contact should be dealt with can be found in *G (Adoption: Contact)* [2003] 1 FLR 270.

[301]

47 Conditions for making adoption orders

(1)   An adoption order may not be made if the child has a parent or guardian unless one of the following three conditions is met; but this section is subject to section 52 (parental etc consent).

(2)   The first condition is that, in the case of each parent or guardian of the child, the court is satisfied—

(a)   that the parent or guardian consents to the making of the adoption order,

(b)   that the parent or guardian has consented under section 20 (and has not withdrawn the consent) and does not oppose the making of the adoption order, or

(c)   that the parent's or guardian's consent should be dispensed with.

(3)   A parent or guardian may not oppose the making of an adoption order under subsection (2)(b) without the court's leave.

(4)   The second condition is that—

(a)   the child has been placed for adoption by an adoption agency with the prospective adopters in whose favour the order is proposed to be made,

(b)   either—

(i)   the child was placed for adoption with the consent of each parent or guardian and the consent of the mother was given when the child was at least six weeks old, or

(ii)   the child was placed for adoption under a placement order, and

(c)   no parent or guardian opposes the making of the adoption order.

(5)   A parent or guardian may not oppose the making of an adoption order under the second condition without the court's leave.

(6)   The third condition is that the child is free for adoption by virtue of an order made—

(a)   in Scotland, under section 18 of the Adoption (Scotland) Act 1978 (c 28), or

(b)   in Northern Ireland, under Article 17(1) or 18(1) of the Adoption (Northern Ireland) Order 1987 (SI 1987/2203 (NI 22)).

(7)   The court cannot give leave under subsection (3) or (5) unless satisfied that there has been a change in circumstances since the consent of the parent or guardian was given or, as the case may be, the placement order was made.

(8)   An adoption order may not be made in relation to a person who is or has been married.

[(8A)   An adoption order may not be made in relation to a person who is or has been a civil partner.]

(9)   An adoption order may not be made in relation to a person who has attained the age of 19 years.

NOTES

Initial Commencement

To be appointed

To be appointed: see s 148(1), (2).

Appointment

Appointment: 30 December 2005: see SI 2005/2213, art 2(c).

Extent

This section does not extend to Scotland: see s 149(2).

Amendment

Sub-s (8A): inserted by the Civil Partnership Act 2004, s 79(1), (3); date in force: 30 December 2005: see SI 2005/3175, art 2(9).

See Further

See further, the application of this section, with modifications, in relation to an external adoption order effected within the period of six months of the making of the adoption, and in respect of adoptions under the 1993 Hague Convention on Protection of Children and Co-operation in respect of Intercountry Adoption: the Adoptions with a Foreign Element Regulations 2005, SI 2005/392, regs 11(1)(l), 52, 55.

General

[302]

This section contains key provisions within ACA 2002. Depending on the facts, an 'agency placement' (s 20) may fall to be considered either under the first or second conditions. A change in circumstances is a pre-condition to obtaining leave to oppose the application for a parent who has previously given consent either to a placement or an adoption (s 47(3), (5), (7)). Presumably, such an application for leave to oppose will be dealt with as a preliminary issue prior to the main hearing.

Parent

[303]

For definition see s 52(6) and comment thereon.

Guardian

[304]

For definition see s 144(1).

Section 47(7)

[305]

There is no indication as to exactly what 'a change in circumstances' means nor what the test is to determine that such a change has taken place so as to justify granting leave to oppose the application for adoption. Clearly, to a large extent each case will depend on its own facts and the impact of any 'change' will vary from case to case. However, it is hoped that at some point the courts will offer some guidance as to the kind of circumstances that will or will not amount to a change which justifies the granting of leave. This is particularly important as a refusal of leave will effectively determine the application for adoption so far as the parent's involvement is concerned, except in relation to questions of contact (s 46(6)).

[306]

48   Restrictions on making adoption orders

(1)   The court may not hear an application for an adoption order in relation to a child, where a previous application to which subsection (2) applies made in relation to the child by the same persons was refused by any court, unless it appears to the court that, because of a change in circumstances or for any other reason, it is proper to hear the application.

(2)   This subsection applies to any application—

(a)   for an adoption order or a Scottish or Northern Irish adoption order, or
(b)   for an order for adoption made in the Isle of Man or any of the Channel Islands.

NOTES

Initial Commencement

To be appointed
To be appointed: see s 148(1), (2).

Appointment
Appointment: 30 December 2005: see SI 2005/2213, art 2(c).

Extent
This section does not extend to Scotland: see s 149(2).

See Further
See further, the application of this section, with modifications, in relation to an external adoption order effected within the period of six months of the making of the adoption, and in respect of adoptions under the 1993 Hague Convention on Protection of Children and Co-operation in respect of Intercountry Adoption: the Adoptions with a Foreign Element Regulations 2005, SI 2005/392, regs 11(1)(m), 52, 55.

General

[307]

For explanation concerning 'a change of circumstances', see note to s 47(7).

'… or for any other reason …': similar comments apply to this phrase as to 'a change of circumstances' (see note to s 47(7) above). There is no clarification as to what kind of reason would justify hearing an adoption application under the circumstances envisaged by the section.

[308]

49   Applications for adoption

(1)   An application for an adoption order may be made by—

(a)   a couple, or
(b)   one person,

but only if it is made under section 50 or 51 and one of the following conditions is met.

(2)   The first condition is that at least one of the couple (in the case of an application under section 50) or the applicant (in the case of an application under section 51) is domiciled in a part of the British Islands.

(3)   The second condition is that both of the couple (in the case of an application under section 50) or the applicant (in the case of an application under section 51) have been habitually resident in a part of the British Islands for a period of not less than one year ending with the date of the application.

(4)   An application for an adoption order may only be made if the person to be adopted has not attained the age of 18 years on the date of the application.

(5)   References in this Act to a child, in connection with any proceedings (whether or not concluded) for adoption, (such as 'child to be adopted' or 'adopted child') include a person who has attained the age of 18 years before the proceedings are concluded.

NOTES

Initial Commencement

To be appointed
To be appointed: see s 148(1), (2).

Appointment
Appointment: 30 December 2005: see SI 2005/2213, art 2(c).

Extent
This section does not extend to Scotland: see s 149(2).

See Further
See further, the application of this section, with modifications, in respect of adoptions under the 1993 Hague Convention on Protection of Children and Co-operation in respect of Intercountry Adoption: the Adoptions with a Foreign Element Regulations 2005, SI 2005/392, regs 52, 58.

General

[309]

Under the old law only a married couple could apply. Now a couple is defined by s 144(4) as either a married couple, or as two people of the same or different sexes who are living, as partners, in an 'enduring family relationship'. What amounts to such a relationship is not defined but clearly each case will depend on its own facts.

[310]

50   Adoption by couple

(1)   An adoption order may be made on the application of a couple where both of them have attained the age of 21 years.

(2)   An adoption order may be made on the application of a couple where—

(a)   one of the couple is the mother or the father of the person to be adopted and has attained the age of 18 years, and

(b)   the other has attained the age of 21 years.

NOTES

Initial Commencement

To be appointed
To be appointed: see s 148(1), (2).

Appointment
Appointment: 30 December 2005: see SI 2005/2213, art 2(c).

Extent
This section does not extend to Scotland: see s 149(2).

See Further
See further, the application of this section, with modifications, in relation to an external adoption order effected within the period of six months of the making of the adoption, and in respect of

adoptions under the 1993 Hague Convention on Protection of Children and Co-operation in respect of Intercountry Adoption: the Adoptions with a Foreign Element Regulations 2005, SI 2005/392, regs 11(1)(n), 52, 55.

General

[311]

For further comment on couples, see the note to s 49 above (para [309]).

Section 50(2)(a) provides the first of two alternatives where the 'couple' in question consists of a natural parent of the child to be adopted and one other adult, aged at least 21. Either both the natural parent and the partner can apply together to adopt the child under s 50 or just the partner can apply under s 51 (below). Although s 46(3) extinguishes parental responsibility for any person if an adoption order is made, this does not apply to a parent of a partner who applies on their own for adoption under s 51(2) (see s 46(3)(b)).

[312]

51 Adoption by one person

(1) An adoption order may be made on the application of one person who has attained the age of 21 years and is not married [or a civil partner].

(2) An adoption order may be made on the application of one person who has attained the age of 21 years if the court is satisfied that the person is the partner of a parent of the person to be adopted.

(3) An adoption order may be made on the application of one person who has attained the age of 21 years and is married if the court is satisfied that—

(a) the person's spouse cannot be found,

(b) the spouses have separated and are living apart, and the separation is likely to be permanent, or

(c) the person's spouse is by reason of ill-health, whether physical or mental, incapable of making an application for an adoption order.

[(3A) An adoption order may be made on the application of one person who has attained the age of 21 years and is a civil partner if the court is satisfied that—

(a) the person's civil partner cannot be found,

(b) the civil partners have separated and are living apart, and the separation is likely to be permanent, or

(c) the person's civil partner is by reason of ill-health, whether physical or mental, incapable of making an application for an adoption order.]

(4) An adoption order may not be made on an application under this section by the mother or the father of the person to be adopted unless the court is satisfied that—

(a) the other natural parent is dead or cannot be found,

(b) by virtue of section 28 of the Human Fertilisation and Embryology Act 1990 (c 37) [(disregarding subsections (5A) to (5I) of that section)], there is no other parent, or

(c) there is some other reason justifying the child's being adopted by the applicant alone,

and, where the court makes an adoption order on such an application, the court must record that it is satisfied as to the fact mentioned in paragraph (a) or (b) or, in the case of paragraph (c), record the reason.

NOTES

Initial Commencement

To be appointed

To be appointed: see s 148(1), (2).

Appointment

Appointment: 30 December 2005: see SI 2005/2213, art 2(c).

PART B – Statutes

Extent
This section does not extend to Scotland: see s 149(2).

Amendment
Sub-s (1): words 'or a civil partner' in square brackets inserted by the Civil Partnership Act 2004, s 79(1), (4); date in force: 30 December 2005: see SI 2005/3175, art 2(9); sub-s (3A): inserted by the Civil Partnership Act 2004, s 79(1), (5); date in force: 30 December 2005: see SI 2005/3175, art 2(9); sub-s (4): in para (b) words '(disregarding subsections (5A) to (5I) of that section)' in square brackets inserted by the Human Fertilisation and Embryology (Deceased Fathers) Act 2003, s 2(1), Schedule, para 18; date in force: 1 December 2003: see SI 2003/3095, art 2; for retrospective, transitional and transitory provision see the Human Fertilisation and Embryology (Deceased Fathers) Act 2003, s 3(1).

See Further
See further, the application of this section, with modifications, in relation to an external adoption order effected within the period of six months of the making of the adoption, and in respect of adoptions under the 1993 Hague Convention on Protection of Children and Co-operation in respect of Intercountry Adoption: the Adoptions with a Foreign Element Regulations 2005, SI 2005/392, regs 11(1)(o), 52, 55.

General

[313]

This section envisages four circumstances in which an application for adoption may be made by one person – a single person who is not married (s 51(1)); the partner of a parent (s 51(2)); a married person separated from their spouse or whose spouse is suffering from a condition which prevents them from applying for adoption (s 51(3)). In addition, and rather oddly, an application may also be made by a natural parent of the child but only if the conditions contained in s 51(4) are satisfied.

A 'civil partner' is someone who has entered into a formal civil partnership agreement pursuant to the Civil Partnership Act 2004 (s 51(3A) added by s 79(1), (4), (5) of the 2004 Act). The Civil Partnership Act 2004 was created to give legal form similar to marriage to persons of the same sex provided they comply with the formalities provided for by the Act.

Section 51(2)

[314]

As included in this section, 'the partner' is defined by ACA 2002, s 144(7) as someone who is in a couple with the child's parent but is not themselves a parent of the child. As to parental responsibility, see note to s 50(2)(a) above.

Section 51(4)(c)

[315]

See note to s 48 above. Clearly the reason must involve the benefits of the child being adopted by one person rather than by that person and a parent. Each case will depend on its own circumstances.

[316]

Placement and adoption: general

52 Parental etc consent

(1) The court cannot dispense with the consent of any parent or guardian of a child to the child being placed for adoption or to the making of an adoption order in respect of the child unless the court is satisfied that—

(a)   the parent or guardian cannot be found or <u>*is incapable of giving consent* [lacks capacity (within the meaning of the Mental Capacity Act 2005) to give consent]</u>, or

(b)   the welfare of the child requires the consent to be dispensed with.

(2)   The following provisions apply to references in this Chapter to any parent or guardian of a child giving or withdrawing—

(a)   consent to the placement of a child for adoption, or

(b)   consent to the making of an adoption order (including a future adoption order).

(3)   Any consent given by the mother to the making of an adoption order is ineffective if it is given less than six weeks after the child's birth.

(4)   The withdrawal of any consent to the placement of a child for adoption, or of any consent given under section 20, is ineffective if it is given after an application for an adoption order is made.

(5)   'Consent' means consent given unconditionally and with full understanding of what is involved; but a person may consent to adoption without knowing the identity of the persons in whose favour the order will be made.

(6)   'Parent' (except in subsections (9) and (10) below) means a parent having parental responsibility.

(7)   Consent under section 19 or 20 must be given in the form prescribed by rules, and the rules may prescribe forms in which a person giving consent under any other provision of this Part may do so (if he wishes).

(8)   Consent given under section 19 or 20 must be withdrawn—

(a)   in the form prescribed by rules, or

(b)   by notice given to the agency.

(9)   Subsection (10) applies if—

(a)   an agency has placed a child for adoption under section 19 in pursuance of consent given by a parent of the child, and

(b)   at a later time, the other parent of the child acquires parental responsibility for the child.

(10)   The other parent is to be treated as having at that time given consent in accordance with this section in the same terms as those in which the first parent gave consent.

NOTES

Initial Commencement

To be appointed

To be appointed: see s 148(1), (2).

Appointment

Appointment: 30 December 2005: see SI 2005/2213, art 2(c).

Extent

This section does not extend to Scotland: see s 149(2).

Amendment

Sub-s (1): in para (a) words 'is incapable of giving consent' in italics repealed and subsequent words in square brackets substituted by the Mental Capacity Act 2005, s 67(1), Sch 6, para 45; date in force: to be appointed: see the Mental Capacity Act 2005, s 68(1).

See Further

See further, the application of this section, with modifications, in relation to an external adoption order effected within the period of six months of the making of the adoption, and in respect of adoptions under the 1993 Hague Convention on Protection of Children and Co-operation in respect of Intercountry Adoption: the Adoptions with a Foreign Element Regulations 2005, SI 2005/392, regs 11(1)(p), 52, 55.

Subordinate Legislation

Family Procedure (Adoption) Rules 2005, SI 2005/2795 (made under sub-ss (7), (8)).

General

[317]

The provisions for consent and dispensing with consent are integral to the making of an adoption order. The net effect of the provisions means that only birth parents with parental responsibility can consent. An unmarried father who does not have parental responsibility cannot consent but he may be joined as a respondent to the application for adoption (see FP(A) Rules 2005, r 23(3)). A guardian or special guardian can also consent. The consent must be in a prescribed form.

Section 52(1)

[318]

Three circumstances apply. They are: missing parent or guardian; incapable (eg, by reasons of mental illness) parent or guardian; or the welfare of the child. In all three instances any application will need to be supported by evidence sufficient to justify dispensing with the consent. In the case of an incapable parent or guardian, regard should be had to the question of the appointment of a litigation friend (as to which see FP(A) Rules 2005, r 55). In the last instance, the 'welfare of the child', the approach will be similar to that under CA 1989, s 1, where the best interests of the child are considered. In addition the welfare checklist at s 1(4) will also need to be taken into account.

Procedure for dispensing with consent

[319]

See FP(A) Rules 2005, r 27.

Section 52(8)

[320]

Forms of consent are at A100–106 of the Practice Direction Forms.

[321]

53 Modification of 1989 Act in relation to adoption

(1) Where—

(a)   a local authority are authorised to place a child for adoption, or

(b)   a child who has been placed for adoption by a local authority is less than six weeks old,

regulations may provide for the following provisions of the 1989 Act to apply with modifications, or not to apply, in relation to the child.

(2) The provisions are—

(a)   section 22(4)(b), (c) and (d) and (5)(b) (duty to ascertain wishes and feelings of certain persons),

(b)   paragraphs 15 and 21 of Schedule 2 (promoting contact with parents and parents' obligation to contribute towards maintenance).

(3) Where a registered adoption society is authorised to place a child for adoption or a child who has been placed for adoption by a registered adoption society is less than six weeks old, regulations may provide—

(a)   for section 61 of that Act to have effect in relation to the child whether or not he is accommodated by or on behalf of the society,

> (b)   for subsections (2)(b) to (d) and (3)(b) of that section (duty to ascertain wishes and feelings of certain persons) to apply with modifications, or not to apply, in relation to the child.
>
> (4) Where a child's home is with persons who have given notice of intention to adopt, no contribution is payable (whether under a contribution order or otherwise) under Part 3 of Schedule 2 to that Act (contributions towards maintenance of children looked after by local authorities) in respect of the period referred to in subsection (5).
>
> (5) That period begins when the notice of intention to adopt is given and ends if—
>
> (a)   the period of four months beginning with the giving of the notice expires without the prospective adopters applying for an adoption order, or
>
> (b)   an application for such an order is withdrawn or refused.
>
> (6) In this section, 'notice of intention to adopt' includes notice of intention to apply for a Scottish or Northern Irish adoption order.
>
> **NOTES**
>
> **Initial Commencement**
>
> ***To be appointed***
>
> Sub-ss (1)–(3): to be appointed: see s 148(6); sub-ss (4)–(6): to be appointed: see s 148(1), (2).
>
> **Appointment**
>
> Sub-ss (1)–(3): appointment (in relation to Wales): 7 February 2004: see SI 2004/252, art 2(b); sub-s (1)–(3): appointment (in relation to England): 7 December 2004: see SI 2004/3203, art 2(1)(h); sub-ss (4)–(6): appointment: 30 December 2005: see SI 2005/2213, art 2(c).
>
> **Extent**
>
> This section does not extend to Scotland: see s 149(2).
>
> **See Further**
>
> See further, the application of this section, with modifications, in relation to an external adoption order effected within the period of six months of the making of the adoption, and in respect of adoptions under the 1993 Hague Convention on Protection of Children and Co-operation in respect of Intercountry Adoption: the Adoptions with a Foreign Element Regulations 2005, SI 2005/392, regs 11(1)(q), 52, 55.
>
> **Subordinate Legislation**
>
> Adoption Agencies Regulations 2005, SI 2005/389 (made under sub-ss (1)–(3)); Adoption Agencies (Wales) Regulations 2005, SI 2005/1313; Adoption and Children (Miscellaneous Amendments) Regulations 2005, SI 2005/3482 (made under sub-ss (1)–(3)).

General

[322]

By this section regulations may be made which modify certain provisions of the Children Act 1989 where a child is placed for adoption by a local authority. At the date of writing, such regulations have not yet been made.

Section 53(2)(a)

[323]

By the sections referred to in ACA 2002, s 53(2)(a), a local authority must, as far as is reasonably practicable, ascertain the wishes and feelings of the parents, anyone who has parental responsibility and any other person they consider to be relevant.

Section 53(2)(b)

[324]

Under CA 1989, Sch 2, para 15, the local authority is required, so far as is reasonably practicable, to promote contact between the child and the parents, anyone who has parental responsibility and any relative, friend or other person connected with the child. Under CA

1989, Sch 2, para 21, certain persons may be called upon to pay contributions towards the child's maintenance, including each of the parents and the child himself, if 16 or over.

Section 53(3)

[325]

The CA 1989, s 61, places obligations on the voluntary organisation to care for the child in order to promote the child's welfare. By CA 1989, s 61(2)(b)–(d) and (3)(b) the voluntary organisation must, before making a decision with regard to the child, as far as is reasonably practicable, ascertain the wishes and feelings of the parents, anyone who has parental responsibility and any other person they consider to be relevant.

[326]

54 Disclosing information during adoption process

Regulations under section 9 may require adoption agencies in prescribed circumstances to disclose in accordance with the regulations prescribed information to prospective adopters.

NOTES

Initial Commencement

To be appointed
To be appointed: see s 148(6).

Appointment
Appointment (in relation to Wales): 7 February 2004: see SI 2004/252, art 2(b); appointment (in relation to England): 7 December 2004: see SI 2004/3203, art 2(1)(i).

Extent
This section does not extend to Scotland: see s 149(2).

Subordinate Legislation
Adoption Agencies Regulations 2005, SI 2005/389; Adoption Agencies (Wales) Regulations 2005, SI 2005/1313; Adoption and Children (Miscellaneous Amendments) Regulations 2005, SI 2005/3482.

General

[327]

Disclosure is dealt with in more detail in the notes to ss 56–65 below (paras [328]–[365]).

[328]

55 Revocation of adoptions on legitimation

(1) Where any child adopted by one natural parent as sole adoptive parent subsequently becomes a legitimated person on the marriage of the natural parents, the court by which the adoption order was made may, on the application of any of the parties concerned, revoke the order.
(2) In relation to an adoption order made by a magistrates' court, the reference in subsection (1) to the court by which the order was made includes a court acting for the same [local justice] area.

NOTES

Initial Commencement

To be appointed
To be appointed: see s 148(1), (2).

Appointment
Appointment: 30 December 2005: see SI 2005/2213, art 2(c).

Extent
This section does not extend to Scotland: see s 149(2).

Amendment

Sub-s (2): words 'local justice' in square brackets substituted by the Courts Act 2003, s 109(1), Sch 8, para 412; date in force: 1 April 2005: see SI 2005/910, art 3(y); for transitional provisions see SI 2005/911, arts 2–5.

General

[329]

The marriage of the natural parents which causes a child adopted by just one of them to be legitimized may result in the adoption order being revoked, provided an application is made to the court to do so. The relevant rules for the application are contained in the FP(A) Rules 2005, Pt 9 and the form to use is F2.

[330]

Disclosure of information in relation to a person's adoption

56   Information to be kept about a person's adoption

(1)   In relation to an adopted person, regulations may prescribe—

(a)   the information which an adoption agency must keep in relation to his adoption,

(b)   the form and manner in which it must keep that information.

(2)   Below in this group of sections (that is, this section and sections 57 to 65), any information kept by an adoption agency by virtue of subsection (1)(a) is referred to as section 56 information.

(3)   Regulations may provide for the transfer in prescribed circumstances of information held, or previously held, by an adoption agency to another adoption agency.

NOTES

Initial Commencement

To be appointed

To be appointed: see s 148(6).

Appointment

Sub-ss (1), (3): Appointment (in relation to Wales): 7 February 2004: see SI 2004/252, art 2(b); appointment (in relation to England for the purpose of making regulations): 7 December 2004: see SI 2004/3203, art 2(1)(m)(v); appointment (in relation to England for remaining purposes): 30 December 2005: see SI 2005/2213, art 3(k); sub-s (2): appointment (in relation to Wales): 30 December 2005: see SI 2005/3112, art 2(e).

Extent

This section does not extend to Scotland: see s 149(2).

Subordinate Legislation

Disclosure of Adoption Information (Post-Commencement Adoptions) Regulations 2005, SI 2005/888; Access to Information (Post-Commencement Adoptions) (Wales) Regulations 2005, SI 2005/2689; Adoption and Children (Miscellaneous Amendments) Regulations 2005, SI 2005/3482.

General

[331]

Under the Act, access to information is filtered through adoption agencies (see s 57). This provides an intermediary safeguard before disclosure is made.

Information

[332]

The following sections deal with different types of information – information for prospective adopters (s 54) (see above); 'protected' information (ss 56 and 57); and 'background' information (s 58).

Disclosure

[333]

ACA 2002, ss 60–62 deal with persons to whom information may be given, s 63 deals with the provision of counselling services for those seeking information.

'Protected' information

[334]

ACA 2002, ss 56 and 57 deal with 'protected' information, which the adoption agency must keep in relation to a person's adoption, including information as to birth parents, siblings, adoptive parents and siblings and other relatives. In addition, the protected information includes any information kept by the adoption agency which is necessary to enable the adopted person to obtain a certified copy of his birth certificate (s 79(3) and (5)) or in relation to an entry in the Adoption Contact Register (see s 57).

Regulations

[335]

The Disclosure of Adoption Information (Post-Commencement Adoptions) Regulations 2005 (SI 2005/888) (DAIPCAR) and Access to Information (Post Commencement Adoptions) (Wales) Regulations 2005 (SI 2005/2689) (AIPCAWR) govern adoptions taking place on or after 30 December 2005. For information concerning adoptions before that date, see the note to s 98 (para **[482]**).

In England, the adoption agency placing a person for adoption, and any such agency to whom records are later transferred, must retain the case records set up for that person, information provided by his/her natural family or other significant persons for future availability to him/her, information from the adoptive parents relevant to post-adoption order issues, information the adopted person has asked should be retained, information from the Registrar General or Adoption Contact Register, and other information arising from the operation of these Regulations. These records must be safely stored, and retained for 100 years from the date of the adoption order (DAIPCAR, regs 3–6).

Similar provisions apply in Wales, save that the records to be retained must include information provided by any of the child's former foster-carers (AIPCAWR, regs 3–5).

There is a slight difference between England and Wales regarding exceptions to the requirements to retain records. In England, a record need not be kept if it is considered prejudicial to the adopted person's welfare, or if it is not reasonably practicable, to keep it. In Wales, there is no 'welfare' exception, but there is an exception allowing the non-retention of 'objects and momentoes' that are not reasonably practicable to store, and with a record to be kept of the items not retained.

Regulations 7 (England) and 6 (Wales) provide for the transfer of records if an agency intends to cease to act or exist as such an agency.

[336]

57 Restrictions on disclosure of protected etc information

(1) Any section 56 information kept by an adoption agency which—

(a) is about an adopted person or any other person, and
(b) is or includes identifying information about the person in question,

may only be disclosed by the agency to a person (other than the person the information is about) in pursuance of this group of sections.

(2) Any information kept by an adoption agency—

(a) which the agency has obtained from the Registrar General on an application under section 79(5) and any other information which would enable the adopted person to obtain a certified copy of the record of his birth, or
(b) which is information about an entry relating to the adopted person in the Adoption Contact Register,

may only be disclosed to a person by the agency in pursuance of this group of sections.

(3) In this group of sections, information the disclosure of which to a person is restricted by virtue of subsection (1) or (2) is referred to (in relation to him) as protected information.
(4) Identifying information about a person means information which, whether taken on its own or together with other information disclosed by an adoption agency, identifies the person or enables the person to be identified.
(5) This section does not prevent the disclosure of protected information in pursuance of a prescribed agreement to which the adoption agency is a party.
(6) Regulations may authorise or require an adoption agency to disclose protected information to a person who is not an adopted person.

NOTES
Initial Commencement
To be appointed
To be appointed: see s 148(6).

Appointment
Appointment (in relation to England for the purpose of making regulations): 7 December 2004: see SI 2004/3203, art 2(1)(m)(v); appointment (in relation to England for remaining purposes): 30 December 2005: see SI 2005/2213, art 3(k); sub-ss (1)–(4): appointment (in relation to Wales): 30 December 2005: see SI 2005/3112, art 2(e); sub-s (5): appointment (in relation to Wales for the purpose of making regulations): 7 February 2004: see SI 2004/252, art 2(c); sub-s (5): appointment (in relation to Wales for remaining purposes): 30 December 2005: see SI 2005/3112, art 2(e); sub-s (6): appointment (in relation to Wales): 7 February 2004: see SI 2004/252, art 2(b).

Extent
This section does not extend to Scotland: see s 149(2).

Subordinate Legislation
Disclosure of Adoption Information (Post-Commencement Adoptions) Regulations 2005, SI 2005/888; Access to Information (Post-Commencement Adoptions) (Wales) Regulations 2005, SI 2005/2689; Adoption and Children (Miscellaneous Amendments) Regulations 2005, SI 2005/3482.

General

[337]

For further explanation of 'protected information', see the note to s 56 above (in particular, para [334]). The protected information includes information which identifies the person or enables the person to be identified (s 57(4) as to which, see note below).

Section 57(4)

[338]

'Identifying information' includes residence, educational and employment addresses, photographic or audiovisual material, case records and legal and medical information held by adoption agencies.

Regulations

[339]

The Disclosure of Adoption Information (Post-Commencement Adoptions) Regulations 2005 (SI 2005/888) (DAIPCAR) and Access to Information (Post Commencement Adoptions) (Wales) Regulations 2005 (SI 2005/2689) (AIPCAWR) govern adoptions taking place on or after 30 December 2005. For information concerning adoptions before that date, see the note to s 98 (para [482]).

An adoption agency may disclose such non-protected information (see s 57(3) for definition), as it sees fit, for the purposes of carrying out its functions. It may also disclose any information (including protected information) to another adoption agency or a registered adoption support agency in connection with its functions under ss 61 and 62 or for research authorised by the Secretary of State/National Assembly for Wales. It must disclose any information (protected or otherwise) required by certain inquiries, the Secretary of State/Children's Commissioner for Wales, CSCI/National Assembly, Ombudsman, a Panel under s 12 of the Act considering a qualifying determination regarding s 56 information, (in Wales only) CAFCASS or a Welsh Family Proceedings Officer, or to a court having power to make orders under the Act or the CA 1989. Records of disclosure, with reasons, must be kept (DAIPCAR, regs 8–10/AIPCAWR, regs 7–9).

A 'prescribed agreement' for the purposes of s 57(5) is one between the adoption agency and an adult, or with the adoptive parent (both, if a couple) and every parent having parental responsibility prior to the adoption order, for the disclosure of protected information (about the adopted person in the first case, and either them or the adopted person in the second case). Records must be kept, with reasons (DAIPCAR, reg 11/AIPCAWR, reg 10).

[340]

58 Disclosure of other information

(1) This section applies to any section 56 information other than protected information.

(2) An adoption agency may for the purposes of its functions disclose to any person in accordance with prescribed arrangements any information to which this section applies.

(3) An adoption agency must, in prescribed circumstances, disclose prescribed information to a prescribed person.

NOTES

Initial Commencement

To be appointed
To be appointed: see s 148(6).

Appointment
Appointment (in relation to England for the purpose of making regulations): 7 December 2004: see SI 2004/3203, art 2(1)(m)(v); appointment (in relation to England for remaining purposes): 30 December 2005: see SI 2005/2213, art 3(k); sub-s (1): appointment (in relation to Wales): 30 December 2005: see SI 2005/3112, art 2(e); sub-ss (2), (3): appointment (in relation to Wales for the purpose of making regulations): 7 February 2004: see SI 2004/252, art 2(c); sub-ss (2), (3): appointment (in relation to Wales for remaining purposes): 30 December 2005: see SI 2005/3112, art 2(e).

Extent
This section does not extend to Scotland: see s 149(2).

Subordinate Legislation
Disclosure of Adoption Information (Post-Commencement Adoptions) Regulations 2005, SI 2005/888; Access to Information (Post-Commencement Adoptions) (Wales) Regulations 2005, SI 2005/2689; Adoption and Children (Miscellaneous Amendments) Regulations 2005, SI 2005/3482.

General

[341]

'Background information' includes information such as the child's birth details, medical history, interests, any special needs and progress which (i) will help adopters and (ii) can be disclosed to the birth family without compromising the adoptee's new identity or whereabouts.

Regulations

[342]

See the note to s 57 (para [337]) for information about the disclosure provisions.

[343]

---

59 Offence

Regulations may provide that a registered adoption society which discloses any information in contravention of section 57 is to be guilty of an offence and liable on summary conviction to a fine not exceeding level 5 on the standard scale.

NOTES

Initial Commencement
To be appointed
To be appointed: see s 148(6).

Appointment
Appointment (in relation to Wales): 7 February 2004: see SI 2004/252, art 2(b); appointment (in relation to England for the purpose of making regulations): 7 December 2004: see SI 2004/3203, art 2(1)(m)(v); appointment (in relation to England for remaining purposes): 30 December 2005: see SI 2005/2213, art 3(k).

Extent
This section does not extend to Scotland: see s 149(2).

Subordinate Legislation
Disclosure of Adoption Information (Post-Commencement Adoptions) Regulations 2005, SI 2005/888; Access to Information (Post-Commencement Adoptions) (Wales) Regulations 2005, SI 2005/2689; Adoption and Children (Miscellaneous Amendments) Regulations 2005, SI 2005/3482.

General

[344]

If a matter is 'liable on summary conviction' it can only be tried by a magistrates' court. 'Level 5' is the highest level of fine, the amount of which is periodically reviewed. At present it is £5,000.

[345]

> ## 60 Disclosing information to adopted adult
>
> (1) This section applies to an adopted person who has attained the age of 18 years.
> (2) The adopted person has the right, at his request, to receive from the appropriate adoption agency—
>
> (a) any information which would enable him to obtain a certified copy of the record of his birth, unless the High Court orders otherwise,
> (b) any prescribed information disclosed to the adopters by the agency by virtue of section 54.
>
> (3) The High Court may make an order under subsection (2)(a), on an application by the appropriate adoption agency, if satisfied that the circumstances are exceptional.
> (4) The adopted person also has the right, at his request, to receive from the court which made the adoption order a copy of any prescribed document or prescribed order relating to the adoption.
> (5) Subsection (4) does not apply to a document or order so far as it contains information which is protected information.
>
> **NOTES**
> **Initial Commencement**
> *To be appointed*
> To be appointed: see s 148(6).
>
> **Appointment**
> Sub-ss (1), (3), (5): appointment (in relation to England): 30 December 2005: see SI 2005/2213, art 3(k); sub-ss (1), (3), (5): appointment (in relation to Wales): 30 December 2005: see SI 2005/3112, art 2(f); sub-ss (2), (4): appointment (in relation to Wales for the purpose of making regulations): 7 February 2004: see SI 2004/252, art 2(c); sub-ss (2), (4): appointment (in relation to England for the purpose of making regulations): 7 December 2004: see SI 2004/3203, art 2(1)(m)(v); sub-ss (2), (4): appointment (in relation to England for remaining purposes): 30 December 2005: see SI 2005/2213, art 3(k); sub-ss (2), (4): appointment (in relation to Wales for remaining purposes): 30 December 2005: see SI 2005/3112, art 2(f).
>
> **Extent**
> This section does not extend to Scotland: see s 149(2).
>
> **Subordinate Legislation**
> Disclosure of Adoption Information (Post-Commencement Adoptions) Regulations 2005, SI 2005/888; Access to Information (Post-Commencement Adoptions) (Wales) Regulations 2005, SI 2005/2689; Family Procedure (Adoption) Rules 2005, SI 2005/2795 (made under sub-s (4)); Adoption and Children (Miscellaneous Amendments) Regulations 2005, SI 2005/3482.

General

[346]

Any 'prescribed document or prescribed order' (s 60(4)) will include the application form for an adoption order (but not the documents attached); any other orders relating to the adoption proceedings; orders allowing a person contact with the child after the adoption order was made; any document or order referred to in the relevant practice direction (Pt 8B, supplementing Pt 8, FP(A) Rules 2005, r 84(1)(d)). The court will remove any protected information from any such copy document or order before it is given to the adopted person.

[347]

> ## 61 Disclosing protected information about adults
>
> (1) This section applies where—
>
> (a) a person applies to the appropriate adoption agency for protected information to be disclosed to him, and
> (b) none of the information is about a person who is a child at the time of the application.

(2)   The agency is not required to proceed with the application unless it considers it appropriate to do so.

(3)   If the agency does proceed with the application it must take all reasonable steps to obtain the views of any person the information is about as to the disclosure of the information about him.

(4)   The agency may then disclose the information if it considers it appropriate to do so.

(5)   In deciding whether it is appropriate to proceed with the application or disclose the information, the agency must consider—

(a)   the welfare of the adopted person,

(b)   any views obtained under subsection (3),

(c)   any prescribed matters,

and all the other circumstances of the case.

(6)   This section does not apply to a request for information under section 60(2) or to a request for information which the agency is authorised or required to disclose in pursuance of regulations made by virtue of section 57(6).

NOTES

Initial Commencement

To be appointed

To be appointed: see s 148(6).

Appointment

Sub-ss (1)–(4), (6): appointment (in relation to England): 30 December 2005: see SI 2005/2213, art 3(k); sub-ss (1)–(4), (5)(a), (b), (6): appointment (in relation to Wales): 30 December 2005: see SI 2005/3112, art 2(f); sub-s (5): appointment (in relation to England for the purpose of making regulations): 7 December 2004: see SI 2004/3203, art 2(1)(m)(v); sub-s (5): appointment (in relation to England for remaining purposes): 30 December 2005: see SI 2005/2213, art 3(k); sub-s (5)(c): appointment (in relation to Wales for the purpose of making regulations): 7 February 2004: see SI 2004/252, art 2(c); sub-s (5)(c): appointment (in relation to Wales for remaining purposes): 30 December 2005: see SI 2005/3112, art 2(f).

Extent

This section does not extend to Scotland: see s 149(2).

Subordinate Legislation

Disclosure of Adoption Information (Post-Commencement Adoptions) Regulations 2005, SI 2005/888; Access to Information (Post-Commencement Adoptions) (Wales) Regulations 2005, SI 2005/2689; Adoption and Children (Miscellaneous Amendments) Regulations 2005, SI 2005/3482.

General

[348]

Other persons may be interested in information concerning an adopted adult. This will be of particular interest to a natural parent who gave a child up for adoption in the first place. Naturally safeguards will need to be built in to such a process. Thus, in two places in the one section we find an exhortation to the adoption agency not to proceed with the application unless it considers it 'appropriate to do so' (s 61(2) and (4)). It is also not surprising to find a requirement that the views of the subject of the enquiry must first be obtained, by taking 'all reasonable steps' to do so (s 61(3)). The implication seems to be that if, after taking reasonable steps, the agency is unable to trace the adopted adult, they may still release information, if 'appropriate', and if the considerations in s 61(5) are taken into account.

Regulations

[349]

The Disclosure of Adoption Information (Post-Commencement Adoptions) Regulations 2005 (SI 2005/888) (DAIPCAR) and Access to Information (Post Commencement

Adoptions) (Wales) Regulations 2005 (SI 2005/2689) (AIPCAWR) govern adoptions taking place on or after 30 December 2005. For information concerning adoptions before that date, see note to s 98.

An application for disclosure of protected information (see s 57(3)) must be in writing, with reasons, and upon receipt the agency must take steps to confirm identity, the authorisation of any third party acting, and (in Wales only) that the agency has enough information about the applicants reasons to enable it to fulfil its duties under ss 61 or 62. It must record the views of those consulted under those sections (DAIPCAR, regs 12–14/AIPCAWR, regs 11–13).

In England only, in certain circumstances a decision under s 61 is a 'qualifying determination' for the purposes of s 12 and the right to request an independent determination of that decision; see note to s 12 (paras [158]–[162]) (DAIPCAR, reg 15). Those are where the agency does not proceed with the application, discloses information against the express wishes of the subject, or where information about a third party is not disclosed to an applicant despite the third party's wish that it should be disclosed.

Information must be made available about counselling, to those seeking information under ss 60, 61 or 62, anyone whose views are canvassed under ss 61(3) or 62 (3) or (4), and anyone considering entering into an agreement with the agency (see note to s 57, paras [337]–[339]) and, if requested, the agency must secure such counselling for that person. To that end, the agency can disclose information (including protected information) to that counsellor (DAIPCAR, regs 16–18/AIPCAWR, regs 14–16).

If an adult adopted person asks the agency for information, which it does not have, to enable him/her to obtain a copy of his/her record of birth, the agency must seek it from the Registrar General, and the Registrar General must disclose information to the agency in relation to applications under ss 60, 61, 62 or entries in the Adoption Contact Register (see note to s 80, paras [386]–[390]). He must also disclose information to any person to help that person locate the appropriate adoption agency (DAIPCAR, regs 19 and 20/AIPCAWR, regs 17 and 18).

[350]

62 Disclosing protected information about children

(1) This section applies where—

(a) a person applies to the appropriate adoption agency for protected information to be disclosed to him, and

(b) any of the information is about a person who is a child at the time of the application.

(2) The agency is not required to proceed with the application unless it considers it appropriate to do so.

(3) If the agency does proceed with the application, then, so far as the information is about a person who is at the time a child, the agency must take all reasonable steps to obtain—

(a) the views of any parent or guardian of the child, and

(b) the views of the child, if the agency considers it appropriate to do so having regard to his age and understanding and to all the other circumstances of the case,

as to the disclosure of the information.

(4) And, so far as the information is about a person who has at the time attained the age of 18 years, the agency must take all reasonable steps to obtain his views as to the disclosure of the information.

(5) The agency may then disclose the information if it considers it appropriate to do so.

(6)   In deciding whether it is appropriate to proceed with the application, or disclose the information, where any of the information is about a person who is at the time a child—

(a)   if the child is an adopted child, the child's welfare must be the paramount consideration,

(b)   in the case of any other child, the agency must have particular regard to the child's welfare.

(7)   And, in deciding whether it is appropriate to proceed with the application or disclose the information, the agency must consider—

(a)   the welfare of the adopted person (where subsection (6)(a) does not apply),

(b)   any views obtained under subsection (3) or (4),

(c)   any prescribed matters,

and all the other circumstances of the case.

(8)   This section does not apply to a request for information under section 60(2) or to a request for information which the agency is authorised or required to disclose in pursuance of regulations made by virtue of section 57(6).

NOTES

Initial Commencement

To be appointed
To be appointed: see s 148(6).

Appointment
Sub-ss (1)–(6), (8): appointment (in relation to England): 30 December 2005: see SI 2005/2213, art 3(k); sub-ss (1)–(6), (7)(a), (b), (8): appointment (in relation to Wales): 30 December 2005: see SI 2005/3112, art 2(f); sub-s (7): appointment (in relation to England for the purpose of making regulations): 7 December 2004: see SI 2004/3203, art 2(1)(m)(v); sub-s (7): appointment (in relation to England for remaining purposes): 30 December 2005: see SI 2005/2213, art 3(k); sub-s (7)(c): appointment (in relation to Wales for the purpose of making regulations): 7 February 2004: see SI 2004/252, art 2(c); sub-s (7)(c): appointment (in relation to Wales for remaining purposes): 30 December 2005: see SI 2005/3112, art 2(f).

Extent
This section does not extend to Scotland: see s 149(2).

Subordinate Legislation
Disclosure of Adoption Information (Post-Commencement Adoptions) Regulations 2005, SI 2005/888; Access to Information (Post-Commencement Adoptions) (Wales) Regulations 2005, SI 2005/2689; Adoption and Children (Miscellaneous Amendments) Regulations 2005, SI 2005/3482.

General

[351]

This section makes a similar provision to that in s 61 (above). As a child is involved, not only must the views of the child be sought first, if appropriate to do so (s 62(3)(b)) but also those of any parent or guardian (s 62(3)(a)). In addition the paramountcy provisions of CA 1989, s 1 apply – ie the welfare of the child.

Regulations

[352]

See note to s 61 (paras [348]–[349]).

[353]

63   Counselling

(1)   Regulations may require adoption agencies to give information about the availability of counselling to persons—

(a)   seeking information from them in pursuance of this group of sections,

(b)   considering objecting or consenting to the disclosure of information by the agency in pursuance of this group of sections, or

(c)   considering entering with the agency into an agreement prescribed for the purposes of section 57(5).

(2)   Regulations may require adoption agencies to make arrangements to secure the provision of counselling for persons seeking information from them in prescribed circumstances in pursuance of this group of sections.

(3)   The regulations may authorise adoption agencies—

(a)   to disclose information which is required for the purposes of such counselling to the persons providing the counselling,

(b)   where the person providing the counselling is outside the United Kingdom, to require a prescribed fee to be paid.

(4)   The regulations may require any of the following persons to provide counselling for the purposes of arrangements under subsection (2)—

(a)   a local authority, a council constituted under section 2 of the Local Government etc (Scotland) Act 1994 (c 39) or a Health and Social Services Board established under Article 16 of the Health and Personal Social Services (Northern Ireland) Order 1972 (SI 1972/1265 (NI 14)),

(b)   a registered adoption society, an organisation within section 144(3)(b) or an adoption society which is registered under Article 4 of the Adoption (Northern Ireland) Order 1987 (SI 1987/2203 (NI 22)),

(c)   an adoption support agency in respect of which a person is registered under Part 2 of the Care Standards Act 2000 (c 14).

(5)   For the purposes of subsection (4), where the functions of a Health and Social Services Board are exercisable by a Health and Social Services Trust, the reference in sub-paragraph (a) to a Board is to be read as a reference to the Health and Social Services Trust.

NOTES

Initial Commencement

To be appointed

To be appointed: see s 148(6).

Appointment

Appointment (in relation to Wales): 7 February 2004: see SI 2004/252, art 2(b); appointment (in relation to England): 7 December 2004: see SI 2004/3203, art 2(1)(j); sub-ss (2)–(5): appointment (in relation to Scotland and Northern Ireland): 7 December 2004: see SI 2004/3203, arts 1(5), 2(1)(j).

Extent

Sub-s (1) does not extend to Scotland: see s 149(2).

Subordinate Legislation

Disclosure of Adoption Information (Post-Commencement Adoptions) Regulations 2005, SI 2005/888; Access to Information (Post-Commencement Adoptions) (Wales) Regulations 2005, SI 2005/2689; Adoption and Children (Miscellaneous Amendments) Regulations 2005, SI 2005/3482.

General

[354]

An integral part of the provision of information about adopted persons is the availability of counselling services both for the person seeking the information and for the subject of the search. Section 2(1) of the Act provides for the setting up of adoption support services which will be responsible for counselling, advice, information and other services subject to the regulations.

Regulations

[355]

See note to s 61 (paras **[348]**–**[349]**).

[356]

64 Other provision to be made by regulations

(1) Regulations may make provision for the purposes of this group of sections, including provision as to—

(a) the performance by adoption agencies of their functions,
(b) the manner in which information may be received, and
(c) the matters mentioned below in this section.

(2) Regulations may prescribe—

(a) the manner in which agreements made by virtue of section 57(5) are to be recorded,
(b) the information to be provided by any person on an application for the disclosure of information under this group of sections.

(3) Regulations may require adoption agencies—

(a) to give to prescribed persons prescribed information about the rights or opportunities to obtain information, or to give their views as to its disclosure, given by this group of sections,
· (b) to seek prescribed information from, or give prescribed information to, the Registrar General in prescribed circumstances.

(4) Regulations may require the Registrar General—

(a) to disclose to any person (including an adopted person) at his request any information which the person requires to assist him to make contact with the adoption agency which is the appropriate adoption agency in the case of an adopted person specified in the request (or, as the case may be, in the applicant's case),
(b) to disclose to the appropriate adoption agency any information which the agency requires about any entry relating to the adopted person on the Adoption Contact Register.

(5) Regulations may provide for the payment of a prescribed fee in respect of the disclosure in prescribed circumstances of any information in pursuance of section 60, 61 or 62; but an adopted person may not be required to pay any fee in respect of any information disclosed to him in relation to any person who (but for his adoption) would be related to him by blood (including half-blood)[, marriage or civil partnership].
(6) Regulations may provide for the payment of a prescribed fee by an adoption agency obtaining information under subsection (4)(b).

NOTES
Initial Commencement
To be appointed
To be appointed: see s 148(6).

Appointment
Appointment (in relation to Wales): 7 February 2004: see SI 2004/252, art 2(b); appointment (in relation to England): 7 December 2004: see SI 2004/3203, art 2(1)(j).

Extent
This section does not extend to Scotland: see s 149(2).

Amendment
Sub-s (5): words ', marriage or civil partnership' in square brackets substituted by the Civil Partnership Act 2004, s 79(1), (6); date in force: 30 December 2005: see SI 2005/3175, art 2(9).

Subordinate Legislation
Disclosure of Adoption Information (Post-Commencement Adoptions) Regulations 2005, SI 2005/888; Access to Information (Post-Commencement Adoptions) (Wales) Regulations 2005, SI 2005/2689; Adoption and Children (Miscellaneous Amendments) Regulations 2005, SI 2005/3482.

General

[357]

See the note to s 63 above. This section suggests the content of the regulations for counselling. Note the use of the word 'may'. The section is not prescriptive.

Regulations

[358]

See note to s 61 (paras **[348]**–**[349]**).

[359]–**[360]**

65 Sections 56 to 65: interpretation

(1) In this group of sections—

'appropriate adoption agency', in relation to an adopted person or to information relating to his adoption, means—

    (a)   if the person was placed for adoption by an adoption agency, that agency or (if different) the agency which keeps the information in relation to his adoption,

    (b)   in any other case, the local authority to which notice of intention to adopt was given,

'prescribed' means prescribed by subordinate legislation,
'regulations' means regulations under section 9,
'subordinate legislation' means regulations or, in relation to information to be given by a court, rules.

(2) But—

    (a)   regulations under section 63(2) imposing any requirement on a council constituted under section 2 of the Local Government etc (Scotland) Act 1994 (c 39), or an organisation within section 144(3)(b), are to be made by the Scottish Ministers,

    (b)   regulations under section 63(2) imposing any requirement on a Health and Social Services Board established under Article 16 of the Health and Personal Social Services (Northern Ireland) Order 1972 (SI 1972/ 1265 (NI 14)), or an adoption society which is registered under Article 4 of the Adoption (Northern Ireland) Order 1987 (SI 1987/2203 (NI 22)), are to be made by the Department of Health, Social Services and Public Safety.

(3) The power of the Scottish Ministers or of the Department of Health, Social Services and Public Safety to make regulations under section 63(2) includes power to make—

    (a)   any supplementary, incidental or consequential provision,

    (b)   any transitory, transitional or saving provision,

which the person making the regulations considers necessary or expedient.

(4) Regulations prescribing any fee by virtue of section 64(6) require the approval of the Chancellor of the Exchequer.

(5) Regulations making any provision as to the manner in which any application is to be made for the disclosure of information by the Registrar General require his approval.

NOTES

Initial Commencement

To be appointed

To be appointed: see s 148(6).

Appointment

Appointment (in relation to Wales): 7 February 2004: see SI 2004/252, art 2(b); appointment (in relation to England): 7 December 2004: see SI 2004/3203, art 2(1)(j); sub-ss (2)(a), (3): appointment (in relation to Scotland): 7 December 2004: see SI 2004/3203, arts 1(5)(a), 2(1)(j); sub-ss (2)(b), (3): appointment (in relation to Northern Ireland): 7 December 2004: see SI 2004/3203, arts 1(5)(b), 2(1)(j).

Extent

Sub-ss (1), (4), (5) do not extend to Scotland: see s 149(2).

Chapter 4
Status of Adopted Children

66 Meaning of adoption in Chapter 4

(1)   In this Chapter 'adoption' means—

(a)   adoption by an adoption order or a Scottish or Northern Irish adoption order,

(b)   adoption by an order made in the Isle of Man or any of the Channel Islands,

(c)   an adoption effected under the law of a Convention country outside the British Islands, and certified in pursuance of Article 23(1) of the Convention (referred to in this Act as a 'Convention adoption'),

(d)   an overseas adoption, or

(e)   an adoption recognised by the law of England and Wales and effected under the law of any other country;

and related expressions are to be interpreted accordingly.

(2)   But references in this Chapter to adoption do not include an adoption effected before the day on which this Chapter comes into force (referred to in this Chapter as 'the appointed day').

(3)   Any reference in an enactment to an adopted person within the meaning of this Chapter includes a reference to an adopted child within the meaning of Part 4 of the Adoption Act 1976 (c 36).

NOTES

Initial Commencement

To be appointed

To be appointed: see s 148(1), (2).

Appointment

Appointment: 30 December 2005: see SI 2005/2213, art 2(d).

Extent

This section does not extend to Scotland: see s 149(2).

General

[361]

In this section, 'a convention country' refers to the 1993 Hague Convention on Protection of Children and Co-operation with respect to Intercountry Adoption. For details of the Convention and countries who are bound by it see http://hcch.e-vision.nl/index_en.php?act=conventions.text&cid=69.

An 'overseas adoption' is one covered under the Adoption (Designation of Overseas Adoption) Order 1973, mainly covering Commonwealth and UK dependent territories plus others specifically listed.

In addition to the other adoptions referred to in the previous paragraphs, the courts in this jurisdiction will recognise foreign adoptions provided they satisfy common law criteria. Any other adoption not covered by the provisions of s 66 will not be recognised and a fresh application for an adoption will need to be made within this jurisdiction

[362]

67 Status conferred by adoption

(1) An adopted person is to be treated in law as if born as the child of the adopters or adopter.

(2) An adopted person is the legitimate child of the adopters or adopter and, if adopted by—

(a) a couple, or
(b) one of a couple under section 51(2),

is to be treated as the child of the relationship of the couple in question.

(3) An adopted person—

(a) if adopted by one of a couple under section 51(2), is to be treated in law as not being the child of any person other than the adopter and the other one of the couple, and
(b) in any other case, is to be treated in law, subject to subsection (4), as not being the child of any person other than the adopters or adopter;

but this subsection does not affect any reference in this Act to a person's natural parent or to any other natural relationship.

(4) In the case of a person adopted by one of the person's natural parents as sole adoptive parent, subsection (3)(b) has no effect as respects entitlement to property depending on relationship to that parent, or as respects anything else depending on that relationship.

(5) This section has effect from the date of the adoption.

(6) Subject to the provisions of this Chapter and Schedule 4, this section—

(a) applies for the interpretation of enactments or instruments passed or made before as well as after the adoption, and so applies subject to any contrary indication, and
(b) has effect as respects things done, or events occurring, on or after the adoption.

NOTES
Initial Commencement
To be appointed
To be appointed: see s 148(1), (2).

Appointment
Appointment: 30 December 2005: see SI 2005/2213, art 2(d).

Extent
This section does not extend to Scotland: see s 149(2).

General

[363]

On adoption the child becomes the legitimate child of the adopters and they assume full parental responsibility. Another other person who had parental responsibility, including a natural parent, loses it (see s 46), unless the adoption is by the partner of a natural parent (see s 51(2)) in which case that natural parent retains parental responsibility (s 67(3)(a)). Note that s 88 modifies the effect of this section in relation to Hague Convention adoptions, disapplying or qualifying the effect of s 67(3).

PART B – Statutes

Section 67(3)(b)

[364]

If a natural parent is not one of the couple envisaged by s 67(3)(a) and is not an adoptive parent, then the adoption extinguishes their parental responsibility and the adopted child has no dependent claim on that parent (s 67(4)).

Section 67(6)

[365]

Note that this section has retrospective effect.

[366]

68 Adoptive relatives

(1) A relationship existing by virtue of section 67 may be referred to as an adoptive relationship, and—

(a) an adopter may be referred to as an adoptive parent or (as the case may be) as an adoptive father or adoptive mother,

(b) any other relative of any degree under an adoptive relationship may be referred to as an adoptive relative of that degree.

(2) Subsection (1) does not affect the interpretation of any reference, not qualified by the word 'adoptive', to a relationship.

(3) A reference (however expressed) to the adoptive mother and father of a child adopted by—

(a) a couple of the same sex, or

(b) a partner of the child's parent, where the couple are of the same sex,

is to be read as a reference to the child's adoptive parents.

NOTES

Initial Commencement

To be appointed
To be appointed: see s 148(1), (2).

Appointment
Appointment: 30 December 2005: see SI 2005/2213, art 2(d).

Extent
This section does not extend to Scotland: see s 149(2).

69 Rules of interpretation for instruments concerning property

(1) The rules of interpretation contained in this section apply (subject to any contrary indication and to Schedule 4) to any instrument so far as it contains a disposition of property.

(2) In applying section 67(1) and (2) to a disposition which depends on the date of birth of a child or children of the adoptive parent or parents, the disposition is to be interpreted as if—

(a) the adopted person had been born on the date of adoption,

(b) two or more people adopted on the same date had been born on that date in the order of their actual births;

but this does not affect any reference to a person's age.

(3) Examples of phrases in wills on which subsection (2) can operate are—

1 Children of A 'living at my death or born afterwards'.

2 Children of A 'living at my death or born afterwards before any one of such children for the time being in existence attains a vested interest and who attain the age of 21 years'.

3 As in example 1 or 2, but referring to grandchildren of A instead of children of A.

4 A for life 'until he has a child', and then to his child or children.

> *Note* Subsection (2) will not affect the reference to the age of 21 years in example 2.

(4)   Section 67(3) does not prejudice—

(a)   any qualifying interest, or
(b)   any interest expectant (whether immediately or not) upon a qualifying interest. 'Qualifying interest' means an interest vested in possession in the adopted person before the adoption.

(5)   Where it is necessary to determine for the purposes of a disposition of property effected by an instrument whether a woman can have a child—

(a)   it must be presumed that once a woman has attained the age of 55 years she will not adopt a person after execution of the instrument, and
(b)   if she does so, then (in spite of section 67) that person is not to be treated as her child or (if she does so as one of a couple) as the child of the other one of the couple for the purposes of the instrument.

(6)   In this section, 'instrument' includes a private Act settling property, but not any other enactment.

NOTES

Initial Commencement
To be appointed
To be appointed: see s 148(1), (2).

Appointment
Appointment: 30 December 2005: see SI 2005/2213, art 2(d).

Extent
This section does not extend to Scotland: see s 149(2).

General

[367]

Paragraphs 69–76 cover the effect of an adoption on various legal transactions where a child may have a benefit or, at least, an effect on any disposition. Section 69 covers the effect of adoption on deeds relating to property. Wills and trusts may refer to dispositions and rights that involve children of the grantor. By this section adopted children are now brought within the definition of children for the purposes of succeeding to the benefit of property dispositions or affect those dispositions, where appropriate

[368]

70   Dispositions depending on date of birth

(1)   Where a disposition depends on the date of birth of a person who was born illegitimate and who is adopted by one of the natural parents as sole adoptive parent, section 69(2) does not affect entitlement by virtue of Part 3 of the Family Law Reform Act 1987 (c 42) (dispositions of property).
(2)   Subsection (1) applies for example where—

(a)   a testator dies in 2001 bequeathing a legacy to his eldest grandchild living at a specified time,
(b)   his unmarried daughter has a child in 2002 who is the first grandchild,
(c)   his married son has a child in 2003,
(d)   subsequently his unmarried daughter adopts her child as sole adoptive parent.

In that example the status of the daughter's child as the eldest grandchild of the testator is not affected by the events described in paragraphs (c) and (d).

NOTES
Initial Commencement
To be appointed
To be appointed: see s 148(1), (2).

Appointment
Appointment: 30 December 2005: see SI 2005/2213, art 2(d).

Extent
This section does not extend to Scotland: see s 149(2).

71 Property devolving with peerages etc

(1) An adoption does not affect the descent of any peerage or dignity or title of honour.

(2) An adoption does not affect the devolution of any property limited (expressly or not) to devolve (as nearly as the law permits) along with any peerage or dignity or title of honour.

(3) Subsection (2) applies only if and so far as a contrary intention is not expressed in the instrument, and has effect subject to the terms of the instrument.

NOTES
Initial Commencement
To be appointed
To be appointed: see s 148(1), (2).

Appointment
Appointment: 30 December 2005: see SI 2005/2213, art 2(d).

Extent
This section does not extend to Scotland: see s 149(2).

72 Protection of trustees and personal representatives

(1) A trustee or personal representative is not under a duty, by virtue of the law relating to trusts or the administration of estates, to enquire, before conveying or distributing any property, whether any adoption has been effected or revoked if that fact could affect entitlement to the property.

(2) A trustee or personal representative is not liable to any person by reason of a conveyance or distribution of the property made without regard to any such fact if he has not received notice of the fact before the conveyance or distribution.

(3) This section does not prejudice the right of a person to follow the property, or any property representing it, into the hands of another person, other than a purchaser, who has received it.

NOTES
Initial Commencement
To be appointed
To be appointed: see s 148(1), (2).

Appointment
Appointment: 30 December 2005: see SI 2005/2213, art 2(d).

Extent
This section does not extend to Scotland: see s 149(2).

73 Meaning of disposition

(1) This section applies for the purposes of this Chapter.

(2) A disposition includes the conferring of a power of appointment and any other disposition of an interest in or right over property; and in this subsection a power of appointment includes any discretionary power to transfer a beneficial interest in property without the furnishing of valuable consideration.

(3) This Chapter applies to an oral disposition as if contained in an instrument made when the disposition was made.

(4) The date of death of a testator is the date at which a will or codicil is to be regarded as made.

(5) The provisions of the law of intestate succession applicable to the estate of a deceased person are to be treated as if contained in an instrument executed by him (while of full capacity) immediately before his death.

NOTES

Initial Commencement

To be appointed
To be appointed: see s 148(1), (2).

Appointment
Appointment: 30 December 2005: see SI 2005/2213, art 2(d).

Extent
This section does not extend to Scotland: see s 149(2).

74 Miscellaneous enactments

(1) Section 67 does not apply for the purposes of—

[(a) section 1 of and Schedule 1 to the Marriage Act 1949 or Schedule 1 to the Civil Partnership Act 2004 (prohibited degrees of kindred and affinity),] [or

(b) sections 64 and 65 of the Sexual Offences Act 2003 (sex with an adult relative)].

(2) Section 67 does not apply for the purposes of any provision of—

(a) the British Nationality Act 1981 (c 61),

(b) the Immigration Act 1971 (c 77),

(c) any instrument having effect under an enactment within paragraph (a) or (b), or

(d) any other provision of the law for the time being in force which determines British citizenship, British overseas territories citizenship, the status of a British National (Overseas) or British Overseas citizenship.

NOTES

Initial Commencement

To be appointed
To be appointed: see s 148(1), (2).

Appointment
Appointment: 30 December 2005: see SI 2005/2213, art 2(d).

Extent
This section does not extend to Scotland: see s 149(2).

Amendment
Sub-s (1): para (a) substituted by the Civil Partnership Act 2004, s 79(1), (7); date in force: 30 December 2005: see SI 2005/3175, art 2(9); sub-s (1): para (b) and word 'or' immediately preceding it substituted, for paras (b), (c) as originally enacted, by the Sexual Offences Act 2003, s 139, Sch 6, para 47; date in force: 1 May 2004: see SI 2004/874, art 2.

75 Pensions

Section 67(3) does not affect entitlement to a pension which is payable to or for the benefit of a person and is in payment at the time of the person's adoption.

NOTES

Initial Commencement

To be appointed
To be appointed: see s 148(1), (2).

Appointment
Appointment: 30 December 2005: see SI 2005/2213, art 2(d).

Extent
This section does not extend to Scotland: see s 149(2).

76 Insurance

(1) Where a child is adopted whose natural parent has effected an insurance with a friendly society or a collecting society or an industrial insurance company for the payment on the death of the child of money for funeral expenses, then—

PART B – Statutes

(a) the rights and liabilities under the policy are by virtue of the adoption transferred to the adoptive parents, and

(b) for the purposes of the enactments relating to such societies and companies, the adoptive parents are to be treated as the person who took out the policy.

(2) Where the adoption is effected by an order made by virtue of section 51(2), the references in subsection (1) to the adoptive parents are to be read as references to the adopter and the other one of the couple.

NOTES

Initial Commencement

To be appointed
To be appointed: see s 148(1), (2).

Appointment
Appointment: 30 December 2005: see SI 2005/2213, art 2(d).

Extent
This section does not extend to Scotland: see s 149(2).

Chapter 5
The Registers

General

[369]

The Registrar General maintains the Adopted Children Register (see s 77), an Index to that Register (see s 78), information linking adoption records to birth records (see s 79) and, in two parts, the Adoption Contact Register (see ss 80 and 81).

[370]

Adopted Children Register etc

77 Adopted Children Register

(1) The Registrar General must continue to maintain in the General Register Office a register, to be called the Adopted Children Register.

(2) The Adopted Children Register is not to be open to public inspection or search.

(3) No entries may be made in the Adopted Children Register other than entries—

(a) directed to be made in it by adoption orders, or
(b) required to be made under Schedule 1.

(4) A certified copy of an entry in the Adopted Children Register, if purporting to be sealed or stamped with the seal of the General Register Office, is to be received as evidence of the adoption to which it relates without further or other proof.

(5) Where an entry in the Adopted Children Register contains a record—

(a) of the date of birth of the adopted person, or
(b) of the country, or the district and sub-district, of the birth of the adopted person,

a certified copy of the entry is also to be received, without further or other proof, as evidence of that date, or country or district and sub-district, (as the case may be) in all respects as if the copy were a certified copy of an entry in the registers of live-births.

(6) Schedule 1 (registration of adoptions and the amendment of adoption orders) is to have effect.

> **NOTES**
>
> **Initial Commencement**
> *To be appointed*
> To be appointed: see s 148(1), (2).
>
> **Appointment**
> Sub-ss (1), (2), (4)–(6): appointment: 30 December 2005: see SI 2005/2213, art 2(e); sub-s (3): appointment (for the purpose of making regulations): 7 December 2004: see SI 2004/3203, art 2(1)(m)(vi); sub-s (3): appointment (for remaining purposes): 30 December 2005: see SI 2005/2213, art 2(e).
>
> **Extent**
> This section does not extend to Scotland: see s 149(2).

General

[371]

This section governs the maintenance of the Adopted Children Register.

Section 77(1) and (2)

Adopted Children Register

[372]

The Registrar General must maintain the Adopted Children Register in the General Register Office, which is not open to the public for search or inspection. An index must be maintained, that is accessible in defined circumstances (see s 78). Anyone may search the index, and anyone may have a certified copy of an entry in the Register for an adopted person aged 18 or over. In defined circumstances, certified copies of entries for adopted persons under the age of 18 may be obtained (see s 78).

Section 77(3) and (6)

Entries

[373]

The only entries that shall be made in the Register are those directed under the terms of an adoption order or those that are required by Sch 1 to the Act.

All adoption orders must contain a direction for the entry of the details prescribed by regulations. Unless the child was previously adopted in England or Wales, then provided that the child's identity is satisfactorily matched to an entry in the register of live births or other records, the adoption order must also direct that those records should record that the child is adopted (Sch 1, para 1(2)). If the child was previously adopted in England or Wales, it is the Adopted Children Register that is amended, by recording the child as 're-adopted' (Sch 1, para 1(3)). Directions are communicated to the Registrar General in a format prescribed by regulations, and bind him to make the relevant entries (Sch 1, para 1(4)).

The form of entry for an English court, or for a registrable foreign adoption if the child lives in England, is contained in the Adopted Children and Adoption Contact Registers Regulations 2005 (SI 2005/924), Sch 1, and in Sch 2 in respect of a Welsh court or registrable foreign adoption where the child lives in Wales (reg 2).

The connections between the entries in the Adopted Children Register and the registers of live births and other records must be traceable (see s 79).

Entries must be cancelled if an adoption order is quashed or an appeal against an adoption order is allowed (Sch 1, para 4(6)).

Directions made in error may be revoked on application, and the amendment must then be communicated by the court to the Registrar General, who must make the necessary amendments (Sch 1, para 4(3), (4) and (5)).

The Adopted Children and Adoption Contact Registers Regulations 2005, Sch 1, para 2, makes provision for the notification to the Registrar General of adoptions in Scotland, Northern Ireland, the Isle of Man or the Channel Islands, and if that information matches the live birth records and there is no existing entry in the Adopted Children Register, the child must be recorded as being adopted. The child must be recorded in the Adopted Children Register as re-adopted, if there is an existing entry. Records must be amended if the adoption order is quashed, revoked or overturned on appeal.

The Adopted Children and Adoption Contact Registers Regulations 2005, Sch 1, para 3, makes provision for the Registrar General, upon application, to record in the Adopted Children Register the details of a child who is subject to a 'registrable foreign adoption', and to secure an entry in the register of live births, provided that he is satisfied that he has sufficient information to do so. Where appropriate, he must also cause an entry to be made in the overseas register of births.

Those who may apply in respect of such a foreign adoption are the adoptive parent (an application may be made by one of a couple) any other person with parental responsibility for the child, or the adopted person if aged 18 or over (Adopted Children and Adoption Contact Registers Regulations 2005, reg 4). The application must be in writing and contain evidence of the adoption together with prescribed information about the child, adoptive parent and birth parents (Adopted Children and Adoption Contact Registers Regulations 2005, reg 5).

A person with 'parental responsibility' for this purpose means as defined in CA 1989, s 3 (Adopted Children and Adoption Contact Register Regulations 2005, reg 4(b)).

A 'registrable foreign adoption' means either a Convention adoption, or an 'overseas adoption', that satisfies the requirements of those regulations (Sch 1, para 3(5)). The requirement is that, at the time the adoption is effected, the adoptive parent is habitually resident in England and Wales (both, if a couple) (Adopted Children and Adoption Contact Registers Regulations 2005, reg 3).

Provision is made for amendments to records concerning foreign adoptions, if the adoption for some reason ceases to have effect, or to correct errors (Sch 1, para 4(9)).

Entries on the register of live births must be re-entered, if a birth is re-registered due the legitimation process (Sch 1, para 5). If an adoption order is revoked under the provisions of s 55(1) (power of court to revoke an adoption order if a child becomes legitimated upon the marriage of the sole adoptive parent), the court must communicate this to the Registrar General, and he must cancel, or secure the cancellation of, the records accordingly (Sch 1, para 6).

Errors in the Register can be corrected upon the application of the adopter or adopted person (Sch 1, para 4(1)).

If the adopted person is given, or takes, a new name within one year of the adoption, either in addition to or instead of existing names, an application may be made to the court for it to exercise its discretion to amend the adoption order accordingly (Sch 1, para 4(2)).

The court must communicate any amended details to the Registrar General, who must then amend the records (Sch 1, para 4(4) and (5)).

Section 77(4) and (5)

[374]

These subsections make provision for certified copies to be accepted as proof of entries in the Register.

'Records' includes certified copies of entries in any registers of birth that are kept by the Registrar General (s 82(1)).

'Register of live births': means the register made under the Births and Deaths Registration Act 1953 (s 82(1)).

[375]

PART B – Statutes

78 Searches and copies

(1)   The Registrar General must continue to maintain at the General Register Office an index of the Adopted Children Register.
(2)   Any person may—

(a)   search the index,
(b)   have a certified copy of any entry in the Adopted Children Register.

(3)   But a person is not entitled to have a certified copy of an entry in the Adopted Children Register relating to an adopted person who has not attained the age of 18 years unless the applicant has provided the Registrar General with the prescribed particulars.

'Prescribed' means prescribed by regulations made by the Registrar General with the approval of the Chancellor of the Exchequer.

(4)   The terms, conditions and regulations as to payment of fees, and otherwise, applicable under the Births and Deaths Registration Act 1953 (c 20), and the Registration Service Act 1953 (c 37), in respect of—

(a)   searches in the index kept in the General Register Office of certified copies of entries in the registers of live-births,
(b)   the supply from that office of certified copies of entries in those certified copies,

also apply in respect of searches, and supplies of certified copies, under subsection (2).

NOTES
Initial Commencement
To be appointed
To be appointed: see s 148(1), (2).

Appointment
Sub-ss (1), (2), (4): appointment: 30 December 2005: see SI 2005/2213, art 2(e); sub-s (3): appointment (for the purpose of making regulations): 7 December 2004: see SI 2004/3203, art 2(1)(m)(vi); sub-s (3): appointment (for remaining purposes): 30 December 2005: see SI 2005/2213, art 2(e).

Extent
This section does not extend to Scotland: see s 149(2).

Subordinate Legislation
Adopted Children and Adoption Contact Registers Regulations 2005, SI 2005/924 (made under sub-s (3)).

General

[376]

This section provides for the maintenance of an index to the Adopted Children Register (see s 77, para [370]), searches of the index and certified copies of entries in the Register.

Section 78(1), (2) and (3)

[377]

The Registrar General must maintain an index to the Adopted Children Register (see s 77 regarding the Register), which any person may search. Anyone may have a certified copy of an entry in the Register for a person aged 18 or over.

Subject to the provision of particulars prescribed by regulations, a person is entitled to have a certified copy of an entry in the Register for a child. The prescribed particulars are the full name and date of birth of the adopted person and the full name of the adoptive parent(s) (Adopted Children and Adoption Contact Registers Regulations 2005, reg 10).

Section 78(4)

[378]

This provides for regulations governing other searches of Registers, such as for births and deaths, to govern searches and certified copies, including the payment of fees.

[379]

79 Connections between the register and birth records

(1) The Registrar General must make traceable the connection between any entry in the registers of live-births or other records which has been marked 'Adopted' and any corresponding entry in the Adopted Children Register.

(2) Information kept by the Registrar General for the purposes of subsection (1) is not to be open to public inspection or search.

(3) Any such information, and any other information which would enable an adopted person to obtain a certified copy of the record of his birth, may only be disclosed by the Registrar General in accordance with this section.

(4) In relation to a person adopted before the appointed day the court may, in exceptional circumstances, order the Registrar General to give any information mentioned in subsection (3) to a person.

(5) On an application made in the prescribed manner by the appropriate adoption agency in respect of an adopted person a record of whose birth is kept by the Registrar General, the Registrar General must give the agency any information relating to the adopted person which is mentioned in subsection (3).

'Appropriate adoption agency' has the same meaning as in section 65.

(6) In relation to a person adopted before the appointed day, Schedule 2 applies instead of subsection (5).

(7) On an application made in the prescribed manner by an adopted person a record of whose birth is kept by the Registrar General and who—

(a) is under the age of 18 years, and
(b) intends to be married [or form a civil partnership],

the Registrar General must inform the applicant whether or not it appears from information contained in the registers of live-births or other records that the applicant and [the intended spouse or civil partner] may be within the prohibited degrees of relationship for the purposes of the Marriage Act 1949 (c 76) [or for the purposes of the Civil Partnership Act 2004 (c 33)].

(8)   Before the Registrar General gives any information by virtue of this section, any prescribed fee which he has demanded must be paid.

(9)   In this section—

'appointed day' means the day appointed for the commencement of sections 56 to 65,

'prescribed' means prescribed by regulations made by the Registrar General with the approval of the Chancellor of the Exchequer.

NOTES

Initial Commencement

To be appointed
To be appointed: see s 148(1), (2).

Appointment
Sub-ss (1)–(4), (6): appointment: 30 December 2005: see SI 2005/2213, art 2(e); sub-ss (5), (7)–(9): appointment (for the purpose of making regulations): 7 December 2004: see SI 2004/3203, art 2(1)(m)(vi); sub-ss (5), (7)–(9): appointment (for remaining purposes): 30 December 2005: see SI 2005/2213, art 2(e).

Extent
This section does not extend to Scotland: see s 149(2).

Amendment
Sub-s (7): in para (b) words 'or form a civil partnership' in square brackets inserted by the Civil Partnership Act 2004, s 79(1), (8)(a); date in force: 30 December 2005: see SI 2005/3175, art 2(9); sub-s (7): words 'the intended spouse or civil partner' in square brackets substituted by the Civil Partnership Act 2004, s 79(1), (8)(b); date in force: 30 December 2005: see SI 2005/3175, art 2(9); sub-s (7): words 'or for the purposes of the Civil Partnership Act 2004 (c 33)' in square brackets inserted by SI 2005/3542, art 4; date in force: 30 December 2005: see SI 2005/3542, art 1(2).

Subordinate Legislation
Adopted Children and Adoption Contact Registers Regulations 2005, SI 2005/924 (made under sub-ss (5), (7), (8)).

PART B – Statutes

General

[380]

This section provides the mechanism for linking records in the Adopted Children Register with other records such as those of live births.

Section 79(1) and (2)

[381]

The Registrar General must make the connection traceable between any entries in the Adopted Children Register and corresponding entries in the registers of live births and other records where a person is marked as 'adopted', although information kept for this purpose is not open to public inspection or search.

Section 79(3) and (4)

[382]

Any of this information, and any other information that would enable an adopted person to obtain a certified copy of his/her birth record, can only be disclosed in accordance with this section, although in exceptional circumstances a court can order the Registrar General to give such information regarding an adoption that took place before 30 December 2005.

Section 79(5) and (6)

[383]

Two regimes for tracing birth records are created, one for those adopted before 30 December 2005, and the other for those adopted on or after that date.

For those adopted before 30 December 2005, the procedure is set out in Sch 2, whereby an adopted person, aged 18 or over, can apply to the Registrar General, provided he/she holds a record of the birth, for information held that is necessary to enable the applicant to obtain a certified copy of his/her birth record (Sch 2, para 1). The Registrar General must then provide the information, provided the person was adopted between 12 November 1975 and 30 December 2005, and counselling services are available as set out below (Sch 2, paras 1 and 4). If the person was adopted before 12 November 1975, it is obligatory for the person first to attend an interview with a counsellor arranged by a person or body set out below, although if the person is living outside the UK the Registrar has a discretion to release the information to a body suitable and willing to provide counselling (Sch 2, para 4).

In all cases of pre-30 December 2005 adoptions, before any information under s 79 is given, the applicant must be told by the Registrar General of the availability of counselling services from adoption societies, local authorities or registered adoption support agencies. The Registrar, a local authority, or a registered adoption society must also provide counselling upon request for an adopted person living in England or Wales who seeks similar information on these links in Scotland or Northern Ireland (Sch 2, para 3). If a person chooses to receive counselling, the Registrar must also send a copy of the information to that person or body (Sch 2, para 2).

For those adopted on or after 30 December 2005, the appropriate adoption agency makes the application to the Registrar General for the s 79 information, in writing, as required by the Adopted Children and Adoption Contact Regulations 2005 (SI 2005/924), reg 11. The Registrar must then disclose to the agency the information that he holds tracing the connection between adoption and birth records as set out above and any other information that would enable the adopted person to obtain his/her birth record.

'Appropriate adoption agency': if the person was placed for adoption by an adoption agency, either that agency or the one holding his/her adoption records; in all other cases, the local authority to whom notice of intention to adopt was given under s 44 (s 44(5) and s 65(1)).

Section 79(7)

[384]

An adopted person under the age of 18 who intends to marry or form a civil partnership is entitled to be told by the Registrar General if the intended spouse or civil partner appears to be within a prohibited degree of relationship. The application must be in writing, and signed (Adopted Children and Adoption Contact Registers Regulations 2005, reg 13).

Fees are payable for applications under this section.

[385]

> ### Adoption Contact Register
>
> ### 80   Adoption Contact Register
>
> (1)   The Registrar General must continue to maintain at the General Register Office in accordance with regulations a register in two Parts to be called the Adoption Contact Register.

(2)   Part 1 of the register is to contain the prescribed information about adopted persons who have given the prescribed notice expressing their wishes as to making contact with their relatives.

(3)   The Registrar General may only make an entry in Part 1 of the register for an adopted person—

(a)   a record of whose birth is kept by the Registrar General,
(b)   who has attained the age of 18 years, and
(c)   who the Registrar General is satisfied has such information as is necessary to enable him to obtain a certified copy of the record of his birth.

(4)   Part 2 of the register is to contain the prescribed information about persons who have given the prescribed notice expressing their wishes, as relatives of adopted persons, as to making contact with those persons.

(5)   The Registrar General may only make an entry in Part 2 of the register for a person—

(a)   who has attained the age of 18 years, and
(b)   who the Registrar General is satisfied is a relative of an adopted person and has such information as is necessary to enable him to obtain a certified copy of the record of the adopted person's birth.

(6)   Regulations may provide for—

(a)   the disclosure of information contained in one Part of the register to persons for whom there is an entry in the other Part,
(b)   the payment of prescribed fees in respect of the making or alteration of entries in the register and the disclosure of information contained in the register.

NOTES

Initial Commencement
To be appointed
To be appointed: see s 148(1), (2).

Appointment
Sub-ss (1), (3), (5): appointment: 30 December 2005: see SI 2005/2213, art 2(e); sub-ss (2), (4), (6): appointment (for the purpose of making regulations): 7 December 2004: see SI 2004/3203, art 2(1)(m)(vi); sub-ss (2), (4), (6): appointment (for remaining purposes): 30 December 2005: see SI 2005/2213, art 2(e).

Extent
This section does not extend to Scotland: see s 149(2).

Subordinate Legislation
Adopted Children and Adoption Contact Registers Regulations 2005 SI 2005/924 (made under sub-ss (2), (4), (6)).

PART B – Statutes

General

[386]

This section provides for the maintenance of the Adoption Contact Register.

Section 80(1)

[387]

The Registrar General must maintain the Adoption Contact Register at the General Register Office, divided into two parts, which is not open to public inspection or search (s 81(1)).

Section 80(2) and (3)

[388]

Part 1 contains information prescribed by regulations about adopted persons who have given notice that they wish to make contact with relatives. The Registrar must have a record of that person's birth, must be satisfied that the person has the information necessary to obtain a certified copy of his/her birth record, and the adopted person must be aged 18 or over.

The prescribed information is the name, address and date of birth of the adopted person and information about relatives (with names, if known) with whom they wish to have contact or do not wish to have contact (Adopted Children and Adoption Contact Registers Regulations 2005 (SI 2005/924), reg 6 and Sch 3). The form makes it clear that the adopted person may withdraw the notice at any time.

Section 80(4) and (5)

[389]

Part 2 contains information prescribed by regulations about relatives of adopted persons who have given notice that they wish to make contact with those adopted persons. The Registrar must be satisfied that he/she is such a relative and has the information necessary to obtain a certified copy of the adopted person's birth record. The relative must also be aged 18 or over.

The notice must contain the name, address and date of birth of the relative, and contain information that he/she would like to have contact with a named adopted person, or that he/she does not wish to have such contact (Adopted Children and Adoption Contact Registers Regulations 2005, reg 7).

Section 80(6)

[390]

Regulations may make provision for the disclosure of information in one Part of the Adoption Contact Register to persons whose names are entered in the other Part. The Adopted Children and Adoption Contact Registers Regulations 2005, reg 8, places a duty on the Registrar to give an adopted person, whose name is recorded in Part 1, the name, and the address by which contact can be made, of any relative recorded in Part 2 who wishes to have contact with the adopted person.

'Records' includes certified copies of entries in any registers of birth that are kept by the Registrar General (s 82(1)).

'Relative' for an adopted person means any person who would, but for the adoption, be related to him/her by blood (including half-blood), marriage, or civil partnership (see s 81(2), as amended by the Civil Partnership Act 2004, s 79).

[391]

81　Adoption Contact Register: supplementary

(1)　The Adoption Contact Register is not to be open to public inspection or search.
(2)　In section 80, 'relative', in relation to an adopted person, means any person who (but for his adoption) would be related to him by blood (including half-blood)[, marriage or civil partnership].

(3)   The Registrar General must not give any information entered in the register to any person except in accordance with subsection (6)(a) of that section or regulations made by virtue of section 64(4)(b).

(4)   In section 80, 'regulations' means regulations made by the Registrar General with the approval of the Chancellor of the Exchequer, and 'prescribed' means prescribed by such regulations.

NOTES

Initial Commencement

To be appointed

To be appointed: see s 148(1), (2).

Appointment

Sub-ss (1)–(3): Appointment: 30 December 2005: see SI 2005/2213, art 2(e); sub-s (4): Appointment: 7 December 2004: see SI 2004/3203, art 2(1)(m)(vi).

Extent

This section does not extend to Scotland: see s 149(2).

Amendment

Sub-s (2): words ', marriage or civil partnership' in square brackets substituted by the Civil Partnership Act 2004, s 79(1), (9); date in force: 30 December 2005: see SI 2005/3175, art 2(9).

General

[392]

This section provides for confidentiality for the Adoption Contact Register, and certain definitions for the purposes of s 80.

The Adoption Contact Register is closed to public inspection and search. The Registrar may not disclose any information contained in that Register except in conformity with the provisions of s 80(6) and the Regulations, or, as set out in Regulations made under s 64(4)(b), to an appropriate adoption agency as required by the agency.

[393]

General

82   Interpretation

(1)   In this Chapter—

'records' includes certified copies kept by the Registrar General of entries in any register of births,

'registers of live-births' means the registers of live-births made under the Births and Deaths Registration Act 1953 (c 20).

(2)   Any register, record or index maintained under this Chapter may be maintained in any form the Registrar General considers appropriate; and references (however expressed) to entries in such a register, or to their amendment, marking or cancellation, are to be read accordingly.

NOTES

Initial Commencement

To be appointed

To be appointed: see s 148(1), (2).

Appointment

Appointment: 30 December 2005: see SI 2005/2213, art 2(e).

Extent

This section does not extend to Scotland: see s 149(2).

General

[394]

Registers, records and the index that are maintained by the Registrar General under Chapter 5 can be in the form of his choice.

[395]

Chapter 6
Adoptions with a Foreign Element

Bringing children into and out of the United Kingdom

General

[396]

This chapter deals with the six sections of the Adoption and Children Act 2002 that deal specifically with adoptions with a foreign element. They deal with the provisions for sending a child out of the UK for adoption, for bringing a child into the UK for adoption, and with cases falling within and outside the provisions of the Convention on Protection of Children and Co-operation in respect of Intercountry Adoption, concluded at the Hague on 29th May 1993, ('the Hague Convention'). That was given statutory force by the Adoption (Intercountry Aspects) Act 1999.

The Adoption with a Foreign Element Regulations 2005 set out comprehensive procedural guides for both Hague Convention and non-Hague Convention cases, and in relation to bringing in and sending out cases.

The Adoption with a Foreign Elements Regulations 2005 contain more than the procedural regulations within this topic, as the power to apply or dis-apply provisions applicable to domestic adoption law are found in the delegated legislation, as well as in the main statute itself.

The legislative development of this topic is covered in the introductory chapter of this work, which also covers future reform.

Within this chapter the following statutory provisions are considered:

Adoption and Children Act 2002 (ACA 2002)

Adoption (Intercountry Aspects) Act 1999 (AIAA 1999)

Adoptions with a Foreign Element Regulations 2005 (SI 2005/392) (AWAFE Regulations 2005)

Adoption Agencies Regulations 2005 (SI 2005/389) (AAR) and Adoption Agencies (Wales) Regulations 2005 (SI 2005/1313) (AAWR)

Family Procedure (Adoption) Rules 2005 (SI 2005/2795).

[397]

83   Restriction on bringing children in

(1)   This section applies where a person who is habitually resident in the British Islands (the 'British resident')—

(a)   brings, or causes another to bring, a child who is habitually resident outside the British Islands into the United Kingdom for the purpose of adoption by the British resident, or

(b)   at any time brings, or causes another to bring, into the United Kingdom a child adopted by the British resident under an external adoption effected within the period of *six* [twelve] months ending with that time.

The references to adoption, or to a child adopted, by the British resident include a reference to adoption, or to a child adopted, by the British resident and another person.

(2)   But this section does not apply if the child is intended to be adopted under a Convention adoption order.

(3)   An external adoption means an adoption, other than a Convention adoption, of a child effected under the law of any country or territory outside the British Islands, whether or not the adoption is—

(a)   an adoption within the meaning of Chapter 4, or

(b)   a full adoption (within the meaning of section 88(3)).

(4)   Regulations may require a person intending to bring, or to cause another to bring, a child into the United Kingdom in circumstances where this section applies—

(a)   to apply to an adoption agency (including a Scottish or Northern Irish adoption agency) in the prescribed manner for an assessment of his suitability to adopt the child, and

(b)   to give the agency any information it may require for the purpose of the assessment.

(5)   Regulations may require prescribed conditions to be met in respect of a child brought into the United Kingdom in circumstances where this section applies.

(6)   In relation to a child brought into the United Kingdom for adoption in circumstances where this section applies, regulations may—

(a)   provide for any provision of Chapter 3 to apply with modifications or not to apply,

(b)   if notice of intention to adopt has been given, impose functions in respect of the child on the local authority to which the notice was given.

(7)   If a person brings, or causes another to bring, a child into the United Kingdom at any time in circumstances where this section applies, he is guilty of an offence if—

(a)   he has not complied with any requirement imposed by virtue of subsection (4), or

(b)   any condition required to be met by virtue of subsection (5) is not met,

before that time, or before any later time which may be prescribed.

(8)   A person guilty of an offence under this section is liable—

(a)   on summary conviction to imprisonment for a term not exceeding six months, or a fine not exceeding the statutory maximum, or both,

(b)   on conviction on indictment, to imprisonment for a term not exceeding twelve months, or a fine, or both.

(9)   In this section, 'prescribed' means prescribed by regulations and 'regulations' means regulations made by the Secretary of State, after consultation with the Assembly.

NOTES

Initial Commencement

To be appointed

To be appointed: see s 148(1), (2).

Appointment

Sub-ss (1)–(7), (9): appointment (for the purpose of making regulations): 7 December 2004: see SI 2004/3203, art 2(1)(m)(vii); sub-ss (1)–(7), (9): appointment (for remaining purposes): 30 December 2005: see SI 2005/2213, art 2(f); sub-s (8): appointment: 30 December 2005: see SI 2005/2213, art 2(f).

Extent

This section does not extend to Scotland: see s 149(2).

PART B – Statutes

Amendment
Sub-s (1); in para (b) word 'six' in italics repealed and subsequent word in square brackets substituted by the Children and Adoption Act 2006, s 14(1); for effect see s 14(2) thereof; date in force: to be appointed: see the Children and Adoption Act 2006, s 17(2).

Subordinate Legislation
Adoptions with a Foreign Element Regulations 2005, SI 2005/392 (made under sub-ss (4)–(7)).

General

[398]

This section makes it an offence to bring a child into United Kingdom for adoption without having first complied with AWAFE Regulations 2005, which provide for the assessment and approval of prospective adopters of a child from overseas, and for a formal matching process between prospective adopters and a child via appropriate agencies both within the UK and in the overseas territory. This section applies to non-Convention adoptions and in two circumstances. First, where the child is to be adopted in England and Wales after being brought in, and second, where the child is adopted overseas and then brought in.

Section 83(1)

Person who is habitually resident

[399]

Habitual residence is not separately defined in the ACA 2002. Habitual residence in this context is therefore likely to be defined using the test set out in *Shah v Barnet London BC* [1983] 1 All ER 226, [1983] 2 AC 309, [1983] 2 WLR 16, HL, and further developed in *Mark v Mark* [2005] UKHL 42, [2005] 2 FCR 467. Habitual residence may need to be defined particularly within the context of the ACA 2002, including consideration as to whether the unlawfulness of a person's habitual residence is relevant. Bearing in mind the policy considerations relating to the protection of children, it is submitted that the unlawfulness of the status of a British resident within this section would not exempt such a person from the provisions of the section.

In the British Islands

[400]

British Islands means the UK together with the Channel Islands and the Isle of Man (Interpretation Act 1978, Sch 1).

Causes another to bring

[401]

There is no territorial restriction on the location of the a person who would be 'another' within the context of this phrase. Case law relating to provisions under the Adoption Act 1976 (eg, *Re AW* [1993] 1 FLR 62) demonstrates debate as to the extent of the reach of the provisions relating to adoption offences.

A child who is habitually resident outside the British Islands

[402]

'Child' is defined by ACA 2002, s 144. A child's habitual residence will be influenced by the dependence of the child on those with, or acting with, parental responsibility for the child. *Re KM (A Minor) (Habitual Residence)* [1996] 2 FCR 333. In the context of preventing irregularities, including the trafficking of children, it can be seen that the factual basis for decisions on a child's habitual residence becomes of prime importance.

External adoption

[403]

External adoption is a new term within international adoption. An external adoption is one where the process is completed outside the UK, in a state or territory that is not a signatory to the Hague Convention.

Six months

[404]

This provision is subject to amendment by the Children and Adoption Act 2006 (not yet in force) extending the period from 6 to 12 months.

British resident and another person

[405]

There is no requirement that the other person need be a British resident. If the child is to be brought in to the UK for the purpose of adoption, an adoption order can only be made in favour of a single person or a couple (ACA 2002, ss 50–51).

Section 83(2)

Convention adoption order

[406]

Defined in ACA 2002, s 144. This is an adoption order made in England and Wales, Convention procedures having been followed (either for a child brought in from a Convention country, or where the UK is the state of origin). The procedures within the AWAFE Regulations 2005 (or their predecessors) will need to have been followed. The procedure for making a Convention adoption order is the same as for a domestic adoption (see paras **[279]**–**[294]** and the FP(A) Rules 2005).

Section 83(3)

Whether or not

[407]

This provision enables simple adoptions to be dealt with, ie those where there is not a complete severance of the legal ties to birth parents.

Convention adoption

[408]

This is defined in ACA 2002, s 66(1)(c). A Convention adoption is one where the procedures for assessment and approval by a local authority within the AWAFE Regulations 2005 have been followed in relation to a child in a Convention country, but the adoption itself takes place outside the British Islands within the home state of the child concerned.

Adoption within the meaning of Chapter 4

[409]

ACA 2002, s 66, and subsequent sections deal with a range of adoptions that give the child adopted status, ie, the status of being the legal children of the adopters and no other person or persons (see paras [360]–[369]).

Section 83(4)

Regulations governing assessment and provision of information

[410]

AWAFE 2005, reg 3, require that the British resident who intends to bring a child in to the United Kingdom must apply in writing to an adoption agency for assessment and provide all information that the adoption agency requires for the purpose of the assessment.

Section 83(5)

Regulations prescribing conditions to be met on bringing a child in

[411]

There are 3 conditions are set out in the AWAFE 2005, reg 4. The prospective adopters must (1) comply with certain requirements prior to visiting an identified child within its state of origin, including being in possession of a certificate of eligibility dealing with approval to be adopters and immigration considerations (2) to accompany the child into the UK (or one of the members of the couple must accompany the child) and (3) comply with certain requirements after bringing the child in.

Section 83(6)

Regulations as to the applicability of Chapter 3

[412]

Regulations 6–9 of the AWAFE Regs 2005 deal with ACA 2002, Ch 3 (Placement for Adoption and Adoption Orders: see para [181] ff). The effect of reg 7 is to forbid the removal of a child who has been brought in under s 83(1)(a) from the UK, or allowing a name change, without consent of each parent or guardian or without the leave of the court. The effect of reg 8 is to compel a local authority to receive a child whose prospective adopters give notice that they do not wish to go ahead with the adoption. Regulation 9 has the effect of setting the length of time that a child has lived with prospective adopters before an application for an adoption order is made at 6 months (in cases where regs 3 and 4 of the AWAFE Regs have been complied with). In cases where regs 3 and 4 of the AWAFE Regs 2005 have not been complied, the residence requirement is 12 months (see para [1003] ff).

Regulations as to the functions of local authorities

[413]

The duties and responsibilities of an adoption agency in relation to assessment, record keeping and panel approval are the same as for domestic adoption approval and contained within Pts 4 and 5 [respectively] AAR/AAWR, regs 21–34/21–35 (see paras [844]–[871]). Of particular relevance are regs 30 and 34 (in England) and regs 31 and 35 (in Wales) dealing with s 83 cases. AWAFE Regs 2005, reg 5, provides for specific functions in relation to children brought in to the UK (see para [1003]).

Section 83(7) and (8)

Offence of bringing in

[414]

There is no specific statutory defence to an offence under this section. For fines on summary conviction see Criminal Justice Act 1991, ss 17 and 18. The fine on conviction on indictment is unlimited.

[415]

84 Giving parental responsibility prior to adoption abroad

(1) The High Court may, on an application by persons who the court is satisfied intend to adopt a child under the law of a country or territory outside the British Islands, make an order giving parental responsibility for the child to them.

(2) An order under this section may not give parental responsibility to persons who the court is satisfied meet those requirements as to domicile, or habitual residence, in England and Wales which have to be met if an adoption order is to be made in favour of those persons.

(3) An order under this section may not be made unless any requirements prescribed by regulations are satisfied.

(4) An application for an order under this section may not be made unless at all times during the preceding ten weeks the child's home was with the applicant or, in the case of an application by two people, both of them.

(5) Section 46(2) to (4) has effect in relation to an order under this section as it has effect in relation to adoption orders.

(6) Regulations may provide for any provision of this Act which refers to adoption orders to apply, with or without modifications, to orders under this section.

(7) In this section, 'regulations' means regulations made by the Secretary of State, after consultation with the Assembly.

NOTES

Initial Commencement

To be appointed

To be appointed: see s 148(1), (2).

Appointment

Appointment (for the purpose of making regulations): 7 December 2004: see SI 2004/3203, art 2(1)(m)(vii); appointment (for remaining purposes): 30 December 2005: see SI 2005/2213, art 2(f).

Extent

This section does not extend to Scotland: see s 149(2).

Subordinate Legislation

Adoptions with a Foreign Element Regulations 2005, SI 2005/392 (made under sub-ss (3), (6)).

PART B – Statutes

General

[416]

This section is linked to s 85 and deals with the removal of children for adoption outside the British Islands. It is thought that it will be rare for children to be sent outside the British Islands for adoption unless there is a family or friends connection, or particular cultural considerations apply. In this respect it is important to note that there are not yet any specific regulations in force under s 86 that make family adoptions subject to any less stringent conditions than stranger adoptions, other than the provisions of s 92 (where an offence of making arrangements to adopt a child does not apply to birth-family arrangements). AWAFE Regulations, 2005, reg 11 deals with s 84(6). Although the regulations are reproduced in full within this work, the annotation below refers in detail to each provision in an attempt to aid the task of cross-referencing between areas of the legislation.

Section 84(1)

Intention to adopt a child under the law of a country or territory outside the British Islands

[417]

This section applies to both Convention and non-Convention cases. British Islands are the UK and the Isle of Man and the Channel Islands (Sch 1, Interpretation Act 1978)

Section 84(2)

Excluded applicants for parental responsibility

[418]

Those who are domiciled in or habitually resident in England and Wales will be subject to domestic adoption procedures.

Section 84(3)

Regulations

[419]

The FP(A) Regs 2005, reg 23 deal with prescribed applicants and respondents in relation to an application for parental responsibility. The AWAFE Regulations 2005, reg 10 deals with compliance with assessments and reports in both the UK and the country of the intended adoption.

Section 84(4)

Child's home with the applicant(s) for 10 weeks

[420]

This provision mirrors the time limit provisions for many adoptions in the domestic context under ACA 2002, s 42. In international cases however, the 10-week provision may provide practical obstacles to a placement going ahead. Given that there is a prohibition on removing a child without s 84 parental responsibility being granted, it is not hard to conceive of cases where practical, immigration or financial difficulties may arise that would make compliance with the 10 weeks' residence requirement impracticable or even impossible, where that residence provision has to be complied with within the UK. For family placements, unless adoption is the only route that will meet a child's needs, a child could be moved outside the UK under the provisions of CA 1989, Sch 2, para 19 as a fostered child subject to CA 1989, Pt IV orders. This could lead, for example to an application being made for a special guardianship order. There may also be scope for an adoption application to be made in the overseas state at a future date, providing that no intention to adopt existed at the date of removal of the child (unless of course s 84 has been complied with). For an example of judicial pragmatism in a case under previous provisions, see *A London Borough Council v M and another* [2006] EWHC 1907 (Fam), where the timing of adoption approval was managed in order to find a legitimate way to achieving an adoption outside the UK. This route however will not be available where there is an expressed intention to adopt, due to the necessity of having a parental responsibility order under s 84. There is no easy route through the requirements of this section: effort and care will need to be taken to avoid falling foul of the 10-week residence provision. In particular, where a Convention country is involved, the intention to adopt is present from the very start.

Section 84(5)

Applicability of s 46(2)–(4)

[421]

These provisions make the parental responsibility granted under this section an extremely powerful form of parental responsibility: it can be said to be an adoption in all but name. A s 84 parental responsibility order operates to extinguish all previously existing parental responsibility.

Section 84(6)

Applicability of other sections of the Act to s 84 orders

[422]

AWAFE 2005, reg 11 makes 19 sections of the ACA 2002 apply to s 84 parental responsibility orders. These are:

(1)   Regulation 11(1)(a) applies ACA 2002, s 1 relating to welfare and the adoption checklist, applicable wherever a court or an adoption agency is making a decision relating to a s 84 parental responsibility order (see paras [101]–[116]).

(2)   Regulation 11(1)(b) applies ACA 2002, s 18(4) to s 84 applications. This provision has the effect of preventing a child, who has been placed with those who have applied for a s 84 parental responsibility order, from being moved to other prospective adopters before the s 84 application has been dealt with (and see para [184]).

(3)   Regulation 11(1)(c) applies ACA 2002, 21(4)(b) with the effect that the making of a s 84 parental responsibility extinguishes a placement order made in relation to the child.

(4)   Regulation 11(1)(d) applies ACA 2002, s 22(5)(a) and (b) (which deal with local authority duties to apply for a placement order (see para [206] ff)) to s 84 cases. This has the effect that those parts of that section that deal with the duty on a local authority to apply for placement orders do not apply when notice of intention to apply for a s 84 order has been given, or that an application for a s 84 order has been made. This provision needs to be read alongside s 44(2) as it applies to s 84 orders (see para [286]).

(5)   Regulation 11(1)(e) applies ACA 2002, s 24(4) (dealing with the revocation of placement orders). The effect is that where a court, following an application for a s 84 parental responsibility order, does not make a s 84 order, it may revoke a placement order that was in place in respect of the child subject of the s 84 application (and see para [224]).

(6)   Regulation 11(1)(f) applies ACA 2002, s 28(1). Where a child is placed or a local authority is authorised to place a child, a parent or guardian may not apply for, respectively, residence and special guardianship orders unless the court's leave has been given and an application for a s 84 order has been made (and see para [239]).

(7)   Regulation 11(1)(g) deals with the application of ACA 2002, s 29(4)(a) and 29(5)(a). Where a child is subject to a placement order, and a parent has the leave of the court, and a s 84 parental responsibility application has been made, the parent may apply for a residence order. There is equivalent provision for special guardians.

(8)   Regulation 11(1)(h) applies ACA 2002, s 32(5) to cases where a child is placed with parental consent and parental consent is withdrawn. Usually withdrawal of consent to placement will compel a local authority to return the child, but where prospective adopters have applied for s 84 parental responsibility, and before the application is determined, the prospective adopters are not required to return the child unless ordered to do so by the court (and see paras [254]–[255]).

PART B – Statutes

(9) Regulation 11(1)(i) deals with the application of ACA 2002, s 42(7). This requires the court to be satisfied that there has been sufficient opportunity to see the child with the proposed adopter(s) in the home environment. This provision does not appear to limit the observation opportunities to the actual home, and so would include a home that the applicants had established within the UK for the purpose of fulfilling the 10-week residence requirement made by s 84 (and see para [283]).

(10) Regulation 11(1)(j) applies the provisions of ACA 2002, s 43, requiring agency reports to the court to be provided dealing with s 1 (and any other relevant matters) in cases where that agency has placed the child and an application for s 84 parental responsibility has been made (and see para [285]).

(11) Regulation 11(1)(k) applies ACA 2002, s 44(2) in relation cases where a child is not placed by an agency. Prospective adopters must give notice of their intention to seek s 84 parental responsibility. Upon receipt of such notice, the case is dealt with, in terms of investigation, report writing and liaison with other local authorities as if the notice of intention is to apply for an adoption order (and see para [288]).

(12) Regulation 11(1)(l) applies ACA 2002, s 47(1), the provisions that require either parental/guardian's consent or dispensation with that with consent, and that no s 84 parental responsibility order may be made where the subject person is or has been married or who has reached 19 years of age (see para [301] ff).

(13) Regulation 11(1)(m) applies ACA 2002, s 48(1) which limits repeat applications for s 84 parental responsibility (see para [307]).

(14) Regulation 11(1)(n) applies ACA 2002, s 50(1) and (2), permitting the making of a s 84 parental responsibility order to a couple on the same criteria as apply in domestic adoptions (see para [310]).

(15) Regulation 11(1)(o) applies ACA 2002, s 51(1)–(4), setting out the criteria needed prior to the making of a s 84 parental responsibility order by a single person (see para [312]).

(16) Regulation 11(1)(p) applies ACA 2002, s 52(1)–(4), being the conditions that must be met before parental or guardian's consent is dispensed with prior to the making of a s 84 parental responsibility order (see para [316]).

(17) Regulation 11 (1)(q) applies ACA 2002, s 53(5), being the circumstances in which a contribution to maintenance for a child is payable after a notice of intention to adopt has been given.

(18) Regulation 11(1)(r) applies ACA 2002, s 141(3) and (4)(c), leading to the application of the rules of procedure to s 84 cases as they apply to applications for an adoption order.

(19) Regulation 11(2) applies ACA 2002, s 35(5). The result is that after an application for s 84 parental responsibility has been made, prospective adopters are not required to return a child unless ordered to do so by the court (see para [261]).

[423]

85 Restriction on taking children out

(1) A child who—

(a) is a Commonwealth citizen, or
(b) is habitually resident in the United Kingdom,

must not be removed from the United Kingdom to a place outside the British Islands for the purpose of adoption unless the condition in subsection (2) is met.

(2) The condition is that—

(a) the prospective adopters have parental responsibility for the child by virtue of an order under section 84, or

(b) the child is removed under the authority of an order under section 49 of the Adoption (Scotland) Act 1978 (c 28) or Article 57 of the Adoption (Northern Ireland) Order 1987 (SI 1987/2203 (NI 22)).

(3) Removing a child from the United Kingdom includes arranging to do so; and the circumstances in which a person arranges to remove a child from the United Kingdom include those where he—

(a) enters into an arrangement for the purpose of facilitating such a removal of the child,

(b) initiates or takes part in any negotiations of which the purpose is the conclusion of an arrangement within paragraph (a), or

An arrangement includes an agreement (whether or not enforceable).

(4) A person who removes a child from the United Kingdom in contravention of subsection (1) is guilty of an offence.

(5) A person is not guilty of an offence under subsection (4) of causing a person to take any step mentioned in paragraph (a) or (b) of subsection (3) unless it is proved that he knew or had reason to suspect that the step taken would contravene subsection (1).

But this subsection only applies if sufficient evidence is adduced to raise an issue as to whether the person had the knowledge or reason mentioned.

(6) A person guilty of an offence under this section is liable—

(a) on summary conviction to imprisonment for a term not exceeding six months, or a fine not exceeding the statutory maximum, or both,

(b) on conviction on indictment, to imprisonment for a term not exceeding twelve months, or a fine, or both.

(7) In any proceedings under this section—

(a) a report by a British consular officer or a deposition made before a British consular officer and authenticated under the signature of that officer is admissible, upon proof that the officer or the deponent cannot be found in the United Kingdom, as evidence of the matters stated in it, and

(b) it is not necessary to prove the signature or official character of the person who appears to have signed any such report or deposition.

NOTES

Initial Commencement

To be appointed

To be appointed: see s 148(1), (2).

Appointment

Appointment: 30 December 2005: see SI 2005/2213, art 2(f).

Extent

This section does not extend to Scotland: see s 149(2).

General

[424]

This section makes it an offence to remove, or arrange to remove, a child from the UK for the purpose of adoption, without a parental responsibility order made under s 84. Provisions under the Adoption Act 1976 enabled court permission to be given for overseas placement (see *Re A (Adoption: Placement outside jurisdiction)* [2004] EWCA Civ 515; [2004] 2 FLR 337) but that provision is not available under the new legislation. The CA 1989, Sch 2, para 19, may provide a useful route through where other forms of permanency are available, but *Re A* (supra) provides an apposite warning in relation to reading CA 1989, Sch 2, para 19 in isolation. Sections 84 and 85, while entirely valuable in policy terms of providing stability and protection for children, run the risk of limiting the availability of overseas adoption for British children to an extent that may mean adoption overseas as the appropriate form of permanency is not available for some children. There was no parliamentary consideration as to need for or impact of this provision, so there is no assistance from that source as to the relationship of, for example, ACA 2002, s 28(3). Although there is provision for regulations to be made to disapply or modify this restriction in relation to family placements, no such regulations have as yet been made.

Section 85(3)

Making arrangements

[425]

Making arrangements can constitute an offence in itself; ACA 2002, ss 92, 93 and 138 (see paras [454]–[460]).

Relevance of ACA 2002, s 92

[426]

ACA 2002, s 92 provides a more extensive list of activities that constitute 'making arrangements', which goes further than the definition contained within this section.

[427]

86 Power to modify sections 83 and 85

(1) Regulations may provide for section 83 not to apply if—

(a) the adopters or (as the case may be) prospective adopters are natural parents, natural relatives or guardians of the child in question (or one of them is), or

(b) the British resident in question is a partner of a parent of the child,

and any prescribed conditions are met.

(2) Regulations may provide for section 85(1) to apply with modifications, or not to apply, if—

(a) the prospective adopters are parents, relatives or guardians of the child in question (or one of them is), or

(b) the prospective adopter is a partner of a parent of the child,

and any prescribed conditions are met.

(3) On the occasion of the first exercise of the power to make regulations under this section—

(a) the statutory instrument containing the regulations is not to be made unless a draft of the instrument has been laid before, and approved by a resolution of, each House of Parliament, and

(b) accordingly section 140(2) does not apply to the instrument.

(4) In this section, 'prescribed' means prescribed by regulations and 'regulations' means regulations made by the Secretary of State after consultation with the Assembly.

NOTES

Initial Commencement

To be appointed
To be appointed: see s 148(1), (2).

Appointment
Appointment (for the purpose of making regulations): 7 December 2004: see SI 2004/3203, art 2(1)(m)(vii); appointment (for remaining purposes): 30 December 2005: see SI 2005/2213, art 2(f).

> **Extent**
> This section does not extend to Scotland: see s 149(2).

General

[428]

No regulations have as yet been made to enable family/guardian/partner of parent adoptions to be subject to any different provisions than exist within the ACA 2002 and the AWAFE 2005 Regulations.

Relevance of ACA 2002, s 92

[429]

Although no specific regulations are yet made under s 86, the offence of making arrangements for the adoption of a child does not apply to relatives or the partner of a parent of a child. This enables the common-sense situation of making enquiries within families to take place without fear of an offence being committed (see para **[454]**).

[430]

Overseas adoptions

87 Overseas adoptions

(1) In this Act, 'overseas adoption'—

(a) means an adoption of a description specified in an order made by the Secretary of State, being a description of adoptions effected under the law of any country or territory outside the British Islands, but

(b) does not include a Convention adoption.

(2) Regulations may prescribe the requirements that ought to be met by an adoption of any description effected after the commencement of the regulations for it to be an overseas adoption for the purposes of this Act.

(3) At any time when such regulations have effect, the Secretary of State must exercise his powers under this section so as to secure that subsequently effected adoptions of any description are not overseas adoptions for the purposes of this Act if he considers that they are not likely within a reasonable time to meet the prescribed requirements.

(4) In this section references to this Act include the Adoption Act 1976 (c 36).

(5) An order under this section may contain provision as to the manner in which evidence of any overseas adoption may be given.

(6) In this section—

'adoption' means an adoption of a child or of a person who was a child at the time the adoption was applied for,

'regulations' means regulations made by the Secretary of State after consultation with the Assembly.

NOTES

Initial Commencement

To be appointed

To be appointed: see s 148(1), (2).

Appointment

Sub-ss (1)(a), (2), (5), (6): appointment (for the purpose of making regulations): 7 December 2004: see SI 2004/3203, art 2(1)(m)(vii); sub-ss (1)(a), (2), (5), (6): appointment (for remaining purposes): 30 December 2005: see SI 2005/2213, art 2(f); sub-ss (1)(b), (4): appointment: 1 June 2003: see SI 2003/366, art 2(5)(a); sub-s (3): appointment: 30 December 2005: see SI 2005/2213, art 2(f).

General

[431]

This section enables an adoption that occurred entirely outside the UK in one of a list of countries and territories to be recognised as valid.

Section 87(1)(a)

Description

[432]

The requirements under the Adoption (Designation of Overseas Adoptions) Order 1973 are that the child was under 18 at the date of the adoption and the adoption was not one at common or customary law

Specified in an order

[433]

In the absence of any new order specifying which countries or territories, the list remains that set out in the Adoption (Designation of Overseas Adoptions) Order 1973.

Outside the British Islands

[434]

The British Islands comprise the UK, the Isle of Man and the Channel Islands (Interpretation Act 1978).

Section 87(1)(b)

Does not include a Convention adoption

[435]

There is considerable overlap between the countries and territories in the schedule to the Adoption (Designation of Overseas Adoption) Order 1973 and those who have acceded to the Hague Convention (22 appear in both categories). It will be a matter of the date – 23rd January 2003 being the date on which the Hague Convention took effect in English law. Adoptions after that date will have had to comply with Convention provisions and will be recognised as such.

Section 87(2)

Regulations to designate overseas adoptions

[436]

There was Parliamentary comment on the need for a revised designated list at Committee stage but no new regulations have yet been made.

Section 87(4)

Inclusion of Adoption Act 1976

[437]

This enables the existing list to remain applicable.

[438]

PART B – Statutes

Miscellaneous

88 Modification of section 67 for Hague Convention adoptions

(1) If the High Court is satisfied, on an application under this section, that each of the following conditions is met in the case of a Convention adoption, it may direct that section 67(3) does not apply, or does not apply to any extent specified in the direction.

(2) The conditions are—

(a) that under the law of the country in which the adoption was effected, the adoption is not a full adoption,

(b) that the consents referred to in Article 4(c) and (d) of the Convention have not been given for a full adoption or that the United Kingdom is not the receiving State (within the meaning of Article 2 of the Convention),

(c) that it would be more favourable to the adopted child for a direction to be given under subsection (1).

(3) A full adoption is an adoption by virtue of which the child is to be treated in law as not being the child of any person other than the adopters or adopter.

(4) In relation to a direction under this section and an application for it, sections 59 and 60 of the Family Law Act 1986 (c 55) (declarations under Part 3 of that Act as to marital status) apply as they apply in relation to a direction under that Part and an application for such a direction.

NOTES

Initial Commencement

To be appointed

To be appointed: see s 148(1), (2).

Appointment

Appointment: 30 December 2005: see SI 2005/2213, art 2(f).

Extent

This section does not extend to Scotland: see s 149(2).

General

[439]

Section 67 deals with the absolute nature of the status of adoption in forming an exclusive legal relationship between adopted child and adoptive parents. In cases where a legal relationship still exists between a child and natural parent in Convention adoption cases, the High Court may direct that the absolute nature of status of the adopted child is modified or suspended. Unless a s 88 direction is made, every Convention adoption will be regarded as a full adoption.

Section 88(2)(b)

Article 4(c) and 4(d) consents

[440]

The Articles of the Hague Convention appear as Sch 1 to the AIAA 1999. Article 4(c) consent deals with consent including parental consent and the need for understanding as to the extent to which existing legal ties are broken. Article 4(d) consent relates to the child in the light of the child's age and maturity.

The UK is not the receiving State

[441]

If the UK is not the receiving State, then the case will be one of a Convention adoption between two other Convention states. The UK will be the receiving State in all cases where the child is to be brought into the UK, with a Convention order having been made, or with the intention of a Convention Adoption order being made. In those cases, there is no scope for an adoption other than a full adoption.

More favourable

[442]

This wording is directly related to art 26(3) of the Hague Convention.

Section 88(4)

Family Law Act 1986, s 59

[443]

This section enables the Attorney-General to intervene in proceedings. Under the FP(A) Regulations 2005, reg 23, the Attorney-General is an automatic respondent to an application for a s 88 direction.

[444]

89 Annulment etc of overseas or Hague Convention adoptions

(1) The High Court may, on an application under this subsection, by order annul a Convention adoption or Convention adoption order on the ground that the adoption is contrary to public policy.

(2) The High Court may, on an application under this subsection—

(a) by order provide for an overseas adoption or a determination under section 91 to cease to be valid on the ground that the adoption or determination is contrary to public policy or that the authority which purported to authorise the adoption or make the determination was not competent to entertain the case, or

(b) decide the extent, if any, to which a determination under section 91 has been affected by a subsequent determination under that section.

(3) The High Court may, in any proceedings in that court, decide that an overseas adoption or a determination under section 91 is to be treated, for the purposes of those proceedings, as invalid on either of the grounds mentioned in subsection (2)(a).

(4) Subject to the preceding provisions, the validity of a Convention adoption, Convention adoption order or overseas adoption or a determination under section 91 cannot be called in question in proceedings in any court in England and Wales.

NOTES

Initial Commencement

To be appointed
To be appointed: see s 148(1), (2).

Appointment
Appointment: 30 December 2005: see SI 2005/2213, art 2(f).

Extent
This section does not extend to Scotland: see s 149(2).

General

[445]

The Adoption Act 1976 contained annulment provisions. It is not thought that any annulments were made under the previous provisions.

Application

[446]

FP(A) Regulations 2005, reg 23 sets out who may apply and the identity of the respondents.

Convention adoption or Convention adoption order

[447]

See above in the commentary to s 83 (see paras [407]–[408]).

Overseas adoptions

[448]

See above in the commentary to s 87 (see para [431] ff]).

[449]

90   Section 89: supplementary

(1)   Any application for an order under section 89 or a decision under subsection (2)(b) or (3) of that section must be made in the prescribed manner and within any prescribed period.

'Prescribed' means prescribed by rules.

(2)   No application may be made under section 89(1) in respect of an adoption unless immediately before the application is made—

(a)   the person adopted, or
(b)   the adopters or adopter,

habitually reside in England and Wales.

(3)   In deciding in pursuance of section 89 whether such an authority as is mentioned in section 91 was competent to entertain a particular case, a court is bound by any finding of fact made by the authority and stated by the authority to be so made for the purpose of determining whether the authority was competent to entertain the case.

NOTES

Initial Commencement
To be appointed
To be appointed: see s 148(1), (2).

Appointment
Appointment: 30 December 2005: see SI 2005/2213, art 2(f).

Extent
This section does not extend to Scotland: see s 149(2).

Subordinate Legislation
Family Procedure (Adoption) Rules 2005, SI 2005/2795 (made under sub-s (1)).

General

Limitation period

[450]

The Family Procedure (Adoption) Rules 2005 (FP(A) Rules 2005), r 109 has the effect of excluding any application for an annulment more than 2 years after the date of making the Convention adoption order, Convention adoption, overseas adoption or s 91 determination.

[451]

91 Overseas determinations and orders

(1) Subsection (2) applies where any authority of a Convention country (other than the United Kingdom) or of the Channel Islands, the Isle of Man or any British overseas territory has power under the law of that country or territory—

(a) to authorise, or review the authorisation of, an adoption order made in that country or territory, or

(b) to give or review a decision revoking or annulling such an order or a Convention adoption.

(2) If the authority makes a determination in the exercise of that power, the determination is to have effect for the purpose of effecting, confirming or terminating the adoption in question or, as the case may be, confirming its termination.

(3) Subsection (2) is subject to section 89 and to any subsequent determination having effect under that subsection.

NOTES

Initial Commencement

To be appointed

To be appointed: see s 148(1), (2).

Appointment

Appointment: 30 December 2005: see SI 2005/2213, art 2(f).

Extent

This section does not extend to Scotland: see s 149(2).

General

[452]

This section makes the recognition within English law of determinations in relation to adoptions in Convention countries, the Channel Islands, the Isle of Man and any British overseas territory.

[453]

[91A Power to charge]

[(1) This section applies to adoptions to which—

(a) section 83 applies, or

(b) regulations made under section 1 of the Adoption (Intercountry Aspects) Act 1999 apply.

(2) The Secretary of State may charge a fee to adopters for services provided or to be provided by him in relation to adoptions to which this section applies.

(3) The Assembly may charge a fee to adopters for services provided or to be provided by it as the Central Authority in relation to adoptions to which this section applies by virtue of subsection (1)(b).

(4) The Secretary of State and the Assembly may determine the level of fee as he or it sees fit, and may in particular—

(a)   charge a flat fee or charge different fees in different cases or descriptions of case, and

(b)   in any case or description of case, waive a fee.

(5)   But the Secretary of State and the Assembly must each secure that, taking one financial year with another, the income from fees under this section does not exceed the total cost to him or, as the case may be, to it of providing the services in relation to which the fees are imposed.

(6)   In this section—

references to adoptions and adopters include prospective adoptions and prospective adopters,

'Central Authority' is to be construed in accordance with section 2 of the Adoption (Intercountry Aspects) Act 1999,

'financial year' means a period of twelve months ending with 31st March.]

NOTES

Extent

This section does not extend to Scotland: see s 149(2).

Amendment

Inserted by the Children and Adoption Act 2006, s 13; date in force: to be appointed: see the Children and Adoption Act 2006, s 17(2), (3).

Chapter 7
Miscellaneous

Restrictions

92   Restriction on arranging adoptions etc

(1)   A person who is neither an adoption agency nor acting in pursuance of an order of the High Court must not take any of the steps mentioned in subsection (2).

(2)   The steps are—

(a)   asking a person other than an adoption agency to provide a child for adoption,

(b)   asking a person other than an adoption agency to provide prospective adopters for a child,

(c)   offering to find a child for adoption,

(d)   offering a child for adoption to a person other than an adoption agency,

(e)   handing over a child to any person other than an adoption agency with a view to the child's adoption by that or another person,

(f)   receiving a child handed over to him in contravention of paragraph (e),

(g)   entering into an agreement with any person for the adoption of a child, or for the purpose of facilitating the adoption of a child, where no adoption agency is acting on behalf of the child in the adoption,

(h)   initiating or taking part in negotiations of which the purpose is the conclusion of an agreement within paragraph (g),

(i)   causing another person to take any of the steps mentioned in paragraphs (a) to (h).

(3)   Subsection (1) does not apply to a person taking any of the steps mentioned in paragraphs (d), (e), (g), (h) and (i) of subsection (2) if the following condition is met.

(4)   The condition is that—

(a)   the prospective adopters are parents, relatives or guardians of the child (or one of them is), or

(b)   the prospective adopter is the partner of a parent of the child.

(5)   References to an adoption agency in subsection (2) include a prescribed person outside the United Kingdom exercising functions corresponding to those of an adoption agency, if the functions are being exercised in prescribed circumstances in respect of the child in question.

(6)   The Secretary of State may, after consultation with the Assembly, by order make any amendments of subsections (1) to (4), and any consequential amendments of this Act, which he considers necessary or expedient.

(7)   In this section—

(a)   'agreement' includes an arrangement (whether or not enforceable),

(b)   'prescribed' means prescribed by regulations made by the Secretary of State after consultation with the Assembly.

NOTES

Initial Commencement

To be appointed

To be appointed: see s 148(1), (2).

Appointment

Appointment (for the purpose of making regulations): 7 December 2004: see SI 2004/3203, art 2(1)(m)(viii); appointment (for remaining purposes): 30 December 2005: see SI 2005/2213, art 2(g).

Extent

This section does not extend to Scotland: see s 149(2).

General

[454]

This section imposes prohibitions on any person taking a variety of steps connected with adoption, unless it is an adoption agency or he/she is acting under the provisions of a High Court Order. In addition, some, but not all, of those steps may lawfully be taken by certain persons connected with the child. To act in breach of these prohibitions is a criminal offence (see s 93).

Section 92(1) and (2)

[455]

The general prohibitions are: asking third parties who are not adoption agencies to provide a child for adoption or prospective adopters for a child, offering to find a child for adoption, offering a child for adoption to anyone other than an adoption agency, both parties to any handover of a child for adoption where an adoption agency is not arranging the placement, and entering into agreements or participating in preparatory negotiations, which do not involve an adoption agency, concerning a child's adoption. In addition, it is prohibited to cause another person to take any of these steps.

Section 92(3) and (4)

[456]

Some of the above steps may lawfully be taken without a High Court Order or the involvement of an adoption agency if the child's prospective adopters (or one of them) is a parent, relative or guardian of the child, or is the partner of one of the child's parents. These steps are: offering the child for adoption, handing the child over for adoption, initiating and participating in negotiations about an agreement for adoption, entering into such an agreement, and causing another person to take any of these steps. In addition, as the person receiving the child would not be doing so in breach of s 92(2)(e), that would also not be prohibited.

It is arguable that the drafting of s 92(3) may have inadvertently made it possible for a person within these degrees of relationship to the child to circumvent the other prohibitions in s 92(2) by causing a third party to take any of those steps – the restriction in s 92(2)(i) is relaxed for all steps – although that third party would him/herself be committing a criminal act.

Section 92(6)

[457]

After consultation with the Welsh Assembly, the Secretary of State may amend these provisions by Parliamentary Order (s 92(6)).

An 'agreement' includes any arrangement, even if not legally enforceable (s 92(7)(a)).

'Payment' includes payments for reward, and therefore does not necessarily have to contain an element of reward (s 97(b)).

'Prescribed' means by regulations (s 97(7)(b)).

'Registered adoption society' is defined in s 2(2) (Sch 6).

[458]

---

93 Offence of breaching restrictions under section 92

(1) If a person contravenes section 92(1), he is guilty of an offence; and, if that person is an adoption society, the person who manages the society is also guilty of the offence.

(2) A person is not guilty of an offence under subsection (1) of taking the step mentioned in paragraph (f) of section 92(2) unless it is proved that he knew or had reason to suspect that the child was handed over to him in contravention of paragraph (e) of that subsection.

(3) A person is not guilty of an offence under subsection (1) of causing a person to take any of the steps mentioned in paragraphs (a) to (h) of section 92(2) unless it is proved that he knew or had reason to suspect that the step taken would contravene the paragraph in question.

(4) But subsections (2) and (3) only apply if sufficient evidence is adduced to raise an issue as to whether the person had the knowledge or reason mentioned.

(5) A person guilty of an offence under this section is liable on summary conviction to imprisonment for a term not exceeding six months, or a fine not exceeding £10,000, or both.

NOTES

Initial Commencement

To be appointed
To be appointed: see s 148(1), (2).

Appointment
Appointment: 30 December 2005: see SI 2005/2213, art 2(g).

Extent
This section does not extend to Scotland: see s 149(2).

General

[459]

This section creates criminal offences for acting in breach of s 92 (see the note to s 92 above, paras [454]–[457]).

PART B – Statutes

Section 93(1)–(5)

[460]

The breach of a prohibition in s 92 is a criminal offence, for which a person is liable on summary conviction to imprisonment of up to six months, a fine of up to £10,000, or both. If an adoption society breaches such a prohibition, the manager is guilty of that offence.

However, in two cases no criminal offence will be committed, although these exceptions will not apply unless sufficient evidence is adduced to raise the relevant defence.

First, a person receiving a child for adoption in breach of the prohibition in s 92(2)(f) will not be guilty unless it is proved that he/she knew or had reason to suspect that the child was being handed over by a person who was not acting as an adoption agency or under a High Court Order, and thus in breach of s 92(2)(e).

Second, causing a third party to take any of the steps prohibited in s 92, in breach of s 92(2)(i), will not render that person guilty of a criminal offence unless it is proved that he/she knew or had reason to suspect that such a step would contravene the relevant prohibition.

[461]

94   Restriction on reports

(1)   A person who is not within a prescribed description may not, in any prescribed circumstances, prepare a report for any person about the suitability of a child for adoption or of a person to adopt a child or about the adoption, or placement for adoption, of a child.

'Prescribed' means prescribed by regulations made by the Secretary of State after consultation with the Assembly.

(2)   If a person—

(a)   contravenes subsection (1), or
(b)   causes a person to prepare a report, or submits to any person a report which has been prepared, in contravention of that subsection,

he is guilty of an offence.

(3)   If a person who works for an adoption society—

(a)   contravenes subsection (1), or
(b)   causes a person to prepare a report, or submits to any person a report which has been prepared, in contravention of that subsection,

the person who manages the society is also guilty of the offence.

(4)   A person is not guilty of an offence under subsection (2)(b) unless it is proved that he knew or had reason to suspect that the report would be, or had been, prepared in contravention of subsection (1).
But this subsection only applies if sufficient evidence is adduced to raise an issue as to whether the person had the knowledge or reason mentioned.

(5)   A person guilty of an offence under this section is liable on summary conviction to imprisonment for a term not exceeding six months, or a fine not exceeding level 5 on the standard scale, or both.

NOTES

Initial Commencement

To be appointed
To be appointed: see s 148(1), (2).

Appointment
Sub-s (1): appointment (for the purpose of making regulations): 7 December 2004: see SI 2004/3203, art 2(1)(m)(ix); sub-s (1): appointment (for remaining purposes): 30 December 2005: see SI 2005/2213, art 2(g); sub-ss (2)–(5): appointment: 30 December 2005: see SI 2005/2213, art 2(g).

Extent
This section does not extend to Scotland: see s 149(2).

Subordinate Legislation
Restriction on the Preparation of Adoption Reports Regulations 2005, SI 2005/1711 (made under sub-s (1)).

General

[462]

This section permits regulations to be made restricting the preparation of reports concerning adoption, following a number of high profile reports in the press and critical judgments in the High Court concerning the previous lack of regulation.

Section 94(1)

[463]

Regulations may prohibit anyone outside of a prescribed description from preparing reports, in 'prescribed circumstances', concerning the suitability of a person to adopt a child, the suitability of a child for adoption, the placement of a child for adoption, or a child's adoption. The relevant Regulations are the Restriction on the Preparation of Adoption Reports Regulations 2005 (RPARR) (SI 2005/1711). These restrictions do not apply to CAFCASS/Welsh Family Proceedings officers writing reports in adoption and placement proceedings.

The prescribed circumstances are reports concerning: (i) whether a child should be placed for adoption, under the Adoption Agencies Regulations 2005 (SI 2005/389), reg 17(1)/ Adoption Agencies (Wales) Regulations 2005 (SI 2005/1313), reg 17(1); (ii) the suitability of prospective adopters, under regs 25(5)/26 (respectively) of those Regulations; (iii) the match of a child with prospective adopters, under reg 31(2)(d)/reg 32 of those Regulations; (iv) visits to children placed for adoption but not yet adopted, under reg 36(4)(b)/reg 37 of those Regulations; (v) visits to, and reviews of, children brought into the UK for the purposes of adoption, under the Adoptions with a Foreign Element Regulations 2005 (SI 2005/392), reg 5(1)(h)(ii); (vi) the review of the case of a child brought into the UK for the purposes of adoption, where an application to adopt has not been made within two years of giving notice, as required by the Adoptions with a Foreign Element Regulations 2005, reg 5(3); (vii) pre- and post-adoption reports produced at the request of a relevant foreign authority (as defined in reg 2 of those regulations), which are not made in accordance with the Adoption Agencies Regulations; (viii) Court reports for the purposes of ss 43 or 44(5) (agency and non-agency cases); and (ix) Reports for the High Court under s 84, where the court is considering granting parental responsibility to a person intending to adopt a child under non-British law (RPARR, reg 4).

The following persons are prescribed for this purpose: (i) a social worker employed by a local authority or registered adoption society and who has either three years' post-qualification experience in child care social work, including direct experience of adoption work, or is supervised by such a person (RPARR, reg 3(1)(a)); (ii) a social worker acting on behalf of a local authority or registered adoption society who satisfies such requirements of experience (RPARR, reg 3(1)(c)); and (iii) a student social worker on an approved course who is employed by, or placed with, a local authority or registered adoption society as part of that course, and is supervised by a social worker employed by the relevant local authority or adoption society and with the requisite experience (RPARR, reg 3(1)(b)).

Section 94(2) and (3)

[464]

It is a criminal offence to prepare a report in contravention of these restrictions, cause such a report to be prepared, or submit to any person a report prepared in such breach. If the breach is committed by an adoption society, the manager is also guilty of the offence.

Section 94(4)

[465]

To prove the offences of causing the report to be prepared or submitting it to a third party, it is necessary to prove that the person knew of, or had reasonable cause to suspect, the breach, provided that sufficient evidence is adduced to raise such a defence as an issue.

Section 94(5)

[466]

Upon conviction, the offences may be punished by imprisonment of up to six months, a fine not exceeding level 5, or both.

Definitions

[467]

A 'social worker' means a person registered with the General Social Care Council, or the Scottish or Northern Irish equivalent (RPARR, reg 2).

[468]

95 Prohibition of certain payments

(1) This section applies to any payment (other than an excepted payment) which is made for or in consideration of—

(a) the adoption of a child,
(b) giving any consent required in connection with the adoption of a child,
(c) removing from the United Kingdom a child who is a Commonwealth citizen, or is habitually resident in the United Kingdom, to a place outside the British Islands for the purpose of adoption,
(d) a person (who is neither an adoption agency nor acting in pursuance of an order of the High Court) taking any step mentioned in section 92(2),
(e) preparing, causing to be prepared or submitting a report the preparation of which contravenes section 94(1).

(2) In this section and section 96, removing a child from the United Kingdom has the same meaning as in section 85.

(3) Any person who—

(a) makes any payment to which this section applies,
(b) agrees or offers to make any such payment, or
(c) receives or agrees to receive or attempts to obtain any such payment,

is guilty of an offence.

(4) A person guilty of an offence under this section is liable on summary conviction to imprisonment for a term not exceeding six months, or a fine not exceeding £10,000, or both.

NOTES

Initial Commencement

To be appointed

To be appointed: see s 148(1), (2).

Appointment

Appointment: 30 December 2005: see SI 2005/2213, art 2(g).

Extent

This section does not extend to Scotland: see s 149(2).

General

[469]

This section makes it a criminal offence to make payments in connection with adoption, save for the exceptions which are contained in s 96.

Section 95(1) and (2)

[470]

Other than 'excepted payments', criminal sanctions apply to a range of payments relating to the adoption of a child. This is where payment is made for the adoption of a child, for a person's consent to adoption, for a child to be removed from the UK for adoption outside the British Islands (if the child is habitually resident in the UK or a citizen of the Commonwealth), for any of the steps prohibited by s 92(2), or in connection with the preparation of reports in breach of s 94(1).

See notes to ss 92(2) and 94(1) (paras [454]–[457] and [463]).

'Adoption' in this context means under any law and wherever the child is habitually resident (see s 97).

'Excepted payments': see s 96.

'Payment': includes payment for reward (see s 97), and therefore does not necessarily have to be payment for reward.

'Removing a child from the UK': this is defined in s 85(3).

Section 95(3)

[471]

The criminal offence covers offering to pay, agreeing to pay, agreeing to receive payment, attempting to obtain payment, making payment and receiving payment.

See s 96(4) for some limited exceptions concerning a child being removed from the UK for adoption.

'Payment': see notes to s 95(1) and (2) (see para [470]).

Section 95(4)

[472]

The offence is a summary one, carrying a maximum sentence of six months' imprisonment or a fine of £10,000, or a combination of both.

[473]

96 Excepted payments

(1) A payment is an excepted payment if it is made by virtue of, or in accordance with provision made by or under, this Act, the Adoption (Scotland) Act 1978 (c 28) or the Adoption (Northern Ireland) Order 1987 (SI 1987/2203 (NI 22)).

(2) A payment is an excepted payment if it is made to a registered adoption society by—

(a) a parent or guardian of a child, or

(b) a person who adopts or proposes to adopt a child,

in respect of expenses reasonably incurred by the society in connection with the adoption or proposed adoption of the child.

(3) A payment is an excepted payment if it is made in respect of any legal or medical expenses incurred or to be incurred by any person in connection with an application to a court which he has made or proposes to make for an adoption order, a placement order, or an order under section 26 or 84.

(4) A payment made as mentioned in section 95(1)(c) is an excepted payment if—

(a) the condition in section 85(2) is met, and

(b) the payment is made in respect of the travel and accommodation expenses reasonably incurred in removing the child from the United Kingdom for the purpose of adoption.

NOTES

Initial Commencement

To be appointed
To be appointed: see s 148(1), (2).

Appointment
Appointment: 30 December 2005: see SI 2005/2213, art 2(g).

Extent
This section does not extend to Scotland: see s 149(2).

General

[474]

Section 95 creates criminal offences in connection with payments concerning the adoption of a child, subject to the three exceptions set out in this section.

Section 96(1)

[475]

The first exception is a payment made under a specific provision of this Act or the adoption legislation in Scotland or Northern Ireland.

Section 96(2)

[476]

The second exception is a payment to a registered adoption society for its reasonable expenses in connection with the adoption, or proposed adoption, of a child, and where the payments are made either by the parent or guardian of the child or by the adopter or prospective adopter.

Section 96(3)

[477]

The third exception is a payment for the legal or medical expenses of a person applying for an adoption order, placement order, s 26 contact order or parental responsibility under s 84 prior to a child entering the UK for adoption.

Section 96(4)

[478]

A person may lawfully agree to receive, attempt to obtain, or receive payment in connection with reasonable travelling and accommodation expenses where a child is removed from the UK for adoption, if the prospective adopters have parental responsibility under s 84 or remove the child under the authority of the relevant sections of Scottish or Northern Irish statutes.

'Adoption': see note to s 95 (para **[470]**).

'Payment': see note to s 95 (para **[470]**).

[479]

> **97   Sections 92 to 96: interpretation**
>
> In sections 92 to 96—
>
> (a)   'adoption agency' includes a Scottish or Northern Irish adoption agency,
> (b)   'payment' includes reward,
> (c)   references to adoption are to the adoption of persons, wherever they may be habitually resident, effected under the law of any country or territory, whether within or outside the British Islands.
>
> **NOTES**
> **Initial Commencement**
> *To be appointed*
> To be appointed: see s 148(1), (2).
>
> **Appointment**
> Appointment: 30 December 2005: see SI 2005/2213, art 2(g).
>
> **Extent**
> This section does not extend to Scotland: see s 149(2).

General

[480]

This section provides specific interpretation provisions for ss 92–96 concerning the restrictions on arranging adoptions, writing reports and making payments in connection with adoption.

[481]

> ## *Information*
>
> **98   Pre-commencement adoptions: information**
>
> (1)   Regulations under section 9 may make provision for the purpose of—
>
> (a)   assisting persons adopted before the appointed day who have attained the age of 18 to obtain information in relation to their adoption, and

(b)   facilitating contact between such persons and their relatives.

(2)   For that purpose the regulations may confer functions on—

(a)   registered adoption support agencies,

(b)   the Registrar General,

(c)   adoption agencies.

(3)   For that purpose the regulations may—

(a)   authorise or require any person mentioned in subsection (2) to disclose information,

(b)   authorise or require the disclosure of information contained in records kept under section 8 of the Public Records Act 1958 (c 51) (court records),

and may impose conditions on the disclosure of information, including conditions restricting its further disclosure.

(4)   The regulations may authorise the charging of prescribed fees by any person mentioned in subsection (2) or in respect of the disclosure of information under subsection (3)(b).

(5)   An authorisation or requirement to disclose information by virtue of subsection (3)(a) has effect in spite of any restriction on the disclosure of information in Chapter 5.

(6)   The making of regulations by virtue of subsections (2) to (4) which relate to the Registrar General requires the approval of the Chancellor of the Exchequer.

(7)   In this section—

'appointed day' means the day appointed for the commencement of sections 56 to 65,

'registered adoption support agency' means an adoption support agency in respect of which a person is registered under Part 2 of the Care Standards Act 2000 (c 14),

'relative', in relation to an adopted person, means any person who (but for his adoption) would be related to him by blood (including half-blood)[, marriage or civil partnership].

NOTES

Initial Commencement

To be appointed

To be appointed: see s 148(6).

Appointment

Appointment (in relation to Wales): 7 February 2004: see SI 2004/252, art 2(b); appointment (in relation to England): 7 December 2004: see SI 2004/3203, art 2(1)(j).

Extent

This section does not extend to Scotland: see s 149(2).

Amendment

Sub-s (7): in definition 'relative' words ', marriage or civil partnership' in square brackets substituted by the Civil Partnership Act 2004, s 79(1), (10); date in force: 30 December 2005: see SI 2005/3175, art 2(9).

Subordinate Legislation

Adoption Information and Intermediary Services (Pre-Commencement Adoptions) Regulations 2005, SI 2005/890; Adoption Information and Intermediary Services (Pre-Commencement Adoptions) (Wales) Regulations 2005, SI 2005/2701; Adoption Support Agencies (England) and Adoption Agencies (Miscellaneous Amendments) Regulations 2005, SI 2005/2720; Adoption Information and Intermediary Services (Pre-Commencement Adoptions) (Wales) (Amendment) Regulations 2005, SI 2005/3293.

Adoption and Children (Miscellaneous Amendments) Regulations 2005, SI 2005/3482.

General

[482]

The Adoption Information and Intermediary Services (Pre-Commencement Adoptions) Regulations 2005 (SI 2005/890) (AIISPCAR) apply in England, and the Adoption Information and Intermediary Services (Pre-Commencement Adoptions) (Wales) Regulations 2005 (SI 2005/2701) (AIISPCAWR) apply in Wales.

Intermediary services may be provided by an adoption agency or adoption support agency and, if provided, are 'adoption support services' for the purposes of s 2 of the Act. They are services to help those (the applicant) aged 18 or over, who were adopted before 30 December 2005, to obtain information about their adoption or to facilitate contact between that person and their relatives (the subject). Written information about counselling services must be provided, and counselling may be provided, including to relatives who apply as referred to below (AIISPCAR, regs 3, 4 and 10/AIISPCAWR, regs 3, 4 and 10).

A relative of an adopted person (the applicant) can seek help in contacting an adopted person (the subject). The adopted relative whom they seek to contact must be aged 18 or over, and if there is a high demand for these services priority must be given to those adopted before 12 November 1975. There is a discretion for the agency to decline to act, having regard to the welfare of the applicant, subject of the request and any third parties (especially if under the age of 18) who might be identified or affected by the request (AIISPCAR, regs 5 and 6/AIISPCAWR, regs 5 and 6).

Fees may be charged (AIISPCAR, reg 18/AIISPCAWR, reg 18).

The agency cannot give the applicant information about the subject without the subject's consent, unless the subject is dead or lacks capacity, in which case the agency has a discretion but subject to the above-mentioned welfare test (AIISPCAR, reg 7/AIISP-CAWR, reg 7). If the subject is the adopted person, he/she has a veto on any application by a relative, if he/she has given notification that no contact with an intermediary agency is desired (or only desired in specified circumstances). If consent is refused, or a veto exists, non-identifying information can be given. (AIISPCAR, regs 8 and 9/AIISPCAWR, regs 8 and 9).

Regulations 11–16 set out the procedure for the intermediary agency to obtain information from the Registrar General or a court, both of whom have an obligation to provide information.

[483]

Proceedings

99 Proceedings for offences

Proceedings for an offence by virtue of section 9 or 59 may not, without the written consent of the Attorney General, be taken by any person other than [the Commission for Social Care Inspection] or the Assembly.

NOTES
Initial Commencement
To be appointed
To be appointed: see s 148(1), (2).

Appointment
Appointment: 30 December 2005: see SI 2005/2213, art 2(h).

Extent
This section does not extend to Scotland: see s 149(2).

Amendment
Words 'the Commission for Social Care Inspection' in square brackets substituted by the Health and Social Care (Community Health and Standards) Act 2003, s 147, Sch 9, para 32; date in force: 1 April 2004: see SI 2004/759, art 4(2)(b).

General

[484]

This section was amended to change the names of the authorities referred to by the Health and Social Care (Community Health and Standards) Act 2003, s 147, Sch 9, para 32. Section 9 prescribes an offence when regulations governing adoption agencies and the like are not adhered to. Section 59 prescribes an offence if such an agency discloses information in contravention of s 57 of the Act

[485]

100 Appeals

In section 94 of the 1989 Act (appeals under that Act), in subsections (1)(a) and (2), after 'this Act' there is inserted 'or the Adoption and Children Act 2002'.

NOTES

Initial Commencement

To be appointed
To be appointed: see s 148(1), (2).

Appointment
Appointment: 30 December 2005: see SI 2005/2213, art 2(h).

Extent
This section does not extend to Scotland: see s 149(2).

General

[486]

The sections of CA 1989 referred to relate to appeals to the High Court against the making or refusal of an order (CA 1989, s 94(1)). However, no appeal lies against the decision by a magistrates' court to decline jurisdiction because it feels that the case is better dealt with by another court (CA 1989, s 94(2)).

[487]

101 Privacy

(1)   Proceedings under this Act in the High Court or a County Court may be heard and determined in private.
(2)   In section 12 of the Administration of Justice Act 1960 (c 65) (publication of information relating to proceedings in private), in subsection (1)(a)(ii), after '1989' there is inserted 'or the Adoption and Children Act 2002'.
(3)   In section 97 of the 1989 Act (privacy for children involved in certain proceedings), after 'this Act' in subsections (1) and (2) there is inserted 'or the Adoption and Children Act 2002'.

NOTES

Initial Commencement

To be appointed
To be appointed: see s 148(1), (2).

Appointment
Appointment: 30 December 2005: see SI 2005/2213, art 2(h).

Extent
This section does not extend to Scotland: see s 149(2).

General

[488]

ACA 2002, s 101 and Sch 3 paras 36–39, deal with public access to and reporting of proceedings under the ACA 2002. Proceedings under sections inserted by the ACA 2002 into other Acts, in particular by Pt 2 amendments of the CA 1989, are proceedings under the Act into which they are inserted and not proceedings under the ACA 2002.

Section 101(1) provides for ACA 2002 proceedings in the High Court or a county court to be heard in private. Section 101(2) brings ACA 2002 proceedings within the special protection afforded by the Administration of Justice Act 1960, s 12(1)(a) regarding the reporting of proceedings before any court sitting in private. ACA 2002, s 101(3) extends the privacy protection in the CA 1989, s 97(1) and (2) to proceedings under the ACA 2002. Consequential amendments are made by Sch 3, paras 36–39 regarding ACA 2002 proceedings in the magistrates' family proceedings court.

Section 101(1)

Privacy of proceedings

[489]

In the High Court or a county court, proceedings under the ACA 2002 may, by virtue of s 101(1), be heard and determined in private. It is usual practice for them to be so, save in so far as there is some point of law of significance for the future. The subsection replaced similar provisions in the Adoption Act 1976, s 64 regarding adoption proceedings under that Act.

In the magistrates' family proceedings court, proceedings under the ACA 2002 are family proceedings within the Magistrates' Courts Act 1980, s 65 (as amended by ACA 2002, Sch 3, paras 36 and 37) and governed by the MCA 1980, s 69, as were proceedings under the Adoption Act 1976. Appropriate substitution amendments have been made to the MCA 1980, s 69 by ACA 2002, Sch 3, para 38. Hence the previous practice of access restricted to those directly concerned with the proceedings in accordance with s 69(2)(a), (b) and (3) continues. The rule-making power in the CA 1989, s 97(1), for magistrates' courts to sit in private in proceedings when exercising powers under the CA 1989, has been extended by s 101(3) to include ACA 2002 proceedings.

Reporting of proceedings

[490]

The AJA 1960, s 12(1) prohibits publication of information relating to proceedings before any court sitting in private in a number of specified instances, to which the ACA 2002, s 101(2) has added proceedings brought under the Act, in a like manner to proceedings brought under the CA 1989. The amendments have assimilated the relevant statutory jurisdictions with the inherent jurisdiction for the purposes of contempt of court, see Laws LJ in *Her Majesty's Attorney General v Pelling* [2005] EWHC 414 (Admin) at 54, [2006] 1 FLR 93. The Family Procedure (Adoption) Rules 2005 (SI 2005/2795), r 78, sets out, for the purposes of the law relating to contempt, the circumstances in which information relating to proceedings heard in private may be communicated.

Additionally with regard to reporting of proceedings under the ACA 2002 in the magistrates' family proceedings court, the MCA 1980, s 71, has been amended by ACA 2002, Sch 3, para 39, so as to limit the particulars permitted to be published by MCA 1980, s 71(1)(1A) to submissions on any point of law arising in the proceedings, the decision of the court and any observations made by the court in giving it.

The prohibition in the CA 1989, s 97(2), on publishing material likely to identify any child involved in any proceedings before the High Court, a county court or a magistrates' court has been extended by the ACA 2002, s 101(3) to proceedings in which any power under the ACA 2002 may be exercised. It should be noted that in *Clayton v Clayton* [2006] EWCA Civ 878, [2006] 2 FCR 405, the Court of Appeal held that the CA 1989, s 97(2) prohibition on publication ceases to operate after the conclusion of the proceedings, but the court can intervene where a child's welfare is put at risk by inappropriate identification for publicity purposes. The court can make appropriate orders, notably an injunction (in accordance with *Re Z (a minor)(freedom of publication)* [1995] 4 All ER 961) or a CA 1989, s 8, prohibited steps order, to protect the privacy of the child beyond the end of the proceedings. Moreover, the limitations imposed by the Administration of Justice Act 1960, s 12 remain.

[491]

The Children and Family Court Advisory and Support Service

102   Officers of the Service

(1)   For the purposes of—

(a)   any relevant application,

(b)   the signification by any person of any consent to placement or adoption,

rules must provide for the appointment in prescribed cases of an officer of the Children and Family Court Advisory and Support Service ('the Service') [or a Welsh family proceedings officer].

(2)   The rules may provide for the appointment of such an officer in other circumstances in which it appears to the Lord Chancellor to be necessary or expedient to do so.

(3)   The rules may provide for the officer—

(a)   to act on behalf of the child upon the hearing of any relevant application, with the duty of safeguarding the interests of the child in the prescribed manner,

(b)   where the court so requests, to prepare a report on matters relating to the welfare of the child in question,

(c)   to witness documents which signify consent to placement or adoption,

(d)   to perform prescribed functions.

(4)   A report prepared in pursuance of the rules on matters relating to the welfare of a child must—

(a)   deal with prescribed matters (unless the court orders otherwise), and

(b)   be made in the manner required by the court.

(5)   A person who—

(a)   in the case of an application for the making, varying or revocation of a placement order, is employed by the local authority which made the application,

(b)   in the case of an application for an adoption order in respect of a child who was placed for adoption, is employed by the adoption agency which placed him, or

(c)   is within a prescribed description,

is not to be appointed under subsection (1) or (2).

(6)   In this section, 'relevant application' means an application for—

(a)   the making, varying or revocation of a placement order,

(b)   the making of an order under section 26, or the varying or revocation of such an order,

(c)   the making of an adoption order, or

(d)   the making of an order under section 84.

(7)   Rules may make provision as to the assistance which the court may require an officer of the Service [or a Welsh family proceedings officer] to give to it.

[(8) In this section and section 103 'Welsh family proceedings officer' has the meaning given by section 35 of the Children Act 2004.]

NOTES

Initial Commencement

To be appointed
To be appointed: see s 148(1), (2).

Appointment
Appointment: 30 December 2005: see SI 2005/2213, art 2(i).

Extent
This section does not extend to Scotland: see s 149(2).

Amendment
Sub-s (1): words 'or a Welsh family proceedings officer' in square brackets inserted by the Children Act 2004, s 40, Sch 3, paras 15, 16(1), (2); date in force: 1 April 2005: by virtue of SI 2005/700, art 2(2); sub-s (7): words 'or a Welsh family proceedings officer' in square brackets inserted by the Children Act 2004, s 40, Sch 3, paras 15, 16(1), (3); date in force: 1 April 2005: by virtue of SI 2005/700, art 2(2); sub-s (8): inserted by the Children Act 2004, s 40, Sch 3, paras 15, 16(1), (4); date in force: 1 April 2005: by virtue of SI 2005/700, art 2(2).

Subordinate Legislation
Family Procedure (Adoption) Rules 2005, SI 2005/2795.

General

[492]

This section governs the requirement for the Rules, in specified circumstances, to provide for the appointment of a CAFCASS officer or Welsh Family Proceedings Officer to protect the interests of the child, and for the duties of those officers. See ACA 2002, s 103 for the right of such officers to have access to records held by an adoption agency.

'Rules': see the Family Procedure (Adoption) Rules 2005.

Section 102(1)

[493]

For the purposes of a 'relevant application', or where a person gives consent to a child's placement for adoption or the making of an adoption order, the Rules must provide for the appointment of a CAFCASS officer or Welsh Family Proceedings Officer in 'prescribed cases'.

'Prescribed cases': as provided for in the Family Procedure (Adoption) Rules 2005 (see Pt 7 of those rules).

'Relevant application': see ACA 2002, s 102(6).

Section 102(2)

[494]

Those rules may also permit the appointment of a CAFCASS officer or Welsh Family Proceedings Officer in other circumstances, additional to those in 'relevant applications'.

See also the Family Procedure (Adoption) Rules 2005, r 59.

'Relevant application': see ACA 2002, s 102(6).

Section 102(3) and (7)

[495]

The Rules may provide for the duties of the CAFCASS officer or Welsh Family Proceedings Officer in relation to acting for the child and safeguarding his/her welfare, preparing reports for Court, witnessing consent to adoption or placement of a child for adoption, other assistance required by the Court, and other prescribed functions.

See the Family Procedure (Adoption) Rules 2005, Pt 7.

Section 102(3) and (7)

[496]

Any CAFCASS or Welsh Family Proceedings Officer's report must comply with the Family Procedure (Adoption) Rules 2005, Pt 7, unless the court gives a direction to the contrary, and must also be in any format required by the court.

Section 102(5)

[497]

Restrictions are placed upon appointing a person as a CAFCASS officer or Welsh Family Proceedings Officer who is employed by an organisation connected to certain cases. These are local authority officers where that authority is applying for a placement order, or its variation or discharge, and adoption agency officers in the context of an adoption application where that agency placed the child for adoption.

Rules may also prescribe other persons who may not act as the CAFCASS officer or Welsh Family Proceedings Officer. The Family Procedure (Adoption) Rules 2005, r 75, provides for such further prohibitions.

Section 102(6)

[498]

A 'relevant application', where Rules must provide for the appointment of a CAFCASS officer or Welsh Family Proceedings Officer (see s 120(1) above), is one for an adoption order, placement order (or variation/discharge), s 26 contact order (or variation/discharge), or parental responsibility for a child under the provisions of s 84.

Section 102(6)

[499]

See above.

[500]

> ### 103 Right of officers of the Service to have access to adoption agency records
>
> (1) Where an officer of the Service [or a Welsh family proceedings officer] has been appointed to act under section 102(1), he has the right at all reasonable times to examine and take copies of any records of, or held by, an adoption agency which were compiled in connection with the making, or proposed making, by any person of any application under this Part in respect of the child concerned.

(2)   Where an officer of the Service [or a Welsh family proceedings officer] takes a copy of any record which he is entitled to examine under this section, that copy or any part of it is admissible as evidence of any matter referred to in any—

(a)   report which he makes to the court in the proceedings in question, or
(b)   evidence which he gives in those proceedings.

(3)   Subsection (2) has effect regardless of any enactment or rule of law which would otherwise prevent the record in question being admissible in evidence.

NOTES

Initial Commencement

To be appointed
To be appointed: see s 148(1), (2).

Appointment
Appointment: 30 December 2005: see SI 2005/2213, art 2(i).

Extent
This section does not extend to Scotland: see s 149(2).

Amendment
Sub-ss (1), (2): words 'or a Welsh family proceedings officer' in square brackets inserted by the Children Act 2004, s 40, Sch 3, paras 15, 17; date in force: 1 April 2005: by virtue of SI 2005/700, art 2(2).

General

[501]

This section complements similar provisions in CA 1989, giving CAFCASS officers and Welsh Family Proceedings Officers a right to gain access to, and copy, certain records held by an adoption agency.

Section 103(1)

[502]

Where a CAFCASS officer or Welsh Family Proceedings Officer is appointed under the Family Procedure (Adoption) Rules 2005 (see s 102) regarding a relevant application, or in connection with consent to adoption or placement for adoption, he/she has a right to examine and take copies of records of, or held by, an adoption agency, but only insofar as those records were compiled in connection with any application, or proposed application, under this Part of the Act.

'Relevant application': see s 102(6).

'This Part', means ACA 2002, Pt I, covering all relevant applications concerning adoption, since that Part extends from s 1 to s 110.

It is submitted that this statutory right of access will not extend to information held about prospective adopters where the application is for a placement order, if that information was not specifically compiled 'in connection with' the placement order application.

Section 103(2) and (3)

[503]

Such copies, or parts of those copies, are admissible as evidence in relation to the evidence, or contents of the Report, of the CAFCASS officer or Welsh Family Proceedings Officer, regardless of any other rule of law or statute that would otherwise render the record inadmissible.

[504]

Evidence

104 Evidence of consent

(1) If a document signifying any consent which is required by this Part to be given is witnessed in accordance with rules, it is to be admissible in evidence without further proof of the signature of the person by whom it was executed.

(2) A document signifying any such consent which purports to be witnessed in accordance with rules is to be presumed to be so witnessed, and to have been executed and witnessed on the date and at the place specified in the document, unless the contrary is proved.

NOTES

Initial Commencement
To be appointed
To be appointed: see s 148(1), (2).

Appointment
Appointment: 30 December 2005: see SI 2005/2213, art 2(j).

Extent
This section does not extend to Scotland: see s 149(2).

General

[505]

This is defined by s 52(5) as meaning consent that is given unconditionally and with full understanding of what is involved.

[506]

Scotland, Northern Ireland and the Islands

105 Effect of certain Scottish orders and provisions

(1) A Scottish adoption order or an order under section 25 of the Adoption (Scotland) Act 1978 (c 28) (interim adoption orders) has effect in England and Wales as it has in Scotland, but as if references to the parental responsibilities and the parental rights in relation to a child were to parental responsibility for the child.

(2) An order made under section 18 of the Adoption (Scotland) Act 1978 (freeing orders), and the revocation or variation of such an order under section 20 or 21 of that Act, have effect in England and Wales as they have effect in Scotland, but as if references to the parental responsibilities and the parental rights in relation to a child were to parental responsibility for the child.

(3) Any person who—

(a) contravenes section 27(1) of that Act (removal where adoption agreed etc), or
(b) contravenes section 28(1) or (2) of that Act (removal where applicant provided home),

is guilty of an offence and liable on summary conviction to imprisonment for a term not exceeding three months, or a fine not exceeding level 5 on the standard scale, or both.

(4) Orders made under section 29 of that Act (order to return or not to remove child) are to have effect in England and Wales as if they were orders of the High Court under section 41 of this Act.

NOTES

Initial Commencement
To be appointed
To be appointed: see s 148(1), (2).

Appointment
Appointment: 30 December 2005: see SI 2005/2213, art 2(j).

Extent
This section does not extend to Scotland: see s 149(2).

106 Effect of certain Northern Irish orders and provisions

(1) A Northern Irish adoption order or an order under Article 26 of the Adoption (Northern Ireland) Order 1987 (SI 1987/2203 (NI 22)) (interim orders) has effect in England and Wales as it has in Northern Ireland.

(2) An order made under Article 17 or 18 of the Adoption (Northern Ireland) Order 1987 (freeing orders), or the variation or revocation of such an order under Article 20 or 21 of that Order, have effect in England and Wales as they have in Northern Ireland.

(3) Any person who—

(a) contravenes Article 28(1) or (2) of the Adoption (Northern Ireland) Order 1987 (removal where adoption agreed etc), or

(b) contravenes Article 29(1) or (2) of that Order (removal where applicant provided home),

is guilty of an offence and liable on summary conviction to imprisonment for a term not exceeding three months, or a fine not exceeding level 5 on the standard scale, or both.

(4) Orders made under Article 30 of that Order (order to return or not to remove child) are to have effect in England and Wales as if they were orders of the High Court under section 41 of this Act.

NOTES

Initial Commencement
To be appointed
To be appointed: see s 148(1), (2).

Appointment
Appointment: 30 December 2005: see SI 2005/2213, art 2(j).

Extent
This section does not extend to Scotland: see s 149(2).

107 Use of adoption records from other parts of the British Islands

Any document which is receivable as evidence of any matter—

(a) in Scotland under section 45(2) of the Adoption (Scotland) Act 1978 (c 28),

(b) in Northern Ireland under Article 63(1) of the Adoption (Northern Ireland) Order 1987, or

(c) in the Isle of Man or any of the Channel Islands under an enactment corresponding to section 77(3) of this Act,

is also receivable as evidence of that matter in England and Wales.

NOTES

Initial Commencement
To be appointed
To be appointed: see s 148(1), (2).

Appointment
Appointment: 30 December 2005: see SI 2005/2213, art 2(j).

Extent
This section does not extend to Scotland: see s 149(2).

108 Channel Islands and the Isle of Man

(1) Regulations may provide—

(a) for a reference in any provision of this Act to an order of a court to include an order of a court in the Isle of Man or any of the Channel Islands which appears to the Secretary of State to correspond in its effect to the order in question,

(b) for a reference in any provision of this Act to an adoption agency to include a person who appears to the Secretary of State to exercise functions under the law of the Isle of Man or any of the Channel Islands which correspond to those of an adoption agency and for any reference in any provision of this Act to a child placed for adoption by an adoption agency to be read accordingly,

(c)　for a reference in any provision of this Act to an enactment (including an enactment contained in this Act) to include a provision of the law of the Isle of Man or any of the Channel Islands which appears to the Secretary of State to correspond in its effect to the enactment,

(d)　for any reference in any provision of this Act to the United Kingdom to include the Isle of Man or any of the Channel Islands.

(2) Regulations may modify any provision of this Act, as it applies to any order made, or other thing done, under the law of the Isle of Man or any of the Channel Islands.

(3) In this section, 'regulations' means regulations made by the Secretary of State after consultation with the Assembly.

NOTES

Initial Commencement

To be appointed
To be appointed: see s 148(1), (2).

Appointment
Appointment: 7 December 2004: see SI 2004/3203, art 2(1)(k).

Extent
This section does not extend to Scotland: see s 149(2).

General

109 Avoiding delay

(1)　In proceedings in which a question may arise as to whether an adoption order or placement order should be made, or any other question with respect to such an order, the court must (in the light of any rules made by virtue of subsection (2))—

(a)　draw up a timetable with a view to determining such a question without delay, and

(b)　give such directions as it considers appropriate for the purpose of ensuring that the timetable is adhered to.

(2)　Rules may—

(a)　prescribe periods within which prescribed steps must be taken in relation to such proceedings, and

(b)　make other provision with respect to such proceedings for the purpose of ensuring that such questions are determined without delay.

NOTES

Initial Commencement

To be appointed
To be appointed: see s 148(1), (2).

Appointment
Appointment: 30 December 2005: see SI 2005/2213, art 2(j).

Extent
This section does not extend to Scotland: see s 149(2).

Subordinate Legislation
Family Procedure (Adoption) Rules 2005, SI 2005/2795 (made under sub-s (2)).

General

[507]

The requirement for a court to set out a timetable for matters to be resolved is not without precedent. It is common in civil matters where, for example, fast track matters must be set down in a timetable which does not extend beyond 30 weeks from allocation to trial. Similarly in care proceedings in which a protocol provides for a prescribed timetable which is not supposed to go beyond 40 weeks from the date that directions are first given.

[508]

> ### 110 Service of notices etc
>
> Any notice or information required to be given by virtue of this Act may be given by post.
>
> **NOTES**
>
> **Initial Commencement**
> *To be appointed*
> To be appointed: see s 148(1), (2).
>
> **Appointment**
> Appointment: 30 December 2005: see SI 2005/2213, art 2(j).
>
> **Extent**
> This section does not extend to Scotland: see s 149(2).

General

[509]

The section does not say whether it is first class or second class post nor the period for presumed service. Using the Civil Procedure Rules 1998, r 6, as a guide shows that service is usually by first class post. As for dates of presumed service, reference might be had to CPR 1998, r. 6.7, whereby documents sent by first class post are presumed served on the second day after posting.

[510]

> ## Part 2
> ## Amendments of the Children Act 1989
>
> ### 111 Parental responsibility of unmarried father
>
> (1) Section 4 of the 1989 Act (acquisition of responsibility by the father of a child who is not married to the child's mother) is amended as follows.
> (2) In subsection (1) (cases where parental responsibility is acquired), for the words after 'birth' there is substituted
>
> > ', the father shall acquire parental responsibility for the child if—
> >
> > (a) he becomes registered as the child's father under any of the enactments specified in subsection (1A);
> > (b) he and the child's mother make an agreement (a "parental responsibility agreement") providing for him to have parental responsibility for the child; or
> > (c) the court, on his application, orders that he shall have parental responsibility for the child.'
>
> (3) After that subsection there is inserted—
>
> > '(1A) The enactments referred to in subsection (1)(a) are—
> >
> > (a) paragraphs (a), (b) and (c) of section 10(1) and of section 10A(1) of the Births and Deaths Registration Act 1953;
> > (b) paragraphs (a), (b)(i) and (c) of section 18(1), and sections 18(2)(b) and 20(1)(a) of the Registration of Births, Deaths and Marriages (Scotland) Act 1965; and
> > (c) sub-paragraphs (a), (b) and (c) of Article 14(3) of the Births and Deaths Registration (Northern Ireland) Order 1976.

> (1B) The Lord Chancellor may by order amend subsection (1A) so as to add further enactments to the list in that subsection.'

(4) For subsection (3) there is substituted—

> '(2A) A person who has acquired parental responsibility under subsection (1) shall cease to have that responsibility only if the court so orders.
>
> (3) The court may make an order under subsection (2A) on the application—
>
>> (a) of any person who has parental responsibility for the child; or
>> (b) with the leave of the court, of the child himself,
>
> subject, in the case of parental responsibility acquired under subsection (1)(c), to section 12(4).'

(5) Accordingly, in section 2(2) of the 1989 Act (a father of a child who is not married to the child's mother shall not have parental responsibility for the child unless he acquires it in accordance with the provisions of the Act), for the words from 'shall not' to 'acquires it' there is substituted 'shall have parental responsibility for the child if he has acquired it (and has not ceased to have it)'.

(6) In section 104 of the 1989 Act (regulations and orders)—

(a) in subsection (2), after 'section' there is inserted '4(1B),', and
(b) in subsection (3), after 'section' there is inserted '4(1B) or'.

(7) Paragraph (a) of section 4(1) of the 1989 Act, as substituted by subsection (2) of this section, does not confer parental responsibility on a man who was registered under an enactment referred to in paragraph (a), (b) or (c) of section 4(1A) of that Act, as inserted by subsection (3) of this section, before the commencement of subsection (3) in relation to that paragraph.

NOTES

Initial Commencement

To be appointed
To be appointed: see s 148(1), (2).

Appointment
Appointment: 1 December 2003: see SI 2003/3079, art 2(2)(a).

Extent
This section does not extend to Scotland: see s 149(2).

General

[511]

The major substantive change that s 111 makes in amending s 4 of the Children Act 1989, is to provide an additional means whereby a father who is not married to the mother at the time of the child's birth can acquire parental responsibility, namely, if he becomes registered as the child's father under the Births and Deaths Registration Act 1953 or the equivalent provisions for Scotland and Northern Ireland. Thus, in accordance with the relevant provisions of the 1953 Act the circumstances in which the father may be registered or, where his name was not originally entered in the register, re-registered, as the child's father are:

(a) at the joint request of the mother and father, in which case both must sign the register, or

(b) at the request of either the mother or the father, on the production of statutory declarations of paternity and the mother's acknowledgement of it.

Section 111(7)

[512]

The new rule enabling acquisition of parental responsibility by registration is not retroactive. A person registered as father before 1 December 2003, when the new rule came into force (Adoption and Children Act 2002 (Commencement No 4) Order 2003, (SI 2003/3079)), does not acquire parental responsibility in this way, and will have to rely, if he can, on obtaining a parental responsibility agreement or a parental responsibility order.

Termination of parental responsibility

[513]

As with the other means of acquiring parental responsibility, parental responsibility granted to an unmarried father as a result of registration may only be terminated by an order of the court. Application for termination may be made by a person who has parental responsibility for the child or, with leave, by the child, which may only be granted if he has sufficient understanding to make the proposed application.

[514]

112 Acquisition of parental responsibility by step-parent

NOTE
This section inserts a new s 4A into the Children Act 1989. The text of this section will be found at para **[701]**.

113 Section 8 orders: local authority foster parents

In section 9 of the 1989 Act (restrictions on making section 8 orders)—

(a)   in subsection (3)(c), for 'three years' there is substituted 'one year', and
(b)   subsection (4) is omitted.

NOTES
Initial Commencement
To be appointed
To be appointed: see s 148(1), (2).

Appointment
Appointment: 30 December 2005: see SI 2005/2213, art 2(k).

Extent
This section does not extend to Scotland: see s 149(2).

General

[515]

This section amends CA 1989, s 9(3)(c) in relation to the time that must elapse before a local authority foster-parent can seek leave to apply for a s 8 (Children Act) Order without being a relative of the child or having the consent of the local authority. This provision concerns a person who either fostered the child in the last six months, or is currently the child's foster-parent. The period of time that the parent must have fostered the child, prior to the application for leave, is reduced from three years to 12 months.

CA 1989, s 9(4) is repealed. This governed the calculation of the previous three-year period.

[516]

114 Residence orders: extension to age of 18

(1) In section 12 of the 1989 Act (residence orders and parental responsibility), after subsection (4) there is inserted—

'(5) The power of a court to make a residence order in favour of any person who is not the parent or guardian of the child concerned includes power to direct, at the request of that person, that the order continue in force until the child reaches the age of eighteen (unless the order is brought to an end earlier); and any power to vary a residence order is exercisable accordingly.

(6) Where a residence order includes such a direction, an application to vary or discharge the order may only be made, if apart from this subsection the leave of the court is not required, with such leave'.

(2) In section 9 of that Act (restrictions on making section 8 orders), at the beginning of subsection (6) there is inserted 'Subject to section 12(5)'.

(3) In section 91 of that Act (effect and duration of orders), in subsection (10), after '9(6)' there is inserted 'or 12(5)'.

NOTES

Initial Commencement

To be appointed

To be appointed: see s 148(1), (2).

Appointment

Appointment: 30 December 2005: see SI 2005/2213, art 2(k).

Extent

This section does not extend to Scotland: see s 149(2).

General

[517]

This section adds non-parents and guardians to the list of those who may apply under CA 1989, s 12, for residence and parental responsibility orders to be extended until the child's 18th birthday

[518]

115 Special guardianship

(1) After section 14 of the 1989 Act there is inserted:
[Not reproduced here]

(2) The 1989 Act is amended as follows.

(3) In section 1 (welfare of the child), in subsection (4)(b), after 'discharge' there is inserted 'a special guardianship order or '.

(4) In section 5 (appointment of guardians) –

(a) in subsection (1) –

(i) in paragraph (b), for 'or guardian' there is substituted ', guardian or special guardian', and

(ii) at the end of paragraph (b) there is inserted '; or

(c) paragraph (b) does not apply, and the child's only or last surviving special guardian dies.';

(b) in subsection (4), at the end there is inserted '; and a special guardian of a child may appoint another individual to be the child's guardian in the event of his death', and

(c) in subsection (7), at the end of paragraph (b) there is inserted 'or he was the child's only (or last surviving) special guardian'.'

> **NOTE**
> This section inserts new ss 14A–G into the Children Act 1989. The text of these sections will be found at para **[703]-[779]**.

General

[519]

Section 115 must be read with Sch 3, paras 56–64, 68, and 70–72, which collectively amend the CA 1989 by adding the new concept of special guardianship to the range of orders available in the 1989 Act, so as to widen the range of options for providing permanence for children (see President's Direction March 2006 *Adoption: the New Law and Procedure*, para 4(vi)).

Section 115(1) inserts ss 14A–14G into the 1989 Act which provide for the additional concept of special guardianship, see paras **[704]-[780]**.

Section 115(2)–(4) further amend the CA 1989 so as to apply the s 1 welfare checklist when the court is considering whether to make, vary or discharge a special guardianship order (SGO) and to amend s 5 relating to the appointment of guardians to include special guardians.

The analysis of the very extensive s 115, which is very much the innovative heart of the Children Act Part of the ACA 2002, begins with an overview of special guardianship as introduced by s 115(1), before the later individual consideration of the CA 1989 ss 14A–G as inserted by s 115(1) (see paras **[704]-[780]**). The analysis is necessarily extensive in view of capacious nature of s 14A–G. Subsequent amendments to, and repeals of, those sections have been incorporated. The analysis of s 115 concludes with s 115(2)–(4), (see paras **[519.2]-[519.3]**, and the Sch 3 amendments to the CA 1989 relating to special guardianship, see para **[519.4]**.

This extensive section, together with Sch 3, paras 46–48, provides for the power of the court to make a SGO; who may apply; notification of intended application; local authority investigations and reports; and the application process. A SGO will only be available in respect of minor children (see CA 1989, ss 14A(1) and 105(1)). Since, however, it relates to the exercise of parental responsibility and will cease in any event when the child attains majority, it will rarely be sought, or made, once he attains the age of 16. It seems likely that the child's marriage or civil partnership will preclude the making of a SGO.

Section 115(1)

[519.1]

This inserts ss 14A–14G into the CA 1989 to provide for the nature and scope of special guardianship; the making and effect of SGOs; their variation and discharge and for local authority support services for special guardians. Those sections are supplemented by the Special Guardianship Regulations 2005 (SI 2005/1109) (see paras **[1101]-[1155]**), and the Special Guardianship (Wales) Regulations 2005 (SI 2005/1513) (see paras **[1201]-[1238]**). The Department for Education and Skills and the Welsh Assembly Government have issued respectively *Special Guardianship Guidance* (DfES, 2005) and *Guidance to Support: The Special Guardianship (Wales) Regulations* 2005 (NAFW, 2006) designed to support the introduction of SGOs and provide guidance on the interpretation of the regulations.

Special guardianship is conferred by a private law court order but is intended for use primarily in the public law context. It has its origins in chapter five of the White Paper *Adoption: a new approach*, (Cm 5017), where the Government set out its proposals 'to

PART B – Statutes

197

achieve permanence for looked after children'. Its nature and scope need to be considered in the context of the range of options for looked after children who are unable to return to their birth parents. It is based upon the premise that such children:

> 'need new families as quickly as possible. In the short term, a foster family will care for them. In the longer term, the Government must provide a range of options for permanence to deliver high quality outcomes for looked after children. There are many already, including family and friends, residence orders, long-term fostering and adoption. But this list is not complete. There is no status which provides legal permanence, but lacks the complete legal break with birth parents of adoption.' (Cm 5017 para 5.2)

A private law order conferring special guardianship is thus intended to fill that lacuna and provide, primarily, a new hybrid option in the public law context, to meet the needs of looked-after children for whom rehabilitation with the birth parents is not considered an option. In many such cases the irrevocable severance of all connection between the child and his birth family consequent upon adoption will not best meet the child's needs. Special guardianship may also be of benefit to a child who is being looked after on a long-term basis who is being accommodated with a member of his wider family (see *A Local Authority v Y, Z* [2006] 2 FLR 41). The child may be a member of a minority ethnic family that has religious and cultural difficulties with adoption. 'Unaccompanied asylum-seeking children may also need secure, permanent homes, but have strong attachments to their families abroad' (DfES, 2005, para 6). The child's carers may be members of his birth family, hence adoption would distort existing relationships. His carers may not wish to uproot legally the child from his family by adoption. From a human rights perspective, the making of a SGO in cases such as these is likely to be a more necessary and proportionate response than the making of an adoption order.

Special guardianship is very similar to the authority conferred by guardianship and slightly more than the authority conferred by a residence order. Like guardianship, but not a residence order, it also confers a title on the office holder. Like a residence order, it requires public ordering in the form of a court order, unlike guardianship which is not confined to court order and can be by private appointment. Like both guardianship and a residence order, it is closely allied to the concept of parental responsibility, but not parenthood, which is unaffected. The latter distinction makes special guardianship of notably less legal and practical significance than adoption in terms of parental autonomy.

Contrary to the impression given in the White Paper, special guardianship does not provide 'legal permanence'. It provides, by virtue of the CA 1989, s 14C (see para [735]), quasi-exclusive parental responsibility which ends at the very latest when the child attains the age of 18 and is susceptible to earlier variation or discharge (see s 14D at para [751]). Moreover, during a child's minority the law does not recognise any rule of absolute parental responsibility as the House of Lords made clear in *Gillick v West Norfolk Area Health Authority* [1986] AC 112. Rather parental responsibility is an authority of dwindling significance, which diminishes as the child acquires sufficient understanding and intelligence to be capable of determining the matter in issue. Hence, special guardianship is of considerably less significance than adoption, which is the termination of the legal relationship with the birth family and the irrevocable transfer of exclusive parental responsibility and, more particularly, parenthood, to the adopters. Special guardianship preserves the legal relationship with the birth family and is about providing the child with a *feeling* of permanence, rather than providing legal permanence. Special guardianship law places more emphasis than adoption law upon continuing contact with the birth family (see, eg, s 14B(1)(a) at para [729]).

The similarities between guardianship and special guardianship are marked. Both a guardian and a special guardian have parental responsibility for the child until termination of the appointment. Both have the right to consent, or refuse to consent, to the making of an adoption order in respect of the child and to the child's being placed for adoption under the ACA 2002, because 'guardian' has the same meaning as in the 1989 Act and includes a special guardian (see ACA 2002, s 144(1)). Both may appoint a guardian (see CA 1989, s 5(4) as substituted by ACA, s 115(4)). Both become substitutes for a parent rather than a substitute parent. Both are to be distinguished from a parent because:

(1)   neither a guardian nor a special guardian has rights of intestate succession on the child's death;

(2)   the child has no right to take British citizenship from either a guardian or special guardian;

(3)   parenthood is for life whereas both guardianship and special guardianship must end, at the very latest, when the child attains majority;

(4)   neither a guardian nor a special guardian is personally liable financially to maintain the child.

Special guardianship is the revocable transfer of parental responsibility to a person other than a parent of the child, by court order. While the order is in force the special guardian appointed has parental responsibility for the child in respect of whom it is made (see s 14C(1)(a) at para [736]). In that regard, the order is identical in effect to a residence order in favour of a person who is not the child's parent for, in addition to settling the arrangements to be made as to the person with whom the child is to live in accordance with the CA 1989, s 8, a residence order also confers parental responsibility for the child (see CA 1989, s 12(2)). Where it differs from a residence order is that subject to any other order in force with respect to the child under the CA 1989, a special guardian is entitled to exercise parental responsibility to the exclusion of anyone else with parental responsibility for the child, apart from another special guardian (see s 14C(1)(b) at para [735]). In contrast, a residence order is based upon the concurrent, rather than exclusive, exercise of parental responsibility.

A special guardian may be entitled, under s 14F, to local authority support services (see para [768]), whereas a person with a residence order is not. If the person with a residence order is a local authority foster parent, however, the local authority may be willing to support their former foster child in terms of financial and other support. Such support has proved to be central to foster parents' decisions whether or not to apply for a residence order and is likely to be central to any decision by foster parents to seek a SGO.

Both a SGO and a residence order may continue until the child's majority (but not thereafter). Special guardianship is more extensive than a residence order, which normally ceases when the child reached the age of 16, unless either the court is satisfied that the circumstances of the case are exceptional (see CA 1989, s 9(6)), or it has directed, at the request of the person in whose favour the residence order operates, that the order continues in force until the child attains majority, (see CA 1989, s 12(5) as inserted by ACA 2002, s 114(1)).

A key feature of a SGO is that it is less easily revoked or varied on application by third parties, especially the child's parents (see s 14D at para [751]), than is the case with a residence order.

A special guardian may appoint a guardian to act in the event of his death, whereas parental responsibility passing with a residence order is not assignable on death (see CA 1989, s 12(3)(c)).

Section 115(2) and (3)

[519.2]

These subsections further amend the CA 1989 so as to apply the welfare checklist in s 1(3) when the court is considering whether to make, vary or discharge a SGO.

In all special guardianship cases the child's welfare is foremost. Where a court hears an application for a SGO under CA 1989, s 14A(3) or (6)(a), see para **[706]**, or considers, under s 14A(6)(b), see para **[705]**, that a SGO should be made, notwithstanding the absence of an application, it must decide the case in accordance with the welfare principle in the CA 1989, s 1. The same principle applies to an application under s 14D, either to vary or discharge a SGO. That well known principle has three parts, the paramountcy principle in s 1(1); the avoidance of delay principle in s 1(2) and the 'no-order' principle in s 1(5).

The insertion by the ACA 2002, s 115(3) of a SGO into the CA 1989, s 1(4)(b) has to be read in the context of the paramountcy principle in s 1(1) of that Act. In applying that principle the court in practice has to ask itself what is best for the child. Where there is more than one child the subject of a special guardianship application, for example siblings, each application is to be decided on the basis that the particular child's welfare is paramount. If the paramount interests of each child produce incompatible and irreconcilable results then, by analogy with the Court of Appeal decision in *Re D (minors)(appeal)* [1995] 1 FCR 301, the court should undertake a balancing exercise and achieve a result of least detriment to all the children.

In discharging its duty to decide what is best for the child, the court must consider, in accordance with the CA 1989, s 1(4)(b), as applied by ACA 2002, s 115 (2) and (3), the matters in the so-called welfare checklist in CA 1989, s 1(3) of the 1989 Act. This is so as to identify the child's needs and, in the light thereof, to reach its decision. It must do so when dealing with any application for a SGO and not just, as with CA 1989, s 8 orders, opposed applications. In deciding whether to make, vary or discharge a SGO, the same weight is attached to the checklist as when the court is considering whether to make, vary or discharge a care or supervision order under the CA 1989, Pt IV. In addition to the court, others should pay regard to the checklist, in particular practitioners involved in applications for a SGO, whether as legal advisor, children and family reporter, or children's guardian, as well as the parties themselves.

The CA 1989, s 1(3) requires the court to have regard in particular to:

'(a) the ascertainable wishes and feelings of the child concerned (considered in the light of his age and understanding);

(b) his physical, emotional and educational needs;

(c) the likely effect upon him of any change in his circumstances;

(d) his age, sex, background and any characteristics of his which the court considers relevant;

(e) any harm which he has suffered or is at risk of suffering;

(f) how capable each of his parents and any other person in relation to whom the court considers the question to be relevant, is of meeting his needs;

(g) the range of powers available to the court under this Act in the proceedings in question.'

The prominence given to the child's wishes and feelings by paragraph (a) reflects the emphasis in the CA 1989 upon the child's entitlement to be consulted about, rather than decide upon, matters affecting his upbringing. The child's wishes regarding special guardianship will not be determinative unless the court considers that they accord with his welfare. Where all other factors are evenly balanced, the child's wishes are likely to be determinative. It is recognised that ascertaining the child's wishes and feelings must depend upon the child's age and understanding and will be a key function of the local authority special guardianship report that is required by the CA 1989, s 14A(8) (see para **[717]** and *Special Guardianship Guidance*, para 104).

The factors listed in paragraphs (b)–(f) reflect the fact that the child's welfare is to be understood in the widest sense so as to include not only the physical and mental well being of the child but also his moral spiritual and emotional welfare. The s 14A(8) report will play a key part in providing an objective assessment of the needs of the particular child (factor (b)). The likely effect upon the child of any change in his circumstances (factor (c)) needs to be addressed in the light of the nature and effect of special guardianship, in particular the exclusive allocation of parental responsibility to the special guardian/s. Although, unlike adoption, there is no requirement that the child should live with the applicants before the application is made, it will be rare for him not to have done so. This is because either the applicants aspired to adoption, having had the care of the child; or residence of the child with them is necessary in order for them to qualify as applicants for special guardianship. Hence the court is less likely to be asked to uproot the child (which it is reluctant to do) on an application for a SGO than on an application for a residence order. This so-called status quo factor is more likely to be to the advantage of the applicant, as well as in the child's best interests.

The child's religious persuasion, racial origin, cultural and linguistic background are not listed specifically in s 1(3), but will be significant when the court is considering his background and characteristics (factor (d)), as well as his needs. Where there is evidence of physical, emotional or sexual abuse or neglect by the parent/s, this will weigh heavily against him/them. Particular attention must be paid to the suitability of the applicant/s to be special guardian/s and of meeting the child's needs and how this suitability will contrast with the capability of each of the child's parents in that regard (factor (f)). In addressing the range of powers available to it (factor (g)) the court will need to be mindful of the menu of orders available to it (including giving directions and imposing conditions under the CA 1989, s 11(7) as applied by s 14E(5), see para **[767]**). For example, it may be in the child's best interests to make a residence order rather than a SGO, if it is felt that some degree of shared responsibility with the child's parents would better secure the child's best interests.

The parents' wishes are not included in the factors, but the checklist is not exhaustive ('a court shall have regard in particular to …') and the court may take into account parental wishes, although they are not likely to carry as much influence as the listed factors. Similarly the blood tie should only be relevant in so far as it assists the court in applying the paramountcy principle (see *Re M (child's upbringing)* [1996] 2 FCR 473, CA).

With regard to the avoidance of delay principle in CA 1989, s 1(2), reference is made later to the close relationship between this principle and the court's duty in the CA 1989, s 14E(1)–(3) to draw up a timetable with a view to determining the special guardianship application without delay, and to give directions for ensuring that the timetable is observed (see para **[765]**). All professionals involved with an application for special guardianship should assist the court in meeting its duty of avoiding delay. Solicitors for the parties have a duty to ensure that the case does not drift and is brought to a hearing with minimum delay. The application of s 1(2) may well justify the court refusing to adjourn the proceedings. The court must balance the likely prejudice to the child's welfare, which the delay consequent upon an adjournment of the final hearing would cause, against the prejudice to the proper determination of what would be in the child's best interests. To the same end, directions appointments are not to be regarded as formalities, but used to maximum effect to ensure that the case is tightly time-tabled and prepared for its final hearing at the earliest opportunity. If this guidance is followed, the court will meet the state's obligations under art 6 of the European Convention on Human Rights to ensure a hearing 'within a reasonable time'. Whether or not delay is reasonable has to be considered in the light of all the circumstances of the special guardianship application, particularly the complexity of the proceedings and the conduct of the parties.

CA 1989, s 1(5) requires that the court shall not make any order 'unless it considers that doing so would be better for the child than making no order at all'. This principle requires the court to be satisfied that the making of a SGO will improve things for the child. Hence, the burden is on the applicant to establish that on a balance of probabilities it is in the child's best interests that the SGO should be made. The proper application of s 1(5) is inconsistent with any particular factors being given special importance. The weight and importance to be given to any factor will depend upon, and vary according to, the circumstances of the individual case examined from the point of view of the child. A special guardianship application can only be made by someone other than a parent of the child, (see CA 1989, s 14A(2)(b) and para **[706]**). Hence, different considerations apply from those applicable to proceedings arising from a parental dispute regarding the exercise of parental responsibility. In the latter case, if the parents reach agreement no order will usually be necessary, save where judicial endorsement of the agreement is considered by the court to be better for the child than relying on the agreement itself. In the case of a special guardianship application, however, if it is in the child's best interests for the applicant to acquire exclusive legally secure parental responsibility, an order will be better for the child than making no order at all. Maintaining the status quo by not making an order will not promote the child's welfare to the same degree. It is open to the court to conclude, however, that instead of a SGO, some other order (most likely a s 8 residence order) would be better for the child.

Section 115(2) and (4)

[519.3]

The amendments made to the CA 1989, s 5 by s 115(4), so as to empower a special guardian to appoint a guardian in the event of his death, are discussed in the context of the CA 1989, s 14C(1), (see para **[743]**).

Schedule 3

[519.4]

Further minor and consequential amendments to the CA 1989 are made by ACA 2002, s 139(1) and Sch 3, paras 56–64, 68 and 70–72, so as to accommodate special guardianship within the overall context of the law relating to children provided by the 1989 Act.

Inter alia, and in particular, in the private law context a special guardian, like a parent or guardian, qualifies under s 10(4)(a) to apply for any s 8 order without leave of the court (see para 56(a)). A residence order may be made whilst a SGO order is in force, but the CA 1989, s 10(7)(a) as inserted by para 56(d), provides that an application for a residence order requires leave of the court if, apart from this subsection, such leave is not required. A special guardian may be named in a s 16 family assistance order, (see ACA 2002, Sch 3, para 58).

In the public law context local authorities have a duty to consider whether to provide advice and assistance under s 24, to a former looked after child aged between 16 and 21 with respect to whom a SGO is in force, or, if he has reached the age of 18, was in force when he reached that age (see Sch 3, para 60(a)). The making of a SGO automatically discharges a care order relating to the child by virtue of the CA 1989, s 91(5A)(a) as inserted (see Sch 3, para 68). Special guardianship is intended to create a new family for the child with the special guardian/s, supported by the state, but free from state control over the exercise of parental responsibility. The court must therefore be satisfied, applying the CA 1989, s 1 principle that it is in the child's best interests for the local authority to cease to share parental responsibility with the birth family and for their control over the child's upbringing to pass virtually exclusively to the special guardian/s. A SGO also discharges any contact order in respect of the child under the CA 1989, s 34, see s 91(5A)(b) as inserted, as the care order upon which the s 34 order is based will have been discharged. The court, in carrying out its duty before making a SGO, of considering whether to make a contact order, will need to consider whether it is in the child's interests for an order to be made regarding his contact with anyone with whom he has been having contact under s 34 prior to the making of the SGO. A SGO does not discharge a supervision order regarding the child, but the making of a SGO will be a significant change of circumstances relevant to any application to vary or discharge the supervision order.

A care order may be made while a SGO is in force, in which case the local authority has power to determine the extent to which a special guardian may exercise his parental responsibility, see CA 1989, s 33(3)(b) as amended by Sch 3, para 63(a). Where a child is in the care of a local authority, the authority's duty under CA 1989, s 34(1) to allow the child reasonable contact with his family includes any special guardian of his (see Sch 3 para 64(a)).

[520]

---

116 Accommodation of children in need etc

(1)   In section 17 of the 1989 Act (provision of services for children in need, their families and others), in subsection (6) (services that may be provided in exercise of the functions under that section) after 'include' there is inserted 'providing accommodation and'.

(2)   In section 22 of that Act (general duty of local authority in relation to children looked after by them), in subsection (1) (looked after children include those provided with accommodation, with exceptions) before '23B' there is inserted '17'.

(3)   In section 24A of that Act (advice and assistance for certain children and young persons aged 16 or over), in subsection (5), for 'or, in exceptional circumstances, cash' there is substituted

'and, in exceptional circumstances, assistance may be given—

(a)   by providing accommodation, if in the circumstances assistance may not be given in respect of the accommodation under section 24B, or

(b)   in cash'.

NOTES

Initial Commencement

Royal Assent

Royal Assent: 7 November 2002: (no specific commencement provision).

Extent

This section does not extend to Scotland: see s 149(2).

General

[521]

This section was inserted by Parliament prior to the House of Lords decision in the conjoined appeals in *R v London Borough of Barnet (ex parte G); R v London Borough of Lambeth (ex parte W)* [2003] UKHL 57. Prior to that decision, the majority Court of Appeal decision in the *Lambeth* case (known as *W v London Borough of Lambeth* [2002] EWCA Civ 613) had held, on 3 May 2002, that it was unlawful for a local authority to provide accommodation for a child together with his/her family using the powers contained in CA 1989, s 17. Parliament amended s 17 to make it explicit that local authorities could indeed lawfully provide such accommodation under s 17 powers. Other changes of a similar nature were also made to the CA 1989, as set out below.

Section 116(1)

[522]

The services that may be provided by a Local Authority to children and need and their families, under CA 1989, s 17, may include the provision of accommodation, as well as services in kind and, exceptionally, cash. Although the House of Lords in *R v London Borough of Barnet (ex parte G); R v London Borough of Lambeth (ex parte W)* [2003] UKHL 57 established that local authorities could use s 17 to provide families with children in need with accommodation, the limitations on the enforceability by individual families of such 'target duties' were set out in their Lordships' judgments.

Section 116(2)

[523]

This amendment was also made at the time of the above-mentioned Court of Appeal judgment, to clarify the definition of a 'looked after' child in the Children Act when the family was provided with accommodation under s 17(6), as amended above.

Section 116(3)

[524]

This amends CA 1989, s 24A, so as to empower Local Authorities to provide accommodation for those for whom assistance cannot be given by way of accommodation under CA 1989, s 24B.

This provision concerns those who qualify for 'advice and assistance' under that Part of the Children Act. To qualify in this respect, the person must *either* (a) be aged 16 to 20 and be subject to a special guardianship order (or, if aged 18 to 20, was so subject on reaching the age of 18) *and* also have been looked after by the local authority immediately before the special guardianship order was made, *or* (b) be under the age of 21, and at any time after reaching the age of sixteen was, but no longer is, looked after, fostered or accommodated.

CA 1989, s 24B concerns, in respect of the power to provide accommodation, young people receiving employment, education and training. The amended s 24A therefore extends the power to provide accommodation in other contexts.

[525]

> ### 117 Inquiries by local authorities into representations
>
> (1) In section 24D of the 1989 Act (representations: sections 23A to 24B), after subsection (1) there is inserted—
>
> > '(1A) Regulations may be made by the Secretary of State imposing time limits on the making of representations under subsection (1).'
>
> (2) Section 26 of that Act (procedure for considering other representations) is amended as follows.
> (3) In subsection (3) (which makes provision as to the persons by whom, and the matters in respect of which, representations may be made), for 'functions under this Part' there is substituted 'qualifying functions'.
> (4) After that subsection there is inserted—
>
> > '(3A) The following are qualifying functions for the purposes of subsection (3)—
> >
> > > (a)   functions under this Part,
> > > (b)   such functions under Part 4 or 5 as are specified by the Secretary of State in regulations.
> >
> > (3B) The duty under subsection (3) extends to representations (including complaints) made to the authority by—
> >
> > > (a)   any person mentioned in section 3(1) of the Adoption and Children Act 2002 (persons for whose needs provision is made by the Adoption Service) and any other person to whom

arrangements for the provision of adoption support services (within the meaning of that Act) extend,

(b)   such other person as the authority consider has sufficient interest in a child who is or may be adopted to warrant his representations being considered by them,

about the discharge by the authority of such functions under the Adoption and Children Act 2002 as are specified by the Secretary of State in regulations.'

(5)   In subsection (4) (procedure to require involvement of independent person), after paragraph (b) there is inserted—

'but this subsection is subject to subsection (5A).'

(6)   After that subsection there is inserted—

'(4A)   Regulations may be made by the Secretary of State imposing time limits on the making of representations under this section.'

(7)   After subsection (5) there is inserted—

'(5A)   Regulations under subsection (5) may provide that subsection (4) does not apply in relation to any consideration or discussion which takes place as part of a procedure for which provision is made by the regulations for the purpose of resolving informally the matters raised in the representations.'

NOTES

Initial Commencement

To be appointed

To be appointed: see s 148(1), (2).

Appointment

Appointment (for the purpose of making regulations): 7 December 2004: see SI 2004/3203, art 2(1)(m)(xi); appointment (for remaining purposes): 30 December 2005: see SI 2005/2213, art 2(k).

Extent

This section does not extend to Scotland: see s 149(2).

General

[526]

This section amends CA 1989, ss 24D and 26, so as to alter the legal framework for the complaints procedures governing children and the actions of local authorities, and also to bring within their scope a range of functions under the ACA 2002 and associated regulations.

In England, the Children Act 1989 Representations Procedure (England) Regulations 2006 (SI 2006/1738) (CA1989RPER 2006) came into force on 1 September 2006 and, other than for transitional cases, replace the Representations Procedure (England) Regulations 1991 (SI 1991/894). *Getting the Best from Complaints: Social Care Complaints and Representations for Children, Young People and Others* is guidance issued in August 2006 by the DfES, under the Local Authority Social Services Act 1970, s 7.

In Wales, the Representations Procedure (Children) (Wales) Regulations 2005 (SI 2005/3365) (RPCWR 2005) came into force on 1 April 2006.

Section 117(1)

[527]

This inserts a new s 24D(1A) into the CA 1989, to enable the creation of regulations that impose time limits on making complaints. In England, the CA1989RPER 2006, reg 9, imposes a general deadline of 12 months, with a discretion for the local authority to extend that limit if it would not be reasonable to expect the complaint to have been made within 12 months and it is still possible to consider the complaint 'effectively and fairly'. In Wales, there is no deadline.

Section 117(2)

[528]

See s 117(3)–(7) for the amendments to the CA 1989, s 26.

Section 117(3)

[529]

This amends CA 1989, s 26(3) so that the definition of the persons who can make complaints, and the matters about which complaints may be made, are defined by reference to 'qualifying functions', which are then referred to in the remainder of the amended s 26 and either, for England, the CA1989RPER 2006, or for Wales, the RPCWR 2005. See below.

Section 117(4)

[530]

This inserts a new s 26(3A) and (3B) into the CA 1989.

CA 1989, s 26(3A) allows complaints to be made about functions under CA 1989, Pt III, and also about 'specified functions' under CA 1989, Pts IV and V. In England, unlike the revised procedures for complaints about adult social services (see the Local Authority Social Services Complaints (England) Regulations 2006 (SI 2006/1681)), there are fewer restrictions on complaints being made within the context of ongoing litigation in public law cases under the Children Act. It remains to be seen how this will operate in practice, with the potential for overlap with the functions of CAFCASS, Welsh Family Proceedings Officers, and the court.

England

[531]

Under the CA1989RPER 2006, reg 3, the specified functions under CA 1989, Pts IV and V are applications for care and supervision orders, the way the local authority exercises its parental responsibility under care orders (including interim care orders: see CA 1989, s 31(11)), the way it carries out its functions under supervision orders (including interim supervision orders), local authority suspension of, or departure from, its obligations regarding contact imposed by a court order or under the duties imposed by s 34, child assessment orders, applications for emergency protection orders, and the exercise of its power to return the child to his/her carer, while the EPO is in force, under the provisions of CA 1989, s 44(1) and (11).

Wales

[532]

Under RPCWR 2005, reg 7, the qualifying functions are wider than in England regarding the CA 1989, but do not include functions under the ACA 2002 (see below for England). They cover all functions under CA 1989, ss 31, 33, 34, 35, 43, 44 and 47. So, for example, they cover s 47 enquiries, and all aspects of the local authority's functions under s 34 in relation to contact.

England only

[533]

Section 26(3B) defines the persons who may complain about the exercise of powers and duties under the ACA 2002 and associated regulations, and the regulations define the specified functions about which they may complain.

Any person mentioned in ACA 2002, s 3(1) may complain, as may any other person to whom arrangements for the provision of adoption support services extend (see notes to ACA 2002, ss 3 and 4 (paras **[120]**–**[124]** and **[126]**–**[134]**)). Others may complain, if the local authority considers they have 'sufficient interest' in a child who is adopted, or may be adopted, to justify the complaint being considered – a wide power.

In England, CA1989RPER 2006, reg 4, defines the specified functions about which they may complain:

(a)   the provision of prescribed adoption support services as defined in the Adoption Support Services Regulations 2005 (SI 2005/691), reg 3 (see note to ACA 2002, s 4, paras **[126]**–**[134]**), save that it excludes discussion groups for adoptive parents, natural parents or former guardians;

(b)   assessments, plans and reviews of adoption support;

(c)   the powers and duties to place children for adoption under ACA 2002, ss 18–29, including applications for placement orders and the way parental responsibility is shared and exercised under ACA 2002, s 25;

(d)   the powers and duties to remove children who are, or may be, placed for adoption, under ACA 2002, ss 30–35;

(e)   the powers and duties to remove children in non-agency cases, under ACA 2002, ss 36–40;

(f)   functions under the AAR Adoption Agencies Regulations 2005 (SI 2005/389), Pts 3, 5, 6, 7, and reg 46 and 47 (duties of adoption agency when considering adoption; duties regarding proposed match; placement and review of adoptive children; case records; and contact for children once a decision has been taken to place for adoption or where the s 27 power is used to depart from contact obligations under the Act); and

(g)   functions under the AWFER Adoptions with a Foreign Element Regulations 2005 (SI 2005/392), reg 10 and Pt 3, Ch 3 (parental responsibility prior to adoption abroad, and various powers relating to Convention adoptions).

Section 117(5)

[534]

CA 1989, s 26(4), governing requirements to have independent involvement when local authorities are considering complaints, is now amended to enable regulations to place restrictions on this duty. See note to s 117(7) below (para **[536]**).

Section 117(6)

[535]

This inserts a new s 26(4A) into the CA 1989, to enable the regulations to impose time limits on making complaints. See note to s 117(1) above (para **[527]**).

Section 117(7)

[536]

This inserts a new s 26(5A) into the CA 1989, and enables the regulations to exclude the requirements of independent involvement when complaints are considered within the context of informal resolution. In England, under the CA1989RPER 2006, at the formal stage an independent person must be appointed under reg 17. CA1989RPER 2006, regs 14–16 govern the initial procedure for attempting local resolution prior to that stage, and there is now no requirement to appoint an independent person at that stage. In Wales, under RPCWR 2005, reg 17, an independent person must be appointed at the formal stage. Under the Social Services Complaints Procedure (Wales) Regulations 2005 (SI 2005/3366), reg 22, a person dissatisfied with the outcome of such investigations can request that the Welsh Assembly appoints an independent panel. Plans to provide access to such panels in England have currently been abandoned.

[537]

118 Review of cases of looked after children

(1) In section 26 of the 1989 Act (review of cases of looked after children, etc), in subsection (2) (regulations as to reviews)—

(a) in paragraph (e), 'to consider' is omitted and after 'their care' there is inserted—

'(i) to keep the section 31A plan for the child under review and, if they are of the opinion that some change is required, to revise the plan, or make a new plan, accordingly,

(ii) to consider',

(b) in paragraph (f), 'to consider' is omitted and after the second mention of 'the authority' there is inserted—

'(i) if there is no plan for the future care of the child, to prepare one,

(ii) if there is such a plan for the child, to keep it under review and, if they are of the opinion that some change is required, to revise the plan or make a new plan, accordingly,

(iii) to consider',

(c) after paragraph (j) there is inserted—

'(k) for the authority to appoint a person in respect of each case to carry out in the prescribed manner the functions mentioned in subsection (2A) and any prescribed function'.

(2) After that subsection there is inserted—

'(2A) The functions referred to in subsection (2)(k) are—

(a) participating in the review of the case in question,

(b) monitoring the performance of the authority's functions in respect of the review,

(c) referring the case to an officer of the Children and Family Court Advisory and Support Service, if the person appointed under subsection (2)(k) considers it appropriate to do so.

(2B) A person appointed under subsection (2)(k) must be a person of a prescribed description.

> (2C) In relation to children whose cases are referred to officers under subsection (2A)(c), the Lord Chancellor may by regulations—
>
> (a) extend any functions of the officers in respect of family proceedings (within the meaning of section 12 of the Criminal Justice and Court Services Act 2000) to other proceedings,
>
> (b) require any functions of the officers to be performed in the manner prescribed by the regulations.'
>
> **NOTES**
>
> **Initial Commencement**
>
> **To be appointed**
>
> To be appointed: see s 148(1), (2).
>
> **Appointment**
>
> Appointment: 21 May 2004: see SI 2004/1403, art 2.
>
> **Extent**
>
> This section does not extend to Scotland: see s 149(2).

General

[538]

CA 1989, s 26(2) and the Review of Children's Cases Regulations 1991 (SI 1991/895) govern the duties of local authorities to hold reviews of the cases of looked after children and the manner in which those reviews are held. This is part of a framework of planning for children who are looked after by local authorities and to avoid drift and delay. They are often referred to as LAC Reviews, or statutory reviews. The system was brought in at the same time as the implementation of the Children Act 1989 in October 1991.

However, the chair of such reviews was often a person who worked for the same local authority, and there was a lack of independence, or perceived lack of independence, of that person.

At the same time, Local Authorities were obliged to prepare a written plan for each looked after child, under the Arrangements for Placement of Children (General) Regulations 1991 (SI 1991/890), which became universally known as a care plan because of the terminology in the s 7 *Guidance to the Children Act 1989* (Vols 3 and 4) produced by the Department of Health. Guidance on the content of such care plans was subsequently published, to try to ensure uniformity, but the obligation to create a care plan remained rooted in the regulations and Guidance – albeit statutory guidance – rather than statute, and there was no explicit statutory restriction on a court making a care order, even if the care plan was deficient or even non-existent.

After the implementation of the Human Rights Act 1998, the House of Lords in *Re S (minors) (Care Order: Implementation of Care Plan); Re W (Minors) (Care Order: Adequacy of Care Plan)* [2002] UKHL 10, [2002] 1 FLR 815 accepted the criticisms made by the Court of Appeal of local authorities breaching the human rights of families in some cases within the care planning process and provision of resources, but rejected the Court of Appeal solution. Instead, their Lordships decided that a significant part of the solution lay in the hands of Parliament. This led to legislative changes in the new Act.

The Act now provides for statutory obligations in respect of care plans (see s 121 and the new ss 31(3A) and 31A to the CA 1989).

In addition, it provides for amendments to the Review of Children's Cases Regulations 1991, by changes introduced by s 118.

See also the Adoption Agencies Regulations 2005 (SI 2005/389), regs 36 and 37 and the Adoption Agencies (Wales) Regulations 2005 (SI 2005/1313), regs 37 and 38 (paras [971] and [973]), in the context of children authorised to be placed for adoption, where similar provisions are made to those for children looked after under the CA 1989.

Section 118(1)

[539]

CA 1989, s 26(2) is amended. The regulations (see below) can provide that the LAC review must consider, review, and, as necessary, amend or replace, the s 31A care plan for the child. They may also create an obligation to make a care plan if none exists, and to provide for the consideration, review, amendment or replacement of any Plan.

In addition, a new CA 1989, s 26(2)(k) provides a power for regulations to require the appointment of a person for each child's case to perform 'prescribed functions', in addition to the functions set out in a new s 26(2A): see below.

The Review of Children's Cases (Amendment) (England) Regulations 2004 (SI 2004/1419) came into force in England on 27 September 2004, and amend the Review of Children's Cases Regulations 1991 (SI 1991/895). In Wales, the Review of Children's Cases (Amendment) (Wales) Regulations (SI 2004/1449) came into force on 1 September 2004. These regulations apply to looked after children.

Similar provisions are made in the context of adoption, once a child is authorised to be placed (see the Adoption Agencies Regulations 2005 (SI 2005/389), reg 37 and the Adoption Agencies (Wales) Regulations 2005 (SI 2005/1313), reg 38.

Section 118(2)

[540]

The Review of Children's Cases Regulations 1991 (SI 1991/895), reg 2A (as amended), requires the local authority to appoint an independent reviewing officer (IRO) for each case of a looked after child. A new CA 1989, s 26(2A) requires the IRO to participate in each review, monitor the performance by the local authority of all of that authority's functions in respect of that review, and if he/she considers it appropriate to do so, refer the case to CAFCASS. The duty in relation to monitoring encompasses all aspects of the preparation for reviews, the conduct of reviews, and the subsequent implementation of the decisions of the review and care plan, and therefore requires a much higher degree of active involvement by the IRO than before September 2004. Reciprocal duties are placed upon the case-holding social workers to keep the IRO informed between reviews: see below. The reviewing duties are now to be seen as a dynamic process, rather than a one to hold a sequence of reviews on specific dates.

[541]

Under a new s 26(2B) and reg 2A, the IRO must be a General Social Care Council-registered social worker with adequate experience (in Wales, must hold a DipSW, Social Work degree or similar qualification recognised by the Care Council for Wales), and no person involved in the management of the case may be appointed as IRO, nor a person under the direct management of such a person (nor, in turn, their line manager), nor a person under the direct management of a person with control of resources allocated to the case (reg 2A(2), (3) and (4)). In the context of children authorised to be placed for adoption, see the requirement for experience in adoption work in Adoption Agencies Regulations 2005, reg 37(3)/the Adoption Agencies (Wales) Regulations 2005, reg 38, and the cross-reference (by reg 37(1)/reg 38(1)) to CA 1989, s 26(2A) of the Act.

[542]

The IRO must ensure that reviews are carried out in accordance with the regulations, and in particular ensure that the child's views are understood and taken into account, and that the Review identifies the persons responsible for implementing each decision. He/she must ensure that any failure properly to review a case, or to take proper steps to make arrangements in accordance with the Review of Children's Cases Regulations 1991, reg 8 (implementation of decisions arising out of Reviews), is brought to the attention of senior management (reg 2A(6)).

If the child wishes to commence Children Act proceedings, the IRO must assist him/her to obtain legal advice or find out whether there is a suitable adult willing and able to assist or bring proceedings on behalf of the child (reg 2A(7)).

[543]

The IRO has the power to direct that a review is held earlier than the date previously fixed or the date chosen by the social worker (new reg 3(3)).

In addition to the obligations of the IRO, those holding responsibility for the child's case within the authority – social worker and line management – have a duty to inform the IRO of any significant failure in the care planning arrangements or any 'significant change in circumstances' in the case that affect the plan (new reg 8A).

[544]

A new CA 1989, s 26(2C) created a power to make regulations governing the actions of CAFCASS upon receipt of a referral by the IRO under CA 1989, s 26(2A) and SI 1991/895, reg 2A. The Regulations are the Children and Family Court Advisory and Support Service (Reviewed Case Referral) Regulations 2004 (SI 2004/2187). Regulation 3 extends the powers of CAFCASS to bring claims for judicial review, under the Human Rights Act 1998, s 7, or to pursue 'other procedures', following an IRO referral. Regulation 5 governs the procedure to be followed, and CAFCASS should aim for a report to be completed within two weeks and send a copy to the IRO, the chief executive of the local authority and anybody else specified by the IRO or considered appropriate by CAFCASS. If CAFCASS feel that the referral was inappropriate, they can refer it back to the IRO for further information or make a decision on the case in any event (reg 6). If deciding to take legal action, the officer should aim to do so within six weeks of the referral. The outcome of the proceedings brought by CAFCASS should then be the subject of a further report to those above (reg 7).

[545]

---

119 Advocacy services

NOTE
This section inserts new s 26A into the Children Act 1989. The text of this section will be found at para **[781]**.

General

[546]

This section creates a new s 26A in the CA 1989, to impose duties in relation to the provision of advocacy services and publicity about those arrangements (see paras **[781]**–**[782]**).

[547]

120 Meaning of 'harm' in the 1989 Act

In section 31 of the 1989 Act (care and supervision orders), at the end of the definition of 'harm' in subsection (9) there is inserted 'including, for example, impairment suffered from seeing or hearing the ill-treatment of another'.

NOTES

Initial Commencement

To be appointed
To be appointed: see s 148(1), (2).

Appointment
Appointment: 31 January 2005: see SI 2004/3203, art 2(2).

Extent
This section does not extend to Scotland: see s 149(2).

General

[548]

This section gives the court power to make care and supervision orders. Being a witness to cruelty inflicted on another is now included in the definition of 'harm' as a ground for consideration provided the witness has suffered or is at risk of suffering some 'impairment' as a result.

[549]–[550]

121 Care plans

NOTE
This section inserts new s 31(3A) and 31A into the Children Act 1989. The text of these sections will be found at para **[783]**.

122 Interests of children in proceedings

(1) In section 41 of the 1989 Act (specified proceedings)—

(a) in subsection (6), after paragraph (h) there is inserted—

'(hh) on an application for the making or revocation of a placement order (within the meaning of section 21 of the Adoption and Children Act 2002);',

(b) after that subsection there is inserted—

'(6A) The proceedings which may be specified under subsection (6)(i) include (for example) proceedings for the making, varying or discharging of a section 8 order.'

(2) In section 93 of the 1989 Act (rules of court), in subsection (2), after paragraph (b) there is inserted—

'(bb) for children to be separately represented in relevant proceedings,'.

NOTES

Initial Commencement

To be appointed
To be appointed: see s 148(1), (2).

Appointment
Sub-s (1)(a): appointment: 30 December 2005: see SI 2005/2213, art 2(k); sub-ss (1)(b), (2): appointment: 7 December 2004: see SI 2004/3203, art 2(1)(l).

Extent
This section does not extend to Scotland: see s 149(2).

General

[551]

CA 1989, s 41 deals with separate representation for children in appropriate cases. Adoption and placement proceedings are now added to the list of applications where this may be considered.

[552]

Part 3
Miscellaneous and Final Provisions

Chapter 1
Miscellaneous

Advertisements in the United Kingdom

123 Restriction on advertisements etc

(1) A person must not—

(a) publish or distribute an advertisement or information to which this section applies, or

(b) cause such an advertisement or information to be published or distributed.

(2) This section applies to an advertisement indicating that—

(a) the parent or guardian of a child wants the child to be adopted,

(b) a person wants to adopt a child,

(c) a person other than an adoption agency is willing to take any step mentioned in paragraphs (a) to (e), (g) and (h) and (so far as relating to those paragraphs) (i) of section 92(2),

(d) a person other than an adoption agency is willing to receive a child handed over to him with a view to the child's adoption by him or another, or

(e) a person is willing to remove a child from the United Kingdom for the purposes of adoption.

(3) This section applies to—

(a) information about how to do anything which, if done, would constitute an offence under section 85 or 93, section 11 or 50 of the Adoption (Scotland) Act 1978 (c 28) or Article 11 or 58 of the Adoption (Northern Ireland) Order 1987 (SI 1987/2203 (NI 22)) (whether or not the information includes a warning that doing the thing in question may constitute an offence),

(b) information about a particular child as a child available for adoption.

(4) For the purposes of this section and section 124—

(a) publishing or distributing an advertisement or information means publishing it or distributing it to the public and includes doing so by electronic means (for example, by means of the internet),

(b) the public includes selected members of the public as well as the public generally or any section of the public.

(5) Subsection (1) does not apply to publication or distribution by or on behalf of an adoption agency.

(6) The Secretary of State may by order make any amendments of this section which he considers necessary or expedient in consequence of any developments in technology relating to publishing or distributing advertisements or other information by electronic or electro-magnetic means.

(7) References to an adoption agency in this section include a prescribed person outside the United Kingdom exercising functions corresponding to those of an adoption agency, if the functions are being exercised in prescribed circumstances.

'Prescribed' means prescribed by regulations made by the Secretary of State.

(8) Before exercising the power conferred by subsection (6) or (7), the Secretary of State must consult the Scottish Ministers, the Department of Health, Social Services and Public Safety and the Assembly.

(9) In this section—

(a) 'adoption agency' includes a Scottish or Northern Irish adoption agency,

(b) references to adoption are to the adoption of persons, wherever they may be habitually resident, effected under the law of any country or territory, whether within or outside the British Islands.

NOTES

Initial Commencement

To be appointed

To be appointed: see s 148(1)–(3).

Appointment

Appointment: 30 December 2005: see SI 2005/2213, art 2(l).

General

[553]

This is part of the court's general control of the process of adoption. Only recognised adoption agencies may advertise. This section is intended to prevent others from offering children for adoption and to deter those who are seeking a child for adoption. Unfortunately the restriction can only apply within the jurisdiction and it does not operate to prevent such steps being taken by persons or organisations outside of the United Kingdom. However, by ACA 2002, s 123(9)(b) the restriction does cover those within the jurisdiction unlawfully advertising adoption details in relation to the adoption of persons who reside outside the jurisdiction, wherever they are. Note that ACA 2002, s 123(6) contemplates rules being made to prevent unlawful publication on electronic media, such as the internet.

[554]

124 Offence of breaching restriction under section 123

(1) A person who contravenes section 123(1) is guilty of an offence.

(2) A person is not guilty of an offence under this section unless it is proved that he knew or had reason to suspect that section 123 applied to the advertisement or information.

But this subsection only applies if sufficient evidence is adduced to raise an issue as to whether the person had the knowledge or reason mentioned.

(3) A person guilty of an offence under this section is liable on summary conviction to imprisonment for a term not exceeding three months, or a fine not exceeding level 5 on the standard scale, or both.

NOTES

Initial Commencement

To be appointed

To be appointed: see s 148(1)–(3).

Appointment

Appointment: 30 December 2005: see SI 2005/2213, art 2(l).

General

[555]

Proving that someone is in breach may not be straightforward because it must be proved that the defendant knew or had reason to suspect that what they were doing was wrong.

This is allied to a degree of knowledge of the provisions of ACA 2002, s 123. Also note that the subsection is only relevant where there is sufficient evidence to suggest there may be an issue as to such knowledge or reason.

A fine on level 5 means a fine up to £5,000.

[556]

Adoption and Children Act Register

125 Adoption and Children Act Register

(1)   Her Majesty may by Order in Council make provision for the Secretary of State to establish and maintain a register, to be called the Adoption and Children Act Register, containing—

(a)   prescribed information about children who are suitable for adoption and prospective adopters who are suitable to adopt a child,

(b)   prescribed information about persons included in the register in pursuance of paragraph (a) in respect of things occurring after their inclusion.

(2)   For the purpose of giving assistance in finding persons with whom children may be placed for purposes other than adoption, an Order under this section may—

(a)   provide for the register to contain information about such persons and the children who may be placed with them, and

(b)   apply any of the other provisions of this group of sections (that is, this section and sections 126 to 131), with or without modifications.

(3)   The register is not to be open to public inspection or search.

(4)   An Order under this section may make provision about the retention of information in the register.

(5)   Information is to be kept in the register in any form the Secretary of State considers appropriate.

NOTES

Initial Commencement

To be appointed

To be appointed: see s 148(1), (2), (4).

General

[557]

The Secretary of State has the power to maintain the Adoption and Children Act Register to seek to match children with prospective adopters and other prospective carers.

Section 125(1)

[558]

The Adoption and Children Act Register can be established and maintained by the Secretary of State, upon the appropriate Order being made, containing 'prescribed information' about children suitable for adoption and prospective adopters who are suitable to adopt them. As they must already be 'suitable' this means they must already have been approved by the relevant adoption agencies (see s 131(2)). The Register can then be updated with new information.

'Order in Council' means one approved by resolution of both Houses of Parliament (see s 131(4)) and, if it extends to Wales, the draft must be approved by the Welsh Assembly (see s 131(6)).

'prescribed information' means as required by the Order (see s 131(1)).

Section 125(2)

[559]

The above Order may extend the use of the Register beyond adoption, for the purposes of finding matches for other purposes such as long term fostering. To this end, the Register may contain the details of prospective non-adoptive carers and children looking for such matches and may apply the provisions of ss 126–131 to this end, perhaps with modifications.

Section 125(3)

[560]

The Register cannot be examined or searched by the public.

Section 125(4) and (5)

[561]

The order may contain requirements in respect of retaining information, and can be kept in any appropriate format as required by the Secretary of State.

[562]

---

126   Use of an organisation to establish the register

(1)   The Secretary of State may make an arrangement with an organisation under which any function of his under an Order under section 125 of establishing and maintaining the register, and disclosing information entered in, or compiled from information entered in, the register to any person is performed wholly or partly by the organisation on his behalf.

(2)   The arrangement may include provision for payments to be made to the organisation by the Secretary of State.

(3)   If the Secretary of State makes an arrangement under this section with an organisation, the organisation is to perform the functions exercisable by virtue of this section in accordance with any directions given by the Secretary of State and the directions may be of general application (or general application in any part of Great Britain) or be special directions.

(4)   An exercise of the Secretary of State's powers under subsection (1) or (3) requires the agreement of the Scottish Ministers (if the register applies to Scotland) and of the Assembly (if the register applies to Wales).

(5)   References in this group of sections to the registration organisation are to any organisation for the time being performing functions in respect of the register by virtue of arrangements under this section.

NOTES

Initial Commencement

To be appointed

To be appointed: see s 148(1), (2), (4).

General

[563]

This Section enables the Secretary of State to use the services of an organisation in creating and operating the Adoption and Children Act Register, and that body is then in that respect subject to the directions of the Secretary of State.

With effect from 1 December 2004, the organisation is the British Association for Adoption and Fostering, and the relevant arrangements for England are set out in Circular LAC (2004) 27, which is Section 7 Guidance to Local Authorities. It is to be cancelled on 1 December 2007. The arrangements for Wales are set out in National Assembly for Wales Circular 53/2004.

A child can be referred after a local search of three months' duration or if the child is the subject of an ICO and the relevant consents and court agreement have been obtained. Prospective adopters can be referred immediately after approval or at the end of a three months' 'holding period', at the end of which the prospective adopter can self-refer. There is no longer a requirement to refer a child to the Register if the agency is actively considering a local match, as defined in the circular.

The agencies must ensure that all relevant staff and all adopters are aware of these provisions.

References to adoption agencies within the context of the Register are to agencies in England and Wales (see note to s 130, para [590]).

Section 126(1)

[564]

The Secretary of State can arrange for an organisation, in whole or in part, to perform his functions under s 125 regarding the Adoption and Children Act Register, and to disclose information from the Register to third parties.

See general note above for the current arrangements.

'organisation' means a public body, private organisation or voluntary organisation (see s 131(1)).

Section 126(2)

[565]

To this end, payments can be made by the Secretary of State to that organisation.

Section 126(3)

[566]

The organisation must carry out those functions in accordance with the Secretary of State's directions. These can be general, or general in one part of Great Britain, or special directions.

Section 126(4)

[567]

The Welsh Assembly or Scottish Ministers must agree to any arrangement for the organisation to extend its role to Wales or Scotland. It currently extends to Wales (see National Assembly for Wales Circular 53/2004).

PART B – Statutes

Section 126(5)

[568]

Any reference in ss 125–131 to 'the registration organisation' means the organisation (currently BAAF) operating the Register under these powers.

[569]

---

127   Use of an organisation as agency for payments

(1)   An Order under section 125 may authorise an organisation with which an arrangement is made under section 126 to act as agent for the payment or receipt of sums payable by adoption agencies to other adoption agencies and may require adoption agencies to pay or receive such sums through the organisation.

(2)   The organisation is to perform the functions exercisable by virtue of this section in accordance with any directions given by the Secretary of State; and the directions may be of general application (or general application in any part of Great Britain) or be special directions.

(3)   An exercise of the Secretary of State's power to give directions under subsection (2) requires the agreement of the Scottish Ministers (if any payment agency provision applies to Scotland) and of the Assembly (if any payment agency provision applies to Wales).

NOTES

Initial Commencement

To be appointed
To be appointed: see s 148(1), (2), (4).

General

[570]

This section allows the organisation authorised to operate the Adoption and Children Act Register to act as the agent for payments passing between adoption agencies. See note to s 125 (paras **[557]**–**[561]**) for the details of the Register. See note to s 126 for the details of the organisation (currently BAAF) operating the Register (para **[563]**). References to adoption agencies within this context are to those in England and Wales (see note to s 130, paras **[590]**–**[593]**).

Section 127(1)

[571]

The Order in Council creating the Register (see note to s 125, paras **[557]**–**[561]**) can authorise the body operating the Register (see note to s 126, para **[563]**) to act as the agent for the receipt or provision of payments from one adoption agency to another, and can require those agencies to make such payments in this way. This allows for payments to be made where matches are made between prospective adopters (and other permanent carers: see note to s 125(2), para **[559]**) and children who are to be placed for adoption or in long-term foster care.

Section 127(2)

[572]

The organisation operating the Register must fulfil these duties under the directions of the Secretary of State, for which see the note to s 126(3) (para **[566]**).

Section 127(3)

[573]

As for s 126(4) (see note above, para [567]), the relevant consent is necessary if the scheme extends to Wales or Scotland. The scheme currently extends to Wales (see National Assembly for Wales Circular 53/2004).

[574]

---

128 Supply of information for the register

(1) An Order under section 125 may require adoption agencies to give prescribed information to the Secretary of State or the registration organisation for entry in the register.

(2) Information is to be given to the Secretary of State or the registration organisation when required by the Order and in the prescribed form and manner.

(3) An Order under section 125 may require an agency giving information which is entered on the register to pay a prescribed fee to the Secretary of State or the registration organisation.

(4) But an adoption agency is not to disclose any information to the Secretary of State or the registration organisation—

(a) about prospective adopters who are suitable to adopt a child, or persons who were included in the register as such prospective adopters, without their consent,

(b) about children suitable for adoption, or persons who were included in the register as such children, without the consent of the prescribed person.

(5) Consent under subsection (4) is to be given in the prescribed form.

NOTES
Initial Commencement
To be appointed
To be appointed: see s 148(1), (2), (4).

General

[575]

This section makes provision for adoption agencies to give information to either the Secretary of State or the organisation operating the Adoption and Children Act Register, for inclusion in that Register. See the note to s 125 for the Register (paras [557]–[561]) and the note to s 126 for the organisation (currently BAAF) operating the Register (para [563]). References to adoption agencies are to those in England and Wales (see note to s 130, paras [590]–[593]).

The provision relates to children who are suitable for adoption or prospective adopters who are suitable to adopt. It can only apply once an adoption agency has determined that the child ought to be placed for adoption, or that the adopters are suitable to have a child placed with them, under the provisions of the Adoption Agencies Regulations 2005 (SI 2005/389)/Adoption Agencies (Wales) Regulations 2005 (SI 2005/1313) (see s 131(2)).

Section 128(1)

[576]

The Order in Council establishing the Register (see note to s 125, paras [557]–[561]) may require adoption agencies to give information for inclusion in the Register. LAC Circular

27/2004 for England and National Assembly for Wales Circular 53/2004 set out the relevant arrangements. See these circulars for the detailed information required in the referral form.

Section 128(2)

[577]

See the above circulars for the forms to contain the prescribed information.

Section 128(3)

[578]

The Order in Council can require the payment of a fee by the adoption agency giving information for inclusion in the Register.

Section 128(4) and (5)

[579]

Information about prospective adopters cannot be given for inclusion in the Register without their consent. The consent of a prescribed person within the adoption agency must be given before information about children who are suitable to be adopted can be given for inclusion in the Register. Any consent must be given in a prescribed format.

'Registration organisation' means an organisation appointed under the provisions of s 126 to fulfil duties in relation to the Register: s 126(5) (see note to s 126, para [563]).

[580]

---

129 Disclosure of information

(1) Information entered in the register, or compiled from information entered in the register, may only be disclosed under subsection (2) or (3).

(2) Prescribed information entered in the register may be disclosed by the Secretary of State or the registration organisation—

(a) where an adoption agency is acting on behalf of a child who is suitable for adoption, to the agency to assist in finding prospective adopters with whom it would be appropriate for the child to be placed,

(b) where an adoption agency is acting on behalf of prospective adopters who are suitable to adopt a child, to the agency to assist in finding a child appropriate for adoption by them.

(3) Prescribed information entered in the register, or compiled from information entered in the register, may be disclosed by the Secretary of State or the registration organisation to any prescribed person for use for statistical or research purposes, or for other prescribed purposes.

(4) An Order under section 125 may prescribe the steps to be taken by adoption agencies in respect of information received by them by virtue of subsection (2).

(5) Subsection (1) does not apply—

(a) to a disclosure of information with the authority of the Secretary of State, or

(b) to a disclosure by the registration organisation of prescribed information to the Scottish Ministers (if the register applies to Scotland) or the Assembly (if the register applies to Wales).

(6) Information disclosed to any person under subsection (2) or (3) may be given on any prescribed terms or conditions.

(7) An Order under section 125 may, in prescribed circumstances, require a prescribed fee to be paid to the Secretary of State or the registration organisation—

(a)   by a prescribed adoption agency in respect of information disclosed under subsection (2), or

(b)   by a person to whom information is disclosed under subsection (3).

(8) If any information entered in the register is disclosed to a person in contravention of subsection (1), the person disclosing it is guilty of an offence.

(9) A person guilty of an offence under subsection (8) is liable on summary conviction to imprisonment for a term not exceeding three months, or a fine not exceeding level 5 on the standard scale, or both.

NOTES

Initial Commencement

To be appointed

To be appointed: see s 148(1), (2), (4).

General

[581]

This section governs the powers of the Secretary of State, or organisation acting on his behalf, to disclose information from the Adoption and Children Act Register. See the note to s 125 for the Register (paras [557]–[561]), and the note to s 126 for the organisation (currently BAAF) operating the Register (para [563]). It makes unauthorised disclosure a criminal offence. References to adoption agencies within this context are to those in England and Wales (see note to s 130, paras [590]–[593]).

Section 129(1)

[582]

Subject to disclosure made under the provisions of s 129(5), information from the Register, whether provided verbatim or in a format complied from the Register, can only be disclosed in accordance with s 129(2) and (3).

Section 129(2) and (4)

[583]

This is the principal disclosure provision. The Secretary of State or organisation operating the Register on his behalf may disclose information about prospective adopters to an adoption agency seeking to find a match for a child, and vice versa for information about such a child to an agency who may have a potential match by way of prospective adopter(s). It can be on prescribed terms and conditions (see s 129(6) below). The Order in Council may determine the steps that an agency must take upon receipt of the information.

Section 129(3)

[584]

The secondary disclosure provision permits the release of information from the Register, whether verbatim or compiled from the records, to a prescribed person for statistical or research purposes, or for other purposes that are prescribed. It can be on prescribed terms and conditions (see s 129(6) below).

Section 129(5)

[585]

Prescribed information from the Register can be provided by the organisation (currently BAAF) to the Welsh Assembly, without breaching s 129(1). The same would apply to provision to the Scottish Minister if the Register were extended to Scotland. The same applies to any information, not just prescribed information, if this is expressly authorised by the Secretary of State.

Section 129(6)

[586]

The provision of information to adoption agencies, researchers or for statistical purposes may be given on prescribed terms and conditions.

Section 129(7)

[587]

The Order in Council creating the Register may require the payment of a fee for the receipt of information.

Section 129(8) and (9)

[588]

Unauthorised disclosure of information from the Register is a criminal offence, punishable with a maximum sentence of three months' imprisonment or a fine no higher than level 5 (or both).

'Prescribed' means by the Order in Council creating the Register (see s 131(1)).

'Registration organisation' means an organisation appointed under the provisions of s 126 to fulfil duties in relation to the Register: s 126(5) (see note to s 126, paras [563]–[568]).

[589]

---

130 Territorial application

(1) In this group of sections, 'adoption agency' means—

(a)   a local authority in England,
(b)   a registered adoption society whose principal office is in England.

(2) An Order under section 125 may provide for any requirements imposed on adoption agencies in respect of the register to apply—

(a)   to Scottish local authorities and to voluntary organisations providing a registered adoption service,
(b)   to local authorities in Wales and to registered adoption societies whose principal offices are in Wales,

and, in relation to the register, references to adoption agencies in this group of sections include any authorities or societies mentioned in paragraphs (a) and (b) to which an Order under that section applies those requirements.

(3)   For the purposes of this group of sections, references to the register applying to Scotland or Wales are to those requirements applying as mentioned in paragraph (a) or, as the case may be, (b) of subsection (2).

(4)   An Order under section 125 may apply any provision made by virtue of section 127—

> (a) to Scottish local authorities and to voluntary organisations providing a regis-tered adoption service,
> (b) to local authorities in Wales and to registered adoption societies whose principal offices are in Wales.
>
> (5) For the purposes of this group of sections, references to any payment agency provision applying to Scotland or Wales are to provision made by virtue of sec-tion 127 applying as mentioned in paragraph (a) or, as the case may be, (b) of subsection (4).
>
> **NOTES**
> **Initial Commencement**
> *To be appointed*
> To be appointed: see s 148(1), (2), (4).

General

[590]

This section governs the applicability of ss 125–131, concerning the Adoption and Children Act Register, to England, Scotland and Wales. See the note to s 125 for details of the Register (paras [557]–[561]).

Section 130(1)

[591]

Where there is a reference to an adoption agency, this means all local authorities in England and all registered adoption societies with their principal offices located in England, irrespective of any other provision made in relation to Wales or Scotland (see below).

Section 130(2) and (3)

[592]

The Order in Council creating the Register can extend any of the provisions regarding the Register to Wales or Scotland, in which case the definition of adoption agency for the purposes of the Register is extended to the relevant country. At the moment, it extends to Wales (see the note to s 126, (paras [563]–[568])).

Section 130(4) and (5)

[593]

The Order in Council can provide that the s 127 authorisation for the organisation operating the Register (currently BAAF), to act as the agent for the receipt or payment of money, can extend to Wales or Scotland as appropriate (see the note to s 127, (paras [570]–[573])).

[594]

> **131 Supplementary**
>
> (1) In this group of sections—
>
> (a) 'organisation' includes a public body and a private or voluntary organisation,
> (b) 'prescribed' means prescribed by an Order under section 125,
> (c) 'the register' means the Adoption and Children Act Register,
> (d) 'Scottish local authority' means a local authority within the meaning of the Regulation of Care (Scotland) Act 2001 (asp 4),

(e) 'voluntary organisation providing a registered adoption service' has the same meaning as in section 144(3).

(2) For the purposes of this group of sections—

(a) a child is suitable for adoption if an adoption agency is satisfied that the child ought to be placed for adoption,

(b) prospective adopters are suitable to adopt a child if an adoption agency is satisfied that they are suitable to have a child placed with them for adoption.

(3) Nothing authorised or required to be done by virtue of this group of sections constitutes an offence under section 93, 94 or 95.

(4) No recommendation to make an Order under section 125 is to be made to Her Majesty in Council unless a draft has been laid before and approved by resolution of each House of Parliament.

(5) If any provision made by an Order under section 125 would, if it were included in an Act of the Scottish Parliament, be within the legislative competence of that Parliament, no recommendation to make the Order is to be made to Her Majesty in Council unless a draft has been laid before, and approved by resolution of, the Parliament.

(6) No recommendation to make an Order under section 125 containing any provision in respect of the register is to be made to Her Majesty in Council if the register applies to Wales or the Order would provide for the register to apply to Wales, unless a draft has been laid before, and approved by resolution of, the Assembly.

(7) No recommendation to make an Order under section 125 containing any provision by virtue of section 127 is to be made to Her Majesty in Council if any payment agency provision applies to Wales or the Order would provide for any payment agency provision to apply to Wales, unless a draft has been laid before, and approved by resolution of, the Assembly.

NOTES

Initial Commencement

To be appointed

To be appointed: see s 148(1), (2), (4).

General

[595]

This section provides a number of definitions for interpreting ss 125–131 regarding the Adoption and Children Act Register, and for further delineating the scope of those sections.

Section 131(1)

[596]

A series of definitions in relation to the Register.

Section 131(2)

[597]

This limits the provisions of the Act regarding the Register, and the provision of information, to those children or prospective adopters whose status for the purposes of adoption has been determined in the affirmative by the relevant adoption agency. Information about children or prospective adopters cannot be provided to the Register until such approval has been given.

Section 131(3)

[598]

For the avoidance of doubt, nothing that is authorised to be done regarding the Register under ss 125–131, such as providing information, or making payments in respect of information, in order to facilitate an adoptive match, is to be construed as a criminal offence under ss 93–95. Those sections make it a criminal offence under certain circumstances to ask a person to find prospective adopters, offer to find a child for adoption, enter into an agreement to facilitate a child's adoption, etc (see notes to ss 93–95, paras [459]–[460], [462]–[467] and paras [469]–[472]).

Section 131(4), (5), (6) and (7)

[599]

Each House of Parliament in England must approve the Order in Council creating the power for the Secretary of State to create the Register. Similar provision is made regarding the Scottish Parliament or Welsh Assembly if the powers are to extend to either of those countries. At present, they apply to Wales: see note to s 125 (paras [557]–[561]).

'Section 144(3)' defines a Scottish adoption agency, and the need for a Scottish voluntary body to be registered in relation to the provision of particular services.

'This group of Sections' means ss 125–131: s 125(2)(b).

[600]

Other miscellaneous provisions

132 Amendment of Adoption (Scotland) Act 1978: contravention of sections 30 to 36 of this Act

After section 29 of the Adoption (Scotland) Act 1978 (c 28) there is inserted—

'**29A Contravention of sections 30 to 36 of Adoption and Children Act 2002**

(1) A person who contravenes any of the enactments specified in subsection (2) is guilty of an offence and liable on summary conviction to imprisonment for a term not exceeding three months, or a fine not exceeding level 5 on the standard scale, or both.

(2) Those enactments are—

(a) section 30(1), (2) and (3) (removal of child placed or who may be placed for adoption),

(b) sections 32(2)(b), 33(2) and 35(2) (return of child by prospective adopters),

(c) section 34(1) (removal of child in contravention of placement order),

(d) section 36(1) (removal of child in non-agency case), and

(e) section 36(5) (return of child to parent or guardian),

of the Adoption and Children Act 2002.'

NOTES

Initial Commencement

To be appointed
To be appointed: see s 148(5)(b).

Appointment
Appointment: 30 December 2005: see SSI 2005/643, art 2(b).

133 Scottish restriction on bringing children into or out of United Kingdom

(1) In section 50 of the Adoption (Scotland) Act 1978 (restriction on removal of children for adoption outside Great Britain)—

(a) in subsection (1), 'not being a parent or guardian or relative of the child' is omitted,

(b) after subsection (3) there is inserted—

'(4) The Scottish Ministers may by regulations provide for subsection (1) to apply with modifications, or not to apply, if—

(a) the prospective adopters are parents, relatives or guardians of the child (or one of them is), or

(b) the prospective adopter is a step-parent of the child,

and any conditions prescribed by the regulations are met.

(5) On the occasion of the first exercise of the power to make regulations under subsection (4)—

(a) the regulations shall not be made unless a draft of the regulations has been approved by a resolution of the Scottish Parliament, and

(b) accordingly section 60(2) does not apply to the statutory instrument containing the regulations.'

(2) For section 50A of that Act (restriction on bringing children into the United Kingdom for adoption) there is substituted—

'50A Restriction on bringing children into the United Kingdom

(1) This section applies where a person who is habitually resident in the British Islands (the "British resident")—

(a) brings, or causes another to bring, a child who is habitually resident outside the British Islands into the United Kingdom for the purpose of adoption by the British resident; or

(b) at any time brings, or causes another to bring, into the United Kingdom a child adopted by the British resident under an external adoption effected within the period of six months ending with that time.

(2) In subsection (1) above the references to adoption, or to a child adopted, by the British resident include a reference to adoption, or to a child adopted, by the British resident and another person.

(3) This section does not apply if the child is intended to be adopted under a Convention adoption order.

(4) An external adoption means an adoption, other than a Convention adoption, of a child effected under the law of any country or territory outside the British Islands, whether or not the adoption is—

(a) an adoption within the meaning of Part IV; or

(b) a full adoption (as defined in section 39(2A)).

(5) Regulations may require a person intending to bring, or to cause another to bring, a child into the United Kingdom in circumstances where this section applies—

(a) to apply to an adoption agency in the prescribed manner for an assessment of his suitability to adopt the child; and

(b) to give the agency any information it may require for the purpose of the assessment.

(6) Regulations may require prescribed conditions to be met in respect of a child brought into the United Kingdom in circumstances where this section applies.

(7) In relation to a child brought into the United Kingdom for adoption in

circumstances where this section applies, regulations may provide for any provision of Part II of this Act to apply with modifications or not to apply.

(8)   If a person brings, or causes another to bring, a child into the United Kingdom at any time in circumstances where this section applies, he is guilty of an offence if—

(a)   he has not complied with any requirement imposed by virtue of subsection (5); or

(b)   any condition required to be met by virtue of subsection (6) is not met,

before that time, or before any later time which may be prescribed.

(9)   A person guilty of an offence under this section is liable—

(a)   on summary conviction to imprisonment for a term not exceeding six months, or a fine not exceeding the statutory maximum, or both;

(b)   on conviction on indictment, to imprisonment for a term not exceeding twelve months, or a fine, or both.

(10)   Regulations may provide for this section not to apply if—

(a)   the adopters or (as the case may be) prospective adopters are natural parents (whether or not they have parental responsibilities or parental rights in relation to the child), natural relatives or guardians of the child in question (or one of them is), or

(b)   the British resident in question is a step-parent of the child,

and any prescribed conditions are met.

(11)   On the occasion of the first exercise of the power to make regulations under subsection (10)—

(a)   the regulations shall not be made unless a draft of the regulations has been approved by a resolution of the Scottish Parliament, and

(b)   accordingly section 60(2) does not apply to the statutory instrument containing the regulations.

(12)   In this section, "prescribed" means prescribed by regulations and "regulations" means regulations made by the Scottish Ministers.'

(3)   In section 65 of that Act (interpretation), in subsection (1), in the definition of 'adoption agency', for 'and 27' there is substituted ', 27 and 50A'.

NOTES

Initial Commencement

To be appointed

To be appointed: see s 148(5)(b).

134 Amendment of Adoption (Scotland) Act 1978: overseas adoptions

In section 65 of the Adoption (Scotland) Act 1978 (c 28) (interpretation), for subsection (2) there is substituted—

'(2)   In this Act, "overseas adoption"—

(a)   means an adoption of a description specified in an order made by the Scottish Ministers, being a description of adoptions effected under the law of any country or territory outside the British Islands, but

(b)   does not include a Convention adoption.

(2A)   The Scottish Ministers may by regulations prescribe the requirements that ought to be met by an adoption of any description effected after the commencement of the regulations for it to be an overseas adoption for the purposes of this Act.

(2B)   At any time when such regulations have effect, the Scottish Ministers

> must exercise their power under subsection (2) so as to secure that subsequently effected adoptions of any description are not overseas adoptions for the purposes of this Act if they consider that such adoptions are not likely within a reasonable time to meet the prescribed requirements.
>
> (2C) An order under subsection (2) may contain provision as to the manner in which evidence of any overseas adoption may be given.
>
> (2D) In subsections (2) to (2C), "adoption" means the adoption of a child or of a person who was a child at the time the adoption was applied for.'

NOTES

Initial Commencement

To be appointed

To be appointed: see s 148(5)(b).

135 ...

...

NOTES

Amendment

Repealed by the Serious Organised Crime and Police Act 2005, s 174(2), Sch 17, Pt 2; date in force: 6 April 2006: see SI 2006/378, art 7(f)(vii).

General

[601]

This section was repealed by s 174 of and Sch 17 to of the Serious Organised Crime and Police Act 2005. However, case law on the subject of enhanced criminal record certificates is still relevant.

The Court of Appeal, in *R (on application of X) v Chief Constable of West Midlands Police* [2004] EWCA Civ 168, allowed an appeal by the police against a decision by Wall J (as he then was) that they had breached the human rights of a social worker, and breached the common law, in disclosing information about allegations of sexually abusive behaviour to a prospective employer even though he had been acquitted in a criminal court.

The Court of Appeal held that the police were under a duty to disclose relevant information if it might be relevant, unless there were good reasons not to do so. Parliament had intended, for the protection of children and vulnerable adults (a 'pressing social need'), that information should be disclosed even if it only might be true. The prospective employee should as a matter of good practice disclose that information in any event, and could make representations to any prospective employer about why it should be disregarded.

This judgment will equally be of relevance in respect of prospective adopters, foster-carers and their families.

[602]

136 Payment of grants in connection with welfare services

(1) Section 93 of the Local Government Act 2000 (c 22) (payment of grants for welfare services) is amended as follows.

(2) In subsection (1) (payment of grants by the Secretary of State), for the words from 'in providing' to the end there is substituted—

> '(a) in providing, or contributing to the provision of, such welfare services as may be determined by the Secretary of State, or
>
> (b) in connection with any such welfare services.'

(3)   In subsection (2) (payment of grants by the Assembly), for the words from 'in providing' to the end there is substituted—

'(a)   in providing, or contributing to the provision of, such welfare services as may be determined by the Assembly, or

(b)   in connection with any such welfare services.'

(4)   After subsection (6) there is inserted—

'(6A)   Before making any determination under subsection (3) or (5) the Secretary of State must obtain the consent of the Treasury.'

NOTES

Initial Commencement

Royal Assent

Royal Assent: 7 November 2002: (no specific commencement provision).

Extent

This section does not extend to Scotland: see s 149(2).

General

[603]

This section makes minor amendments to the Local Government Act 2000, s 93. That section allows the Secretary of State to pay grants to local authorities in England, and the National Assembly to pay grants to local authorities in Wales, towards expenditure made in providing, or contributing to providing, certain welfare services as determined by the Secretary of State or National Assembly.

Section 136(2)

[604]

This allows the payment of grants 'in connection' with English local authority expenditure on the specified welfare services, rather than just where the local authority has provided, or contributed to, a welfare service.

Section 136(3)

[605]

This makes the same amendment as in s 136(2), for Welsh local authorities.

Section 136(4)

[606]

The fixing of such grants, and the attachment of any terms and conditions, are now to be subject to the Treasury's consent.

[607]–[700]

137   Extension of the Hague Convention to British overseas territories

(1)   Her Majesty may by Order in Council provide for giving effect to the Convention in any British overseas territory.

(2)   An Order in Council under subsection (1) in respect of any British overseas territory may, in particular, make any provision corresponding to provision which in

relation to any part of Great Britain is made by the Adoption (Intercountry Aspects) Act 1999 (c 18) or may be made by regulations under section 1 of that Act.

(3) The British Nationality Act 1981 (c 61) is amended as follows.

(4) In section 1 (acquisition of British citizenship by birth or adoption)—

(a) in subsection (5), at the end of paragraph (b) there is inserted 'effected under the law of a country or territory outside the United Kingdom',

(b) at the end of subsection (5A)(b) there is inserted 'or in a designated territory',

(c) in subsection (8), the words following 'section 50' are omitted.

(5) In section 15 (acquisition of British overseas territories citizenship)—

(a) after subsection (5) there is inserted—

'(5A) Where—

(a) a minor who is not a British overseas territories citizen is adopted under a Convention adoption,

(b) on the date on which the adoption is effected—

(i) the adopter or, in the case of a joint adoption, one of the adopters is a British overseas territories citizen, and

(ii) the adopter or, in the case of a joint adoption, both of the adopters are habitually resident in a designated territory, and

(c) the Convention adoption is effected under the law of a country or territory outside the designated territory,

the minor shall be a British overseas territories citizen as from that date.',

(b) in subsection (6), after 'order' there is inserted 'or a Convention adoption'.

(6) In section 50 (interpretation), in subsection (1)—

(a) after the definition of 'company' there is inserted—

'"Convention adoption" means an adoption effected under the law of a country or territory in which the Convention is in force, and certified in pursuance of Article 23(1) of the Convention',

(b) after the definition of 'Crown service under the government of the United Kingdom' there is inserted—

"designated territory' means a qualifying territory, or the Sovereign Base Areas of Akrotiri and Dhekelia, which is designated by Her Majesty by Order in Council under subsection (14)'.

(7) After subsection (13) of that section there is inserted—

'(14) For the purposes of the definition of "designated territory" in subsection (1), an Order in Council may—

(a) designate any qualifying territory, or the Sovereign Base Areas of Akrotiri and Dhekelia, if the Convention is in force there, and

(b) make different designations for the purposes of section 1 and section 15;

and, for the purposes of this subsection and the definition of "Convention adoption" in subsection (1), "the Convention" means the Convention on the Protection of Children and Co-operation in respect of Intercountry Adoption, concluded at the Hague on 29th May 1993.

An Order in Council under this subsection shall be subject to annulment in pursuance of a resolution of either House of Parliament.'

NOTES

Initial Commencement

To be appointed

To be appointed: see s 148(1), (2).

Appointment

Appointment: 30 December 2005: see SI 2005/2213, art 2(m).

138 Proceedings in Great Britain

Proceedings for an offence by virtue of section 9, 59, 93, 94, 95 or 129—

(a) may not be brought more than six years after the commission of the offence but, subject to that,

(b) may be brought within a period of six months from the date on which evidence sufficient in the opinion of the prosecutor to warrant the proceedings came to his knowledge.

In relation to Scotland, 'the prosecutor' is to be read as 'the procurator fiscal'.

NOTES

Initial Commencement

To be appointed

To be appointed: see s 148(1), (2).

Appointment

Appointment: 30 December 2005: see SI 2005/2213, art 2(n).

Amendments etc

139 Amendments, transitional and transitory provisions, savings and repeals

(1) Schedule 3 (minor and consequential amendments) is to have effect.

(2) Schedule 4 (transitional and transitory provisions and savings) is to have effect.

(3) The enactments set out in Schedule 5 are repealed to the extent specified.

NOTES

Initial Commencement

To be appointed

To be appointed: see s 148(1), (2), (5)(c)–(f), (6).

Appointment

Sub-s (1): appointment (for certain purposes): 3 February 2003: see SI 2003/288, art 2(a); sub-s (1): appointment (in relation to England for certain purposes): 25 February 2003: see SI 2003/366, art 2(1)(b); sub-s (1): appointment (in relation to England for certain purposes): 30 April 2003: see SI 2003/366, art 2(4)(b)–(d); sub-s (1): appointment (in relation to Wales for certain purposes): 28 November 2003: see SI 2003/3079, art 2(1)(b), (c); sub-s (1): appointment (for certain purposes): 1 December 2003: see SI 2003/3079, art 2(2)(b); sub-s (1): appointment (for certain purposes): 7 December 2004: see SI 2004/3203, art 2(1)(m)(x); sub-s (1): appointment (for certain purposes): 30 December 2005: see SI 2005/2213, art 2(o); sub-s (1): appointment (in relation to England for certain purposes): 30 December 2005: see SI 2005/2213, art 3(l); sub-s (2): appointment (for certain purposes): 30 December 2005: see SI 2005/2897, art 2(a); for transitional provisions and savings see arts 3–16 thereof; sub-s (1): appointment (in relation to Wales for certain purposes): 30 December 2005: see SI 2005/3112, art 2(g); sub-s (1): appointment (in relation to Scotland for certain purposes): 30 December 2005: see SSI 2005/643, art 2(f); sub-s (2): appointment (for certain purposes): 3 February 2003: see SI 2003/288, art 2(b); sub-s (2): appointment (for certain purposes): 25 February 2003: see SI 2003/366, art 2(1)(c); sub-s (2): appointment (in relation to England for certain purposes): 10 March 2003: see SI 2003/366, art 2(2)(a); sub-s (2): appointment (for certain purposes): 1 April 2003: see SI 2003/366, art 2(3); sub-s (2): appointment (for certain purposes): 1 June 2003: see SI 2003/366, art 2(5)(c); sub-s (2): appointment (in relation to England for certain purposes): 6 October 2003: see SI 2003/366, art 2(6)(a); sub-s (2): appointment (in relation to England for certain purposes): 1 December 2003: see SI 2003/3079, art 2(2)(c); sub-s (2): appointment (in relation to England for certain purposes): 1 April 2004: see SI 2003/3079, art 2(4)(a); sub-s (2): appointment (in relation to Wales): 7 February 2004: see SI 2004/252, art 2(d); sub-s (2): appointment (in relation to Scotland for certain purposes): 30 December 2005: see SSI 2005/643, art 2(f); sub-s (3): appointment (for certain purposes): 28 November 2003: see SI 2003/3079, art 2(1)(d); sub-s (3): appointment (for certain purposes): 30 December 2005: by virtue of SI 2005/2213, art 2(m), (o); sub-s (3): appointment (in relation to England for certain purposes): 30 December 2005: see SI 2005/2213, art 3(l); sub-s (3): appointment (for certain purposes): 30 December 2005: see SI 2005/2897, art 2(b); for transitional provisions and savings see arts 3–16 thereof; sub-s (3): appointment (in relation to Scotland for certain purposes): 30 December 2005: see SSI 2005/643, art 2(f).

Chapter 2
Final Provisions

140 Orders, rules and regulations

(1) Any power to make subordinate legislation conferred by this Act on the Lord Chancellor, the Secretary of State, the Scottish Ministers, the Assembly or the Registrar General is exercisable by statutory instrument.

(2) A statutory instrument containing subordinate legislation made under any provision of this Act (other than section 14 or 148 or an instrument to which subsection (3) applies) is to be subject to annulment in pursuance of a resolution of either House of Parliament.

(3) A statutory instrument containing subordinate legislation—

(a)   under section 9 which includes provision made by virtue of section 45(2),

(b)   under section 92(6), 94 or 123(6), or

(c)   which adds to, replaces or omits any part of the text of an Act,

is not to be made unless a draft of the instrument has been laid before, and approved by resolution of, each House of Parliament.

(4) Subsections (2) and (3) do not apply to an Order in Council or to subordinate legislation made—

(a)   by the Scottish Ministers, or

(b)   by the Assembly, unless made jointly by the Secretary of State and the Assembly.

(5) A statutory instrument containing regulations under section 63(2) made by the Scottish Ministers is to be subject to annulment in pursuance of a resolution of the Scottish Parliament.

(6) The power of the Department of Health, Social Services and Public Safety to make regulations under section 63(2) is to be exercisable by statutory rule for the purposes of the Statutory Rules (Northern Ireland) Order 1979 (SI 1979/ 1573 (NI 12)); and any such regulations are to be subject to negative resolution within the meaning of section 41(6) of the Interpretation Act (Northern Ireland) 1954 (c 33 (NI)) as if they were statutory instruments within the meaning of that Act.

(7) Subordinate legislation made under this Act may make different provision for different purposes.

(8) A power to make subordinate legislation under this Act (as well as being exercisable in relation to all cases to which it extends) may be exercised in relation to—

(a)   those cases subject to specified exceptions, or

(b)   a particular case or class of case.

(9) In this section, 'subordinate legislation' does not include a direction.

NOTES

Initial Commencement

Royal Assent
Royal Assent: 7 November 2002: (no specific commencement provision).

Subordinate Legislation
Adoption and Children Act 2002 (Consequential Amendment to Statutory Adoption Pay) Order 2006, SI 2006/2012 (made under sub-s (7)).

141 Rules of procedure

(1) [Family Procedure Rules may make provision] in respect of any matter to be prescribed by rules made by virtue of this Act and dealing generally with all matters of procedure.

(2) ...

(3) In the case of an application for a placement order, for the variation or revocation of such an order, or for an adoption order, the rules must require any person mentioned in subsection (4) to be notified—

(a)   of the date and place where the application will be heard, and

(b)   of the fact that, unless the person wishes or the court requires, the person need not attend.

(4)   The persons referred to in subsection (3) are—

(a)   in the case of a placement order, every person who can be found whose consent to the making of the order is required under subsection (3)(a) of section 21 (or would be required but for subsection (3)(b) of that section) or, if no such person can be found, any relative prescribed by rules who can be found,

(b)   in the case of a variation or revocation of a placement order, every person who can be found whose consent to the making of the placement order was required under subsection (3)(a) of section 21 (or would have been required but for subsection (3)(b) of that section),

(c)   in the case of an adoption order—

    (i)   every person who can be found whose consent to the making of the order is required under subsection (2)(a) of section 47 (or would be required but for subsection (2)(c) of that section) or, if no such person can be found, any relative prescribed by rules who can be found,

    (ii)   every person who has consented to the making of the order under section 20 (and has not withdrawn the consent) unless he has given a notice under subsection (4)(a) of that section which has effect,

    (iii)   every person who, if leave were given under section 47(5), would be entitled to oppose the making of the order.

(5)   Rules made in respect of magistrates' courts may provide—

(a)   for enabling any fact tending to establish the identity of a child with a child to whom a document relates to be proved by affidavit, and

(b)   for excluding or restricting in relation to any facts that may be so proved the power of a justice of the peace to compel the attendance of witnesses.

[(6)   Rules may, for the purposes of the law relating to contempt of court, authorise the publication in such circumstances as may be specified of information relating to proceedings held in private involving children.]

NOTES

Initial Commencement

Royal Assent

Royal Assent: 7 November 2002: (no specific commencement provision).

Extent

This section does not extend to Scotland: see s 149(2).

Amendment

Sub-s (1): words 'Family Procedure Rules may make provision' in square brackets substituted by the Courts Act 2003, s 109(1), Sch 8, para 413(1), (2); date in force: 1 April 2005: see SI 2005/910, art 3(y); for transitional provisions see SI 2005/911, arts 2–5; sub-s (2): repealed by the Courts Act 2003, s 109(1), (3), Sch 8, para 413(1), (3), Sch 10; date in force: 1 April 2005: see SI 2005/910, art 3(y), (aa); for transitional provisions see SI 2005/911, arts 2–5; sub-s (6): inserted by the Children Act 2004, s 62(6); date in force: 12 April 2005: see SI 2005/847, art 2.

See Further

See further, the application of this section, with modifications, in relation to an external adoption order effected within the period of six months of the making of the adoption, and in respect of adoptions under the 1993 Hague Convention on Protection of Children and Co-operation in respect of Intercountry Adoption: the Adoptions with a Foreign Element Regulations 2005, SI 2005/392, regs 11(1)(r), 52, 55.

Subordinate Legislation

Family Procedure (Adoption) Rules 2005, SI 2005/2795 (made under sub-s (1), (3)).

142 Supplementary and consequential provision

(1)   The appropriate Minister may by order make—

(a)   any supplementary, incidental or consequential provision,

(b)   any transitory, transitional or saving provision,

which he considers necessary or expedient for the purposes of, in consequence of or for giving full effect to any provision of this Act.

(2)   For the purposes of subsection (1), where any provision of an order extends to England and Wales, and Scotland or Northern Ireland, the appropriate Minister in relation to the order is the Secretary of State.

(3)   Before making an order under subsection (1) containing provision which would, if included in an Act of the Scottish Parliament, be within the legislative competence of that Parliament, the appropriate Minister must consult the Scottish Ministers.

(4)   Subsection (5) applies to any power of the Lord Chancellor, the Secretary of State or the Assembly to make regulations, rules or an order by virtue of any other provision of this Act or of Her Majesty to make an Order in Council by virtue of section 125.

(5)   The power may be exercised so as to make—

(a)   any supplementary, incidental or consequential provision,

(b)   any transitory, transitional or saving provision,

which the person exercising the power considers necessary or expedient.

(6)   The provision which may be made under subsection (1) or (5) includes provision modifying Schedule 4 or amending or repealing any enactment or instrument.

In relation to an Order in Council, 'enactment' in this subsection includes an enactment comprised in, or in an instrument made under, an Act of the Scottish Parliament.

(7)   The power of the Registrar General to make regulations under Chapter 5 of Part 1 may, with the approval of the Chancellor of the Exchequer, be exercised so as to make—

(a)   any supplementary, incidental or consequential provision,

(b)   any transitory, transitional or saving provision,

which the Registrar General considers necessary or expedient.

NOTES

Initial Commencement

Royal Assent

Royal Assent: 7 November 2002: (no specific commencement provision).

Subordinate Legislation

Adoption and Children Act 2002 (Consequential Amendments) Order 2005, SI 2005/3504 (made under sub-ss (1), (2), (6)); Adoption and Children Act 2002 (Consequential Amendment to Statutory Adoption Pay) Order 2006, SI 2006/2012 (made under sub-s (1)).

143   Offences by bodies corporate and unincorporated bodies

(1)   Where an offence under this Act committed by a body corporate is proved to have been committed with the consent or connivance of, or to be attributable to any neglect on the part of, any director, manager, secretary or other similar officer of the body, or a person purporting to act in any such capacity, that person as well as the body is guilty of the offence and liable to be proceeded against and punished accordingly.

(2)   Where the affairs of a body corporate are managed by its members, subsection (1) applies in relation to the acts and defaults of a member in connection with his functions of management as it applies to a director of a body corporate.

(3)   Proceedings for an offence alleged to have been committed under this Act by an unincorporated body are to be brought in the name of that body (and not in that of any of its members) and, for the purposes of any such proceedings in England and Wales or Northern Ireland, any rules of court relating to the service of documents have effect as if that body were a corporation.

(4)   A fine imposed on an unincorporated body on its conviction of an offence under this Act is to be paid out of the funds of that body.

(5)   If an unincorporated body is charged with an offence under this Act—

(a)   in England and Wales, section 33 of the Criminal Justice Act 1925 (c 86) and Schedule 3 to the Magistrates' Courts Act 1980 (c 43) (procedure on charge of an offence against a corporation),

(b)   in Northern Ireland, section 18 of the Criminal Justice Act (Northern Ireland) 1945 (c 15 (NI)) and Schedule 4 to the Magistrates' Courts (Northern Ireland) Order 1981 (SI 1981/1675 (NI 26)) (procedure on charge of an offence against a·corporation), have effect in like manner as in the case of a corporation so charged.

(6)   Where an offence under this Act committed by an unincorporated body (other than a partnership) is proved to have been committed with the consent or connivance of, or to be attributable to any neglect on the part of, any officer of the body or any member of its governing body, he as well as the body is guilty of the offence and liable to be proceeded against and punished accordingly.

(7)   Where an offence under this Act committed by a partnership is proved to have been committed with the consent or connivance of, or to be attributable to any neglect on the part of, a partner, he as well as the partnership is guilty of the offence and liable to be proceeded against and punished accordingly.

NOTES

Initial Commencement

Royal Assent

Royal Assent: 7 November 2002: (no specific commencement provision).

144   General interpretation etc

(1)   In this Act—

'appropriate Minister' means—

(a)   in relation to England, Scotland or Northern Ireland, the Secretary of State,

(b)   in relation to Wales, the Assembly,

and in relation to England and Wales means the Secretary of State and the Assembly acting jointly,

'the Assembly' means the National Assembly for Wales,

'body' includes an unincorporated body,

'by virtue of' includes 'by' and 'under',

'child', except where used to express a relationship, means a person who has not attained the age of 18 years,

'the Convention' means the Convention on Protection of Children and Co-operation in respect of Intercountry Adoption, concluded at the Hague on 29th May 1993,

'Convention adoption order' means an adoption order which, by virtue of regulations under section 1 of the Adoption (Intercountry Aspects) Act 1999 (c 18) (regulations giving effect to the Convention), is made as a Convention adoption order,

'Convention country' means a country or territory in which the Convention is in force,

'court' means, subject to any provision made by virtue of Part 1 of Schedule 11 to the 1989 Act, the High Court, a county court or a magistrates' court,

'enactment' includes an enactment comprised in subordinate legislation,

'fee' includes expenses,

'guardian' has the same meaning as in the 1989 Act and includes a special guardian within the meaning of that Act,

'information' means information recorded in any form,

'local authority' means any unitary authority, or any county council so far as they are not a unitary authority,

'Northern Irish adoption agency' means an adoption agency within the meaning of Article 3 of the Adoption (Northern Ireland) Order 1987 (SI 1987/2203 (NI 22)),

'Northern Irish adoption order' means an order made, or having effect as if made, under Article 12 of the Adoption (Northern Ireland) Order 1987,

'notice' means a notice in writing,

'registration authority' (in Part 1) has the same meaning as in the Care Standards Act 2000 (c 14),

'regulations' means regulations made by the appropriate Minister, unless they are required to be made by the Lord Chancellor, the Secretary of State or the Registrar General,

'relative', in relation to a child, means a grandparent, brother, sister, uncle or aunt, whether of the full blood or half-blood or by marriage [or civil partnership],

['rules' means Family Procedure Rules made by virtue of section 141(1),]

'Scottish adoption order' means an order made, or having effect as if made, under section 12 of the Adoption (Scotland) Act 1978 (c 28), 'subordinate legislation' has the same meaning as in the Interpretation Act 1978 (c 30),

'unitary authority' means—

    (a)   the council of any county so far as they are the council for an area for which there are no district councils,

    (b)   the council of any district comprised in an area for which there is no county council,

    (c)   the council of a county borough,

    (d)   the council of a London borough,

    (e)   the Common Council of the City of London.

(2)   Any power conferred by this Act to prescribe a fee by Order in Council or regulations includes power to prescribe—

(a)   a fee not exceeding a prescribed amount,

(b)   a fee calculated in accordance with the Order or, as the case may be, regulations,

(c)   a fee determined by the person to whom it is payable, being a fee of a reasonable amount.

(3)   In this Act, 'Scottish adoption agency' means—

(a)   a local authority, or

(b)   a voluntary organisation providing a registered adoption service;

but in relation to the provision of any particular service, references to a Scottish adoption agency do not include a voluntary organisation unless it is registered in respect of that service or a service which, in Scotland, corresponds to that service.

Expressions used in this subsection have the same meaning as in the Regulation of Care (Scotland) Act 2001 (asp 4) and 'registered' means registered under Part 1 of that Act.

(4)   In this Act, a couple means—

(a)   a married couple, or

[(aa)   two people who are civil partners of each other, or]

(b)   two people (whether of different sexes or the same sex) living as partners in an enduring family relationship.

(5)   Subsection (4)(b) does not include two people one of whom is the other's parent, grandparent, sister, brother, aunt or uncle.

(6)   References to relationships in subsection (5)—

(a)   are to relationships of the full blood or half blood or, in the case of an adopted person, such of those relationships as would exist but for adoption, and

(b)   include the relationship of a child with his adoptive, or former adoptive, parents,

but do not include any other adoptive relationships.

(7)   For the purposes of this Act, a person is the partner of a child's parent if the person and the parent are a couple but the person is not the child's parent.

NOTES

Initial Commencement

Royal Assent

Royal Assent: 7 November 2002: (no specific commencement provision).

Amendment

Sub-s (1): in definition 'relative' words 'or civil partnership' in square brackets inserted by the Civil Partnership Act 2004, s 79(1), (11); date in force: 30 December 2005: see SI 2005/3175, art 2(9); sub-s (1): definition 'rules' substituted by the Courts Act 2003, s 109(1), Sch 8, para 414; date in force: 1 April 2005: see SI 2005/910, art 3(y); for transitional provisions see SI 2005/911, arts 2–5; sub-s (4): para (aa) inserted by the Civil Partnership Act 2004, s 79(1), (12); date in force: 30 December 2005: see SI 2005/3175, art 2(9).

145 Devolution: Wales

(1) The references to the Adoption Act 1976 (c 36) and to the 1989 Act in Schedule 1 to the National Assembly for Wales (Transfer of Functions) Order 1999 (SI 1999/672) are to be treated as referring to those Acts as amended by virtue of this Act.

(2) This section does not affect the power to make further Orders varying or omitting those references.

(3) In Schedule 1 to that Order, in the entry for the Adoption Act 1976, '9' is omitted.

(4) The functions exercisable by the Assembly under sections 9 and 9A of the Adoption Act 1976 (by virtue of paragraphs 4 and 5 of Schedule 4 to this Act) are to be treated for the purposes of section 44 of the Government of Wales Act 1998 (c 38) (parliamentary procedures for subordinate legislation) as if made exercisable by the Assembly by an Order in Council under section 22 of that Act.

NOTES

Initial Commencement

Royal Assent

Royal Assent: 7 November 2002: (no specific commencement provision).

Extent

This section does not extend to Scotland: see s 149(2).

146 Expenses

There shall be paid out of money provided by Parliament—

(a)   any expenditure incurred by a Minister of the Crown by virtue of this Act,

(b)   any increase attributable to this Act in the sums payable out of money so provided under any other enactment.

NOTES

Initial Commencement

Royal Assent

Royal Assent: 7 November 2002: (no specific commencement provision).

147 Glossary

Schedule 6 (glossary) is to have effect.

NOTES

Initial Commencement

Royal Assent

Royal Assent: 7 November 2002: (no specific commencement provision).

148 Commencement

(1) This Act (except sections 116 and 136, this Chapter and the provisions mentioned in subsections (5) and (6)) is to come into force on such day as the Secretary of State may by order appoint.

(2) Before making an order under subsection (1) (other than an order bringing paragraph 53 of Schedule 3 into force) the Secretary of State must consult the Assembly.

(3) Before making an order under subsection (1) bringing sections 123 and 124 into force, the Secretary of State must also consult the Scottish Ministers and the Department of Health, Social Services and Public Safety.

(4) Before making an order under subsection (1) bringing sections 125 to 131 into force, the Secretary of State must also consult the Scottish Ministers.

(5) The following are to come into force on such day as the Scottish Ministers may by order appoint—

(a)   section 41(5) to (9), so far as relating to Scotland,

(b)   sections 132 to 134,

(c)   paragraphs 21 to 35 and 82 to 84 of Schedule 3,

(d)   paragraphs 15 and 23 of Schedule 4,

(e)   the entries in Schedule 5, so far as relating to the provisions mentioned in paragraphs (c) and (d),

(f)   section 139, so far as relating to the provisions mentioned in the preceding paragraphs.

(6)   Sections 2(6), 3(3) and (4), 4 to 17, 27(3), 53(1) to (3), 54, 56 to 65 and 98, paragraphs 13, 65, 66 and 111 to 113 of Schedule 3 and paragraphs 3 and 5 of Schedule 4 are to come into force on such day as the appropriate Minister may by order appoint.

NOTES

Initial Commencement

Royal Assent
Royal Assent: 7 November 2002: (no specific commencement provision).

Subordinate Legislation

UK
Adoption and Children Act 2002 (Commencement No 1) (Wales) Order 2003, SI 2003/181 (made under sub-s 6)); Adoption and Children Act 2002 (Commencement No 2) Order 2003, SI 2003/288 (made under sub-s (1)); Adoption and Children Act 2002 (Commencement No 3) Order 2003, SI 2003/366 (made under sub-ss (1), (6)).

Adoption and Children Act 2002 (Commencement No 4) Order 2003, SI 2003/3079 (made under sub-ss (1), (6)); Adoption and Children Act 2002 (Commencement No 5) (Wales) Order 2004, SI 2004/252 (made under sub-s (6)); Adoption and Children Act 2002 (Commencement No 6) Order 2004, SI 2004/1403 (made under sub-s (1)).

Adoption and Children Act 2002 (Commencement No 7) Order 2004, SI 2004/3203 (made under sub-ss (1), (6)); Adoption and Children Act 2002 (Commencement No 8) (Wales) Order 2005, SI 2005/1206 (made under sub-s (6)); Adoption and Children Act 2002 (Commencement No 9) Order 2005, SI 2005/2213 (made under sub-ss (1), (6)).

Adoption and Children Act 2002 (Commencement No 10 Transitional and Savings Provisions) Order 2005, SI 2005/2897 (made under sub-s (1)); Adoption and Children Act 2002 (Commencement No 11) (Wales) Order 2005, SI 2005/3112 (made under sub-s (6)).

Scotland
Adoption and Children Act 2002 (Commencement No 1) (Scotland) Order 2005, SSI 2005/643 (made under sub-s (5)).

149   Extent

(1)   The amendment or repeal of an enactment has the same extent as the enactment to which it relates.

(2)   Subject to that and to the following provisions, this Act except section 137 extends to England and Wales only.

(3)   The following extend also to Scotland and Northern Ireland—

(a)   sections 63(2) to (5), 65(2)(a) and (b) and (3), 123 and 124,
(b)   this Chapter, except sections 141 and 145.

(4)   The following extend also to Scotland—

(a)   section 41(5) to (9),
(b)   sections 125 to 131,
(c)   section 138,
(d)   section 139, so far as relating to provisions extending to Scotland.

(5)   In Schedule 4, paragraph 23 extends only to Scotland.

NOTES

Initial Commencement

Royal Assent
Royal Assent: 7 November 2002: (no specific commencement provision).

150   Short title

This Act may be cited as the Adoption and Children Act 2002.

NOTES

Initial Commencement

Royal Assent
Royal Assent: 7 November 2002: (no specific commencement provision).

SCHEDULE 1
Registration of Adoptions

Section 77(6)

Registration of adoption orders

1 (1) Every adoption order must contain a direction to the Registrar General to make in the Adopted Children Register an entry in the form prescribed by regulations made by the Registrar General with the approval of the Chancellor of the Exchequer.
(2) Where, on an application to a court for an adoption order in respect of a child, the identity of the child with a child to whom an entry in the registers of live-births or other records relates is proved to the satisfaction of the court, any adoption order made in pursuance of the application must contain a direction to the Registrar General to secure that the entry in the register or, as the case may be, record in question is marked with the word 'Adopted'.
(3) Where an adoption order is made in respect of a child who has previously been the subject of an adoption order made by a court in England or Wales under Part 1 of this Act or any other enactment—

(a) sub-paragraph (2) does not apply, and
(b) the order must contain a direction to the Registrar General to mark the previous entry in the Adopted Children Register with the word 'Re-adopted'.

(4) Where an adoption order is made, the prescribed officer of the court which made the order must communicate the order to the Registrar General in the prescribed manner; and the Registrar General must then comply with the directions contained in the order.

'Prescribed' means prescribed by rules.

Registration of adoptions in Scotland, Northern Ireland, the Isle of Man and the Channel Islands

2 (1) Sub-paragraphs (2) and (3) apply where the Registrar General is notified by the authority maintaining a register of adoptions in a part of the British Islands outside England and Wales that an order has been made in that part authorising the adoption of a child.
(2) If an entry in the registers of live-births or other records (and no entry in the Adopted Children Register) relates to the child, the Registrar General must secure that the entry is marked with—

(a) the word 'Adopted', followed by
(b) the name, in brackets, of the part in which the order was made.

(3) If an entry in the Adopted Children Register relates to the child, the Registrar General must mark the entry with—

(a) the word 'Re-adopted', followed by
(b) the name, in brackets, of the part in which the order was made.

(4) Where, after an entry in either of the registers or other records mentioned in sub-paragraphs (2) and (3) has been so marked, the Registrar General is notified by the authority concerned that—

(a) the order has been quashed,
(b) an appeal against the order has been allowed, or
(c) the order has been revoked,

the Registrar General must secure that the marking is cancelled.

(5) A copy or extract of an entry in any register or other record, being an entry the marking of which is cancelled under sub-paragraph (4), is not to be treated as an accurate copy unless both the marking and the cancellation are omitted from it.

Registration of other adoptions

3 (1) If the Registrar General is satisfied, on an application under this paragraph, that he has sufficient particulars relating to a child adopted under a registrable foreign adoption to enable an entry to be made in the Adopted Children Register for the child he must make the entry accordingly.

(2) If he is also satisfied that an entry in the registers of live-births or other records relates to the child, he must—

(a) secure that the entry is marked 'Adopted', followed by the name, in brackets, of the country in which the adoption was effected, or

(b) where appropriate, secure that the overseas registers of births are so marked.

(3) An application under this paragraph must be made, in the prescribed manner, by a prescribed person and the applicant must provide the prescribed documents and other information.

(4) An entry made in the Adopted Children Register by virtue of this paragraph must be made in the prescribed form.

(5) In this Schedule 'registrable foreign adoption' means an adoption which satisfies prescribed requirements and is either—

(a) adoption under a Convention adoption, or

(b) adoption under an overseas adoption.

(6) In this paragraph—

(a) 'prescribed' means prescribed by regulations made by the Registrar General with the approval of the Chancellor of the Exchequer,

(b) 'overseas register of births' includes—

(i) a register made under regulations made by the Secretary of State under section 41(1)(g), (h) or (i) of the British Nationality Act 1981 (c 61),

(ii) a record kept under an Order in Council made under section 1 of the Registration of Births, Deaths and Marriages (Special Provisions) Act 1957 (c 58) (other than a certified copy kept by the Registrar General).

Amendment of orders and rectification of Registers and other records

4 (1) The court by which an adoption order has been made may, on the application of the adopter or the adopted person, amend the order by the correction of any error in the particulars contained in it.

(2) The court by which an adoption order has been made may, if satisfied on the application of the adopter or the adopted person that within the period of one year beginning with the date of the order any new name—

(a) has been given to the adopted person (whether in baptism or otherwise), or

(b) has been taken by the adopted person,

either in place of or in addition to a name specified in the particulars required to be entered in the Adopted Children Register in pursuance of the order, amend the order by substituting or, as the case may be, adding that name in those particulars.

(3) The court by which an adoption order has been made may, if satisfied on the application of any person concerned that a direction for the marking of an entry in the registers of live-births, the Adopted Children Register or other records included in the order in pursuance of paragraph 1(2) or (3) was wrongly so included, revoke that direction.

(4) Where an adoption order is amended or a direction revoked under sub-paragraphs (1) to (3), the prescribed officer of the court must communicate the amendment in the prescribed manner to the Registrar General.

'Prescribed' means prescribed by rules.

(5) The Registrar General must then—

(a)   amend the entry in the Adopted Children Register accordingly, or

(b)   secure that the marking of the entry in the registers of live-births, the Adopted Children Register or other records is cancelled,

as the case may be.

(6) Where an adoption order is quashed or an appeal against an adoption order allowed by any court, the court must give directions to the Registrar General to secure that—

(a)   any entry in the Adopted Children Register, and

(b)   any marking of an entry in that Register, the registers of live-births or other records as the case may be, which was effected in pursuance of the order,

is cancelled.

(7) Where an adoption order has been amended, any certified copy of the relevant entry in the Adopted Children Register which may be issued pursuant to section 78(2)(b) must be a copy of the entry as amended, without the reproduction of—

(a)   any note or marking relating to the amendment, or

(b)   any matter cancelled in pursuance of it.

(8) A copy or extract of an entry in any register or other record, being an entry the marking of which has been cancelled, is not to be treated as an accurate copy unless both the marking and the cancellation are omitted from it.

(9) If the Registrar General is satisfied—

(a)   that a registrable foreign adoption has ceased to have effect, whether on annulment or otherwise, or

(b)   that any entry or mark was erroneously made in pursuance of paragraph 3 in the Adopted Children Register, the registers of live-births, the overseas registers of births or other records,

he may secure that such alterations are made in those registers or other records as he considers are required in consequence of the adoption ceasing to have effect or to correct the error.

'Overseas register of births' has the same meaning as in paragraph 3.

(10) Where an entry in such a register is amended in pursuance of sub-paragraph (9), any copy or extract of the entry is not to be treated as accurate unless it shows the entry as amended but without indicating that it has been amended.

Marking of entries on re-registration of birth on legitimation

5   (1) Without prejudice to paragraphs 2(4) and 4(5), where, after an entry in the registers of live-births or other records has been marked in accordance with paragraph 1 or 2, the birth is re-registered under section 14 of the Births and Deaths Registration Act 1953 (c 20) (re-registration of births of legitimated persons), the entry made on the re-registration must be marked in the like manner.

(2) Without prejudice to paragraph 4(9), where an entry in the registers of live-births or other records is marked in pursuance of paragraph 3 and the birth in question is subsequently re-registered under section 14 of that Act, the entry made on re-registration must be marked in the like manner.

Cancellations in registers on legitimation

6   (1) This paragraph applies where an adoption order is revoked under section 55(1).

(2) The prescribed officer of the court must communicate the revocation in the prescribed manner to the Registrar General who must then cancel or secure the cancellation of—

(a)   the entry in the Adopted Children Register relating to the adopted person, and

(b)   the marking with the word 'Adopted' of any entry relating to the adopted person in the registers of live-births or other records.

'Prescribed' means prescribed by rules.

(3)   A copy or extract of an entry in any register or other record, being an entry the marking of which is cancelled under this paragraph, is not to be treated as an accurate copy unless both the marking and the cancellation are omitted from it.

NOTES

Initial Commencement

To be appointed

To be appointed: see s 148(1), (2).

Appointment

Paras 1, 3: appointment (for the purpose of making regulations): 7 December 2004: see SI 2004/3203, art 2(1)(m)(vi); paras 1, 3: appointment (for remaining purposes): 30 December 2005: see SI 2005/2213, art 2(e); paras 2, 4–6: appointment: 30 December 2005: see SI 2005/2213, art 2(e).

Extent

This Schedule does not extend to Scotland: see s 149(2).

Subordinate Legislation

Adopted Children and Adoption Contact Registers Regulations 2005, SI 2005/924 (made under paras 1(1), 3(3)–(5)); Family Procedure (Adoption) Rules 2005, SI 2005/2795 (made under paras 1(4), 4(4), 6(2)).

SCHEDULE 2
Disclosure of Birth Records by Registrar General

Section 79(6)

1   On an application made in the prescribed manner by an adopted person—

(a)   a record of whose birth is kept by the Registrar General, and

(b)   who has attained the age of 18 years,

the Registrar General must give the applicant any information necessary to enable the applicant to obtain a certified copy of the record of his birth.

'Prescribed' means prescribed by regulations made by the Registrar General with the approval of the Chancellor of the Exchequer.

2   (1)   Before giving any information to an applicant under paragraph 1, the Registrar General must inform the applicant that counselling services are available to the applicant—

(a)   from a registered adoption society, an organisation within section 144(3)(b) or an adoption society which is registered under Article 4 of the Adoption (Northern Ireland) Order 1987 (SI 1987/2203 (NI 22)),

(b)   if the applicant is in England and Wales, at the General Register Office or from any local authority or registered adoption support agency,

(c)   if the applicant is in Scotland, from any council constituted under section 2 of the Local Government etc (Scotland) Act 1994 (c 39),

(d)   if the applicant is in Northern Ireland, from any Board.

(2)   In sub-paragraph (1)(b), 'registered adoption support agency' means an adoption support agency in respect of which a person is registered under Part 2 of the Care Standards Act 2000 (c 14).

(3)   In sub-paragraph (1)(d), 'Board' means a Health and Social Services Board established under Article 16 of the Health and Personal Social Services (Northern Ireland) Order 1972 (SI 1972/1265 (NI 14)); but where the functions of a Board are exercisable by a Health and Social Services Trust, references in that sub-paragraph to a Board are to be read as references to the Health and Social Services Trust.

(4)   If the applicant chooses to receive counselling from a person or body within sub-paragraph (1), the Registrar General must send to the person or body the information to which the applicant is entitled under paragraph 1.

3   (1)   Where an adopted person who is in England and Wales—

(a)   applies for information under paragraph 1 or Article 54 of the Adoption (Northern Ireland) Order 1987, or

(b)   is supplied with information under section 45 of the Adoption (Scotland) Act 1978 (c 28),

the persons and bodies mentioned in sub-paragraph (2) must, if asked by the applicant to do so, provide counselling for the applicant.

(2)   Those persons and bodies are—

(a)   the Registrar General,
(b)   any local authority,
(c)   a registered adoption society, an organisation within section 144(3)(b) or an adoption society which is registered under Article 4 of the Adoption (Northern Ireland) Order 1987.

4   (1)   Where a person—

(a)   was adopted before 12th November 1975, and
(b)   applies for information under paragraph 1,

the Registrar General must not give the information to the applicant unless the applicant has attended an interview with a counsellor arranged by a person or body from whom counselling services are available as mentioned in paragraph 2.

(2)   Where the Registrar General is prevented by sub-paragraph (1) from giving information to a person who is not living in the United Kingdom, the Registrar General may give the information to any body which—

(a)   the Registrar General is satisfied is suitable to provide counselling to that person, and
(b)   has notified the Registrar General that it is prepared to provide such counselling.

NOTES

Initial Commencement
To be appointed
To be appointed: see s 148(1), (2).

Appointment
Para 1: appointment (for the purpose of making regulations): 7 December 2004: see SI 2004/3203, art 2(1)(m)(vi); para 1: appointment (for remaining purposes): 30 December 2005: see SI 2005/2213, art 2(e); paras 2–4: appointment: 30 December 2005: see SI 2005/2213, art 2(e).

Extent
This Schedule does not extend to Scotland: see s 149(2).

SCHEDULE 3
Minor and Consequential Amendments

Section 139

The Marriage Act 1949 (c 76)

1   Section 3 of the Marriage Act 1949 (marriage of person aged under eighteen) is amended as follows.

2   In subsection (1), for 'person or persons specified in subsection (1A) of this section' there is substituted 'appropriate persons'.

3   For subsection (1A) there is substituted—

'(1A)   The appropriate persons are—

(a)   if none of paragraphs (b) to (h) apply, each of the following—
    (i)   any parent of the child who has parental responsibility for him; and
    (ii)   any guardian of the child;

> (b)   where a special guardianship order is in force with respect to a child, each of the child's special guardians, unless any of paragraphs (c) to (g) applies;
>
> (c)   where a care order has effect with respect to the child, the local authority designated in the order, and each parent, guardian or special guardian (in so far as their parental responsibility has not been restricted under section 33(3) of the Children Act 1989), unless paragraph (e) applies;
>
> (d)   where a residence order has effect with respect to the child, the persons with whom the child lives, or is to live, as a result of the order, unless paragraph (e) applies;
>
> (e)   where an adoption agency is authorised to place the child for adoption under section 19 of the Adoption and Children Act 2002, that agency or, where a care order has effect with respect to the child, the local authority designated in the order;
>
> (f)   where a placement order is in force with respect to the child, the appropriate local authority;
>
> (g)   where a child has been placed for adoption with prospective adopters, the prospective adopters (in so far as their parental responsibility has not been restricted under section 25(4) of the Adoption and Children Act 2002), in addition to those persons specified in paragraph (e) or (f);
>
> (h)   where none of paragraphs (b) to (g) apply but a residence order was in force with respect to the child immediately before he reached the age of sixteen, the persons with whom he lived, or was to live, as a result of the order.'

4   For subsection (1B) there is substituted—

> '(1B)   In this section—
>
> "guardian of a child", "parental responsibility", "residence order", "special guardian", "special guardianship order" and "care order" have the same meaning as in the Children Act 1989;
>
> "adoption agency", "placed for adoption", "placement order" and "local authority" have the same meaning as in the Adoption and Children Act 2002;
>
> "appropriate local authority" means the local authority authorised by the placement order to place the child for adoption.'

5   In subsection (2), for 'The last foregoing subsection' there is substituted 'Subsection (1)'.

The Births and Deaths Registration Act 1953 (*c 20*)

6   In section 10 of the Births and Deaths Registration Act 1953 (registration of father where parents not married)—

(a)   in subsection (1)(d)(i), for 'a parental responsibility agreement made between them in relation to the child' there is substituted 'any agreement made between them under section 4(1)(b) of the Children Act 1989 in relation to the child',

(b)   in subsection (1)(d)(ii), for 'the Children Act 1989' there is substituted 'that Act',

(c)   in subsection (3), the words following 'the Family Law Reform Act 1987' are omitted.

7   In section 10A of the Births and Deaths Registration Act 1953 (re-registration of father where parents not married)—

(a)   in subsection (1)(d)(i), for 'a parental responsibility agreement made between them in relation to the child' there is substituted 'any agreement made between them under section 4(1)(b) of the Children Act 1989 in relation to the child',

(b)   in subsection (1)(d)(ii), for 'the Children Act 1989' there is substituted 'that Act'.

The Sexual Offences Act 1956 (*c 69*)

8   In section 28 of the Sexual Offences Act 1956 (causing or encouraging prostitution of, intercourse with, or indecent assault on, girl under sixteen), in subsection (4), the 'or' at the end of paragraph (a) is omitted, and after that paragraph there is inserted—

> '(aa)   a special guardianship order under that Act is in force with respect to her and he is not her special guardian; or'.

The Health Services and Public Health Act 1968 (*c 46*)

9   The Health Services and Public Health Act 1968 is amended as follows.

10   In section 64 (financial assistance by the Secretary of State to certain voluntary organisations), in subsection (3)(a)(xviii), for 'the Adoption Act 1976' there is substituted 'the Adoption and Children Act 2002'.

11   In section 65 (financial and other assistance by local authorities to certain voluntary organisations), in subsection (3)(b), for 'the Adoption Act 1976' there is substituted 'the Adoption and Children Act 2002'.

The Local Authority Social Services Act 1970 (*c 42*)

12   The Local Authority Social Services Act 1970 is amended as follows.

13   In section 7D (default powers of Secretary of State as respects social services functions of local authorities), in subsection (1), after 'the Children Act 1989' there is inserted 'section 1 or 2(4) of the Adoption (Intercountry Aspects) Act 1999 or the Adoption and Children Act 2002'.

14   In Schedule 1 (enactments conferring functions assigned to social services committee)—

(a)   the entry relating to the Adoption Act 1976 is omitted,
(b)   in the entry relating to the Children Act 1989, after 'Consent to application for residence order in respect of child in care' there is inserted 'Functions relating to special guardianship orders',
(c)   in the entry relating to the Adoption (Intercountry Aspects) Act 1999—

> (i)   in the first column, for 'Section' there is substituted 'Sections 1 and',
> (ii)   in the second column, for 'Article 9(a) to (c) of' there is substituted 'regulations made under section 1 giving effect to' and at the end there is inserted 'and functions under Article 9(a) to (c) of the Convention',

and at the end of the Schedule there is inserted—

'Adoption and Children Act 2002	Maintenance of Adoption Service; functions of local authority as adoption agency.'

The Immigration Act 1971 (*c 77*)

15   In section 33(1) of the Immigration Act 1971 (interpretation)—

(a)   in the definition of 'Convention adoption', after '1978' there is inserted 'or in the Adoption and Children Act 2002',
(b)   in the definition of 'legally adopted', for 'section 72(2) of the Adoption Act 1976' there is substituted 'section 87 of the Adoption and Children Act 2002'.

The Legitimacy Act 1976 (*c 31*)

16   The Legitimacy Act 1976 is amended as follows.

PART B – Statutes

17 In section 4 (legitimation of adopted child)—

(a)   in subsection (1), after '1976' there is inserted 'or section 67 of the Adoption and Children Act 2002',

(b)   in subsection (2)—

    (i)   in paragraph (a), after '39' there is inserted 'or subsection (3)(b) of the said section 67',

    (ii)   in paragraph (b), after '1976' there is inserted 'or section 67, 68 or 69 of the Adoption and Children Act 2002'.

18 In section 6 (dispositions depending on date of birth), at the end of subsection (2) there is inserted 'or section 69(2) of the Adoption and Children Act 2002'.

The Adoption Act 1976 (*c 36*)

19 In section 38 of the Adoption Act 1976 (meaning of 'adoption' in Part 4), in subsection (2), after '1975' there is inserted 'but does not include an adoption of a kind mentioned in paragraphs (c) to (e) of subsection (1) effected on or after the day which is the appointed day for the purposes of Chapter 4 of Part 1 of the Adoption and Children Act 2002'.

The National Health Service Act 1977 (*c 49*)

20 In section 124A(3) of the National Health Service Act 1977 (information provided by the Registrar General to the Secretary of State), the 'or' at the end of paragraph (a) is omitted and after that paragraph there is inserted—

    '(aa)   entered in the Adopted Children Register maintained by the Registrar General under the Adoption and Children Act 2002; or'.

The Adoption (*Scotland*) Act 1978 (*c 28*)

21 The Adoption (Scotland) Act 1978 is amended as follows.

22 In section 11 (restriction on arranging adoptions and placing of children)—

(a)   in subsection (2)—

    (i)   for paragraph (a) there is substituted—

        '(a)   a registered adoption society (within the meaning of section 2(2) of the Adoption and Children Act 2002)'; and

    (ii)   for 'section 1' there is substituted 'section 3(1)', and

(b)   after subsection (2) there is inserted—

    '(2A)   In relation to the provision of any particular service by an adoption society, the reference in subsection (2)(a) to a registered adoption society does not include a voluntary organisation unless it is registered under Part 2 of the Care Standards Act 2000 in respect of that service or a service which, in England, corresponds to that service.'

23 In section 16 (parental agreement to adoption order)—

(a)   in subsection (1), after paragraph (a) there is inserted—

    '(aa)   each parent or guardian of the child has consented under section 20 of the Adoption and Children Act 2002 (advance consent to adoption), has not withdrawn the consent and does not oppose the making of the adoption order;

    (ab)   subsection (3A) applies and no parent or guardian of the child opposes the making of the adoption order', and

(b)   after subsection (3) there is inserted—

'(3A) This subsection applies where—

(a) the child has been placed for adoption by an adoption agency (within the meaning of section 2(1) of the Adoption and Children Act 2002) with the prospective adopters in whose favour the adoption order is proposed to be made; and

(b) the child was placed for adoption—

(i) under section 19 of that Act (placing children with parental consent) with the consent of each parent or guardian and the consent of the mother was given when the child was at least six weeks old; or

(ii) under an order made under section 21 of that Act (placement orders) and the child was at least six weeks old when that order was made.

(3B) A parent or guardian may not oppose the making of an adoption order under subsection (1)(aa) or (ab) without the leave of the court.

(3C) The court shall not give leave under subsection (3B) unless satisfied that there has been a change of circumstances since the consent of the parent or guardian was given or, as the case may be, the order under section 21 of that Act was made.

(3D) The withdrawal of—

(a) any consent to the placement of a child for adoption—

(i) under section 19; or

(ii) under an order made under section 21,

of the Adoption and Children Act 2002; or

(b) any consent given under section 20 of that Act,

is ineffective if it is given after an application for an adoption order is made.'

24 In section 29 (return of children taken away in breach of section 27 or 28)—

(a) in subsection (1), for 'section 27 or 28 of the Adoption Act 1976' there is substituted 'section 30, 34, 35 or 36 of the Adoption and Children Act 2002', and

(b) in subsection (2), for 'section 27 or 28 of the Adoption Act 1976', in both places where those words occur, there is substituted 'section 30, 34, 35 or 36 of the Adoption and Children Act 2002'.

25 In section 45 (Adopted Children Register)—

(a) in subsection (6)(d), for sub-paragraph (ii) there is substituted—

'(ii) registered under Part II of the Care Standards Act 2000;';

(b) in subsection (6A)(b), for sub-paragraph (i) there is substituted—

'(i) Schedule 2 to the Adoption and Children Act 2002;'.

26 In section 47 (annulment etc of overseas adoptions), in subsection (4), for 'section 53 of the Adoption Act 1976' there is substituted 'section 89(2) of the Adoption and Children Act 2002'.

27 In section 50 (restriction on removal of children for adoption outside Great Britain), in subsection (1), for 'section 55 of the Adoption Act 1976' there is substituted 'section 84 of the Adoption and Children Act 2002'.

28 Section 52 (restriction on advertisements) is omitted.

29 In section 53 (effect of determination and orders made in England and Wales and overseas in adoption proceedings), in subsection (2), the words 'England and Wales or' are omitted.

30 After section 53 there is inserted—

'53A Effect of certain orders made in England and Wales

(1)   An adoption order (within the meaning of section 46(1) of the Adoption and Children Act 2002) has effect in Scotland as it has in England and Wales but as if any reference to the parental responsibility for the child were to the parental responsibilities and parental rights in relation to the child.

(2)   An order made under section 21 of that Act (placement orders), and the variation or revocation of such an order under section 23 or 24 of that Act, have effect in Scotland as they have in England and Wales but as if any reference to the parental responsibility for the child were to the parental responsibilities and parental rights in relation to the child.

53B   Effect of placing for adoption etc under Adoption and Children Act 2002

(1)   If—

    (a)   a child is placed for adoption under section 19 of the Adoption and Children Act 2002 (placing children with parental consent); or

    (b)   an adoption agency is authorised to place a child for adoption under that section,

sections 25 (parental responsibility) and 28(2) to (4) (further consequences of placement) of that Act have effect in Scotland as they have in England and Wales but with the modifications specified in subsection (2).

(2)   Those modifications are—

    (a)   in section 25, any reference to the parental responsibility for the child is to be read as a reference to the parental responsibilities and parental rights in relation to the child; and

    (b)   in section 28(2), the reference to the court is to be read as a reference to the authorised court.

53C   Further consequences of placement and placement orders

(1)   Subsection (2) applies where—

    (a)   a child is placed for adoption under section 19 of the Adoption and Children Act 2002 (placing children with parental consent); or

    (b)   an adoption agency is authorised to place the child for adoption under that section.

(2)   No order under subsection (1) of section 11 of the Children (Scotland) Act 1995 (court orders relating to parental responsibilities etc) of a kind referred to in subsection (2)(c) (residence orders) of that section may be made in respect of the child.

(3)   On the making of an order under section 21 of the Adoption and Children Act 2002 (a "placement order") in respect of a child, any order under subsection (1) of section 11 of the Children (Scotland) Act 1995 of a kind referred to in subsection (2)(c) to (f) (residence orders, contact orders, specific issue orders and interdicts in relation to parental responsibilities) of that section in respect of the child ceases to have effect.

(4)   Where a placement order is in force—

    (a)   no such order as is referred to in subsection (3) of this section; and

    (b)   no order under section 55 of the Children (Scotland) Act 1995 (child assessment orders),

may be made in respect of the child.'

31   In section 54 (evidence of adoption in England, Wales and Northern Ireland), in paragraph (a), for 'section 50(2) of the Adoption Act 1976' there is substituted 'section 77(4) and (5) of the Adoption and Children Act 2002'.

32   In section 56 (authorised courts), in subsection (3), for 'Great Britain' there is substituted 'Scotland'.

33   In section 59 (rules of procedure)—

(a)   in subsection (2)—

(i)   for the words from 'in relation to' to 'adoption', where it secondly occurs, there is substituted '(except where an order has been made freeing the child for adoption)'; and

(ii)   for the words from 'every' to 'Act' there is substituted 'any person mentioned in subsection (2A)'; and

(b)   after subsection (2) there is inserted—

'(2A)   The persons referred to in subsection (2) are—

(a)   every person who can be found and whose agreement or consent to the making of the order is required to be given or dispensed with under this Act or, if no such person can be found, any relative prescribed by rules who can be found;

(b)   every person who has consented to the making of the order under section 20 of the Adoption and Children Act 2002 (and has not withdrawn the consent) unless he has given a notice under subsection (4)(a) of that section which has effect;

(c)   every person who, if leave were given under section 16(3B), would be entitled to oppose the making of the order.'

34   In section 60 (orders, rules and regulations), after subsection (3) there is inserted—

'(3A)   An order under section 65(2) shall be subject to annulment in pursuance of a resolution of the Scottish Parliament.'

35   In section 65 (interpretation), in subsection (1)—

(a)   in the definition of 'adoption agency', for 'section 1 of the Adoption Act 1976' there is substituted 'section 2(1) of the Adoption and Children Act 2002',

(b)   in the definition of 'adoption order'—

(i)   in paragraph (b), for 'section 12 of the Adoption Act 1976' there is substituted 'section 46 of the Adoption and Children Act 2002',

(ii)   in paragraph (c), for 'section 55 of the Adoption Act 1976' there is substituted 'section 84 of the Adoption and Children Act 2002', and

(c)   in the definition of 'order freeing a child for adoption', paragraph (a) and the word 'and' immediately following that paragraph are omitted.

The Magistrates' Courts Act 1980 (c 43)

36   The Magistrates' Courts Act 1980 is amended as follows.

37   In section 65 (meaning of family proceedings), in subsection (1), for paragraph (h) there is substituted—

'(h)   the Adoption and Children Act 2002;'.

38   In section 69 (sitting of magistrates' courts for family proceedings), in subsections (2) and (3), for 'the Adoption Act 1976' there is substituted 'the Adoption and Children Act 2002'.

39   In section 71 (newspaper reports of family proceedings)—

(a)   in subsection (1), '(other than proceedings under the Adoption Act 1976)' is omitted,

(b)   in subsection (2)—

(i)   for 'the Adoption Act 1976' there is substituted 'the Adoption and Children Act 2002',

(ii)   the words following '(a) and (b)' are omitted.

40   In Part 1 of Schedule 6 (fees to be taken by justices' chief executives), in the entry relating to family proceedings—

(a)   for 'the Adoption Act 1976, except under section 21 of that Act', there is substituted 'the Adoption and Children Act 2002, except under section 23 of that Act',

(b)   in paragraph (c), for 'section 21 of the Adoption Act 1976' there is substituted 'section 23 of the Adoption and Children Act 2002'.

The Mental Health Act 1983 (*c 20*)

41   In section 28 of the Mental Health Act 1983 (nearest relative of minor under guardianship, etc), in subsection (3), after '"guardian" ' there is inserted 'includes a special guardian (within the meaning of the Children Act 1989), but'.

The Child Abduction Act 1984 (*c 37*)

42   (1)   Section 1 of the Child Abduction Act 1984 (offence of abduction of child by parent, etc) is amended as follows.

(2)   In subsection (2), after paragraph (c) there is inserted—

'(ca)   he is a special guardian of the child; or'.

(3)   In subsection (3)(a), after sub-paragraph (iii) there is inserted—

'(iiia)   any special guardian of the child;'.

(4)   In subsection (4), for paragraphs (a) and (b) there is substituted—

'(a)   he is a person in whose favour there is a residence order in force with respect to the child, and he takes or sends the child out of the United Kingdom for a period of less than one month; or

(b)   he is a special guardian of the child and he takes or sends the child out of the United Kingdom for a period of less than three months.'

(5)   In subsection (5A), the 'or' at the end of sub-paragraph (i) of paragraph (a) is omitted, and after that sub-paragraph there is inserted—

'(ia)   who is a special guardian of the child; or'.

(6)   In subsection (7)(a), after '"guardian of a child," ' there is inserted '"special guardian," '.

43   (1)   The Schedule to that Act (modifications of section 1 for children in certain cases) is amended as follows.

(2)   In paragraph 3 (adoption and custodianship), for sub-paragraphs (1) and (2) there is substituted—

'(1)   This paragraph applies where—

(a)   a child is placed for adoption by an adoption agency under section 19 of the Adoption and Children Act 2002, or an adoption agency is authorised to place the child for adoption under that section; or

(b)   a placement order is in force in respect of the child; or

(c)   an application for such an order has been made in respect of the child and has not been disposed of; or

(d)   an application for an adoption order has been made in respect of the child and has not been disposed of; or

(e)   an order under section 84 of the Adoption and Children Act 2002 (giving parental responsibility prior to adoption abroad) has been made in respect of the child, or an application for such an order in respect of him has been made and has not been disposed of.

(2)   Where this paragraph applies, section 1 of this Act shall have effect as if—

(a)　the reference in subsection (1) to the appropriate consent were—

    (i)　in a case within sub-paragraph (1)(a) above, a reference to the consent of each person who has parental responsibility for the child or to the leave of the High Court;

    (ii)　in a case within sub-paragraph (1)(b) above, a reference to the leave of the court which made the placement order;

    (iii)　in a case within sub-paragraph (1)(c) or (d) above, a reference to the leave of the court to which the application was made;

    (iv)　in a case within sub-paragraph (1)(e) above, a reference to the leave of the court which made the order or, as the case may be, to which the application was made;

(b)　subsection (3) were omitted;

(c)　in subsection (4), in paragraph (a), for the words from "in whose favour" to the first mention of "child" there were substituted "who provides the child's home in a case falling within sub-paragraph (1)(a) or (b) of paragraph 3 of the Schedule to this Act"; and

(d)　subsections (4A), (5), (5A) and (6) were omitted.'

(3)　In paragraph 5 (interpretation), in sub-paragraph (a), for the words from 'and 'adoption order' to the end there is substituted ', "adoption order", "placed for adoption by an adoption agency" and "placement order" have the same meaning as in the Adoption and Children Act 2002; and'.

...

44　...

The Child Abduction and Custody Act 1985 (*c 60*)

45　In Schedule 3 to the Child Abduction and Custody Act 1985 (custody orders), in paragraph 1, the 'and' at the end of paragraph (b) is omitted and after that paragraph there is inserted—

'(bb)　a special guardianship order (within the meaning of the Act of 1989); and',

and paragraph (c)(v) is omitted.

The Family Law Act 1986 (*c 55*)

46　The Family Law Act 1986 is amended as follows.

47　In section 1 (orders to which Part 1 applies), in subsection (1), after paragraph (a) there is inserted—

'(aa)　a special guardianship order made by a court in England and Wales under the Children Act 1989;

(ab)　an order made under section 26 of the Adoption and Children Act 2002 (contact), other than an order varying or revoking such an order'.

4　In section 2 (jurisdiction: general), after subsection (2) there is inserted—

'(2A)　A court in England and Wales shall not have jurisdiction to make a special guardianship order under the Children Act 1989 unless the condition in section 3 of this Act is satisfied.

(2B)　A court in England and Wales shall not have jurisdiction to make an order under section 26 of the Adoption and Children Act 2002 unless the condition in section 3 of this Act is satisfied.'

49　In section 57 (declarations as to adoptions effected overseas)—

(a) for subsection (1)(a) there is substituted—

'(a) a Convention adoption, or an overseas adoption, within the meaning of the Adoption and Children Act 2002, or',

(b) in subsection (2)(a), after '1976' there is inserted 'or section 67 of the Adoption and Children Act 2002'.

The Family Law Reform Act 1987 (*c 42*)

50 The Family Law Reform Act 1987 is amended as follows.

51 In section 1 (general principle), for paragraph (c) of subsection (3) there is substituted—

'(c) is an adopted person within the meaning of Chapter 4 of Part 1 of the Adoption and Children Act 2002'.

52 In section 19 (dispositions of property), in subsection (5), after '1976' there is inserted 'or section 69 of the Adoption and Children Act 2002'.

The Adoption (Northern Ireland) Order 1987 (*SI 1987/2203 (NI 22)*)

53 In Article 2(2) (interpretation), in the definition of 'prescribed', for 'Articles 54' there is substituted 'Articles 53(3B) and (3D), 54'.

The Children Act 1989 (*c 41*)

54 The Children Act 1989 is amended as follows.

55 In section 8 (residence, contact and other orders with respect to children), in subsection (4), for paragraph (d) there is substituted—

'(d) the Adoption and Children Act 2002;'.

56 In section 10 (power of court to make section 8 orders)—

(a) in subsection (4)(a), for 'or guardian' there is substituted ', guardian or special guardian',

(b) after subsection (4)(a) there is inserted—

'(aa) any person who by virtue of section 4A has parental responsibility for the child;',

(c) after subsection (5) there is inserted—

'(5A) A local authority foster parent is entitled to apply for a residence order with respect to a child if the child has lived with him for a period of at least one year immediately preceding the application.',

(d) after subsection (7) there is inserted—

'(7A) If a special guardianship order is in force with respect to a child, an application for a residence order may only be made with respect to him, if apart from this subsection the leave of the court is not required, with such leave.'

57 In section 12 (residence orders and parental responsibility), in subsection (3)—

(a) paragraph (a) is omitted,
(b) in paragraph (b), for 'section 55 of the Act of 1976' there is substituted 'section 84 of the Adoption and Children Act 2002'.

58 In section 16 (family assistance orders), in subsection (2)(a), for 'or guardian' there is substituted ', guardian or special guardian'.

59 In section 20 (provision of accommodation for children: general), in subsection (9), the 'or' at the end of paragraph (a) is omitted and after that paragraph there is inserted—

'(aa) who is a special guardian of the child; or'.

60 In section 24 (persons qualifying for advice and assistance)—

(a) for subsection (1) there is substituted—

'(1) In this Part "a person qualifying for advice and assistance" means a person to whom subsection (1A) or (1B) applies.

(1A) This subsection applies to a person—

(a) who has reached the age of sixteen but not the age of twenty-one;

(b) with respect to whom a special guardianship order is in force (or, if he has reached the age of eighteen, was in force when he reached that age); and

(c) who was, immediately before the making of that order, looked after by a local authority.

(1B) This subsection applies to a person to whom subsection (1A) does not apply, and who—

(a) is under twenty-one; and

(b) at any time after reaching the age of sixteen but while still a child was, but is no longer, looked after, accommodated or fostered.',

(b) in subsection (2), for 'subsection (1)(b)' there is substituted 'subsection (1B)(b)',

(c) in subsection (5), before paragraph (a) there is inserted—

'(za) in the case of a person to whom subsection (1A) applies, a local authority determined in accordance with regulations made by the Secretary of State;'.

61 In section 24A (advice and assistance for qualifying persons)—

(a) in subsection (2)(b), after 'a person' there is inserted 'to whom section 24(1A) applies, or to whom section 24(1B) applies and',

(b) in subsection (3)(a), after 'if' there is inserted 'he is a person to whom section 24(1A) applies, or he is a person to whom section 24(1B) applies and'.

62 In section 24B (assistance with employment, education and training), in each of subsections (1) and (3)(b), after 'of' there is inserted 'section 24(1A) or'.

63 In section 33 (effect of care order)—

(a) in subsection (3)(b), for 'a parent or guardian of the child' there is substituted

'—

(i) a parent, guardian or special guardian of the child; or

(ii) a person who by virtue of section 4A has parental responsibility for the child,',

(b) in subsection (5), for 'a parent or guardian of the child who has care of him' there is substituted 'a person mentioned in that provision who has care of the child',

(c) in subsection (6)(b)—

(i) sub-paragraph (i) is omitted,

(ii) in sub-paragraph (ii), for 'section 55 of the Act of 1976' there is substituted 'section 84 of the Adoption and Children Act 2002',

(d)   in subsection (9), for 'a parent or guardian of the child' there is substituted 'a person mentioned in that provision'.

64   In section 34 (parental contact etc with children in care)—

(a)   in subsection (1)(b), after 'guardian' there is inserted 'or special guardian', and
(b)   after subsection (1)(b) there is inserted—

'(ba)   any person who by virtue of section 4A has parental responsibility for him;'.

65   In section 80 (inspection of children's homes by persons authorised by Secretary of State), in subsection (1), paragraphs (e) and (f) are omitted.

66   In section 81 (inquiries), in subsection (1), paragraph (b) is omitted.

67   In section 88 (amendments of adoption legislation), subsection (1) is omitted.

68   In section 91 (effect and duration of orders, etc)—

(a)   after subsection (5) there is inserted—

'(5A)   The making of a special guardianship order with respect to a child who is the subject of—

(a)   a care order; or
(b)   an order under section 34,

discharges that order.',

(b)   in subsection (7), after '4(1)' there is inserted '4A(1)',
(c)   in subsection (8)(a), after '4' there is inserted 'or 4A'.

69   In section 102 (power of constable to assist in exercise of certain powers to search for children or inspect premises), in subsection (6), paragraph (c) is omitted.

70   In section 105 (interpretation), in subsection (1)—

(a)   in the definition of 'adoption agency', for 'section 1 of the Adoption Act 1976' there is substituted 'section 2 of the Adoption and Children Act 2002',
(b)   at the appropriate place there is inserted—

"section 31A plan' has the meaning given by section 31A(6);',

(c)   in the definition of 'parental responsibility agreement', for 'section 4(1)' there is substituted 'sections 4(1) and 4A(2)',
(d)   the definition of 'protected child' is omitted,
(e)   after the definition of 'special educational needs' there is inserted—

'"special guardian" and "special guardianship order" have the meaning given by section 14A;'.

71   In Schedule 1 (financial provision for children)—

(a)   in paragraph 1 (orders for financial relief against parents)—

(i)   in sub-paragraph (1), for 'or guardian' there is substituted ', guardian or special guardian', and
(ii)   in sub-paragraph (6), after 'order' there is inserted 'or a special guardianship order',

(b)   in paragraph 6 (variation etc of orders for periodical payments), in sub-paragraph (8), after 'guardian' there is inserted 'or special guardian',
(c)   in paragraph 8 (financial relief under other enactments), in sub-paragraph (1) and in sub-paragraph (2)(b), after 'residence order' there is inserted 'or a special guardianship order',

(d)   in paragraph 14 (financial provision for child resident in country outside England and Wales), in sub-paragraph (1)(b), after 'guardian' there is inserted 'or special guardian'.

72   In Schedule 2, in paragraph 19 (arrangements by local authorities to assist children to live abroad)—

(a)   in sub-paragraph (4) (arrangements to assist children to live abroad), after 'guardian,' there is inserted 'special guardian,',
(b)   in sub-paragraph (6), for the words from the beginning to 'British subject)' there is substituted 'Section 85 of the Adoption and Children Act 2002 (which imposes restrictions on taking children out of the United Kingdom)',
(c)   after sub-paragraph (8) there is inserted—

'(9)   This paragraph does not apply to a local authority placing a child for adoption with prospective adopters.'

73   In Schedule 8 (privately fostered children), in paragraph 5, for sub-paragraphs (a) and (b) there is substituted

'he is placed in the care of a person who proposes to adopt him under arrangements made by an adoption agency within the meaning of—

(a)   section 2 of the Adoption and Children Act 2002;
(b)   section 1 of the Adoption (Scotland) Act 1978; or
(c)   Article 3 of the Adoption (Northern Ireland) Order 1987'.

74   Part 1 of Schedule 10 is omitted.

75   In Schedule 11 (jurisdiction), in paragraphs 1 and 2, for the words 'the Adoption Act 1976', wherever they occur, there is substituted 'the Adoption and Children Act 2002'.

The Human Fertilisation and Embryology Act 1990 (*c 37*)

76   The Human Fertilisation and Embryology Act 1990 is amended as follows.

77   In section 27 (meaning of mother), in subsection (2), for 'child of any person other than the adopter or adopters' there is substituted 'woman's child'.

78   In section 28 (meaning of father), in subsection (5)(c), for 'child of any person other than the adopter or adopters' there is substituted 'man's child'.

79   In section 30 (parental orders in favour of gamete donors), in subsection (10) for 'Adoption Act 1976' there is substituted 'Adoption and Children Act 2002'.

The Courts and Legal Services Act 1990 (*c 41*)

80   In section 58A of the Courts and Legal Services Act 1990 (conditional fee agreements: supplementary), in subsection (2), for paragraph (b) there is substituted—

'(b)   the Adoption and Children Act 2002;'.

The Child Support Act 1991 (*c 48*)

81   In section 26 of the Child Support Act 1991 (disputes about parentage), in subsection (3), after '1976' there is inserted 'or Chapter 4 of Part 1 of the Adoption and Children Act 2002'.

The Children (Scotland) Act 1995 (c 36)

82   Section 86 of the Children (Scotland) Act 1995 (parental responsibilities order: general) is amended as follows.

83   In subsection (3), in paragraph (a), for 'section 18 (freeing for adoption) or 55 (adoption abroad) of the Adoption Act 1976' there is substituted 'section 19 (placing children with parental consent) or 84 (giving parental responsibility prior to adoption abroad) of the Adoption and Children Act 2002'.

84   In subsection (6), in paragraph (b), for the words from the beginning to 'Adoption Act 1976' there is substituted—

'(b)   he becomes the subject of an adoption order within the meaning of the Adoption (Scotland) Act 1978;

(bb)   an adoption agency, within the meaning of section 2 of the Adoption and Children Act 2002, is authorised to place him for adoption under section 19 of that Act (placing children with parental consent) or he becomes the subject of an order under section 21 of that Act (placement orders) or under section 84 of that Act (giving parental responsibility prior to adoption abroad)'.

The Family Law Act 1996 (c 27)

85   The Family Law Act 1996 is amended as follows.

86   In section 62 (meaning of 'relevant child' etc)—

(a)   in subsection (2), in paragraph (b), after 'the Adoption Act 1976' there is inserted ', the Adoption and Children Act 2002',

(b)   in subsection (5), for the words from 'has been freed' to '1976' there is substituted 'falls within subsection (7)'.

87   At the end of that section there is inserted—

'(7)   A child falls within this subsection if—

(a)   an adoption agency, within the meaning of section 2 of the Adoption and Children Act 2002, has power to place him for adoption under section 19 of that Act (placing children with parental consent) or he has become the subject of an order under section 21 of that Act (placement orders), or

(b)   he is freed for adoption by virtue of an order made—
  (i)   in England and Wales, under section 18 of the Adoption Act 1976,
  (ii)   in Scotland, under section 18 of the Adoption (Scotland) Act 1978, or
  (iii)   in Northern Ireland, under Article 17(1) or 18(1) of the Adoption (Northern Ireland) Order 1987.'

88   In section 63 (interpretation of Part 4)—

(a)   in subsection (1), for the definition of 'adoption order', there is substituted—

'"adoption order" means an adoption order within the meaning of section 72(1) of the Adoption Act 1976 or section 46(1) of the Adoption and Children Act 2002;',

(b)   in subsection (2), after paragraph (h) there is inserted—

'(i)   the Adoption and Children Act 2002.'

The Housing Act 1996 (c 52)

89   Section 178 of the Housing Act 1996 (meaning of associated person) is amended as follows.

90   In subsection (2), for the words from 'has been freed' to '1976' there is substituted 'falls within subsection (2A)'.

91   After that subsection there is inserted—

'(2A)   A child falls within this subsection if—

(a)   an adoption agency, within the meaning of section 2 of the Adoption and Children Act 2002, is authorised to place him for adoption under section 19 of that Act (placing children with parental consent) or he has become the subject of an order under section 21 of that Act (placement orders), or

(b)   he is freed for adoption by virtue of an order made—

(i)   in England and Wales, under section 18 of the Adoption Act 1976,

(ii)   in Scotland, under section 18 of the Adoption (Scotland) Act 1978, or

(iii)   in Northern Ireland, under Article 17(1) or 18(1) of the Adoption (Northern Ireland) Order 1987.'

92   In subsection (3), for the definition of 'adoption order', there is substituted—

'"adoption order" means an adoption order within the meaning of section 72(1) of the Adoption Act 1976 or section 46(1) of the Adoption and Children Act 2002;'.

...

93   ...

The Protection of Children Act 1999 (c 14)

94   In section 2B of the Protection of Children Act 1999 (individuals named in the findings of certain inquiries), in subsection (7), after paragraph (a) there is inserted—

'(vi)   section 17 of the Adoption and Children Act 2002;'.

The Adoption (Intercountry Aspects) Act 1999 (c 18)

95   The following provisions of the Adoption (Intercountry Aspects) Act 1999 cease to have effect in relation to England and Wales: sections 3, 6, 8, 9 and 11 to 13.

96   Section 2 of that Act (accredited bodies) is amended as follows.

97   In subsection (2A)—

(a)   for the words from the beginning to '2000' there is substituted 'A registered adoption society',

(b)   for 'agency' there is substituted 'society'.

98   For subsection (5) there is substituted—

'(5)   In this section, "registered adoption society" has the same meaning as in section 2 of the Adoption and Children Act 2002 (basic definitions); and expressions used in this section in its application to England and Wales which are also used in that Act have the same meanings as in that Act.'

99 In subsection (6)—

(a) the words 'in its application to Scotland' are omitted,

(b) after 'expressions' there is inserted 'used in this section in its application to Scotland'.

100 Section 14 (restriction on bringing children into the United Kingdom for adoption) is omitted.

101 In section 16(1) (devolution: Wales), the words ', or section 17 or 56A of the 1976 Act,' are omitted.

The Access to Justice Act 1999 (*c 22*)

102 In Schedule 2 to the Access to Justice Act 1999 (Community Legal Service: excluded services), in paragraph 2(3)(c)—

(a) for 'section 27 or 28 of the Adoption Act 1976' there is substituted 'section 36 of the Adoption and Children Act 2002',

(b) for 'an order under Part II or section 29 or 55' there is substituted 'a placement order or adoption order (within the meaning of the Adoption and Children Act 2002) or an order under section 41 or 84'.

The Care Standards Act 2000 (*c 14*)

103 The Care Standards Act 2000 is amended as follows.

104 In section 4 (basic definitions), in subsection (7), for 'the Adoption Act 1976' there is substituted 'the Adoption and Children Act 2002'.

105 At the end of section 5 (registration authorities) there is inserted—

'(2) This section is subject to section 36A.'

106 In section 11 (requirement to register), in subsection (3), for 'reference in subsection (1) to an agency does' there is substituted 'references in subsections (1) and (2) to an agency do'.

107 In section 14 (2) (offences conviction of which may result in cancellation of registration), for paragraph (d) there is substituted—

'(d) an offence under regulations under section 1(3) of the Adoption (Intercountry Aspects) Act 1999,

(e) an offence under the Adoption and Children Act 2002 or regulations made under it'.

108 In section 16(2) (power to make regulations providing that no application for registration may be made in respect of certain agencies which are unincorporated bodies), 'or a voluntary adoption agency' is omitted.

109 In section 22(10) (disapplication of power to make regulations in the case of voluntary adoption agencies), at the end there is inserted 'or adoption support agencies'.

110 In section 23 (standards), at the end of subsection (4)(d) there is inserted 'or proceedings against a voluntary adoption agency for an offence under section 9(4) of the Adoption Act 1976 or section 9 of the Adoption and Children Act 2002'.

111 In section 31 (inspections by authorised persons), in subsection (3)(b), for 'section 9(2) of the Adoption Act 1976' there is substituted 'section 9 of the Adoption and Children Act 2002'.

112 In section 43 (introductory), in subsection (3)(a)—

(a) for 'the Adoption Act 1976' there is substituted 'the Adoption and Children Act 2002',

(b) after 'children' there is inserted 'or the provision of adoption support services (as defined in section 2(6) of the Adoption and Children Act 2002)'.

113 In section 46 (inspections: supplementary), in subsection (7)(c), for 'section 9(3) of the Adoption Act 1976' there is substituted 'section 9 of the Adoption and Children Act 2002'.

114 In section 48 (regulation of fostering functions), at the end of subsection (1) there is inserted—

'(f) as to the fees or expenses which may be paid to persons assisting local authorities in making decisions in the exercise of such functions'.

115 In section 55(2)(b) (definition of 'social care worker'), for 'or a voluntary adoption agency' there is substituted ', a voluntary adoption agency or an adoption support agency'.

116 In section 121 (general interpretation)—

(a) in subsection (1), in the definition of 'voluntary organisation', for 'the Adoption Act 1976' there is substituted 'the Adoption and Children Act 2002',

(b) in subsection (13), in the appropriate place in the table there is inserted—

'Adoption support   Section 4'.
agency

117 In Schedule 4 (minor and consequential amendments), paragraph 27(b) is omitted.

The Criminal Justice and Court Services Act 2000 (c 43)

118 In section 12(5) of the Criminal Justice and Court Services Act 2000 (meaning of 'family proceedings' in relation to CAFCASS), paragraph (b) (supervision orders under the 1989 Act) and the preceding 'and' are omitted.

NOTES

Initial Commencement

To be appointed
Paras 1–12, 14–20, 36–52, 54–64, 67–81, 85–110, 114–118: To be appointed: see s 148(1), (2); paras 13, 65, 66, 111–113: to be appointed: see s 148(6); paras 21–35, 82–84: to be appointed: see s 148(5)(c); para 53: to be appointed: see s 148(1).

Appointment
Paras 1–5, 9–12, 14–20, 36–43, 45–52, 54–59, 61–64, 67–81, 85–93, 95–99, 101, 102, 104, 107–109, 114–117: appointment: 30 December 2005: see SI 2005/2213, art 2(o); paras 6, 7: appointment: 1 December 2003: see SI 2003/3079, art 2(2)(b); paras 13, 65, 111–113: appointment (in relation to England): 30 December 2005: see SI 2005/2213, art 3(l); paras 13, 65, 111–113: appointment (in relation to Wales): 30 December 2005: see SI 2005/3112, art 2(g); paras 21–35, 82–84: appointment: 30 December 2005: see SSI 2005/643, art 2(c); para 53: appointment: 3 February 2003: see SI 2003/288, art 2(a); para 60: appointment (for the purpose of making regulations): 7 December 2004: see SI 2004/3203, art 2(1)(m)(x); para 60: appointment (for remaining purposes): 30 December 2005: see SI 2005/2213, art 2(o); para 103: appointment (in relation to England for certain purposes): 25 February 2003: see SI 2003/366, art 2(1)(b); para 103: appointment (in relation to England for certain purposes): 30 April 2003: see SI 2003/366, art 2(4)(b)–(d); para 103: appointment (in relation to Wales): 28 November 2003: see SI 2003/3079, art 2(1)(b); para 103: appointment (in relation to England for remaining purposes): 30 December 2005: see SI 2005/2213, art 2(o); paras 105, 106: appointment (in relation to England for certain purposes): 25 February 2003: see SI 2003/366, art 2(1)(b); paras 105, 106: appointment (in relation to England for remaining purposes): 30 April 2003: see SI 2003/366, art 2(4)(b); paras 105, 106: appointment (in relation to Wales): 28 November 2003: see SI 2003/3079, art 2(1)(b); para 110: appointment (in relation to England in so far as it relates to the Adoption Act 1976): 30 April 2003: see SI 2003/366, art 2(4)(c); para 110: appointment (in relation to Wales in so far as it relates to the Adoption Act 1976): 28 November 2003: see

SI 2003/3079, art 2(1)(b); para 110: appointment (for remaining purposes): 30 December 2005: see SI 2005/2213, art 2(o); para 118: appointment: 28 November 2003: see SI 2003/3079, art 2(1)(c).

Amendment
Para 44: repealed by the Courts Act 2003, s 109(3), Sch 10.; date in force: 1 April 2005: see SI 2005/910, art 3(aa); for transitional provisions see SI 2005/911, arts 2–5; para 93: repealed by the Serious Organised Crime and Police Act 2005, s 174(2), Sch 17, Pt 2; date in force: 6 April 2006: see SI 2006/378, art 7(f)(vii).

SCHEDULE 4
Transitional and Transitory Provisions and Savings

Section 139

General rules for continuity

1   (1)   Any reference (express or implied) in Part 1 or any other enactment, instrument or document to—

(a)   any provision of Part 1, or
(b)   things done or falling to be done under or for the purposes of any provision of Part 1,

must, so far as the nature of the reference permits, be construed as including, in relation to the times, circumstances or purposes in relation to which the corresponding provision repealed by this Act had effect, a reference to that corresponding provision or (as the case may be) to things done or falling to be done under or for the purposes of that corresponding provision.

(2)   Any reference (express or implied) in any enactment, instrument or document to—

(a)   a provision repealed by this Act, or
(b)   things done or falling to be done under or for the purposes of such a provision,

must, so far as the nature of the reference permits, be construed as including, in relation to the times, circumstances or purposes in relation to which the corresponding provision of Part 1 has effect, a reference to that corresponding provision or (as the case may be) to things done or falling to be done under or for the purposes of that corresponding provision.

General rule for old savings

2   (1)   The repeal by this Act of an enactment previously repealed subject to savings does not affect the continued operation of those savings.
(2)   The repeal by this Act of a saving made on the previous repeal of an enactment does not affect the operation of the saving in so far as it is not specifically reproduced in this Act but remains capable of having effect.

...

3   ...

4   ...

5   ...

Pending applications for freeing orders

6   Nothing in this Act affects any application for an order under section 18 of the Adoption Act 1976 (freeing for adoption) where—

(a) the application has been made and has not been disposed of immediately before the repeal of that section, and

(b) the child in relation to whom the application is made has his home immediately before that repeal with a person with whom he has been placed for adoption by an adoption agency.

Freeing orders

7 (1) Nothing in this Act affects any order made under section 18 of the Adoption Act 1976 (c 36) and—

(a) sections 19 to 21 of that Act are to continue to have effect in relation to such an order, and

(b) Part 1 of Schedule 6 to the Magistrates' Courts Act 1980 (c 43) is to continue to have effect for the purposes of an application under section 21 of the Adoption Act 1976 in relation to such an order.

(2) Section 20 of that Act, as it has effect by virtue of this paragraph, is to apply as if, in subsection (3)(c) after '1989' there were inserted—

'(iia) any care order, within the meaning of that Act'.

(3) Where a child is free for adoption by virtue of an order made under section 18 of that Act, the third condition in section 47(6) is to be treated as satisfied.

Pending applications for adoption orders

8 Nothing in this Act affects any application for an adoption order under section 12 of the Adoption Act 1976 where—

(a) the application has been made and has not been disposed of immediately before the repeal of that section, and

(b) the child in relation to whom the application is made has his home immediately before that repeal with a person with whom he has been placed for adoption by an adoption agency.

Notification of adoption applications

9 Where a notice given in respect of a child by the prospective adopters under section 22(1) of the Adoption Act 1976 is treated by virtue of paragraph 1(1) as having been given for the purposes of section 44(2) in respect of an application to adopt the child, section 42(3) has effect in relation to their application for an adoption order as if for 'six months' there were substituted 'twelve months'.

...

10 ...

11 ...

12 ...

13 ...

14 ...

15 ...

16 ...

Status

17 (1) Section 67—

(a) does not apply to a pre-1976 instrument or enactment in so far as it contains a disposition of property, and

(b) does not apply to any public general Act in its application to any disposition of property in a pre-1976 instrument or enactment.

(2) Section 73 applies in relation to this paragraph as if this paragraph were contained in Chapter 4 of Part 1; and an instrument or enactment is a pre-1976 instrument or enactment for the purposes of this Schedule if it was passed or made at any time before 1st January 1976.

18 Section 69 does not apply to a pre-1976 instrument.

19 In section 70(1), the reference to Part 3 of the Family Law Reform Act 1987 (c 42) includes Part 2 of the Family Law Reform Act 1969 (c 46).

Registration of adoptions

20 (1) The power of the court under paragraph 4(1) of Schedule 1 to amend an order on the application of the adopter or adopted person includes, in relation to an order made before 1st April 1959, power to make any amendment of the particulars contained in the order which appears to be required to bring the order into the form in which it would have been made if paragraph 1 of that Schedule had applied to the order.

(2) In relation to an adoption order made before the commencement of the Adoption Act 1976 (c 36), the reference in paragraph 4(3) of that Schedule to paragraph 1(2) or (3) is to be read—

(a) in the case of an order under the Adoption of Children Act 1926 (c 29), as a reference to section 12(3) and (4) of the Adoption of Children Act 1949 (c 98),

(b) in the case of an order under the Adoption Act 1950 (c 26), as a reference to section 18(3) and (4) of that Act,

(c) in the case of an order under the Adoption Act 1958 (c 5), as a reference to section 21(4) and (5) of that Act.

The Child Abduction Act 1984 (c 37)

21 Paragraph 43 of Schedule 3 does not affect the Schedule to the Child Abduction Act 1984 in its application to a child who is the subject of—

(a) an order under section 18 of the Adoption Act 1976 freeing the child for adoption,

(b) a pending application for such an order, or

(c) a pending application for an order under section 12 of that Act.

The Courts and Legal Services Act 1990 (c 41)

22 Paragraph 80 of Schedule 3 does not affect section 58A(2)(b) of the Courts and Legal Services Act 1990 in its application to proceedings under the Adoption Act 1976 (c 36).

The Children (Scotland) Act 1995 (c 36)

23 Paragraph 84 of Schedule 3 does not affect section 86(6) of the Children (Scotland) Act 1995 in its application to a child who becomes the subject of an order under section 18 or 55 of the Adoption Act 1976 by virtue of an application made before the repeal of that section.

PART B – Statutes

NOTES

Initial Commencement

To be appointed

Paras 1, 2, 4, 6–14, 16–22: to be appointed: see s 148(1), (2); paras 3, 5: To be appointed: see s 148(6); paras 15, 23: to be appointed: see s 148(5)(d).

Appointment

Paras 1, 2, 6–8, 17–22: appointment: 30 December 2005: see SI 2005/2897, art 2(a); for transitional provisions and savings see arts 3–16 thereof; para 3: appointment (in relation to England for the purposes of making regulations): 10 March 2003: see SI 2003/366, art 2(2)(a); para 3: appointment (in relation to England for remaining purposes): 6 October 2003: see SI 2003/366, art 2(6)(a); paras 3, 5: appointment (in relation to Wales): 7 February 2004: see SI 2004/252, art 2(d); para 5: appointment (in relation to England for the purposes of making regulations): 1 December 2003: see SI 2003/3079, art 2(2)(c); para 5: appointment (in relation to England for remaining purposes): 1 April 2004: see SI 2003/3079, art 2(4)(a); paras 10, 11(a), 13, 14: appointment: 1 June 2003: see SI 2003/366, art 2(5)(c)(i)–(iii); para 12: appointment (in so far as it inserts the Adoption Act 1976, s 56A(1)–(8), (11) for the purposes of making regulations): 1 April 2003: see SI 2003/366, art 2(3); para 12: appointment (in so far as it inserts the Adoption Act 1976, s 56A(1)–(8), (11) for remaining purposes): 1 June 2003: see SI 2003/366, art 2(5)(c)(i); para 23: appointment: 30 December 2005: see SSI 2005/643, art 2(d).

Extent

Para 23 applies to Scotland only: see s 149(5).

Amendment

Paras 3–5, 10–16: repealed by s 139(3), Sch 5 hereto; date in force: 30 December 2005: see SI 2005/2897, art 2(b).

SCHEDULE 5
Repeals

Section 139

Short title and chapter	Extent of repeal
Births and Deaths Registration Act 1953 (c 20)	In section 10(3), the words following 'the Family Law Reform Act 1987'.
Sexual Offences Act 1956 (c 69)	In section 28(4), the 'or' at the end of paragraph (a).
Local Authority Social Services Act 1970 (c 42)	In Schedule 1, the entry relating to the Adoption Act 1976.
Adoption Act 1976 (c 36)	The whole Act, except Part 4 and paragraph 6 of Schedule 2.
Criminal Law Act 1977 (c 45)	In Schedule 12, the entries relating to the Adoption Act 1976.
National Health Service Act 1977 (c 49)	In section 124A(3), the 'or' at the end of paragraph (a).
Domestic Proceedings and Magistrates' Courts Act 1978 (c 22)	Sections 73(2), 74(2) and 74(4).
Adoption (Scotland) Act 1978 (c 28)	In section 50, the words 'not being a parent or guardian or relative of the child'.
	Section 52.
	In section 53(2), the words 'England and Wales or'.
	In section 65(1), in the definition of 'order freeing a child for adoption', paragraph (a) and the word 'and' immediately following that paragraph.

Magistrates' Courts Act 1980 (c 43)	In section 71(1) the words '(other than proceedings under the Adoption Act 1976)'.
	In section 71(2) the words following '(a) and (b)'.
	In Schedule 7, paragraphs 141 and 142.
British Nationality Act 1981 (c 61)	In section 1(8), the words following 'section 50'.
Mental Health Act 1983 (c 20)	In Schedule 4, paragraph 45.
Health and Social Services and Social Security Adjudications Act 1983 (c 41)	In Schedule 2, paragraphs 29 to 33, 35 and 36.
	In Schedule 9, paragraph 19.
County Courts Act 1984 (c 28)	In Schedule 2, paragraph 58.
Child Abduction Act 1984 (c 37)	In section 1(5A)(a), the 'or' at the end of sub-paragraph (i).
Matrimonial and Family Proceedings Act 1984 (c 42)	In section 40(2)(a), after 'the Adoption Act 1968', the word 'or'.
	In Schedule 1, paragraph 20.
Child Abduction and Custody Act 1985 (c 60)	In Schedule 3, in paragraph 1, the 'and' at the end of paragraph (b).
	In Schedule 3, in paragraph 1(c), paragraph (v).
Family Law Reform Act 1987 (c 42)	In Schedule 3, paragraphs 2 to 5.
Children Act 1989 (c 41)	Section 9(4).
	Section 12(3)(a).
	In section 20(9), the 'or' at the end of paragraph (a).
	In section 26(2)(e) and (f), the words 'to consider'.
	Section 33(6)(b)(i).
	Section 80(1)(e) and (f).
	Section 81(1)(b).
	Section 88(1).
	Section 102(6)(c).
	In section 105(1), the definition of 'protected child'.
	In Schedule 10, Part 1.
National Health Service and Community Care Act 1990 (c 19)	In Schedule 9, paragraph 17.

Human Fertilisation and Embryology Act 1990 (c 37)	In Schedule 4, paragraph 4.
Courts and Legal Services Act 1990 (c 41)	In Schedule 16, paragraph 7.
Local Government (Wales) Act 1994 (c 19)	In Schedule 10, paragraph 9.
Health Authorities Act 1995 (c 17)	In Schedule 1, paragraph 101.
Adoption (Intercountry Aspects) Act 1999 (c 18)	In section 2(6), the words 'in its application to Scotland'.
	Section 7(3).
	Section 14.
	In section 16(1), the words ', or section 17 or 56A of the 1976 Act,'.
	In Schedule 2, paragraph 3.
Access to Justice Act 1999 (c 22)	In Schedule 13, paragraph 88.
Care Standards Act 2000 (c 14)	In section 16(2), the words 'or a voluntary adoption agency'.
	In Schedule 4, paragraphs 5 and 27(b).
Local Government Act 2000 (c 22)	In Schedule 5, paragraph 16.
Criminal Justice and Court Services Act 2000 (c 43)	Section 12(5)(b) and the preceding 'and'.
	In Schedule 7, paragraphs 51 to 53.
This Act	In Schedule 4, paragraphs 3 to 5 and 10 to 16.

NOTES

Initial Commencement

To be appointed

To be appointed (in so far as relating to the repeals in the Adoption (Scotland) Act 1978): see s 148(5)(e).

To be appointed (remainder): see s 148(1), (2).

Appointment

Appointment (in part): 1 June 2003: by virtue of SI 2003/366, art 2(5)(c)(i).

Appointment (in part): 28 November 2003: see SI 2003/3079, art 2(1)(d).

Appointment (in part): 1 December 2003: by virtue of SI 2003/3079, art 2(2)(b).

Appointment (in part): 30 December 2005: by virtue of SI 2005/2213, art 2(m), (o).

Appointment (in relation to England in part): 30 December 2005: by virtue of SI 2005/2213, art 3(l).

Appointment (in part): 30 December 2005: see SI 2005/2897, art 2(b); for transitional provisions and savings see arts 3–16 thereof.

Appointment (in relation to Scotland in part): 30 December 2005: see SSI 2005/643, art 2(e).

Miscellaneous

It is understood that the reference above to the Courts and Legal Services Act 1990, Sch 16, para 7 is incorrect; para 7 has already been repealed by the Criminal Justice and Court Services Act 2000, s 75, Sch 8.

SCHEDULE 6
Glossary

Section 147

In this Act, the expressions listed in the left-hand column below have the meaning given by, or are to be interpreted in accordance with, the provisions of this Act or (where stated) of the 1989 Act listed in the right-hand column.

Expression	Provision
the 1989 Act	section 2(5)
Adopted Children Register	section 77
Adoption and Children Act Register	section 125
adoption (in relation to Chapter 4 of Part 1)	section 66
adoption agency	section 2(1)
adoption agency placing a child for adoption	section 18(5)
Adoption Contact Register	section 80
adoption order	section 46(1)
Adoption Service	section 2(1)
adoption society	section 2(5)
adoption support agency	section 8
adoption support services	section 2(6)
appointed day (in relation to Chapter 4 of Part 1)	section 66(2)
appropriate Minister	section 144
Assembly	section 144
body	section 144
by virtue of	section 144
care order	section 105(1) of the 1989 Act
child	sections 49(5) and 144
child assessment order	section 43(2) of the 1989 Act
child in the care of a local authority	section 105(1) of the 1989 Act
child looked after by a local authority	section 22 of the 1989 Act
child placed for adoption by an adoption agency	section 18(5)
child to be adopted, adopted child	section 49(5)
consent (in relation to making adoption orders or placing for adoption)	section 52

the Convention	section 144
Convention adoption	section 66(1)(c)
Convention adoption order	section 144
Convention country	section 144
couple	section 144(4)
court	section 144
disposition (in relation to Chapter 4 of Part 1)	section 73
enactment	section 144
fee	section 144
guardian	section 144
information	section 144
interim care order	section 38 of the 1989 Act
local authority	section 144
local authority foster parent	section 23(3) of the 1989 Act
Northern Irish adoption agency	section 144
Northern Irish adoption order	section 144
notice	section 144
notice of intention to adopt	section 44(2)
overseas adoption	section 87
parental responsibility	section 3 of the 1989 Act
partner, in relation to a parent of a child	section 144(7)
placement order	section 21
placing, or placed, for adoption	sections 18(5) and 19(4)
prohibited steps order	section 8(1) of the 1989 Act
records (in relation to Chapter 5 of Part 1)	section 82
registered adoption society	section 2(2)
registers of live-births (in relation to Chapter 5 of Part 1)	section 82
registration authority (in Part 1)	section 144
regulations	section 144
relative	section 144, read with section 1(8)
residence order	section 8(1) of the 1989 Act

rules	section 144
Scottish adoption agency	section 144(3)
Scottish adoption order	section 144
specific issue order	section 8(1) of the 1989 Act
subordinate legislation	section 144
supervision order	section 31(11) of the 1989 Act
unitary authority	section 144
voluntary organisation	section 2(5)

NOTES

Initial Commencement

Royal Assent

Royal Assent: 7 November 2002: (no specific commencement provision).

Children Act 1989

1989 CHAPTER 41

An Act to reform the law relating to children; to provide for local authority services for children in need and others; to amend the law with respect to children's homes, community homes, voluntary homes and voluntary organisations; to make provision with respect to fostering, child minding and day care for young children and adoption; and for connected purposes
[16th November 1989]

BE IT ENACTED by the Queen's most Excellent Majesty, by and with the advice and consent of the Lords Spiritual and Temporal, and Commons, in this present Parliament assembled, and by the authority of the same, as follows:–

[701]

4 Acquisition of parental responsibility by father

(1) Where a child's father and mother were not married to each other at the time of his birth([, the father shall acquire parental responsibility for the child if—

(a) he becomes registered as the child's father under any of the enactments specified in subsection (1A);

(b) he and the child's mother make an agreement (a 'parental responsibility agreement') providing for him to have parental responsibility for the child; or

(c) the court, on his application, orders that he shall have parental responsibility for the child.]

[(1A) The enactments referred to in subsection (1)(a) are—

(a) paragraphs (a), (b) and (c) of section 10(1) and of section 10A(1) of the Births and Deaths Registration Act 1953;

(b) paragraphs (a), (b)(i) and (c) of section 18(1), and sections 18(2)(b) and 20(1)(a) of the Registration of Births, Deaths and Marriages (Scotland) Act 1965; and

(c) sub-paragraphs (a), (b) and (c) of Article 14(3) of the Births and Deaths Registration (Northern Ireland) Order 1976.

(1B) The [Secretary of State] may by order amend subsection (1A) so as to add further enactments to the list in that subsection.]

(2) No parental responsibility agreement shall have effect for the purposes of this Act unless—

(a) it is made in the form prescribed by regulations made by the Lord Chancellor; and

(b) where regulations are made by the Lord Chancellor prescribing the manner in which such agreements must be recorded, it is recorded in the prescribed manner.

[(2A) A person who has acquired parental responsibility under subsection (1) shall cease to have that responsibility only if the court so orders.

(3) The court may make an order under subsection (2A) on the application—

(a) of any person who has parental responsibility for the child; or

(b) with the leave of the court, of the child himself,

subject, in the case of parental responsibility acquired under subsection (1)(c), to section 12(4).]

(4) The court may only grant leave under subsection (3)(b) if it is satisfied that the child has sufficient understanding to make the proposed application.

NOTES

Initial Commencement

To be appointed

To be appointed: see s 108(2).

Appointment

Appointment: 14 October 1991: see SI 1991/828, art 3(2).

Extent

This section does not extend to Scotland: see s 108(11).

Amendment

Sub-s (1): words from ', the father shall' to 'for the child.' in square brackets substituted by the Adoption and Children Act 2002, s 111(1), (2); for further provision in relation to parental responsibility conferred on a man registered under the enactments referred to in sub-s (1A) above see sub-s (7) thereof; Date in force: 1 December 2003: see SI 2003/3079, art 2(2)(a); Sub-ss (1A), (1B): inserted by the Adoption and Children Act 2002, s 111(1), (3); Date in force: 1 December 2003: see SI 2003/3079, art 2(2)(a); Sub-s (1B): words 'Secretary of State' in square brackets substituted by SI 2003/3191, arts 3(a), 6, Schedule, para 1; Date in force: 12 January 2004: see SI 2003/3191, art 1(2); Sub-ss (2A), (3): substituted, for sub-s (3) as originally enacted, by the Adoption and Children Act 2002, s 111(1), (4) Date in force: 1 December 2003: see SI 2003/3079, art 2(2)(a).

Subordinate Legislation

Parental Responsibility Agreement Regulations 1991, SI 1991/1478 (made under sub-s (2)); Parental Responsibility Agreement (Amendment) Regulations 2005, SI 2005/2808 (made under sub-s (2)).

[4A   Acquisition of parental responsibility by step-parent]

[(1)   Where a child's parent ('parent A') who has parental responsibility for the child is married to[, or a civil partner of,] a person who is not the child's parent ('the step-parent')—

(a)   parent A or, if the other parent of the child also has parental responsibility for the child, both parents may by agreement with the step-parent provide for the step-parent to have parental responsibility for the child; or

(b)   the court may, on the application of the step-parent, order that the step-parent shall have parental responsibility for the child.

(2)   An agreement under subsection (1)(a) is also a 'parental responsibility agreement', and section 4(2) applies in relation to such agreements as it applies in relation to parental responsibility agreements under section 4.

(3)   A parental responsibility agreement under subsection (1)(a), or an order under subsection (1)(b), may only be brought to an end by an order of the court made on the application—

(a)   of any person who has parental responsibility for the child; or

(b)   with the leave of the court, of the child himself.

(4)   The court may only grant leave under subsection (3)(b) if it is satisfied that the child has sufficient understanding to make the proposed application.]

NOTES

Extent

This section does not extend to Scotland: see s 108(11).

Amendment

Inserted by the Adoption and Children Act 2002, s 112; date in force: 30 December 2005: see SI 2005/2213, art 2(k); sub-s (1): words ', or a civil partner of,' in square brackets inserted by the Civil Partnership Act 2004, s 75(1), (2); date in force: 30 December 2005: see SI 2005/3175, art 2(9).

General

[702]

Section 112 inserts a new s 4A into the CA 1989. It enables a step–parent to acquire parental responsibility for a child of his spouse or of his civil partner (CA 1989, s 4A(1), as amended by the Civil Partnership Act 2004, s 75(2)). This may be done either by agreement between the step-parent and the parents who have parental responsibility for the child, or by order of the court. An agreement is a 'parental responsibility agreement', and the rules governing form and recording apply as they do to a parental responsibility agreement made between the mother and unmarried father of a child.

An agreement or an order automatically ends when the child reaches 18 (see CA 1989, s 91(7) and (8), as amended by the Adoption and Children Act 2002, Sch 3, para 68(b) and (c)) or if earlier adopted. Otherwise an agreement or order may only be brought to an end by an order of the court and the same rules apply as they do in respect of termination of a parental responsibility agreement made between a mother and unmarried father.

The new rule (operative since 1 December 2003) is intended to provide an alternative to adoption where a step-parent wishes to acquire parental responsibility for his or her step-child. It has the advantage of not removing parental responsibility from the other birth parent and does not legally separate the child from membership of the family of the other birth parent (see the *Explanatory Notes on the Adoption and Children Act 2002*, para 268, issued by the government).

[703]

[Special guardianship]

NOTES

Amendment
Inserted by the Adoption and Children Act 2002, s 115(1); date in force (for certain purposes): 7 December 2004: see SI 2004/3203, art 2(1)(m)(x); date in force (for remaining purposes): 30 December 2005: see SI 2005/2213, art 2(k).

[14A Special guardianship orders]

[(1) A 'special guardianship order' is an order appointing one or more individuals to be a child's 'special guardian' (or special guardians).
(2) A special guardian—

(a)   must be aged eighteen or over; and
(b)   must not be a parent of the child in question,

and subsections (3) to (6) are to be read in that light.

(3) The court may make a special guardianship order with respect to any child on the application of an individual who—

(a)   is entitled to make such an application with respect to the child; or
(b)   has obtained the leave of the court to make the application,

or on the joint application of more than one such individual.

(4) Section 9(3) applies in relation to an application for leave to apply for a special guardianship order as it applies in relation to an application for leave to apply for a section 8 order.
(5) The individuals who are entitled to apply for a special guardianship order with respect to a child are—

(a)   any guardian of the child;
(b)   any individual in whose favour a residence order is in force with respect to the child;
(c)   any individual listed in subsection (5)(b) or (c) of section 10 (as read with subsection (10) of that section);
(d)   a local authority foster parent with whom the child has lived for a period of at least one year immediately preceding the application.

(6) The court may also make a special guardianship order with respect to a child in any family proceedings in which a question arises with respect to the welfare of the child if—

PART B – Statutes

271

(a)   an application for the order has been made by an individual who falls within subsection (3)(a) or (b) (or more than one such individual jointly); or

(b)   the court considers that a special guardianship order should be made even though no such application has been made.

(7) No individual may make an application under subsection (3) or (6)(a) unless, before the beginning of the period of three months ending with the date of the application, he has given written notice of his intention to make the application—

(a)   if the child in question is being looked after by a local authority, to that local authority, or

(b)   otherwise, to the local authority in whose area the individual is ordinarily resident.

(8) On receipt of such a notice, the local authority must investigate the matter and prepare a report for the court dealing with—

(a)   the suitability of the applicant to be a special guardian;

(b)   such matters (if any) as may be prescribed by the Secretary of State; and

(c)   any other matter which the local authority consider to be relevant.

(9) The court may itself ask a local authority to conduct such an investigation and prepare such a report, and the local authority must do so.

(10) The local authority may make such arrangements as they see fit for any person to act on their behalf in connection with conducting an investigation or preparing a report referred to in subsection (8) or (9).

(11) The court may not make a special guardianship order unless it has received a report dealing with the matters referred to in subsection (8).

(12) Subsections (8) and (9) of section 10 apply in relation to special guardianship orders as they apply in relation to section 8 orders.

(13) This section is subject to section 29(5) and (6) of the Adoption and Children Act 2002.]

NOTES

Extent
This section does not extend to Scotland: see s 108(11).

Amendment
Inserted by the Adoption and Children Act 2002, s 115(1); for further effect in relation to applications for special guardianship orders see s 29(6) thereof; date in force (for the purpose of making regulations): 7 December 2004: see SI 2004/3203, art 2(1)(m)(x); date in force (for remaining purposes): 30 December 2005: see SI 2005/2213, art 2(k).

Subordinate Legislation
Special Guardianship Regulations 2005, SI 2005/1109 (made under sub-s (8)(b)); Special Guardianship (Wales) Regulations 2005, SI 2005/1513 (made under sub-s (8)(b)).

General

[704]

The background to s 14A is contained in the commentary on the ACA 2002, s 115(1) (see para [519.1]). This extensive section, together with Sch 3, paras 46–48, provide for the power of the court to make a special guardianship order (SGO); who may apply; notification of intended application; local authority investigations and reports; and the application process. A SGO will only be available in respect of minor children see CA 1989, ss 14A(1) and 105(1). Since, however, it relates to the exercise of parental responsibility and will cease in any event when the child attains majority, it will rarely be sought, or made, once he attains the age of 16. It seems likely that the child's marriage or civil partnership will preclude the making of a SGO.

Section 14A(1)(3) and (6)

Power of the court

[705]

The court's power to make a SGO (ie an order appointing one or more individuals to be a child's special guardian/s see s 14A(1)) usually, but not necessarily, arises upon an application being made for such an order. The powers in s 14A correspond to those in CA 1989, s 10 to make a s 8 order (in particular a residence order) under the 1989 Act.

The court may make an order on a free standing application, made solely for the purpose of seeking a SGO, by an applicant who either is qualified to apply, under s 14A(5), or has obtained the court's leave to do so in accordance with s 14A(3). The court also has power to make a SGO order in any family proceedings (as defined in CA 1989, s 8(3)(4)) in which a question arises with respect to the welfare of the child, either if an application has been made by either a qualified applicant, or one who has obtained the court's leave, see s 14A(6)(a) or of its own motion, if it considers that an order should be made even though there has been no application, see s 14A(6)(b).

Special guardianship is intended to meet the needs of children who will benefit from a secure placement but for whom adoption is not appropriate. Adoption proceedings, being family proceedings, are thus likely to be a particular context in which the court will need to consider whether to exercise its power in s 14A(6)(b) and make a SGO of its own motion, rather than the adoption order sought. The court is expressly directed by the ACA 2002, s 1(6) always to consider the whole range of powers available to it, whether under that Act or the CA 1989. Hence, it will need to be mindful in all adoption proceedings under the ACA 2002 of its power in CA 1989, s 14A(6) and the option of special guardianship in those cases where the permanent and irrevocable transfer of parental responsibility as well parenthood, associated with adoption, will not best serve the child's interests.

When the court makes a SGO order, whether on application or of its own motion, it also has the power to make directions, conditions, and incidental, supplemental or consequential provisions in accordance with the CA 1989, s 11(7)(a)(b) and (d) as applied by s 14E(5).

Section 14A(1)–(6) and (12)

Who may apply

[706]

As with adoption, only individuals may apply and be appointed a special guardian, see s 14A(1). There is no question of the state, or an individual representing the state such as a Director of children's services, becoming special guardian. If a local authority wish to take over the exercise of parental responsibility they must seek a care order under the CA 1989, Pt IV. A court may only exercise parental responsibility under its inherent jurisdiction, in particular wardship.

Not all individuals are qualified, however, to apply for special guardianship. Special guardianship is intended to meet the needs of children who cannot be looked after by their parents, hence it follows that a special guardian must not be a parent of the child in question, see s 14A(2)(b), and s 14A(3)–(6) are to be read in that light. Parents (biological or adoptive) already have a special relationship with the child by virtue of parenthood. Additionally any mother has parental responsibility, as does any father if he either is married to the mother at the time of the child's birth, or has acquired it in accordance with CA 1989, s 4. In all cases a special guardian must be an adult, see s 14A(2)(a). Section 14A(3)–(6) are again to be read in that light. Although a minor cannot be appointed special guardian, there is no prohibition on a minor making an application, (save that leave to apply would normally be required), provided any appointment takes effect after he attains majority. In applying the principle of paramountcy of the child's welfare in accordance with CA 1989, s 1(1), however, the court will be reluctant to appoint someone who has just attained majority to be a special guardian. As with applications for CA 1989, s 8 orders, certain individuals may apply as of right, while other applicants require leave of the court, see s 14A(3).

(A) PERSONS ENTITLED TO APPLY WITHOUT LEAVE, S 14A(5)

[707]

In recognition of their particularly close connection with the child the following are entitled by s 14A(5) to apply for a SGO:

[708]

(*i*)   *Any guardian of the child*

Such applicants are likely to be rare. Any guardian will already have parental responsibility, including the authority to consent to the child's being adopted or placed for adoption. If the applicant is a sole guardian and both the child's parents are dead he will have exclusive parental responsibility and hence nothing is to be gained for the child by the guardian additionally becoming special guardian. If he is not sole guardian, or a parent with parental responsibility for the child has survived the other parent (who must have had a residence order for the guardianship to become effective, see CA 1989, s 5(7), (8)), the court will need some convincing that it is in the child's best interests for a guardian to have quasi exclusive parental responsibility. If there is a dispute about a particular aspect of the exercise of parental responsibility could this be better resolved by way of a specific issue or prohibited steps order under CA 1989, s 8? If there is a dispute as to where the child is to live, the better order would seem to be a s 8 residence order. A guardian is disqualified from applying for a SGO where the child is placed for adoption under the ACA 2002, s 19, or an adoption agency is authorised to place the child for adoption under that section, and an application has been made for an adoption order, unless he has obtained the court's leave under ACA 2002, s 47(3) or (5) to oppose the making of the adoption order, see ACA 2002, s 28(1)(b).

[709]

(*ii*)   *Anyone with a residence order with respect to the child*

The earlier comparison of special guardianship and a residence order (see para [519.1]), demonstrated that a residence order is based upon the concurrent, rather than the exclusive, exercise of parental responsibility. Although a person with a residence order is in a stronger position compared with the others with whom he shares parental responsibility, there is an expectation that all those with parental responsibility will be involved in important matters relating to the child's upbringing. Hence, a non-parent with a residence order who seeks a more exclusive exercise of parental responsibility has the option of applying for a SGO. If he seeks a legal relationship that is fully exclusive, permanent and irrevocable, special guardianship is none of those, and he will instead need to consider adoption.

If a SGO is made in favour of one holder of a joint residence order, then any other joint holder of the order does not cease to have parental responsibility. This is because a residence order is not automatically terminated by the making of a SGO. The other joint holder's exercise of parental responsibility will however be significantly curtailed because of the SGO. When making the SGO, the court will need to consider whether the child's best interests require also a revocation or variation of the residence order.

[710]

(*iii*) *Anyone with whom the child has lived for a period of at least three out of the last five years*

Section 14A(5)(c) enables long term carers of a child to apply for a SGO, in a like manner to their being qualified to apply for a CA 1989, s 8 residence or contact order under CA 1989, s 10(5)(b). Although, theoretically, the category includes local authority foster parents, they qualify in less time, under s 14A(5)(d), after caring for the child for one year. A private foster parent, however, must have had the child living with him for at least three out of the last five years. The period must not have ended more than three months before the making of the application, see CA 1989, s 10(10) as applied by s 14A(5)(c).

[711]

(*iv*) *Where a residence order is in force, any person who has the consent of each of the persons in whose favour the residence order was made (see s 14A(5)(c) applying s 10(5)(c)(i))*

Such consent is sufficient, notwithstanding that if a SGO is made the applicant will receive more extensive parental responsibility than that associated with the residence order. The residence order will not be discharged by the making of a SGO.

[712]

(*v*) *Where the child is in the care of a local authority (ie under a care order (CA 1989, s 105(1)), any person who has the consent of the local authority, see s 14A(5)(c) applying s 10(5)(c)(ii)*

In view of special guardianship being intended primarily to meet the needs of looked-after children for whom rehabilitation with the birth parents is not considered to be an option, this is likely to be a major category of applicants. Persons most likely to apply with the consent of a local authority are its foster parents. Usually they will be the child's foster parents, but there is no limitation to that effect if the local authority consent to the application, so applicants could include, for example, a member of the child's wider family other than a carer. If the local authority do not consent to the child's foster parents' application, they can apply without consent under s 14A(5)(d) once the child has lived with them for a year immediately preceding the application.

[713]

(*vi*) *In any other case, any person who has the consent of each of those (if any) who has parental responsibility for the child, see s 14A(5)(c) applying s 10(5)(c)(iii)*

In the case of a marital child, the applicant will need the consent of both parents. In the case of a non-marital child whether or not the father's consent is required will depend upon his having parental responsibility, see CA 1989, s 4. Others who will have parental responsibility and hence whose consent is required, are any guardian and, of course, any special guardian. A step-parent may also have acquired parental responsibility under the CA 1989, s 4A as inserted by ACA 2002, s 112.

[714]

(*vii*) *A local authority foster parent with whom the child has lived for a period of at least one year immediately preceding the application*

Section 14A(5)(d) greatly enhances the entitlement of local authority foster parents to seek special guardianship in comparison to other carers, who must have had the child living with them for a period (or periods) of at least three years. No distinction is made between children who are the subject of a care order and those being provided with accommodation under a voluntary arrangement. The one-year period must, it is submitted, be a single period and hence continuous as no provision is made to the contrary, as there is in the CA 1989, s 10(10). Anything less would seem unlikely to provide sufficient opportunity for the relationship between the foster parent and child to have developed sufficiently to justify the enhanced entitlement.

The rationale behind the time restrictions is that without it, local authorities would be hesitant and tentative in planning arrangements for looked-after children in view of the real risk of foster parents applying for a SGO soon after the child has been placed with them. In view of that risk, parents would also be reluctant to place their child with local authorities under voluntary arrangements. As it is, parents who agree to their child being accommodated under the CA 1989, s 20 will need to be made aware, as part of the accommodation agreement, that any foster parent with whom the child lives for at least a year will be entitled to apply for special guardianship.

Section 14A(5)(d) renders otiose, in the context of an application for special guardianship, the provision in s 9(3)(c) (applied by s 14A(4)) entitling a local authority foster parent with whom the child has lived for a year to apply for leave to apply for a SGO. Such a foster parent is qualified to apply without leave.

(B) APPLICANTS REQUIRING LEAVE TO APPLY, S 14A(3)(B)(4) AND (12)

[715]

The general policy of the CA 1989 is an 'open door' one allowing almost anyone who is not qualified to apply for a SGO, to seek the court's leave to make an application. Section 14A(3)(b) is in line with the thinking behind the CA 1989, s 10(1)(a)(ii) regarding leave to apply for a s 8 order and is modelled upon it. As with such applications for leave, the interests of justice require that notice of an application for leave is given to parties likely to be affected, see *Re M (prohibited steps order: application for leave)* [1993] 1 FCR 78; *Re W (a child) (contact: leave to apply)* [2000] 1 FCR 185.

Special restrictions apply to local authority foster parents who wish to seek leave to apply, whether the child is the subject of a care order or, more particularly, provided with accommodation under the CA 1989, Pt III, see *Re P (a minor)(leave to apply: foster-parents)* [1994] 2 FCR 1093. In such cases CA 1989, s 14A(4) applies s 9(3) which disqualifies from seeking leave any person who is, or was at anytime within the last six months, a local authority foster parent unless:

(a)   he has the consent of the authority;

(b)   he is a relative of the child;

(c)   the child has lived with him for at least one year preceding the application.'

'Relative' means a grandparent, brother, sister, uncle or aunt (whether of the full blood or half blood or by marriage or civil partnership) or step-parent, see CA 1989, s 105(1) as amended. The connection between such a relative foster parent and the child is presumed to be sufficiently close to justify the court, rather than the local authority, deciding whether or not he should be able to apply for a SGO.

The guidance in the CA 1989, s 10(9), on how the court should exercise its discretion when considering an application for leave, applies in relation to special guardianship, in the same way as it does to an application for leave to apply for a s 8 order, see s 14A(12). So, where the applicant is a person other than the child, the court in deciding whether or not to grant leave must have particular regard to:

(a)   the nature of the proposed application for a SGO;

(b)   the applicant's connection with the child;

(c)   any risk there might be of that proposed application disrupting the child's life to such an extent that he would be harmed by it; and

(d)   where the child is being looked after by a local authority (ie either voluntarily or compulsorily, see CA 1989, s 22(1)) –

      (i)   the authority's plans for the child's future;

      (ii)   the wishes and feelings of the child's parents.

Where the applicant is a local authority foster parent, it is likely that a relevant consideration under s 10(9)(b) and (c) will be that the making of a SGO will maintain and enhance the existing connection between the child and the applicant, see *Re P (a minor)(leave to apply: foster-parents)* [1994] 2 FCR 1093 at 1098. Much will depend upon how the placement with the foster parent fitted within the local authority's overall plans for the child's future in accordance with the CA 1989, s 10(9)(d)(i). The plans should have been designed, in accordance with CA 1989, s 22(3), to safeguard and promote the child's welfare. If the placement with the foster-parent was intended to be short-term, rather than long-term, the grant of the application for leave may necessitate a departure from those plans. Such departure might well disrupt the child's life to such an extent that he would be harmed by it. Conversely, if the placement was intended to be long-term, the granting of the application for leave may be more consistent with the authority's plans for the child's future.

Although, a child who, in the words of CA 1989, s 10(8) (as applied by s 14A(12)), is 'the child concerned' may seek leave under s 14A(3)(b) to apply for a SGO, it will be extremely rare that the circumstances will warrant the granting of leave to a child to seek a person's appointment as his special guardian. As with any other applicant for leave, the court should consider particularly whether there is a reasonable prospect of the substantive application succeeding, rather than whether a SGO is in the child's best interests which is a matter for the substantive application, see *Re SC (a minor) (leave to seek a residence)* [1994] 1 FLR 96; *Re C (residence: child's application for leave)* [1996] 1 FCR 461; *Re H (residence order: child's application for leave)* [2000] 1 FLR 780.

In view of the nature of special guardianship, see para **[519]** above, it is suggested that a child's application for leave should be approached cautiously if there is either no qualified applicant willing to apply for an order or no-one willing to seek leave to apply. If there is such an applicant it seems likely that the interests of the child concerned will coincide sufficiently with those of a person who is already a party to the proceedings, so that leave to apply should not be granted to the child. In considering any such application for leave the court must be 'satisfied that he has sufficient understanding to make the proposed application'. The court is likely to need satisfying that the child has sufficient understanding to be able to instruct a solicitor independently, see *Re S (a minor)(independent representation)* [1993] Fam 263, CA; *Re H (residence order: child's application for leave)* [2000] 1 FLR 780. The legislation offers no other guidance regarding factors that the court should take into account in deciding whether or not to grant him leave.

If the person seeking leave to apply for a SGO is a child other than the child concerned the provisions of s 10(9), rather than 10(8) apply, see *Re S (a minor)(adopted child: contact)* [1999] Fam 283. In view of a SGO not being open to minors, see s 14A(2)(a), the court is likely to be particularly reluctant to grant a child leave to apply for such an order.

(c) Joint applicants, s 14A(3)

[715.1]

Section 14A(3) allows a joint application to be made by more than one individual who is either entitled to apply without leave, or has obtained leave. An obvious example of the former is a married couple with whom the child has lived for at least three years in accordance with the CA 1989, s 10(5)(b) as applied by s 14A(5)(c). Joint applicants for special guardianship, like joint applicants for adoption, will not, however, be restricted to married couples. Hence, civil partners and an unmarried cohabiting couple (whether of different sexes or the same sex) can apply for a SGO, as, less likely, can applicants who are not cohabiting. The nature, duration and stability of the joint applicants' relationship with each other and with the child will, of course, be relevant factors when the court is applying the principle of the paramountcy of the child's welfare in accordance with CA 1989, s 1(1). Where there is more than one applicant, the court may choose only one (or some) of them to be special guardian, depending upon what it considers to be in the child's best interests.

Section 14A(7) and (13)

Notice of intended application

[716]

A special guardianship application cannot be made, whether free standing under s 14A(3) or in any family proceedings under s 14A(6), unless each applicant has given written notice in accordance with s 14A(7), to the relevant local authority, of his intention to make the application. The relevant local authority in the case of a child who is in the care of, or being provided with accommodation by, a local authority (see CA 1989, s 22(1)) is that local authority, see s 14A(7)(a). Otherwise, it is the local authority in whose area the applicant is ordinarily resident see s 14A(7)(b). With one exception, notice must be given at least 3 months before the date of the application. The duty to notify is comparable with the duty imposed on prospective adopters who wish to adopt a child who is not placed with them by an adoption agency. The notice of intended application is essential to enable the local authority to discharge its duties in s 14A(8) to investigate the matter and provide the court with a report on the suitability of the applicant to be a special guardian and other related matters.

Where a placement order under ACA 2002, s 21 is in force in respect of the child and the person applying for special guardianship has obtained the court's leave to do so under ACA 2002, s 29(5) or, if he is a guardian of the child has obtained the court's leave under s 47(5), the notice required by s 14A(7) can be given at any time before the date of the application, see ACA 2002, s 29(6). CA 1989, s 14A is subject to ACA 2002, s 29(5) and (6), see s 14A(13).

Where a court considers, in accordance with s 14A(6)(b) that a SGO should be made in the absence of an application, it will obviously not possible for the applicant to notify the local authority. The relevant local authority's investigative and reporting functions remain.

Section 14A(8)(9)(10) and (11)

Local authority investigation and report

[717]

On receipt of the notice of the intended application required by s 14A(7), the notified local authority are under a duty, by virtue of s 14A(8), to investigate the matter and prepare a report for the court. The court may not make a SGO unless it has received a report, see s 14A(11). In requiring a report under s 14A(8), there is an inquisitorial element to the court's function (see *A Local Authority v Y, Z & ors* [2006] 2 FLR 41 at 10). The s 14A(8) duties upon the relevant local authority to investigate and report distinguish applications for a SGO from applications for a CA 1989, s 8 order, and may dissuade some potential applicants from seeking special guardianship rather than a residence order. In s 8 proceedings there are no corresponding duties and any investigation is dependent upon the court exercising its power in CA 1989, s 7 to call for a welfare report from either a children and family reporter or welfare officer appointed by a local authority. That general discretion applies also in proceedings for a SGO, as the court is considering a 'question with respect to a child under [the Children] Act'. The requirement of the local authority's pre-hearing report under CA 1989, s 14A(8) is, however, likely to obviate the need for the court to invoke s 7. If it considers there to be any matter which the local authority ought to investigate and has not done so, it may exercise its power in s 14A(9) to ask the local authority to conduct a (further) investigation and prepare a report. If so requested the local authority are under a duty to investigate and report. The court could use that power also, for example, where a local authority other than the one looking after the child, or in whose area the applicant is ordinarily resident, has already been involved with the child and is better able to conduct an investigation and prepare a report than the authority which is required to report under s 14A(8).

The legislation is opaque regarding the matters to be included within a special guardianship report. Section 14A(8) particularises only the suitability of the applicant to be a special guardian. It leaves other matters to be prescribed in regulations, or determined by the local authority as being relevant, including the desirability of making a SGO. The Special Guardianship Regulations 2005, reg 21 and Schedule and the Special Guardianship (Wales) Regulations 2005, reg 2 and Schedule prescribe the matters to be dealt with in reports. They include comprehensive particulars in respect of the child; his family; the prospective special guardian/s and the wishes and feelings of the child and others. The local authority which completed the report must give details, inter alia, of any past involvement with the prospective special guardians and the assessment for and provision of support services. The report must also give details of the implications of the making of an order for the child, his parent/s, the prospective special guardians and his family and any other person the local authority consider relevant. The report should comment on whether a SGO should be made, and the relative merits of an order and other orders which may be made under either the CA 1989 or the ACA 2002. In all cases the reporting local authority will be free to include any matter it considers to be relevant in assisting the court to reach its decision.

Where a court considers that a SGO should be made in the absence of an application, it will obviously not be possible for the applicant to notify the local authority. The relevant local authority's investigative and reporting functions remain, however, as s 14A(11) prohibits the court from making a SGO, unless it has received a report dealing with the matters in CA 1989, s 14A(8). Hence, it has an independent power in s 14A(9) to ask 'a local authority' to conduct a s 14A(8) investigation and prepare such a report. If the child in question is being looked after by a local authority the court is likely (but not mandated) to ask that local authority. The court is free, however, to nominate whichever local authority it feels is best able to meet the duty in s 14A(8) and the nominated local authority must accept the nomination. The local authority are free, however, to delegate their investigative and reporting functions imposed upon them by s 14A(8) or (9) as they see fit (see s 14A(10)), for example by agreement to the NSPCC.

The court will set the timetable within which the relevant local authority must file the report under s 14A(8) or (9), see Family Proceedings Court (Children Act 1989) Rules 1991, r 17A(1) and Family Proceedings Rules 1991, r 4.17A(1). In doing so the court will need to have regard to the avoidance of delay principle in the Children Act 1989, s 1(2). The justices' clerk or the court must consider whether to give a direction that the report under s 14A(8) or (9) be disclosed to each party to the proceedings (see r 17A(2) and r 4.17A(2)) and may direct that the report will not be disclosed to a party (see r 17A(4) and r 4.17A(4)). Before giving a direction for disclosure, the justices' clerk or the court must consider whether any information should be deleted including information which reveals the party's address in a case where he has declined to reveal it in accordance with the rules (see r 17A(3) and r 4.17A(3)). The designated, or proper, officer must serve a copy of the report in accordance with any direction for disclosure and on any children's guardian, welfare officer or children and family reporter, see rr17A(5) and r 4.17A(5). At the hearing at which the report is considered, a party to whom the report, or part thereof, has been disclosed, may question the person who prepared the report about it (see FPC(CA 1989) R 1991, r 21(3) and FPR 1991, r 4.21(2A)).

Application process

(a) *Jurisdiction*

[718]

A SGO is a 'Part I order' within the Family Law Act 1986 (see s 1(a)(a) as inserted by ACA 2002, Sch 3, paras 46–47). A court does not have jurisdiction to make a SGO unless the condition relating to habitual residence or presence of the child in s 3 is satisfied (see FLA 1986, s 2(2A) as inserted by ACA 2002, Sch 3, para 48).

No SGO may be made in respect of a child who is the subject of a placement order under the ACA 2002 unless an application has been made for an adoption order and the applicant for special guardianship has obtained the court's leave under the ACA 2002, s 29(5), or if he is a guardian of the child under ACA 2002, s 47(5). The CA 1989, s 14A is subject to ACA 2002, s 29(5), see s 14A(13).

(b) *Authorised courts*

[719]

The courts authorised to hear applications relating to special guardianship are the magistrates' family proceedings court, the county court and the Family Division of the High Court. The rules governing the allocation of proceedings are those applicable generally to Children Act 1989 proceedings, ie the Children (Allocation of Proceedings) Order 1991, SI 1991/1677 as amended. Where a SGO is in force an application for leave to change the child's surname or remove him from the United Kingdom under s 14C(3) must be commenced in the court which made the SGO, see SI 1991/1677, art 3C(1) as inserted.

(c) *Procedure*

[720]

The procedure is governed by the Family Proceedings (Children Act 1989) Rules 1991 (FPC (CA) R 1991) (SI 1991/1395), as amended by the Magistrates' Courts (Miscellaneous Amendments) Rules 2005 (SI 2005/2930), paras 33–47 and 49–51, in the magistrates' family proceedings court and the Family Proceedings Rules 1991 (FPR 1991) (SI 1991/1247), Pt IV, as amended by the Family Proceedings (Amendment)(No 5) Rules, 2005 (SI 2005/2922), rr 75–89, in the county court and High Court.

(d) *Fees*

[721]

The fees to be taken are prescribed by the Magistrates' Courts Fees Order 2005 (SI 2005/3444), arts 2–6 and Schedule, and the Family Proceedings Fees Order 2004, SI 2004/3114 arts 2 and 4, and Sch 1.

(e) *Application*

[722]

The application procedure is set out in the FPC (CA 1989) R 1991, r 4 as amended and FPR 1991, r 4.4 as amended. The applicant must file Form C1 and Supplement for an application for a Special Guardianship Order in Form C13A, together with sufficient copies for one to be served on each respondent (see rr 4(1)(a) and (1A) and FPR 1991, rr 4.4(1)(a) and (1A)).

(f) Parties

[723]

The respondents to an application under CA 1989, s 14A (for a SGO), s14(C)(3) (for leave to change the child's surname or remove him from the UK) and s 14D (to vary or discharge a SGO) are prescribed by the FPC (CA 1989) R 1991, r 7(1) and Sch 2 as amended and FPR 1991, r 4.7(1) and App 3 as amended. The rules relating to joinder as, and ceasing to be, a party are set out in r 7(2)–(5) as amended and r 4.7(2)–(5) as amended.

(g) Hearing

[724]

The justices' clerk or the appropriate court officer will fix the hearing date in accordance with the FPC (CA 1989) R 1991, r 15 as amended, and FPR 1991, r 4.15 as amended, and notify the parties, any local authority that is preparing, or has prepared, a report under s 14A(8) or (9) and such of the following as may have been appointed, the children's guardian, children and family reporter or the welfare officer.

There is no provision currently in the legislation for the child to be independently represented in special guardianship proceedings. They have not been included within 'specified proceedings' under CA 1989, s 41(6) for the purpose of the appointment of a children's guardian. The Government envisaged, subject to consultation, 'that a CAF-CASS officer will be appointed in most cases where the court is considering a special guardianship order' per Lord Hunt, HL Grand Committee, 18 July 2002, col CWH 348, and that provision would be made in the court rules for such appointment. The court may require a welfare report to be prepared under the CA 1989, s 7.

(h) The order

[725]

If the court makes a SGO it must be recorded in Form C43A and a copy served as soon as practicable by the designated or proper officer on the parties, any person with whom the child is living, and where applicable the local authority that prepared the report under s 14A(8) or (9), in accordance with the FPC (CA 1989) R 1991, r 21(7) and Sch 1 as amended, and FPR 1991, r 4.21(5) and (6) and App 1 as amended.

(i) Enforcement

[726]

Where a person in whose favour a special guardianship order made in the magistrates' court, is in force wishes to enforce it, the FPC (CA 1989) R 1991, r 24 as amended, requires that he shall file a written statement describing the alleged breach of the order, whereupon the justices' clerk will fix a date, time and place for the hearing and the designated officer will give notice, as soon as practicable, to the person wishing to enforce the order and to any person whom it is alleged is in breach of it. In the county court the FPR 1991, r 4.21A as substituted applies CCR Ord 29, r 1 (committal for breach of order or undertaking) as varied to orders under ss 14A, 14B(2)(b), 14C(3)(b) or 14D. The judge or district judge may, on the application of the person entitled to enforce the order, direct that the proper officer issue a copy of the order, endorsed with or incorporating a notice as to the consequences of disobedience, for service in accordance with Ord 29, r 1(2).

[727]

> ### [14B Special guardianship orders: making]
>
> [(1)   Before making a special guardianship order, the court must consider whether, if the order were made—
>
> (a)   a contact order should also be made with respect to the child, *and*
> (b)   any section 8 order in force with respect to the child should be varied or discharged,
> [(c)   where a contact order made with respect to the child is not discharged, any enforcement order relating to that contact order should be revoked, and
> (d)   where a contact activity direction has been made as regards contact with the child and is in force, that contact activity direction should be discharged].
>
> (2)   On making a special guardianship order, the court may also—
>
> (a)   give leave for the child to be known by a new surname;
> (b)   grant the leave required by section 14C(3)(b), either generally or for specified purposes.]
>
> **NOTES**
> **Extent**
> This section does not extend to Scotland: see s 108(11).
>
> **Amendment**
> Inserted by the Adoption and Children Act 2002, s 115(1); date in force (for the purpose of making regulations): 7 December 2004: see SI 2004/3203, art 2(1)(m)(x); date in force (for remaining purposes): 30 December 2005: see SI 2005/2213, art 2(k); sub-s (1): in para (a) word 'and' in italics repealed by the Children and Adoption Act 2006, s 15, Sch 2, paras 7, 8(a), Sch 3; date in force: to be appointed: see the Children and Adoption Act 2006, s 17(2); sub-s (1): paras (c), (d) inserted by the Children and Adoption Act 2006, s 15(1), Sch 2, paras 7, 8(b); date in force: to be appointed: see the Children and Adoption Act 2006, s 17(2).

General

[728]

Section 14B(1), as amended by the Children and Adoption Act 2006, Sch 2 paras 7 and 8, imposes certain duties upon the court (regarding the making of a contact order; the variation or discharge of any CA 1989, s 8 order; the revocation of any enforcement order relating to a contact order and the discharge of a contact activity direction) *before* it makes a SGO (see s 115(1)).

Section 14B(2) confers two powers upon the court, (regarding change of the child's surname and his removal from the United Kingdom) *when* it makes a SGO.

Section 14B(1)(a)

Contact

[729]

The security afforded by a SGO to both the child and the applicants in terms of the special guardian's exercise of parental responsibility independently of the birth parents, may well mean that it is in the child's best interests for a SGO to be made. Contact between the child and, inter alia, his birth family, may nevertheless also be in his best interests. Special guardianship is not a closed relationship and provides a significant alternative to adoption where continuing contact with the birth family is in the child's best interests. It may well be in the child's best interests for a SGO to be made and for the court to recognise, or vary, existing contact arrangements. Hence the court is mandated by s 14B(1)(a) *before* making a SGO, to consider whether, if the order were made, a contact order should also be made with respect to the child. There is no statutory presumption in favour of reasonable contact between a child who is the subject of a SGO and his parents, as there is, by virtue of CA 1989, s 34(1), where a child is the subject of a care order. This is justified on the basis that a SGO, unlike a care order, is not based on the partnership principle of shared (although not equal) parental responsibility (see CA 1989, s 33(3)(4)) The courts have nevertheless classified contact variously as a basic right of the child to have contact with his parent (see *M v M (child access)* [1973] 2 All ER 81 at 85 per Wrangham J), as well as a right of the parent (see Lord Oliver in *Re KD (a minor)(ward: termination of access)* [1988] AC 806 at 817) such that it is appropriate to treat contact as conferring mutual rights on the child and his parent to each other's companionship, of which each can only be deprived if the child's welfare exceptionally so warrants. In recognition of this presumption in favour of contact, it is appropriate that s 14B(1)(a) should require consideration (but not a presumption) of a contact order with respect to the child before the court makes a SGO. Any such order will be made under the CA 1989, s 8, provided that a SGO is made, and can be subject to directions and conditions under s 11(7).

If the child has been benefiting from contact prior to the application for special guardian-ship, it will normally be in his interests for contact to continue if a SGO is made. The decision will, of course, be based upon the tri-partite welfare principle in CA 1989, s 1, see para **[519.2]**. The making of a SGO does not, it is submitted, detract from the premise that it is the child's right to know both his parents and his interests are best served by providing for contact between him and the parent/s with whom he is not living, even though the parent in question has failed to discharge parental responsibility adequately (see Willmer LJ in *S v S and P* [1962] 2 All ER 1 at 3). To deny the child contact is to deprive him of an important contribution to his emotional and material development in the long term. In all cases, however, the child's welfare is paramount and if the fundamental need for the child to have an enduring relationship with his parents is outweighed by the harm to the child's welfare if a contact order is made, then no order for contact should be made.

Most of the reasons for not making a contact order relate to the conduct or condition of the parent. These include: his past cruelty to, or sexual abuse of, the child; the parent's bad criminal record, mental illness or unstable condition. The case for refusing contact will be the stronger if the conduct or condition has made the child afraid of the parent (see, eg, *Cheshire County Council v M* [1992] 2 FCR 817; *Re G (a child)(domestic violence: direct contact)* [2001] 2 FCR 134), or has been such as poses the risk of destabilising the special guardianship relationship. The courts need to have a heightened awareness of the existence of, and consequences upon a child of, exposure to domestic violence. As the Court of Appeal held in *Re L (a child)(contact: domestic violence); Re V (a child)(contact: domestic violence); Re M (a child)(contact: domestic violence); Re H (a child)(contact: domestic violence)* [2000] 4 All ER 609, as a matter of principle domestic violence cannot of itself constitute a bar to contact, but is a factor when the court is applying the welfare principle in CA 1989, s 1. In cases of proved domestic violence the court must weigh in the balance the seriousness of that violence, the risks involved and the impact on the child, against the positive factors, if any, of contact between the parent proved to have been violent and the child.

One option open to the court, is to make an order for indirect contact so that the parents may either renew, or build up, a relationship with their child, if such is in the child's best interests. A contact order may also impose on those listed in CA 1989, s 11(7)(b) conditions under which contact with the child is to be allowed.

Sometimes parental conduct or condition is not in question and the reasons for making no order relate to the child. For example, where contact seriously affects his health (*Re C and V (minors)(parental responsibility and contact)* [1998] 1 FCR 52), or is acutely distressing to him (*Re M (minors)* [1995] 1 FCR 753, CA), or would otherwise be harmful to him, or where his opposition is so marked that to allow contact would similarly harm him. Another relevant factor is the strength, or, more likely in a special guardianship application, the weakness, of the bond between the child and parent. It may be so tenuous that in addition to justifying a SGO, it also justifies refusing contact. This is especially so where the child has established a close relationship with the applicant for the SGO or where there is no relationship between the child and his parent/s and to establish one would be emotionally disturbing to the child.

Consideration of contact under s 14B(1)(a) is not limited to parental contact and extends to anyone (whether or not related to the child) with whom it is in the child's interests for contact to be continued or established, for example siblings with whom the child is not living, grandparents and former carers.

Where there are practical difficulties which prevent contact, save for which contact with the parent or other person would be in the child's best interests, future contact should not be ruled out, but instead should be (re)established, if possible, as soon as the difficulties are removed (*Re M(minors)* (1990) Times, 22 February, CA) There might be cogent reasons for denying contact in the short term, for example allowing the child to settle in with the special guardian, but not in the long term, in which case it may be appropriate to adjourn the consideration of contact until after the SGO has been made. Alternatively, it may be appropriate to grant supervised contact as an interim measure on making the SGO (eg, because of the parent's unsatisfactory lifestyle or lack of suitability) but with the medium- or long-term view in mind of unsupervised contact. The court has the power to grant contact subject to carefully controlled conditions imposed under CA 1989, s 11(7), or supervision. Alternatively, the court may allow contact by way of visits but not staying contact.

Where there is more than one child the subject of a special guardianship application, for example siblings, the question of contact must be considered in relation to each of them individually and not collectively (*Corkett v Corkett* [1985] FLR 708, CA). If the paramount interests of each produce incompatible results, the court may find it necessary not to make a contact order with respect to one child, but grant it in respect of his sibling.

Section 14B(1)(b)

Variation or discharge of any CA 1989, s 8 order

[730]

A SGO does not automatically operate to discharge any CA 1989, s 8 order (ie residence, contact, prohibited steps or specific issue) in force with respect to the child. Instead, s 14B(1)(b) requires the court before it makes a SGO, to consider whether, if an order were made, any s 8 order should be varied or discharged. The court will need to apply the welfare principle in CA 1989, s 1, see para [519.2]. In doing so it must consider whether it will be in the child's best interests for the s 8 order to continue, rather than for the special guardian to exercise parental responsibility unencumbered by an existing order. If the court decides that the existing order should remain in force, it has the option of varying it, and must consider whether or not to vary it would be in the child's best interests. If an existing s 8 order is not varied or discharged, the SGO will take effect subject to the s 8 order (CA 1989, s 14C(1)(b)) and the special guardian's exclusive exercise of parental responsibility will be affected accordingly.

Section 14B(1)(c)

Revocation of any enforcement order relating to a contact order

[731]

This subsection was inserted into the CA 1989, s 14B(1) by the Children and Adoption Act 2006 (CAA 2006), s 15(1) and Sch 2, paras 7 and 8, to provide for the case where a contact order is not discharged under s 14B(1)(b) and an enforcement order (ie, an order imposing an unpaid work requirement for breach of a contact order) made under CA 1989, ss 11J–11L (as inserted by CAA 2006, s 4), relating to that contact order is in force. Before making a SGO the court must revoke any enforcement order relating to any continuing contact order. In the event of further non-compliance with the contact order, it will be open to a qualified applicant under s 11J(5) to apply subsequently for an enforcement order and seek to establish the statutory criteria for the making of such an order.

Section 14B(1)(d)

Discharge of any contact activity direction

[732]

This subsection was also inserted into s 14B(1) by the CAA 2006, s 15(1) and Sch 2, paras 7 and 8. It applies where a contact activity direction (ie, a direction requiring a party to proceedings to take part in an activity that promotes contact with the child) made under CA 1989, ss 11A and 11B (as inserted by CAA 2006, s 1) is in force. During proceedings in which a court is considering making, varying or discharging a contact order, it can make a contact activity direction and if it does so, it cannot finally dispose of the contact proceedings, see s 11A(1)(2)(7). Any contact activity direction which is in force must be discharged, however, by the special guardianship proceedings court before it makes a SGO. If there is a continuing dispute regarding contact, the court is empowered, by s 11A(1) and (2), to address the need for such a direction as part of its consideration whether to make a contact order with respect to the child in accordance with s 14B(1)(a); or vary or discharge an existing order in accordance with s 14B(1)(b). In making its decision the child's welfare is the court's paramount consideration see s 11A(9). If it does make a direction it may not finally dispose of the proceedings relating to contact, see s 11A(7).

Section 14B(2)(a)

Change of surname

[733]

On making a SGO this subsection empowers the court to authorise the child to be known by a new surname. The court's leave is similarly required by s 14C(3)(a) to any such change while a SGO is in force. In deciding whether or not to grant leave, applying the House of Lords decision in *Dawson v Wearmouth* [1999] AC 308, the welfare of the child is paramount in accordance with CA 1989, s 1(1). The court should not make an order to change the child's surname unless there is some evidence that to do so would lead to an improvement in his welfare. Although the welfare checklist in s 1(3) does not strictly apply to the granting of leave under s 14B(2)(a), as it does to an opposed application for a CA 1989, s 8 specific issue order regarding a change of surname, it provides a useful guide to the factors which may impinge upon the child's welfare. Of particular relevance in favour of allowing the change of surname are factors such as lack of parental commitment and attachment to the child or a history of parental misconduct towards the child. The age and understanding of the child are relevant in terms of the extent to which the child has come to identify himself with the current name and how far that identity is in his interests. In the case of the mature child, particular regard should be paid to his views regarding any proposed new surname in line with the principle in *Gillick v West Norfolk Area Health Authority* [1986] AC 112.

Section 14B(2)(b)

Removal of the child from the United Kingdom

[734]

This subsection confers on the court a discretion on making a SGO to grant the leave required by s 14C(3)(b), for the child's removal from the United Kingdom, either generally or for specified purposes. It may grant leave not only to a special guardian but also to some other person, for example to a parent or other relative to take the child out of the United Kingdom annually during the summer holidays (s 14(3)(b) does not prevent removal of a child by his special guardian for a period of less than three months, see s 14C(4)). In deciding whether or not to grant the leave required by s 14C(3)(b), either on the making of a SGO, under s 14B(2)(b), or thereafter under s 14C(3)(b), the court must apply the principle of the paramountcy of the child's welfare in accordance with the CA 1989, s 1(1), see para **[519.2]**. In so doing, it should, as when deciding whether or not to give leave to change the child's surname, be guided by the checklist of factors in the CA 1989, s 1(3), notwithstanding that it does not strictly apply. As the child's removal from the jurisdiction is a particular incident of the power to determine where the child spends his time, it is submitted that the principle applicable where there is a disagreement between parents regarding the child's removal, applies equally to granting the leave required by s 14C(3)(b). That long standing principle, traceable to *P (LM)(otherwise E) v P (GE)* [1970] 3 All ER 659, affirmed by the Court of Appeal in *Payne v Payne* [2001] 1 FCR 425, requires there to be some compelling reason to justify a court preventing the person with whom the child is living from taking a reasonable decision to live outside the jurisdiction. As the Court of Appeal made clear in *Payne*, care must be taken, however, to avoid the creation of presumptions, otherwise there is a risk of infringing the European Convention on Human Rights, art 8 (right to respect for private and family life). That risk is met provided that the primary judicial task is to apply the principle of paramountcy of the child's welfare.

Hence, applying the case law applicable to parental disputes regarding a child's removal from the jurisdiction, a proposal for permanent removal by a special guardian must be realistic and sensible (see e g *Re W (minors)(removal from jurisdiction)* [1994] 1 FCR 842; *Re S (children: application for removal from jurisdiction)* [2004] EWCA Civ 1724, [2005] 1 FCR 471; *Re G (removal from jurisdiction)* [2005] EWCA Civ 170, [2005] 2 FLR 166) and must be fully supported by evidence (*K v K* [1992] 2 FCR 61). If it is, refusal of leave should only be ordered if it is clearly shown that the removal would be against the child's best interests. A highly relevant factor will be the relationship between the child and his parents. Where removal would substantially reduce contact between the child and his parents, the issue is whether the benefit of taking the child abroad outweighs the disadvantage to him of losing contact with his parents. As with change of surname, considerable weight should be given to the wishes and feelings of the mature child (*M v M (removal from jurisdiction)* [1993] 1 FCR 5). The considerations relevant to leave to relocate permanently are not automatically applicable in cases of temporary removal (see *Re A* [2004] EWCA Civ 1587, [2005] 1 FLR 639).

[735]

[14C Special guardianship orders: effect]

[(1) The effect of a special guardianship order is that while the order remains in force—

(a)   a special guardian appointed by the order has parental responsibility for the child in respect of whom it is made; and

(b)   subject to any other order in force with respect to the child under this Act, a special guardian is entitled to exercise parental responsibility to the exclusion of any other person with parental responsibility for the child (apart from another special guardian).

(2)   Subsection (1) does not affect—

(a)   the operation of any enactment or rule of law which requires the consent of more than one person with parental responsibility in a matter affecting the child; or

(b)   any rights which a parent of the child has in relation to the child's adoption or placement for adoption.

(3) While a special guardianship order is in force with respect to a child, no person may—

(a)   cause the child to be known by a new surname; or
(b)   remove him from the United Kingdom,

without either the written consent of every person who has parental responsibility for the child or the leave of the court.

(4) Subsection (3)(b) does not prevent the removal of a child, for a period of less than three months, by a special guardian of his.
(5) If the child with respect to whom a special guardianship order is in force dies, his special guardian must take reasonable steps to give notice of that fact to—

(a)   each parent of the child with parental responsibility; and
(b)   each guardian of the child,

but if the child has more than one special guardian, and one of them has taken such steps in relation to a particular parent or guardian, any other special guardian need not do so as respects that parent or guardian.

(6) This section is subject to section 29(7) of the Adoption and Children Act 2002.]

NOTES
Extent
This section does not extend to Scotland: see s 108(11).

Amendment
Inserted by the Adoption and Children Act 2002, s 115(1); date in force (for the purpose of making regulations): 7 December 2004: see SI 2004/3203, art 2(1)(m)(x); date in force (for remaining purposes): 30 December 2005: see SI 2005/2213, art 2(k).

General

[736]

This major section provides for the effect of a special guardianship order (SGO) regarding the entitlement to exclusive exercise of parental responsibility by the special guardian/s, and the limitations upon that entitlement with particular reference to the child's adoption, placement for adoption, surname and removal from the United Kingdom. It also provides for the duties of the special guardian to notify the child's parents if the child dies.

Section 14C(1)(2)

Parental responsibility

[737]

Special guardianship leaves parenthood unaffected, but is closely related to parental responsibility. Section 14C(1)(a) confers parental responsibility for the child on the special guardian and, subject to any other CA 1989 order with respect to the child, he is entitled to exercise that responsibility to the exclusion of any other person with parental responsibility for the child (apart from another special guardian), see s 14C(1)(b). Hence, an understanding of the effect of a SGO calls for a consideration of the nature and scope of parental responsibility both generally and, more particularly, as entrusted to a special guardian. The CA 1989, s 3(1), cryptically defines parental responsibility, as 'all the rights, duties, powers, responsibilities and authority which by law a parent of a child has in relation to the child and his property'. It focuses upon the day-to-day care and responsibility of bringing up a child rather than any right to do so. Most so-called parental rights are powers, and their exercise is to be seen as part of the wider concept of parental responsibility. They are supportive of the discharge of parental duties, which are primarily associated with responsibility. Neither statute nor common law provides a formulated exhaustive list of the rights, duties, powers and responsibilities included within the concept of parental responsibility. The following responsibilities and authority have been suggested as falling within its scope: care and control of the child; discipline; protection and maintenance; contact; secular education; religious upbringing; protection from publicity; medical treatment; determination of surname; removal from the jurisdiction; representation in legal proceedings; consent to marriage; agreement to adoption; appointment of a guardian; administration of property and burial or cremation of a deceased child. For a full analysis see *Butterworths Family Law Service*, Vol 3I, Children, Ch 3.

All are subject to the general principle that the law does not recognise any rule of absolute parental responsibility. Rather, as the House of Lords made clear in *Gillick v West Norfolk and Wisbech Area Health Authority* [1986] AC 112, parental responsibility exists only so long as is needed for the protection of the child. It diminishes as he becomes '*Gillick*' competent, ie, acquires sufficient understanding and intelligence to be capable of making up his own mind on the matter in question. Additionally if a placement order is in force under the ACA 2002, a special guardian's exercise of parental responsibility by virtue of s 14C(1)(b) may be restricted by the adoption agency vested with parental responsibility to the extent specified in any determination made by the agency under the ACA 2002, s 25(4), see CA 1989, s 14C(6) and ACA 2002, s 29(7)(a).

Consideration will now be given to the application and scope of those incidents of parental responsibility calling for particular comment in the context of special guardianship.

1 CARE AND CONTROL

[738]

This major parental responsibility attaching to special guardianship encompasses the duty to look after and bring up the child and, in order to do that properly, the power to control him both physically and by determining how and where he spends his time. Care and control vests in the special guardian/s to the exclusion of others with parental responsibility, in particular the child's parents, save where a residence order survives the making of the SGO, see s 14B(1)(b). 'The intention is that the special guardian has clear responsibility for all the day-to-day decisions about caring for the child or young person and for taking decisions about his upbringing. But the order retains the basic legal link with the birth parents, unlike adoption. They remain legally the child's parents, though their ability to exercise their parental responsibility is limited' (see *Explanatory Notes to the ACA 2002*, para 278). Hence the following parental responsibilities do not necessarily vest exclusively in the special guardian and may either remain to some degree with parents, whether with parental responsibility (eg, consent to adoption), whether with or without it (eg, the duty to maintain); or are likely to be subject to court order (eg, contact).

2 PROTECTION AND MAINTENANCE

[739]

A corollary to the special guardian's duty to care for the child and the power to control him are the duties to protect and maintain him. They are now chiefly governed by statute, for example the Children and Young Persons Act 1933, Pt I. Any enforceable duty to provide financial support is not, however, most closely related to parental responsibility, but parenthood. Thus, the CA 1989, s 3(4)(a), makes clear that the fact that a person does, or does not, have parental responsibility for a child does not affect 'any obligation which he may have in relation to the child (such as a statutory duty to maintain him)'. Responsibility does not include liability. Thus the making of a SGO, unlike an adoption order, does not absolve the child's parents from their liability to maintain their child. This is so whether under the child support legislation (which targets non-residential parents, see Child Support Act 1991, s 1); the matrimonial legislation (which targets those in respect of whom the child is a child of the family); or the CA 1989, s 15 and Sch 1 (which targets parents). Nor does the making of a SGO impose such liability upon the special guardian.

So, like a guardian, but unlike the mother or father (by birth or adoption) a special guardian is not liable for the child under the Child Support Act 1991. Neither is he liable under the social security legislation, so that if benefit is paid for the child it cannot be recovered from the special guardian. Nor, unlike a parent, is he liable under the CA 1989, s 29(4), to contribute either to the costs of services provided by a local authority for a child in need, or towards the maintenance of the child under Sch 2, should the child, subsequent to the SGO, be looked after by a local authority. The only possible financial personal liability is in proceedings consequent upon his marriage or civil partnership having broken down and the child being a child of the family under the matrimonial legislation, the Civil Partnership Act 2004 (CPA 2004) or the CA 1989, Sch 1. Special guardianship is, however, recognised parri passu with parenthood, guardianship and a residence order for the purpose of conferring eligibility to seek financial relief in respect of the child against parents under the CA 1989, s 15 and Sch 1. This is so either on application, or, in the absence of an application, by the court of its own motion when it makes, varies or discharges a SGO, see CA 1989, Sch 1, para 1(1), (6) as amended by ACA 2002, Sch 3, para 72.

3 CONTACT

[740]

An incident of parental responsibility to control the child vested in the special guardian is the power to decide with whom he shall have contact. This power must be seen in the context of the court's duty in CA 1989, s 14B(1)(a), before making a SGO, to consider whether a contact order should be made with respect to the child. If more than one special guardian is appointed and the child is not living with all of them, it is submitted that the resident special guardian/s are under a duty to allow the child to have contact with the non-resident special guardian/s, in view of their shared parental responsibility. This presumption in favour of allowing a child to have contact with a non-resident special guardian extends to a child subject to a SGO who is subsequently looked after by a local authority. The local authority are under a duty to promote contact between the child and, inter alia, any person who has parental responsibility for the child, see CA 1989, Sch 2, para 15, where they are looking after the child, whether or not under a care order. The expectation is that the child's contacts should continue undisturbed save where such contact is not in his interests, see Department of Health, *The Children Act 1989 Guidance and Regulations, Volume 3, Family Placements* Ch 6 (1991).

Where the child is the subject of a care order (rather than provided with accommodation) the CA 1989, s 34(1)(b) as amended by ACA 2002, Sch 3, para 64, gives a presumption of the child being allowed 'reasonable contact' by the local authority with, inter alia, any special guardian. Good practice requires that the local authority endeavour to reach agreement with any special guardian regarding reasonable contact, the terms of which are recorded and a copy given to the parties as part of the sharing of parental responsibility associated with a care order. If a special guardian is dissatisfied with the extent of his contact with the child, he can apply to the court, under the CA 1989, s 34(3)(a), which may make such order as it considers appropriate based on the tri-partite welfare principle in the CA 1989, s 1.

4 CONSENT TO MARRIAGE/CIVIL PARTNERSHIP

[741]

Consent to the marriage of a person aged 16 or 17 is governed by the Marriage Act 1949 (MA 1949), s 3. Consent to the civil partnership of a person of that age is governed by the Civil Partnerships Act 2004 (CPA 2004), Sch 2. Normally each parent who has parental responsibility for the child must consent by virtue of the parental responsibility. Where a

PART B – Statutes

SGO has been made, however, the power is entrusted instead to each of the special guardians save in the following cases, see MA 1949, s 3(1A)(b)(c)–(g) as substituted by ACA 2002, Sch 3, paras 1–3, CPA 2004, Sch 2, Pt 1. Where the child is the subject of a care order, the consent of the following is required in addition to the consent of the special guardians, provided that the consent of each parent, guardian or special guardian has not been restricted by the local authority under the CA 1989, s 33(3). The designated local authority and each parent or guardian must consent, save where an adoption agency is authorised to place the child for adoption under ACA 2002, s 19, in which case the consent required is that of the agency, or the local authority if the child is the subject of a care order. If a residence order has been made in addition to the SGO, only the consent of the person with whom the child lives, or is to live, as a result of the order is required, save where an adoption agency is authorised to place the child for adoption when the above caveat applies. If a placement order is in force with respect to the child, the appropriate local authority's consent is required. Where the child has been placed for adoption with prospective adopters (insofar as their parental responsibility has not been restricted under ACA 2002, s 25(4)) their consent is required in addition to that of the agency or appropriate local authority.

The legislation is silent regarding the effect of the marriage or civil partnership of a 16- or 17-year old upon any SGO. On one view the effect of the silence is for the order to continue as normal until the child attains majority. Even if it does, it will be rare for circumstances to arise which justify giving effect to it for the child's protection. The special guardian will be in no better position than where there are no court orders in respect of a child and a parent seeks to exercise parental responsibility over his married or civil-partnered child. The law is unlikely to countenance such exercise in the absence of compelling evidence that it is in the child's best interests to do so. An alternative view is that marriage or civil partnership terminates the special guardianship. It is regretted that the Children Act 1989 does not resolve the uncertainty. The suggested solution is a pragmatic one, namely that the special guardianship order continues but in abeyance after the child's marriage or civil partnership. The office of special guardian remains, but the onus is on anyone seeking to exercise parental responsibility to discharge the considerable burden of proving that it is the child's best interests. If he seeks to do so in the face of opposition, the matter may be referred to the court which may well be favourably disposed to make an order discharging the SGO.

5 CONSENT TO ADOPTION

[742]

A special guardian, like a guardian, is required to consent to the child's adoption and to the child being placed for adoption. Subject to the court's power in the ACA 2002, s 52 to dispense with consent, s 47 makes the consent of each parent with parental responsibility, or guardian (including a special guardian, see ACA 2002, s 144(1)), a prerequisite to the making of an adoption order. Similarly the consent required to a child being placed for adoption in accordance with ACA 2002, s 19, is that of each parent with parental responsibility, or guardian (including special guardian), subject to the court's power of dispensation. The CA 1989, s 14C(2)(b) makes clear that a SGO does not affect any rights which a parent of the child has in relation to the child's adoption or placement for adoption. An adoption order extinguishes a SGO as it does all Children Act 1989 orders (see ACA 2002, s 46(2)). If a placement order is made in respect of the child any special guardianship order continues, but the special guardian's exercise of parental responsibility may be restricted by the adoption agency in accordance with ACA 2002, s 25(4).

6 APPOINTMENT OF A GUARDIAN

[743]

The CA 1989, s 14C(1) must be read with the amendments made to CA 1989, s 5 by the ACA 2002, s 115(4) regarding the appointment of guardians. The special guardian is again equated with a guardian in terms of being empowered to appoint an individual to be the child's guardian in the event of his death, see CA 1989, s 5(4) as amended by ACA 2002, s 115(4)(b). In line with the principle of minimal intervention in the birth family, the appointment will only come into effect on the special guardian's death if the child has no parent with parental responsibility, see CA 1989, s 5(7)(a) and (8), or if the special guardian had a residence order regarding the child in his favour when he died (unless the residence order was also in favour of a surviving parent, see s 5(9)), or he was the child's only or last surviving special guardian, see s 5(7)(b) as amended by ACA 2002, s 115(4)(c). The exception in CA 1989, s 5(7)(b) to the minimal intervention principle where there is a residence order in favour of the special guardian, rests on the questionable notion that since a court has shown a preference for the special guardian in making the residence order, that preference extends beyond the special guardian's lifetime to his appointee. Equally questionable in terms of contravening the minimal intervention principle, is the exception, also in s 5(7)(b), which makes effective the child's only or last surviving special guardian's appointment of a guardian, notwithstanding that the child has a parent with parental responsibility for him. The same criticism can be levelled at the court's power in s 5(1)(b) as amended by ACA 2002, s 115(4)(a)(i), on application, to appoint a guardian on the death of a special guardian who had a residence order regarding the child, in his favour at his death (unless the residence order was also in favour of a surviving parent, s 5(9)), or where there is no residence order in favour of a special guardian (or in favour of a parent or guardian) and the child's only or last surviving special guardian dies (see s 5(1)(c) as inserted by ACA 2002, s 115(4)(a)(ii)). Where one of the exceptions to the minimal intervention principle operates, the question of with whom the child is to live may be in dispute. If so, either the surviving parent or the guardian appointed by the special guardian can apply for a residence order. The dispute will be determined by the court applying the principle of paramountcy of the child's welfare.

7   ADMINISTRATION OF THE CHILD'S PROPERTY

[744]

Parental responsibility means 'all the rights, duties, powers, responsibilities and authority which by law a parent of a child has in relation to the child and his property', see CA 1989, s 3(1), and includes the rights, powers and duties which a guardian of the child's estate would have had in relation to the child and his property if appointed before the Children Act 1989 came into force (see s 3(2)). These rights include by virtue of s 3(3) 'in particular, the right of the guardian to receive or recover in his own name, for the benefit of the child, property of whatever description and wherever situated which the child is entitled to receive or recover'. On the making of a SGO they are entrusted exclusively to the special guardian. If there should be a dispute over the administration of the child's property or the application of income arising from it, the court must, in accordance with CA 1989, s 1, apply the principle that the child's welfare is the paramount consideration.

8   SUCCESSION

[745]

The special guardian's power to administer the child's property does not extend to inheriting it in the event of the child's death. The CA 1989, s 3(4) is quite explicit: 'The fact that a person has, or does not have, parental responsibility for a child shall not affect – ... (b) any rights which, in the event of the child's death, he (or any other person) may have in relation to the child's property'. Rights of intestate succession are incidents of parenthood and vest in the child's mother and father (whether or not he has parental responsibility) in accordance with the Administration of Estates Act 1925, Pt IV. Conversely, unlike adoption, the relationship of special guardian and child is not recognised for the purpose of inheritance on the special guardian's death. If the special guardian wishes the child in respect of whom he is, or was, special guardian to inherit on his death, he must provide accordingly by will.

9   CHANGE TO CHILD'S SURNAME OR REMOVAL FROM THE UNITED KINGDOM

[746]

The CA 1989, s 14C(3) makes special provision such that the written consent of everyone with parental responsibility or leave of the court is required to either any change of the child's surname or his removal from the United Kingdom, see para [747].

The exclusive exercise of parental responsibility conferred on a special guardian by CA 1989, s 14C(1)(b) is subject to a number of further significant qualifications. In addition to the required judicial consideration, before a SGO is made, of contact with respect to the child if an order were made and whether any CA 1989, s 8 order with respect to the child should be varied or discharged (see s 14B(1)), CA 1989, s 14C(2)(a) qualifies s 14C(1) so that it does not affect any rights which a parent of the child has in relation to the child's adoption or placement for adoption (s 14C(2)(b)), for example consent, see above, or the operation of any enactment or rule of law which requires the consent of more than one person with parental responsibility in a matter affecting the child (s 14C(2)(a)). For example, consent of the special guardian per se under the Child Abduction Act 1984, s 1 (as amended by ACA Sch 3, para 42) to the child's being taken out of the United Kingdom is insufficient authorisation (see further Child Abduction Act 1984, s 1(3)–(6) as amended, save for a period of less than three months, see CAA 1984, s 1(4)(b) as inserted).

In day-to-day matters affecting the child, the special guardian has the advantage of being entitled to the exclusive exercise of parental responsibility. Similarly in an emergency, for example the giving of consent to urgent medical treatment, he may act alone in a like manner to a person with a residence order who is exercising the right of independent action conferred by CA 1989, s 2(7), which provides that where more than one person has parental responsibility, each may act alone and without the other/s in meeting that responsibility. The courts, however, have interpreted s 2(7) restrictively, as not encompassing 'important' matters such as change of education, see Glidewell LJ obiter in *Re G (a minor)(parental responsibility: education)* [1995] 2 FCR 53, and the decision to circumcise a child, see *Re J (child's religious upbringing and circumcision)* [2000] 1 FCR 307. It is submitted that this restriction applies equally to a special guardian's exclusive exercise and discharge of parental responsibility regarding other important medical decisions relating to the child, which fall outside urgent medical treatment. The example given in the *Explanatory Notes to the ACA 2002*, para 277, of a matter requiring the consent of all parties with parental responsibility, is that of sterilisation of the child. Indeed such action may require court approval. The judicial view (see Lord Templeman in *Re B (a minor)(wardship: sterilisation)* [1988] AC 199 at 205–6; Lord Goff in *Re F (mental patient: sterilisation)* [1990] 2 AC 1 at 79–80, which is confirmed by a *Practice Note* [1996] 3 FCR 95, [1996] 2 FLR 375, is that such a drastic step as an operation to achieve sterilisation of a child is not to be performed without a court order after a full and informed investigation. Court authorisation would also be required if important medical treatment is to be carried out against the wishes of a *Gillick*-competent child, whose opposition is such as may require the use of force to enable the operation to be performed, in a case where a serious deterioration to the child's physical or mental health may occur if appropriate medical treatment is not administered.

The exclusive exercise of parental responsibility by a special guardian is expressly disapplied by CA 1989, s 14C (1)(b), where the special guardianship appointment extended to more than one special guardian. Although all special guardians will have parental responsibility, they will be subject to the right of independent action in CA 1989, s 2(7). This is the case, save in the small group of important matters affecting the child where there should be both consultation with, and the agreement of, all special guardians, as well as others with parental responsibility. Where there is disagreement between the holders of parental responsibility, the important matter should be referred to court for determination under CA 1989, s 8, by way of a prohibited steps order or, if appropriate, a specific issue order. Such determination will be made on the basis of the paramountcy of the child's welfare in accordance with CA 1989, s 1. Section 14C(1)(b) also requires that the special guardian's exercise and discharge of parental responsibility must be compatible with any other order made under the CA 1989 with respect to the child, for example a prohibited steps order. The other CA 1989 order may have been made either before, or after, the SGO.

Section 14C(3)(a)

Change of child's surname

[747]

One or both of the child's parents, depending upon their marital status and the stability of their relationship, will already have made the initial choice of surname for the child. Any later change on or after the making of a SGO is made expressly dependent, by CA 1989, s 14C(3)(a), upon either the written consent of *every* person who has parental responsibility for the child, or leave of the court, save if a placement order is in force regarding the child, whereupon s 14C(3)(a) does not apply see CA 1989, s 14C(6) and ACA 2002, s 29(7)(b). Thus the general principle in CA 1989, s 14C(1)(b) that a special guardian is entitled to exercise parental responsibility to the exclusion of any other person (apart from another special guardian) does not affect the need for consent or judicial leave, to change the child's surname. The consent of all those with parental responsibility prior to the making of a SGO and who retained residual parental responsibility after the making of the order, is required. This will include the child's mother, the child's father if he had acquired parental responsibility either by marriage to the mother or under CA 1989, s 4, any step-parent who has acquired parental responsibility under s 4A, any guardian and any other special guardian. If the child was the subject of a care order at the time the SGO was made, it will have been discharged (see CA 1989, s 91(5A)(a) as inserted by ACA 2002, Sch 3, para 68) and hence the local authority's consent is not required. A CA 1989, s 8 residence order is not automatically discharged by a SGO and is dependent upon the court expressly doing so in accordance with CA 1989, s 14B(1)(b). If it does, parental responsibility and the need for consent to a change of surname will also have been extinguished. If full consent is not forthcoming, the court's leave is required, in which case, the applicable principles are the same as those when the court is exercising its power under s 14B(2)(a), see para [733]. Although the welfare checklist in CA 1989, s 1(3) does not strictly apply to an application under s 14(C)(3)(a) as it does to an opposed application for a s 8 specific issue order regarding a change of surname, it provides a useful guide to the factors which may impinge upon the child's welfare.

Section 14C(3)(b)(4)

Removal of the child from the United Kingdom

[748]

The parental power to give or withhold consent to a child being taken out of the jurisdiction is a particular incident of the power to determine the place and manner in which the child spends his time, which passes to a special guardian on the making of a SGO. As with the power to determine the child's surname, it does not pass exclusively. The CA 1989, s 14C(3)(b), prohibits the child's removal from the United Kingdom save with either the written consent of every person who has parental responsibility for the child (as to which see s 14(3)(a)) or the leave of the court (as to which see s 14B(2)(b)). Section 14C(3)(b) does not apply if a placement order made under the ACA 2002 is in force regarding the child (see CA 1989, s 14C(6) and ACA 2002, s 29(7)(b)).

The rule against removal in CA 1989, s 14C(3)(b) is modified by s 14C(4) to the extent that a special guardian (but no one else) may remove the child for a period of less than three months, save where a placement order is in force regarding the child (see CA 1989, s 14C(6) and ACA 2002, s 29(7)(b)). The main purpose of the s 14C(4) modification is to allow for holiday or educational trips abroad, although there is no limit imposed upon their number.

If someone, for example a parent or a non-resident special guardian, is concerned about their frequency, or there is a risk of abduction, application should be made for either a CA 1989, s 8 specific issue order, or a variation of the SGO, imposing restrictions on travel abroad.

Section 14C(5)

Notice to parents of the child's death

[749]

A SGO does not transfer parenthood, but 'retains the basic legal link with the birth parents, unlike adoption. They remain legally the child's parents, though their ability to exercise their parental responsibility is limited' (*Explanatory Notes to the ACA 2002*, para 278). Hence it is appropriate that s 14C(5) requires that if the child dies, his special guardian must take reasonable steps to give notice of the fact to each of his parents with parental responsibility and each of the child's guardians. If the child has more than one special guardian, and one of them has taken such steps to notify a particular parent or guardian, any other special guardian need not do so as respects that parent or guardian. The CA 1989 is thereafter silent regarding the child's burial or cremation. In so far as that is an incident of parental responsibility, it is submitted that one (but not the only) purpose of notifying parents with parental responsibility is so as to give them the opportunity to meet the duty upon a parent who has the means to do so, recognised at common law, to provide for the burial, or presumably the cremation, of the child. Moreover, following *R v Gwynedd County Council, ex parte B* [1992] 3 All ER 317, sub nom *Re B* [1991] 1 FCR 800, CA, it is further submitted that where parental responsibility has been transferred (in that case to a local authority under the pre-CA 1989 care jurisdiction) from the parents, then on the child's death the parental duty and right to bury the child reverts to the child's parents. Only if they cannot be found, or are unwilling to exercise their right, does it not revert so as to empower (but not require) the special guardian to bury or cremate the child.

Section 14C(6)

[750]

The effect of s 14C being subject to the ACA 2002, s 29(7) has been considered in the context of ss 14C(1)(b), 14C(3) and 14C(4) to which it relates.

[751]

[14D Special guardianship orders: variation and discharge]

[(1) The court may vary or discharge a special guardianship order on the application of—

(a) the special guardian (or any of them, if there are more than one);
(b) any parent or guardian of the child concerned;
(c) any individual in whose favour a residence order is in force with respect to the child;
(d) any individual not falling within any of paragraphs (a) to (c) who has, or immediately before the making of the special guardianship order had, parental responsibility for the child;
(e) the child himself; or
(f) a local authority designated in a care order with respect to the child.

(2) In any family proceedings in which a question arises with respect to the welfare of a child with respect to whom a special guardianship order is in force, the court may also vary or discharge the special guardianship order if it considers that the order should be varied or discharged, even though no application has been made under subsection (1).

---

(3)   The following must obtain the leave of the court before making an application under subsection (1)—

(a)   the child;
(b)   any parent or guardian of his;
(c)   any step-parent of his who has acquired, and has not lost, parental responsibility for him by virtue of section 4A;
(d)   any individual falling within subsection (1)(d) who immediately before the making of the special guardianship order had, but no longer has, parental responsibility for him.

(4)   Where the person applying for leave to make an application under subsection (1) is the child, the court may only grant leave if it is satisfied that he has sufficient understanding to make the proposed application under subsection (1).
(5)   The court may not grant leave to a person falling within subsection (3)(b)(c) or (d) unless it is satisfied that there has been a significant change in circumstances since the making of the special guardianship order.]

NOTES

Extent

This section does not extend to Scotland: see s 108(11).

Amendment

Inserted by the Adoption and Children Act 2002, s 115(1); date in force (for the purpose of making regulations): 7 December 2004: see SI 2004/3203, art 2(1)(m)(x); date in force (for remaining purposes): 30 December 2005: see SI 2005/2213, art 2(k).

General

[752]

Unlike adoption, special guardianship is neither permanent nor irrevocable. As it involves the exercise of parental responsibility, special guardianship, like guardianship, cannot in any event extend beyond the child's 18th birthday, see CA 1989, s 91(13). A SGO, unlike a residence order, cannot be made for a specified period because the CA 1989, s 11(7)(c) is disapplied by s 14E(5), although may contain provisions which are to have effect for a specified period (see s 14E(4)). Although a SGO can last until the child attains majority, it must be remembered that there is no rule of absolute parental authority. Parental responsibility exists only so long as it is needed for the protection of the child and diminishes once the child is competent to make up his own mind on the matter in question (see para [519.1]). Hence, for the mature teenager, special guardianship is of diminishing relevance. The purpose of s 14D is to provide a qualified opportunity for the variation or discharge of a SGO, before the child attains 18. This may be either on application under s 14D(1), or by a court of its own motion under s 14D(2) in any family proceedings. It is important to note, however, the restrictions which s 14D places upon many categories of applicants in terms of the need for leave of the court and evidence of a significant change in circumstances (see s 14D(3) and (5)). These restrictions provide special guardians with a considerable degree of protection against subsequent challenge to their entitlement to exclusive exercise of parental responsibility for the child, particularly and significantly by his parents. The onus is very much on the applicant to justify an application being allowed to proceed to a hearing. This protection contrasts with the more liberal regime applicable to applications to vary or discharge a CA 1989, s 8 residence order. Bainham has suggested that 'these restrictions will in due course be challenged on the basis that they prevent access to the court as required by Article 6 of the ECHR. It remains to be seen whether they will be found sufficiently watertight to survive such a challenge' (*Children – The Modern Law*, 3rd edn, p 254, *Family Law*, 2005).

Section 14D(1)

Variation or discharge on application

[753]

Section 14D(1) lists six categories of applicant qualified to seek a variation or discharge of a SGO.

1 ANY SPECIAL GUARDIAN OF THE CHILD

[754]

Any special guardian may apply, for example, where there has been a change of circumstances since the making of the original order which has led him to conclude that he can no longer properly exercise parental responsibility to the exclusion of others. No leave of the court is required and the application can proceed to be determined in accordance with the welfare principle. A special guardian may seek to be discharged or for an additional special guardian to be appointed if, for example, he has married, entered a civil partnership or formed a stable relationship since the original order was made. The change of circumstances may relate to another special guardian, such that a variation or discharge of that appointment is in the child's best interests.

2 ANY PARENT (WITH OR WITHOUT PARENTAL RESPONSIBILITY) OR GUARDIAN OF THE CHILD

[755]

The important restriction that such an applicant must have obtained leave of the court before making the application in accordance with s 14D(3)(b) has already been mentioned (see para [752]). The requirement of leave should allow the special guardianship relationship to develop and pre-empt premature challenges to it by a parent or guardian. For the same reason the court may not grant leave to a parent or guardian, unless it is satisfied that there has been a significant change in the circumstances since the making of the SGO, see s 14D(5). The latter puts beyond doubt that the reason for any variation or discharge is change of circumstances and that an application must not merely be an attack on the original order because it is alleged that the evidence did not support the court's decision. The appropriate remedy in the latter situation is to seek leave to appeal the original order. The burdens of obtaining leave and establishing a significant change in circumstances, obviate the need for any temporal restriction on an application by a parent or guardian for variation or discharge, as had been provided for at one time in the Adoption and Children Bill, clause 14D(6).

3 ANY PERSON IN WHOSE FAVOUR A RESIDENCE ORDER IS IN FORCE WITH RESPECT TO THE CHILD

[756]

Such an applicant does not require either leave of the court or to establish that there has been a significant change in circumstances since the making of the SGO in order to be able to apply. The need to show a change of circumstances will, however, be relevant when the court is determining the application in accordance with the welfare principle. The residence order may have been made either before, or after, the making of the SGO. If the residence order is made after the SGO, the issue of variation or discharge of the SGO may need to be addressed at that time. For example, whether the person in whose favour the residence order is made should also be appointed special guardian.

4   ANY OTHER PERSON WHO HAS, OR IMMEDIATELY BEFORE THE MAKING OF THE SGO HAD, PARENTAL RESPONSIBILITY FOR THE CHILD

[757]

This would include a step-parent of the child who has acquired, and not lost, parental responsibility under CA 1989, s 4A as inserted by ACA 2002, s 112. He must also obtain the leave of the court before making an application as required by s 14D(3)(c). Similarly, any individual who had parental responsibility for the child immediately before the making of SGO, but no longer has it, for example under a discharged s 4A agreement or CA 1989, s 8 residence order, must obtain the court's leave in accordance with s 14D(3)(d). Leave in such cases will, again, only be granted if the court is satisfied that there has been a significant change in circumstances since the making of the SGO, see s 14D(5).

5   THE CHILD

[758]

The child must also obtain the court's leave before making the application in accordance with s 14D(3)(a) and the court may only grant leave if it is satisfied, in accordance with s 14D(4), that the child has sufficient understanding to make the proposed application. The court does not have to be satisfied that there has been a significant change in circumstances since the SGO was made.

6   A LOCAL AUTHORITY DESIGNATED IN A CARE ORDER WITH RESPECT TO THE CHILD

[759]

The care order will have to have been made after the SGO, for a prior care order will have been discharged on the making of the SGO in accordance with CA 1989, s 91(5A)(a), as inserted by the ACA 2002, Sch 3, para 68. The fact that a court has been satisfied that a child who is the subject of a SGO is suffering, or is likely to suffer, significant harm, such that it is in his best interests to be the subject of a care order, raises the issue whether the child's welfare also demands either the variation, or particularly, the discharge, of the SGO. If the special guardian had had a residence order rather than a SGO, it would automatically have been discharged on the making of the care order in accordance with CA 1989, s 91(2). This is because decisions relating to where the child shall live vest in the local authority by virtue of the care order. On making the care order the court will need to address whether it is in the child's best interests for the special guardian to retain a degree of residual parental responsibility in conjunction with the dominant role to be played by the local authority in the child's future upbringing.

Criteria

[760]

The criteria to be applied on hearing *any* application to vary or discharge a SGO are those in the CA 1989, s 1 welfare principle, see para **[519.2]**. The court will need to be satisfied that there has been a significant change of circumstances since the making of the order, which justifies a variation or discharge of it in the child's best interests, applying the paramountcy principle in CA 1989, s 1(1). The court is also mandated to pay regard to the checklist in s 1(3) if the application is opposed (see CA 1989, s 1(4)(b) as amended by the ACA 2002, s 115(3)), and is likely to be guided by it in all cases. In applying the paramountcy principle the court will need to consider in particular, who is to exercise parental responsibility if the SGO is varied or discharged. Where the appointment of one of joint special guardians is terminated, is it in the child's best interests for the remaining special guardian/s to continue to act? Where the appointment of a sole special guardian is terminated, is it in the child's best interests for the parental responsibility of those who would have exercised it but for the order to revive, bearing in mind that any care order will have been discharged by the SGO?

Section 14D(2)

Variation or discharge by the court of its own motion

[761]

The court may vary or discharge a SGO of its own motion in any family proceedings in which a question arises with regard to the welfare of the child subject to the SGO, notwithstanding the absence of an application under s 14D(1), in a like manner to the court's power to make a SGO order in any family proceedings of its own motion under CA 1989, s 14A(6)(b). Family proceedings are listed in the CA 1989, s 8(3) and (4). There have been, and will continue to be, modifications to the list from time to time. This power ceases to be available if the family proceedings have ended, see *Re C (minors)(contact: jurisdiction)* (1995) Times, 15 February, CA. The criteria applicable when this court exercises the power in s 14D(2) are again those in CA 1989, s 1.

When the court makes a variation order, whether on application or of its own motion, it also has the power to make directions, conditions, and incidental, supplemental or consequential provisions in accordance with CA 1989, s 11(7)(a)(b) and (d), in the same way as it can when making a SGO (see s 14E(5)). A variation order may also contain provisions which are to have effect for a specified period in accordance with s 14E(4).

Proceedings to discharge a SGO are themselves family proceedings, hence the court is empowered by s 14A(6) to make a SGO in favour of one or more new special guardians. It may do so, either on the application of a person who either is qualified to apply, or has obtained the court's leave to do so under the Children Act, or of its own motion. The court may also, or instead, make a CA 1989, s 8 order in like circumstances, in accordance with CA 1989, s 10(1), if such accords with the welfare principle in CA 1989, s 1.

Section 14D(3)–(5)

Leave of the court to make an application for variation or discharge

[762]

Section 14(3) lists those who must obtain the leave of the court before making an application under s 14D(1). The effect of this subsection was considered in relation to the four affected categories in the context of s 14D(1), where it was noted that in all relevant categories, save the child, s 14D(5) prohibits the court from granting leave unless it is satisfied that there has been a significant change of circumstances since the making of the SGO. In the case of an application by the child, in addition to the need for the child to obtain the court's leave before the application is made (see s 14D(3)(a)), the court must be satisfied in accordance with s 14D(4), that the child has sufficient understanding to make the proposed application. The test is the same as that applicable to the granting of leave to a child to apply for a SGO (see s 14A(12) applying CA 1989, s 10(8)). The case law applicable to a child's understanding to make an application for leave in other CA 1989 proceedings, for example a s 8 order, will be relevant (see, eg, *Re C (residence: child's application for leave)* [1996] 1 FCR 461; *Re H (residence order: child's application for leave)* [2000] 1 FLR 780; *Re N (contact: minor seeking leave to defend and removal of guardian)* [2003] 1 FLR 652).

[763]

[14E Special guardianship orders: supplementary]

[(1) In proceedings in which any question of making, varying or discharging a special guardianship order arises, the court shall (in the light of any rules made by virtue of subsection (3))—

(a) draw up a timetable with a view to determining the question without delay; and

(b) give such directions as it considers appropriate for the purpose of ensuring, so far as is reasonably practicable, that the timetable is adhered to.

(2) Subsection (1) applies also in relation to proceedings in which any other question with respect to a special guardianship order arises.

(3) The power to make rules in subsection (2) of section 11 applies for the purposes of this section as it applies for the purposes of that.

(4) A special guardianship order, or an order varying one, may contain provisions which are to have effect for a specified period.

(5) Section 11(7) (apart from paragraph (c)) applies in relation to special guardianship orders and orders varying them as it applies in relation to section 8 orders.]

NOTES

Extent

This section does not extend to Scotland: see s 108(11).

Amendment

Inserted by the Adoption and Children Act 2002, s 115(1); date in force (for the purpose of making regulations): 7 December 2004: see SI 2004/3203, art 2(1)(m)(x); date in force (for remaining purposes): 30 December 2005: see SI 2005/2213, art 2(k).

General

[764]

This section makes supplementary provision in three contexts. Section 14E(1)–(3) provide for the court in special guardianship proceedings to draw up a timetable to determine the issue without delay and give appropriate directions. Section 14E(4) enables provisions to be included in a SGO and orders varying a SGO for a specified period. Section 14E(5) applies CA 1989, s 11(7)(a), (b) and (d) to SGOs and orders varying a SGO, in a like manner to CA 1989, s 8 orders.

Section 14E(1)–(3)

Timetable and directions

[765]

In line with CA 1989, ss 11(1)–(2) (in relation to s 8 orders) and 32 (in relation to care and supervision orders), s 14E (1)–(3) impose a duty upon the court in proceedings in which *any* question with respect to a special guardianship order arises (see s 14E(1) and (2)), to draw up a timetable for the progress of proceedings, with a view to determining the question without delay and to give the necessary directions for ensuring that the timetable is observed in accordance with the rules. The FPC(CA 1989)R 1991, r 15, as amended and the FPR 1991, r 4.15, as amended (which apply for the purposes of s 14E as they do to s 11, see s 14E(3)) impose time limits within which certain acts must be performed. The period may not be extended except by direction of the court. The rules applicable to directions and attendance at directions appointments and the hearing are in the FPC(CA 1989)R 1991, rr 14 and 16 as amended and the FPR 1991, rr 4.14 and 4.16 as amended. The court's duty to draw up a timetable and give directions is an important part of the avoidance of delay principle in CA 1989, s 1(2), which applies to special guardianship proceedings, see para **[519.2]**. Nevertheless, the need to avoid or minimise delay must yield to the paramountcy of the child's welfare.

Section 14E(4)

Provisions for a specified period

[766]

Reference has already been made to the court's power to include in a SGO, or an order under s 14D varying an SGO, provisions which are to have effect for a specified period. This power corresponds to that in CA 1989, s 11(7)(c) applicable to s 8 orders, which is disapplied generally by s 14E(5) in the context of special guardianship.

Section 14E(5)

Directions and conditions in special guardianship orders

[767]

This subsection applies the extensive powers in CA 1989, s 11(7)(a)(b) and (d) to SGOs and orders varying them in a like manner to CA 1989, s 8 orders. Although s 14E(4) provides that SGOs, like CA 1989, s 8 orders (see s 11(7)(c)), may contain provisions which are to have effect for a specified period, a SGO, unlike a s 8 order in particular a residence order, cannot itself be made for a specified period, because it is intended to offer a greater degree of permanence regarding the exercise of parental responsibility than a residence order. Hence, s 14E(5) disapplies CA 1989, s 11(7)(c) which enables orders to be of specified duration. That apart, s 11(7) is applied in full in the context of special guardianship proceedings, so that when the court makes or varies a SGO, whether on application or of its own motion, it also has the power to make directions about how the order is to be carried into effect, conditions, and incidental, supplemental or consequential provisions, which may, by virtue of s 14E(4), have effect for a specified period. This is to enable orders to be as flexible as possible.

There are, however, limits to flexibility. Thus, the court should not impose a condition, for example, as to where the special guardian and the child are to live within the United Kingdom. In the context of the CA 1989, s 8, it has been held that the court should not include a condition the effect of which is to interfere with a party's right of occupation of property, see *D v D (ouster order)* [1996] 2 FCR 496; *Re D (minors)(residence: conditions)* [1996] 2 FCR 820. Similarly, the power should not be used to impose injunctive-type conditions which essentially relate to the protection of a special guardian from harassment from a parent. Where appropriate, remedies lie in orders under the statutory or inherent jurisdictions. The flexibility is limited also in terms of those upon whom conditions may be imposed. Section 11(7)(b) identifies four categories of persons who can be required to comply with conditions imposed by a SGO, and in each case the conditions must be expressed to apply to that person. They are:

(1)   any person is whose favour the order is made;

(2)   a parent of the child, including therefore the unmarried father who has not acquired parental responsibility for his child;

(3)   a person who is not a parent but who has parental responsibility for the child, for example, a guardian or a person with a residence order;

(4)   a person with whom the child is living.

[768]

> ### [14F   Special guardianship support services]
>
> [(1)   Each local authority must make arrangements for the provision within their area of special guardianship support services, which means—
>
> (a)   counselling, advice and information; and

(b)   such other services as are prescribed,

in relation to special guardianship.

(2)   The power to make regulations under subsection (1)(b) is to be exercised so as to secure that local authorities provide financial support.
(3)   At the request of any of the following persons—

(a)   a child with respect to whom a special guardianship order is in force;
(b)   a special guardian;
(c)   a parent;
(d)   any other person who falls within a prescribed description,

a local authority may carry out an assessment of that person's needs for special guardianship support services (but, if the Secretary of State so provides in regulations, they must do so if he is a person of a prescribed description, or if his case falls within a prescribed description, or if both he and his case fall within prescribed descriptions).

(4)   A local authority may, at the request of any other person, carry out an assessment of that person's needs for special guardianship support services.
(5)   Where, as a result of an assessment, a local authority decide that a person has needs for special guardianship support services, they must then decide whether to provide any such services to that person.
(6)   If—

(a)   a local authority decide to provide any special guardianship support services to a person, and
(b)   the circumstances fall within a prescribed description,

the local authority must prepare a plan in accordance with which special guardianship support services are to be provided to him, and keep the plan under review.

(7)   The Secretary of State may by regulations make provision about assessments, preparing and reviewing plans, the provision of special guardianship support services in accordance with plans and reviewing the provision of special guardianship support services.
(8)   The regulations may in particular make provision—

(a)   about the type of assessment which is to be carried out, or the way in which an assessment is to be carried out;
(b)   about the way in which a plan is to be prepared;
(c)   about the way in which, and the time at which, a plan or the provision of special guardianship support services is to be reviewed;
(d)   about the considerations to which a local authority are to have regard in carrying out an assessment or review or preparing a plan;
(e)   as to the circumstances in which a local authority may provide special guardianship support services subject to conditions (including conditions as to payment for the support or the repayment of financial support);
(f)   as to the consequences of conditions imposed by virtue of paragraph (e) not being met (including the recovery of any financial support provided);
(g)   as to the circumstances in which this section may apply to a local authority in respect of persons who are outside that local authority's area;
(h)   as to the circumstances in which a local authority may recover from another local authority the expenses of providing special guardianship support services to any person.

(9)   A local authority may provide special guardianship support services (or any part of them) by securing their provision by—

(a)   another local authority; or
(b)   a person within a description prescribed in regulations of persons who may provide special guardianship support services,

and may also arrange with any such authority or person for that other authority or that person to carry out the local authority's functions in relation to assessments under this section.

PART B – Statutes

> (10)   A local authority may carry out an assessment of the needs of any person for the purposes of this section at the same time as an assessment of his needs is made under any other provision of this Act or under any other enactment.
>
> (11)   Section 27 (co-operation between authorities) applies in relation to the exercise of functions of a local authority under this section as it applies in relation to the exercise of functions of a local authority under Part 3.]
>
> **NOTES**
>
> **Extent**
> This section does not extend to Scotland: see s 108(11).
>
> **Amendment**
> Inserted by the Adoption and Children Act 2002, s 115(1); date in force (for the purpose of making regulations): 7 December 2004: see SI 2004/3203, art 2(1)(m)(x); date in force (for remaining purposes): 30 December 2005: see SI 2005/2213, art 2(k).
>
> **Subordinate Legislation**
> Special Guardianship Regulations 2005, SI 2005/1109; Special Guardianship (Wales) Regulations 2005, SI 2005/1513.

General

[769]

The hybrid nature of special guardianship is reflected in the duty placed upon each local authority by CA 1989, s 14F, to make arrangements for the provision, within their area, of special guardianship support services. Hence the private law SGO may be supported by the provision of public services so as to ease the transfer in particular of the looked after child from public to private responsibility.

Special guardianship support services are loosely defined in s 14F(1) as counselling, advice and information; and such other prescribed services, including financial support, see s 14F(2). Like adoption support services under ACA 2002, s 2(6) (see para [118], the Act is skeletal regarding detail of special guardianship support services). That detail is again provided in regulations, namely the Special Guardianship Regulations 2005 (SI 2005/1109), Pt 2, and the Special Guardianship (Wales) Regulations 2005 (SI 2005/1513), Pt 3 (see paras [1107]–[1207]), which, in line with s 14F(7) and (8), particularise the provision of support services in accordance with special guardianship support services plans and the assessment for, and review of, such service provision. Guidance on the interpretation of the Special Guardianship Regulations 2005 is provided in *Special Guardianship Guidance* issued by the Department for Education and Skills and on the Special Guardianship (Wales) Regulations 2005 in the *Guidance to Support The Special Guardianship (Wales) Regulations 2005* issued by the Welsh Assembly Government.

The Government, in the White Paper *Adoption: a new approach*, promised that special guardianship 'will be accompanied by proper access to a full range of support services including, where appropriate, financial support' (Cm 5017, para 5.10) and during passage of the Adoption and Children Bill through Parliament it was 'anticipated that the support services 'will operate in a similar manner to adoption support services' (Lord Hunt, HL Grand Committee, 18 July 2002, col CWH 347). The provision of support is likely to be crucial to the success of special guardianship. Without it, many foster parents who might otherwise apply for a SGO may be dissuaded from doing so. 'Nevertheless the Government believe that, because of the fundamental difference between adoption and special guardianship, access to support for special guardianship should be more restricted than access to similar services for adoption' (The Minister of State, Department of Health (Jacqui Smith), HC Special Standing Committee, 15 January 2002, col 826). For provision of adoption support services see ACA 2002, s 4 and para [126].

Section 14F(1), (2), (9)

Local authority duty to make arrangements for the provision of special guardianship support services, including financial support

[770]

Section 14F(1) imposes a duty on each local authority to make arrangements for the provision of special guardianship support services within their area. Such services are loosely defined as meaning counselling, advice and information; and such other additional services as are prescribed, in relation to special guardianship, including, in accordance with s 14F(2), the provision of financial support. The Special Guardianship Regulations 2005 (SI 2005/1109), reg 3, see para **[1108]** and the Special Guardianship (Wales) Regulations 2005 (SI 2005/1513), reg 3, see para **[1208]**, prescribe similar, but not the same, additional prescribed services for the purposes of s 14F(1)(b). They are broadly:

(a)   financial support, in accordance with section 14F(2), payable conditionally under regs 6–10 in England, see paras **[1115]**–**[1126]**, and reg 4(2) in Wales, see para **[1210]**;

(b)   services to enable groups of relevant children, their parents, and actual and prospective special guardians to discuss matters relating to special guardianship (relevant child and prospective special guardian are defined in regs 2(1) and 1(1) respectively);

(c)   assistance in relation to contact arrangements between such a child and his parents, relatives and certain other persons as set out, with differences as to detail, in reg 3(1)(c) respectively;

(d)   therapeutic needs services for a relevant child;

(e)   assistance to ensure the continuance of the relationship between such a child and an actual or prospective special guardian, including training for that person to meet any special needs of the child; respite care (defined in the English reg 3(3)) and mediation.

Services described in paras (b)–(e) above may include assistance in cash (see English reg 3(2)). For example, giving a special guardian money to pay a babysitter or for petrol where a contact visit has been arranged. Such payment 'should not be means tested as it is being provided as part of a service rather than as financial support' see *Special Guardianship Guidance*, para 27.

A local authority may either make such provision itself or, as s 14F(9) makes clear, and in line with the partnership principle which underpins the CA 1989, secure provision of services (or part thereof) by others. They are other local authorities, local education authorities, adoption support agencies, Local Health Boards and Primary Care Trusts; certain fostering agencies; certain adoption agencies and societies, the details of which are prescribed in the Special Guardianship Regulations 2005, reg 4, and the Special Guardianship (Wales) Regulations 2005, reg 3(3) – the latter also includes NHS Trusts (see paras **[1110]** and **[1208]**), for the respective agencies in the two countries. It is envisaged that the provision of services by others may be appropriate where there is a low demand for a particular service in an area or to avoid duplication of provision, see *Special Guardianship Guidance*, para 30. The Guidance indicates, at paras 25 and 26 that:

'**The local authority should take into account the similar services already being delivered in their area, such as adoption support services, and plan the provision of special guardianship support services accordingly.**

Special guardianship support services should not be seen in isolation from mainstream services. It is vital to ensure that children and families involved in special guardianship arrangements are assisted in accessing mainstream services and are aware of their entitlement to social security benefits and tax credits as appropriate.'

PART B – Statutes

Section 14(9) also applies to s 14F assessments. Section 14F(11) further facilitates inter-agency co-operation (see para [778]).

Section 14F(3), (4), (9) and (10)

Assessments for special guardianship support services

[771]

Availability of support services is subject to tight control as the regulations make clear (see, eg, the Special Guardianship Regulations 2005, reg 7 and the Special Guardianship (Wales) Regulations 2005, reg 4). Services are targeted primarily, as s 14F(3) indicates, at children who are the subject of a SGO, special guardians and parents, and additionally other prescribed persons, but will not automatically be available. It is open to those categories to ask the local authority, ie, usually the local authority within whose area the special guardian lives, see *Special Guardianship Guidance*, para 31 and para [1113], to carry out an assessment of his needs for special guardianship support services. Section 14F(3) gives the local authority a discretion, however, whether to carry out an assessment, save in cases prescribed by the Special Guardianship Regulations 2005, reg 11(1) (see para [1127]), and the Special Guardianship (Wales) Regulations 2005, reg 5(1)(2) (see para [1212]), which specify differing categories of those at whose request an assessment must be carried out. If the support services to be provided are counselling, advice or information, in accordance with s 14F(1)(a), it will not always be necessary to undertake an assessment before making provision. If, however, the local authority are considering providing any of the s 14F(1)(b) prescribed services (see para [770]), including financial support an assessment should be carried out, see *Special Guardianship Guidance*, para 55.

Assessment entitlement

[772]

The English reg 11(1) prescribes the following as persons at whose request an assessment is mandatory: a relevant child (as defined in reg 2(1)) who is looked after by the local authority or was looked after immediately before the making of a SGO; an actual or prospective special guardian of such a child and a parent of such a child. The *Special Guardianship Guidance*, at para 51, acknowledges that: 'It is important that children who are not (or were not) looked after are not unfairly disadvantaged by this approach. In many cases the only reason that the child is not looked after is that relatives stepped in quickly to take on the responsibility for the child when a parent could no longer do so.'

Regulation 11(2) additionally prescribes others who *may* seek an assessment by making a written request of the local authority. They are a child with respect to whom a SGO is in force and who is not looked after so as to fall within reg 11(1); an actual or prospective special guardian or parent not falling within reg 11(1); a child of a special guardian (whether the special guardianship child is looked after or not); and any person whom the local authority consider to have a significant and ongoing relationship with a relevant child (whether the child is looked after or not).

Where either an assessment request relates to a particular service, or it appears to the local authority that a person's needs may be adequately assessed by reference to a particular service, they may carry an assessment limited to that service in accordance with reg 11(4).

If the local authority are minded not to carry out an assessment where they have a discretion, they must give the person notice of the proposed decision (and the reasons) and allow him a reasonable opportunity of at least 28 days to make representations in relation to that decision (see reg 11(3) and *Special Guardianship Guidance*, para 53).

The Special Guardianship (Wales) Regulations 2005 (SI 2005/1513), reg 5(1)(2) (see para [1212]), make different provision, regarding those persons at whose request a local authority must carry out an assessment, and those who are prescribed for the purposes of s 14F(3)(d).

Local authorities have a residual discretion under s 14F(4), at the request of any other person, to assess his needs for special guardianship support services. If they do so assess, they should follow the same procedure as they would use for those entitled to an assessment (see *Special Guardianship Guidance*, para 54).

Assessment procedure

[773]

The nature and scope of, and procedure for, assessment are prescribed by the Special Guardianship Regulations 2005, regs 12 and 13, subject to reg 19 in urgent cases (see para [1129]), and the Special Guardianship (Wales) Regulations 2005, regs 6–10 (see paras [1214]–[1222]). They provide, inter alia, for their type and manner, including the matters to which the local authority are to have regard in accordance with s 14F(7)(8)(a) and (d) and reflect those which are considered under the *Framework for the Assessment of Children in Need and their Families* (Department of Health, 2000) in the context of the provision of services under the CA 1989, Pt III, for children in need and their families. Assessments should recognise, however, 'that the context is different from that for birth families. This takes into account the child's developmental needs, the parenting capacity of the special guardian and consideration of the family and environmental factors that together help to explain the child's life so far and what life might be like with the new family. Taking this approach means that past assessments for a child who has previously been a child in need or looked after by a local authority, can inform the assessment of special guardianship support needs'. *Special Guardianship Guidance*, para 58. The assessment procedure should be flexible and not delay the provision of appropriate services (see para 62). After the assessment the local authority must prepare a written report of the assessment (see reg 12(4) and reg 6(2)(b) respectively).

Section 14F(9) enables local authorities to arrange for other prescribed authorities and persons, including other local authorities, to carry out needs assessments, in a like manner to their power to secure the provision by others of special guardianship support services under that subsection, see para [770]. Section 14F(11) further facilitates such co-operation (see para [778]).

In order to minimise the number of assessments, a special guardianship support services needs assessment may, in accordance with s 14F(10), be carried out at the same time as an assessment of that person's needs for any other purpose under the CA 1989 or any other Act, for example for adoption support services (see ACA 2002, s 4, the Adoption Support Services Regulations 2005 (SI 2005/691) and the Adoption Support Services (Local Authorities) (Wales) Regulations 2005 (SI 2005/1512), at para [125]).

Section 14F(5

Local authority decision regarding provision of special guardianship support services

[774]

The largely discretionary nature of the local authorities' responsibilities continues where the outcome of an assessment is a decision that a person needs special guardianship support services. Thereafter their duty under s 14F(5) is to decide whether to provide him with any such services. Local authorities are not under a duty to provide services but rather, as with CA 1989, Pt III services, they may be expected to act as a reasonable authority would in the light of their resources and competing claims upon them. Unless an authority act unreasonably, so as to be liable to judicial review, it is submitted that their decision whether or not to provide a person with special guardianship support services is not subject to judicial control or scrutiny. An aggrieved party should use the local authority's complaints procedure (see para [780]). The Special Guardianship Regulations 2005, regs 15 and 16 (see paras [1135]–[1138]), and the Special Guardianship (Wales) Regulations 2005, regs 8–10 (see paras [1218]–[1223]), make additional, but different, provision regarding the s 14F(5) duty, including allowing an opportunity to make representations and the giving of notice of the decision and the reasons for it.

Section 14F(6)–(8)

Provision of services in accordance with a special guardianship support services plan

[775]

If the outcome of an assessment is that an authority decide in favour of providing a person with special guardianship support services on more than one occasion, then in accordance with s 14F(6) and 14F(8)(b)–(d) and the Special Guardianship Regulations 2005, reg 14 (if the services are not limited to the provision of advice or information) (see para [1133]), and the Special Guardianship (Wales) Regulations 2005, reg 11 (see para [1224]), they must prepare and keep under review a special guardianship support services plan. The services should then be provided in accordance with that plan and the regulations, see s 14F(7) and (8), and under the English reg 14(4), a person should be nominated by the local authority to monitor that provision. Where it appears to the local authority that the person may need services from a Local Health Board, Primary Care Trust or local education authority, they must consult with the relevant agency before preparing the plan, see reg 14(3) and reg 11(3) respectively, the latter also includes an NHS Trust. The plan should set out the services to be provided, the objectives and criteria for evaluating success, time scales for provision, procedures for review and the name of the person nominated to monitor the provision. The plan should be set out in writing in a way that everyone affected can understand (see *Special Guardianship Guidance*, paras 71–72).

The Special Guardianship Regulations 2005, reg 10 (see para [1125]) and the Special Guardianship (Wales) Regulations 2005, reg 4(2) see para [1210], provide, in accordance with s 14F(8)(e), that financial support may be conditional. The regulations provide that financial support that is payable periodically is not payable until the special guardian, or prospective special guardian, agrees:

(i)   immediately to inform the local authority, with details, if any of the listed change in circumstances occurs, and where the information is given orally, that he will confirm it in writing within seven days; and

(ii)   that he will provide the authority with an annual statement of, inter alia, his financial circumstances and the financial needs and resources of the child.

The Special Guardianship Regulations 2005, reg 10(2) also provides, in accordance with s 14F(8)(e)(f), that financial support may be subject to any other conditions that the local authority consider appropriate, including the timescale within which, and the purposes for which such support should be used. Where any such condition is not complied with, the local authority may suspend or terminate financial support and seek to recover all or part of the money paid, provided that where the non-compliance is failure to provide the annual statement, before they take such steps, they have sent a written reminder and 28 days have passed, see reg 10(3), (4). Local authorities should ensure that their repayment policy is publicised to those likely to be affected, so that they may make an informed choice when seeking special guardianship support services in the light of the potential consequences if conditions are not met.

Support services for persons outside the local authority's area

[776]

The local authority within whose area the special guardian lives is responsible for undertaking any assessment that is required to be carried out (see *Special Guardianship Guidance*, para 31), and arranging the provision of any special guardianship support services that are required in response to that assessment, see para [771].

Section 14F(8)(g) enables regulations to provide for the circumstances in which s 14F may apply to a local authority in respect of persons outside their area. Such provision has been made in England by the Special Guardianship Regulations 2005, reg 5, regarding a relevant child (see reg 2(1)), who is looked after by the local authority or was looked after immediately before the SGO was made; an actual or prospective special guardian of such a child; and a child of such a special guardian or prospective special guardian. In order to ensure continuity for such a child and his special guardianship family in the early stages of a SGO, the assessment for, and provision of, support services remain the responsibility of the local authority where the child was last looked after. This is so for three years from the date of the SGO, wherever the child and his family live during that period. The *Special Guardianship Guidance*, para 32, advises that: 'If the family do move during the three years or there is any other significant change in their circumstances, the local authority may wish to undertake a re-assessment and alter the support plan accordingly, including any contact arrangements that are part of the plan'. The reference to contact arrangements relates, it is submitted, to assistance in relation to such arrangements as prescribed in reg 3(1)(c), and not the arrangements themselves. At the end of the three-year period, s 14F ceases to apply except in a case where the local authority are providing financial support under regs 6–10 and the decision to provide that support was made before the SGO was made (see reg 5(2)). As the *Special Guardianship Guidance*, para 35, explains: 'A distinction is made between ongoing financial support (financial support that is paid on a regular basis) which was agreed before the special guardianship order was made and other support services. The assessment and provision of such financial support will remain the responsibility of the local authority who originally agreed it for as long as the family in question qualify for payments. This distinction has been made because financial support can be paid without direct contact'. In other respects, the local authority where the special guardian lives will be responsible for assessing and providing support services after the three-year period (see para 33).

Where the child was not looked after, the local authority where the special guardian lives is always responsible for assessment and support, including assessment and any support that is need by the child's relatives who may live elsewhere. If the special guardian and his family move the responsibility passes to the new authority (see *Special Guardianship Guidance*, para 34).

Regulation 5 does not prevent a local authority from providing special guardianship support services to persons outside their area where they consider it appropriate to do so, see reg 5(3). The example given in the *Special Guardianship Guidance*, para 36, is transitional arrangements by the originating authority where a family move to allow time for the new authority to review the existing special guardianship support services plan without a break in service provision.

In Wales, the regulations merely provide that the fact that a person is outside a local authority's area does not prevent the provision of special guardianship support services (see reg 3(2) and para [1208]).

Section 14F(8)(h) enables regulations to provide for the circumstances in which one local authority may recover from another the cost of providing special guardianship support services.

PART B – Statutes

Reviews

[777]

'Regular reviews enable the local authority and the service user to review the effectiveness of any services provided and consider whether it is appropriate to continue that service or change the provision in some way' (*Special Guardianship Guidance*, para 82). The Special Guardianship Regulations 2005, regs 17 and 18 (see paras [1141]–[1144]), and the Special Guardianship (Wales) Regulations 2005, reg 12 (see para [1226]), make detailed provision regarding reviews and require, inter alia, that the authority review the provision of such services in the light of any change in the recipient's circumstances and in any event at least annually in England and from time to time in Wales.

There is no independent review mechanism for those dissatisfied with a local authority's provision of special guardianship support services. Any concerns which the child, special guardian, parent or anyone else who may be provided with special guardianship support services, has regarding a local authority's discharge of their s 14F special guardianship support services functions, should be raised with the local authority using their special guardianship support services complaints procedure (see para [780]).

Section 14F(11)

Co-operation between authorities

[778]

Co-operation between authorities is facilitated by s 14F(11) which applies CA 1989, s 27 to the provision of special guardianship support services. Section 27, as amended, enables a local authority to seek the help of any other local authority, any local education authority, local housing authority, Health Authority, Special Health Authority, Primary Care Trust, NHS Trust or NHS Foundation Trust and any person authorised by the Secretary of State, when it appears to the local authority that the other authority can help in the provision of special guardianship support services. The requested authority must comply if the request is compatible with their statutory or other duties and does not unduly prejudice the discharge of any of their functions (see s 27(2)). It is up to the authorities, however, to decide the nature of that co-operation and judicial review does not lie as a means to challenge that decision.

[779]

[14G ...]

[...]

NOTES

Amendment

Inserted by the Adoption and Children Act 2002, s 115(1); date in force: 30 December 2005: see SI 2005/2213, art 2(k); repealed by the Health and Social Care (Community Health and Standards) Act 2003, ss 117(2), 196, Sch 14, Pt 2; date in force (in relation to England): 17 January 2005: see SI 2005/38, art 2(b); date in force (in relation to Wales): 30 December 2005: see SI 2005/3285, art 2(1).

General

[780]

Section 14G, as enacted, required every local authority to establish a procedure for considering representations, including complaints, about the discharge of their s 14F functions. The detail was to be in regulations. As the section was modelled upon the CA 1989, s 26 complaints procedure (see further ACA 2002, s 117, at para [525]), it seems appropriate that prior to its implementation, s 14G was repealed by the Health and Social Care (Community Health and Standards) Act 2003, and the CA 1989, s 26 procedure extended (by s 117(1) of the 2003 Act) to any representations which are made to a local authority by:

'(a)   a child with respect to whom a special guardianship order is in force,

(b)   a special guardian or a parent of such a child,

(c)   any other person the authority consider has a sufficient interest in the welfare of such a child to warrant his representations being considered by them, or

(d)   any person who has applied for an assessment under section 14F(3) or (4),

about the discharge by the authority of such functions under section 14F as may be specified by the Secretary of State in regulations.'

(See CA 1989, s 26(3C) as inserted.)

The Children Act 1989 Representations Procedure (England) Regulations 2006, SI 2006/1738 reg 5, identifies the following, in relation to England only, as specified functions under s 14F for the purposes of CA 1989, s 26(3C):

(a)   the provision of financial support payable under the Special Guardianship Regulations 2005, Pt 2, Ch 2 (see para [1115]);

(b)   services to enable groups of relevant children (see para [1104]) to discuss matters relating to special guardianship;

(c)   assistance, including mediation services, in relation to arrangements for contact between a relevant child and (i) his parent or a relative of his; or (ii) any other person with whom such a child has a relationship which appears to the local authority to be beneficial to the welfare of the child having regard to the factors specified in CA 1989, s 1(3);

(d)   services in relation to the therapeutic needs of a relevant child;

(e)   assistance for the purpose of ensuring the continuance of the relationship between a relevant child and a special guardian or prospective special guardian, including (i) training for that person to meet any special needs of that child; (ii) respite care (see para [1108]) and (iii) mediation in relation to matters relating to special guardianship orders (see reg 5(a)); and

(f)   functions under the Special Guardianship Regulations 2005, Part 2, Chapter 2 in so far as they relate to the above support services (see reg 5(b)).

The Special Guardianship (Wales) Regulations 2005, reg 14 makes similar, but not identical, provision in relation to Wales (see para [1233]).

[781]

Supplemental

[26A   Advocacy services]

[(1)   Every local authority shall make arrangements for the provision of assistance to—

(a)   persons who make or intend to make representations under section 24D; and
(b)   children who make or intend to make representations under section 26.

(2)   The assistance provided under the arrangements shall include assistance by way of representation.

[(2A)   The duty under subsection (1) includes a duty to make arrangements for the provision of assistance where representations under section 24D or 26 are further considered under section 26ZA or 26ZB.]

(3)   The arrangements—

(a)   shall secure that a person may not provide assistance if he is a person who is prevented from doing so by regulations made by the Secretary of State; and

(b)   shall comply with any other provision made by the regulations in relation to the arrangements.

(4)   The Secretary of State may make regulations requiring local authorities to monitor the steps that they have taken with a view to ensuring that they comply with regulations made for the purposes of subsection (3).

(5)   Every local authority shall give such publicity to their arrangements for the provision of assistance under this section as they consider appropriate.]

NOTES

Amendment

Inserted by the Adoption and Children Act 2002, s 119; date in force (for the purposes of making regulations): 30 January 2004: see SI 2003/3079, art 2(3); date in force (for remaining purposes): 1 April 2004: see SI 2003/3079, art 2(4)(b); sub-s (2A): inserted by the Health and Social Care (Community Health and Standards) Act 2003, s 116(3); date in force (in relation to Wales): 1 April 2006: see SI 2005/3285, art 2(2)(b); date in force (in relation to England): to be appointed: see the Health and Social Care (Community Health and Standards) Act 2003, s 199(1)–(3).

Subordinate Legislation

Advocacy Services and Representations Procedure (Children) (Amendment) Regulations 2004, SI 2004/719 (made under sub-ss (3), (4)); Advocacy Services and Representations Procedure (Children) (Wales) Regulations 2004, SI 2004/1448 (made under sub-ss (3), (4)); Representations Procedure (Children) (Wales) Regulations 2005, SI 2005/3365 (made under sub-s (3)); Social Services Complaints Procedure (Wales) Regulations 2005, SI 2005/3366; Children Act 1989 Representations Procedure (England) Regulations 2006, SI 2006/1738 (made under sub-s 3(b)).

General

[782]

Each local authority must make arrangements to provide assistance, including representation, for those wishing to make complaints under CA 1989, ss 24D and 26. Regulations can govern the way these arrangements are made, and prohibit certain persons from providing this assistance. They may also require the local authority to monitor compliance.

Each local authority must publicise the arrangements, to the extent that it considers appropriate (s 26A(5)).

The Advocacy Services and Representations Procedure (Children) (Amendment) Regulations 2004 (SI 719/2004)/Advocacy Services and Representations Procedure (Children) (Wales) Regulations 2004 (SI 2004/1448) came into force on 1 April 2004. A child or recipient of after-care services who complains or wishes to do so must be provided with information about advocacy services and offered help in obtaining an advocate. That advocate then has a right to be involved in the complaint process, to refer the matter to a panel, to be heard on the complaint, and for the person to have a choice of representation between the advocate or another person of his/her choice. The advocate must be given notice of the panel's recommendation.

Some degree of independence is introduced by prohibiting the following from providing the advocacy arrangements: the subject of the complaint and his/her managers; those managing a service which is or may be the subject of the complaint; those who control resources allocated to the service in question; and anyone who may become involved in considering the complaint .

Guidance has been issued by the DfES (2004) on the provision of advocacy services: *Getting it Sorted: Guidance on Providing Effective Advocacy Services for Children and Young People making a Complaint under the Children Act 1989*. The National Assembly for Wales has published *Providing Effective Advocacy Services for Children and Young People making a Representation or Complaint under the Children Act 1989*.

[783]

Part IV
Care and Supervision

General

31 Care and supervision orders

(1) On the application of any local authority or authorised person, the court may make an order—

(a) placing the child with respect to whom the application is made in the care of a designated local authority; or

(b) putting him under the supervision of a designated local authority < ... >.

(2) A court may only make a care order or supervision order if it is satisfied—

(a) that the child concerned is suffering, or is likely to suffer, significant harm; and

(b) that the harm, or likelihood of harm, is attributable to—

(i) the care given to the child, or likely to be given to him if the order were not made, not being what it would be reasonable to expect a parent to give to him; or

(ii) the child's being beyond parental control.

(3) No care order or supervision order may be made with respect to a child who has reached the age of seventeen (or sixteen, in the case of a child who is married).

[(3A) No care order may be made with respect to a child until the court has considered a section 31A plan.]

(4) An application under this section may be made on its own or in any other family proceedings.

(5) The court may—

(a) on an application for a care order, make a supervision order;

(b) on an application for a supervision order, make a care order.

(6) Where an authorised person proposes to make an application under this section he shall—

(a) if it is reasonably practicable to do so; and

(b) before making the application,

consult the local authority appearing to him to be the authority in whose area the child concerned is ordinarily resident.

(7) An application made by an authorised person shall not be entertained by the court if, at the time when it is made, the child concerned is—

(a) the subject of an earlier application for a care order, or supervision order, which has not been disposed of; or

(b) subject to—

(i) a care order or supervision order;

(ii) an order under [section 63(1) of the Powers of Criminal Courts (Sentencing) Act 2000]; or

(iii) a supervision requirement within the meaning of [Part II of the Children (Scotland) Act 1995].

(8) The local authority designated in a care order must be—

(a) the authority within whose area the child is ordinarily resident; or

(b)   where the child does not reside in the area of a local authority, the authority within whose area any circumstances arose in consequence of which the order is being made.

(9)   In this section—

'authorised person' means—

(a)   the National Society for the Prevention of Cruelty to Children and any of its officers; and

(b)   any person authorised by order of the Secretary of State to bring proceedings under this section and any officer of a body which is so authorised;

'harm' means ill-treatment or the impairment of health or development [including, for example, impairment suffered from seeing or hearing the ill-treatment of another];
'development' means physical, intellectual, emotional, social or behavioural development;
'health' means physical or mental health; and
'ill-treatment' includes sexual abuse and forms of ill-treatment which are not physical.

(10)   Where the question of whether harm suffered by a child is significant turns on the child's health or development, his health or development shall be compared with that which could reasonably be expected of a similar child.
(11)   In this Act—

'a care order' means (subject to section 105(1)) an order under subsection (1)(a) and (except where express provision to the contrary is made) includes an interim care order made under section 38; and
'a supervision order' means an order under subsection (1)(b) and (except where express provision to the contrary is made) includes an interim supervision order made under section 38.

NOTES
Initial Commencement
To be appointed
To be appointed: see s 108(2).

Appointment
Appointment: 14 October 1991: see SI 1991/828, art 3(2).

Extent
This section does not extend to Scotland: see s 108(11).

Amendment
Sub-s (1): in para (b) words omitted repealed by the Criminal Justice and Court Services Act 2000, ss 74, 75, Sch 7, Pt II, paras 87, 90, Sch 8.

Date in force: 1 April 2001: see SI 2001/919, art 2(f)(ii), (g).

Sub-s (3A): inserted by the Adoption and Children Act 2002, s 121(1).

Date in force (for the purpose of making regulations): 7 December 2004: see SI 2004/3203, art 2(1)(m)(xii).

Date in force (for remaining purposes): 30 December 2005: see SI 2005/2213, art 2(k).

Sub-s (7): in para (b)(ii) words 'section 63(1) of the Powers of Criminal Courts (Sentencing) Act 2000' in square brackets substituted by the Powers of Criminal Courts (Sentencing) Act 2000, s 165(1), Sch 9, para 127.

Date in force: 25 August 2000: see the Powers of Criminal Courts (Sentencing) Act 2000, s 168(1).

Sub-s (7): in para (b)(iii) words 'Part II of the Children (Scotland) Act 1995' in square brackets substituted by the Children (Scotland) Act 1995, s 105(4), Sch 4, para 48(2).

Sub-s (9): in definition 'harm' words from 'including, for example,' to 'ill-treatment of another' in square brackets inserted by the Adoption and Children Act 2002, s 120.

Date in force: 31 January 2005: see SI 2004/3203, art 2(2).

Transfer of Functions
Functions of the Secretary of State, so far as exercisable in relation to Wales, transferred to the National Assembly for Wales, by the National Assembly for Wales (Transfer of Functions) Order 1999, SI 1999/672, art 2, Sch 1.

[31A   Care orders: care plans]

[(1)   Where an application is made on which a care order might be made with respect to a child, the appropriate local authority must, within such time as the court may direct, prepare a plan ('a care plan') for the future care of the child.
(2)   While the application is pending, the authority must keep any care plan prepared by them under review and, if they are of the opinion some change is required, revise the plan, or make a new plan, accordingly.
(3)   A care plan must give any prescribed information and do so in the prescribed manner.
(4)   For the purposes of this section, the appropriate local authority, in relation to a child in respect of whom a care order might be made, is the local authority proposed to be designated in the order.
(5)   In section 31(3A) and this section, references to a care order do not include an interim care order.
(6)   A plan prepared, or treated as prepared, under this section is referred to in this Act as a 'section 31A plan'.]

NOTES

Amendment

Inserted by the Adoption and Children Act 2002, s 121(2); date in force (for the purpose of making regulations): 7 December 2004: see SI 2004/3203, art 2(1)(m)(xii); for transitional provision see the Adoption and Children Act 2002, s 121(3); date in force (for remaining purposes): 30 December 2005: see SI 2005/2213, art 2(k); for provision as to care orders made before that date see the Adoption and Children Act 2002, s 121(3).

General

[784]

The background to s 31A is contained in the note to ACA 2002, s 118 (see para [538]).

For the first time, it puts the requirement for local authorities to prepare a care plan for each looked after child on a statutory footing, rather than a requirement of regulations and guidance. It imposes a restriction upon the court, in the absence of a care plan, and imposes obligations in respect of the content of a s 31A care plan.

Section 31A(1)

[785]

A new s 31(3A) is inserted in CA 1989. It prohibits the court from making a final care order (by virtue of CA 1989, ss 31(11) and 31A(5) this does not include an interim care order) unless the court has considered a s 31A care plan.

Section 31A(2)

[786]

The new CA 1989, s 31A imposes a duty on a local authority to prepare a care plan for the future care of the child, within a timescale directed by the court, in any proceedings where a care order might be made (sub-s (1)). Since a care order might be made within an application for a supervision order, or on a s 31 application where the local authority then proposes adjourning or concluding the case with no order, this is a wider obligation than the existing requirements under the Arrangements for Placement of Children (General) Regulations 1991 (SI 1991/890), under which the only express requirement for a 'care plan' ('the arrangements') is where the child is looked after or it is actively proposed that the child should be looked after. It only includes a final hearing and care order (see ss 31(11) and 31A(5)).

The care plan must contain any prescribed information, and during the proceedings, the local authority must keep that care plan under review, and revise or change it as necessary (s 31A(2) and (3)).

The local authority with responsibility for the care plan is the one proposed to be designated in the order (s 31A(4)). This pre-supposes, in cases where two local authorities are in dispute over which should be the designated authority, that the court has determined that issue by the time directions are given under s 31A(1). This provision will therefore require an earlier determination of such disputes than hitherto.

By virtue of s 31A(6), a court may treat a care plan produced under the Arrangements for Placement of Children (General) Regulations 1991 as a 's 31A care plan'.

Section 31A(3)

[787]–[800]

If a child is subject to a care order made before s 121(2) of this Act (and therefore CA 1989, s 31A) came into force, then if that order was made based upon a plan for the child's future care – whatever the document in question may be called – that plan is to have effect as a s 31A care plan. This includes a care order that does not currently have effect due to the existence of a placement order under the provisions of s 29(1) of this Act.

Part C   Statutory Instruments

Adoption Agencies Regulations 2005

(SI 2005/389)

Made	*23rd February 2005*
Laid before Parliament	*2nd March 2005*
Coming into force	*30th December 2005*

The Secretary of State for Education and Skills, in exercise of the powers conferred on her by sections 26(1) to (2B), 59(4)(a) and (5) and 104(4) of the Children Act 1989 and sections 9(1)(a), 11(1)(b), 27(3), 53(1) to (3), 54, 140(7) and (8) and 142(4) and (5) of the Adoption and Children Act 2002, and all other powers enabling her in that behalf, hereby makes the following Regulations:

General

[801]

These regulations govern the functions of adoption agencies and adoption panels in England. For Wales, see the Adoption Agencies (Wales) Regulations 2005 (SI 2005/1313).

Adoption Guidance: Adoption and Children Act 2002 [2005], issued by the DfES, contains important guidance on the functions of adoption agencies and adoption panels. It is issued under the Local Authority Social Services Act 1970, s 7, though the annexes to it are issued only as good practice guidance.

An 'adoption agency' can be a local authority or a registered adoption society (see ACA 2002, s 2(1)). A 'registered adoption society' is a voluntary organisation registered as an adoption society under the Care Standards Act 2000 (see ACA 2002, s 2(2)).

It is important to note that the Adoption Panel makes recommendations to the adoption agency, and that decisions are then taken by the agency.

[802]

Part 1
General

1   Citation, commencement and application

(1)   These Regulations may be cited as the Adoption Agencies Regulations 2005 and shall come into force on 30th December 2005.
(2)   These Regulations apply to England only.

NOTES

Initial Commencement

Specified date
Specified date: 30 December 2005: see para (1) above.

Extent
These regulations apply to England only: see para (2) above.

General

[803]

These regulations came into force on 30 December 2005, the same date as the main provisions of the Act. They apply only to England.

[804]

2 Interpretation

(1) In these Regulations—

'the Act' means the Adoption and Children Act 2002;

'the 1989 Act' means the Children Act 1989;

'adoption panel' means a panel established in accordance with regulation 3;

'adoption placement plan' has the meaning given in regulation 35(2);

'adoption placement report' means the report prepared by the adoption agency in accordance with regulation 31(2)(d);

'adoption support services' has the meaning given in section 2(6)(a) of the Act and in any regulations made under section 2(6)(b) of the Act;

'adoptive family' has the meaning given in regulation 31(2)(a);

'CAFCASS' means the Children and Family Court Advisory and Support Service;

'child's case record' has the meaning given in regulation 12;

'child's health report' means the report obtained in accordance with regulation 15(2)(b);

'child's permanence report' means the report prepared by the adoption agency in accordance with regulation 17(1);

'independent member' in relation to an adoption panel has the meaning given in regulation 3(3)(e);

'independent review panel' means a panel constituted under section 12 of the Act;

'joint adoption panel' means an adoption panel established in accordance with regulation 3(5);

'medical adviser' means the person appointed as the medical adviser by the adoption agency in accordance with regulation 9(1);

'proposed placement' has the meaning given in regulation 31(1);

'prospective adopter's case record' has the meaning given in regulation 22(1);

'prospective adopter's report' means the report prepared by the adoption agency in accordance with regulation 25(5);

'prospective adopter's review report' means the report prepared by the adoption agency in accordance with regulation 29(4)(a);

'qualifying determination' has the meaning given in regulation 27(4)(a);

'registration authority' means the Commission for Social Care Inspection;

'relevant foreign authority' means a person, outside the British Islands performing functions in the country in which the child is, or in which the prospective adopter is, habitually resident which correspond to the functions of an adoption agency or to the functions of the Secretary of State in respect of adoptions with a foreign element;

'relevant post-qualifying experience' means post-qualifying experience in child care social work including direct experience in adoption work;

'section 83 case' means a case where a person who is habitually resident in the British Islands intends to bring, or to cause another to bring, a child into the United Kingdom in circumstances where section 83 of the Act (restriction on bringing children into the United Kingdom) applies;

'social worker' means a person who is registered as a social worker in a register maintained by the General Social Care Council or the Care Council for Wales under section 56 of the Care Standards Act 2000 or in a corresponding register maintained under the law of Scotland or Northern Ireland;

'vice chair' has the meaning given in regulation 3(4) or, as the case may be, (5)(c);

'working day' means any day other than a Saturday, Sunday, Christmas Day, Good Friday or a day which is a bank holiday within the meaning of the Banking and Financial Dealings Act 1971.

NOTES

Initial Commencement

Specified date

Specified date: 30 December 2005: see reg 1(1).

Extent

These regulations apply to England only: see reg 1(2).

Part 2
Adoption Agency—Arrangements for Adoption Work

3 Establishment of adoption panel

(1) Subject to paragraph (5) [and regulation 3A], an adoption agency must establish at least one panel, to be known as an adoption panel, in accordance with this regulation.

(2) The adoption agency must appoint to chair the panel a person, not being a disqualified person, who has the skills and experience necessary for chairing an adoption panel.

(3) Subject to paragraph (5), the adoption panel shall consist of no more than ten members, including the person appointed under paragraph (2), and shall include—

(a)   two social workers each with at least three years' relevant post-qualifying experience;

(b)   in the case of a registered adoption society, one person who is a director, manager or other officer and is concerned in the management of that society;

(c)   in the case of a local authority, one member of that authority;

(d)   the medical adviser to the adoption agency (or one of them if more than one medical adviser is appointed);

(e)   at least three other persons (in this regulation referred to as 'independent members') including where reasonably practicable at least two persons with personal experience of adoption.

(4) The adoption agency must appoint one member of the adoption panel as vice chair ('vice chair') who shall act as chair if the person appointed to chair the panel is absent or his office is vacant.

(5) An adoption panel may be established jointly by any two or more local authorities ('joint adoption panel') and if a joint adoption panel is established—

(a)   the maximum number of members who may be appointed to that panel is eleven;

(b)   by agreement between the local authorities there shall be appointed to that panel—

(i)   a person to chair the panel, not being a disqualified person, who has the skills and experience necessary for chairing an adoption panel;

(ii)   two social workers each with at least three years' relevant post-qualifying experience;

(iii) one member of any of the local authorities;

(iv) the medical adviser to one of the local authorities; and

(v)   at least three independent members including where reasonably practicable at least two persons with personal experience of adoption;

(c)   by agreement the local authorities must appoint one member of the panel as vice chair ('vice chair') who shall act as chair if the person appointed to chair the panel is absent or his office is vacant.

(6) A person shall not be appointed as an independent member of an adoption panel if—

(a)   in the case of a registered adoption society, he is or has been within the last year a trustee or employee, or is related to an employee, of that society;

(b)   in the case of a local authority, he—

(i)   is or has been within the last year employed by that authority in their children and family social services;

(ii)   is related to a person falling within head (i); or

(iii) is or has been within the last year a member of that authority; or

(c)   he is the adoptive parent of a child who was—

(i)   placed for adoption with him by the adoption agency ('agency A'); or

(ii)   placed for adoption with him by another adoption agency where he had been approved as suitable to be an adoptive parent by agency A, unless at least twelve months has elapsed since the adoption order was made in respect of the child.

(7) For the purposes of regulation 3(2) and (5)(b)(i) a person is a disqualified person if—

(a)   in the case of a registered adoption society, he is or has been within the last year a trustee or employee, or is related to an employee, of that society; or

[(b)   in the case of a local authority, he—

    (i)   is or has been within the last year employed by that authority in their children and family social services;

    (ii)   is related to a person falling within head (i); or

    (iii)   is or has been within the last year a member of that authority].

(8) For the purposes of paragraphs (6)(a) and (b)(ii) and (7) a person ('person A') is related to another person ('person B') if person A is—

(a)   a member of the household of, or married to or the civil partner of, person B;

(b)   the son, daughter, mother, father, sister or brother of person B; or

(c)   the son, daughter, mother, father, sister or brother of the person to whom person B is married or with whom B has formed a civil partnership.

NOTES

Initial Commencement

Specified date

Specified date: 30 December 2005: see reg 1(1).

Extent

These regulations apply to England only: see reg 1(2).

Amendment

Para (1): words 'and regulation 3A' in square brackets inserted by SI 2005/3482, reg 5(a); date in force: 30 December 2005: see SI 2005/3482, reg 1; para (7): sub-para (b) substituted by SI 2005/3482, reg 5(b); date in force: 30 December 2005: see SI 2005/3482, reg 1.

General

[805]

Each adoption agency must establish at least one adoption panel, with an experienced chair and up to ten members (including the chair), although two or more local authorities may establish joint panels with a maximum of 11 members. Each panel must include the adoption agency's medical advisor (or one of them, if more than one), at least two experienced social workers, and at least three independent members (if possible, at least two to have personal experience of adoption). A vice-chair must be appointed. If the agency is a local authority, one of the members must be an elected member. If it is a registered adoption society, one member must be a director, manager or other officer with management functions. Safeguards are imposed in relation to the degree of independence of the chair, and regarding any connections through employment or in other ways between the agency and any independent member of the panel.

See reg 9 in relation to the medical advisor.

An adoption panel makes recommendations to the adoption agency.

If panel members have serious reservations about the majority view, these should be recorded in the minutes and attached to the recommendations. It should not make conditional or 'in principle' recommendations, but can advise on twin-track or concurrent planning. See also note to reg 18 (para [837]). The panel should be updated on the progress of cases it has considered. (*Adoption Guidance* [2005] DfES, Ch 1)

[806]

[3A

[Where an adoption agency operates only for the purpose of putting persons into contact with other adoption agencies and for the purpose of putting such agencies into contact with each other or for either of such purposes, regulations 3, 8, 10 and, to the extent that it requires consultation with the adoption panel, regulation 7 shall not apply to such an agency.]

NOTES
Extent
These regulations apply to England only: see reg 1(2).

Amendment
Inserted by SI 2005/3482, reg 5(c); date in force: 30 December 2005: see SI 2005/3482, reg 1.

General

[807]

See note to reg 7.

[808]

4   Tenure of office of members of the adoption panel

(1)   Subject to the provisions of this regulation and regulation 10, a member of an adoption panel shall hold office for a term not exceeding three years, and may not hold office for the adoption panel of the same adoption agency for more than three terms in total.
(2)   The medical adviser member of the adoption panel shall hold office only for so long as he is the medical adviser.
(3)   A member of an adoption panel may resign his office at any time by giving one month's notice in writing to the adoption agency.
(4)   Where an adoption agency is of the opinion that any member of the adoption panel is unsuitable or unable to remain in office, it may terminate his office at any time by giving him notice in writing with reasons.
(5)   If the member whose appointment is to be terminated under paragraph (4) is a member of a joint adoption panel, his appointment may only be terminated with the agreement of all the local authorities whose panel it is.

NOTES
Initial Commencement
Specified date
Specified date: 30 December 2005: see reg 1(1).

Extent
These regulations apply to England only: see reg 1(2).

PART C – SIs

General

[809]

The term of office of a member of an adoption panel is a maximum of three years, and he/she can only hold office for a maximum of three terms. A month's notice must be given by a member who resigns, but an agency or agencies that terminate a person's membership may do so without notice if necessary, with written reasons.

[810]

---

5 Meetings of adoption panel

(1) Subject to paragraph (2), no business shall be conducted by the adoption panel unless at least five of its members, including the person appointed to chair the panel or the vice chair and at least one of the social workers and one of the independent members, meet as the panel.

(2) In the case of a joint adoption panel, no business shall be conducted unless at least six of its members, including the person appointed to chair the panel or the vice chair and at least one of the social workers and one of the independent members, meet as the panel.

(3) An adoption panel must make a written record of its proceedings, its recommendations and the reasons for its recommendations.

NOTES

Initial Commencement

Specified date

Specified date: 30 December 2005: see reg 1(1).

Extent

These regulations apply to England only: see reg 1(2).

General

[811]

There must be a quorum of five (six for a joint adoption panel: see reg 3) including the chair or vice-chair. Written minutes must be taken of its discussions and recommendations to the adoption agency, including reasons.

[812]

---

6 Payment of fees to member of local authority adoption panel

A local authority may pay to any member of their adoption panel such fee as they may determine, being a fee of a reasonable amount.

NOTES

Initial Commencement

Specified date

Specified date: 30 December 2005: see reg 1(1).

Extent

These regulations apply to England only: see reg 1(2).

General

[813]

A local authority may pay reasonable fees to its adoption panel members.

[814]

---

7 Adoption agency arrangements for adoption work

An adoption agency must, in consultation with the adoption panel and, to the extent specified in regulation 9(2) with the agency's medical adviser, prepare and implement written policy and procedural instructions governing the exercise of the functions of the agency and the adoption panel in relation to adoption and such instructions shall be kept under review and, where appropriate, revised by the agency.

NOTES
Initial Commencement
Specified date
Specified date: 30 December 2005: see reg 1(1).

Extent
These regulations apply to England only: see reg 1(2).

General

[815]

An adoption agency must prepare, put into effect, review and, where necessary, amend written policies and procedures governing how the adoption panel(s) and the agency carry out their functions. Regulation 3A creates a limited exception to this requirement, for adoption societies with limited functions.

[816]

8 Requirement to appoint an agency adviser to the adoption panel

(1)   The adoption agency must appoint a senior member of staff, or in the case of a joint adoption panel the local authorities whose panel it is must by agreement appoint a senior member of staff of one of them, (referred to in this regulation as the 'agency adviser')—

(a)   to assist the agency with the appointment (including re-appointment), termination and review of appointment of members of the adoption panel;
(b)   to be responsible for the induction and training of members of the adoption panel;
(c)   to be responsible for liaison between the agency and the adoption panel, monitoring the performance of members of the adoption panel and the administration of the adoption panel; and
(d)   to give such advice to the adoption panel as the panel may request in relation to any case or generally.

(2)   The agency adviser must be a social worker and have at least five years' relevant post-qualifying experience and, in the opinion of the adoption agency, relevant management experience.

NOTES
Initial Commencement
Specified date
Specified date: 30 December 2005: see reg 1(1).

Extent
These regulations apply to England only: see reg 1(2).

PART C – SIs

General

[817]

A senior member of staff, who is a qualified social worker with requisite social work and management experience, must be appointed as the agency advisor, who has a number of important functions. These include advising the adoption panel, both in general and on individual cases; assisting with appointments to the panel, the review of panel members, the monitoring of panel members, and the termination of membership of the panel; the induction and training of panel members; administration of the panel; and being responsible for the necessary liaison between the panel(s) and the agency. He/she plays a vital role in the link between the adoption panel(s) and the adoption agency decision-maker (see notes to regs 18, 19, 26, 27, 32 and 33, paras **[837]**, **[839]**, **[855]**, **[857]**, **[868]** and **[870]**).

[818]

9 Requirement to appoint a medical adviser

(1)   The adoption agency must appoint at least one registered medical practitioner to be the agency's medical adviser.

(2)   The medical adviser shall be consulted in relation to the arrangements for access to, and disclosure of, health information which is required or permitted by virtue of these Regulations.

NOTES

Initial Commencement

Specified date

Specified date: 30 December 2005: see reg 1(1).

Extent

These regulations apply to England only: see reg 1(2).

General

[819]

At least one medical advisor must be appointed for the adoption agency. He/she must be consulted about access to, or disclosure of, health information where there is a power or duty to gain or give such access or disclosure under these regulations. See, for example, the requirements to obtain health information about children and prospective adopters under regs 15 and 25.

[820]

10 Establishment of new adoption panels on 30 December 2005

(1)   All members of an adoption panel established before 30th December 2005 (referred to in this regulation as the 'old adoption panel') shall cease to hold office on that date.

(2)   With effect from 30th December 2005 an adoption agency shall establish a new adoption panel in accordance with regulations 3 and 4.

(3)   This paragraph applies where [a person's term of office as] a member of the old adoption panel was extended by the adoption agency in accordance with regulation 5A(1A) of the Adoption Agencies Regulations 1983.

(4)   This paragraph applies where [the person served only one] term of office as a member of the old adoption panel.

(5)   [A person who has been at any time a member of an old adoption panel] may not hold office as a member of the new adoption panel of the same adoption agency—

(a)   where paragraph (3) applies, for more than one term, not exceeding one year;

(b)   where paragraph (4) applies, for more than two terms, each term not exceeding three years;

(c)   in any other case, for more than one term, not exceeding three years.

NOTES

Initial Commencement

Specified date

Specified date: 30 December 2005: see reg 1(1).

Extent

These regulations apply to England only: see reg 1(2).

Amendment

Para (3): words 'a person's term of office as' in square brackets substituted by SI 2005/3482, reg 5(d)(i); date in force: 30 December 2005: see SI 2005/3482, reg 1; para (4): words 'the person served only one' in square brackets substituted by SI 2005/3482, reg 5(d)(ii); date in force:

> 30 December 2005: see SI 2005/3482, reg 1; para (5): words 'A person who has been at any time a member of an old adoption panel' in square brackets substituted by SI 2005/3482, reg 5(d)(iii); date in force: 30 December 2005: see SI 2005/3482, reg 1.

General

[821]

All members of adoption panels prior to 30 December 2005 ceased to hold office on that date, and the new panels required under these regulations were then to be constituted from that date. It provides for the calculation of the maximum terms of office from 30 December 2005 for those who previously held membership of a panel, depending on their length of previous tenure.

[822]

Part 3
Duties of Adoption Agency where the Agency is Considering Adoption for a Child

11 Application of regulations [12] to 17

Regulations [12] to 17 apply where the adoption agency is considering adoption for a child.

NOTES

Initial Commencement

Specified date
Specified date: 30 December 2005: see reg 1(1).

Extent
These regulations apply to England only: see reg 1(2).

Amendment
Reference to '12' in square brackets substituted by virtue of SI 2005/3482, reg 5(e); date in force: 30 December 2005: see SI 2005/3482, reg 1; reference to '12' in square brackets substituted by SI 2005/3482, reg 5(e); date in force: 30 December 2005: see SI 2005/3482, reg 1.

General

[823]

Regulations 12–17 govern the procedures to be followed when an adoption agency is considering whether a child should be adopted.

[824]

12 Requirement to open the child's case record

(1) The adoption agency must set up a case record ('the child's case record') in respect of the child and place on it—

(a) the information and reports obtained by the agency by virtue of this Part;

(b) the child's permanence report;

(c) the written record of the proceedings of the adoption panel under regulation 18, its recommendation and the reasons for its recommendation and any advice given by the panel to the agency;

(d) the record of the agency's decision and any notification of that decision under regulation 19;

(e) any consent to placement for adoption under section 19 of the Act (placing children with parental consent);

> (f)   any consent to the making of a future adoption order under section 20 of the Act (advance consent to adoption);
>
> (g)   any form or notice withdrawing consent under section 19 or 20 of the Act or notice under section 20(4)(a) or (b) of the Act;
>
> (h)   a copy of any placement order in respect of the child; and
>
> (i)   any other documents or information obtained by the agency which it considers should be included in that case record.
>
> (2) Where an adoption agency places on the child's case record a notice under section 20(4)(a) or (b) of the Act, the agency must send a copy of that notice to a court which has given the agency notice of the issue of an application for an adoption order.
>
> **NOTES**
>
> **Initial Commencement**
>
> *Specified date*
> Specified date: 30 December 2005: see reg 1(1).
>
> **Extent**
> These regulations apply to England only: see reg 1(2).

General

[825]

Once an adoption agency is considering whether a child should be adopted, it must open a case record for that child, containing, as time unfolds, the following: the information and reports that the agency must obtain as required by regs 12–20 (see below); the child's permanence report (see reg 17); the written minutes of the adoption panel, including its recommendations, reasons, and any advice given to the agency (see reg 18); the record of the adoption agency's decision and any notification of that decision (see reg 19); any consent to placement for adoption given by a parent under ACA 2002, s 19; any advance consent to adoption given by a parent under ACA 2002, s 20; any withdrawal of s 19 or s 20 consent; any notice under ACA 2002, s 20(4) expressing a wish not to be notified of an adoption application or withdrawing such notice (and a copy of this document must be sent to the court which has notified the agency of the issue of an adoption application for the child); any placement order made by the court; and any other relevant information.

The child's need for a permanent home should be considered at the four-month LAC review, and the adoption panel's recommendation on whether the child should be placed for adoption should be made within two months of the review identifying adoption as the plan for the child. It seems clear that this means the review determining that adoption is the sole plan, and all relevant twin-track planning and assessments have been completed, concluding with an adoption plan. At the review, the parent should be given written information about the implications of the different permanence options (*Adoption Guidance* [2005] DfES, Ch 2).

[826]

> ### 13 Requirement to provide counselling and information for, and ascertain wishes and feelings of, the child
>
> (1) The adoption agency must, so far as is reasonably practicable—
>
> (a)   provide a counselling service for the child;
>
> (b)   explain to the child in an appropriate manner the procedure in relation to, and the legal implications of, adoption for the child and provide him with appropriate written information about these matters; and
>
> (c)   ascertain the child's wishes and feelings regarding—
>
>   (i)   the possibility of placement for adoption with a new family and his adoption;

    (ii)   his religious and cultural upbringing; and
    (iii)   contact with his parent or guardian or other relative or with any other person the agency considers relevant.

(2) Paragraph (1) does not apply if the adoption agency is satisfied that the requirements of that paragraph have been carried out in respect of the child by another adoption agency.

NOTES

Initial Commencement

Specified date
Specified date: 30 December 2005: see reg 1(1).

Extent
These regulations apply to England only: see reg 1(2).

General

[827]

As far as reasonably practicable, the adoption agency must – unless done by another adoption agency – explain adoption procedures and the legal implications of adoption to the child, and provide a counselling service for him/her. It must ascertain his/her wishes and feelings about adoption, contact, and religious and cultural upbringing.

[828]

14   Requirement to provide counselling and information for, and ascertain wishes and feelings of, the parent or guardian of the child and others

(1)   The adoption agency must, so far as is reasonably practicable—

(a)   provide a counselling service for the parent or guardian of the child;
(b)   explain to him—

    (i)   the procedure in relation to both placement for adoption and adoption;
    (ii)   the legal implications of—

        (aa)   giving consent to placement for adoption under section 19 of the Act;
        (bb)   giving consent to the making of a future adoption order under section 20 of the Act; and
        (cc)   a placement order; and

    (iii)   the legal implications of adoption,

    and provide him with written information about these matters; and

(c)   ascertain the wishes and feelings of the parent or guardian of the child and, of any other person the agency considers relevant, regarding—

    (i)   the child;
    (ii)   the placement of the child for adoption and his adoption, including any wishes and feelings about the child's religious and cultural upbringing; and
    (iii)   contact with the child if the child is authorised to be placed for adoption or the child is adopted.

(2)   Paragraph (1) does not apply if the agency is satisfied that the requirements of that paragraph have been carried out in respect of the parent or guardian and any other person the agency considers relevant by another adoption agency.
(3)   This paragraph applies where the father of the child does not have parental responsibility for the child and the father's identity is known to the adoption agency.
(4)   Where paragraph (3) applies and the adoption agency is satisfied it is appropriate to do so, the agency must—

(a)   carry out in respect of the father the requirements of paragraph (1)(a), (b)(i) and (iii) and (c) as if they applied to him unless the agency is satisfied that the requirements have been carried out in respect of the father by another agency; and

(b)   ascertain so far as possible whether the father—

    (i)   wishes to acquire parental responsibility for the child under section 4 of the 1989 Act (acquisition of parental responsibility by father); or

    (ii)   intends to apply for a residence order or contact order with respect to the child under section 8 of the 1989 Act (residence, contact and other orders with respect to children) or, where the child is subject to a care order, an order under section 34 of the 1989 Act (parental contact etc with children in care).

NOTES

Initial Commencement

Specified date

Specified date: 30 December 2005: see reg 1(1).

Extent

These regulations apply to England only: see reg 1(2).

General

[829]

Unless carried out by another adoption agency, the adoption agency must provide a counselling service for the parents or guardian of the child, explain the procedures for placement for adoption and adoption, and explain the legal implications of ss 19 or 20 consent, placement orders and adoption. These explanations must be accompanied by written material.

Unless carried out by another adoption agency, the adoption agency must ascertain the wishes and feelings of the parents or guardian of the child, and any other 'relevant' person, about the child, the proposed placement for adoption, adoption, religious and cultural upbringing and post-adoptive placement and post-adoption contact. Although the judgment of who, other than the parent or guardian, is 'relevant' is that of the agency, it is submitted that this should include significant people in the child's life, including siblings and close relatives. See also the Adoption Agencies (Wales) Regulations 2005 (SI 2005/1313), reg 14 (see para [924]), where the word 'significant' is used.

Fathers without parental responsibility, whose identities are known, are owed a number of duties, subject to the adoption agency being satisfied that it is appropriate to meet these requirements. These are as set out above for parents or guardians, with the exclusion of the requirement to explain the legal implications of consent under ss 19 or 20 and a placement order. In addition, it must find out whether he wishes to acquire parental responsibility, or apply for a residence order or contact order (CA 1989, ss 8 or 34).

In fulfilling these duties, the agency should explain why it considers that the child should not return to their care, and provide clear written explanations of all of these matters. It should offer the services of either an independent person, or at least someone who is not from the social work team with responsibility for the child's case. If counselling is refused, the agency should inform the parent's solicitors and explain the situation (*Adoption Guidance* [2005] DfES, Ch 2).

Annex B (non-statutory) to that Guidance advises that, when counselling mothers, the agency should advise her of its obligations under human rights legislation to counsel and seek the views of the father. Where it is in the child's best interests, the agency should then 'take all reasonable steps to trace and counsel' the father, if his identity is known.

[830]

15 Requirement to obtain information about the child

(1) The adoption agency must obtain, so far as is reasonably practicable, the information about the child which is specified in Part 1 of Schedule 1.

(2) Subject to paragraph (4), the adoption agency must—

(a) make arrangements for the child to be examined by a registered medical practitioner; and

(b) obtain from that practitioner a written report ('the child's health report') on the state of the child's health which shall include any treatment which the child is receiving, any need for health care and the matters specified in Part 2 of Schedule 1,

unless the agency has received advice from the medical adviser that such an examination and report is unnecessary.

(3) Subject to paragraph (4), the adoption agency must make arrangements—

(a) for such other medical and psychiatric examinations of, and other tests on, the child to be carried out as are recommended by the agency's medical adviser; and

(b) for written reports of such examinations and tests to be obtained.

(4) Paragraphs (2) and (3) do not apply if the child is of sufficient understanding to make an informed decision and refuses to submit to the examinations or other tests.

NOTES

Initial Commencement

Specified date
Specified date: 30 December 2005: see reg 1(1).

Extent
These regulations apply to England only: see reg 1(2).

General

[831]

The agency must, as far as reasonably practicable, obtain the information about the child set out in Sch 1, Pt 1 to the regulations. Subject to the child's consent if of sufficient understanding, and the medical advisor advising that these are necessary, the agency must arrange for a medical examination of the child and obtain a written medical report with the information contained in Sch 1, Pt 2, and arrange any further examinations or tests recommended by the doctor.

[832]

16 Requirement to obtain information about the child's family

(1) The adoption agency must obtain, so far as is reasonably practicable, the information about the child's family which is specified in Part 3 of Schedule 1.

(2) The adoption agency must obtain, so far as is reasonably practicable, the information about the health of each of the child's natural parents and his brothers and sisters (of the full blood or half-blood) which is specified in Part 4 of Schedule 1.

NOTES

Initial Commencement

Specified date
Specified date: 30 December 2005: see reg 1(1).

Extent
These regulations apply to England only: see reg 1(2).

PART C – SIs

General

[833]

The agency must, as far as is reasonably practicable, obtain information about the child's family set out Sch 1, Pt 3. This includes parents, siblings, other relatives and others considered relevant by the agency, and must include consideration of the father if his identity or whereabouts are unknown or uncertain and any steps taken to establish paternity. It should contain some analysis of the parents' relationship.

In addition, it must as far as practicable obtain information about the health of the parents and siblings, as set out in Sch 1, Pt 4

[834]

17 Requirement to prepare child's permanence report for the adoption panel

(1) The adoption agency must prepare a written report ('the child's permanence report') which shall include—

(a)   the information about the child and his family as specified in Parts 1 and 3 of Schedule 1;

(b)   a summary, written by the agency's medical adviser, of the state of the child's health, his health history and any need for health care which might arise in the future;

(c)   the wishes and feelings of the child regarding the matters set out in regulation 13(1)(c);

(d)   the wishes and feelings of the child's parent or guardian, and where regulation 14(4)(a) applies, his father, and any other person the agency considers relevant, regarding the matters set out in regulation 14(1)(c);

(e)   the views of the agency about the child's need for contact with his parent or guardian or other relative or with any other person the agency considers relevant and the arrangements the agency proposes to make for allowing any person contact with the child;

(f)   an assessment of the child's emotional and behavioural development and any related needs;

(g)   an assessment of the parenting capacity of the child's parent or guardian and, where regulation 14(4)(a) applies, his father;

(h)   a chronology of the decisions and actions taken by the agency with respect to the child;

(i)   an analysis of the options for the future care of the child which have been considered by the agency and why placement for adoption is considered the preferred option; and

(j)   any other information which the agency considers relevant.

(2) [Subject to paragraph (2A),] the adoption agency must send—

(a)   the child's permanence report;

(b)   the child's health report and any other reports referred to in regulation 15; and

(c)   the information relating to the health of each of the child's natural parents,

to the adoption panel.

[(2A) The adoption agency shall only send the documents referred to in paragraph (2)(b) and (c) to the adoption panel if the agency's medical adviser advises it to do so.]

(3) The adoption agency must obtain, so far as is reasonably practicable, any other relevant information which may be requested by the adoption panel and send that information to the panel.

NOTES

Initial Commencement

Specified date

Specified date: 30 December 2005: see reg 1(1).

Extent
These regulations apply to England only: see reg 1(2).

Amendment
Para (2): words 'Subject to paragraph (2A),' in square brackets inserted by SI 2005/3482, reg 5(f); date in force: 30 December 2005: see SI 2005/3482, reg 1; para (2A): inserted by SI 2005/3482, reg 5(g); date in force: 30 December 2005: see SI 2005/3482, reg 1.

General

[835]

The adoption agency must then prepare the child's permanence report, including: the non-health information obtained under regs 15 and 16; a summary from the medical advisor of the state of the child's health and future health needs; the wishes and feelings of the child, parents (including fathers without parental responsibility if his their views were obtained under reg 14), and other significant persons who were consulted under reg 14; the agency's views and plans regarding contact; an assessment of the parents' parenting capacity; an assessment of the child's emotional and behavioural development; a chronology; and an analysis of alternative options for future care with reasons why adoption is the preferred plan.

The agency then has to send the child's permanence report to adoption panel, and as far as possible obtain other information requested by the panel members. Originally, it was also to be obliged to send the health reports on the child, parents and siblings (see regs 15 and 16) to the adoption panel, but amendments to the Regulations (by the Adoption Support Agencies (England) and Adoption Agencies (Miscellaneous Amendments) Regulations 2005 (SI 2005/2720)) now state that these can only be sent to the panel if the agency is advised to do so by the medical advisor. This reflects the significance attached to confidentiality concerning health information, and the fact that it will normally be sufficient for a panel to read the child's health summary prepared for the permanence report and hear orally from the advisor at the panel.

The adoption panel should receive all relevant reports within six weeks of the permanence report being completed. Where the agency considers it appropriate, it should give the parents a copy of either the whole report, or at least that part relating to themselves, and the same for the child if of sufficient age and understanding, and invite their comments. The agency should inform the panel whether the child's parents have seen the child's permanence report, or parts of that report, and pass to the panel any views the parents have expressed on the report (*Adoption Guidance* [2005] DfES, Ch 2).

[836]

18 Function of the adoption panel in relation to a child referred by the adoption agency

(1) The adoption panel must consider the case of every child referred to it by the adoption agency and make a recommendation to the agency as to whether the child should be placed for adoption.

(2) In considering what recommendation to make the adoption panel must have regard to the duties imposed on the adoption agency under section 1(2), (4), (5) and (6) of the Act (considerations applying to the exercise of powers in relation to the adoption of a child) and—

(a) must consider and take into account the reports and any other information passed to it in accordance with regulation 17;

(b) may request the agency to obtain any other relevant information which the panel considers necessary; and

(c) must obtain legal advice in relation to the case.

PART C – SIs

331

(3) Where the adoption panel makes a recommendation to the adoption agency that the child should be placed for adoption, it must consider and may at the same time give advice to the agency about—

(a) the arrangements which the agency proposes to make for allowing any person contact with the child; and

(b) where the agency is a local authority, whether an application should be made by the authority for a placement order in respect of the child.

NOTES

Initial Commencement

Specified date

Specified date: 30 December 2005: see reg 1(1).

Extent

These regulations apply to England only: see reg 1(2).

General

[837]

When a case is referred to the adoption panel, it is the panel's duty to consider the case, having regard to the agency's duties under ACA 2002, s 1 to treat the child's welfare throughout his/her life as paramount, to consider the s 1(4) welfare checklist, to have regard to race, language, culture and religion, and to consider the full range of powers open to the court under the ACA 2002 and the CA 1989. It must consider the permanence report and any other reports received, receive legal advice on the case, and may adjourn the case to obtain more information.

Before the adoption panel considers a child's case, that case should already have been considered at a Looked After Child (LAC) review, under the Review of Children's Cases Regulations 1991 (SI 1991/895), and a decision taken in principle at that review that adoption should be the child's permanency plan. If, at the date of the panel, there are outstanding assessments still to be received that are likely to inform the views of the panel or the adoption agency, it is likely that consideration at the panel will need to be deferred. Prior to the new Act, adoption agency practice varied in this context, but the new guidance is clear. 'The panel's recommendation should not be conditional and it should not make any 'in principle' recommendations', although the panel can offer guidance on parallel, twin-track or concurrent planning (*Adoption Guidance* [2005] DfES, Ch 1).

In Wales, the *Adoption Agencies (Wales) Regulations 2005 Guidance*: [April 2006] National Assembly for Wales, states (para 52): 'Recommendations made by the panel must not be conditional and must not be 'in principle' recommendations, as neither have any legal force. Where adoption panels need further information, or where rehabilitation with the birth family has yet to be ruled out, panels must defer making a recommendation as to whether a child should be placed for adoption until the additional information is available, or any plan for rehabilitation is ruled out.' The child's case should only be referred to the panel when 'the local authority has eliminated rehabilitation as an option', and leave of the court should have been sought in good time for the disclosure of reports to the panel (para 102).

The explanatory note in the Welsh Guidance is confusing, since in contrast it advises that the social worker should inform the panel of any other assessments that may still be underway, if the core assessment at least has been completed, and 'The panel may be confronted with situations where there is uncertainty about the outcome of further assessments. Panel members must recommend whether a child should be placed for adoption based on the information available, taking account of panel members' and the key Social Worker's professional experience and personal knowledge'. Insofar as this may conflict with the English Guidance, and the Welsh Guidance above, it is submitted that the English and the principle Welsh Guidance should prevail.

The panel is then obliged to recommend whether or not the child should be placed for adoption, replacing the former recommendation, under the old regulations, of whether adoption was in the child's best interests (inelegantly, now referred to as SHOPA, instead of AIBI, as shorthand).

If it does so recommend, then it is under a duty to consider the contact plans and whether the agency (if it is a local authority) should apply for a placement order, although the panel has a discretion whether to give advice on these issues.

See note to reg 19 (para [839]) for the case of *In the Matter of P-B (a Child)* [2006] EWCA Civ 1016, where the Court of Appeal, in the context of a contested application for a placement order, emphasised the mandatory nature of the regulations.

[838]

---

19   Adoption agency decision and notification

(1)   The adoption agency must take into account the recommendation of the adoption panel in coming to a decision about whether the child should be placed for adoption.
(2)   No member of the adoption panel shall take part in any decision made by the adoption agency under paragraph (1).
(3)   The adoption agency must, if their whereabouts are known to the agency, notify in writing the parent or guardian and, where regulation 14(3) applies and the agency considers it is appropriate, the father of the child of its decision.

NOTES
Initial Commencement
Specified date
Specified date: 30 December 2005: see reg 1(1).

Extent
These regulations apply to England only: see reg 1(2).

General

[839]

The adoption agency will appoint a senior person to make decisions on its behalf – often referred to as the agency decision-maker – and that person must make a decision about whether the child should be placed for adoption, taking into account the views of the panel. No-one from the panel can participate in that decision. The agency must then give written notification of the decision to the parents (including fathers without parental responsibility, if consulted under reg 14 and the agency considers it appropriate) or guardian, if their whereabouts are known.

When a decision is taken that a child should be placed for adoption, see reg 46 for the requirements in relation to contact.

There should be no presumption for or against contact (*Adoption Guidance* [2005] DfES, Ch 7).

In *In the Matter of P-B (a Child)* [2006] EWCA Civ 1016, the Court of Appeal had no doubt that the local authority was right in submitting that it had separate functions under the Act from those under the CA 1989, when considering whether it should apply for a placement order, that adoption panels are 'a crucial component of the decision-making process', and that the panel's recommendation had to be considered independently by the local authority in its role as an adoption agency. There had to be 'complete compliance with the requirements of the regulations', and until that had been done it could not issue the placement order application, even though the social worker had filed a care plan proposing adoption.

In the same case, Arden LJ stressed the fact that the agency could not just pay lip service to the views of the adoption panel, and that it was open to the agency to take a different view, provided it had 'strong grounds' for doing so. See, in the context of a fostering panel, the decision in *R (on application of Raines) v Orange Grove Foster Care Agency* [2006] EWHC 1887 (Admin) [2006] 2 FCR 746.

Where the decision-maker is minded not to accept the adoption panel's recommendation, he or she should discuss this with another senior person in the agency who is not a member of the panel. The outcome of that discussion should be recorded on the child's case record. (*Adoption Guidance* [2005] DfES, Ch 2).

The agency decision should be made within seven working days of the panel meeting. If the whereabouts of the parent or guardian is known, they should be told within two working days of the decision, and notified in writing within five working days (*Adoption Guidance* [2005] DfES, Ch 2).

[840]

20 Request to appoint an officer of the Service or a Welsh family proceedings officer

Where the parent or guardian of the child [resides in England and Wales and] is prepared to consent to the placement of the child for adoption under section 19 of the Act and, as the case may be, to consent to the making of a future adoption order under section 20 of the Act, the adoption agency must request the CAFCASS to appoint an officer of the Service or the National Assembly for Wales to appoint a Welsh family proceedings officer for the purposes of the signification by that officer of the consent to placement or to adoption by that parent or guardian and send with that request the information specified in Schedule 2.

NOTES

Initial Commencement

Specified date
Specified date: 30 December 2005: see reg 1(1).

Extent
These regulations apply to England only: see reg 1(2).

Amendment
Words 'resides in England and Wales and' in square brackets inserted by SI 2005/3482, reg 5(h); date in force: 30 December 2005: see SI 2005/3482, reg 1.

General

[841]

This regulation governs the procedure where a parent lives in England or Wales and is prepared to give consent to placement for adoption, or adoption, under ACA 2002, ss 19 or 20.

The adoption agency must request the appointment of a CAFCASS officer or Welsh Family Proceedings Officer, including with the request the information set out in Sch 2 to the regulations. The officer's duty is to ensure that the consent is given unconditionally and with full understanding, and witness the signing of the consent.

[842]

[20A

[(1) Where the parent or guardian resides outside England and Wales and is prepared to consent to the placement of the child for adoption under section 19 of the Act and, as the case may be, to consent to the making of a future adoption order under section 20 of the Act, the adoption agency must arrange for the appointment of an authorised person to witness the execution of the form of consent to placement or to adoption by that parent or guardian and send to that person the information specified in Schedule 2.

(2) 'Authorised person' for the purposes of this regulation means in relation to a form of consent executed—

(a)   in Scotland, a Justice of the Peace or a Sheriff;
(b)   in Northern Ireland, a Justice of the Peace;
(c)   outside the United Kingdom, any person for the time being authorised by law in the place where the document is executed to administer an oath for any judicial or other legal purpose; a British Consular officer; a notary public; or, if the person executing the document is serving in any of the regular armed forces of the Crown, an officer holding a commission in any of those forces.]

NOTES
Extent
These regulations apply to England only: see reg 1(2).

Amendment
Inserted by SI 2005/3482, reg 5(i); date in force: 30 December 2005: see SI 2005/3482, reg 1.

General

[843]

This regulation was added by the Adoption Support Agencies (England) and Adoption Agencies (Miscellaneous Amendments) Regulations 2005 (SI 2005/2720).

This provides for the agency to arrange for an 'authorised person' to witness the parent's consent under ss 19 or 20, if living outside of England and Wales.

[844]

Part 4
Duties of Adoption Agency in Respect of a Prospective Adopter

21 Requirement to provide counselling and information

(1) Where an adoption agency is considering a person's suitability to adopt a child, the agency must—

(a)   provide a counselling service for the prospective adopter;
(b)   in a section 83 case, explain to the prospective adopter the procedure in relation to, and the legal implications of, adopting a child from the country from which the prospective adopter wishes to adopt;
(c)   in any other case, explain to him the procedure in relation to, and the legal implications of, placement for adoption and adoption; and
(d)   provide him with written information about the matters referred to in sub-paragraph (b) or, as the case may be, (c).

(2) Paragraph (1) does not apply if the adoption agency is satisfied that the requirements set out in that paragraph have been carried out in respect of the prospective adopter by another adoption agency.

PART C – SIs

NOTES

Initial Commencement

Specified date
Specified date: 30 December 2005: see reg 1(1).

Extent
These regulations apply to England only: see reg 1(2).

General

[845]

This regulation sets out the preliminary duties of the adoption agency when a person expresses a wish to be approved as an adoptive parent. Another adoption agency can meet these requirements instead.

The agency must provide a counselling and information service, and either explain the procedures and legal implications of placement for adoption and adoption, or, if he/she wishes to adopt from a country outside of the British Isles, explain the issues affecting an adoption within that context.

Written information on the process should be sent within five working days of the initial enquiry (*Adoption Guidance* [2005] DfES, Ch 3).

[846]

---

22 Requirement to consider application for an assessment of suitability to adopt a child

(1) Where the adoption agency, following the procedures referred to in regulation 21, receives an application in writing in the form provided by the agency from a prospective adopter for an assessment of his suitability to adopt a child, the agency must set up a case record in respect of that prospective adopter ('the prospective adopter's case record') and consider his suitability to adopt a child.

(2) The adoption agency may ask the prospective adopter to provide any further information in writing the agency may reasonably require.

(3) The adoption agency must place on the prospective adopter's case record—

(a) the application by the prospective adopter for an assessment of his suitability to adopt a child referred to in paragraph (1);

(b) the information and reports obtained by the agency by virtue of this Part;

(c) the prospective adopter's report and his observations on that report;

(d) the written record of the proceedings of the adoption panel under regulation 26 (and, where applicable, regulation 27(6)), its recommendation and the reasons for its recommendation and any advice given by the panel to the agency;

(e) the record of the agency's decision under regulation 27(3), (5) or, as the case may be, (9);

(f) where the prospective adopter applied to the Secretary of State for a review by an independent review panel the recommendation of that review panel;

(g) where applicable, the prospective adopter's review report and his observations on that report; and

(h) any other documents or information obtained by the agency which it considers should be included in that case record.

NOTES

Initial Commencement

Specified date
Specified date: 30 December 2005: see reg 1(1).

Extent
These regulations apply to England only: see reg 1(2).

General

[847]

Upon receiving a written application for an assessment of suitability to adopt, the adoption agency must set up a case record, incrementally including the application, reports obtained for this purpose, a report on the applicant with his/her response, the minutes of the adoption panel considering his/her case including the recommendation with reasons and any advice given by the panel to the agency, the agency decision, the recommendation of any independent review (if initially unsuccessful with the adoption agency and the applicant's case if it has been to such a review), and subsequent review reports on the adopter with responses, and any other relevant information.

The adoption panel should make a recommendation within eight months of the formal application to be considered as an adopter. Applications should not be automatically refused on the grounds of age, health or other factors, save for certain specified criminal convictions (see reg 23 below) (*Adoption Guidance* [2005] DfES, Ch 3).

[848]

23 Requirement to carry out police checks

(1) An adoption agency must take steps to obtain—

(a) in respect of the prospective adopter, an enhanced criminal record certificate within the meaning of section 115 of the Police Act 1997 including the matters specified in subsection (6A) of that section; and

(b) in respect of any other member of his household aged 18 or over, an enhanced criminal record certificate under section 115 of that Act including the matters specified in subsection (6A) of that section.

(2) An adoption agency may not consider a person suitable to adopt a child if he or any member of his household aged 18 or over—

(a) has been convicted of a specified offence committed at the age of 18 or over; or

(b) has been cautioned by a constable in respect of any such offence which, at the time the caution was given, he admitted.

(3) In paragraph (2), 'specified offence' means—

(a) an offence against a child;

(b) an offence specified in Part 1 of Schedule 3;

(c) an offence contrary to section 170 of the Customs and Excise Management Act 1979 in relation to goods prohibited to be imported under section 42 of the Customs Consolidation Act 1876 (prohibitions and restrictions relating to pornography) where the prohibited goods included indecent photographs of children under the age of 16;

(d) any other offence involving bodily injury to a child, other than an offence of common assault or battery,

and the expression 'offence against a child' has the meaning given to it by section 26(1) of the Criminal Justice and Court Services Act 2000 except that it does not include an offence contrary to section 9 of the Sexual Offences Act 2003 (sexual activity with a child) in a case where the offender was under the age of 20 and the child was aged 13 or over at the time the offence was committed.

(4) An adoption agency may not consider a person suitable to adopt a child if he or any member of his household aged 18 or over—

(a) has been convicted of an offence specified in paragraph 1 of Part 2 of Schedule 3 committed at the age of 18 or over or has been cautioned by a constable in respect of any such offence which, at the time the caution was given, was admitted; or

(b) falls within paragraph 2 or 3 of Part 2 of Schedule 3,

notwithstanding that the statutory offences specified in Part 2 of Schedule 3 have been repealed.

(5) Where an adoption agency becomes aware that a prospective adopter or a member of his household falls within paragraph (2) or (4), the agency must notify the prospective adopter as soon as possible that he cannot be considered suitable to adopt a child.

NOTES

Initial Commencement

Specified date

Specified date: 30 December 2005: see reg 1(1).

Extent

These regulations apply to England only: see reg 1(2).

General

[849]

An enhanced criminal record certificate must be obtained in respect of the prospective adopter and all adults in the household. See note to ACA 2002, s 135 (para [601]) (now repealed by s 174 of and Sch 17 to the Serious Organised Crime and Police Act 2005).

The adoption agency is prohibited from approving a person if he/she, or any adult member of the household, has a specified criminal conviction, or caution (where the offence was admitted), within the category set out in reg 23(2). These are offences against children (with a limited exception for sexual activity with a child over 12 when the person convicted was under the age of 20), a wide range of sexual offences against adults, and importation of child pornography. Regulation 23(4) covers convictions and cautions under repealed legislation of a broadly similar nature.

If a person is unsuitable to adopt because of relevant convictions or cautions of his/her own or a household member, the agency must give that person written notification as soon as possible. It should be borne in mind that he/she may not necessarily know of the conviction or caution of another household member. This regulation overcomes any potential data protection problems.

[850]

24 Requirement to provide preparation for adoption

(1) Where an adoption agency is considering a person's suitability to adopt a child, the agency must make arrangements for the prospective adopter to receive such preparation for adoption as the agency considers appropriate.

(2) In paragraph (1) 'preparation for adoption' includes the provision of information to the prospective adopter about—

(a) the age range, sex, likely needs and background of children who may be placed for adoption by the adoption agency;

(b) the significance of adoption for a child and his family;

(c) contact between a child and his parent or guardian or other relatives where a child is authorised to be placed for adoption or is adopted;

(d) the skills which are necessary for an adoptive parent;

(e) the adoption agency's procedures in relation to the assessment of a prospective adopter and the placement of a child for adoption; and

(f) the procedure in relation to placement for adoption and adoption.

(3) Paragraph (1) does not apply if the adoption agency is satisfied that the requirements set out in that paragraph have been carried out in respect of the prospective adopter by another adoption agency.

NOTES

Initial Commencement

Specified date

Specified date: 30 December 2005: see reg 1(1).

Extent

These regulations apply to England only: see reg 1(2).

General

[851]

The adoption agency must provide the applicant with preparation for adoption, unless another agency has already done so.

[852]

25 Prospective adopter's report

(1)   This regulation applies where the adoption agency ... consider the prospective adopter may be suitable to adopt a child.

(2)   The adoption agency must obtain the information about the prospective adopter which is specified in Part 1 of Schedule 4.

(3)   The adoption agency must obtain—

(a)   a written report from a registered medical practitioner about the health of the prospective adopter following a full examination which must include matters specified in Part 2 of Schedule 4 unless the agency has received advice from its medical adviser that such an examination and report is unnecessary; and

(b)   a written report of each of the interviews with the persons nominated by the prospective adopter to provide personal references for him.

(4)   The adoption agency must ascertain whether the local authority in whose area the prospective adopter has his home have any information about the prospective adopter which may be relevant to the assessment and if so obtain from that authority a written report setting out that information.

(5)   The adoption agency must prepare a written report ('the prospective adopter's report') which shall include—

(a)   the information about the prospective adopter and his family which is specified in Part 1 of Schedule 4;

(b)   a summary, written by the agency's medical adviser, of the state of health of the prospective adopter;

(c)   any relevant information the agency obtains under paragraph (4);

(d)   any observations of the agency on the matters referred to in regulations 21, 23 and 24;

(e)   the agency's assessment of the prospective adopter's suitability to adopt a child; and

(f)   any other information which the agency considers to be relevant.

(6)   In a section 83 case, the prospective adopter's report shall also include—

(a)   the name of the country from which the prospective adopter wishes to adopt ('country of origin');

(b)   confirmation that the prospective adopter meets the eligibility requirements to adopt from the country of origin;

(c)   additional information obtained as a consequence of the requirements of the country of origin; and

(d)   the agency's assessment of the prospective adopter's suitability to adopt a child who is habitually resident outside the British Islands.

(7)   Where the adoption agency receives information under paragraph (2), (3) or (4) or other information in relation to the assessment of the prospective adopter and is of the opinion that a prospective adopter is unlikely to be considered suitable to adopt a

PART C – SIs

child, it may make the prospective adopter's report under paragraph (5) notwithstanding that the agency may not have obtained all the information about the prospective adopter which may be required by this regulation.

[(7A)   The report shall not be completed until the adoption agency has carried out police checks in accordance with regulation 23 and made arrangements for the prospective adopter to receive preparation for adoption in accordance with regulation 24.]

(8)   The adoption agency must notify the prospective adopter that his application is to be referred to the adoption panel and give him a copy of the prospective adopter's report, inviting him to send any observations in writing to the agency within 10 working days, beginning with the date on which the notification is sent.

(9)   At the end of the period of 10 working days referred to in paragraph (8) (or earlier if any observations made by the prospective adopter are received before that period has expired) the adoption agency must send—

(a)   the prospective adopter's report and the prospective adopter's observations;

(b)   the written reports referred to in paragraphs (3) and (4) [but in the case of reports obtained in accordance with paragraph (3)(a), only if the agency's medical adviser advises it to do so]; and

(c)   any other relevant information obtained by the agency,

to the adoption panel.

(10)   The adoption agency must obtain, so far as is reasonably practicable, any other relevant information which may be required by the adoption panel and send that information to the panel.

NOTES

Initial Commencement

Specified date
Specified date: 30 December 2005: see reg 1(1).

Extent
These regulations apply to England only: see reg 1(2).

Amendment
Para (1): words omitted revoked by SI 2005/3482, reg 5(j)(i); date in force: 30 December 2005: see SI 2005/3482, reg 1; para (7A): inserted by SI 2005/3482, reg 5(j)(ii); date in force: 30 December 2005: see SI 2005/3482, reg 1; para (9): in sub-para (b) words from 'but in the' to 'to do so' in square brackets inserted by SI 2005/3482, reg 5(j)(iii); date in force: 30 December 2005: see SI 2005/3482, reg 1.

General

[853]

After the counselling, advice and preparation service has been provided to potential applicants for approval, the agency then decides whether or not to provide them with an application form to complete.

On receiving a written application for an assessment of suitability to adopt, the adoption agency must set up a case record, incrementally including the application, reports obtained for this purpose, a report on the applicant with his/her response, the minutes of the adoption panel considering his/her case including the recommendation with reasons, and any advice given by the panel to the agency, the agency decision, the recommendation of any independent review if initially unsuccessful and the applicant's case has been to such a review, and subsequent review reports on the adopter (with responses), and any other relevant information.

Once the procedures have been followed for enhanced criminal record certificates (which might have been completed during the preparation stages) and the preparation, if the agency considers the applicant to be a suitable adopter it must prepare a report containing: a breadth of information about the applicant and family covering the matters in Pt 1 of

Sch 4 to the regulations; a medical summary concerning their health; written information from the local authority (only if the applicant lives outside their area where the agency is a local authority, but in all cases where the agency is a voluntary agency); observations from the initial counselling, criminal record certificates or preparation work; an assessment of their suitability to adopt; and any other relevant information.

The agency must also obtain a written medical report, and written reports on the interviews of those giving references.

Further particulars are required for those seeking to bring a child into the UK from abroad for the purposes of adoption, under s 83 of the Act.

The regulation permits a foreshortened procedure if the agency is of the preliminary view that the applicant is unlikely to prove suitable, even though not all information has yet been received. It must then prepare a brief prospective adopter's report, notwithstanding the incomplete nature of the document.

This provision is subject to the Suitability of Adopters Regulations 2005 (SI 2005/1712), reg 5, whereby the matters to be taken into account may be limited to information received under reg 25(2), (3) or (4) (the obligatory information being compiled under Pt 1 of Sch 4 to the regulations: the medical report, the references, and the information obtained from the local authority for the applicant's area). This provision may also be applied if the agency receives information in any other context leading the agency to form the view that that person is unlikely to be suitable. It is submitted that, where necessary, not all of the information required by Sch 4 need be obtained, if the incomplete information engenders a reasonable belief that that person is unlikely to be suitable to be an adopter. The test is a subjective one.

In all cases, when the report is prepared the applicant must be sent a copy of it and given at least 10 working days before the adoption panel to make representations on it is sent a copy. After this time, the report, the applicant's comments, the medical report, the interviews with those giving references, and the report from a local authority under reg 25(4) (if applicable) must be sent to the adoption panel. See the note to ACA 2002, s 12 (paras [158]–[162]), for the powers of a panel conducting an independent review to recommend that the agency conducts a full assessment instead.

The panel may also ask the agency to obtain further information.

By virtue of the Suitability of Adopters Regulations 2005, reg 3, when preparing the report on the prospective adopter, the agency must take account of: information obtained from the counselling provided to that person under reg 21 above, or the Adoptions with a Foreign Element Regulations 2005 (SI 2005/392), reg 14; information from the enhanced criminal record certificate procedures under reg 23 above; information from the preparatory work under reg 24 above; information obtained under this regulation [reg 25]; in Convention adoption cases, further information obtained under the Adoptions with a Foreign Element Regulations 2005, reg 15(4); the written reports on the person's health, and references, obtained under this regulation; and any information from the local authority in whose area that person lives, under reg 25(4).

[854]

> ## 26 Function of the adoption panel
>
> (1) Subject to [paragraphs (2) and (2A)], the adoption panel must consider the case of the prospective adopter referred to it by the adoption agency and make a recommendation to the agency as to whether the prospective adopter is suitable to adopt a child.
> (2) In considering what recommendation to make the adoption panel—

(a)   must consider and take into account all the information and reports passed to it in accordance with regulation 25;

(b)   may request the adoption agency to obtain any other relevant information which the panel considers necessary; and

(c)   may obtain legal advice as it considers necessary in relation to the case.

[(2A)   In relation to the case of a prospective adopter in respect of whom a report has been prepared in accordance with regulation 25(7), the adoption panel must either—

(a)   request the adoption agency to prepare a further prospective adopter's report, covering all the matters set out in regulation 25(5); or

(b)   recommend that the prospective adopter is not suitable to adopt a child.]

(3)   Where the adoption panel makes a recommendation to the adoption agency that the prospective adopter is suitable to adopt a child, the panel may consider and give advice to the agency about the number of children the prospective adopter may be suitable to adopt, their age range, sex, likely needs and background.

(4)   Before making any recommendation, the adoption panel must invite the prospective adopters to attend a meeting of the panel.

NOTES

Initial Commencement

Specified date

Specified date: 30 December 2005: see reg 1(1).

Extent

These regulations apply to England only: see reg 1(2).

Amendment

Para (1): words 'paragraphs (2) and (2A)' in square brackets substituted by SI 2005/3482, reg 5(k); date in force: 30 December 2005: see SI 2005/3482, reg 1; para (2A): inserted by SI 2005/3482, reg 5(k)(ii); date in force: 30 December 2005: see SI 2005/3482, reg 1.

General

[855]

As with children, the adoption panel makes recommendations to the adoption agency. See notes to regs 18 and 19 (paras **[837]** and **[839]**).

When considering a person's suitability to adopt, there is a discretion whether to obtain legal advice: see the duty to do so regarding children under reg 18. The panel must consider all reports received, decide whether to request further information, and invite the applicant(s) to attend the panel. It must make a recommendation to the agency, whether positive or adverse. The panel has a discretion to offer the agency advice about the number of children he/she could adopt and other factors such as the children's age range, gender and background, but this is not a formal recommendation and does not bind the agency or prospective adopters.

[856]

27 Adoption agency decision and notification

(1)   The adoption agency must make a decision about whether the prospective adopter is suitable to adopt a child.

(2)   No member of the adoption panel shall take part in any decision made by the adoption agency under paragraph (1).

(3)   Where the adoption agency decides to approve the prospective adopter as suitable to adopt a child, it must notify him in writing of its decision.

(4)   Where the adoption agency considers that the prospective adopter is not suitable to adopt a child, it must—

(a) notify the prospective adopter in writing that it proposes not to approve him as suitable to adopt a child ('qualifying determination');

(b) send with that notification its reasons together with a copy of the recommendation of the adoption panel if that recommendation is different;

(c) advise the prospective adopter that within 40 working days beginning with the date on which the notification was sent he may—

   (i)   submit any representations he wishes to make to the agency; or

   (ii) apply to the Secretary of State for a review by an independent review panel of the qualifying determination.

(5) If, within the period of 40 working days referred to in paragraph (4), the prospective adopter has not made any representations or applied to the Secretary of State for a review by an independent review panel, the adoption agency shall proceed to make its decision and shall notify the prospective adopter in writing of its decision together with the reasons for that decision.

(6) If, within the period of 40 working days referred to in paragraph (4), the adoption agency receives further representations from the prospective adopter, it may refer the case together with all the relevant information to the adoption panel for further consideration.

(7) The adoption panel must consider any case referred to it under paragraph (6) and make a fresh recommendation to the adoption agency as to whether the prospective adopter is suitable to adopt a child.

(8) The adoption agency must make a decision on the case but—

(a) if the case has been referred to the adoption panel under paragraph (6), the agency must make the decision only after taking into account the recommendations of the adoption panel made under both paragraph (7) and regulation 26; or

(b) if the prospective adopter has applied to the Secretary of State for a review by an independent review panel of the qualifying determination, the agency must make the decision only after taking into account the recommendation of the independent review panel and the recommendation of the adoption panel made under regulation 26.

(9) As soon as possible after making its decision under paragraph (8), the adoption agency must notify the prospective adopter in writing of its decision stating its reasons for that decision if they do not consider the prospective adopter suitable to adopt a child, and of the adoption panel's recommendation under paragraph (7), if this is different from the agency's decision.

(10) In a case where an independent review panel has made a recommendation, the adoption agency shall send to the Secretary of State a copy of the notification referred to in paragraph (9).

NOTES

Initial Commencement

Specified date

Specified date: 30 December 2005: see reg 1(1).

Extent

These regulations apply to England only: see reg 1(2).

General

[857]

The agency decision-maker must then decide, without the involvement of any panel member, whether the applicant is suitable to adopt a child. If in the affirmative, he/she must be notified in writing. Where the decision-maker is minded not to accept the adoption panel's recommendation, he or she should discuss this with another senior person in the agency who is not a member of the panel. The outcome of that discussion should be recorded on the child's case record. (*Adoption Guidance* [2005] DfES, Ch 3). See also the case of *R (on application of Raines) v Orange Grove Foster Care Agency* [2006] EWHC 1887 (Admin), [2006] 2 FCR 746, if the decision-maker departs from the panel's recommendation

By virtue of the Suitability of Adopters Regulations 2005 (SI 2005/1712), reg 4, the agency must have regard to: the prospective adopter's report, medical report and references under reg 25; the adoption panel's recommendation under reg 26; any other 'relevant information' obtained by the agency under reg 26(2)(b); and, in Convention adoption cases, any extra information obtained under the Adoptions with a Foreign Element Regulations 2005 (SI 2005/392), regs 12–34.

In addition, if the prospective adopters are a couple, the agency, in making its decision, must have 'proper regard' to the need for there to be stability and permanence in that relationship (Suitability of Adopters Regulations 2005, reg 4(2)).

The decision should be taken within seven working days of the panel recommendation, and then that decision communicated orally within two working days and in writing within five working days (*Adoption Guidance* [2005] DfES, Ch 3).

If minded to refuse the application, the agency must provide that decision (the 'qualifying determination') to the applicant, with reasons, and any recommendation from the panel if that differs. He/she must be notified of the right *either* to make representations to the agency *or* to apply for a review by an independent review panel. If neither right is exercised, the agency must notify the applicant with its decision in writing. If the applicant makes representations, there is a discretion to refer the case back to the adoption panel for further consideration (and then a further recommendation back to the agency again), or the decision-maker may make a final decision without a referral back to panel.

The procedure for an independent review is set out in the Independent Review of Determinations (Adoption) Regulations 2005 (SI 2005/3332). See the note to ACA 2002, s 12 (paras [158]–[162]) for the detailed procedure.

If the independent review procedure is pursued, the agency cannot take a final decision until the recommendation of that independent review panel has been considered by the agency decision-maker.

If the decision is still negative, the applicant must be told so in writing with reasons, and provided with the recommendation of any reconvened adoption panel if that differs.

In all cases where the independent panel has made a recommendation, whether positive or negative, a copy of the agency decision-maker's final decision must be sent to the Secretary of State.

[858]

---

28 Information to be sent to the independent review panel

(1) If the adoption agency receives notification from the Secretary of State that a prospective adopter has applied for a review by an independent review panel of the qualifying determination, the agency must, within 10 working days of receipt of that notification, send to the Secretary of State the information specified in paragraph (2).

(2) The following information is specified for the purposes of paragraph (1)—

(a) all of the documents and information which were passed to the adoption panel in accordance with regulation 25;

(b) any relevant information in relation to the prospective adopter which was obtained by the agency after the date on which the documents and information referred to in sub-paragraph (a) were passed to the adoption panel; and

(c) the documents referred to in regulation 27(4)(a) and (b).

NOTES

Initial Commencement

Specified date

Specified date: 30 December 2005: see reg 1(1).

Extent

These regulations apply to England only: see reg 1(2).

General

[859]

This sets out the information that the agency must provide to the Secretary of State where an unsuccessful applicant for approval as an adopter pursues his/her right to seek an independent review of that 'qualifying determination': see note to reg 27 (para [857]).

[860]

29 Review and termination of approval

(1)   The adoption agency must review the approval of each prospective adopter in accordance with this regulation, unless—

(a)   in a section 83 case, the prospective adopter has visited the child in the country in which the child is habitually resident and has confirmed in writing that he wishes to proceed with the adoption; and

(b)   in any other case, a child is placed for adoption with the prospective adopter [or the agency is considering placing a child with the prospective adopter in accordance with regulations 31 to 33].

(2)   A review must take place whenever the adoption agency considers it necessary but otherwise not more than one year after approval and thereafter at intervals of not more than a year.

(3)   When undertaking such a review the adoption agency must—

(a)   make such enquiries and obtain such information as it considers necessary in order to review whether the prospective adopter continues to be suitable to adopt a child; and

(b)   seek and take into account the views of the prospective adopter.

(4)   If at the conclusion of the review, the adoption agency considers that the prospective adopter may no longer be suitable to adopt a child, it must—

(a)   prepare a written report ('the prospective adopter's review report') which shall include the agency's reasons;

(b)   notify the prospective adopter that his case is to be referred to the adoption panel; and

(c)   give him a copy of the report inviting him to send any observations to the agency within 10 working days beginning with the date on which that report is [given to him].

(5)   At the end of the period of 10 working days referred to in paragraph (4)(c) (or earlier if the prospective adopter's comments are received before that period has expired), the adoption agency must send the prospective adopter's review report together with the prospective adopter's observations to the adoption panel.

(6)   The adoption agency must obtain, so far as is reasonably practicable, any other relevant information which may be required by the adoption panel and send that information to the panel.

(7)   The adoption panel must consider the prospective adopter's review report, the prospective adopter's observations and any other information passed to it by the adoption agency and make a recommendation to the agency as to whether the prospective adopter continues to be suitable to adopt a child.

(8)   The adoption agency must make a decision as to whether the prospective adopter continues to be suitable to adopt a child and regulation 27(2) to (10) shall apply in relation to that decision by the agency.

NOTES

Initial Commencement

Specified date

Specified date: 30 December 2005: see reg 1(1).

Extent

These regulations apply to England only: see reg 1(2).

Amendment

Para (1): in sub-para (b) words from 'or the agency' to 'regulations 31 to 33' in square brackets inserted by SI 2005/3482, reg 5(l); date in force: 30 December 2005: see SI 2005/3482, reg 1; para (4): in sub-para (c) words 'given to him' in square brackets substituted by SI 2005/3482, reg 5(m); date in force: 30 December 2005: see SI 2005/3482, reg 1.

General

[861]

This provides for reviews of prospective adopters who have been approved but have not yet had a child placed (or, in s 83 cases of adoption from abroad, he/she has not yet visited the child in that country and given written confirmation of intention to proceed).

Their status must be reviewed by the adoption agency at least annually or if there is a significant change in circumstances.

If it is concluded that he/she is no longer suitable to adopt, a report must be prepared, namely the prospective adopter's review report. This report must be sent to the prospective adopter with at least 10 working days notice to enable him/her to make representations before the adoption panel meeting. The prospective adopter's review report, and any comments he/she makes, must be sent to the adoption panel. The panel must then make a fresh recommendation, and the agency decision-maker must make a fresh decision. All of the procedural requirements in reg 27 apply to this process. Therefore if the agency proposes to terminate the approval the prospective adopters have an entitlement to a review by the IRM.

By virtue of the Suitability of Adopters Regulations 2005 (SI 2005/1712), reg 3, when preparing the report on the prospective adopter, the agency must take account of: information obtained from the counselling provided to that person under reg 21 above, or the Adoptions with a Foreign Element Regulations 2005 (SI 2005/392), reg 14; information from the enhanced criminal record certificate procedures under reg 23 above; information from the preparatory work under reg 24 above; information obtained under reg 25(2); in Convention adoption cases, further information obtained under the Adoptions with a Foreign Element Regulations 2005, reg 15(4); the written reports on the person's health, and references, obtained under reg 25; and any information from the local authority in whose area that person lives, under reg 25(4).

[862]

30 Duties of the adoption agency in a section 83 case

Where the adoption agency decides in a section 83 case to approve a prospective adopter as suitable to adopt a child, the agency must send to the Secretary of State—

(a)   written confirmation of the decision and any recommendation the agency may make in relation to the number of children the prospective adopter may be suitable to adopt, their age range, sex, likely needs and background;

(b)   all the documents and information which were passed to the adoption panel in accordance with regulation 25;

(c)   the record of the proceedings of the adoption panel, its recommendation and the reasons for its recommendation;

(d) if the prospective adopter applied to the Secretary of State for a review by an independent review panel of a qualifying determination, the record of the proceedings of that panel, its recommendation and the reasons for its recommendation; and

(e) any other information relating to the case which the Secretary of State or the relevant foreign authority may require.

NOTES

Initial Commencement

Specified date

Specified date: 30 December 2005: see reg 1(1).

Extent

These regulations apply to England only: see reg 1(2).

General

[863]

In all s 83 cases (proposals for a child to be brought to the UK to be adopted) the adoption agency must provide the Secretary of State with prescribed information.

[864]

Part 5
Duties of Adoption Agency in Respect of Proposed Placement of Child with Prospective Adopter

31 Proposed placement

(1) Where an adoption agency is considering placing a child for adoption with a particular prospective adopter ('the proposed placement') the agency must—

(a) provide the prospective adopter with a copy of the child's permanence report and any other information the agency considers relevant;

(b) meet with the prospective adopter to discuss the proposed placement;

(c) ascertain the views of the prospective adopter about—

  (i) the proposed placement; and
  (ii) the arrangements the agency proposes to make for allowing any person contact with the child; and

(d) provide a counselling service for, and any further information to, the prospective adopter as may be required.

(2) Where the adoption agency considers that the proposed placement should proceed, the agency must—

(a) where the agency is a local authority, carry out an assessment of the needs of the child and the prospective adopter and any children of the prospective adopter ('the adoptive family') for adoption support services in accordance with regulations made under section 4(6) of the Act;

(b) where the agency is a registered adoption society, notify the prospective adopter that he may request the local authority in whose area he has his home ('the relevant authority') to carry out an assessment of his needs for adoption support services under section 4(1) of the Act and pass to the relevant authority, at their request, a copy of the child's permanence report and a copy of the prospective adopter's report;

(c) consider the arrangements for allowing any person contact with the child; and

(d) prepare a written report ('the adoption placement report') which shall include—

  (i) the agency's reasons for proposing the placement;
  (ii) the information obtained by the agency by virtue of paragraph (1);

(iii)   where the agency is a local authority, their proposals for the provision of adoption support services for the adoptive family;

(iv)   the arrangements the agency proposes to make for allowing any person contact with the child; and

(v)   any other relevant information.

(3) [Where the adoption agency remains of the view that the proposed placement should proceed, it] must notify the prospective adopter that the proposed placement is to be referred to the adoption panel and give him a copy of the adoption placement report, inviting him to send any observations in writing to the agency within 10 working days, beginning with the date on which the notification is sent.

(4) At the end of the period of 10 working days referred to in paragraph (3) (or earlier if observations are received before the 10 working days has expired) the adoption agency must send—

(a)   the adoption placement report;

(b)   the child's permanence report; and

(c)   the prospective adopter's report and his observations,

to the adoption panel.

(5) The adoption agency must obtain so far as is reasonably practicable any other relevant information which may be requested by the adoption panel in connection with the proposed placement and send that information to the panel.

(6) This paragraph applies where an adoption agency ('agency A') intends to refer a proposed placement to the adoption panel and another agency ('agency B') made the decision (in accordance with these Regulations) that—

(a)   the child should be placed for adoption; or

(b)   the prospective adopter is suitable to be an adoptive parent.

(7) Where paragraph (6) applies agency A may only refer the proposed placement to the adoption panel if it has consulted agency B about the proposed placement.

(8) Agency A must—

(a)   where paragraph (6)(a) applies, open a child's case record; or

(b)   where paragraph (6)(b) applies, open a prospective adopter's case record,

and place on the appropriate record, the information and documents received from agency B.

NOTES

Initial Commencement

Specified date

Specified date: 30 December 2005: see reg 1(1).

Extent

These regulations apply to England only: see reg 1(2).

Amendment

Para (3): words 'Where the adoption agency remains of the view that the proposed placement should proceed, it' in square brackets substituted by SI 2005/3482, reg 5(n); date in force: 30 December 2005: see SI 2005/3482, reg 1.

General

[865]

Regulations 31–33 concern the match of a child with a prospective adopter, who are both separately approved under the procedures set out in regs 11–19 (the child) and regs 21–29 (prospective adopters).

A proposed match should be identified within six months of the agency deciding that the child should be placed for adoption (*Adoption Guidance* [2005] DfES, Ch 4). Under the previous adoption guidance in England, and in the new Welsh Guidance (see para [961]), where there are Court proceedings the time-limit is six months from the final hearing. It is unclear whether this is simply an unintended omission from the English guidance.

The child cannot actually be placed before authorisation by the granting of a placement order or the giving of s 19 consent. The agency is no longer, under the new Act, required to satisfy the Court that is considering a placement order application as to the likelihood of placement.

The regulation

[866]

Three stages are contemplated. When there is a provisional view that a match is viable, the agency must give the prospective adopter a copy of the child's permanence report and other relevant information, meet him/her and discuss the match, take into account his/her views (including about the contact and support proposals), and provide any necessary counselling to that person.

Prior to the present legislation, the Court of Appeal gave judgment in *A and Another v Essex County Council* [2003] EWCA Civ 1848 and partially allowed an appeal by the local authority against a judgment that it was liable in damages to adopters who claimed that they had been given insufficient or misleading information about the child prior to placement. The Court of Appeal held that any duty of care (if one existed at all) was owed to the child, not to the prospective adopters, but that liability would arise if a decision was taken to provide specific information to the adopters and then the agency failed to provide it.

It is thus now possible that a breach of the duties arising under this regulation will potentially give rise to a cause of action in damages, given the much more detailed requirements in the regulation of the information that must be given to the applicant.

Hale LJ (as she then was) noted that any placement was provisional, prior to adoption, and that both the agency and the prospective adopters were 'actors in the story'. She observed that there was a 'delicate balance to be struck between pessimism and optimism', in imparting information, that excessive pessimism might render a child unadoptable, and that part of the assessment process was of the resilience of prospective adopters.

The Court of Appeal was of the view that, even if there was liability, there was a cut-off point in respect of damage after adoption. Prior to adoption, the placement was 'probationary', and there was a duty of candour on both sides.

Once satisfied that the match should proceed, the adoption agency – if a local authority – must carry out an assessment of any need of the child, prospective adopter, and any other children of the prospective adopter, for adoption support services from the placing local authority. If the agency is a registered adoption society, it must notify him/her of the right to request an assessment of any need for adoption support services. The agency must consider the contact and support plans, and then prepare an adoption placement report on the match and invite comments from the prospective adopter about the report at least 10 working days before the matching adoption panel meeting.

The report and accompanying response from the prospective adopter are then referred to the adoption panel. If another adoption agency has approved the relevant status of the child or prospective adopter, that agency must first be consulted about the proposed match.

PART C – SIs

[867]

32 Function of the adoption panel in relation to proposed placement

(1)   The adoption panel must consider the proposed placement referred to it by the adoption agency and make a recommendation to the agency as to whether the child should be placed for adoption with that particular prospective adopter.

(2)   In considering what recommendation to make the adoption panel shall have regard to the duties imposed on the adoption agency under section 1(2), (4) and (5) of the Act (considerations applying to the exercise of powers in relation to the adoption of a child) and—

(a)   must consider and take into account all information and the reports passed to it in accordance with regulation 31;

(b)   may request the agency to obtain any other relevant information which the panel considers necessary; and

(c)   may obtain legal advice as it considers necessary in relation to the case.

(3)   The adoption panel must consider—

(a)   in a case where the adoption agency is a local authority, the authority's proposals for the provision of adoption support services for the adoptive family;

(b)   the arrangements the adoption agency proposes to make for allowing any person contact with the child; and

(c)   whether the parental responsibility of any parent or guardian or the prospective adopter should be restricted and if so the extent of any such restriction.

(4)   Where the adoption panel makes a recommendation to the adoption agency that the child should be placed for adoption with the particular prospective adopter, the panel may at the same time give advice to the agency about any of the matters set out in paragraph (3).

(5)   An adoption panel may only make the recommendation referred to in paragraph (1) if—

(a)   that recommendation is to be made at the same meeting of the adoption panel at which a recommendation has been made that the child should be placed for adoption; or

(b)   the adoption agency, or another adoption agency, has already made a decision in accordance with regulation 19 that the child should be placed for adoption,

and in either case that recommendation is to be made at the same meeting of the panel at which a recommendation has been made that the prospective adopter is suitable to adopt a child or the adoption agency, or another adoption agency, has made a decision in accordance with regulation 27 that the prospective adopter is suitable to adopt a child.

NOTES

Initial Commencement

Specified date
Specified date: 30 December 2005: see reg 1(1).

Extent
These regulations apply to England only: see reg 1(2).

General

[868]

The adoption panel considers the information and makes a recommendation to the adoption agency. See the notes to regs 18 and 19 (paras **[837]** and **[839]**) regarding the separate functions of the panel and adoption agency.

In doing so, there is a discretion to take legal advice or to seek further information.

A match can only be recommended if it has already been decided that the child should be placed for adoption, either previously (by any adoption agency), or that is recommended at the same panel. Likewise, the prospective adopter must either already be approved, or be approved at the same panel.

Before making its recommendation, the panel must consider the proposed adoption support services for the adoptive family (if the agency is a local authority), the contact proposals, and, given that parental responsibility will be shared, the extent (if any) to which that of the prospective adopter or the parent or guardian of the child should be restricted. If the panel recommends a match, it can give the agency advice on any of these matters.

[869]

33 Adoption agency decision in relation to proposed placement

(1) The adoption agency must take into account the recommendation of the adoption panel in coming to a decision about whether the child should be placed for adoption with the particular prospective adopter.

(2) No member of the adoption panel shall take part in any decision made by the adoption agency under paragraph (1).

(3) As soon as possible after making its decision the adoption agency must notify in writing—

(a) the prospective adopter of its decision; and

(b) if their whereabouts are known to the agency, the parent or guardian and, where regulation 14(3) applies and the agency considers it is appropriate, the father of the child, of the fact that the child is to be placed for adoption.

(4) If the adoption agency decides that the proposed placement should proceed, the agency must, in an appropriate manner and having regard to the child's age and understanding, explain its decision to the child.

(5) The adoption agency must place on the child's case record—

(a) the prospective adopter's report;

(b) the adoption placement report and the prospective adopter's observations on that report;

(c) the written record of the proceedings of the adoption panel under regulation 32, its recommendation, the reasons for its recommendation and any advice given by the panel to the agency; and

(d) the record and notification of the agency's decision under this regulation.

NOTES

Initial Commencement

Specified date

Specified date: 30 December 2005: see reg 1(1).

Extent

These regulations apply to England only: see reg 1(2).

PART C – SIs

General

[870]

The agency decision-maker, without any involvement by panel members, decides whether the match should proceed, and must give written notification to the prospective adopter of the decision. The parent or guardian, and any father without parental responsibility falling within the terms of reg 14, must also be notified in writing if their whereabouts are known. If the decision is negative, there is no formal requirement for reasons to be given to the adopter or parent/guardian.

Note the provisions of reg 46(5), (6) and (7) in relation to contact.

There must be no presumption for or against contact (*Adoption Guidance* [2005] DfES, Ch 7).

The decision should be taken within seven working days of the panel recommendation, and the decision communicated orally within two working days and in writing within five working days (*Adoption Guidance* [2005] DfES, Ch 4).

Any decision to proceed with a match must be explained to the child.

Records from this process are added to the child's case records.

[871]

> ### 34 Function of the adoption agency in a section 83 case
>
> (1) This paragraph applies where in a section 83 case the adoption agency receives from the relevant foreign authority information about a child to be adopted by a prospective adopter.
> (2) Where paragraph (1) applies, the adoption agency must—
>
> (a) send a copy of the information referred to in paragraph (1) to the prospective adopter unless it is aware that the prospective adopter has received a copy;
> (b) consider that information and meet with the prospective adopter to discuss the information; and
> (c) if appropriate, provide a counselling service for, and any further information to, the prospective adopter as may be required.
>
> **NOTES**
> **Initial Commencement**
> *Specified date*
> Specified date: 30 December 2005: see reg 1(1).
>
> **Extent**
> These regulations apply to England only: see reg 1(2).

General

[872]

This regulation governs the procedure to be followed in s 83 cases (child being brought to the UK to be adopted), where the relevant foreign authority provides the adoption agency with information.

[873]

> ## Part 6
> ## Placement and Reviews
>
> ### 35 Requirements imposed on the adoption agency before the child may be placed for adoption
>
> (1) This paragraph applies where the adoption agency—
>
> (a) has decided in accordance with regulation 33 to place a child for adoption with a particular prospective adopter; and
> (b) has met with the prospective adopter to consider the arrangements it proposes to make for the placement of the child with him.

(2) Where paragraph (1) applies, the adoption agency must, as soon as possible, send the prospective adopter a placement plan in respect of the child which covers the matters specified in Schedule 5 ('the adoption placement plan').

(3) Where the prospective adopter notifies the adoption agency that he wishes to proceed with the placement and the agency is authorised to place the child for adoption or, subject to paragraph (4), the child is less than 6 weeks old, the agency may place the child for adoption with the prospective adopter.

(4) Unless there is a placement order in respect of the child, the adoption agency may not place for adoption a child who is less than six weeks old unless the parent or guardian of the child has agreed in writing with the agency that the child may be placed for adoption.

(5) Where the child already has his home with the prospective adopter, the adoption agency must notify the prospective adopter in writing of the date on which the child is placed for adoption with him by that agency.

(6) The adoption agency must before the child is placed for adoption with the prospective adopter—

(a) send to the prospective adopter's general practitioner written notification of the proposed placement and send with that notification a written report of the child's health history and current state of health;

(b) send to the local authority (if that authority is not the adoption agency) and Primary Care Trust or Local Health Board (Wales), in whose area the prospective adopter has his home, written notification of the proposed placement; and

(c) where the child is of compulsory school age, send to the local education authority, in whose area the prospective adopter has his home, written notification of the proposed placement and information about the child's educational history and whether he has been or is likely to be assessed for special educational needs under the Education Act 1996.

(7) The adoption agency must notify the prospective adopter in writing of any change to the adoption placement plan.

(8) The adoption agency must place on the child's case record—

(a) in the case of a child who is less than 6 weeks old and in respect of whom there is no placement order, a copy of the agreement referred to in paragraph (4); and

(b) a copy of the adoption placement plan and any changes to that plan.

NOTES

Initial Commencement

Specified date

Specified date: 30 December 2005: see reg 1(1).

Extent

These regulations apply to England only: see reg 1(2).

PART C – SIs

General

[874]

Once the adoption agency decision-maker has approved a match and the agency has discussed with him/her the proposed plans for placement, the agency must prepare the written 'adoption placement plan', setting out the details required by Sch 5 to the regulations, including any adoption support services, details of the contact arrangements and the extent to which the prospective adopter will be permitted to exercise parental responsibility. The adoption placement plan must be provided to the prospective adopters before placement.

There must be a placement planning meeting, using a draft adoption placement plan as a basis for discussion, which should include discussions about any arrangements for contact and adoption support services (*Adoption Guidance* [2005] DfES, Ch 5).

Note the obligation on the agency to keep the contact plans under review, under reg 46, and the duty to have consulted any person who was previously the subject of a contact decision when the agency decided that the child should be placed for adoption.

Prior to any placement, notification must be given to the prospective adopter's GP with a health report on the child, other notifications given to the local authority and primary care trust where the child is to live, and if of school age, notification to the local education authority.

Provided the agency is authorised to place the child for adoption (or the child is under six weeks of age and the parent or guardian has given written agreement to placement), and the prospective adopters have agreed to the placement, the agency can then place the child for adoption.

If an existing carer is approved as the prospective adopter and authorisation to place for adoption has been achieved (by placement order or s 19 consent), his/her status changes to that of prospective adopter, and the date of the formal 'placement for adoption' must be notified in writing to the carer.

Documents are added to the child's case record.

[875]

36 Reviews

(1) Where an adoption agency is authorised to place a child for adoption but the child is not for the time being placed for adoption the agency must carry out a review of the child's case—

(a) not more than 3 months after the date on which the agency first has authority to place; and

(b) thereafter not more than 6 months after the date of the previous review ('6 months review'),

until the child is placed for adoption.

(2) Paragraphs (3) and (4) apply where a child is placed for adoption.

(3) The adoption agency must carry out a review of the child's case—

(a) not more than 4 weeks after the date on which the child is placed for adoption ('the first review');

(b) not more than 3 months after the first review; and

(c) thereafter not more than 6 months after the date of the previous review,

unless the child is returned to the agency by the prospective adopter or an adoption order is made.

(4) The adoption agency must—

(a) ensure that the child and the prospective adopter are visited within one week of the placement and thereafter at least once a week until the first review and thereafter at such frequency as the agency decides at each review;

(b) ensure that written reports are made of such visits; and

(c) provide such advice and assistance to the prospective adopter as the agency considers necessary.

(5) When carrying out a review the adoption agency must consider each of the matters set out in paragraph (6) and must, so far as is reasonably practicable, ascertain the views of—

(a) the child, having regard to his age and understanding;

(b) if the child is placed for adoption, the prospective adopter; and

(c) any other person the agency considers relevant,

in relation to such of the matters set out in paragraph (6) as the agency considers appropriate.

(6)   The matters referred to in paragraph (5) are—

(a)   whether the adoption agency remains satisfied that the child should be placed for adoption;

(b)   the child's needs, welfare and development, and whether any changes need to be made to meet his needs or assist his development;

(c)   the existing arrangements for contact, and whether they should continue or be altered;

(d)   … the arrangements in relation to the exercise of parental responsibility for the child, and whether they should continue or be altered;

(e)   [where the child is placed for adoption] the arrangements for the provision of adoption support services for the adoptive family and whether there should be any re-assessment of the need for those services;

(f)   in consultation with the appropriate agencies, the arrangements for assessing and meeting the child's health care and educational needs;

(g)   subject to paragraphs (1) and (3), the frequency of the reviews.

(7)   Where the child is subject to a placement order and has not been placed for adoption at the time of the first 6 months review, the local authority must at that review—

(a)   establish why the child has not been placed for adoption and consider what further steps the authority should take in relation to the placement of the child for adoption; and

(b)   consider whether it remains satisfied that the child should be placed for adoption.

(8)   The adoption agency must, so far as is reasonably practicable, notify—

(a)   the child, where the agency considers he is of sufficient age and understanding;

(b)   the prospective adopter; and

(c)   any other person whom the agency considers relevant,

of … any decision taken by the agency in consequence of that review.

(9)   The adoption agency must ensure that—

(a)   the information obtained in the course of a review or visit in respect of a child's case including the views expressed by the child;

(b)   the details of the proceedings of any meeting arranged by the agency to consider any aspect of the review of the case; and

(c)   details of any decision made in the course of or as a result of the review,

are recorded in writing and placed on the child's case record.

(10)   Where the child is returned to the adoption agency in accordance with section 35(1) or (2) of the Act, the agency must conduct a review of the child's case no earlier than 28 days, or later than 42 days, after the date on which the child is returned to the agency and when carrying out that review the agency must consider the matters set out in paragraph (6)(a), (b), (c) and (f).

NOTES
Initial Commencement
Specified date
Specified date: 30 December 2005: see reg 1(1).

Extent
These regulations apply to England only: see reg 1(2).

Amendment
Para (6): in sub-para (d) words omitted revoked by SI 2005/3482, reg 5(o)(i); date in force: 30 December 2005: see SI 2005/3482, reg 1; para (6): in sub-para (e) words 'where the child is placed for adoption' in square brackets inserted by SI 2005/3482, reg 5(o)(ii); date in force: 30 December 2005: see SI 2005/3482, reg 1; para (8): words omitted revoked by SI 2005/3482, reg 5(o)(iii); date in force: 30 December 2005: see SI 2005/3482, reg 1.

PART C – SIs

> **See Further**
> See further, in relation to the application of this regulation, with modifications, in respect of a child who on or after 30 December 2005 is free for adoption by virtue of a freeing order under the Adoption Act 1976, s 18 but is not placed for adoption: the Adoption and Children Act 2002 (Commencement No 10 Transitional and Savings Provisions) Order 2005, SI 2005/2897, art 4.

General

[876]

This regulation makes detailed provision for the review of adoptive children's cases, both where the agency is authorised to place but has not yet placed the child, and where the child is placed for adoption but not yet adopted.

Where not yet placed, a review must be held within three months of authorisation, and at least six-monthly thereafter, until placed for adoption.

If a child is subject to a placement order, and not yet placed, at the first six-monthly review (ie, no more than ten months after the placement order was granted), the local authority and Independent Reviewing Officer must actively consider and analyse why the child is not yet placed, consider what further steps are required to achieve that, and consider whether adoption remains the correct plan for the future.

Once placed for adoption, the case must be reviewed within four weeks, then within three months, and then at least six-monthly thereafter, until adopted or returned to the adoption agency if the placement is unsuccessful.

In preparing for reviews, the child must be consulted if of sufficient age and understanding, as must the prospective adopters (if placed), and any other 'relevant' person. It is arguable in many cases that this should include members of the birth family, at least until the child is placed for adoption. However, by virtue of reg 45 and the amendments that makes to the CA 1989, this is a discretion and not a duty, albeit one to be exercised under the usual public law principles.

There is a checklist of matters that must be discussed at each review, including the child's progress and needs, any contact arrangements, whether adoption remains the correct plan, and any adoption support services.

The outcome and decisions of each review must be notified to the child (if of sufficient age and understanding), any prospective adopter, and any other 'relevant' person. It is submitted that this is an important aspect of the safeguards for parents once a placement order is made but the child is not yet placed for adoption, and that it should be the norm for natural parents to be identified by the agency as 'relevant' persons for this purpose, and provided with such information as would enable them to make an informed decision about whether to seek legal advice for an application to revoke the placement order or other order under the Act.

If a child is returned to the agency under s 35 of the Act, the first review must be between 28 and 42 days of that date.

Provision is made for the minimum frequency of social work visits to the placement, the provision of advice, and recordings.

[877]

> ## 37 Independent reviewing officers
>
> (1) An adoption agency which is—

(a)   a local authority; or
(b)   a registered adoption society which is a voluntary organisation who provide accommodation for a child,

must appoint a person ('the independent reviewing officer') in respect of the case of each child authorised to be placed for adoption by the agency to carry out the functions mentioned in section 26(2A) of the 1989 Act.

(2)   The independent reviewing officer must be registered as a social worker in a register maintained by the General Social Care Council or by the Care Council for Wales under section 56 of the Care Standards Act 2000 or in a corresponding register maintained under the law of Scotland or Northern Ireland.

(3)   The independent reviewing officer must, in the opinion of the adoption agency, have sufficient relevant social work experience to undertake the functions referred to in paragraph (1) in relation to the case.

(4)   A person who is an employee of the adoption agency may not be appointed as an independent reviewing officer in a case if he is involved in the management of the case or is under the direct management of—

(a)   a person involved in the management of the case;
(b)   a person with management responsibilities in relation to a person mentioned in sub-paragraph (a); or
(c)   a person with control over the resources allocated to the case.

(5)   The independent reviewing officer must—

(a)   as far as is reasonably practicable attend any meeting held in connection with the review of the child's case; and
(b)   chair any such meeting that he attends.

(6)   The independent reviewing officer must, as far as is reasonably practicable, take steps to ensure that the review is conducted in accordance with regulation 36 and in particular to ensure—

(a)   that the child's views are understood and taken into account;
(b)   that the persons responsible for implementing any decision taken in consequence of the review are identified; and
(c)   that any failure to review the case in accordance with regulation 36 or to take proper steps to make the arrangements agreed at the review is brought to the attention of persons at an appropriate level of seniority within the adoption agency.

(7)   If the child whose case is reviewed wishes to take proceedings on his own account, for example, to apply to the court for revocation of a placement order, it is the function of the independent reviewing officer—

(a)   to assist the child to obtain legal advice; or
(b)   to establish whether an appropriate adult is able and willing to provide such assistance or bring the proceedings on the child's behalf.

(8)   The adoption agency must inform the independent reviewing officer of—

(a)   any significant failure to make the arrangements agreed at a review; and
(b)   any significant change in the child's circumstances after a review.

NOTES
Initial Commencement
Specified date
Specified date: 30 December 2005: see reg 1(1).

Extent
These regulations apply to England only: see reg 1(2).

PART C – SIs

General

[878]

As with children who are looked after under the CA 1989, an Independent Reviewing Officer must be appointed for each child who is authorised to be placed for adoption.

See the note to s 118 of the Act (paras [538]–[544]) for the new provisions in the CA 1989 and associated regulations concerning the powers and duties of the IRO.

This regulation provides similar powers and duties in the case of children who are authorised to be placed for adoption, and the IRO is responsible for ensuring that reg 36 is complied with. The adoption agency, as with social workers in Children Act cases, is placed under an obligation to inform the IRO of any significant change in the child's circumstances or failure to carry out the agreed plans.

If a child wishes to take legal action, such as for the revocation of a placement order or discharge of a s 26 contact order, the IRO must provide assistance to achieve this.

[879]

38 Withdrawal of consent

(1)   This paragraph applies where consent given under section 19 or 20 of the Act in respect of a child is withdrawn in accordance with section 52(8) of the Act.

(2)   Where paragraph (1) applies and the adoption agency is a local authority, on receipt of the form or notice given in accordance with section 52(8) of the Act the authority must immediately review their decision to place the child for adoption and where, in accordance with section 22(1) to (3) of the Act, the authority decide to apply for a placement order in respect of the child, they must notify as soon as possible—

(a)   the parent or guardian of the child;

(b)   where regulation 14(3) applies and the agency considers it is appropriate, the child's father; and

(c)   if the child is placed for adoption, the prospective adopter with whom the child is placed.

(3)   Where paragraph (1) applies and the adoption agency is a registered adoption society, the agency must immediately consider whether it is appropriate to inform the local authority in whose area the child is living.

NOTES

Initial Commencement

Specified date

Specified date: 30 December 2005: see reg 1(1).

Extent

These regulations apply to England only: see reg 1(2).

General

[880]

When consent to placement for adoption or adoption, under ACA 2002, ss 19 or 20, is withdrawn under the s 52(8) procedure, and the agency is a local authority, the decision to place for adoption must immediately be reviewed. If the agency is a registered adoption society it must immediately decide whether to inform the local authority.

If an adoption agency that is a local authority decides to apply for a placement order, the agency must notify the parents (including a father without parental responsibility if reg 14 applies and it is appropriate) and, if the child is already placed, the prospective adopter.

[881]

Part 7
Case Records

39 Storage of case records

The adoption agency must ensure that the child's case record and the prospective adopter's case record and the contents of those case records are at all times kept in secure conditions and in particular that all appropriate measures are taken to prevent the theft, unauthorised disclosure, loss or destruction of, or damage to, the case record or its contents.

NOTES

Initial Commencement

Specified date
Specified date: 30 December 2005: see reg 1(1).

Extent
These regulations apply to England only: see reg 1(2).

40 Preservation of case records

An adoption agency must keep the child's case record and the prospective adopter's case record for such period as it considers appropriate.

NOTES

Initial Commencement

Specified date
Specified date: 30 December 2005: see reg 1(1).

Extent
These regulations apply to England only: see reg 1(2).

General

[882]

Guidance for the CA 1989 requires records for looked after children to be retained for 75 years from birth, or 15 years after death, whichever is earlier (*Adoption Guidance* [2005] DfES, Ch 6).

[883]

41 Confidentiality of case records

Subject to regulation 42, the contents of the child's case record and the prospective adopter's case record shall be treated by the adoption agency as confidential.

NOTES

Initial Commencement

Specified date
Specified date: 30 December 2005: see reg 1(1).

Extent
These regulations apply to England only: see reg 1(2).

42 Access to case records and disclosure of information

(1) Subject to paragraph (3), an adoption agency shall provide such access to its case records and disclose such information in its possession, as may be required—

(a) to those holding an inquiry under [sections 3 and 4 of the Children Act 2004 (inquiries held by the Children's Commissioner) or under the Inquiries Act 2005] for the purposes of such an inquiry;

(b) to the Secretary of State;

PART C – SIs

(c)   to the registration authority;

(d)   subject to the provisions of sections 29(7) and 32(3) of the Local Government Act 1974 (investigations and disclosure), to the Commission for Local Administration in England, for the purposes of any investigation conducted in accordance with Part 3 of that Act;

(e)   to any person appointed by the agency for the purposes of the consideration by the agency of any representations (including complaints);

(f)   by and to the extent specified in these Regulations;

(g)   to an officer of the Service or a Welsh family proceedings officer for the purposes of the discharge of his duties under the Act; and

(h)   to a court having power to make an order under the Act or the 1989 Act.

(2)   Subject to paragraph (3), an adoption agency may provide such access to its case records and disclose such information in its possession, as it thinks fit for the purposes of carrying out its functions as an adoption agency.

(3)   A written record shall be kept by an adoption agency of any access provided or disclosure made by virtue of this regulation.

NOTES

Initial Commencement

Specified date

Specified date: 30 December 2005: see reg 1(1).

Extent

These regulations apply to England only: see reg 1(2).

Amendment

Para (1): in sub-para (a) words 'sections 3 and 4 of the Children Act 2004 (inquiries held by the Children's Commissioner) or under the Inquiries Act 2005' in square brackets substituted by SI 2005/3482, reg 5(p); date in force: 30 December 2005: see SI 2005/3482, reg 1.

General

[884]

This regulation specifies certain bodies who have a right of access to adoption case records and information. In addition, it must provide such access as is required by these regulations themselves. Third, the adoption agency has a discretion to make such disclosure as it thinks fit for the purpose of carrying out its functions, provided it keeps a record of such disclosure.

See also reg 44 and the note thereto (para **[886]**).

[885]

43   Transfer of case records

(1)   An adoption agency may transfer a copy of a child's case record or prospective adopter's case record (or part of that record) to another adoption agency when it considers this to be in the interests of the child or prospective adopter to whom the record relates, and a written record shall be kept of any such transfer.

(2)   Subject to paragraph (3), a registered adoption society which intends to cease to act or exist as such shall forthwith either transfer its case records to another adoption agency having first obtained the registration authority's approval for such transfer, or transfer its case records—

(a)   to the local authority in whose area the society's principal office is situated; or

(b)   in the case of a society which amalgamates with another registered adoption society to form a new registered adoption society, to the new body.

(3)   An adoption agency to which case records are transferred by virtue of paragraph (2)(a) or (b) shall notify the registration authority in writing of such transfer.

NOTES
Initial Commencement
Specified date
Specified date: 30 December 2005: see reg 1(1).

Extent
These regulations apply to England only: see reg 1(2).

44 Application of regulations 40 to 42

Nothing in this Part applies to the information which an adoption agency must keep in relation to an adopted person by virtue of regulations made under section 56 of the Act.

NOTES
Initial Commencement
Specified date
Specified date: 30 December 2005: see reg 1(1).

Extent
These regulations apply to England only: see reg 1(2).

General

[886]

Section 56 of the Act, and associated regulations, govern the retention of adoption records. Nothing in regs 40–42 applies to records covered by those duties.

[887]

Part 8
Miscellaneous

45 Modification of 1989 Act in relation to adoption

(1) This paragraph applies where—

(a) a local authority are authorised to place a child for adoption; or
(b) a child who has been placed for adoption by a local authority is less than 6 weeks old.

(2) Where paragraph (1) applies—

(a) section 22(4)(b) of the 1989 Act shall not apply;
(b) section 22(4)(c) of the 1989 Act shall apply as if for that sub-paragraph there were inserted '(c) any prospective adopter with whom the local authority has placed the child for adoption[;]';
(c) section 22(5)(b) of the 1989 Act shall apply as if for the words '(4)(b) to (d)' there were inserted '(4)(c) and (d)'; and
(d) paragraphs 15 and 21 of Schedule 2 to the 1989 Act shall not apply.

(3) This paragraph applies where a registered adoption society is authorised to place a child for adoption or a child who has been placed for adoption by a registered adoption society is less than 6 weeks old.
(4) Where paragraph (3) applies—

(a) section 61... of the 1989 Act is to have effect in relation to the child whether or not he is accommodated by or on behalf of the society;
(b) section 61(2)(b) of the 1989 Act shall not apply; and
(c) section 61(2)(c) of the 1989 Act shall apply as if for that sub-paragraph there were inserted '(c) any prospective adopter with whom the registered adoption society has placed the child for adoption[;]'.

PART C – SIs

NOTES

Initial Commencement

Specified date

Specified date: 30 December 2005: see reg 1(1).

Extent

These regulations apply to England only: see reg 1(2).

Amendment

Para (2): in sub-para (b) semi-colon substituted by SI 2005/3482, reg 5(q)(i); date in force: 30 December 2005: see SI 2005/3482, reg 1; para (4): in sub-para (a) reference omitted revoked by SI 2005/3482, reg 5(q)(ii); date in force: 30 December 2005: see SI 2005/3482, reg 1; para (4): in sub-para (c) semi-colon substituted by SI 2005/3482, reg 5(q)(iii); date in force: 30 December 2005: see SI 2005/3482, reg 1.

General

[888]

This regulation makes important modifications to the CA 1989 once a child is authorised to be placed for adoption or a child under six weeks of age has been placed for adoption.

Decisions can be made without consulting parents, and the obligation to take their views into account when making decisions ceases. Instead, any prospective adopter must be consulted. The obligation to promote contact to the birth family and the obligation to notify them of the child's whereabouts (if in CA 1989, s 20 accommodation, or if in care and it is safe to do so) ceases. If the child is in care, the obligation on the parents under the CA 1989, to keep the local authority informed of where they live ceases, as does their liability to pay maintenance for the child.

Similar amendments about consultation and notification are made if it is a registered adoption society that is in this position.

Adoption Guidance [2005] DfES, Ch 7, notes that, as a result, once the agency is authorised to place the child for adoption: 'there should be no general presumption for or against contact ... Contact arrangements should be focused on and shaped around the child's needs ... There should be no presumption for or against contact'.

[889]

46 Contact

(1) This paragraph applies where an adoption agency decides that a child should be placed for adoption.

(2) Where paragraph (1) applies and subject to paragraph (3), the adoption agency must consider what arrangements it should make for allowing any person contact with the child once the agency is authorised to place the child for adoption ('the contact arrangements').

(3) The adoption agency must—

(a) take into account the wishes and feelings of the parent or guardian of the child and, where regulation 14(3) applies and the agency considers it is appropriate, the father of the child;

(b) take into account any advice given by the adoption panel in accordance with regulation 18(3); and

(c) have regard to the considerations set out in section 1(2) and (4) of the Act,

in coming to a decision in relation to the contact arrangements.

(4) The adoption agency must notify—

(a) the child, if the agency considers he is of sufficient age and understanding;

(b)   if their whereabouts are known to the agency, the parent or guardian, and, where regulation 14(3) applies and the agency considers it is appropriate, the father of the child;

(c)   any person in whose favour there was a provision for contact under the 1989 Act which ceased to have effect by virtue of section 26(1) of the Act; and

(d)   any other person the agency considers relevant,

of the contact arrangements.

(5)   Where an adoption agency decides that a child should be placed for adoption with a particular prospective adopter, the agency must review the contact arrangements in light of the views of the prospective adopter and any advice given by the adoption panel in accordance with regulation 32(3).

(6)   If the adoption agency proposes to make any change to the contact arrangements which affects any person mentioned in paragraph (4), it must seek the views of that person and take those views into account in deciding what arrangements it should make for allowing any person contact with the child while he is placed for adoption with the prospective adopter.

(7)   The adoption agency must—

(a)   set out the contact arrangements in the placement plan; and

(b)   keep the contact arrangements under review.

NOTES

Initial Commencement .

Specified date

Specified date: 30 December 2005: see reg 1(1).

Extent

These regulations apply to England only: see reg 1(2).

General

[890]

When an adoption agency, pursuant to reg 19, decides that a child should be placed for adoption, the agency must consider what arrangements should be made for contact with any person at the point that the agency is authorised to place the child for adoption. In determining this question, the agency must take into account the wishes and feelings of the parents or guardian (including a father without parental responsibility where reg 14 applies and the agency considers it appropriate), have regard to any advice on contact offered by the adoption panel, and have regard to the requirements of ACA 2002, s 1(2) (paramountcy of child's welfare for rest of his/her life) and ACA 2002, s 1(4) (welfare checklist); the agency is under a duty to have regard to ACA 2002, s 1(2) and (4) by virtue of ACA 2002, s 1(1).

So if there is to be an application for a placement order, for example, the agency must at this point take a decision about contact in respect of any person who is significant to the child, and record that decision, although it is subject to possible subsequent modification under reg 46(5) once there is a match.

The agency's decisions on contact – even if no contact is proposed – must be communicated by the agency in writing, to the parents or guardian if their whereabouts are known, the child, if of sufficient age and understanding, any person who had a contact order under the provisions of the CA 1989 which ceased to have effect under ACA 2002, s 26(1) (the point at which an agency is authorised to place a child for adoption, or where the child has been placed prior to the age of six weeks), and to any other person the agency considers relevant.

When the child is matched by the agency decision-maker under reg 33, these contact decisions must be reviewed, taking into account the views of the panel at the stage the match was recommended under reg 32 and the views of the prospective adopters (which one would presume the panel will already have considered when considering the plans under reg 32). If the agency is minded to change the contact plans at this stage, it must first consult the person affected by the proposal, and he/she must take their views into account before making a decision at this review.

At all stages, the agency must keep contact plans under review, and include those plans in the placement plan (see reg 35, for the requirement to have a placement plan prior to placement for adoption).

There should be no presumption for or against contact (*Adoption Guidance* [2005] DfES, Ch 7).

[891]

---

47 Contact: supplementary

(1) Where an adoption agency has decided under section 27(2) of the Act to refuse to allow the contact that would otherwise be required by virtue of an order under section 26 of the Act, the agency must, as soon as the decision is made, inform the persons specified in paragraph (3) and notify them of the decision, the date of the decision, the reasons for the decision and the duration of the period.

(2) The terms of an order under section 26 of the Act may be departed from by agreement between the adoption agency and any person for whose contact with the child the order provides subject to the following conditions—

(a) where the child is of sufficient age and understanding, subject to his agreement;

(b) where the child is placed for adoption, subject to consultation before the agreement is reached, with the prospective adopter with whom the child is placed for adoption; and

(c) written confirmation by the agency to the persons specified in paragraph (3) of the terms of that agreement.

(3) The following persons are specified for the purposes of paragraphs (1) and (2)—

(a) the child, if the adoption agency considers he is of sufficient age and understanding;

(b) the person in whose favour the order under section 26 was made; and

(c) if the child is placed for adoption, the prospective adopter.

NOTES
Initial Commencement
Specified date
Specified date: 30 December 2005: see reg 1(1).

Extent
These regulations apply to England only: see reg 1(2).

General

[892]

This regulation makes provision for adoption agencies to depart from s 26 contact orders in an emergency, and also allows the agency and others to reach agreement to depart from such a court order.

Section 27(2) makes provision in an emergency for contact to be suspended for up to seven days, despite the existence of a court order, where necessary to safeguard and promote the child's welfare. This mirrors similar provisions under the CA 1989, s 34.

The Children Act powers are regulated, and likewise the power in ACA 2002, s 27(2) subject to the provisions of reg 47.

When it has made the decision, the agency must inform the following persons of the decision, with the date of the decision, the reasons for it, and the period of suspension (up to seven days): the child if of sufficient age and understanding, the person with the benefit of the s 26 order and, if the child is placed for adoption, the prospective adopter. The agency will need to return the matter to court if a period longer than seven days is considered necessary.

The adoption agency and a person with the benefit of a s 26 contact order can agree to depart from the terms of that order, provided the child agrees if he/she is of sufficient age and understanding, the prospective adopter has been consulted – if the child is already placed – and written confirmation is subsequently given to those who would require notification, as above, when a contact order is suspended.

[893]–[900]

SCHEDULE 1
Information

Part 1
Information about the Child

Regulation 15(1)

1   Name, sex, date and place of birth and address including the local authority area.

2   A photograph and physical description.

3   Nationality.

4   Racial origin and cultural and linguistic background.

5   Religious persuasion (including details of baptism, confirmation or equivalent ceremonies).

6   Whether the child is looked after or is provided with accommodation under section 59(1) of the 1989 Act.

7   Details of any order made by a court with respect to the child under the 1989 Act including the name of the court, the order made and the date on which the order was made.

8   Whether the child has any rights to, or interest in, property or any claim to damages under the Fatal Accidents Act 1976 or otherwise which he stands to retain or lose if he is adopted.

9   A chronology of the child's care since birth.

10   A description of the child's personality, his social development and his emotional and behavioural development.

11   Whether the child has any difficulties with activities such as feeding, washing and dressing himself.

PART C – SIs

12 The educational history of the child including—

(a) the names, addresses and types of nurseries or schools attended with dates;
(b) a summary of his progress and attainments;
(c) whether he is subject to a statement of special educational needs under the Education Act 1996;
(d) any special needs he has in relation to learning; and
(e) where he is looked after, details of his personal education plan prepared by the local authority.

13 Information about—

(a) the child's relationship with—

(i) his parent or guardian;
(ii) any brothers or sisters or other relatives he may have; and
(iii) any other person the agency considers relevant;

(b) the likelihood of any such relationship continuing and the value to the child of its doing so; and
(c) the ability and willingness of the child's parent or guardian or any other person the agency considers relevant, to provide the child with a secure environment in which he can develop, and otherwise to meet his needs.

14 The current arrangements for and the type of contact between the child's parent or guardian or other person with parental responsibility for him, his father, and any relative, friend or other person.

15 A description of the child's interests, likes and dislikes.

16 Any other relevant information which might assist the adoption panel and the adoption agency.

17 In this Part 'parent' includes the child's father whether or not he has parental responsibility for the child.

NOTES

Initial Commencement

Specified date
Specified date: 30 December 2005: see reg 1(1).

Extent
These regulations apply to England only: see reg 1(2).

Part 2
Matters to be Included in the Child's Health Report

Regulation 15(2)

1 Name, date of birth, sex, weight and height.

2 A neo-natal report on the child, including—

(a) details of his birth and any complications;
(b) the results of a physical examination and screening tests;
(c) details of any treatment given;
(d) details of any problem in management and feeding;
(e) any other relevant information which may assist the adoption panel and the adoption agency; and
(f) the name and address of any registered medical practitioner who may be able to provide further information about any of the above matters.

3 A full health history of the child, including—

(a) details of any serious illness, disability, accident, hospital admission or attendance at an out-patient department, and in each case any treatment given;

(b) details and dates of immunisations;

(c) a physical and developmental assessment according to age, including an assessment of vision and hearing and of neurological, speech and language development and any evidence of emotional disorder;

(d) for a child over five years of age, the school health history (if available);

(e) how his physical and mental health and medical history have affected his physical, intellectual, emotional, social or behavioural development; and

(f) any other relevant information which may assist the adoption panel and the adoption agency.

NOTES

Initial Commencement

Specified date

Specified date: 30 December 2005: see reg 1(1).

Extent

These regulations apply to England only: see reg 1(2).

Part 3
Information about the Child's Family and Others

Regulation 16(1)

Information about each parent of the child

1   Name, sex, date and place of birth and address including the local authority area.

2   A photograph, if available, and physical description.

3   Nationality.

4   Racial origin and cultural and linguistic background.

5   Religious persuasion.

6   A description of their personality and interests.

Information about the child's brothers and sisters

7   Name, sex, and date and place of birth.

8   A photograph, if available, and physical description.

9   Nationality.

10   Address, if appropriate.

11   If the brother or sister is under the age of 18—

(a) where and with whom he or she is living;

(b) whether he or she is looked after or is provided with accommodation under section 59(1) of the 1989 Act;

(c) details of any court order made with respect to him or her under the 1989 Act, including the name of the court, the order made, and the date on which the order was made; and

(d) whether he or she is also being considered for adoption.

Information about the child's other relatives and any other person the agency considers relevant

PART C – SIs

12 Name, sex and date and place of birth.

13 Nationality.

14 Address, if appropriate.
Family history and relationships

15 Whether the child's parents were married to each other at the time of the child's birth (or have subsequently married) and if so, the date and place of marriage and whether they are divorced or separated.

16 Where the child's parents are not married, whether the father has parental responsibility for the child and if so how it was acquired.

17 If the identity or whereabouts of the child's father are not known, the information about him that has been ascertained and from whom, and the steps that have been taken to establish paternity.

18 Where the child's parents have been previously married or formed a civil partnership, the date of the marriage or, as the case may be, the date and place of registration of the civil partnership.

19 So far as is possible, a family tree with details of the child's grandparents, parents and aunts and uncles with their age (or ages at death).

20 Where it is reasonably practicable, a chronology of each of the child's parents from birth.

21 The observations of the child's parents about their own experiences of being parented and how this has influenced them.

22 The past and present relationship of the child's parents.

23 Details of the wider family and their role and importance to—

(a)   the child's parents; and
(b)   any brothers or sisters of the child.

Other information about each parent of the child

24 Information about their home and the neighbourhood in which they live.

25 Details of their educational history.

26 Details of their employment history.

27 Information about the parenting capacity of the child's parents, particularly their ability and willingness to parent the child.

28 Any other relevant information which might assist the adoption panel and the adoption agency.

29 In this Part 'parent' includes the father of the child whether or not he has parental responsibility for the child.

NOTES

Initial Commencement

Specified date
Specified date: 30 December 2005: see reg 1(1).

Extent
These regulations apply to England only: see reg 1(2).

Part 4
Information Relating to the Health of the Child's Natural Parents and Brothers and Sisters

Regulation 16(2)

1 Name, date of birth, sex, weight and height of each natural parent.

2 A health history of each of the child's natural parents, including details of any serious physical or mental illness, any hereditary disease or disorder, drug or alcohol misuse, disability, accident or hospital admission and in each case any treatment given where the agency consider such information to be relevant.

3 A health history of the child's brothers and sisters (of the full blood or half-blood), and the other children of each parent with details of any serious physical or mental illness and any hereditary disease or disorder.

4 A summary of the mother's obstetric history, including any problems in the ante-natal, labour and post-natal periods, with the results of any tests carried out during or immediately after the pregnancy.

5 Details of any present illness, including treatment and prognosis.

6 Any other relevant information which the adoption agency considers may assist the adoption panel and the agency.

NOTES

Initial Commencement

Specified date

Specified date: 30 December 2005: see reg 1(1).

Extent

These regulations apply to England only: see reg 1(2).

SCHEDULE 2
Information and Documents to be Provided to the CAFCASS or the National Assembly for Wales

Regulation 20

1 A certified copy of the child's birth certificate.

2 Name and address of the child's parent or guardian.

3 A chronology of the actions and decisions taken by the adoption agency with respect to the child.

4 Confirmation by the adoption agency that it has counselled, and explained to the parent or guardian the legal implications of both consent to placement under section 19 of the Act and, as the case may be, to the making of a future adoption order under section 20 of the Act and provided the parent or guardian with written information about this together with a copy of the written information provided to him.

5 Such information about the parent or guardian or other information as the adoption agency considers the officer of the Service or the Welsh family proceedings officer may need to know.

NOTES

Initial Commencement

Specified date

Specified date: 30 December 2005: see reg 1(1).

PART C – SIs

Extent
These regulations apply to England only: see reg 1(2).

SCHEDULE 3

Part 1
Offences Specified for the Purposes of Regulation 23(3)(b)

Regulation 23(3)

Offences in England and Wales

1   Any of the following offences against an adult—

(a)   an offence of rape under section 1 of the Sexual Offences Act 2003;

(b)   an offence of assault by penetration under section 2 of that Act;

(c)   an offence of causing a person to engage in sexual activity without consent under section 4 of that Act, if the activity fell within subsection (4) of that section;

(d)   an offence of sexual activity with a person with a mental disorder impeding choice under section 30 of that Act, if the touching fell within subsection (3) of that section;

(e)   an offence of causing or inciting a person with mental disorder impeding choice to engage in sexual activity under section 31of that Act, if the activity caused or incited fell within subsection (3) of that section;

(f)   an offence of inducement, threat or deception to procure sexual activity with a person with a mental disorder under section 34 of that Act, if the touching involved fell within subsection (2) of that section; and

(g)   an offence of causing a person with a mental disorder to engage in or agree to engage in sexual activity by inducement, threat or deception under section 35 of that Act, if the activity fell within subsection (2) of that section.

Offences in Scotland

2   An offence of rape.

3   An offence specified in Schedule 1 to the Criminal Procedure (Scotland) Act 1995 except, in a case where the offender was under the age of 20 at the time the offence was committed, an offence contrary to section 5 of the Criminal Law (Consolidation) (Scotland) Act 1995 (intercourse with a girl under 16), an offence of shameless indecency between men or an offence of sodomy.

4   An offence of plagium (theft of a child below the age of puberty).

5   Section 52 or 52A of the Civil Government (Scotland) Act 1982 (indecent photographs of children).

6   An offence under section 3 of the Sexual Offences (Amendment) Act 2000 (abuse of trust).

Offences in Northern Ireland

7   An offence of rape.

8   An offence specified in Schedule 1 to the Children and Young Person Act (Northern Ireland) 1968, except offences of common assault or battery or in the case where the offender was under the age of 20 at the time the offence was committed, an offence contrary to section 5 or 11 of the Criminal Law Amendment Act 1885 (unlawful carnal knowledge of a girl under 17 and gross indecency between males).

9 An offence under Article 3 of the Protection of Children (Northern Ireland) Order 1978 (indecent photographs).

10 An offence under Article 9 of the Criminal Justice (Northern Ireland) Order 1980 (inciting girl under 16 to have incestuous sexual intercourse).

11 An offence contrary to Article 15 of the Criminal Justice (Evidence, Etc) (Northern Ireland) Order 1988 (possession of indecent photographs of children).

NOTES

Initial Commencement

Specified date

Specified date: 30 December 2005: see reg 1(1).

Extent

These regulations apply to England only: see reg 1(2).

Part 2
Repealed Statutory Offences

Regulation 23(4)

1 (1) An offence under any of the following sections of the Sexual Offences Act 1956—

(a) section 1 (rape);

(b) section 5 (intercourse with a girl under 13);

(c) subject to paragraph 4, section 6 (intercourse with a girl under 16);

(d) section 19 or 20 (abduction of girl under 18 or 16);

(e) section 25 or 26 of that Act (permitting girl under 13, or between 13 and 16, to use premises for intercourse); and

(f) section 28 (causing or encouraging prostitution of, intercourse with or indecent assault on, girl under 16).

(2) An offence under section 1 of the Indecency with Children Act 1960 (indecent conduct towards young child).

(3) An offence under section 54 of the Criminal Law Act 1977 (inciting girl under sixteen to incest).

(4) An offence under section 3 of the Sexual Offences (Amendment) Act 2000 (abuse of trust).

2 A person falls within this paragraph if he has been convicted of any of the following offences against a child committed at the age of 18 or over or has been cautioned by a constable in respect of any such offence which, at the time the caution was given, he admitted—

(a) an offence under section 2 or 3 of the Sexual Offences Act 1956 Act (procurement of woman by threats or false pretences);

(b) an offence under section 4 of that Act (administering drugs to obtain or facilitate intercourse);

(c) an offence under section 14 or 15 of that Act (indecent assault);

(d) an offence under section 16 of that Act (assault with intent to commit buggery);

(e) an offence under section 17 of that Act (abduction of woman by force or for the sake of her property); and

(f) an offence under section 24 of that Act (detention of woman in brothel or other premises).

3 A person falls within this paragraph if he has been convicted of any of the following offences committed at the age of 18 or over or has been cautioned by a constable in respect of any such offence which, at the time the caution was given, he admitted—

PART C – SIs

(a)   an offence under section 7 of the Sexual Offences Act 1956 (intercourse with defective) by having sexual intercourse with a child;

(b)   an offence under section 9 of that Act (procurement of defective) by procuring a child to have sexual intercourse;

(c)   an offence under section 10 of that Act (incest by a man) by having sexual intercourse with a child;

(d)   an offence under section 11 of that Act (incest by a woman) by allowing a child to have sexual intercourse with her;

(e)   subject to paragraph 4, an offence under section 12 of that Act by committing buggery with a child under the age of 16;

(f)   subject to paragraph 4, an offence under section 13 of that Act by committing an act of gross indecency with a child;

(g)   an offence under section 21 of that Act (abduction of defective from parent or guardian) by taking a child out of the possession of her parent or guardian;

(h)   an offence under section 22 of that Act (causing prostitution of women) in relation to a child;

(i)   an offence under section 23 of that Act (procuration of girl under 21) by procuring a child to have sexual intercourse with a third person;

(j)   an offence under section 27 of that Act (permitting defective to use premise for intercourse) by inducing or suffering a child to resort to or be on premises for the purpose of having sexual intercourse;

(k)   an offence under section 29 of that Act (causing or encouraging prostitution of defective) by causing or encouraging the prostitution of a child;

(l)   an offence under section 30 of that Act (man living on earnings of prostitution) in a case where the prostitute is a child;

(m)   an offence under section 31 of that Act (woman exercising control over prostitute) in a case where the prostitute is a child;

(n)   an offence under section 128 of the Mental Health Act 1959 (sexual intercourse with patients) by having sexual intercourse with a child;

(o)   an offence under section 4 of the Sexual Offences Act 1967 (procuring others to commit homosexual acts) by—

   (i)   procuring a child to commit an act of buggery with any person; or
   (ii)   procuring any person to commit an act of buggery with a child;

(p)   an offence under section 5 of that Act (living on earnings of male prostitution) by living wholly or in part on the earnings of prostitution of a child; and

(q)   an offence under section 9(1)(a) of the Theft Act 1968 (burglary), by entering a building or part of a building with intent to rape a child.

4   Paragraphs 1(c) and 3(e) and (f) do not include offences in a case where the offender was under the age of 20 at the time the offence was committed.

NOTES

Initial Commencement

Specified date

Specified date: 30 December 2005: see reg 1(1).

Extent

These regulations apply to England only: see reg 1(2).

SCHEDULE 4

Part 1
Information about the Prospective Adopter

Regulation 25(2)

Information about the prospective adopter

1   Name, sex, date and place of birth and address including the local authority area.

2   A photograph and physical description.

3   Whether the prospective adopter is domiciled or habitually resident in a part of the British Islands and if habitually resident for how long he has been habitually resident.

4   Racial origin and cultural and linguistic background.

5   Religious persuasion.

6   Relationship (if any) to the child.

7   A description of his personality and interests.

8   If the prospective adopter is married or has formed a civil partnership and is applying alone for an assessment of his suitability to adopt, the reasons for this.

9   Details of any previous family court proceedings in which the prospective adopter has been involved.

10   Names and addresses of three referees who will give personal references on the prospective adopter, not more than one of whom may be a relative.

11   Name and address of the prospective adopter's registered medical practitioner.

12   If the prospective adopter ...—
(a)   [is] married, the date and place of marriage;
(b)   has formed a civil partnership, the date and place of registration of that partnership; or
(c)   has a partner, details of that relationship.

13   Details of any previous marriage, civil partnership or relationship.

14   A family tree with details of the prospective adopter, his siblings and any children of the prospective adopter, with their ages (or ages at death).

15   A chronology of the prospective adopter from birth.

16   The observations of the prospective adopter about his own experience of being parented and how this has influenced him.

17   Details of any experience the prospective adopter has had of caring for children (including as a parent, step-parent, foster parent, child minder or prospective adopter) and an assessment of his ability in this respect.

18   Any other information which indicates how the prospective adopter and anybody else living in his household is likely to relate to a child placed for adoption with the prospective adopter.
Wider family

19   A description of the wider family of the prospective adopter and their role and importance to the prospective adopter and their likely role and importance to a child placed for adoption with the prospective adopter.
Information about the home etc of the prospective adopter

20   Information about the prospective adopter's home and the neighbourhood in which he lives.

PART C – SIs

21   Details of other members of the prospective adopter's household (including any children of the prospective adopter whether or not resident in the household).

22   Information about the local community of the prospective adopter, including the degree of the family's integration with its peer groups, friendships and social networks.

Education and employment

23   Details of the prospective adopter's educational history and attainments and his views about how this has influenced him.

24 . Details of his employment history and the observations of the prospective adopter about how this has influenced him.

25   The current employment of the prospective adopter and his views about achieving a balance between employment and child care.

Income

26   Details of the prospective adopter's income and expenditure.

Other information

27   Information about the prospective adopter's capacity to—

(a)   provide for a child's needs, particularly emotional and behavioural development needs;

(b)   share a child's history and associated emotional issues; and

(c)   understand and support a child through possible feelings of loss and trauma.

28   The prospective adopter's—

(a)   reasons for wishing to adopt a child;

(b)   views and feelings about adoption and its significance;

(c)   views about his parenting capacity;

(d)   views about parental responsibility and what it means;

(e)   views about a suitable home environment for a child;

(f)   views about the importance and value of education;

(g)   views and feelings about the importance of a child's religious and cultural upbringing; and

(h)   views and feelings about contact.

29   The views of other members of the prospective adopter's household and wider family in relation to adoption.

30   Any other relevant information which might assist the adoption panel or the adoption agency.

NOTES

Initial Commencement

Specified date

Specified date: 30 December 2005: see reg 1(1).

Extent

These regulations apply to England only: see reg 1(2).

Amendment

Para 12: word omitted revoked by SI 2005/3482, reg 5(r); date in force: 30 December 2005: see SI 2005/3482, reg 1; para 12: in sub-para (a) word 'is' in square brackets inserted by SI 2005/3482, reg 5(r); date in force: 30 December 2005: see SI 2005/3482, reg 1.

Part 2
Report on the Health of the Prospective Adopter

Regulation 25(3)(a)

1 Name, date of birth, sex, weight and height.

2 A family health history of the parents, any brothers and sisters and the children of the prospective adopter, with details of any serious physical or mental illness and hereditary disease or disorder.

3 Infertility or reasons for deciding not to have children (if applicable).

4 Past health history, including details of any serious physical or mental illness, disability, accident, hospital admission or attendance at an out-patient department, and in each case any treatment given.

5 Obstetric history (if applicable).

6 Details of any present illness, including treatment and prognosis.

7 Details of any consumption of alcohol that may give cause for concern or whether the prospective adopter smokes or uses habit-forming drugs.

8 Any other relevant information which the adoption agency considers may assist the adoption panel and the adoption agency.

NOTES
Initial Commencement
Specified date
Specified date: 30 December 2005: see reg 1(1).

Extent
These regulations apply to England only: see reg 1(2).

SCHEDULE 5
Adoption Placement Plan

Regulation 35(2)

1 Whether [the child is] placed under a placement order or with the consent of the parent or guardian.

2 The arrangements for preparing the child and the prospective adopter for the placement.

3 Date on which it is proposed to place the child for adoption with the prospective adopter.

4 The arrangements for review of the placement.

5 Whether parental responsibility of the prospective adopter for the child is to be restricted, and if so, the extent to which it is to be restricted.

6 Where the local authority has decided to provide adoption support services for the adoptive family, how these will be provided and by whom.

PART C – SIs

7 The arrangements which the adoption agency has made for allowing any person contact with the child, the form of contact, the arrangements for supporting contact and the name and contact details of the person responsible for facilitating the contact arrangements (if applicable).

8 The dates on which the child's life story book and later life letter are to be passed by the adoption agency to the prospective adopter.

9 Details of any other arrangements that need to be made.

10 Contact details of the child's social worker, the prospective adopter's social worker and out of hours contacts.

NOTES

Initial Commencement

Specified date

Specified date: 30 December 2005: see reg 1(1).

Extent

These regulations apply to England only: see reg 1(2).

Amendment

Para 1: words 'the child is' in square brackets inserted by SI 2005/3482, reg 5(s); date in force: 30 December 2005: see SI 2005/3482, reg 1.

Adoption Agencies (Wales) Regulations 2005
(SI 2005/1313)

Made	*10 May 2005*
Coming into force	*30 December 2005*

The National Assembly for Wales in exercise of the powers conferred by sections 26(1) to (2B), 59(4)(a) and (5) and 104(4) of the Children Act 1989 and sections 9(1)(a), 11(1)(b), 27(3), 45(1) and (2), 53, 54 and 140(7) and (8) and 142(4) and (5) of the Adoption and Children Act 2002 hereby makes the following Regulations:

General

[901]

These Regulations govern the functions of adoption agencies and adoption panels in Wales.

Adoption Agencies (*Wales*) *Regulations 2005 Guidance* [April 2006] ('the Welsh Guidance'), issued by the National Assembly for Wales, contains important guidance on the functions of adoption agencies and adoption panels in Wales. It is issued under s 7 of the Local Authority Social Services Act 1970, and unlike *Adoption Guidance* [2005]: DfES ('the English Guidance') does not contain separate 'good practice' guidance.

An 'adoption agency' can be a local authority or a registered adoption society (see s 2(1) of the Act). A 'registered adoption society' is a voluntary organisation registered as an adoption society under the Care Standards Act 2000 (see s 2(2) of the Act).

It is important to note that the Adoption Panel makes recommendations to the adoption agency, and that decisions are then taken by the agency

[902]

Part 1
General

1 Citation, commencement and application

(1) These Regulations may be cited as the Adoption Agencies (Wales) Regulations 2005 and come into force on 30 December 2005.
(2) These Regulations apply to Wales.

NOTES
Initial Commencement
Specified date
Specified date: 30 December 2005: see para (1) above.

General

[903]

These regulations came into force on 30 December 2005, the same date as the main provisions of the Act. They apply only to Wales.

[904]

2 Interpretation

In these Regulations—

'the Act' ('*y Ddeddf*') means the Adoption and Children Act 2002;

'the 1989 Act' ('*Deddf 1989*') means the Children Act 1989;

'adoption agency' ('*asiantaeth fabwysiadu*') has the meaning given in section 2(1) of the Act;

'adoption panel' ('*panel mabwysiadu*') means a panel established in accordance with regulation 3;

'adoption placement plan' ('*cynllun lleoliad mabwysiadu*') has the meaning given in regulation 36;

'adoption service' ('*gwasanaeth mabwysiadu*') has the meaning given in section 2(1) of the Act;

'adoption support services' ('*gwasanaethau cymorth mabwysiadu*') has the meaning given in section 2(6) of the Act and in regulations made under section 2(6)(b) of the Act;

'agency adviser' ('*cynghorydd asiantaeth*') has the meaning given in regulation 8;

'CAFCASS' means the Children and Family Court Advisory and Support Service;

'employed' ('*cyflogi/cyflogaeth*') in these regulations includes employment under a contract of service or a contract for services, or otherwise than under a contract and whether or not for payment;

'independent person ' ('*person annibynnol*') in relation to an adoption panel has the meaning given in regulation 3;

'independent review panel' ('*panel adolygu annibynnol*') means the panel constituted under section 12 of the Act;

'joint adoption panel' ('*panel mabwysiadu ar y cyd*') means an adoption panel established in accordance with regulation 3(5);

'medical adviser' ('*cynghorydd meddygol*') means the person appointed as the medical adviser by the adoption agency in accordance with regulation 9;

'National Assembly' ('*Cynulliad Cenedlaethol*') means the National Assembly for Wales;

'notify' ('*hysbysu*') means notify in writing;

'parent' ('*rhiant*') means, in relation to a child, any parent who has parental responsibility for the child under the 1989 Act;

'placement plan' ('*cynllun lleoliad*') has the meaning given in regulation 36(2);

'proposed placement' ('*lleoliad arfaethedig*') has the meaning given in regulation 32(1);

'qualifying determination' ('*dyfarniad cymwys*') has the meaning given in regulation 28(4)(a);

'registered adoption society' ('*cymdeithas fabwysiadu gofrestredig*') has the meaning given in section 2(2) of the Act;

'registration authority' ('*awdurdod cofrestru*') means the National Assembly for Wales;

'relevant foreign authority' ('*awdurdod tramor perthnasol*') means a person, outside the British Islands performing functions in the country in which the child is, or in which the prospective adopter is habitually resident, which correspond to the functions of an adoption agency or to the functions of the Secretary of State in respect of adoptions with a foreign element;

'section 83 case' ('*achos adran 83*') means a case where a person intends to bring, or to cause another to bring, a child into the United Kingdom in circumstances where section 83 of the Act (restrictions on bringing children into the United Kingdom) applies;

'social worker' ('*gweithiwr cymdeithasol*') means a person who is registered as a social worker in a register maintained by the Care Council for Wales or the General Social Care Council under section 56 of the Care Standards Act 2000 or in a corresponding register maintained under the law of Scotland or Northern Ireland;

'social services functions' ('*swyddogaethau gwasanaethau cymdeithasol*') has the meaning given in section 1A of the Local Authority Social Services Act 1970;

'Welsh family proceedings officer' ('*swyddog achosion teuluol ar gyfer Cymru*') has the meaning given in section 35(4) of the Children Act 2004; and 'working day' ('*diwrnod gwaith*') means any day other than a Saturday, Sunday, Christmas day, Good Friday or a day which is a bank holiday within the meaning of the Banking and Financial Dealings Act 1971.

NOTES

Initial Commencement

Specified date

Specified date: 30 December 2005: see reg 1(1).

Part 2
Adoption Agency—Arrangements for Adoption Work

3   Establishment of adoption panel

(1)   Subject to paragraph (5), the adoption agency must establish at least one panel, to be known as the adoption panel, in accordance with this regulation.

(2)   The adoption agency must appoint to chair the panel a person, not being a person who has been an elected member, trustee, director or employee of the agency within the last 12 months, who has the skills and experience necessary for chairing the adoption panel.

(3)   Subject to paragraph (5), the adoption panel must consist of no more than ten members, including the person appointed under paragraph (2), and must include—

(a)   two social workers;

(b)   in the case of a registered adoption society a person who is a director, manager or other officer of the agency and is concerned in the management of the agency;

(c)   in the case of a local authority, one elected member of the authority;

(d)   the person appointed as the medical adviser to the agency in accordance with regulation 9, (or one of them if more than one medical adviser is appointed), for so long as that person is the medical adviser;

(e)   at least three other persons (in this regulation referred to as 'independent persons') including where reasonably practicable at least two persons with personal experience of adoption.

(4)   The adoption agency must appoint two members of the adoption panel either of whom will act as chair if the person appointed to chair the panel is absent or their office is vacant ('the vice chair').

(5)   The adoption panel may be established jointly by any two but not more than three local authorities ('joint adoption panel') and where a joint adoption panel is established—

(a)   the maximum number of persons who may be appointed to that panel is eleven;

(b)   each local authority must appoint two persons to the panel, one of whom must be a social worker and the other who must be an elected member of that authority;

(c)   by agreement between the local authorities there must be appointed—

(i)   a person to chair the panel who is not an elected member of any of the local authorities whose panel it is and who has the skills and experience necessary for chairing the adoption panel;

(ii)   at least three independent members including where reasonably practicable at least two persons with personal experience of adoption;

(iii)   two members of the panel either of whom will act as chair if the person appointed to chair the panel is absent or their office is vacant ('the vice chair').

(iv)   the medical adviser to one of the authorities.

(6)   A person must not be appointed as an independent person on the adoption panel if that person—

(a)   is or has been within the last year employed—

(i)   in the case of a registered adoption society, by that agency; or

(ii)   in the case of a local authority, by that authority to carry out any of the social services functions of that authority;

(b)   is or has been within the last year in the case of a local authority an elected member of that authority;

(c)   is or has been within the last year in the case of a registered adoption society a trustee or concerned in the management of that agency;

(d)   is an adoptive parent with whom the agency has placed a child for adoption or whom the agency have approved as suitable to be an adoptive parent unless at least two years have elapsed since the adoption order was made in respect of the child;

(e)   is related—

(i)   in the case of a registered adoption society, to a person employed by that agency; or

(ii)   in the case of a local authority, to a person employed by that authority to carry out any of the social services functions of that authority.

(7)   For the purposes of paragraph (6)(e) a person ('person A') is related to another person ('person B') if person A is—

(a)   a member of the household of, or married to or the civil partner of, person B;

(b)   the son, daughter, mother, father, sister or brother of person B; or

(c)   the son, daughter, mother, father, sister or brother of the person to whom person B is married or with whom B has formed a civil partnership.

NOTES
Initial Commencement
Specified date
Specified date: 30 December 2005: see reg 1(1).

General

[905]

Each adoption agency must establish at least one adoption panel, with an experienced chair and up to ten members (including the chair), although two or three local authorities (there is no limit in England) may establish joint panels with a maximum of 11 members. Each panel must include the adoption agency's medical advisor (or one of them, if more than one), at least two experienced social workers (see the table to para 32 in the Welsh Guidance for the requirements of experience in care proceedings and adoption work), and at least three independent members (if possible, at least two to have personal experience of adoption).

There must be enough panels to ensure compliance with the Judicial Protocol for Case Management (Welsh Guidance: Pt III Introduction).

Two vice-chairs must be appointed (one in England). If the agency is a local authority, one of the members must be an elected member. If it is a registered adoption society, one member must be a director, manager or other officer with management functions. Safeguards are imposed in relation to the degree of independence of the chair, and regarding any connections through employment or in other ways between the agency and any independent member of the panel. In Wales, these restrictions are wider than in England, as they encompass previous employment in any of the authority's social care functions. Unlike England, restrictions also apply to those who have been trustees or managers of a registered adoption society, and a longer period of prohibition applies to adopters having a link with the agency.

In Wales, there is a presumption in the Welsh Guidance (para 32) that consideration needs to be given to the Chair's continued role if he/she misses three consecutive panels.

See reg 9 in relation to the medical advisor.

An adoption panel makes recommendations to the adoption agency.

If panel members have serious reservations about the majority view, these should be recorded in the minutes and attached to the recommendations (Welsh Guidance, para 51).

It should not make conditional or 'in principle' recommendations, but can advise on twin-track or concurrent planning. The Welsh Guidance states (para 52): 'Recommendations made by the Panel must not be conditional and must not be 'in principle' recommendations, as neither have any legal force. Where adoption panels need further information, or where rehabilitation with the birth family has yet to be ruled out, panels must defer making a recommendation as to whether a child should be placed for adoption until the additional information is available, or any plan for rehabilitation is ruled out.' See also the note to reg 18 (para [933]).

[906]

4   Tenure of office of members of the adoption panel

(1)   Subject to the provisions of this regulation and regulation 10, a member of the adoption panel must not hold office for a term exceeding 5 years, and may not hold office for the adoption panel of the same adoption agency for more than two consecutive terms without an intervening period of at least three years.
(2)   The medical adviser member of the adoption panel must hold office only for so long as their appointment under regulation 9.
(3)   A member of the adoption panel may resign office at any time by giving one month's notice in writing to the adoption agency.
(4)   Where the adoption agency is of the opinion that any member of the adoption panel is unsuitable or unable to remain in office, their office may be terminated at any time by giving that member notice in writing with reasons.
(5)   Termination of the appointment of a member of a joint adoption panel under paragraph (4) must have the agreement of all the local authorities whose panel it is.

NOTES
Initial Commencement
Specified date
Specified date: 30 December 2005: see reg 1(1).

General

[907]

The term of office of a member of an adoption panel is a maximum of five years, and he/she cannot hold office for more than two consecutive terms without a break of at least three years. Unlike the English regulations, there is no maximum total period of membership that a person can hold in his/her life.

A month's notice must be given by a member who resigns, but an agency or agencies that terminate a person's membership may do so without notice if necessary, with written reasons.

[908]

5   Meetings of adoption panel

(1)   Subject to paragraph (2), no business is to be conducted by the adoption panel unless at least five of its members, including the person appointed to chair the panel or one of the vice chairs, and at least one of the social workers and at least one of the independent persons, meet as the panel.

PART C – SIs

(2)   In the case of a joint adoption panel, no business is to be conducted unless at least six of its members, including the person appointed to chair the panel or one of the vice chairs, and at least one social worker, and at least one of the independent persons, meet as the panel.

(3)   The adoption panel must make a written record of its proceedings, its recommendations and the reason for its recommendations.

NOTES

Initial Commencement

Specified date

Specified date: 30 December 2005: see reg 1(1).

General

[909]

There must be a quorum of five (six for a joint adoption panel: see reg 3) including the chair or one of the vice-chairs. Written minutes must be taken of its discussions and recommendations to the adoption agency, including reasons.

[910]

6   Payment of fees—chair or independent person on local authority adoption panel

A local authority may pay to a person appointed to chair, or to any independent person on, their adoption panel or joint adoption panel such fee as that local authority may determine, being a fee of a reasonable amount.

NOTES

Initial Commencement

Specified date

Specified date: 30 December 2005: see reg 1(1).

General

[911]

A local authority may pay reasonable fees to its chair or independent persons (unlike England, not to all adoption panel members).

[912]

7   Adoption agency arrangements for adoption work

The adoption agency must, in consultation with the adoption panel and, to the extent specified in regulation 9(2), with the agency's medical adviser, prepare and implement written policy and procedural instructions governing the exercise of the agency's and the panel's functions in relation to adoption and such instructions must be kept under review and, where appropriate, revised by the agency.

NOTES

Initial Commencement

Specified date

Specified date: 30 December 2005: see reg 1(1).

General

[913]

An adoption agency must prepare, put into effect, review and, where necessary, amend written policies and procedures governing how the adoption panel(s) and the agency carry out their functions.

[914]

> ### 8 Requirement to appoint an agency adviser to the adoption panel
>
> The adoption agency must appoint a senior member of staff, or in the case of a joint adoption panel the local authorities whose panel it is must by agreement appoint a senior member of staff of one of them, (to be known as the 'agency adviser') with such qualifications, skills and experience as the agency considers appropriate—
>
> (a) to assist the agency with the appointment (including re-appointment), termination and review of appointment of members of the adoption panel;
> (b) to be responsible for the induction and training of members of the adoption panel;
> (c) to be responsible for the administration of the adoption panel including assisting with liaison between the agency and the adoption panel and monitoring the performance of members of the adoption panel; and
> (d) to give such advice to the adoption panel as the panel may request in relation to any case or generally.
>
> **NOTES**
> **Initial Commencement**
> *Specified date*
> Specified date: 30 December 2005: see reg 1(1).

General

[915]

A senior member of staff, with the qualifications, skills and experience determined by the agency (a wider discretion than in England, where he/she must be a qualified social worker with requisite social work and management experience), must be appointed as the agency advisor, who has a number of important functions. These include advising the adoption panel, both in general and on individual cases; assisting with appointments to the panel, the review of panel members, the monitoring of panel members, and the termination of membership of the panel; the induction and training of panel members; administration of the panel; and assisting with [compare the position in England, where he/she is responsible for] the necessary liaison between the panel(s) and the agency. He/she plays a vital role in the link between the adoption panel(s) and the adoption agency decision-maker (see notes to regs 18, 19, 27, 28, 33 and 34, paras [933], [935], [951], [953], [964] and [966]).

In Wales, each Local Authority must establish an adoption panel, as already required by these Regulations, have a training strategy for panel members, and ensure that the panel is properly advised by a suitably qualified person when adoptions with a foreign element are being considered (Local Authority Adoption Service (Wales) Regulations 2006 (SI 2006/xxxx)).

The Local Authority Adoption Services (Wales) Regulations 2006 are expected to come into force on 31 December 2006, when they will revoke the 2005 Regulations of the same name. References in this book are to the 2006 Regulations but at the time of publication the Welsh Assembly and English Parliament had not yet allocated a number for these Regulations.

[916]

9 Requirement to appoint a medical adviser

(1) The adoption agency must appoint at least one registered medical practitioner to be the agency's medical adviser.

(2) The adoption agency's medical adviser must be consulted in relation to the arrangements for, access to, and disclosure of, health information which is required or permitted by virtue of these Regulations.

NOTES

Initial Commencement

Specified date

Specified date: 30 December 2005: see reg 1(1).

General

[917]

At least one medical advisor must be appointed for the adoption agency. He/she must be consulted about access to, or disclosure of, health information where there is a power or duty to gain or give such access or disclosure under these regulations. See, for example, the requirements to obtain health information about children and prospective adopters under regs 15 and 25.

[918]

10 Establishment of new adoption panels on 30 December 2005

(1) All members of an adoption panel established before 30 December 2005 (referred to in this regulation as the 'old adoption panel') will cease to hold office on that date.

(2) With effect from 30 December 2005, the adoption agency must establish a new adoption panel in accordance with regulations 3 and 4.

(3) Where a member of an old adoption panel ceases to hold office under paragraph (1) and whether that member's term of office was extended by the adoption agency in accordance with regulation 5A(1A) of the Adoption Agencies Regulations 1983 or in any other case, that member may be appointed as a member of a new adoption panel of the same adoption agency save that their term of office on the new adoption panel must not exceed that permitted by regulation 4 taking account of the term they have already served as a member of the old adoption panel.

NOTES

Initial Commencement

Specified date

Specified date: 30 December 2005: see reg 1(1).

Part 3
Duties of Adoption Agency where the Agency is Considering Adoption for a Child

11 Application of regulations 11 to 20

Regulations 11 to 20 apply where the adoption agency is considering adoption for a child.

NOTES

Initial Commencement

Specified date

Specified date: 30 December 2005: see reg 1(1).

General

[919]

Regulations 12 to 20 govern the procedures to be followed when an adoption agency is considering whether a child should be adopted.

[920]

---

12 Requirement to open child's case record

(1) The adoption agency must set up a case record in respect of the child and place on it any information obtained and any report, recommendation or decision made by virtue of these Regulations.

(2) Where the child—

(a) is looked after; or
(b) is provided with accommodation under section 59(1) of the 1989 Act (provision of accommodation by voluntary organisations),

the local authority or, as the case may be, the registered adoption society must obtain any information which is required to be obtained by the agency by virtue of this Part, from the records maintained with respect to the child under the 1989 Act, and place that information on the case record referred to in paragraph (1).

NOTES
Initial Commencement
Specified date
Specified date: 30 December 2005: see reg 1(1).

General

[921]

This regulation is very simple in structure, when compared with reg 12 of the English regulations.

The agency must set up a case-record for the child, to contain all relevant information, reports, and records of recommendations and decisions made under these regulations. If the child has been looked after, or accommodated by a voluntary organisation, the agency must seek to obtain any information that it requires from records prepared under CA 1989.

The child's need for a permanent home should be considered at the four-month LAC review. The adoption panel's recommendation on whether the child should be placed for adoption should be made within two months of the review identifying adoption as the plan for the child (Welsh Guidance, paras 17 and 90). It seems clear that this means the review determining that adoption is the sole plan, and all relevant twin-track planning and assessments have been completed, concluding with an adoption plan. Any options for placement within the extended family must be identified at an early stage, to avoid delay (Welsh Guidance, para 91).

It is to be noted that, in Wales, each local authority, in operating the adoption service, once it considers that adoption is 'the preferred option for a child', or a child is relinquished by a parent, must provide a counselling service and advice for the natural parents, and as much information as the parents reasonably require insofar as the authority is in a position to give it (Local Authority Adoption Service (Wales) Regulations 2006 (SI 2006/xxxx), reg (6). This provision therefore applies from the date of the LAC review determining that plan and referring the case to the adoption panel.

PART C – SIs

Birth parents must have access to a person independent of the case-holding social worker, from the point that adoption is identified as the preferred plan for the child (Welsh Guidance, para 116).

The Local Authority Adoption Services (Wales) Regulations 2006 are expected to come into force on 31 December 2006, when they will revoke the 2005 Regulations of the same name. References in this book are to the 2006 Regulations but at the time of publication the Welsh Assembly and English Parliament had not yet allocated a number for these Regulations.

[922]

---

13 Requirement to provide counselling and information for, and ascertain the wishes and feelings of, the child

(1)   The adoption agency must, so far as is reasonably practicable and in the light of the child's age and understanding—

(a)   provide a counselling service for the child;

(b)   explain to the child in an appropriate manner the procedure in relation to, and the legal implications of, their adoption and provide the child with appropriate written information about these matters; and

(c)   ascertain the child's wishes and feelings in relation to—

  (i)   the possibility of placement with a new family and their adoption;

  (ii)   their religious and cultural upbringing; and

  (iii)   contact with their parent, guardian, relative or other significant person.

NOTES

Initial Commencement

Specified date

Specified date: 30 December 2005: see reg 1(1).

General

[923]

As far as reasonably practicable (and having regard to the child's age and understanding, an omission from the English regulations), the adoption agency must explain adoption procedures and the legal implications of adoption to the child, and provide a counselling service for him/her. It must ascertain his/her wishes and feelings about adoption, contact, and religious and cultural upbringing. 'Relative' has a wide definition under the Act, but this regulation, unlike the English regulation, explicitly requires consideration of the child's contact with 'other significant' persons.

[924]

---

14 Requirement to provide counselling and information for, and ascertain the wishes and feelings of, the parent or guardian of the child and others

(1)   The adoption agency must, so far as is reasonably practicable—

(a)   provide a counselling service for the parent or guardian of the child;

(b)   explain and provide written information to the child's parent or guardian on the following matters—

  (i)   the procedure in relation to both placement for adoption and adoption;

  (ii)   the legal implications of—

    (aa)   giving consent to placement for adoption under section 19 of the Act (placing children with parental consent);

> (bb) giving consent to the making of a future adoption order under section 20 of the Act (advance consent to adoption);
>
> (cc) a placement order; and
>
> (iii) the legal implications of adoption; and
>
> (c) ascertain the wishes and feelings of the parent or guardian of the child and of any other significant person the agency considers relevant in relation to—
>
> (i) the matters set out in section 1(4)(f)(ii) and (iii) of the Act (matters the agency must have regard to);
>
> (ii) the placement of the child for adoption and their adoption, including any wishes and feelings about the child's religious and cultural upbringing; and
>
> (iii) contact with the child if the agency is authorised to place the child for adoption or the child is adopted.
>
> (2) This paragraph applies where the father of a child does not have parental responsibility for the child and the father's identity is known to the agency.
>
> (3) Where paragraph (2) applies and the adoption agency is satisfied it is appropriate to do so the agency must—
>
> (a) carry out in respect of the father the requirements of paragraph (1)(a), (b)(i), and (iii) and (c) as if they applied to the father and
>
> (b) ascertain so far as possible whether the father—
>
> (i) wishes to acquire parental responsibility for the child under section 4 of the 1989 Act (acquisition of parental responsibility); or
>
> (ii) intends to apply for a residence order or contact order with respect to the child under section 8 of the 1989 Act (residence, contact and other orders with respect to children) or where the child is subject to a care order, an order under section 34 of the 1989 Act (parental contact with children in care).
>
> **NOTES**
> **Initial Commencement**
> *Specified date*
> Specified date: 30 December 2005: see reg 1(1).

General

[925]

The adoption agency must provide a counselling service for the parents or guardian of the child, explain the procedures for placement for adoption and adoption, and explain the legal implications of ss 19 or 20 consent, placement orders and adoption. These explanations must be accompanied by written material.

Unless carried out by another adoption agency, the adoption agency must ascertain the wishes and feelings of the parents or guardian of the child, and any other 'significant' person (compare in England, where this is 'relevant' persons), about the child, the proposed placement for adoption, adoption, religious and cultural upbringing and post-adoptive placement and post-adoption contact. Although the judgment of who, other than the parent or guardian, is 'significant' is that of the agency, it is submitted that this should include all key people in the child's life, including siblings and close relatives.

Fathers without parental responsibility, whose identities are known, are owed a number of duties, subject to the adoption agency being satisfied that it is appropriate to meet these requirements. These are as set out above for parents or guardians, with the exclusion of the requirement to explain the legal implications of consent under ss 19 or 20 and a placement order. In addition, it must find out whether he wishes to acquire parental responsibility, apply for a residence order or contact order (CA 1989, s 8 or 34).

Under the Welsh Guidance, paras 138 and 139, when counselling mothers, the agency should advise her of its obligations under human rights legislation to counsel and seek the views of the father. The agency must consider the nature of the child's relationship with the child, mother and any siblings. Where it is in the child's best interests, the agency should then 'take all reasonable steps to trace and counsel' the father, if his identity is known.

Parents must be given the chance to give their version of events, and to see and comment upon what is written about them in reports to panel and in information given to prospective adopters (see Welsh Guidance, para 116).

[926]

---

15   Requirement to obtain information (including health information) about the child

(1)   The adoption agency must, so far as is reasonably practicable, obtain the information about the child which is specified in Part 1 of Schedule 1.

(2)   Subject to paragraph (4), the adoption agency must—

(a)   make arrangements for the child to be examined by a registered medical practitioner; and

(b)   obtain from that practitioner a written report on the state of the child's health which must include any treatment which the child is receiving, the child's needs for health care and the matters specified in Part 2 of Schedule 1,

unless the agency has received advice from the medical adviser that such an examination and report is unnecessary.

(3)   Subject to paragraph (4), the adoption agency must make arrangements—

(a)   for such other medical and psychiatric examinations of, and other tests on, the child to be carried out as are recommended by the agency's medical adviser; and

(b)   to obtain written reports of such examinations and tests.

(4)   Paragraphs (2) and (3) do not apply if the child is of sufficient understanding to make an informed decision and refuses to submit to the examinations or other tests.

NOTES
Initial Commencement
Specified date
Specified date: 30 December 2005: see reg 1(1).

General

[927]

The agency must, as far as reasonably practicable, obtain the information about the child set out in Sch 1, Pt 1 to the regulations. Subject to the child's consent if of sufficient understanding, and the medical advisor advising that these are necessary, the agency must arrange for a medical examination of the child and a written medical report with the information contained in Sch 1, Pt 2, and any further examinations or tests recommended by the doctor.

[928]

---

16   Requirement to obtain information (including health information) about the child's family

(1)   The adoption agency must, so far as is reasonably practicable, obtain the information about the child's family which is specified in Parts 3 and 4 of Schedule 1.

> (2) The adoption agency must, so far as is reasonably practicable, obtain the information about the health of each of the child's natural parents and brothers and sisters which is specified in Part 5 of Schedule 1.
>
> **NOTES**
>
> **Initial Commencement**
>
> *Specified date*
>
> Specified date: 30 December 2005: see reg 1(1).

General

[929]

The agency must, as far as is reasonably practicable, obtain information about the child's family set out in Sch 1, Pts 3 and 4. This includes parents, siblings, other relatives and others considered relevant by the agency, and must include consideration of the father if his identity or whereabouts are unknown or uncertain and any steps taken to establish paternity. It should contain some analysis of the parents' relationship.

In addition, it must as far as practicable obtain information about the health of the parents and siblings, as set out in Sch 1, Pt 5.

Parents must be allowed to read, and comment on, what is written about them in reports (Welsh Guidance, para 116).

[930]

17 Requirement to prepare a written report for the adoption panel

(1) Where the adoption agency consider in light of all the information obtained by virtue of regulations 12 to 16 that adoption is the preferred option for permanence for the child, the agency must prepare a written report which must include—

(a) the information about the child and the child's family as specified in Parts 1, 3 and 4 of Schedule 1;

(b) a summary, written by the agency's medical adviser, of the child's state of health, the child's health history and any need for health care which might arise in the future;

(c) the wishes and feelings of the child regarding the matters set out in regulation 13(1)(c);

(d) the wishes and feelings of the child's parent or guardian, and where regulation 14(2) applies, the child's father, and any other person the agency considers relevant, regarding the matters set out in regulation 14(1)(c);

(e) the views of the agency about the child's need for contact with the child's parent or guardian or other relative or with any other person the agency considers relevant (including the child's father where regulation 14(2) applies) and the arrangements the agency proposes to make for allowing any person contact with the child;

(f) an assessment of the child's emotional and behavioural development and any related needs;

(g) an assessment of the parenting capacity of the child's parent or guardian, and if regulation 14(2) applies, the child's father;

(h) a chronology of the decisions and actions taken by the agency with respect to the child;

(i) an analysis of the options for the future care of the child which have been considered by the agency and why placement for adoption is considered the preferred option; and

(j) any other information which the agency considers relevant.

(2) The adoption agency must send the written report together with the other reports required by virtue of regulations 15 and 16 to the adoption panel.

PART C – SIs

(3)   The adoption agency must obtain, so far as is reasonably practicable, any other relevant information which may be requested by the adoption panel and send that information to the panel.

NOTES
Initial Commencement
Specified date
Specified date: 30 December 2005: see reg 1(1).

General

[931]

The adoption agency must then prepare a written report (in England, this is referred to as the child's permanence report), including: the non-health information obtained under regs 15 and 16; a summary from the medical advisor of the state of the child's health and future health needs; the wishes and feelings of the child, parents (including fathers without parental responsibility if their views were obtained under reg 14), and other significant persons who were consulted under reg 14; the agency's views and plans regarding contact; an assessment of the parents' parenting capacity; an assessment of the child's emotional and behavioural development; a chronology; and an analysis of alternative options for future care with reasons why adoption is the preferred plan.

The agency then has to send the report to adoption panel, and as far as possible obtain other information requested by the panel members. It must also send the reports on the health of the child and his/her family required by regs 15 and 16. See note to reg 16 for the right of parents to read and comment upon written material about themselves.

It is to be noted that, in England, amendments to the English regulations (by the Adoption Support Agencies (England) and Adoption Agencies (Miscellaneous Amendments) Regulations 2005 (SI 2005/2720)) now state that the health reports can only be sent to the panel if the agency is advised to do so by the medical advisor. This reflects the significance attached to confidentiality concerning health information, and the fact that it will normally be sufficient for a panel to read the child's health summary prepared for the report and hear orally from the advisor at the panel. No similar changes have yet been made to the Welsh regulations.

[932]

18   Function of the adoption panel in relation to a child referred by the adoption agency

(1)   The adoption panel must consider the case of every child referred to it by the adoption agency and make a recommendation to that agency as to whether the child should be placed for adoption.
(2)   In considering what recommendation to make the adoption panel must have regard to the duties imposed on the adoption agency under section 1(2), (4), (5) and (6) of the Act (considerations applying to the exercise of powers in relation to the adoption of a child) and—

(a)   must consider and take into account all the information and reports passed to it in accordance with regulation 17;
(b)   may request the agency to obtain any other relevant information which the panel considers necessary;
(c)   must obtain legal advice as it considers necessary in relation to the case.

(3)   Where the adoption panel make a recommendation to the adoption agency that the child should be placed for adoption it must consider and may at the same time give advice to the agency about—

(a) the arrangements the agency proposes to make for allowing any person contact with the child;

(b) where the adoption agency is a local authority, whether an application should be made for a placement order in respect of the child.

NOTES

Initial Commencement

Specified date

Specified date: 30 December 2005: see reg 1(1).

General

[933]

When a case is referred to the adoption panel, it is the panel's duty to consider the case, having regard to the agency's duties under ACA 2002, s 1 of the Act to treat the child's welfare throughout his/her life as paramount, to consider the s 1(4) welfare checklist, to have regard to race, language, culture and religion, and to consider the full range of powers open to the Court under the Act and the CA 1989. It must consider the report on the child (see reg 17) and any other reports received, receive any legal advice it considers necessary (in England, legal advice is mandatory) on the case, and may adjourn the case to obtain more information.

A permanency plan should be made at the child's four-month review, where all options for permanence should be considered (Welsh Guidance, para 88).

Before the adoption panel considers a child's case, that case should already have been considered at a Looked After Child (LAC) review, under the Review of Children's Cases Regulations 1991 (SI 1991/895), and a decision taken in principle at that review that adoption should be the child's permanency plan. If, at the date of the panel, there are outstanding assessments still to be received that are likely to inform the views of the panel or the adoption agency, it is likely that consideration at the panel will need to be deferred.

Prior to the new Act, adoption agency practice varied in this context, but both the new Welsh and English guidance are clear. The Welsh guidance states (at para 52): 'Recommendations made by the panel must not be conditional and must not be 'in principle' recommendations, as neither have any legal force. Where adoption panels need further information, or where rehabilitation with the birth family has yet to be ruled out, panels must defer making a recommendation as to whether a child should be placed for adoption until the additional information is available, or any plan for rehabilitation is ruled out.' The child's case should only be referred to the panel when 'the local authority has eliminated rehabilitation as an option', and leave of the Court should have been sought in good time for the disclosure of reports to the panel (para 102).

In England, it is stated that: 'The panel's recommendation should not be conditional and it should not make any 'in principle' recommendations', although the panel can offer guidance on parallel, twin-track or concurrent planning (*Adoption Guidance*, Ch 1 [2005] DfES).

The explanatory note in the Welsh guidance is confusing, since in contrast it advises that the social worker should inform the panel of any other assessments that may still be underway, if the core assessment at least has been completed, and 'The panel may be confronted with situations where there is uncertainty about the outcome of further assessments. Panel members must recommend whether a child should be placed for adoption based on the information available, taking account of panel members' and the key social worker's professional experience and personal knowledge'. Insofar as this may conflict with the other guidance above, it is submitted that the latter should be preferred, particularly with the similar guidance in England referred to above.

The Welsh guidance is stronger, and far more explicit, than the English guidance, on the need for there to be sufficient numbers of panels to accommodate the needs of care planning in the court, including the Judicial Protocol (see explanatory note to the Welsh Guidance, Pt 3), and for the social work team with responsibility for a child's case to keep the adoption team briefed at all stages of a child's case progressing through the looked after system. The authority must have systems in place to ensure that the adoption team is briefed about children's cases as they progress through care proceedings (Welsh Guidance, para 101).

The panel is then obliged to recommend whether or not the child should be placed for adoption, replacing the former recommendation, under the old regulations, of whether adoption was in the child's best interests (inelegantly, now referred to as SHOPA, instead of AIBI, as shorthand).

If it does so recommend, then it is under a duty to consider the contact plans and whether the agency (if it is a local authority) should apply for a placement order, although the panel has a discretion whether to give advice on these issues.

The panel should make its recommendation within two months of the LAC Review determining adoption as the appropriate plan (Welsh Guidance, paras 17 and 90).

In Wales, if a local authority proposes to place a child for adoption in the area of another local authority, it must consult that authority in writing about the placement and the results of the assessments for adoption support services, and a period of 20 days must elapse before the proposed match can be placed before the adoption panel. Any response by that authority must be taken into account by the adoption panel (Adoption Support Services (Local Authorities) (Wales) Regulations 2005 (SI 2005/1512), reg 7(4), (5) and (6)).

See note to reg 19 (para [935]) for the case of *In the Matter of P-B (a Child)* [2006] EWCA Civ 1016, where the Court of Appeal, in the context of a contested application for a placement order, emphasised the mandatory nature of the regulations.

The recommendations must be communicated orally to the children and birth parents within 24 hours (Welsh Guidance, para 17).

[934]

19   Adoption agency decision and notification

(1)   The adoption agency must—

(a)   take into account the recommendation of the adoption panel;
(b)   take into account any advice given by the adoption panel in accordance with regulation 18(3); and
(c)   have regard to the consideration set out in section 1(2) of the Act

in coming to a decision about whether the child should be placed for adoption.

(2)   No member of the adoption panel may take part in any decision made by the adoption agency under paragraph (1).

(3)   The adoption agency must, if their whereabouts are known to the agency, notify its decision about whether the child should be placed for adoption and any decision in relation to contact arrangements in writing to—

(a)   the parent or guardian of the child;
(b)   any relative or other significant person whom the agency consulted under regulation 14(1) including any person in whose favour a contact order under section 8 of the 1989 Act or an order under section 34 of the 1989 Act

(parental contact with children in care) may be in force immediately before the agency is authorised to place the child for adoption; and

(c)   where regulation 14(2) applies, the father; and

(d)   the agency must in an appropriate manner and in the light of the child's age and understanding explain its decision to the child.

(4)   Unless either an application has been made on which a care order might be made in respect of the child which has not been disposed of, or the child is less than 6 weeks old, the agency must ascertain whether the parent or guardian of the child is prepared—

(a)   to consent under section 19 of the Act (placing children with parental consent) to the child being placed for adoption with prospective adopters identified in the consent or being placed for adoption with any prospective adopters who may be chosen by the agency; and

(b)   at the same time to consent to the making of a future adoption order under section 20 of the Act (advance consent to adoption).

(5)   Where the parent or guardian of the child is prepared to consent to the making of a future adoption order under section 20 of the Act, the agency must explain and confirm in writing to the parent or guardian of the child that—

(a)   any consent given under section 20 of the Act may be withdrawn but that the withdrawal of consent is ineffective if it is given after an application for an adoption order is made;

(b)   notice given to the agency may at the same or any subsequent time state their wish not to be informed of any application for an adoption order; and

(c)   such a statement may be withdrawn.

NOTES

Initial Commencement

Specified date

Specified date: 30 December 2005: see reg 1(1).

General

[935]

The adoption agency will appoint a senior person to make decisions on its behalf – often referred to as the agency decision-maker – and that person must make a decision about whether the child should be placed for adoption, taking into account the views of the panel. In addition (especially in England) he/she is formally obliged to consider any advice given by the panel on contact and the question of whether an application should be made for a placement order. He/she is also formally reminded to have regard to ACA 2002, s 1(2) (child's welfare throughout life to be paramount consideration) of the Act when making a decision.

No-one from the panel can participate in that decision. The agency must then give written notification of the decision to the parents (including fathers without parental responsibility, if consulted under reg 14 and the agency considers it appropriate) or guardian, if their whereabouts are known. Unlike in England, there is also a detailed obligation to give written notice to relatives and other 'significant' persons consulted under reg 14, including those with contact orders and fathers without parental responsibility.

When a decision is taken that a child should be placed for adoption, see reg 47 for the requirements in relation to contact, and the absence of a regulatory mechanism to parallel that in England.

In *In the matter of P-B (a Child)* [2006] EWCA Civ 1016, the Court of Appeal had no doubt that the local authority was right in submitting that it had separate functions under the Act from those under CA 1989, when considering whether it should apply for a placement order, that adoption panels are 'a crucial component of the decision-making process', and that the panel's recommendation had to be considered independently by the local authority in its role as an adoption agency. There had to be 'complete compliance with the requirements of the regulations', and until that had been done it could not issue the placement order application, even though the social worker had filed a care plan proposing adoption.

In the same case, Arden LJ stressed the fact that the agency could not just pay lip service to the views of the adoption panel, and that it was open to the agency to take a different view, provided it had 'strong grounds' for doing so. See, in the context of a fostering panel, the decision of *R (on application of Raines) v Orange Grove Foster Care Agency* [2006] EWHC 1887 (Admin) [2006] 2 FCR 746.

In Wales (see also England), the regulations formally require the agency to consider consent issues under ss 19 and 20 of the Act, if the child is less than six weeks old or an application has been made to a court whereby a care order might be made.

[936]

20 Request to appoint a Welsh family proceedings officer or an officer of CAFCASS

(1) Where the parent or guardian of the child is prepared to consent to the placement of the child for adoption under section 19 of the Act (placing children with parental consent) and, as the case may be, to consent to the making of a future adoption order under section 20 of the Act (advance consent to adoption), the adoption agency must request the National Assembly to appoint one of it's Welsh family proceedings officers or, where the child is ordinarily resident in England, the CAFCASS to appoint one of it's officers for the purposes of their signification of the consent to placement or adoption and send with that request the information specified in Schedule 2.

(2) The adoption agency must keep on the case record with respect to the child maintained in accordance with regulation 12—

(a)   the consent form duly signed by the parent or guardian and witnessed by the Welsh family proceedings officer or the officer of CAFCASS;

(b)   any notice given to the agency under section 20(4)(a) of the Act (statement of a wish not to be informed of any application for an adoption order); and

(c)   the withdrawal of any consent or statement given under sections 19 or 20 of the Act.

NOTES
Initial Commencement
Specified date
Specified date: 30 December 2005: see reg 1(1).

General

[937]

This regulation governs the procedure where a parent lives in England or Wales and is prepared to give consent to placement for adoption, or adoption, under ss 19 or 20.

The adoption agency must request the appointment of a Welsh Family Proceedings Officer (or CAFCASS officer, if the child is ordinarily resident in England), including with the request the information set out in Sch 2 to the regulations. The officer's duty is to ensure that the consent is given unconditionally and with full understanding, and witness the signing of the consent.

The relevant consents and notices must be kept on the child's case records.

[938]

Part 4
Duties of Adoption Agency in Respect of a Prospective Adopter

21 Requirement to provide counselling and information

Where the adoption agency is considering a person's suitability to adopt a child, the agency must—

(a) provide a counselling service for the prospective adopter;

(b) in a section 83 case, explain to the prospective adopter the procedure in relation to, and the legal implications of, adopting a child from the country from which the prospective adopter wishes to adopt;

(c) in any other case explain to the prospective adopter the procedure in relation to, and the legal implications of, placement for adoption (including placement by consent under section 19 of the Act, consent to the making of a future adoption order under section 20 of the Act, restriction of parental responsibility and placement orders) and adoption; and

(d) provide the prospective adopter with written information about the matters referred to in sub-paragraph (b) or, as the case may be, (c).

NOTES
Initial Commencement
Specified date
Specified date: 30 December 2005: see reg 1(1).

General

[939]

This regulation sets out the preliminary duties of the adoption agency when a person expresses a wish to be approved as an adoptive parent.

In Wales, each local authority must have a written strategy to recruit adequate numbers of adopters, a written policy and procedure for the process of preparation and approval, and it must provide the prospective adopters with written information about the adoption process, the arrangements for assessment and provision of adoption support services, and the local consortium arrangements (Local Authority Adoption Service (Wales) Regulations 2006 (SI 2006/xxxx, reg 7).

The agency must provide a counselling and information service, and either explain the procedures and legal implications of placement for adoption and adoption, or, if he/she wishes to adopt from a country outside of the British Islands, explain the issues affecting an adoption within that context. In Wales (see also England) the information must include information about s 19 and s 20 consent, placement orders and restrictions on the exercise of parental responsibility.

The Local Authority Adoption Services (Wales) Regulations 2006 are expected to come into force on 31 December 2006, when they will revoke the 2005 Regulations of the same name. References in this book are to the 2006 Regulations but at the time of publication the Welsh Assembly and English Parliament had not yet allocated a number for these Regulations.

[940]

> ### 22 Requirement to consider application for an assessment of suitability to adopt a child
>
> (1) Where the adoption agency, following the procedures referred to in regulation 21, receives an application in writing from a prospective adopter for an assessment of their suitability to adopt a child, the agency must set up a case record in respect of that prospective adopter and consider that person's suitability to adopt a child.
>
> (2) The adoption agency may ask the prospective adopter to provide any further information in writing the agency may reasonably require.
>
> (3) Where paragraph (1) applies in relation to a couple, the assessment of their suitability to adopt a child will be considered jointly and the agency will set up a single case record.
>
> **NOTES**
>
> **Initial Commencement**
>
> *Specified date*
> Specified date: 30 December 2005: see reg 1(1).

General

[941]

Upon receiving a written application for an assessment of suitability to adopt, the adoption agency must set up a case record.

In England, the agency must incrementally include: the application, reports obtained for this purpose, a report on the applicant with his/her response, the minutes of the adoption panel considering his/her case including the recommendation with reasons and any advice given by the panel to the agency, the agency decision, the recommendation of any independent review (if initially unsuccessful with the adoption agency) and the applicant's case has been to such a review, and subsequent review reports on the adopter with responses, and any other relevant information. This is all excluded from the Welsh regulations, and so it is submitted that the English procedure may be seen only as good practice in this context.

The adoption panel should make a recommendation within six months of the formal application to be considered as an adopter (Welsh Guidance, para 201) (in England this time frame is eight months; in Wales, it should be eight months from initial enquiries).

In Wales (but not England) there is a requirement for couples that there is one case record and that their application is considered jointly by the agency.

[942]

> ### 23 Requirement to carry out police checks
>
> (1) The adoption agency must obtain—
>
> (a) in respect of the prospective adopter, an enhanced criminal record certificate within the meaning of section 115 of the Police Act 1997 including the matters specified in subsection (6A) of that section; and
>
> (b) in respect of any other member of the prospective adopter's household aged 18 or over, an enhanced criminal record certificate under section 115 of that Act including the matters specified in subsection (6A) of that section.
>
> (2) The adoption agency must not consider a person suitable to adopt a child or, as the case may be, must consider a person no longer suitable to adopt a child, if the person or any member of the person's household aged 18 or over—

(a)   has been convicted of a specified offence committed at the age of 18 or over; or

(b)   has been cautioned by a constable in respect of any such offence which, at the time the caution was given, the person admitted.

(3)   In paragraph (2) 'specified offence' means—

(a)   an offence against a child;

(b)   an offence specified in Part 1 of Schedule 3;

(c)   an offence contrary to section 170 of the Customs and Excise Management Act 1979 in relation to goods prohibited to be imported under section 42 of the Customs Consolidation Act 1876 (prohibitions and restrictions relating to pornography) where the prohibited goods included indecent photographs of children under the age of 16;

(d)   any other offence involving bodily injury to a child, other than an offence of common assault or battery,

and the expression 'offence against a child' has the meaning given to it by section 26(1) of the Criminal Justice and Court Services Act 2000 except that it does not include an offence contrary to section 9 of the Sexual Offences Act 2003 (sexual activity with a child) in a case where the offender was under the age of 20 and the child was aged 13 or over at the time the offence was committed.

(4)   An adoption agency may not consider a person to be suitable to adopt a child or, as the case may be, must consider a person no longer suitable to adopt a child, if that person or any member of that person's household aged 18 or over—

(a)   has been convicted of an offence specified in paragraph 1 of Part 2 of Schedule 3 committed at the age of 18 or over or has been cautioned by a constable in respect of any such offence which, at the time the caution was given, was admitted; or

(b)   falls within paragraph 2 or 3 of Part 2 of Schedule 3,

notwithstanding that the statutory offences specified in Part 2 of Schedule 3 have been repealed.

NOTES

Initial Commencement

Specified date

Specified date: 30 December 2005: see reg 1(1).

General

[943]

An enhanced criminal record certificate must be obtained in respect of the prospective adopter and all adults in the household. See note to ACA 2002, s 135 (para [601]), (now repealed by s 174 of and Sch 17 to the Serious Organised Crime and Police Act 2005).

The adoption agency is prohibited from approving a person if he/she, or any adult member of the household, has a specified criminal conviction, or caution (where the offence was admitted), within the category set out in reg 23(2). These are offences against children (with a limited exception for sexual activity with a child over 12 when the person convicted was under the age of 20), a wide range of sexual offences against adults, and importation of child pornography. Regulation 23(4) covers convictions and cautions under repealed legislation of a broadly similar nature.

Although it may be stating the obvious, this regulation (unlike the English regulations) formally requires the agency to consider a person, who has previously been approved, unsuitable to adopt if that person, or a household member, is subsequently convicted or cautioned in this way.

[944]

24 Requirement to notify

The adoption agency must notify the prospective adopter in writing as soon as possible after becoming aware that the person is not suitable, or as the case may be, is no longer suitable, to adopt a child by virtue of regulation 23 (2) to (4).

NOTES

Initial Commencement

Specified date
Specified date: 30 December 2005: see reg 1(1).

General

[945]

If a person is unsuitable to adopt because of relevant convictions or cautions of his/her own or a household member, under reg 23, the agency must give that person written notification as soon as possible. It should be borne in mind that he/she may not necessarily know of the conviction or caution of another household member. This regulation overcomes any potential data protection problems.

[946]

25 Requirement to provide preparation for adoption

(1)   Where the adoption agency is considering whether a person may be suitable to adopt a child, the agency must make arrangements for the prospective adopter to receive such preparation for adoption as the agency considers appropriate.
(2)   Paragraph (1) does not apply if the adoption agency is satisfied that the requirements set out in that paragraph have been carried out in respect of the prospective adopter by another adoption agency.
(3)   Where the prospective adopter is not prepared to undertake the preparation for adoption which the adoption agency considers appropriate in their case, the agency may refuse to proceed further with the prospective adopter's application for an assessment of their suitability to adopt.
(4)   In paragraph (1) 'preparation for adoption' includes the provision of information to the prospective adopter about—

(a)   the age range, gender and likely needs and background of children who may be placed for adoption by the adoption agency;
(b)   the significance and legal implications of adoption for a child and his family;
(c)   contact between a child and his natural parents and other relatives where a child is authorised to be placed for adoption or the child is adopted;
(d)   the skills needed to be an adoptive parent;
(e)   the perspective of the child and the child's family;
(f)   the adoption agency's procedures in relation to assessment of prospective adopters and placement of a child for adoption; and
(g)   the procedure in relation to placement for adoption and adoption.

NOTES

Initial Commencement

Specified date
Specified date: 30 December 2005: see reg 1(1).

General

[947]

The adoption agency must provide the applicant with preparation for adoption, unless another agency has already done so.

In Wales (see also England) the agency can decline to progress the application for assessment if the applicant is unwilling to engage in suitable preparation. In addition, although the minimum legal requirements for preparation are similar in Wales and England, in Wales it must also include the legal implications of adoption for the child and family, and consideration of 'the perspective of the child and the child's family'.

[948]

26   Procedure in respect of carrying out an assessment

(1)   Where the adoption agency, after having followed the procedures referred to in regulations 23 and 25, consider the prospective adopter may be suitable to be an adoptive parent, it must carry out an assessment in accordance with this regulation.

(2)   The adoption agency must obtain such particulars about the prospective adopter as are referred to in Part 1 of Schedule 4.

(3)   The adoption agency must obtain—

(a)   a written report from a registered medical practitioner about the health of the prospective adopter which must deal with the matters specified in Part 2 of Schedule 4 unless such a report has been made within 6 months of the panel's consideration of the case under regulation 27 and is available to the agency;

(b)   a written report of each of the interviews with the persons nominated by the prospective adopter as personal referees; and

(c)   a written report from the local authority in whose area the prospective adopter lives, and where the prospective adopter has lived in that area for a period of less than twelve months the agency must obtain a written report also from the local authority in whose area the prospective adopter lived previously.

(4)   The adoption agency must prepare a written report which must include—

(a)   the details of the prospective adopter as set out in Part 1 of Schedule 4;

(b)   a summary, written by the agency's medical adviser, of the state of health of the prospective adopter;

(c)   the agency's assessment of the prospective adopter's suitability to adopt a child, and in determining the suitability of a couple to adopt a child the agency must have proper regard to the need for stability and permanence in their relationship;

(d)   any relevant information the agency obtains under paragraph (3)(c);

(e)   any observations of the agency on the matters referred to in regulations 22, 23, and 25;

(f)   any other information which the agency considers relevant.

(5)   In a section 83 case the report must include—

(a)   the name of the country ('country of origin') from which the prospective adopter wishes to adopt;

(b)   confirmation that the prospective adopter meets the eligibility requirements to adopt from the country of origin;

(c)   additional information obtained as a consequence of the requirements of the country of origin; and

(d)   the agency's assessment of the prospective adopter's suitability to adopt a child who is habitually resident outside the British Islands.

(6)   The adoption agency must notify the prospective adopter their application is to be referred to the adoption panel and at the same time send the prospective adopter a copy of the agency's report referred to in paragraph (4), and invite any observations on the report to be sent in writing to the agency within 10 working days, beginning with the date on which the notification was sent.

(7)   At the end of the period of 10 working days referred to in paragraph (6) (or earlier if any observations made by the prospective adopter are received before the 10 working days have expired) the adoption agency must send—

(a)   the report referred to in paragraph (4), together with any observations provided by the prospective adopter under paragraph (6);

(b)   the written reports referred to in paragraph (3); and

PART C – SIs

> (c)　any other relevant information obtained by the agency under this regulation to the adoption panel.
>
> (8)　The adoption agency must obtain, so far as is reasonably practicable, any other relevant information which may be required by the adoption panel and send that information to the panel.
>
> **NOTES**
> **Initial Commencement**
> *Specified date*
> Specified date: 30 December 2005: see reg 1(1).

General

[949]

After the counselling, advice and preparation service has been provided to potential applicants for approval, the agency then decides whether or not to provide the potential applicants with an application form to complete.

On receiving a written application for an assessment of suitability to adopt, the adoption agency should, as good practice (see note to reg 22, para [941]), set up a case record, incrementally including the application, reports obtained for this purpose, a report on the applicant with his/her response, the minutes of the adoption panel considering his/her case including the recommendation with reasons, and any advice given by the panel to the agency, the agency decision, the recommendation of any independent review if initially unsuccessful and the applicant's case has been to such a review, and subsequent review reports on the adopter (with responses), and any other relevant information.

Once the procedures have been followed for enhanced criminal record certificates (which might have been completed during the preparation stages) and the preparation, if the agency considers the applicant to be a suitable adopter it must prepare a report containing: a breadth of information about the applicant and family covering the matters in Pt 1 of Sch 4 to the regulations; a medical summary concerning their health; written information from the local authority (only if the applicant lives outside their area where the agency is a local authority, but in all cases where the agency is a voluntary agency); observations from the initial counselling, criminal record certificates or preparation work; an assessment of their suitability to adopt; and any other relevant information. Under the Welsh regulations, the information from the other local authority must also be from any previous local authority if the applicant has lived in the present area for less than 12 months.

If a couple, the agency must have 'proper regard to the need for stability and permanence in their relationship' when considering their applications.

The agency must also obtain a written medical report, and written reports on the interviews of those giving references.

Further particulars are required for those seeking to bring a child into the UK from abroad for the purposes of adoption, under ACA 2002, s 83.

(Note that in England, the equivalent regulation permits a foreshortened procedure if the agency is of the preliminary view that the applicant is unlikely to prove suitable, even though not all information has yet been received. It must then prepare a brief prospective adopter's report, notwithstanding the incomplete nature of the document. That provision is subject in England to the Suitability of Adopters Regulations 2005 (SI 2005/1712), reg 5. See the commentary to the Adoption Agencies Regulations 2005 (SI 2005/389), reg 25 (para [853]). In Wales, the closest provision to this is in the guidance, paras 53 and 54, where it permits, as a matter of good practice, a social worker who believes that there are 'any contra indications prior to, or at the start of, an assessment' to refer the matter to panel for immediate consideration. The panel may then offer only advice, not a recommendation, and an agency decision then becomes a qualifying determination (see note to ACA 2002, s 12, paras [158]–[162]).

The panel may also ask the agency to obtain further information.

[950]

---

27 Function of the adoption panel

(1) Subject to paragraph (2), the adoption panel must consider the case of the prospective adopter referred to it by the adoption agency and make a recommendation to that agency as to whether the prospective adopter is suitable to adopt a child.

(2) In considering what recommendation to make, the adoption panel—

(a) must consider and take into account all information and reports passed to it in accordance with regulation 26;

(b) may request the adoption agency to obtain any other relevant information which the panel considers necessary; and

(c) must obtain legal advice as it considers necessary in relation to the case.

(3) Where the adoption panel make a recommendation to the adoption agency that the prospective adopter is suitable to adopt a child, it may consider and at the same time give advice to the agency about the number of children the prospective adopter may be suitable to adopt, their age range, gender and characteristics (health and social).

(4) Before making any recommendation, the adoption panel must invite the prospective adopters to attend the panel meeting.

NOTES

Initial Commencement

Specified date

Specified date: 30 December 2005: see reg 1(1).

General

[951]

As with children, the adoption panel makes recommendations to the adoption agency. See notes to regs 18 and 19.

When considering a person's suitability to adopt, there is a discretion whether to obtain legal advice. The panel must consider all reports received, decide whether to request further information, and invite the applicant(s) to attend the panel. It must make a recommendation to the agency, whether positive or adverse. The panel has a discretion to offer the agency advice about the numbers of children he/she could adopt and other factors such as the children's age range, gender and background, but this is not a formal recommendation and does not bind the agency or prospective adopters.

Recommendations must be communicated orally to the applicants within 24 hours (Welsh Guidance, para 17).

[952]

---

28 Adoption agency decision and notification

(1) The adoption agency must take into account the recommendation of the adoption panel in coming to a decision about whether the prospective adopter is suitable to adopt a child.

---

(2)   No member of the adoption panel is to take part in any decision made by the adoption agency under paragraph (1).

(3)   Where the adoption agency decides to approve the prospective adopter as suitable to adopt a child it must notify the prospective adopter in writing of its decision.

(4)   Where the adoption agency considers that the prospective adopter is not suitable to adopt a child, it must—

(a)   notify the prospective adopter in writing that it proposes not to approve the prospective adopter as suitable to adopt a child ('qualifying determination');

(b)   send with that notification its reasons together with a copy of the recommendation of the adoption panel, if different;

(c)   advise the prospective adopter that within 20 working days beginning with the date on which the notification was sent the prospective adopter may—

(i)   submit any representations to the agency, or

(ii)   apply to the independent review panel for a review of the qualifying determination.

(5)   If, within the period of 20 working days referred to in paragraph (4), the prospective adopter has not made any representations or applied to the independent review panel, the adoption agency must proceed to make its decision and must notify the prospective adopter in writing of its decision together with the reasons for that decision.

(6)   If, within the period of 20 working days referred to in paragraph (4), the adoption agency receive further representations from the prospective adopter, it may refer the case together with all the relevant information back to their adoption panel for further consideration.

(7)   The adoption panel must consider any case referred to it under paragraph (6) and make a fresh recommendation to the adoption agency as to whether the prospective adopter is suitable to adopt a child.

(8)   The adoption agency must make a decision on the case but if the case has been referred to the adoption panel under paragraph (6) or the prospective adopter has applied to the independent review panel for a review of the qualifying determination it must make the decision only after taking into account any recommendation of the adoption panel made under paragraph (7) and regulation 27 or, as the case may be, of the independent review panel.

(9)   As soon as possible after making its decision under paragraph (8), the adoption agency must notify the prospective adopter in writing of its decision, stating its reasons for that decision if it does not consider the prospective adopter to be suitable to adopt a child, and of the adoption panel's recommendation under paragraph (7), if this is different from the adoption agency's decision.

NOTES

Initial Commencement

Specified date

Specified date: 30 December 2005: see reg 1(1).

General

[953]

The agency decision-maker must then decide, without the involvement of any panel member, whether the applicant is suitable to adopt a child. In Wales, he/she is formally required to have regard to the recommendation of the adoption panel.

If the decision is in the affirmative, he/she must be notified in writing.

If minded to refuse the application, the agency must provide that decision (the 'qualifying determination') to the applicant, with reasons, and any recommendation from the panel if that differs. He/she must be notified of the right either to make representations to the agency or to apply for a review by an independent review panel. If neither right is exercised, the agency must notify the applicant with its decision in writing. If the applicant makes representations, there is a discretion to refer the case back to the adoption panel for further consideration (and then a further recommendation back to the agency again), or the decision-maker may make a final decision without a referral back to panel.

The procedure for an independent review is set out in the Independent Review of Determinations (Adoption) (Wales) Regulations 2005 (SI 2005/1819). See note to ACA 2002, s 12 for the detailed procedure (paras [158]–[162]).

If the independent review procedure is pursued, the agency cannot take a final decision until the recommendation of that independent review panel has been considered by the agency decision-maker.

If the decision is still negative, the applicant must be told so in writing with reasons, and provided with the recommendation of any reconvened adoption panel if that differs.

(Unlike in England, where the independent panel has made a recommendation, whether positive or negative, there is no obligation for a copy of the agency decision-maker's final decision to be sent to the Secretary of State).

[954]

29 Information to be sent to the independent review panel

(1) Where the adoption agency receives notification from the independent review panel that a prospective adopter has applied for a review of the qualifying determination, the agency must, within 10 working days of receipt of that notification, send to the independent review panel the information specified in paragraph (2).

(2) The following information is specified for the purposes of paragraph (1)—

(a) all the reports and information which were sent to the adoption panel in accordance with regulation 26;

(b) any written representations made by the prospective adopter in accordance with regulation 26(6);

(c) any other reports or information sent by the adoption agency to the adoption panel; ·

(d) the record of the proceedings of the adoption panel, its recommendations and the reasons for its recommendations;

(e) the notification, together with reasons sent by the adoption agency to the prospective adopter in accordance with 28(4)(a) and (b).

NOTES

Initial Commencement

Specified date
Specified date: 30 December 2005: see reg 1(1).

PART C – SIs

General

[955]

This sets out the information that the agency must provide to the independent review panel where an unsuccessful applicant for approval as an adopter pursues his/her right to seek an independent review of that 'qualifying determination'.

[956]

30 Reviews and termination of approval

(1) The adoption agency must review the approval of each prospective adopter in accordance with this regulation, unless—

(a)   in a section 83 case, the prospective adopter has visited the child in the country in which the child is habitually resident and has confirmed in writing that he wishes to proceed with the adoption; and

(b)   in any other case, the child is placed for adoption with the prospective adopter.

(2)   A review must take place whenever the adoption agency considers it necessary but otherwise not more than two years after approval and thereafter at intervals of not more than two years.

(3)   When undertaking such a review the adoption agency must—

(a)   make such enquiries and obtain such information as it considers necessary in order to review whether the prospective adopter continues to be suitable to adopt a child; and

(b)   seek and take account of the views of the prospective adopter.

(4)   As a part of each review the adoption agency must consider—

(a)   why no child has yet been placed with the prospective adopter;

(b)   any arrangements for the provision of adoption support services and whether they should continue or be modified;

(c)   where a child is returned to the adoption agency in accordance with section 35(1) or (2) of the Act, the reasons for the child's return; and

(d)   whether the prospective adopter is still suitable to adopt a child.

(5)   The adoption agency must—

(a)   set out in writing the arrangements governing the manner in which the review of a prospective adopter is to be carried out and must draw the written arrangements to the attention of—

      (i)   the prospective adopter; and

      (ii)   any other person the agency considers relevant.

(b)   ensure that—

      (i)   the information obtained in respect of the prospective adopter;

      (ii)   details of the proceedings at any meeting arranged by the agency to consider any aspect of the review; and

      (iii) details of any decision made in the course of or as a result of the review,

    are recorded in writing and placed on the prospective adopter's case record.

(6)   If at the conclusion of the review, the adoption agency considers the prospective adopter may no longer be suitable to be an adoptive parent, it must prepare a written report which must include—

(a)   the information obtained on the matters referred to in paragraphs (3) and (4);

(b)   the agency's reasons; and

(c)   any other information which the agency considers relevant.

(7)   The adoption agency must notify the prospective adopter that the report referred to in paragraph (6) is to be referred to the adoption panel and give the prospective adopter a copy of that report and invite any observations on the report to be sent in writing to the agency within 10 working days, beginning with the date on which the notification was sent.

(8)   At the end of the period of 10 working days referred to in paragraph (7) (or earlier if the prospective adopter's comments are received before the 10 working days have expired), the adoption agency must send a copy of the report referred to in paragraph (6) together with the prospective adopter's observations and the report prepared for panel under regulation 26(4).

(9)   The adoption agency must obtain, so far as is reasonably practicable, any other relevant information which may be required by the adoption panel and send that information to the adoption panel.

(10)   The adoption panel must consider the report and any other information passed to it by the adoption agency under this regulation and make a recommendation to the agency as to whether the prospective adopter continues to be suitable to adopt a child.

(11) Regulation 28 will apply in relation to the decision by the adoption agency about whether a prospective adopter continues to be suitable to adopt a child as it applies in relation to the decision by the agency about whether the prospective adopter is suitable to adopt a child.

NOTES

Initial Commencement

Specified date

Specified date: 30 December 2005: see reg 1(1).

General

[957]

This provides for reviews of prospective adopters who have been approved but have not yet had a child placed (or, in s 83 cases of adoption from abroad, he/she has not yet visited the child in that country and given written confirmation of intention to proceed).

Their status must be reviewed by the adoption agency at least every two years (yearly in England) or if there is a significant change in circumstances.

The agency must have written procedures for such reviews, and there are minimum requirements for the written records.

The agency must consider why no child has yet been placed, any adoption support services provided and whether they should change, the reasons why any child was placed then returned, and generally whether he/she remains suitable to adopt.

If it is concluded that he/she is no longer suitable to adopt, a written report must be prepared, and this report must be sent to the prospective adopter with at least 10 working days' notice, to enable him/her to make representations before the adoption panel meeting. The review report, and any comments he/she makes, must be sent to the adoption panel. The panel must then make a fresh recommendation, and the agency decision-maker must make a fresh decision. All of the procedural requirements in reg 28 apply to this process. Therefore if the agency proposes to terminate the approval the prospective adopter has an entitlement to an independent review.

[958]

31 Duties of the adoption agency in a section 83 case following approval of prospective adopter

Where the adoption agency decides in a section 83 case to approve a prospective adopter as suitable to adopt a child, the agency must send to the National Assembly—

(a) written confirmation of the decision and any recommendation the agency may make in relation to the number of children the prospective adopter may be suitable to adopt, their age range, gender, likely needs and background;

(b) all of the documents and information which were passed to the adoption panel in accordance with regulation 26;

(c) the record of the proceedings of the adoption panel, its recommendations and the reasons for its recommendations;

(d) if the prospective adopter had applied for a review by an independent panel of a qualifying determination, the record of the proceedings of that panel, its recommendations and the reasons for its recommendations; and

(e) any other information relating to the case which the National Assembly or the relevant foreign authority may require.

PART C – SIs

NOTES
Initial Commencement
Specified date
Specified date: 30 December 2005: see reg 1(1).

General

[959]

In all s 83 cases (proposals for a child to be brought to the UK to be adopted) the adoption agency must provide the National Assembly with prescribed information.

[960]

Part 5
Duties of Adoption Agency in Respect of Proposed Placement of Child with Prospective Adopter

32 Proposed placement

(1) Where the adoption agency is considering placing a child for adoption with a particular prospective adopter (in this regulation referred to as 'the proposed placement') the agency must—

(a) provide the prospective adopter with a report about the child which must include the information set out in Schedule 5 and any other information which the agency considers relevant;

(b) meet with the prospective adopter to discuss the proposed placement;

(c) ascertain the views of the prospective adopter about—

  (i) the proposed placement;
  (ii) the child's assessed needs for adoption support services and the adoption support plan;
  (iii) the arrangements the agency proposes to make for allowing any person contact with the child; and

  where applicable, any restriction in the exercise of their parental responsibility.

(d) provide a counselling service for, and any further information to, the prospective adopter as may be required.

(2) Where the procedures set out in paragraph (1) have been followed and the prospective adopter has confirmed to the agency in writing their agreement to the proposed placement, the agency must, in such cases as it considers appropriate and so far as is reasonably practicable in the light of the child's age and understanding, counsel the child and tell the child about the prospective adopters, their family circumstances and home environment and ascertain the child's views about the proposed placement, contact arrangements and any restriction of the prospective adopter's parental responsibility.

(3) Where the adoption agency considers that the proposed placement should proceed the agency must—

(a) where the agency is a local authority, carry out an assessment of the needs of the child and the prospective adoptive family for adoption support services in accordance with regulations made under section 4(6) of the Act;

(b) consider the arrangements for allowing any person contact with the child;

(c) consider whether the parental responsibility of any parent or guardian, or of prospective adopters, is to be restricted to any extent;

(d) prepare a written report which must include—

  (i) the agency's reasons for proposing the placement;
  (ii) the information obtained by virtue of paragraphs (1) and (2);

    (iii)   where the agency is a local authority, its proposals for the provision of adoption support services, if any, in accordance with regulations made under section 4(6) of the Act;

    (iv)   the arrangements the agency propose to make for allowing any person contact with the child;

    (v)   the agency's proposals for restricting the parental responsibility of any parent or guardian, or prospective adopter; and

    (vi)   any other information relevant to the proposed placement.

(4) The adoption agency must notify the prospective adopter that the proposed placement is to be referred to the adoption panel and send the prospective adopter a copy of the agency's report referred to in paragraph (3) and invite any observations on the report to be sent in writing to the agency within 10 working days, beginning with the date on which the notification was sent.

(5) At the end of the period of 10 working days referred to in paragraph (4) (or earlier if observations are received before the 10 working days have expired) the adoption agency must send—

(a)   the report referred to in paragraph (3);

(b)   the report referred to in regulation 17;

(c)   the report referred to in regulation 26 and any observations made by the prospective adopter on that report;

(d)   any other relevant information obtained by the agency under this regulation

to the adoption panel.

(6) The adoption agency may only refer to the adoption panel its proposal to place a child for adoption with a particular prospective adopter if any other adoption agency which has made a decision in accordance with these Regulations that the child should be placed for adoption, or that the prospective adopter is suitable to adopt a child, has been consulted about the proposed placement.

(7) Where the adoption agency proposes to place a child for adoption with a particular prospective adopter the agency must set up case records in any case where it has not already set up such records and place on the appropriate record any information, report, recommendation or decision referred to it by another adoption agency together with any other information to be sent to the adoption panel by virtue of this regulation in respect of them.

(8) The adoption agency must obtain so far as is reasonably practicable any other relevant information which may be requested by the adoption panel in connection with the proposed placement and send that information to the panel.

NOTES

Initial Commencement

Specified date

Specified date: 30 December 2005: see reg 1(1).

PART C – SIs

General

[961]

Regulations 32–34 concern the match of a child with a prospective adopter, who are both separately approved under the procedures set out in regs 11–20 (the child) and regs 21–31 (prospective adopters).

A proposed match should be identified within six months of the agency deciding that the child should be placed for adoption or, in care proceedings, within six months of the court's decision (Welsh Guidance, para 90). However, the child cannot actually be placed before authorisation by the granting of a placement order or the giving of s 19 consent. The agency is no longer, under the new Act, required to satisfy the court that is considering a placement order application as to the likelihood of placement.

The regulation

[962]

Three stages are contemplated. When there is a provisional view that a match is viable, the agency must give the prospective adopter a copy of the written report on the child and other relevant information, meet him/her and discuss the match, take into account his/her views (including about the contact and support proposals), and provide any necessary counselling to that person. The information given must include the information in Sch 5 to the regulations.

In Wales (see also England), the agency must explicitly, under this regulation, ascertain the prospective adopter's views on the child's assessed needs for adoption support services, the adoption support plan and any restriction on the exercise of parental responsibility.

Prior to the present legislation, the Court of Appeal gave judgment in *A and Another v Essex County Council* [2003] EWCA Civ 1848 and partially allowed an appeal by the local authority against a judgment that it was liable in damages to adopters who claimed that they had been given insufficient or misleading information about the child prior to placement. The Court of Appeal held that any duty of care (if one existed at all) was owed to the child, not to the prospective adopters, but that liability would arise if a decision was taken to provide specific information to the adopters and then the agency failed to provide it.

It is thus now possible that a breach of the duties arising under this regulation will potentially give rise to a cause of action in damages, given the much more detailed requirements in the regulation of the information that must be given to the applicant.

Hale LJ (as she then was) noted that any placement was provisional, prior to adoption, and that both the agency and the prospective adopters were 'actors in the story'. She observed that there was a 'delicate balance to be struck between pessimism and optimism', in imparting information, that excessive pessimism might render a child unadoptable, and that part of the assessment process was of the resilience of prospective adopters.

The Court of Appeal was of the view that, even if there was liability, there was a cut-off point in respect of damage after adoption. Prior to adoption, the placement was 'probationary', and there was a duty of candour on both sides.

In Wales, but not England, the adopter must confirm to the agency in writing his/her agreement to the placement, and the agency must counsel the child, tell the child about the new family and their circumstances, and seek his/her views on the placement, contact and proposed restrictions on parental responsibility, subject to the child's age and understanding.

Once satisfied that the match should proceed, the adoption agency – if a local authority – must carry out an assessment of any need of the child, prospective adopter, and any other children of the prospective adopter, for adoption support services from the placing local authority. The agency must consider the contact and support plans, and then prepare a written report (in England, called an adoption placement report) on the match and invite comments from the prospective adopter about the report at least 10 working days before the matching adoption panel meeting. In Wales the agency must explicitly consider the extent to which the parental responsibility of the adopters or natural parents or guardians should be restricted, and this must be addressed in the written report.

The report, accompanying response from the prospective adopter, and original report under reg 17 are then referred to the adoption panel. If another adoption agency has approved the relevant status of the child or prospective adopter, that agency must first be consulted about the proposed match.

[963]

33 Function of the adoption panel in relation to the proposed placement

(1) The adoption panel must consider the proposed placement referred to it by the adoption agency and make a recommendation to the agency as to whether the child should be placed for adoption with that particular prospective adopter.

(2) In considering what recommendation to make the adoption panel must have regard to the duties imposed on the adoption agency under section 1(2), (4) and (5) of the Act (considerations applying to the exercise of powers in relation to the adoption of a child) and—

(a) must consider and take into account all information and the reports passed to it in accordance with regulation 32;

(b) may request the adoption agency to obtain any other relevant information which the panel considers necessary; and

(c) must obtain legal advice as it considers necessary in relation to the case.

(3) The adoption panel must also consider and, where the panel makes a recommendation to the agency that the child should be placed for adoption with that particular prospective adopter, the panel may consider and at the same time give advice to the adoption agency about—

(i) where the adoption agency is a local authority, the authority's proposals for the provision of adoption support services;

(ii) the arrangements the adoption agency proposes to make for allowing any person contact with the child;

(iii) whether an application should be made for a placement order; and

(iv) where the agency is authorised to place the child for adoption whether it considers any person's parental responsibility should be restricted and, if so, the extent of any such restriction.

(4) The adoption panel may only make the recommendation in paragraph (1) if—

(a) that recommendation is to be made at the same meeting of the adoption panel at which a recommendation has been made that the child should be placed for adoption; or

(b) the adoption agency or another adoption agency has made a decision in accordance with regulation 19 that the child should be placed for adoption;

and in either case that recommendation is to be made at the same meeting of the panel at which a recommendation has been made that the prospective adopter is suitable to adopt a child or the adoption agency, or another adoption agency, has made a decision in accordance with regulation 28 that the prospective adopter is suitable to adopt a child.

NOTES
Initial Commencement
Specified date
Specified date: 30 December 2005: see reg 1(1).

PART C – SIs

General

[964]

The adoption panel considers the information and makes a recommendation to the adoption agency. See the notes to regs 18 and 19 (paras [933] and [935]) regarding the separate functions of the panel and adoption agency.

In doing so, there is a discretion to take legal advice or to seek further information.

A match can only be recommended if it has already been decided that the child should be placed for adoption, either previously (by any adoption agency), or that is recommended at the same panel. Likewise, the prospective adopter must either already be approved, or be approved at the same panel.

If there are no Court proceedings, the match should be made within six months of the decision that the child should be adopted. If there are Court proceedings, the match should be made within the six months following the Final Hearing. For babies under the age of six months, being adopted by consent, there should be a match within three months (Welsh Guidance, para 90).

Before making its recommendation, the panel must consider the proposed adoption support services (unlike England, not just for the adoptive family) (if the agency is a local authority), the contact proposals, whether a placement order application is required and, given that parental responsibility will be shared, if the authority is authorised to place the child, the extent (if any) to which that of any person should be restricted. If the panel recommends a match, it can give the agency advice on any of these matters.

The decision must be taken within seven working days of the panel's recommendation, communicated orally to the child, birth parents and applicants within one day, and confirmed in writing within seven working days (Welsh Guidance, paras 17, 294 and 297).

[965]

34 Adoption agency's decision in relation to the proposed placement

(1) The adoption agency must—

(a) take into account the recommendation of the adoption panel;
(b) take into account any advice given by the adoption panel in accordance with regulation 33(3); and
(c) have regard to the consideration set out in section 1(2) of the Act,

in coming to a decision about whether the child should be placed for adoption with the particular prospective adopter.

(2) No member of the adoption panel is to take part in any decision made by the adoption agency under paragraph (1).

(3) As soon as possible after making its decision the adoption agency must notify the prospective adopter in writing of its decision about the proposed placement, contact arrangements and the restriction of any person's parental responsibility.

(4) As soon as possible after making its decision, the agency must notify in writing—

(a) the parent or guardian, if their whereabouts are known to the agency; and
(b) where regulation 14(2) applies, the father of the child,

of its decision.

(5) Where the adoption agency decides the proposed placement should proceed the agency must, in an appropriate manner and in the light of the child's age and understanding, explain its decision to the child.

NOTES
Initial Commencement
Specified date
Specified date: 30 December 2005: see reg 1(1).

General

[966]

The agency decision-maker, without any involvement by panel members, decides whether the match should proceed, and must give written notification to the prospective adopter of the decision. He/she must take into account the panel's recommendation under reg 33, any advice given by the panel, and the consideration in ACA 2002, s 1(2) (paramountcy of child's welfare throughout his/her life).

The notification to the prospective adopter must also contain any determination of the future plans for contact and restriction on the exercise of any person's parental responsibility.

The parent or guardian, and any father without parental responsibility falling within the terms of reg 14, must also be notified in writing if their whereabouts are known. If the decision is negative, there is no formal requirement for reasons to be given to the adopter or parent/guardian.

Note the provisions of reg 47 in relation to contact, and the absence of a regulatory mechanism to parallel that in England.

Any decision to proceed with a match must be explained to the child.

[967]

35 Function of the adoption agency in a section 83 case

(1)   This paragraph applies where in a section 83 case the adoption agency receives from the relevant foreign authority information about a child to be adopted by a prospective adopter whom the agency has approved as suitable to adopt a child.
(2)   Where paragraph (1) applies, the adoption agency must—

(a)   send a copy of the information referred to in paragraph (1) to the prospective adopter unless it is aware that the prospective adopter has received a copy;
(b)   consider that information;
(c)   meet with the prospective adopter to discuss the information; and
(d)   if appropriate, provide a counselling service for, and any further information to, the prospective adopter as may be required.

NOTES

Initial Commencement

Specified date
Specified date: 30 December 2005: see reg 1(1).

General

[968]

This regulation governs the procedure to be followed in s 83 cases (child being brought to the UK to be adopted), where the relevant foreign authority provides the adoption agency with information.

[969]

Part 6
Placements and Reviews

36 Requirements imposed on the adoption agency before the child is placed for adoption with prospective adopter

(1)   This paragraph applies where the adoption agency—

(a)   has decided in accordance with regulation 34 to place a child for adoption with a particular prospective adopter; and

(b)   has met with the prospective adopter to consider the arrangements it proposes to make for placing the child with him.

(2)   Where paragraph (1) applies, the adoption agency must, at least 7 days before the child is placed with the prospective adopter, provide the prospective adopter with a placement plan in respect of the child which covers the matters specified in Schedule 6 ('the placement plan').

(3)   Where paragraph (1) applies and the child already lives with the prospective adopter, the adoption agency must provide the prospective adopter with the placement plan in respect of the child within 7 days of its decision to place the child for adoption with the prospective adopter.

(4)   Where paragraph (1) applies, the adoption agency must, before the child is placed for adoption with the prospective adopter—

(a)   notify the prospective adopter's general practitioner in writing of the proposed placement and send with that notification a written report of the child's health history and current state of health;

(b)   notify the local authority (if that authority is not the adoption agency) and Local Health Board or Primary Care Trust (England) in whose area the prospective adopter resides in writing of the proposed placement;

(c)   notify the local education authority in whose area the prospective adopter resides in writing of the proposed placement and information about the child's educational history and whether the child has been or is likely to be assessed for special educational needs under the Education Act 1996.

(5)   The adoption agency must notify the prospective adopter in writing of any change to the placement plan.

(6)   Where paragraph (1) applies the adoption agency must, before the child is placed for adoption with the prospective adopter, arrange for the prospective adopter to meet the child and following that meeting counsel the prospective adopter and, so far as is reasonably practicable in the light of the child's age and understanding, the child about the prospective placement.

(7)   Where, following the procedures referred to in paragraph (6) the prospective adopter confirms in writing their wish to proceed with the placement and the agency is authorised to place the child for adoption or the child is less than 6 weeks old, the adoption agency may place the child for adoption with the prospective adopter.

(8)   Where the child already lives with the prospective adopter, the adoption agency must notify the prospective adopter in writing of the date on which the child is placed there for adoption by the agency.

NOTES
Initial Commencement
Specified date
Specified date: 30 December 2005: see reg 1(1).

General

[970]

Once the adoption agency decision-maker has approved a match and the agency has discussed with him/her the proposed plans for placement, the agency must prepare the written 'placement plan', setting out the details required by Sch 6 to the regulations, including any adoption support services, details of the contact arrangements and the extent to which the prospective adopter will be permitted to exercise parental responsibility. The placement plan must be provided to the prospective adopters at least seven days before placement (there is no timescale in the English regulations, where it is to be done as soon as possible). If the child is already living with the prospective adopter, the plan must be provided within seven days of the decision.

The parents must have the opportunity of reading, and commenting upon, any written material about themselves (Welsh Guidance, para 116).

The plan must include the arrangements for maintaining links, including any contact, with birth families and other significant people (Welsh Guidance, para 273).

Prior to any placement, notification must be given to the prospective adopter's GP with a health report on the child, other notifications given to the local authority, and local health board or primary care trust where the child is to live, and if of school age, notification to the local education authority.

Before the child is placed, the agency must arrange a meeting between the child and the prospective adopter, and then counsel the prospective adopter, and the child (as far as practicable in the light of his/her age and understanding), about the prospective placement. This provision is only in the Welsh regulations.

Provided the agency is authorised to place the child for adoption (or the child is under six weeks of age and the parent or guardian has given written agreement to placement), and the prospective adopters have agreed to the placement, the agency can then place the child for adoption.

If an existing carer is approved as the prospective adopter and authorisation to place for adoption has been achieved (by placement order or s 19 consent), his/her status changes to that of prospective adopter, and the date of the formal 'placement for adoption' must be notified in writing to the carer.

Documents are added to the child's case record.

[971]

37 Reviews

(1)   This paragraph applies where the adoption agency is authorised to place a child for adoption but the child has not been placed for adoption.

(2)   This paragraph applies where a child is placed for adoption.

(3)   Where paragraph (1) applies, the adoption agency must carry out a review of the child's case—

(a)   not more than three months after the date on which the agency first has authority to place; and

(b)   thereafter not more than six months after the date of the previous review ('six months review'),

until the child is placed for adoption.

(4)   Where paragraph (2) applies, the adoption agency must carry out a review of the child's case—

(a)   not more than four weeks after the date on which the child is placed for adoption ('the first review');

(b)   no more than three months after the first review; and

(c)   thereafter not more than six months after the date of the previous review,

unless the child is returned to the agency by the prospective adopter or an adoption order is made.

(5)   Where paragraph (2) applies, the adoption agency must—

(a)   ensure the child and the prospective adopter are visited within one week of the placement and thereafter at least once a week until the first review and thereafter at such frequency as the agency decide at each review;

(b)   ensure that written reports are made of such visits; and

(c)   provide such advice and assistance to the prospective adopter as the agency considers necessary.

(6)   When carrying out a review the adoption agency must visit the child and so far as reasonably practicable ascertain the views of—

(a)   the child in the light of the child's age and understanding;
(b)   if the child is placed for adoption, the prospective adopter; and
(c)   any other person the agency considers relevant,

in relation to each of the matters set out in paragraph (7)(a) to (f).

(7)   As part of each review the adoption agency must consider—

(a)   whether placed or not, whether the adoption agency remain satisfied that the child should still be placed for adoption;
(b)   the child's needs, welfare, progress and development, and whether any changes need to be made to meet the child's needs or assist the child's development;
(c)   the existing arrangements for contact, and whether they should continue or be modified;
(d)   where the child is placed for adoption the arrangements in relation to the exercise of parental responsibility for the child, and whether they should continue or be modified;
(e)   the existing arrangements for the provision of adoption support services and whether there should be any re-assessment of the need for those services;
(f)   in consultation with the appropriate agencies, the arrangements for assessing and meeting the child's health care needs and educational needs;
(g)   subject to paragraphs (3) and (4) the frequency of the reviews.

(8)   Where the child is subject to a placement order and has not been placed for adoption at the time of the first six months review, the local authority must at that review—

(a)   establish why the child has not been placed for adoption and consider what further steps the authority should take in relation to the placement of the child for adoption; and
(b)   in light of that, consider whether it remains satisfied that the child should be placed for adoption.

(9)   The adoption agency must—

(a)   set out in writing the arrangements governing the manner in which the case of each child is to be reviewed and must draw the written arrangements to the attention of—

(i)   the child where reasonably practicable in the light of the child's age and understanding;
(ii)   the prospective adopter; and
(iii)   any other person the agency considers relevant.

(b)   ensure that—

(i)   the information obtained in respect of a child's case including the ascertainable wishes and feelings of the child;
(ii)   details of the proceedings at any meeting arranged by the agency to consider any aspect of the review of the case; and
(iii)   details of any decision made in the course of or as a result of the review (including as to frequency of visits),

are recorded in writing and placed on the child's case record.

(10)   The adoption agency must, so far as is reasonably practicable, notify—

(a)   the child where it considers the child is of sufficient age and understanding;
(b)   the prospective adopter; and
(c)   any other person whom it considers ought to be notified

of the outcome of the review and of any decision taken by it in consequence of the review.

(11)   Where the child is returned to the adoption agency in accordance with section 35(1) or (2) of the Act, the agency must conduct a review of the child's case

as soon as reasonably practicable and in any event no later than 28 days after the date on which the child is returned to the agency.

NOTES

Initial Commencement

Specified date

Specified date: 30 December 2005: see reg 1(1).

See Further

See further, in relation to the application of this regulation, with modifications, in respect of a child who on or after 30 December 2005 is free for adoption by virtue of a freeing order under the Adoption Act 1976, s 18 but is not placed for adoption: the Adoption and Children Act 2002 (Commencement No 10 Transitional and Savings Provisions) Order 2005, SI 2005/2897, art 4.

General

[972]

This regulation makes detailed provision for the review of adoptive children's cases, both where the agency is authorised to place but have not yet placed the child, and where the child is placed for adoption but not yet adopted.

Where not yet placed, a review must be held within three months of authorisation, and at least six-monthly thereafter, until placed for adoption.

The agency must have written procedures for such reviews.

If a child is subject to a placement order, and not yet placed, at the first six-monthly review (i.e. no more than ten months after the placement order was granted), the local authority and Independent Reviewing Officer must actively consider and analyse why the child is not yet placed, consider what further steps are required to achieve that, and consider whether adoption remains the correct plan for the future.

Once placed for adoption, the case must be reviewed within four weeks, then within three months, and then at least six-monthly thereafter, until adopted or returned to the adoption agency if the placement is unsuccessful.

In preparing for reviews, the agency must consult the child if of sufficient age and understanding, the prospective adopters (if placed), and any other 'relevant' person. It is arguable in many cases that this should include members of the birth family, at least until the child is placed for adoption. However, by virtue of reg 46 and the amendments that makes to the CA 1989, this is a discretion and not a duty, albeit one to be exercised under the usual public law principles.

There is a checklist of matters that must be discussed at each review, including the child's progress and needs, any contact arrangements, whether adoption remains the correct plan, and any adoption support services.

The outcome and decisions of each review must be notified to the child (if of sufficient age and understanding), any prospective adopter and any other 'person whom it considers ought to be notified'. It is submitted that this is an important aspect of the safeguards for parents once a placement order is made but the child is not yet placed for adoption, and that it should be the norm for natural parents to be identified by the agency as persons for this purpose, and provided with such information as would enable them to make an informed decision about whether to seek legal advice for an application to revoke the placement order or other order under the Act. The Welsh Guidance (para 315) requires the agency to consider whether this includes the 'parents or wider members of his/her family'.

PART C – SIs

If a child is returned to the agency under s 35 of the Act, the first review must be held as soon as practicable and no later than 28 days after the child is returned (in England it must be held between 28 and 42 days of that date).

Provision is made for the minimum frequency of social work visits to the placement, the provision of advice, and recordings.

[973]

38 Independent reviewing officers

(1) An adoption agency which is a local authority or a registered adoption society which is a voluntary organisation which provides accommodation for a child, must appoint a person ('the independent reviewing officer') in respect of the case of each child authorised to be placed for adoption by the agency to carry out the functions mentioned in section 26(2A) of the 1989 Act.

(2) The independent reviewing officer must have significant experience in social work and hold a Diploma in Social Work or a Social Work Degree or an equivalent qualification recognised by the Care Council for Wales.

(3) Where the independent reviewing officer is an employee of the adoption agency the independent reviewing officer's post within that agency must not be under the direct management of—

(a) a person involved in the management of the case;

(b) a person with management responsibilities in relation to a person mentioned in sub-paragraph (a); or

(c) a person with control over the resources allocated to the case.

(4) The independent reviewing officer must, as far as reasonably practicable chair any meeting held in connection with the review of the child's case.

(5) The independent reviewing officer must, as far as is reasonably practicable, take steps to ensure that the review is conducted in accordance with regulation 37 and in particular to ensure—

(a) that the child's views are understood and taken into account;

(b) that the persons responsible for implementing any decision taken in consequence of the review are identified; and

(c) that any failure to review the case in accordance with regulation 37 or to take proper steps to make or carry out arrangements agreed at the review is brought to the attention of persons at an appropriate level of seniority within the agency.

(6) If the child whose case is reviewed wishes to take proceedings under the Act on his own account, for example, to apply to the court for revocation of a placement order, it is the function of the independent reviewing officer—

(a) to assist the child to obtain legal advice; or

(b) to establish whether an appropriate adult is able and willing to provide such assistance or bring the proceedings on the child's behalf.

(7) The adoption agency must inform the independent reviewing officer of—

(a) any significant failure to make or to carry out arrangements in accordance with a review;

(b) any significant change of circumstances occurring after the review that affects those arrangements.

NOTES
Initial Commencement
Specified date
Specified date: 30 December 2005: see reg 1(1).

General

[974]

As with children who are looked after under the CA 1989, an Independent Reviewing Officer (IRO) must be appointed for each child who is authorised to be placed for adoption.

See the note to ACA 2002, s 118 (paras [538]–[544]), for the new provisions in the Children Act and associated regulations concerning the powers and duties of the IRO.

This regulation provides similar powers and duties in the case of children who are authorised to be placed for adoption, and the IRO is responsible for ensuring that reg 37 is complied with. The adoption agency, as with social workers in Children Act cases, is placed under an obligation to inform the IRO of any significant change in the child's circumstances or failure to carry out the agreed plans.

If a child wishes to take legal action, such as for the revocation of a placement order or discharge of a s 26 contact order, the IRO must provide assistance to achieve this.

[975]

39 Withdrawal of consent

(1) This paragraph applies where consent under section 19, or section 19 and 20, of the Act in respect of a child is withdrawn in accordance with section 52(8) of the Act.

(2) Where paragraph (1) applies and the adoption agency is a local authority, on receipt of the form or notice given in accordance with section 52(8) of the Act, the authority must immediately review its decision to place the child for adoption and where, in accordance with section 22(1) or (2) of the Act, the authority decides to apply for a placement order in respect of the child, it must immediately notify—

(a) the parent or guardian;
(b) if regulation 14(2) applies, the child's father; and
(c) if the child is placed for adoption, the prospective adopter with whom the child is placed.

(3) Where paragraph (1) applies and the adoption agency is a registered adoption society, the agency must immediately consider whether it is appropriate to inform the local authority in whose area the child is living.

NOTES
Initial Commencement
Specified date
Specified date: 30 December 2005: see reg 1(1).

General

[976]

When consent to placement for adoption or adoption, under ACA 2002, ss 19 or 20, is withdrawn under the s 52(8) procedure, and the agency is a local authority, the decision to place for adoption must immediately be reviewed. If the agency is a registered adoption society it must immediately decide whether to inform the local authority.

If an adoption agency that is a local authority decides to apply for a placement order, the agency must notify the parents (including a father without parental responsibility if reg 14 applies and it is appropriate) and, if the child is already placed, the prospective adopter.

[977]

Part 7
Records

40 Storage of case records

The adoption agency must ensure that the case record set up in accordance with regulation 12 or 22 in respect of a child or prospective adopter and the contents of that case record are at all times kept in secure conditions and in particular that all appropriate measures are taken to prevent the theft, unauthorised disclosure, loss or destruction of, or damage to, the case record or its contents.

NOTES
Initial Commencement
Specified date
Specified date: 30 December 2005: see reg 1(1).

41 Preservation of case records

Where an adoption order is made in relation to a child the adoption agency must keep all case records set up in accordance with regulations 12 or 22 for at least 100 years. In any other case the agency must keep the case records for such period as it considers appropriate.

NOTES
Initial Commencement
Specified date
Specified date: 30 December 2005: see reg 1(1).

General

[978]

All case records set up under regs 12 and 22 (records for children and prospective adopters) must be retained for 100 years, which is more prescriptive than the English regulations – they give a general discretion on timescales.

English guidance for CA 1989 also requires records for looked after children to be retained for 75 years from birth, or 15 years after death, whichever is earlier (*Adoption Guidance*: Ch 6 [2005] DfES).

[979]

42 Confidentiality of case records

Subject to regulation 43, any information obtained or reports, recommendations or decisions made by virtue of these Regulations must be treated by the adoption agency as confidential.

NOTES
Initial Commencement
Specified date
Specified date: 30 December 2005: see reg 1(1).

General

[980]

This restriction is wider than that contained in the English regulations.

[981]

43 Access to case records and disclosure of information

(1)   Subject to paragraph (3), the adoption agency must provide such access to its case records and disclose such information in its possession, as may be required—

(a)   to those holding an inquiry under section 81 of the 1989 Act (inquiries) or section 17 of the Act (inquiries) for the purposes of such an inquiry;

(b)   to the National Assembly for Wales;

(c)   subject to the provisions of section 74(5) of the Care Standards Act 2000 (disclosure), to the Children's Commissioner for Wales for the purposes of any examination conducted in accordance with Part V of that Act;

(d)   subject to the provisions of sections 29(7) and 32(3) of the Local Government Act 1974 (investigations and disclosure), to the [Public Services Ombudsman for Wales], for the purposes of any investigation conducted in accordance with Part III of that Act;

(e)   to any person appointed by the adoption agency for the purposes of the consideration by the agency of any representations (including complaints);

(f)   to the persons and authorities by and to the extent specified in these Regulations;

(g)   to a Welsh family proceedings officer or an officer of the CAFCASS for the purposes of the discharge of the officer's duties under the Act;

(h)   to a court having power to make an order under the Act or the 1989 Act.

(2)   Subject to paragraph (3), the adoption agency may provide such access to its case records and disclose such information in its possession as it thinks fit for the purposes of carrying out its functions as an adoption agency.

(3)   A written record must be kept by the adoption agency of any access provided or disclosure made by virtue of this regulation.

NOTES
Initial Commencement
Specified date
Specified date: 30 December 2005: see reg 1(1).

Amendment
Para (1): in sub-para (d) words 'Public Services Ombudsman for Wales' in square brackets substituted by SI 2006/362, art 3, Sch 2, para 13; date in force: 1 April 2006: see SI 2006/362, art 1(1).

General

[982]

This regulation specifies certain bodies who have a right of access to adoption case records and information. In addition, it must provide such access as is required by these regulations themselves. Third, the adoption agency has a discretion to make such disclosure as it thinks fit for the purpose of carrying out its functions, provided it keeps a record of such disclosure.

See also reg 45 and the note thereto (para **[984]**).

[983]

44 Transfer of case records

(1)   Subject to paragraph (4), the adoption agency may transfer a copy of a case record (or part thereof) to another adoption agency when it considers this to be in the interests of a child or prospective adopter to whom the record relates, and a written record must be kept of any such transfer.

(2)   Subject to paragraph (4) a registered adoption society which intends to cease to act or exist as such must forthwith either transfer its case records to another adoption agency having first obtained the registration authority's approval for such transfer, or transfer its case records—

(a)   to the local authority in whose area the society's principal office is situated; or
(b)   in the case of a society which amalgamates with another registered adoption society to form a new registered adoption society, to the new body.

(3)   Where a registered adoption society intends to cease to provide for the adoption of children but is registered to provide adoption support services it may retain all its case records having first obtained the registration authority's approval in writing for such retention.

(4)   The adoption agency to which case records are transferred by virtue of paragraph (2)(a) or (b) must notify the registration authority in writing of such transfer.

NOTES

Initial Commencement

Specified date
Specified date: 30 December 2005: see reg 1(1).

45   Application of regulations 41 to 43

Regulations 41 to 43 do not apply to case records which are subject to the regulations made under sections 56 to 68 of the Act.

NOTES

Initial Commencement

Specified date
Specified date: 30 December 2005: see reg 1(1).

General

[984]

Sections 56 to 68 of the Act, and associated regulations, govern the retention of adoption records. Nothing in regs 41–43 applies to records covered by those duties.

[985]

Part 8
Miscellaneous

46   Modification of the 1989 Act in relation to adoption

(1)   This paragraph applies where—

(a)   a local authority is authorised to place a child for adoption; or
(b)   a child who has been placed for adoption by a local authority is less than six weeks old.

(2)   Where paragraph (1) applies—

(a)   section 22(4)(b) of the 1989 Act shall not apply;
(b)   section 22(4)(c) of the 1989 Act shall apply as if for that sub-paragraph there were inserted ' (c) any prospective adopter with whom the local authority has placed the child for adoption.';
(c)   section 22(5)(b) of the 1989 Act shall apply as if for the words ' (4)(b) to (d)' there were inserted ' (4)(c) and (d)'; and
(d)   paragraphs 15 and 21 of Schedule 2 to the 1989 Act shall not apply.

(3)   This paragraph applies where a registered adoption society is authorised to place a child for adoption or a child who has been placed for adoption by a registered adoption society is less than 6 weeks old.

(4)   Where paragraph (3) applies—

(a)   section 61(2)(a) of the 1989 Act is to have effect in relation to the child whether or not he is accommodated by or on behalf of the society;

(b)   section 61(2)(b) of the 1989 Act shall not apply;

(c)   section 61(2)(c) of the 1989 Act shall apply as if for that sub-paragraph there were inserted ' (c) any prospective adopter with whom the registered adoption society has placed the child for adoption.'.

NOTES

Initial Commencement

Specified date

Specified date: 30 December 2005: see reg 1(1).

General

[986]

This regulation makes important modifications to the CA 1989 once a child is authorised to be placed for adoption or a child under six weeks of age has been placed for adoption.

Decisions can be made without consulting parents, and the obligation to take their views into account when making decisions ceases. Instead, any prospective adopter must be consulted. The obligations to promote contact to the birth family and the obligation to notify them of the child's whereabouts (if CA 1989, s 20 accommodation, or if in care and it is safe to do so) ceases. The obligation on the parents under the CA 1989, regarding a child in care, to keep the local authority informed of where they live, ceases, as does their liability to pay maintenance for the child.

Similar amendments about consultation and notification are made if it is a registered adoption society that is in this position.

[987]

47   Contact

(1)   Where the adoption agency has decided under section 27(2) of the Act to refuse to allow the contact that would otherwise be required by virtue of an order under section 26 of the Act, the agency must, as soon as the decision is made, notify the persons specified in paragraph (4) in writing of those parts of the information specified in paragraph (5) as the agency considers those persons need to know.

(2)   The terms of an order under section 26 of the Act may be departed from by agreement between the adoption agency and any person for whose contact with the child the order provides in the following circumstances and subject to the following conditions—

(a)   where the child is of sufficient age and understanding, subject to the child's agreement;

(b)   where the child is placed for adoption, subject to prior consultation with the prospective adopter with whom the child is placed for adoption; and

(c)   written notification by the agency to the persons specified in paragraph (4) of those parts of the information specified in paragraph (5) as the agency considers those persons need to know, within seven days of the agreement to depart from the terms of the order.

(3)   Where the adoption agency varies or suspends any arrangements made (otherwise than under an order under section 26 of the Act) with a view to allowing any person contact with the child, the agency must notify the persons specified in paragraph (4) in writing of those parts of the information specified in paragraph (5) as the agency considers those persons need to know.

(4)   The following persons are specified for the purposes of paragraphs (1) and (2)—

> (a) the child, if the adoption agency considers the child is of sufficient age and understanding;
> (b) the child's parents;
> (c) any guardian of the child;
> (d) any person for whose contact with the child the order under section 26 of the Act provides;
> (e) any person the agency allowed contact with the child;
> (f) if the child is placed for adoption, the prospective adopter;
> (g) any other person whose wishes and feelings the agency consider to be relevant.
>
> (5) The following information is specified for the purposes of paragraphs 1, 2 and 3—
>
> (a) adoption agency's decision;
> (b) date of the decision;
> (c) reasons for the decision;
> (d) duration (if applicable).
>
> **NOTES**
> **Initial Commencement**
> *Specified date*
> Specified date: 30 December 2005: see reg 1(1).

General

[988]

This regulation makes provision for adoption agencies to depart from s 26 contact orders in an emergency, and also allows the agency and others to reach agreement to depart from such a Court order.

Section 27(2) makes provision in an emergency for contact to be suspended for up to seven days, despite the existence of a court order, where necessary to safeguard and promote the child's welfare. This mirrors similar provisions under CA 1989, s 34.

The Children Act powers are regulated, and likewise the s 27(2) power in ACA 2002 is subject to the provisions of reg 47.

When it has made the decision, the agency must inform certain persons of such of the following as the agency 'considers [they] need to know': the decision, the date of the decision, the reasons for it, and the period of suspension (up to seven days). The persons are: the child if of sufficient age and understanding, the parents and/or guardian, the person with the benefit of the s 26 order, any person who is being allowed by the agency to have contact, any other person whose wishes and feelings are considered relevant, and, if the child is placed for adoption, the prospective adopter. The agency will need to return the matter to court if a period longer than seven days is considered necessary. It is to be noted that there is a discretion about what amount of information is to be provided, when compared with the English regulations' mandatory requirements, but a far wider group of people fall within the scope of this discretion.

The adoption agency and a person with the benefit of a s 26 contact order can agree to depart from the terms of that order, provided the child agrees if he/she is of sufficient age and understanding, the prospective adopter has been consulted – if the child is already placed – and written confirmation is subsequently given within seven days to those who would require notification, as above, when a contact order is suspended.

It is to be noted that the English regulations (reg 46) provide a detailed regulatory mechanism for the consideration by an adoption agency of the contact arrangements for a child when the agency decides that the child should be placed for adoption, and subsequently at the point of a match. This is absent from the Welsh regulations. It is submitted that the safeguards contained within the English regulations should be considered as good practice in Wales. See note to reg 46 of the Adoption Agencies Regulations 2005 (para [890]).

[989]–[1000]

48 Revocation

The Adoption of Children from Overseas (Wales) Regulations 2001, the Adoption of Children from Overseas (Wales) (Amendment) Regulations 2003 and The Adoption Agencies (Amendment) (Wales) Regulations 2003 are hereby revoked.

NOTES

Initial Commencement

Specified date
Specified date: 30 December 2005: see reg 1(1).

SCHEDULE 1

Part 1
Information about the Child

Regulation 15(1)

1   Name, gender, date and place of birth and address including the local authority area.

2   A photograph and physical description.

3   Nationality.

4   Racial origin and cultural and linguistic background.

5   Religious persuasion, if any, (including details of baptism, confirmation or equivalent ceremonies).

6   Whether the child is looked after or is provided with accommodation under section 59(1) of the 1989 Act.

7   Details of any order made by a court with respect to the child under the 1989 Act including the name of the court, the order made and the date on which the order was made.

8   Whether the child has any rights to, or interest in, property or any claim to damages under the Fatal Accidents Act 1976 or otherwise which he or she stands to retain or lose if adopted.

9   A chronology of the child's care since birth.

10   An assessment of the child's personality, social development and emotional and behavioural development.

11   Whether the child has any difficulties with activities such as feeding, washing and dressing him or herself.

12   The educational history of the child including—

(a)   the names, addresses and types of nurseries or schools attended with dates;
(b)   a summary of progress and attainments;
(c)   whether he or she is subject to a statement under the Education Act 1996;
(d)   any special needs he or she has in relation to learning; and
(e)   where he or she is looked after, details of the personal education plan prepared by the local authority.

13   Information about—

(a)   the child's relationship with—

(i)   the child's parent or guardian and, where regulation 14(2) applies, the child's father;
(ii)   any brothers or sisters or other relatives; and
(iii)   any other person the agency considers relevant;

(b)   the likelihood of any such relationship continuing and the value to the child of its doing so; and
(c)   the ability and willingness of any of the child's relatives, or any other person the agency considers relevant, to provide the child with a secure environment in which the child can develop, and otherwise to meet the child's needs.

14   The current arrangements for and the type of contact between the child's parent or guardian or other person with parental responsibility for the child and, where regulation 14(2) applies, the child's father, and any relative, friend or other person.

15   A description of the child's interests, likes and dislikes.

16   Any other relevant information which might assist the adoption panel or the adoption agency.

NOTES
Initial Commencement
Specified date
Specified date: 30 December 2005: see reg 1(1).

Part 2
Matters to be Included in the Child's Health Report

Regulation 15(2)

1   Name, date of birth, gender, weight and height.

2   A neo-natal report on the child, including—

(a)   details of the child's birth, and any complications;
(b)   results of a physical examination and screening tests;
(c)   details of any treatment given;
(d)   details of any problem in management and feeding;
(e)   any other relevant information which may assist the panel;
(f)   the name and address of any doctor who may be able to provide further information about any of the above matters.

3   A full health history of the child, including—

(a)   details of any serious illness, disability, accident, hospital admission or attendance at an out-patient department, and in each case any treatment given;
(b)   details and dates of immunisations;
(c)   a physical and developmental assessment according to age, including an assessment of vision and hearing and of neurological, speech and language development and any evidence of emotional disorder;

(d)   the school health history (if available);

(e)   how the child's physical and mental health and medical history has affected his or her physical, intellectual, emotional, social or behavioural development;

(f)   any other relevant information which may assist the adoption panel.

4   The signature, name, address and telephone number and qualifications of the registered medical practitioner who prepared the report, the date of the report and of the examinations carried out together with the name and address of any other doctor who may be able to provide further information about any of the above matters.

NOTES

Initial Commencement

Specified date

Specified date: 30 December 2005: see reg 1(1).

Part 3
Information about the Child's Family and Others

Regulation 16(1)

Information about each parent of the child (both natural and adoptive) including a father who does not have parental responsibility for the child

1   Name, gender, date and place of birth and address including the local authority area.

2   A photograph, if available, and physical description.

3   Nationality.

4   Racial origin and cultural and linguistic background.

5   Religious persuasion, if any.

6   A description of their personality and interests.

Information about the child's brothers and sisters

7   Name, gender and date and place of birth.

8   A photograph, if available, and physical description.

9   Nationality.

10   Address, if appropriate.

11   If any brother or sister is under the age of 18—

(a)   where and with whom he or she is living;

(b)   whether he or she is looked after or is provided with accommodation under section 59(1) of the 1989 Act;

(c)   details of any court order made with respect to him or her under the 1989 Act, including the name of the court, the order made, and the date on which the order was made; and

(d)   whether he or she is also being considered for adoption.

Information about the child's other relatives and any other person the agency considers relevant

12   Name, gender and date and place of birth.

13   Nationality.

PART C – SIs

14 Address, if appropriate.
Family history and relationships

15 Whether the child's parents were married to each other at the time of the child's birth (or have subsequently married) and if so, the date and place of marriage and whether they are divorced or separated.

16 Where the child's parents were not married to each other at the time of the birth, whether the father has parental responsibility for the child and if so how it was acquired.

17 If the identity or whereabouts of the child's father are not known, the information about him that has been ascertained and from whom, and the steps that have been taken to establish paternity.

18 Where the child's parents have been previously married or formed a civil partnership, the date of the marriage or, as the case may be, the date and place of registration of the civil partnership.

19 So far as is possible, a family tree with details of the child's grandparents, parents and aunts and uncles with their age (or ages at death).

20 Where it is reasonably practicable, a chronology of each of the child's parents from birth.

21 The observations of the child's parents about their own experiences of being parented and of how this has influenced them.

22 The past and present relationship of the child's parents.

23 Details of the wider family and their role and importance to—

(a)   the child's parents; and
(b)   any brothers or sisters of the child.

Other information about each parent of the child and where regulation 14(2) applies, the father

24 Information about their home and the neighbourhood in which they live.

25 Details of their educational history.

26 Details of their employment history.

27 Information about the parenting capacity of the child's mother and father, particularly their ability and willingness to parent the child.

28 Any other relevant information which might assist the adoption panel or the adoption agency.

NOTES
Initial Commencement
Specified date
Specified date: 30 December 2005: see reg 1(1).

Part 4
Particulars Relating to a Guardian

Regulation 16(1)

1

(a)   Name, gender and date and place of birth.
(b)   Nationality.
(c)   Address and telephone number.

2   Their past and present relationship with the child.

3   Religion.

4   Any other relevant information which the agency considers may assist the adoption panel.

NOTES
Initial Commencement
Specified date
Specified date: 30 December 2005: see reg 1(1).

Part 5
Particulars Relating to the Health of the Child's Natural Parents and Brothers and Sisters

Regulation 16(2)

1   Name, date of birth, gender, weight and height of each natural parent.

2   A family health history, covering each of the child's natural parents, the child's brothers and sisters (if any) and the other children (if any) of each parent with details of any serious physical or mental illness and any hereditary disease or disorder.

3   A health history of each of the child's natural parents, including details of any serious physical or mental illness, drug or alcohol misuse, disability, accident or hospital admission and in each case any treatment given where the agency consider such information to be relevant.

4   A summary of the mother's obstetric history, including any problems in the ante-natal, labour and post-natal periods, with the results of any tests carried out during or immediately after pregnancy.

5   Details of any present illness, including treatment and prognosis.

6   Any other relevant information which the agency considers may assist the panel.

7   The signature, name, address, telephone number and qualifications of any registered medical practitioner who supplied any of the information in this Part together with the name and address of any other doctor who may be able to provide further information about any of the above matters.

NOTES
Initial Commencement
Specified date
Specified date: 30 December 2005: see reg 1(1).

SCHEDULE 2
INFORMATION AND DOCUMENTS TO BE PROVIDED TO WELSH FAMILY PROCEEDINGS OFFICER OR OFFICER OF CAFCASS

Regulation 20(1)

1   A copy of the child's birth certificate.

2   Name and address of the parent or guardian.

3   A chronology of the actions and decisions taken by the adoption agency with respect to the child.

4   Confirmation by the agency that it has counselled, and explained to the parent or guardian the legal implications of both consent to placement under section 19 of the Act and, as the case may be, to the making of a future adoption order under section 20 of the Act, and provided the parent or guardian with written information about this together with a copy of the information provided to the parent or guardian.

5   Such information about the parent or guardian or other information as the adoption agency considers the Welsh family proceedings officer or officer of CAFCASS may need to know.

NOTES
Initial Commencement
Specified date
Specified date: 30 December 2005: see reg 1(1).

SCHEDULE 3

Regulation 23 (3)(b)

Part 1
Offences Specified for the Purposes of Regulation 23(3)(b)
Offences in England and Wales

1   An offence of rape of an adult under section 1 of the Sexual Offences Act 2003—

(a)   an offence of rape under section 1 of the Sexual Offences Act 2003;
(b)   an offence of assault by penetration under section 2 of that Act;
(c)   an offence of causing a person to engage in sexual activity without consent under section 4 of that Act if the activity fell within subsection (3);
(d)   an offence of sexual activity with a person with a mental disorder impeding choice under section 30 of that Act if the touching fell within subsection (3);
(e)   an offence of causing or inciting a person with mental disorder impeding choice, to engage in sexual activity under section 31 of that Act, if the activity caused or incited fell within subsection (3);
(f)   an offence of inducement threat or deception to procure sexual activity with a person with a mental disorder under section 34 of that Act, if the touching involved fell within subsection (2); and
(g)   an offence of causing a person with a mental disorder to engage in or agree to engage in sexual activity by inducement, threat or deception if the activity fell within subsection (2).

Offences in Scotland

2   An offence of rape.

3 An offence specified in Schedule 1 to the Criminal Procedure (Scotland) Act 1995 except, in a case where the offender was under the age of 20 at the time the offence was committed, an offence contrary to section 5 of the Criminal Law (Consolidation) (Scotland) Act 1995 (intercourse with a girl under 16), an offence of shameless indecency between men or an offence of sodomy.

4 An offence of plagium (theft of a child below the age of puberty).

5 An offence under section 52 or 52A of the Civil Government (Scotland) Act 1982 (indecent photographs of children).

6 An offence under section 3 of the Sexual Offences (Amendment) Act 2000 (abuse of trust).

Offences in Northern Ireland

7 An offence of rape.

8 An offence specified in Schedule 1 to the Children and Young Person Act (Northern Ireland) 1968, except in the case where the offender was under the age of 20 at the time the offence was committed, an offence contrary to sections 5 or 11 of the Criminal Law Amendment Act 1885 (unlawful carnal knowledge of a girl under 17 and gross indecency between males), or an offence contrary to section 61 of the Offences against the Person Act 1861 (buggery).

9 An offence under Article 3 of the Protection of Children (Northern Ireland) Order 1978 (indecent photographs).

10 An offence under Article 9 of the Criminal Justice (Evidence etc) (Northern Ireland) Order 1980 (inciting girl under 16 to have incestuous sexual intercourse).

11 An offence contrary to Article 15 of the Criminal Justice (Evidence, etc) (Northern Ireland) Order 1988 (possession of indecent photograph of children).

12 An offence under section 3 of the Sexual Offences (Amendment) Act 2000 (abuse of trust).

NOTES

Initial Commencement

Specified date
Specified date: 30 December 2005: see reg 1(1).

Part 2
Repealed Statutory Offences

Regulation 23(4)

1 (1) An offence under any of the following sections of the Sexual Offences Act 1956—

(a)   section 1 (rape);
(b)   section 5 (intercourse with a girl under 13);
(c)   unless paragraph 4 applies, section 6 (intercourse with a girl under 16);
(d)   section 19 or 20 (abduction of girl under 18 or 16);
(e)   section 25 or 26 of that Act (permitting girl under 13, or between 13 and 16, to use premises for intercourse);
(f)   section 28 of that Act (causing or encouraging prostitution of, intercourse with or indecent assault on, girl under 16).

(2) An offence under section 1 of the Indecency with Children Act 1960 (indecent conduct towards young child).

(3)   An offence under section 54 of the Criminal Law Act 1977 (inciting girl under sixteen to incest).

(4)   An offence under section 3 of the Sexual Offences (Amendment) Act 2000 (abuse of trust).

2   A person falls within this paragraph if he has been convicted of any of the following offences against a child committed at the age of 18 or over or has been cautioned by a constable in respect of any such offence which, at the time the caution was given, he admitted—

(a)   an offence under section 2 or 3 of the Sexual Offences Act 1956 Act (procurement of woman by threats or false pretences);

(b)   an offence under section 4 of that Act (administering drugs to obtain or facilitate intercourse);

(c)   an offence under section 14 or 15 of that Act (indecent assault);

(d)   an offence under section 16 of that Act (assault with intent to commit buggery);

(e)   an offence under section 17 of that Act (abduction of woman by force or for the sake of her property);

(f)   an offence under section 24 of that Act (detention of woman in brothel or other premises).

3   A person falls within this paragraph if he has been convicted of any of the following offences committed at the age of 18 or over or has been cautioned by a constable in respect of any such offence which, at the time the caution was given, he admitted—

(a)   an offence under section 7 of the Sexual Offences Act 1956 (intercourse with defective) by having sexual intercourse with a child;

(b)   an offence under section 9 of that Act (procurement of defective) by procuring a child to have sexual intercourse;

(c)   an offence under section 10 of that Act (incest by a man) by having sexual intercourse with a child;

(d)   an offence under section 11 of that Act (incest by a woman) by allowing a child to have sexual intercourse with her;

(e)   unless paragraph 4 applies, an offence under section 12 of that Act by committing buggery with a child under the age of 16;

(f)   unless paragraph 4 applies, an offence under section 13 of that Act by committing an act of gross indecency with a child;

(g)   an offence under section 21 of that Act (abduction of defective from parent or guardian) by taking a child out of the possession of her parent or guardian;

(h)   an offence under section 22 of that Act (causing prostitution of women) in relation to a child;

(i)   an offence under section 23 of that Act (procuration of girl under 21) by procuring a child to have sexual intercourse with a third person;

(j)   an offence under section 27 of that Act (permitting defective to use premise for intercourse) by inducing or suffering a child to resort to or be on premises for the purpose of having sexual intercourse;

(k)   an offence under section 29 of that Act (causing or encouraging prostitution of defective) by causing or encouraging the prostitution of a child;

(l)   an offence under section 30 of that Act (man living on earnings of prostitution) in a case where the prostitute is a child;

(m)   an offence under section 31 of that Act (woman exercising control over prostitute) in a case where the prostitute is a child;

(n)   an offence under section 128 of the Mental Health Act 1959 (sexual intercourse with patients) by having sexual intercourse with a child;

(o)   an offence under section 4 of the Sexual Offences Act 1967 (procuring others to commit homosexual acts) by—

(i)   procuring a child to commit an act of buggery with any person; or
(ii)   procuring any person to commit an act of buggery with a child;

(p)   an offence under section 5 of that Act (living on earnings of male prostitution) by living wholly or in part on the earnings of prostitution of a child;

(q)   an offence under section 9(1)(a) of the Theft Act 1968 (burglary), by entering a building or part of a building with intent to rape a child.

4   Paragraphs 1(c) and 3(e) and (f) do not include offences in a case where the offender was under the age of 20 at the time the offence was committed.

NOTES

Initial Commencement

Specified date

Specified date: 30 December 2005: see reg 1(1).

SCHEDULE 4

Part 1
Information about Prospective Adopter

Regulation 26(2)

Information about the prospective adopter

1   Name, gender, date and place of birth and address including the local authority area.

2   A photograph and physical description.

3 . Whether the prospective adopter is domiciled or habitually resident in a part of the British Islands and if habitually resident for how long he or she has been habitually resident.

4   Racial origin and cultural and linguistic background.

5   Religious persuasion, if any.

6 . Relationship (if any) to the child.

7   An assessment of the prospective adopter's personality and interests.

8   If the prospective adopter is married or in a civil partnership and is applying alone, an assessment of the prospective adopter's suitability to adopt and the reasons for this.

9   Details of any previous family court proceedings in which the prospective adopter has been involved.

10   Names and addresses of three referees who will give personal references on the prospective adopter, not more than one of whom may be a relative.

11   Name and address of the prospective adopter's registered medical practitioner, if any.

12   If the prospective adopter is—

(a)   married, the date and place of marriage;
(b)   has formed a civil partnership, the date and place of registration of that partnership; or
(c)   has a partner, details of that relationship.

13   Details of any previous marriage, civil partnership or relationship.

PART C – SIs

14   A family tree with details of the prospective adopter, their children and any siblings, with their ages (or ages at death).

15   A chronology of the prospective adopter from birth.

16   The observations of the prospective adopter about their own experience of being parented and how this has been an influence.

17   Details of any experience the prospective adopter has had of caring for children (including as a parent, step-parent, foster parent, child-minder or prospective adopter) and an assessment of their ability in this respect.

18   Any other information which indicates how the prospective adopter and anybody else living in their household is likely to relate to a child placed for adoption with the prospective adopter.
Wider family

19   A description of the wider family of the prospective adopter and their role and importance to the prospective adopter and their likely role and importance to a child placed for adoption with the prospective adopter.
Information about the home of the prospective adopter etc

20   An assessment of the prospective adopter's home and the neighbourhood of their home.

21   Details of other members of the prospective adopter's household (including any children of the prospective adopter whether or not resident in the household).

22   The local community of the prospective adopter, including the degree of the family's integration, its peer groups, friendships and social networks.
Education and employment

23   Details of the prospective adopter's educational history and attainments and the observations of the prospective adopter about how this has been an influence.

24   Details of the prospective adopter's employment history and the observations of the prospective adopter about how this has been an influence.

25   The current employment of the prospective adopter and their views about achieving a balance between employment and child care.
Income

26   Details of the prospective adopter's income and expenditure.
Other information

27   The prospective adopter's capacity to—

(a)   share the child's birth history and associated emotional issues;
(b)   understand and support the child through possible feelings of loss and trauma.

28   The prospective adopter's—

(a)   reasons for wishing to adopt a child;
(b)   views and feelings about adoption and its significance;
(c)   views about their parenting capacity;
(d)   views about their parental responsibility and what it means;
(e)   views about a suitable home environment for a child;
(f)   views about the importance and value of education;
(g)   views and feelings about the importance of a child's religious and cultural upbringing;

(h)   views and feelings about contact.

29   The views of other members of the prospective adopter's household and wider family in relation to adoption.

30   Any other relevant information which might assist the adoption panel or the adoption agency.

NOTES

Initial Commencement

Specified date

Specified date: 30 December 2005: see reg 1(1).

Part 2
Information about the Health of the Prospective Adopter

Regulation 26(3)(a)

1   Name, date of birth, gender, weight and height.

2   A family health history of the parents, the brothers and sisters (if any) and the children (if any) of the prospective adopter, with details of any serious physical or mental illness and inherited and congenital disease.

3   Infertility or reasons for deciding not to have children (if applicable).

4   Past health history, including details of any serious physical or mental illness, disability, accident, hospital admission or attendance at an out-patient department, and in each case any treatment given.

5   Obstetric history (if applicable).

6   Details of any present illness, including treatment and prognosis.

7   A full medical examination.

8   Details of any consumption of alcohol that may give cause for concern or whether the prospective adopter smokes or uses habit-forming drugs.

9   Any other relevant information which the agency considers may assist the panel.

10   The signature, name, address and qualifications of the registered medical practitioner who prepared the report, the date of the report and of the examinations carried out together with the name and address of any other doctor who may be able to provide further information about any of the above matters.

NOTES

Initial Commencement

Specified date

Specified date: 30 December 2005: see reg 1(1).

SCHEDULE 5
INFORMATION ABOUT THE CHILD TO BE GIVEN TO THE PROSPECTIVE ADOPTER

Regulation 32(1)

1   Details of the child.

2 Photograph and physical description.

3 Details of the child's family circumstances and home environment, including details of the child's family (parents, siblings and significant others).

4 Chronology of the child's care.

5 The child's behaviour, how the child interacts with other children and relates to adults.

6 Whether the child is looked after by the local authority and, if so, the reasons and why the child is to be placed for adoption.

7 Details of the child's placement history including reasons for any placement breakdowns.

8 Details of the child's state of health, health history and any need for health care which might arise in the future.

9 Details of the child's educational history, a summary of the child's progress to date and whether assessed or likely to be assessed for special educational needs under the Education Act 1996.

10 The child's ascertainable wishes and feelings in relation to adoption, and contact with the child's parent, guardian, relative or other significant person.

11 The wishes and feelings of the child's parent, guardian, relative or other significant person in relation to adoption and contact.

12 The views of the person with whom the child is living about adoption.

13 The assessment of the child's needs for adoption support services and the agency's proposals for meeting those needs.

14 The agency's proposals for allowing any person contact with the child.

15 The proposed time-scale for placement.

16 Any other information which the agency considers relevant.

NOTES
Initial Commencement
Specified date
Specified date: 30 December 2005: see reg 1(1).

SCHEDULE 6
PLACEMENT PLAN

Regulation 36(2)

1 Status of the child and whether placed under a placement order or with the consent of the birth parents.

2 The arrangements for preparing the child and the prospective adopter for the placement.

3 Date on which it is proposed to place the child for adoption with the prospective adopter.

4   The arrangements for review of the placement.

5   Whether parental responsibility of the prospective adopter for the child is to be restricted and if so the extent to which it is to be restricted.

6   The adoption support services the local authority has decided to provide for the child and the adoptive family, how these will be provided and by whom (if applicable).

7   The arrangements which the adoption agency has made for allowing any person contact with the child, the form of contact this will be and the arrangements for supporting contact and the name and contact details of the person responsible for facilitating the contact arrangements (if applicable).

8   The date on which the life story book and later life letter is to be passed to the prospective adopter or the child.

9   Details of any arrangements that need to be made.

10   Contact details of the child's social worker, the prospective adopter's social worker and out of hours contacts.

NOTES
Initial Commencement
Specified date
Specified date: 30 December 2005: see reg 1(1).

Adoptions with a Foreign Element Regulations 2005

(SI 2005/392)

Made	*24th February 2005*
Laid before Parliament	*2nd March 2005*
Coming into force	*30th December 2005*

The Secretary of State for Education and Skills, in exercise of the powers conferred on her by section 1(1), (3) and (5) of the Adoption (Intercountry Aspects) Act 1999 and sections 83(4), (5), (6) and (7), 84(3) and (6), 140(7) and (8), 142(4) and (5) of the Adoption and Children Act 2002, and of all other powers enabling her in that behalf, after consultation with the National Assembly for Wales, hereby makes the following Regulations:—

[1001]

Part 1
General

1 Citation, commencement and application

(1) These Regulations may be cited as the Adoptions with a Foreign Element Regulations 2005 and shall come into force on 30th December 2005.
(2) These Regulations apply to England and Wales.

NOTES

Initial Commencement

Specified date
Specified date: 30 December 2005: see para (1) above.

Extent
These Regulations do not extend to Scotland: see para (2) above.

2 Interpretation

In these Regulations—

'the Act' means the Adoption and Children Act 2002;
'adoption support services' has the meaning given in section 2(6)(a) of the Act and any regulations made under section 2(6)(b) of the Act;
'adoptive family' has the same meaning as in regulation 31(2)(a) of the Agencies Regulations or corresponding Welsh provision;
'adoption panel' means a panel established in accordance with regulation 3 of the Agencies Regulations or corresponding Welsh provision;
'the Agencies Regulations' means the Adoption Agencies Regulations 2005;
'child's case record' has the same meaning as in regulation 12 of the Agencies Regulations or corresponding Welsh provision;
'CA of the receiving State' means, in relation to a Convention country other than the United Kingdom, the Central Authority of the receiving State;
'CA of the State of origin' means, in relation to a Convention country other than the United Kingdom, the Central Authority of the State of origin;
'Convention adoption' is given a meaning by virtue of section 66(1)(c) of the Act;
'Convention country' has the same meaning as in section 144(1) of the Act;
'Convention list' means—

    (a)   in relation to a relevant Central Authority, a list of children notified to that Authority in accordance with regulation 40; or
    (b)   in relation to any other Central Authority within the British Islands, a list of children notified to that Authority in accordance with provisions, which correspond to regulation 40.

'corresponding Welsh provision' in relation to a Part or a regulation of the Agencies Regulations means the provision of regulations made by the Assembly under section 9 of the Act which corresponds to that Part or regulation;

'prospective adopter's case record' has the same meaning as in regulation 22(1) of the Agencies Regulations or corresponding Welsh provision;

'prospective adopter's report' has the same meaning as in regulation 25(5) of the Agencies Regulations or corresponding Welsh provisions;

'receiving State' has the same meaning as in Article 2 of the Convention;

'relevant Central Authority' means—

    (a)   in Chapter 1 of Part 3, in relation to a prospective adopter who is habitually resident in—

        (i)   England, the Secretary of State; and

        (ii)   Wales, the National Assembly for Wales; and

    (b)   in Chapter 2 of Part 3 in relation to a local authority in—

        (i)   England, the Secretary of State; and

        (ii)   Wales, the National Assembly for Wales;

'relevant local authority' means in relation to a prospective adopter—

    (a)   the local authority within whose area he has his home; or

    (b)   in the case where he no longer has a home in England or Wales, the local authority for the area in which he last had his home;

'relevant foreign authority' means a person, outside the British Islands performing functions in the country in which the child is, or in which the prospective adopter is, habitually resident which correspond to the functions of an adoption agency or to the functions of the Secretary of State in respect of adoptions with a foreign element;

'State of origin' has the same meaning as in Article 2 of the Convention.

NOTES

Initial Commencement

Specified date

Specified date: 30 December 2005: see reg 1(1).

Extent

These Regulations do not extend to Scotland: see reg 1(2).

Part 2
Bringing Children into and out of the United Kingdom

Chapter 1
Bringing Children into the United Kingdom

3 Requirements applicable in respect of bringing or causing a child to be brought into the United Kingdom

A person intending to bring, or to cause another to bring, a child into the United Kingdom in circumstances where section 83(1) of the Act applies must—

    (a)   apply in writing to an adoption agency for an assessment of his suitability to adopt a child; and

    (b)   give the adoption agency any information it may require for the purpose of the assessment.

NOTES

Initial Commencement

Specified date

Specified date: 30 December 2005: see reg 1(1).

Extent

These Regulations do not extend to Scotland: see reg 1(2).

4 Conditions applicable in respect of a child brought into the United Kingdom

(1)   This regulation prescribes the conditions for the purposes of section 83(5) of the Act in respect of a child brought into the United Kingdom in circumstances where section 83 applies.

(2)   Prior to the child's entry into the United Kingdom, the prospective adopter must—

(a)   receive in writing, notification from the Secretary of State that she has issued a certificate confirming to the relevant foreign authority—

(i)   that the person has been assessed and approved as eligible and suitable to be an adoptive parent in accordance with Part 4 of the Agencies Regulations or corresponding Welsh provision; and

(ii)   that if entry clearance and leave to enter and remain, as may be necessary, is granted and not revoked or curtailed, and an adoption order is made or an overseas adoption is effected, the child will be authorised to enter and reside permanently in the United Kingdom;

(b)   before visiting the child in the State of origin—

(i)   notify the adoption agency of the details of the child to be adopted;

(ii)   provide the adoption agency with any information and reports received from the relevant foreign authority; and

(iii)   meet with the adoption agency to discuss the proposed adoption and information received from the relevant foreign authority;

(c)   visit the child in the State of origin (and where the prospective adopters are a couple each of them); and

(d)   after that visit—

(i)   confirm in writing to the adoption agency that he has done so and wishes to proceed with the adoption;

(ii)   provide the adoption agency with any additional reports and information received on or after that visit; and

(iii)   notify the adoption agency of his expected date of entry into the United Kingdom with the child.

(3)   The prospective adopter must accompany the child on entering the United Kingdom unless, in the case of a couple, the adoption agency and the relevant foreign authority have agreed that it is necessary for only one of them to do so.

(4)   Except where an overseas adoption is or is to be effected, the prospective adopter must within the period of 14 days beginning with the date on which the child is brought into the United Kingdom give notice to the relevant local authority—

(a)   of the child's arrival in the United Kingdom; and

(b)   of his intention—

(i)   to apply for an adoption order in accordance with section 44(2) of the Act; or

(ii)   not to give the child a home.

(5)   In a case where a prospective adopter has given notice in accordance with paragraph (4) and subsequently moves his home into the area of another local authority, he must within 14 days of that move confirm in writing to that authority, the child's entry into the United Kingdom and that notice of his intention—

(a)   to apply for an adoption order in accordance with section 44(2) of the Act has been given to another local authority; or

(b)   not to give the child a home,

has been given.

NOTES

Initial Commencement

Specified date

Specified date: 30 December 2005: see reg 1(1).

> **Extent**
> These Regulations do not extend to Scotland: see reg 1(2).
>
> **See Further**
> See further, the disapplication of paras (2)(b)–(d), (3) above in relation to a particular case: the Adoption and Children Act 2002 (Commencement No 10 Transitional and Savings Provisions) Order 2005, SI 2005/2897, art 7.

General

[1002]

Paras (2)(b)–(d) and (3) above are modified by the Adoption and Children Act 2002 (Commencement No 10 Transitional and Savings Provisions) Order 2005, SI 2005/2897, art 7 in relation to cases that have reached certificate of eligibility stage before 30th December 2005.

[1003]

5 Functions imposed on the local authority

(1) Where notice of intention to adopt has been given to the local authority, that authority must—

(a) if it has not already done so, set up a case record in respect of the child and place on it any information received from the—

    (i) relevant foreign authority;
    (ii) adoption agency, if it is not the local authority;
    (iii) prospective adopter;
    (iv) entry clearance officer; and
    (v) Secretary of State, or as the case may be, the Assembly;

(b) send the prospective adopter's general practitioner written notification of the arrival in England or Wales of the child and send with that notification a written report of the child's health history and current state of health, so far as is known;

(c) send to the Primary Care Trust or Local Health Board (Wales), in whose area the prospective adopter has his home, written notification of the arrival in England or Wales of the child;

(d) where the child is of compulsory school age, send to the local education authority, in whose area the prospective adopter has his home, written notification of the arrival of the child in England or Wales and information, if known, about the child's educational history and whether he is likely to be assessed for special educational needs under the Education Act 1996;

(e) ensure that the child and the prospective adopter are visited within one week of receipt of the notice of intention to adopt and thereafter not less than once a week until the review referred to in sub-paragraph (f) and thereafter at such frequency as the authority may decide;

(f) carry out a review of the child's case not more than 4 weeks after receipt of the notice of intention to adopt and—

    (i) visit and, if necessary, review not more than 3 months after that initial review; and
    (ii) thereafter not more than 6 months after the date of the previous visit,

unless the child no longer has his home with the prospective adopter or an adoption order is made;

(g) when carrying out a review consider—

    (i) the child's needs, welfare and development, and whether any changes need to be made to meet his needs or assist his development;
    (ii) the arrangements for the provision of adoption support services and whether there should be any re-assessment of the need for those services; and

      (iii)   the need for further visits and reviews; and

(h)   ensure that—

      (i)   advice is given as to the child's needs, welfare and development;

      (ii)   written reports are made of all visits and reviews of the case and placed on the child's case record; and

      (iii)   on such visits, where appropriate, advice is given as to the availability of adoption support services.

(2)   Part 7 of the Agencies Regulations or corresponding Welsh provision (case records) shall apply to the case record set up in respect of the child as a consequence of this regulation as if that record had been set up under the Agencies Regulations or corresponding Welsh provision.

(3)   In a case where the prospective adopter fails to make an application under section 50 or 51 of the Act within two years of the receipt by a local authority of the notice of intention to adopt the local authority must review the case.

(4)   For the purposes of the review referred to in paragraph (3), the local authority must consider—

(a)   the child's needs, welfare and development, and whether any changes need to be made to meet his needs or assist his development;

(b)   the arrangements, if any, in relation to the exercise of parental responsibility for the child;

(c)   the terms upon which leave to enter the United Kingdom is granted and the immigration status of the child;

(d)   the arrangements for the provision of adoption support services for the adoptive family and whether there should be any re-assessment of the need for those services; and

(e)   in conjunction with the appropriate agencies, the arrangements for meeting the child's health care and educational needs.

(5)   In a case where the local authority to which notice of intention to adopt is given ('the original authority') is notified by the prospective adopter that he intends to move or has moved his home into the area of another local authority, the original authority must notify the local authority into whose area the prospective adopter intends to move or has moved, within 14 days of receiving information in respect of that move, of—

(a)   the name, sex, date and place of birth of child;

(b)   the prospective adopter's name, sex and date of birth;

(c)   the date on which the child entered the United Kingdom;

(d)   where the original authority received notification of intention to adopt, the date of receipt of such notification whether an application for an adoption order has been made and the stage of those proceedings; and

(e)   any other relevant information.

NOTES

Initial Commencement

Specified date

Specified date: 30 December 2005: see reg 1(1).

Extent

These Regulations do not extend to Scotland: see reg 1(2).

6 Application of Chapter 3 of the Act

In the case of a child brought into the United Kingdom for adoption in circumstances where section 83 of the Act applies—

(a)   the modifications in regulations 7 to 9 apply;

(b)   section 36(2) and (5) (restrictions on removal) and section 39(3)(a) (partners of parents) of the Act shall not apply.

NOTES

Initial Commencement

Specified date

Specified date: 30 December 2005: see reg 1(1).

PART C – SIs

Extent
These Regulations do not extend to Scotland: see reg 1(2).

7 Change of name and removal from the United Kingdom

Section 28(2) of the Act (further consequences of placement) shall apply as if from the words 'is placed' to 'then', there is substituted 'enters the United Kingdom in the circumstances where section 83(1)(a) of this Act applies'.

NOTES

Initial Commencement

Specified date
Specified date: 30 December 2005: see reg 1(1).

Extent
These Regulations do not extend to Scotland: see reg 1(2).

General

[1004]

The effect of reg 7 is to forbid the removal of a child who has been brought in under s 83(1)(a) from the UK, or allowing a name change, without consent of each parent or guardian or without the leave of the court.

[1005]

8 Return of the child

(1) Section 35 of the Act (return of child) shall apply with the following modifications.
(2) Subsections (1), (2) and (3) shall apply as if in each place where—

(a) the words 'is placed for adoption by an adoption agency' occur there were substituted 'enters the United Kingdom in circumstances where section 83(1) applies';

(b) the words 'the agency' occur there were substituted the words 'the local authority'; and

(c) the words 'any parent or guardian of the child' occur there were substituted 'the Secretary of State or, as the case may be, the Assembly'.

(3) Subsection (5) shall apply as if for the words 'an adoption agency' or 'the agency' there were substituted the words 'the local authority'.

NOTES

Initial Commencement

Specified date
Specified date: 30 December 2005: see reg 1(1).

Extent
These Regulations do not extend to Scotland: see reg 1(2).

General

[1006]

The effect of reg 8 is to compel a local authority to receive a child whose prospective adopters give notice that they do not wish to go ahead with the adoption.

[1007]

9 Child to live with adopters before application

(1) In a case where the requirements imposed by section 83(4) of the Act have been complied with and the conditions required by section 83(5) of the Act have been met, section 42 shall apply as if—

(a) subsection (3) is omitted; and
(b) in subsection (5) the words from 'three years' to 'preceding' there were substituted 'six months'.

(2) In a case where the requirements imposed by section 83(4) of the Act have not been complied with or the conditions required by section 83(5) have not been met, section 42 shall apply as if—

(a) subsection (3) is omitted; and
(b) in subsection (5) the words from 'three years' to 'preceding' there were substituted 'twelve months'.

NOTES

Initial Commencement
Specified date
Specified date: 30 December 2005: see reg 1(1).

Extent
These Regulations do not extend to Scotland: see reg 1(2).

General

[1008]

Regulation 9 has the effect of setting the length of time that a child brought in to the UK has lived with prospective adopters before an application for an adoption order is made at 6 months (in cases where Adoptions with a Foreign Element Regulations 2005 (SI 2005/392) (AWAFE), regs 3 and 4 have been complied with). In cases where the AWAFE Regulations 2005, regs 3 and 4 have not been complied, the residence requirement is 12 months.

[1009]

Chapter 2
Taking Children out of the United Kingdom

10 Requirements applicable in respect of giving parental responsibility prior to adoption abroad

The prescribed requirements for the purposes of section 84(3) of the Act (requirements to be satisfied prior to the making of an order) are that—

(a) in the case of a child placed by an adoption agency, that agency has—

(i) confirmed to the court that it has complied with the requirements imposed in accordance with Part 3 of the Agencies Regulations or corresponding Welsh provision;
(ii) submitted to the court—

(aa) the reports and information referred to in regulation 17(2) and (3) of the Agencies Regulations or corresponding Welsh provision;
(bb) the recommendations made by the adoption panel in accordance with regulations 18 (placing child for adoption) and 33 (proposed placement) of the Agencies Regulations or corresponding Welsh provision;
(cc) the adoption placement report prepared in accordance with regulation 31(2)(d) of the Agencies Regulations or corresponding Welsh provision;

> (dd) the reports of and information obtained in respect of the visits and reviews referred to in regulation 36 of the Agencies Regulations or corresponding Welsh provision; and
>
> (ee) the report referred to in section 43 of the Act as modified by regulation 11;

(b) in the case of a child placed by an adoption agency the relevant foreign authority has—

> (i) confirmed in writing to that agency that the prospective adopter has been counselled and the legal implications of adoption have been explained to him;
>
> (ii) prepared a report on the suitability of the prospective adopter to be an adoptive parent;
>
> (iii) determined and confirmed in writing to that agency that he is eligible and suitable to adopt in the country or territory in which the adoption is to be effected; and
>
> (iv) confirmed in writing to that agency that the child is or will be authorised to enter and reside permanently in that foreign country or territory; and

(c) in the case of a child placed by an adoption agency the prospective adopter has confirmed in writing to the adoption agency that he will accompany the child on taking him out of the United Kingdom and entering the country or territory where the adoption is to be effected, or in the case of a couple, the agency and relevant foreign authority have confirmed that it is necessary for only one of them to do so.

NOTES

Initial Commencement

Specified date
Specified date: 30 December 2005: see reg 1(1).

Extent
These Regulations do not extend to Scotland: see reg 1(2).

11 Application of the Act in respect of orders under section 84

(1) The following provisions of the Act which refer to adoption orders shall apply to orders under section 84 as if in each place where the words 'adoption order' appear there were substituted 'order under section 84'—

(a) section 1(7)(a) (coming to a decision relating to adoption of a child);
(b) section 18(4) (placement for adoption by agencies);
(c) section 21(4)(b) (placement orders);
(d) section 22(5)(a) and (b) (application for placement orders);
(e) section 24(4) (revoking placement orders);
(f) section 28(1) (further consequences of placement);
(g) section 29(4)(a) and (5)(a) (further consequences of placement orders);
(h) section 32(5) (recovery by parent etc where child placed and consent withdrawn);
(i) section 42(7) (sufficient opportunity for adoption agency to see the child);
(j) section 43 (reports where child placed by agency);
(k) section 44(2) (notice of intention to adopt);
(l) section 47(1) to (5), (8) and (9) (conditions for making orders);
(m) section 48(1) (restrictions on making applications);
(n) section 50(1) and (2) (adoption by a couple);
(o) section 51(1) to (4) (adoption by one person);
(p) section 52(1) to (4) (parental etc consent);
(q) section 53(5) (contribution towards maintenance); and
(r) section 141(3) and (4)(c) (rules of procedure).

(2) Section 35(5) of the Act (return of child in other cases) shall apply to orders under section 84 of that Act as if in paragraph (b) of that subsection—

(a) for the first reference to 'adoption order' there were substituted 'order under section 84(1)'; and
(b) the words in brackets were omitted.

NOTES
Initial Commencement
Specified date
Specified date: 30 December 2005: see reg 1(1).

Extent
These Regulations do not extend to Scotland: see reg 1(2).

General

[1010]

This regulation applies 19 sections of the ACA 2002 to applications under s 84 for parental responsibility prior to adoption abroad. Limited descriptions of the effect of each of the sub-paragraphs is given, the intention being to assist with cross-referencing to the main commentary on the Act itself.

[1011]–[1022]

Regulation 1(1)(a) applies the ACA 2002, s 1 relating to welfare and the adoption checklist, applicable wherever a court or an adoption agency is making a decision relating to a s 84 parental responsibility order.

Regulation 11(1)(b) has the effect of preventing a child, who has been placed with those who have applied for a s 84 parental responsibility order, from being moved to other prospective adopters before the s 84 application has been dealt with.

Regulation 11(1)(c) has the effect that the making of a s 84 parental responsibility extinguishes a placement order made in relation to the child.

Regulation 11(1)(d) has the effect that those parts of s 22(5) that deal with the duty on a local authority to apply for placement orders do not apply when notice of intention to apply for a s 84 order has been given, or that an application for a s 84 order has been made. This provision needs to be read along side s 44(2) as it applies to s 84 orders.

Regulation 11(1)(e) has the effect that where a court, following an application for a s 84 parental responsibility order, does not make a s 84 order, it may revoke a placement order that was in place in respect of the child subject of the s 84 application.

Regulation 11(1)(f) has the effect that where a child is placed or a local authority is authorised to place a child, a parent or guardian may not apply for, respectively, residence and special guardianship orders unless the court's leave has been given and an application for a s84 order has been made.

Regulation 11(1(g) has the effect that where a child is subject to a placement order, and a parent has the leave of the court, and a s 84 parental responsibility application has been made, the parent may apply for a residence order. There is equivalent provision for special guardians.

Regulation 11(1)(h) applies where a child is placed with parental consent and parental consent is withdrawn. Usually withdrawal of consent to placement will compel a local authority to return the child, but where prospective adopters have applied for s 84 parental responsibility, and before the application is determined, the prospective adopters are not required to return the child unless ordered to do so by the court.

Regulation 11(1)(i) requires the court to be satisfied that there has been sufficient opportunity to see the child with the proposed adopter(s) in the home environment. This provision does not appear to limit the observation opportunities to the actual home, and so would include a home that the applicants had established within the UK for the purpose of fulfilling the 10-week residence requirement made by s 84.

Regulation 11(1)(j) applies the provisions of ACA 2002, s 43, requiring agency reports to the court to be provided dealing with s 1 (and any other relevant matters) in cases where that agency has placed the child and an application for s 84 parental responsibility has been made.

Regulation 11(1)(k) applies ACA 2002, s 44(2) in relation cases where a child is not placed by an agency. Prospective adopters must give notice of their intention to seek s 84 parental responsibility. Upon receipt of such notice, the case is dealt with, in terms of investigation, report writing and liaison with other local authorities as if the notice of intention is to apply for an adoption order.

Regulation 11(1)(l) applies ACA 2002, s 47(1) (the provisions that require either parental/guardian's consent or dispensation with that with consent), and that no s 84 parental responsibility order may be made where the subject person is or has been married or who has reached 19 years of age.

Regulation 11(1)(m) applies ACA 2002, s 48(1) which limits repeat applications for s 84 parental responsibility. The circumstances in which a repeat application made are made are however broadly set. The renewed application must appear to be a proper one, and based on a change of circumstances or any other reason.

Regulation 11(1)(n) applies ACA 2002, s 50(1) and (2), permitting the making of a s 84 parental responsibility order to a couple on the same criteria as apply to making an adoption order to a couple.

Regulation 11(1)(o) applies ACA 2002, s 51(1)–(4), setting out the criteria needed prior to the making of a s 84 parental responsibility order in favour of a single person.

Regulation 11(1)(p) applies ACA 2002, s 52(1)–(4), being the conditions that must be met before parental or guardian's consent is dispensed with prior to the making of a s 84 parental responsibility order.

Regulation 11(1)(q) applies ACA 2002, s 53(5), being the circumstances in which a contribution to maintenance for a child is payable after a notice of intention to adopt has been given.

Regulation 11(1)(r) applies ACA 2002, s 141(3) and (4)(c), leading to the application of the rules of procedure to s 84 cases as they apply to applications for an adoption order.

Regulation 11(2) applies ACA 2002, s 35(5). The result is that after an application for s 84 parental responsibility has been made, prospective adopters are not required to return a child unless ordered to do so by the court.

[1023]

Part 3
Adoptions under the Convention

Chapter 1
Requirements, Procedure, Recognition and Effect of Adoptions where the United Kingdom is the Receiving State

12 Application of Chapter 1

The provisions in this Chapter shall apply where a couple or a person, habitually resident in the British Islands, wishes to adopt a child who is habitually resident in a Convention country outside the British Islands in accordance with the Convention.

NOTES

Initial Commencement

Specified date

Specified date: 30 December 2005: see reg 1(1).

Extent

These Regulations do not extend to Scotland: see reg 1(2).

13 Requirements applicable in respect of eligibility and suitability

(1) A couple or a person who wishes to adopt a child habitually resident in a Convention country outside the British Islands shall—

(a) apply in writing to an adoption agency for a determination of eligibility, and an assessment of his suitability, to adopt; and

(b) give the agency any information it may require for the purposes of the assessment.

(2) An adoption agency may not consider an application under paragraph (1) unless at the date of that application—

(a) in the case of an application by a couple, they have both—

  (i) attained the age of 21 years; and
  (ii) been habitually resident in a part of the British Islands for a period of not less than one year ending with the date of application; and

(b) in the case of an application by one person, he has—

  (i) attained the age of 21 years; and
  (ii) been habitually resident in a part of the British Islands for a period of not less than one year ending with the date of application.

NOTES

Initial Commencement

Specified date

Specified date: 30 December 2005: see reg 1(1).

Extent

These Regulations do not extend to Scotland: see reg 1(2).

14 Counselling and information

(1) An adoption agency must provide a counselling service in accordance with regulation 21(1)(a) of the Agencies Regulations or corresponding Welsh provision and must—

(a) explain to the prospective adopter the procedure in relation to, and the legal implications of, adopting a child from the State of origin from which the prospective adopter wishes to adopt in accordance with the Convention; and

(b) provide him with written information about the matters referred to in sub-paragraph (a).

(2) Paragraph (1) does not apply if the adoption agency is satisfied that the requirements set out in that paragraph have been carried out in respect of the prospective adopter by another agency.

NOTES

Initial Commencement

Specified date

Specified date: 30 December 2005: see reg 1(1).

Extent

These Regulations do not extend to Scotland: see reg 1(2).

15 Procedure in respect of carrying out an assessment

(1) Regulation 22 of the Agencies Regulations (requirement to consider application for an assessment of suitability) or corresponding Welsh provision shall apply as if the reference to an application in those Regulations or corresponding Welsh provision was to an application made in accordance with regulation 13.

PART C – SIs

(2)   Where the adoption agency is satisfied that the requirements in—

(a)   regulation 14; and
(b)   regulations 23 (police checks) and 24 (preparation for adoption) of the Agencies Regulations or corresponding Welsh provision,

have been meet, regulations 25 (prospective adopter's report) and 26 (adoption panel) of the Agencies Regulations or corresponding Welsh provisions shall apply.

(3)   The adoption agency must place on the prospective adopter's case record any information obtained as a consequence of this Chapter.

(4)   The adoption agency must include in the prospective adopter's report—

(a)   the State of origin from which the prospective adopter wishes to adopt a child;
(b)   confirmation that the prospective adopter is eligible to adopt a child under the law of that State;
(c)   any additional information obtained as a consequence of the requirements of that State; and
(d)   the agency's assessment of the prospective adopter's suitability to adopt a child who is habitually resident in that State.

(5)   The references to information in regulations 25(5) and 26(2) of the Agencies Regulations or corresponding Welsh provisions shall include information obtained by the adoption agency or adoption panel as a consequence of this regulation.

NOTES
Initial Commencement
Specified date
Specified date: 30 December 2005: see reg 1(1).

Extent
These Regulations do not extend to Scotland: see reg 1(2).

16   Adoption agency decision and notification

The adoption agency must make a decision about whether the prospective adopter is suitable to adopt a child in accordance with regulation 27 of the Agencies Regulations and regulations made under section 45 of the Act, or corresponding Welsh provisions.

NOTES
Initial Commencement
Specified date
Specified date: 30 December 2005: see reg 1(1).

Extent
These Regulations do not extend to Scotland: see reg 1(2).

17   Review and termination of approval

The adoption agency must review the approval of each prospective adopter in accordance with regulation 29 of the Agencies Regulations or corresponding Welsh provision unless the agency has received written notification from the relevant Central Authority that the agreement under Article 17(c) of the Convention has been made.

NOTES
Initial Commencement
Specified date
Specified date: 30 December 2005: see reg 1(1).

Extent
These Regulations do not extend to Scotland: see reg 1(2).

General

[1024]

'Relevant Central Authority': see AWAFE Regulations 2005, reg 2. In relation to England, the Central Authority is the Secretary of State for Education and Skills, and in relation to Wales, the National Assembly for Wales.

'Agreement under Article 17(c)': see A(IA)A 1999, Sch 1. This is the agreement of the Central Authority of a child's State of origin that, following assessments, approval and agreements, that the child in question may be entrusted to prospective adopters.

[1025]

18   Procedure following decision as to suitability to adopt

(1)   Where an adoption agency has made a decision that the prospective adopter is suitable to adopt a child in accordance with regulation 16, it must send to the relevant Central Authority—

(a)   written confirmation of the decision and any recommendation the agency may make in relation to the number of children the prospective adopter may be suitable to adopt, their age range, sex, likely needs and background;

(b)   the enhanced criminal record certificate obtained under regulation 23 of the Agencies Regulations or corresponding Welsh provision;

(c)   all the documents and information which were passed to the adoption panel in accordance with regulation 25(9) of the Agencies Regulations or corresponding Welsh provision;

(d)   the record of the proceedings of the adoption panel, its recommendation and the reasons for its recommendation; and

(e)   any other information relating to the case as the relevant Central Authority or the CA of the State of origin may require.

(2)   If the relevant Central Authority is satisfied that the adoption agency has complied with the duties and procedures imposed by the Agencies Regulations or corresponding Welsh provision, and that all the relevant information has been supplied by that agency, the Authority must send to the CA of the State of origin—

(a)   the prospective adopter's report prepared in accordance with regulation 25 of the Agencies Regulations or corresponding Welsh provision;

(b)   ...

(c)   a copy of the adoption agency's decision and the adoption panel's recommendation;

(d)   any other information that the CA of the State of origin may require; ...

[(da)   if the prospective adopter applied to the appropriate Minister for a review under section 12 of the Adoption and Children Act 2002, the record of the proceedings of the panel, its recommendation and the reasons for its recommendation; and]

(e)   a certificate in the form set out in Schedule 1 confirming that the—

(i)   prospective adopter is eligible to adopt;

(ii)   prospective adopter has been assessed in accordance with this Chapter;

(iii)   prospective adopter has been approved as suitable to adopt a child; and

(iv)   child will be authorised to enter and reside permanently in the United Kingdom if entry clearance, and leave to enter or remain as may be necessary, is granted and not revoked or curtailed and a Convention adoption order or Convention adoption is made.

(3)   The relevant Central Authority must notify the adoption agency and the prospective adopter in writing that the certificate and the documents referred to in paragraph (2) have been sent to the CA of the State of origin.

PART C – SIs

> **NOTES**
>
> **Initial Commencement**
>
> *Specified date*
> Specified date: 30 December 2005: see reg 1(1).
>
> **Extent**
> These Regulations do not extend to Scotland: see reg 1(2).
>
> **Amendment**
> Para (2): sub-para (b) revoked by SI 2005/3482, reg 6(a)(i); date in force: 30 December 2005: see
> SI 2005/3482, reg 1; para (2): in sub-para (d) word omitted revoked by SI 2005/3482, reg 6(a)(ii);
> date in force: 30 December 2005: see SI 2005/3482, reg 1; para (2): sub-para (da) inserted by
> SI 2005/3482, reg 6(a)(iii); date in force: 30 December 2005: see SI 2005/3482, reg 1.

General

[1026]

'Relevant Central Authority': see AWAFE Regulations 2005, reg 2.

'CA of the State of origin': see AWAFE Regulations 2005, reg 2.

[1027]

> **19   Procedure following receipt of the Article 16 Information from the CA of the State of origin**
>
> (1)   Where the relevant Central Authority receives from the CA of the State of origin, the Article 16 Information relating to the child whom the CA of the State of origin considers should be placed for adoption with the prospective adopter, the relevant Central Authority must send that Information to the adoption agency.
> (2)   The adoption agency must consider the Article 16 Information and—
>
> (a)   send that Information to the prospective adopter;
> (b)   meet with him to discuss—
>
> (i)   that Information;
> (ii)   the proposed placement;
> (iii)   the availability of adoption support services; and
>
> (c)   if appropriate, offer a counselling service and further information as required.
>
> (3)   Where—
>
> (a)   the procedure in paragraph (2) has been followed;
> (b)   the prospective adopter (and where the prospective adopters are a couple each of them) has visited the child in the State of origin; and
> (c)   after that visit to the child, the prospective adopter has confirmed in writing to the adoption agency that—
>
> (i)   he has visited the child;
> (ii)   he has provided the adoption agency with additional reports and information received on or after that visit; and
> (iii)   he wishes to proceed to adopt that child,
>
> the agency must notify the relevant Central Authority in writing that the requirements specified in sub-paragraphs (a) to (c) have been satisfied and at the same time it must confirm that it is content for the adoption to proceed.
>
> (4)   Where the relevant Central Authority has received notification from the adoption agency under paragraph (3), the relevant Central Authority shall—
>
> (a)   notify the CA of the State of origin that—
>
> (i)   the prospective adopter wishes to proceed to adopt the child;
> (ii)   it is prepared to agree with the CA of the State of origin that the adoption may proceed; and

(b)   confirm to the CA of the State of origin that—

    (i)   in the case where the requirements specified in section 1(5A) of the British Nationality Act 1981 are met that the child will be authorised to enter and reside permanently in the United Kingdom; or

    (ii)   in any other case, if entry clearance and leave to enter and remain, as may be necessary, is granted and not revoked or curtailed and a Convention adoption order or a Convention adoption is made, the child will be authorised to enter and reside permanently in the United Kingdom.

(5)   The relevant Central Authority must inform the adoption agency and the prospective adopter when the agreement under Article 17(c) of the Convention has been made.

(6)   For the purposes of this regulation and regulation 20 'the Article 16 Information' means—

(a)   the report referred to in Article 16(1) of the Convention including information about the child's identity, adoptability, background, social environment, family history, medical history including that of the child's family and any special needs of the child;

(b)   proof of confirmation that the consents of the persons, institutions and authorities whose consents are necessary for adoption have been obtained in accordance with Article 4 of the Convention; and

(c)   the reasons for the CA of the State of origin's determination on the placement.

NOTES

Initial Commencement

Specified date

Specified date: 30 December 2005: see reg 1(1).

Extent

These Regulations do not extend to Scotland: see reg 1(2).

General

[1028]

'Relevant Central Authority': see AWAFE Regulations 2005, reg 2.

'CA of the State of origin': see AWAFE Regulations 2005, reg 2.

'Article 16 information': see A(IA)A 1999, Sch 1, and of course, within this regulation, reg 19(6).

'Agreement under Article 17(c) of the Convention': see A(IA)A 1999, Sch 1. This is the agreement of the Central Authority of a child's State of origin that, following assessments, approval and agreements, that the child in question may be entrusted to prospective adopters.

[1029]

20   Procedure where proposed adoption is not to proceed

(1)   If, at any stage before the agreement under Article 17(c) of the Convention is made, the CA of the State of origin notifies the relevant Central Authority that it has decided the proposed placement should not proceed—

(a)   the relevant Central Authority must inform the adoption agency of the CA of the State of origin's decision;

(b)   the agency must then inform the prospective adopter and return the Article 16 Information to the relevant Central Authority; and

(c) the relevant Central Authority must then return those documents to the CA of the State of origin.

(2) Where at any stage before the adoption agency receives notification of the agreement under Article 17(c) of the Convention the approval of the prospective adopter is reviewed under regulation 29 of the Agencies Regulations or corresponding Welsh provision, and as a consequence, the agency determines that the prospective adopter is no longer suitable to adopt a child—

(a) the agency must inform the relevant Central Authority and return the documents referred to in regulation 19(1);

(b) the relevant Central Authority must notify the CA of the State of origin and return those documents.

(3) If, at any stage before the child is placed with him, the prospective adopter notifies the adoption agency that he does not wish to proceed with the adoption of the child—

(a) that agency must inform the relevant Central Authority and return the documents to that Authority; and

(b) the relevant Central Authority must notify the CA of the State of origin of the prospective adopter's decision and return the documents to the CA of the State of origin.

NOTES

Initial Commencement

Specified date

Specified date: 30 December 2005: see reg 1(1).

Extent

These Regulations do not extend to Scotland: see reg 1(2).

General

[1030]

'Agreement under Article 17(c) of the Convention': See A(IA)A 1999, Sch 1. This is the agreement of the Central Authority of a child's State of origin that, following assessments, approval and agreements, that the child in question may be entrusted to prospective adopters.

'CA of the State of origin': see AWAFE Regulations 2005, reg 2.

'Relevant Central Authority': see AWAFE Regulations 2005, reg 2. In England this is the Secretary of State for Education and Skills and in Wales the National Assembly for Wales.

'Article 16 information': see A(IA)A 1999, Sch 1 and AWAFE Regulations 2005, reg 19(6).

[1031]

21 Applicable requirements in respect of prospective adopter entering the United Kingdom with a child

Following any agreement under Article 17(c) of the Convention, the prospective adopter must—

(a) notify the adoption agency of his expected date of entry into the United Kingdom with the child;

(b) confirm to the adoption agency when the child is placed with him by the competent authority in the State of origin; and

(c) accompany the child on entering the United Kingdom unless, in the case of a couple, the adoption agency and the CA of the State of origin have agreed that it is necessary for only one of them to do so.

> **NOTES**
> **Initial Commencement**
> *Specified date*
> Specified date: 30 December 2005: see reg 1(1).
> **Extent**
> These Regulations do not extend to Scotland: see reg 1(2).

General

[1032]

'Agreement under Article 17(c) of the Convention': see A(IA)A 1999, Sch 1. This is the agreement of the Central Authority of a child's State of origin that, following assessments, approval and agreements, that the child in question may be entrusted to prospective adopters.

'CA of the State of origin': see AWAFE Regulations 2005, reg 2.

'Relevant Central Authority': see AWAFE Regulations 2005, reg 2. In England this is the Secretary of State for Education and Skills and in Wales the National Assembly for Wales.

'Article 16 information': see A(IA)A 1999, Sch 1 and AWAFE Regulations 2005, reg 19(6).

[1033]

> **22 Applicable requirements in respect of an adoption agency before the child enters the United Kingdom**
>
> Where the adoption agency is informed by the relevant Central Authority that the agreement under Article 17(c) of the Convention has been made and the adoption may proceed, before the child enters the United Kingdom that agency must—
>
> (a) send the prospective adopter's general practitioner written notification of the proposed placement and send with that notification a written report of the child's health history and current state of health, so far as it is known;
>
> (b) send the local authority (if that authority is not the adoption agency) and the Primary Care Trust or Local Health Board (Wales), in whose area the prospective adopter has his home, written notification of the proposed arrival of the child into England or Wales; and
>
> (c) where the child is of compulsory school age, send the local education authority, in whose area the prospective adopter has his home, written notification of the proposed arrival of the child into England or Wales and information about the child's educational history if known and whether he is likely to be assessed for special educational needs under the Education Act 1996.
>
> **NOTES**
> **Initial Commencement**
> *Specified date*
> Specified date: 30 December 2005: see reg 1(1).
> **Extent**
> These Regulations do not extend to Scotland: see reg 1(2).

General

[1034]

'Agreement under Article 17(c) of the Convention': see A(IA)A 1999, Sch 1. This is the agreement of the Central Authority of a child's State of origin that, following assessments, approval and agreements, that the child in question may be entrusted to prospective adopters.

'Compulsory school age': Education Act 1996, s 8 – broadly speaking attendance at school is compulsory from the term following a child's fifth birthday until the conclusion of the academic year following their 16th birthday (or their 16th birthday falls before the start of the next academic year).

[1035]

---

23   Applicable provisions following the child's entry into the United Kingdom where no Convention adoption is made

Regulations 24 to 27 apply where—

(a)   following the agreement between the relevant Central Authority and the CA of the State of origin under Article 17(c) of the Convention that the adoption may proceed, no Convention adoption is made, or applied for, in the State of origin; and

(b)   the child is placed with the prospective adopter in the State of origin who then returns to England or Wales with that child.

NOTES
Initial Commencement
Specified date
Specified date: 30 December 2005: see reg 1(1).

Extent
These Regulations do not extend to Scotland: see reg 1(2).

General

[1036]

'Convention adoption': defined in ACA 2002, s 66(1)(c). A Convention adoption is one where the procedures for assessment and approval by a local authority within the AWAFE Regulations 2005 have been followed in relation to a child in a Convention country, but the adoption itself takes place outside the British Islands within the home state of the child concerned.

[1037]

---

24   Applicable requirements in respect of prospective adopter following child's entry into the United Kingdom

(1)   A prospective adopter must within the period of 14 days beginning with the date on which the child enters the United Kingdom give notice to the relevant local authority—

(a)   of the child's arrival in the United Kingdom; and
(b)   of his intention—

  (i)   to apply for an adoption order in accordance with section 44(2) of the Act; or
  (ii)   not to give the child a home.

(2)   In a case where a prospective adopter has given notice in accordance with paragraph (1) and he subsequently moves his home into the area of another local authority, he must within 14 days of that move confirm to that authority in writing the child's entry into the United Kingdom and that notice of his intention—

(a)   to apply for an adoption order in accordance with section 44(2) of the Act has been given to another local authority; or
(b)   not to give the child a home,

has been given.

NOTES
Initial Commencement
Specified date
Specified date: 30 December 2005: see reg 1(1).

Extent
These Regulations do not extend to Scotland: see reg 1(2).

25 Functions imposed on the local authority following the child's entry into the United Kingdom

(1)   Where notice is given to a local authority in accordance with regulation 24, the functions imposed on the local authority by virtue of regulation 5 shall apply subject to the modifications in paragraph (2).
(2)   Paragraph (1) of regulation 5 shall apply as if—

(a)   in sub-paragraph (a)—

(i)   in head (i) for the words 'relevant foreign authority' there is substituted 'CA of the State of origin and competent foreign authority';
(ii)   in head (v) there is substituted 'the relevant Central Authority'; and

(b)   sub-paragraphs (b) to (d) were omitted.

NOTES
Initial Commencement
Specified date
Specified date: 30 December 2005: see reg 1(1).

Extent
These Regulations do not extend to Scotland: see reg 1(2).

General

[1038]

'Relevant foreign authority': see AWAFE Regulations 2005, reg 2.

'Competent foreign authority': this is a term that comes direct from the Hague Convention – see A(IA)A 1999, Sch 1.

'Relevant Central Authority': see AWAFE Regulations 2005, reg 2.

[1039]

[26   Prospective adopter unable to proceed with adoption]

[(1)   Where the prospective adopter gives notice to the relevant local authority that he does not wish to proceed with the adoption and no longer wishes to give the child a home, he must return the child to that authority not later than the end of the period of seven days beginning with the date on which notice was given.
(2)   Where a relevant local authority have received a notice in accordance with paragraph (1), that authority must give notice to the relevant Central Authority of the decision of the prospective adopter not to proceed with the adoption.]

NOTES
Extent
These Regulations do not extend to Scotland: see reg 1(2).

Amendment
Substituted by SI 2005/3482, reg 6(b); date in force: 30 December 2005: see SI 2005/3482, reg 1.

General

[1040]

'Relevant Central Authority': see AWAFE Regulations 2005, reg 2.

[1041]

27 Withdrawal of child from prospective adopter

(1) Where the relevant local authority are of the opinion that the continued placement of the child is not in the child's best interests—

(a) that authority must give notice to the prospective adopter of their opinion and request the return of the child to them; and

(b) subject to paragraph (3), the prospective adopter must, not later than the end of the period of seven days beginning with the date on which notice was given, return the child to that authority.

(2) Where the relevant local authority has given notice under paragraph (1), that authority must at the same time notify the relevant Central Authority that they have requested the return of the child.

(3) Where notice is given under paragraph (1) but—

(a) an application for a Convention adoption order was made prior to the giving of that notice; and

(b) the application has not been disposed of,

the prospective adopter is not required by virtue of paragraph (1) to return the child unless the court so orders.

(4) This regulation does not affect the exercise by any local authority or other person of any power conferred by any enactment or the exercise of any power of arrest.

NOTES

Initial Commencement

Specified date

Specified date: 30 December 2005: see reg 1(1).

Extent

These Regulations do not extend to Scotland: see reg 1(2).

General

[1042]

'Relevant Central Authority': see AWAFE Regulations 2005, reg 2.

A application for a Convention adoption order is an application in the UK for an adoption order, following Hague Convention compliant assessment, matching and placing.

[1043]

28 Breakdown of placement

(1) This regulation applies where—

(a) notification is given by the prospective adopter under regulation 26 (unable to proceed with adoption);

(b) the child is withdrawn from the prospective adopter under regulation 27 (withdrawal of child from prospective adopter);

(c) an application for a Convention adoption order is refused;

(d) a Convention adoption which is subject to a probationary period cannot be made; or

(e)   a Convention adoption order or a Convention adoption is annulled pursuant to section 89(1) of the Act.

(2)   Where the relevant local authority are satisfied that it would be in the child's best interests to be placed for adoption with another prospective adopter habitually resident in the United Kingdom they must take the necessary measures to identify a suitable adoptive parent for that child.

(3)   Where the relevant local authority have identified and approved another prospective adopter who is eligible, and has been assessed as suitable, to adopt in accordance with these Regulations—

(a)   that authority must notify the relevant Central Authority in writing that—

(i)   another prospective adopter has been identified; and
(ii)   the provisions in regulations 14, 15 and 16 have been complied with; and

(b)   the requirements specified in regulations 18 and 19 have been complied with.

(4)   Where the relevant Central Authority has been notified in accordance with paragraph (3)(a)—

(a)   it shall inform the CA of the State of origin of the proposed placement; and
(b)   it shall agree the placement with the CA of the State of origin in accordance with the provisions in this Chapter.

(5)   Subject to paragraph (2), where the relevant local authority is not satisfied it would be in the child's best interests to be placed for adoption with another prospective adopter in England or Wales, it must liaise with the relevant Central Authority to arrange for the return of the child to his State of origin.

(6)   Before coming to any decision under this regulation, the relevant local authority must have regard to the wishes and feelings of the child, having regard to his age and understanding, and where appropriate, obtain his consent in relation to measures to be taken under this regulation.

NOTES

Initial Commencement

Specified date
Specified date: 30 December 2005: see reg 1(1).

Extent
These Regulations do not extend to Scotland: see reg 1(2).

PART C – SIs

General

[1044]

An application for a Convention adoption order is an application in the UK for an adoption order, following Hague Convention compliant assessment

'Convention adoption subject to a probationary period': a Convention adoption is one made in the child's State of origin. For probationary period, see reg 29 below.

'Relevant Central Authority'; 'CA of the State of origin': see AWAFE Regulations 2005, reg 2.

[1045]

29   Convention adoptions subject to a probationary period

(1)   This regulation applies where—

(a)   the child has been placed with the prospective adopters by the competent authority in the State of origin and a Convention adoption has been applied for by the prospective adopters in the State of origin but the child's placement with the prospective adopter is subject to a probationary period before the Convention adoption is made; and

(b)   the prospective adopter returns to England or Wales with the child before that probationary period is completed and the Convention adoption is made in the State of origin.

(2)   The relevant local authority must, if requested by the competent authority of the State of origin, submit a report about the placement to that authority and such a report must be prepared within such timescales and contain such information as the competent authority may reasonably require.

NOTES

Initial Commencement

Specified date

Specified date: 30 December 2005: see reg 1(1).

Extent

These Regulations do not extend to Scotland: see reg 1(2).

General

[1046]

'Competent authority': this is a term that derives from the Hague Convention – see A(IA)A 1999, Sch 1.

[1047]

30   Report of local authority investigation

The report of the investigation which a local authority must submit to the court in accordance with section 44(5) of the Act must include—

(a)   confirmation that the Certificate of eligibility and approval has been sent to the CA of the State of origin in accordance with regulation 18;

(b)   the date on which the agreement under Article 17(c) of the Convention was made; and

(c)   details of the reports of the visits and reviews made in accordance with regulation 5 as modified by regulation 25.

NOTES

Initial Commencement

Specified date

Specified date: 30 December 2005: see reg 1(1).

Extent

These Regulations do not extend to Scotland: see reg 1(2).

31   Convention adoption order

An adoption order shall not be made as a Convention adoption order unless—

(a)   in the case of—

(i)   an application by a couple, both members of the couple have been habitually resident in any part of the British Islands for a period of not less than one year ending with the date of the application; or

(ii)   an application by one person, the applicant has been habitually resident in any part of the British Islands for a period of not less than one year ending with the date of the application;

(b)   the child to be adopted was, on the date on which the agreement under Article 17(c) of the Convention was made, habitually resident in a Convention country outside the British Islands; and

(c)   in a case where one member of a couple (in the case of an application by a couple) or the applicant (in the case of an application by one person) is not a

British citizen, the Home Office has confirmed that the child is authorised to enter and reside permanently in the United Kingdom.

NOTES

Initial Commencement

Specified date

Specified date: 30 December 2005: see reg 1(1).

Extent

These Regulations do not extend to Scotland: see reg 1(2).

32 Requirements following a Convention adoption order or Convention adoption

(1)   Where the relevant Central Authority receives a copy of a Convention adoption order made by a court in England or Wales that Authority must issue a certificate in the form set out in Schedule 2 certifying that the adoption has been made in accordance with the Convention.

(2)   A copy of the certificate issued under paragraph (1) must be sent to the—

(a)   CA of the State of origin;

(b)   adoptive parent; and

(c)   adoption agency and, if different, the relevant local authority.

(3)   Where a Convention adoption is made and the relevant Central Authority receives a certificate under Article 23 of the Convention in respect of that Convention adoption, the relevant Central Authority must send a copy of that certificate to the—

(a)   adoptive parent; and

(b)   adoption agency and, if different, the relevant local authority.

NOTES

Initial Commencement

Specified date

Specified date: 30 December 2005: see reg 1(1).

Extent

These Regulations do not extend to Scotland: see reg 1(2).

33 Refusal of a court in England or Wales to make a Convention adoption order

Where an application for a Convention adoption order is refused by the court or is withdrawn, the prospective adopter must return the child to the relevant local authority within the period determined by the court.

NOTES

Initial Commencement

Specified date

Specified date: 30 December 2005: see reg 1(1).

Extent

These Regulations do not extend to Scotland: see reg 1(2).

34 Annulment of a Convention adoption order or a Convention adoption

Where a Convention adoption order or a Convention adoption is annulled under section 89(1) of the Act and the relevant Central Authority receives a copy of the order from the court, it must forward a copy of that order to the CA of the State of origin.

NOTES

Initial Commencement

Specified date

Specified date: 30 December 2005: see reg 1(1).

Extent

These Regulations do not extend to Scotland: see reg 1(2).

PART C – SIs

Chapter 2
Requirements, Procedure, Recognition and Effect of Adoptions in England and Wales where the United Kingdom is the State of Origin

35 Application of Chapter 2

The provisions in this Chapter shall apply where a couple or a person habitually resident in a Convention country outside the British Islands, wishes to adopt a child who is habitually resident in the British Islands in accordance with the Convention.

NOTES

Initial Commencement

Specified date

Specified date: 30 December 2005: see reg 1(1).

Extent

These Regulations do not extend to Scotland: see reg 1(2).

36 Counselling and information for the child

(1)   Where an adoption agency is considering whether a child is suitable for an adoption in accordance with the Convention, it must provide a counselling service for and information to that child in accordance with regulation 13 of the Agencies Regulations or corresponding Welsh provision and it must—

(a)   explain to the child in an appropriate manner the procedure in relation to, and the legal implications of, adoption under the Convention for that child by a prospective adopter habitually resident in the receiving State; and

(b)   provide him with written information about the matters referred to in sub-paragraph (a).

(2)   Paragraph (1) does not apply if the adoption agency is satisfied that the requirements set out in that paragraph have been carried out in respect of the prospective adopter by another agency.

NOTES

Initial Commencement

Specified date

Specified date: 30 December 2005: see reg 1(1).

Extent

These Regulations do not extend to Scotland: see reg 1(2).

37 Counselling and information for the parent or guardian of the child etc

(1)   An adoption agency must provide a counselling service and information in accordance with regulation 14 of the Agencies Regulations or corresponding Welsh provision for the parent or guardian of the child and, where regulation 14(4) of the Agencies Regulations or corresponding Welsh provision applies, for the father.

(2)   The adoption agency must also—

(a)   explain to the parent or guardian, and, where regulation 14(4) of the Agencies Regulations or corresponding Welsh provision applies, the father the procedure in relation to, and the legal implications of, adoption under the Convention by a prospective adopter in a receiving State; and

(b)   provide him with written information about the matters referred to in sub-paragraph (a).

(3)   Paragraphs (1) and (2) do not apply if the adoption agency is satisfied that the requirements set out in that paragraph have been carried out in respect of the prospective adopter by another agency.

NOTES

Initial Commencement

Specified date

Specified date: 30 December 2005: see reg 1(1).

Extent
These Regulations do not extend to Scotland: see reg 1(2).

38 Requirements in respect of the child's permanence report and information for the adoption panel

(1)   The child's permanence report which the adoption agency is required to prepare in accordance with regulation 17 of the Agencies Regulations or corresponding Welsh provision must include—

(a)   a summary of the possibilities for placement of the child within the United Kingdom; and
(b)   an assessment of whether an adoption by a person in a particular receiving State is in the child's best interests.

(2)   The adoption agency must send—

(a)   if received, the Article 15 Report; and
(b)   their observations on that Report,

together with the reports and information referred to in regulation 17(2) of the Agencies Regulations or corresponding Welsh provision to the adoption panel.

NOTES
Initial Commencement
Specified date
Specified date: 30 December 2005: see reg 1(1).

Extent
These Regulations do not extend to Scotland: see reg 1(2).

General

[1048]

'Article 15 Report': Article 15 of the Hague Convention: see A(IA)A 1999, Sch 1.

[1049]

---

39 Recommendation of adoption panel

Where an adoption panel make a recommendation in accordance with regulation 18(1) of the Agencies Regulations or corresponding Welsh provision it must consider and take into account the Article 15 Report, if available, and the observations thereon together with the information passed to it as a consequence of regulation 38.

NOTES
Initial Commencement
Specified date
Specified date: 30 December 2005: see reg 1(1).

Extent
These Regulations do not extend to Scotland: see reg 1(2).

General

[1050]

'Article 15 Report': Article 15 of the Hague Convention: see A(IA)A 1999, Sch 1.

[1051]

40 Adoption agency decision and notification

Where the adoption agency decides in accordance with regulation 19 of the Agencies Regulations or corresponding Welsh provision that the child should be placed for an adoption in accordance with the Convention it must notify the relevant Central Authority of—

(a) the name, sex and age of the child;

(b) the reasons why they consider that the child may be suitable for such an adoption;

(c) whether a prospective adopter has been identified and, if so, provide any relevant information; and

(d) any other information that Authority may require.

NOTES

Initial Commencement

Specified date

Specified date: 30 December 2005: see reg 1(1).

Extent

These Regulations do not extend to Scotland: see reg 1(2).

General

[1052]

'Relevant Central Authority': see AWAFE Regulations 2005, reg 2.

[1053]

41 Convention list

(1) The relevant Central Authority is to maintain a Convention list of children who are notified to that Authority under regulation 40 and shall make the contents of that list available for consultation by other Authorities within the British Islands.

(2) Where an adoption agency—

(a) places for adoption a child whose details have been notified to the relevant Central Authority under regulation 40; or

(b) determines that an adoption in accordance with the Convention is no longer in the best interests of the child,

it must notify the relevant Central Authority accordingly and that Authority must remove the details relating to that child from the Convention list.

NOTES

Initial Commencement

Specified date

Specified date: 30 December 2005: see reg 1(1).

Extent

These Regulations do not extend to Scotland: see reg 1(2).

General

[1054]

'Convention list': see AWAFE Regulations 2005, reg 2.

'Relevant Central Authority': see AWAFE Regulations 2005, reg 2.

[1055]

42 Receipt of the Article 15 Report from the CA of the receiving State

(1) This regulation applies where—

(a) the relevant Central Authority receives a report from the CA of the receiving State which has been prepared for the purposes of Article 15 of the Convention ('the Article 15 Report');

(b) the Article 15 Report relates to a prospective adopter who is habitually resident in that receiving State; and

(c) the prospective adopter named in the Article 15 Report wishes to adopt a child who is habitually resident in the British Islands.

(2) Subject to paragraph (3), if the relevant Central Authority is satisfied the prospective adopter meets the following requirements—

(a) the age requirements as specified in section 50 of the Act in the case of adoption by a couple, or section 51 of the Act in the case of adoption by one person; and

(b) in the case of a couple, both are, or in the case of adoption by one person, that person is habitually resident in a Convention country outside the British Islands,

that Authority must consult the Convention list and may, if the Authority considers it appropriate, consult any Convention list maintained by another Central Authority within the British Islands.

(3) Where a prospective adopter has already been identified in relation to a proposed adoption of a particular child and the relevant Central Authority is satisfied that prospective adopter meets the requirements referred to in paragraph (2)(a) and (b), that Authority—

(a) need not consult the Convention list; and

(b) must send the Article 15 Report to the local authority which referred the child's details to the Authority.

(4) The relevant Central Authority may pass a copy of the Article 15 Report to any other Central Authority within the British Islands for the purposes of enabling that Authority to consult its Convention list.

(5) Where the relevant Central Authority identifies a child on the Convention list who may be suitable for adoption by the prospective adopter, that Authority must send the Article 15 Report to the local authority which referred the child's details to that Authority.

NOTES

Initial Commencement

Specified date

Specified date: 30 December 2005: see reg 1(1).

Extent

These Regulations do not extend to Scotland: see reg 1(2).

General

[1056]

'Article 15 Report': Article 15 of the Hague Convention: see A(IA)A 1999, Sch 1.

'Relevant Central Authority': see AWAFE Regulations 2005, reg 2.

'Age requirements of s 50 and 51': Applicants will need to be 21 (or if one of a couple is a parent of the child, that parent to be 18).

'Convention list': see AWAFE Regulations 2005, reg 2.

[1057]

---

43 Proposed placement and referral to adoption panel

(1) Where the adoption agency is considering whether a proposed placement should proceed in accordance with the procedure provided for in regulation 31 of the Agencies Regulations or corresponding Welsh provision it must take into account the Article 15 Report.

(2) Where the adoption agency refers the proposal to place the child with the particular prospective adopter to the adoption panel in accordance with regulation 31 of the Agencies Regulations or corresponding Welsh provision, it must also send the Article 15 Report to the panel.

NOTES

Initial Commencement

Specified date

Specified date: 30 December 2005: see reg 1(1).

Extent

These Regulations do not extend to Scotland: see reg 1(2).

General

[1058]

'Article 15 Report': Article 15 of the Hague Convention: see A(IA)A 1999, Sch 1.

[1059]

---

44 Consideration by adoption panel

The adoption panel must take into account when considering what recommendation to make in accordance with regulation 32(1) of the Agencies Regulations or corresponding Welsh provision the Article 15 Report and any other information passed to it as a consequence of the provisions in this Chapter.

NOTES

Initial Commencement

Specified date

Specified date: 30 December 2005: see reg 1(1).

Extent

These Regulations do not extend to Scotland: see reg 1(2).

General

[1060]

'Article 15 Report': Article 15 of the Hague Convention: see A(IA)A 1999, Sch 1.

[1061]

---

45 Adoption agency's decision in relation to the proposed placement

(1) Regulation 33 of the Agencies Regulations or corresponding Welsh provision shall apply as if paragraph (3) of that regulation or corresponding Welsh provision was omitted.

(2) As soon as possible after the agency makes its decision, it must notify the relevant Central Authority of its decision.

---

(3) If the proposed placement is not to proceed—

(a) the adoption agency must return the Article 15 Report and any other documents or information sent to it by the relevant Central Authority to that Authority; and

(b) the relevant Central Authority must then send that Report, any such documents or such information to the CA of the receiving State.

NOTES

Initial Commencement

Specified date

Specified date: 30 December 2005: see reg 1(1).

Extent

These Regulations do not extend to Scotland: see reg 1(2).

General

[1062]

'Relevant Central Authority'/'CA of the receiving State': see AWAFE Regulations 2005, reg 2.

'Article 15 Report': Article 15 of the Hague Convention: see A(IA)A 1999, Sch 1.

[1063]

46 Preparation of the Article 16 Information

(1) If the adoption agency decides that the proposed placement should proceed, it must prepare a report for the purposes of Article 16(1) of the Convention which must include—

(a) the information about the child which is specified in Schedule 1 to the Agencies Regulations or corresponding Welsh provision; and

(b) the reasons for their decision.

(2) The adoption agency must send the following to the relevant Central Authority—

(a) the report referred to in paragraph (1);

(b) details of any placement order or other orders, if any, made by the courts; and

(c) confirmation that the parent or guardian consents to the proposed adoption.

(3) The relevant Central Authority must then send the documents referred to in paragraph (2) to the CA of the receiving State.

NOTES

Initial Commencement

Specified date

Specified date: 30 December 2005: see reg 1(1).

Extent

These Regulations do not extend to Scotland: see reg 1(2).

General

[1064]

'Article 16 Information': Article 16 of the Hague Convention: see A(IA)A 1999, Sch 1.

'Relevant Central Authority'/'CA of the receiving State': see AWAFE Regulations 2005, reg 2.

[1065]

47 Requirements to be met before the child is placed for adoption with prospective adopter

(1)   The relevant Central Authority may notify the CA of the receiving State that it is prepared to agree that the adoption may proceed provided that CA has confirmed that—

(a)   the prospective adopter has agreed to adopt the child and has received such counselling as may be necessary;

(b)   the prospective adopter has confirmed that he will accompany the child to the receiving State, unless in the case of a couple, the adoption agency and the CA of the receiving State have agreed that it is only necessary for one of them to do so;

(c)   it is content for the adoption to proceed;

(d)   in the case where a Convention adoption is to be effected, it has explained to the prospective adopter the need to make an application under section 84(1) of the Act; and

(e)   the child is or will be authorised to enter and reside permanently in the Convention country if a Convention adoption is effected or a Convention adoption order is made.

(2)   The relevant Central Authority may not make an agreement under Article 17(c) of the Convention with the CA of the receiving State unless—

(a)   confirmation has been received in respect of the matters referred to in paragraph (1); and

(b)   the adoption agency has confirmed to the relevant Central Authority that—

(i)   it has met the prospective adopter and explained the requirement to make an application for an order under section 84 of the Act before the child can be removed from the United Kingdom;

(ii)   the prospective adopter has visited the child; and

(iii)   the prospective adopter is content for the adoption to proceed.

(3)   An adoption agency may not place a child for adoption unless the agreement under Article 17(c) of the Convention has been made and the relevant Central Authority must advise that agency when that agreement has been made.

(4)   In this regulation, the reference to 'prospective adopter' means in the case of a couple, both of them.

NOTES

Initial Commencement

Specified date

Specified date: 30 December 2005: see reg 1(1).

Extent

These Regulations do not extend to Scotland: see reg 1(2).

General

[1066]

'relevant Central Authority'/'CA of the receiving State': see AWAFE Regulations 2005, reg 2.

'Agreement under Article 17(c)': Agreement under Art 17(c) of the Convention: see A(IA)A 1999, Sch 1. This is the agreement of the Central Authority of a child's State of origin (in this case the UK) that, following assessments, approval and agreements, that the child in question may be entrusted to prospective adopters.

[1067]

48 Requirements in respect of giving parental responsibility prior to a proposed Convention adoption

In the case of a proposed Convention adoption, the prescribed requirements for the purposes of section 84(3) of the Act (requirements to be satisfied prior to making an order) are—

(a) the competent authorities of the receiving State have—

    (i) prepared a report for the purposes of Article 15 of the Convention;

    (ii) determined and confirmed in writing that the prospective adoptive parent is eligible and suitable to adopt;

    (iii) ensured and confirmed in writing that the prospective adoptive parent has been counselled as may be necessary; and

    (iv) determined and confirmed in writing that the child is or will be authorised to enter and reside permanently in that State;

(b) the report required for the purposes of Article 16(1) of the Convention has been prepared by the adoption agency;

(c) the adoption agency confirms in writing that it has complied with the requirements imposed upon it under Part 3 of the Agencies Regulations or corresponding Welsh provision and this Chapter;

(d) the adoption agency has obtained and made available to the court—

    (i) the reports and information referred to in regulation 17(1) and (2) of the Agencies Regulations or corresponding Welsh provision;

    (ii) the recommendation made by the adoption panel in accordance with regulations 18 and 33 of the Agencies Regulations or corresponding Welsh provisions; and

    (iii) the adoption placement report prepared in accordance with regulation 31(2) of the Agencies Regulations or corresponding Welsh provision;

(e) the adoption agency includes in their report submitted to the court in accordance with section 43(a) or 44(5) of the Act as modified respectively by regulation 11, details of any reviews and visits carried out as consequence of Part 6 of the Agencies Regulations or corresponding Welsh provision; and

(f) the prospective adopter has confirmed in writing that he will accompany the child on taking the child out of the United Kingdom to travel to the receiving State or in the case of a couple the agency and competent foreign authority have confirmed that it is necessary for only one of them to do so.

NOTES

Initial Commencement

Specified date

Specified date: 30 December 2005: see reg 1(1).

Extent

These Regulations do not extend to Scotland: see reg 1(2).

General

[1068]

Article 15 Report: Article 15 of the Hague Convention: see A(IA)A 1999, Sch 1. This is the report on the adopters.

'competent authorities of the receiving State': term derived from the Hague Convention – see A(IA)A 1999, Sch 1.

Article 16 report: Article 16 Information: Article 16 of the Hague Convention. See A(IA)A 1999, Sch 1. This is the report on the child.

[1069]

---

49 Local authority report

In the case of a proposed application for a Convention adoption order, the report which a local authority must submit to the court in accordance with section 43(a) or 44(5) of the Act must include a copy of the—

(a)   Article 15 Report;

(b)   report prepared for the purposes of Article 16(1); and

(c)   written confirmation of the agreement under Article 17(c) of the Convention.

NOTES

Initial Commencement

Specified date

Specified date: 30 December 2005: see reg 1(1).

Extent

These Regulations do not extend to Scotland: see reg 1(2).

General

[1070]

'Article 15 Report': Article 15 of the Hague Convention: see A(IA)A 1999, Sch 1. This is the report on the adopters.

'report prepared for the purposes of Article 16(1)': Article 16 information: Article 16 of the Hague Convention: see A(IA)A 1999, Sch 1. This is the report on the child.

'agreement under Article 17(c)': Agreement under Art 17(c) of the Convention: See A(IA)A 1999, Sch 1. This is the agreement of the Central Authority of a child's State of origin (in this case the UK) that, following assessments, approval and agreements, that the child in question may be entrusted to prospective adopters.

[1071]

---

50 Convention adoption order

An adoption order shall not be made as a Convention adoption order unless—

(a)   in the case of—

      (i)   an application by a couple, both members of the couple have been habitually resident in a Convention country outside the British Islands for a period of not less than one year ending with the date of the application; or

      (aa)   an application by one person, the applicant has been habitually resident in a Convention country outside the British Islands for a period of not less than one year ending with the date of the application;

(b)   the child to be adopted was, on the date on which the agreement under Article 17(c) of the Convention was made, habitually resident in any part of the British Islands; and

(c)   the competent authority has confirmed that the child is authorised to enter and remain permanently in the Convention country in which the applicant is habitually resident.

NOTES

Initial Commencement

Specified date

Specified date: 30 December 2005: see reg 1(1).

> **Extent**
> These Regulations do not extend to Scotland: see reg 1(2).

General

[1072]

'habitually resident': see note to ACA 2002, s 83 (para **[399]**).

'agreement under Article 17(c) of the Convention': see A(IA)A 1999, Sch 1. This is the agreement of the Central Authority of a child's State of origin (in this case the UK) that, following assessments, approval and agreements, that the child in question may be entrusted to prospective adopters.

[1073]

> ### 51 Requirements following a Convention adoption order or Convention adoption
>
> (1) Where the relevant Central Authority receives a copy of a Convention adoption order made by a court in England or Wales, that Authority must issue a certificate in the form set out in Schedule 2 certifying that the adoption has been made in accordance with the Convention.
> (2) A copy of the certificate must be sent to the—
>
> (a) CA of the receiving State; and
> (b) the relevant local authority.
>
> (3) Where a Convention adoption is made and the Central Authority receives a certificate under Article 23 in respect of that Convention adoption, the relevant Central Authority must send a copy of that certificate to the relevant local authority.
>
> **NOTES**
> **Initial Commencement**
> *Specified date*
> Specified date: 30 December 2005: see reg 1(1).
>
> **Extent**
> These Regulations do not extend to Scotland: see reg 1(2).

General

[1074]

'Relevant Central Authority'/'CA of the receiving State': see AWAFE Regulations 2005, reg 2.

[1075]

> ### Chapter 3
> ### Miscellaneous Provisions
>
> ### 52 Application, with or without modifications, of the Act
>
> (1) Subject to the modifications provided for in this Chapter, the provisions of the Act shall apply to adoptions within the scope of the Convention so far as the nature of the provision permits and unless the contrary intention is shown.

53 Change of name and removal from the United Kingdom

In a case falling within Chapter 1 of this Part, section 28(2) of the Act shall apply as if—

(a) at the end of paragraph (a), 'or' was omitted;
(b) at the end of paragraph (b) there were inserted 'or (c) a child is placed by a competent foreign authority for the purposes of an adoption under the Convention,'; and
(c) at the end of subsection (2) there were inserted 'or the competent foreign authority consents to a change of surname.'.

General

[1076]

This regulation concerns cases where the UK is the Receiving State of a child under the provisions of the Hague Convention. Under the provisions of ACA 2002, s 28(2) a child may not be removed from the UK (for a period of one month or more (s 28(4))) or known by a new surname without the leave of the court or the written consent of each parent or guardian being given. The competent foreign authority may give consent to a change of surname, but would appear not to be required to be part of arrangements for the child to be removed from the UK for a month or longer.

[1077]

54 Removal of children

(1) In a case falling within Chapter 1 of this Part, sections 36 to 40 of the Act shall not apply.
(2) In a case falling within Chapter 2 of this Part—

(a) section 36 of the Act shall apply, as if—

(i) for the words 'an adoption order' in paragraphs (a) and (c) in subsection (1) there were substituted 'a Convention adoption order'; and
(ii) subsection (2) was omitted; and

(b) section 39 of the Act shall apply as if subsection (3)(a) was omitted.

General

[1078]

Chapter 1 cases are Convention cases where the UK is the receiving state. ACA 2002, ss 36–40 deal with restrictions on removal of a child from a prospective adoptive home in non-agency cases.

Chapter 2 cases are those where the UK is the State of Origin in a case where prospective adopters from another Convention country seek the adoption of a child. This regulation makes ACA 2002,ss 37–40 applicable to Chapter 2 cases.

[1079]

---

55 Modifications of the Act in respect of orders under section 84 where child is to be adopted under the Convention

The modifications set out in regulation 11 shall apply in the case where a couple or person habitually resident in a Convention country outside the British Islands intend to adopt a child who is habitually resident in England or Wales in accordance with the Convention.

NOTES
Initial Commencement
Specified date
Specified date: 30 December 2005: see reg 1(1).

Extent
These Regulations do not extend to Scotland: see reg 1(2).

General

[1080]

Regulation 11 contains a number of modifications of the Act. For the sake of economy they are not repeated here.

[1081]

---

56 Child to live with adopters before application for a Convention adoption order

Section 42 of the Act shall apply as if—

(a)   subsections (1)(b) and (3) to (6) were omitted; and
(b)   in subsection (2) from the word 'If' to the end of paragraph (b) there were substituted 'In the case of an adoption under the Convention,'.

NOTES
Initial Commencement
Specified date
Specified date: 30 December 2005: see reg 1(1).

Extent
These Regulations do not extend to Scotland: see reg 1(2).

57 Notice of intention to adopt

Section 44 of the Act shall apply as if subsection (3) was omitted.

NOTES
Initial Commencement
Specified date
Specified date: 30 December 2005: see reg 1(1).

> **Extent**
> These Regulations do not extend to Scotland: see reg 1(2).

General

[1082]

ACA 2002, s 44(3) prescribes the timing of an application for an application to adopt following notice of intention to proceed.

[1083]

> ### 58 Application for Convention adoption order
>
> Section 49 of the Act shall apply as if—
>
> (a)   in subsection (1), the words from 'but only' to the end were omitted;
> (b)   subsections (2) and (3) were omitted.
>
> **NOTES**
> **Initial Commencement**
> *Specified date*
> Specified date: 30 December 2005: see reg 1(1).
>
> **Extent**
> These Regulations do not extend to Scotland: see reg 1(2).

General

[1084]

The omissions permitted under this regulation enable applicants from outside the UK to apply for a Convention adoption order.

[1085]

> ### 59 Offences
>
> Any person who contravenes or fails to comply with—
>
> [(a)   regulation 24 (requirements in respect of prospective adopter following child's entry into the United Kingdom);
> (b)   regulation 26(1) (return of child to relevant local authority where prospective adopter does not wish to proceed);
> (c)   regulation 27(1)(b) (return of child to relevant local authority on request of local authority or by order of court); or
> (d)   regulation 33 (refusal of a court in England or Wales to make a Convention adoption order)]
>
> is guilty of an offence and liable on summary conviction to imprisonment for a term not exceeding three months, or a fine not exceeding level 5 on the standard scale, or both.
>
> **NOTES**
> **Initial Commencement**
> *Specified date*
> Specified date: 30 December 2005: see reg 1(1).
>
> **Extent**
> These Regulations do not extend to Scotland: see reg 1(2).
>
> **Amendment**
> Paras (a)–(d) substituted, for paras (a)–(c) as originally enacted, by SI 2005/3482, reg 6(c); date in force: 30 December 2005: see SI 2005/3482, reg 1.

General

[1086]

Regulation 33 requires the return of the child where a court in England or Wales refuses to make a Convention adoption order.

[1087]–[1100]

SCHEDULE 1
Certificate of Eligibility and Approval

Regulation 18

To the Central Authority of the State of origin

Re ... [name of applicant]

In accordance with Article 5 of the Convention, I hereby certify on behalf of the Central Authority for [England] [Wales] that ... ... [name of applicant] has been counselled, is eligible to adopt and has been assessed and approved as suitable to adopt a child from ... ... [State of origin] by ... ... [public authority or accredited body for the purposes of the Convention].

The attached report has been prepared in accordance with Article 15 of the Convention for presentation to the competent authority in ... . [State of origin].

This certificate of eligibility and approval and the report under Article 15 of the Convention are provided on the condition that a Convention adoption or Convention adoption order will not be made until the agreement under Article 17(c) of the Convention has been made.

I confirm on behalf of the Central Authority that if following the agreement under Article 17(c) of the Convention that—

[in the case, where the requirements specified in section 1(5A) of the British Nationality Act 1981 are met that the child ... ... [name] will be authorised to enter and reside permanently in the United Kingdom]; or

[in any other case, if entry clearance and leave to enter and remain, as may be necessary, is granted and not revoked, or curtailed and a Convention adoption order or Convention adoption is made, the child ... ... [name] will be authorised to enter and reside permanently in the United Kingdom.]

Name

[On behalf of the Secretary of State, the Central Authority for England]

Date

[the National Assembly for Wales, the Central Authority for Wales]

NOTES

Initial Commencement

Specified date

Specified date: 30 December 2005: see reg 1(1).

Extent

These Regulations do not extend to Scotland: see reg 1(2).

SCHEDULE 2
Certificate that the Convention Adoption Order has been made in Accordance with the Convention

Regulations 32 and 51

1 The Central Authority as the competent authority for [England] [Wales] being the country in which the Convention adoption order was made hereby certifies, in accordance with Article 23(1) of the Convention, that the child:

(a)   name ... ... [name on birth certificate, also known as/now known as ... . .]

  sex: ... ...

  date and place of birth: ... ...

  habitual residence at the time of the adoption: ... ...

State of origin: ... ...

(b)   was adopted on: ... ...

by order made by: ... ... court in [England] [Wales]

(c)   by the following person(s):

(i) family name and first name(s): ... ...
sex: ... .
date and place of birth: ... ...
Habitual residence at the time adoption order was made: ... ...
(ii)family name and first name(s): ... ...
sex: ... .
date and place of birth: ... ...
habitual residence at the time adoption order made: ... ...

2   The competent authority for [England] [Wales] in pursuance of Article 23(1) of the Convention hereby certifies that the adoption was made in accordance with the Convention and that the agreement under Article 17(c) was given by:

(a)   name and address of the Central Authority in State of origin: ... ...

date of the agreement: ... ...

(b)   name and address of the Central Authority of receiving State: ... ...

date of the agreement: ... ...

Signed
Date

NOTES

Initial Commencement

Specified date

Specified date: 30 December 2005: see reg 1(1).

Extent

These Regulations do not extend to Scotland: see reg 1(2).

Special Guardianship Regulations 2005

(SI 2005/1109)

Made	*4th April 2005*
Laid before Parliament	*6th April 2005*
Coming into force	*20th December 2005*

The Secretary of State for Education and Skills, in exercise of the powers conferred on her by sections 14A(8)(b), 14F, 24(5)(za), and 104(4) of the Children Act 1989, hereby makes the following Regulations:—

General

[1101]

The Special Guardianship Regulations 2005 (the regulations) supplement CA 1989, ss 14A–14G as inserted by ACA 2002, s 115(1), regarding special guardianship orders in relation to England. Part 2 forms the bulk of the regulations and makes detailed provision regarding special guardianship support services (SGSS) (see regs 3–20). Part 3 prescribes the matters to be included in a report to the court under s 14A(8) (reg 21 and Schedule) and specifies, for the purposes of the CA 1989, ss 24A and 24B, the relevant authority in relation to a child in respect of whom a special guardianship order (SGO) is in force and who was immediately before the making of the order looked after by a local authority (reg 22).

Special Guardianship Guidance (the Guidance) designed to provide guidance on the interpretation of the regulations has been issued by the Department for Education and Skills (DfES). The guidance does not have statutory force 'but should be complied with unless local circumstances indicate exceptional reasons which justify a variation', see para 2. Appropriate reference is made to the Guidance throughout the commentary on the regulations.

[1102]

Part 1
Introductory

1 Citation, commencement and application

(1)   These Regulations may be cited as the Special Guardianship Regulations 2005 and shall come into force on 30th December 2005.

(2)   These Regulations apply to England only.

NOTES

Initial Commencement

Specified date

Specified date: 30 December 2005: see para (1) above.

Extent

These Regulations apply to England only: see para (2) above.

General

[1103]

The Regulations apply to England only. For the Welsh Regulations see the Special Guardianship (Wales) Regulations 2005(SI 2005/1513 (W 117)) at para [1201].

[1104]

2 Interpretation

(1) In these Regulations—

'the Act' means the Children Act 1989;
'couple' has the same meaning as in section 144(4) of the Adoption and Children Act 2002;
'Local Health Board' means a Local Health Board established by the National Assembly for Wales under section 16BA of the National Health Service Act 1977;
'prospective special guardian' means a person—

    (a)   who has given notice to a local authority under section 14A(7) of the Act of his intention to make an application for a special guardianship order in accordance with section 14A(3) of the Act; or

    (b)   in respect of whom a court has requested that a local authority conduct an investigation and prepare a report pursuant to section 14A(9) of the Act;

'relevant child' means a child in respect of whom—

    (a)   a special guardianship order is in force;

    (b)   a person has given notice to a local authority under section 14A(7) of the Act of his intention to make an application for a special guardianship order in accordance with section 14A(3) of the Act; or

    (c)   a court is considering whether a special guardianship order should be made and has asked a local authority to conduct an investigation and prepare a report pursuant to section 14A(9) of the Act.

(2) In any case where—

    (a)   a person aged 18 or over is in full-time education or training; and

    (b)   immediately before he reached the age of 18, financial support was payable in relation to him under Chapter 2 of Part 2 of these Regulations,

then, for the purposes of the continued provision of financial support and any review of financial support, these Regulations shall have effect in relation to him as if he were still a child.

NOTES
Initial Commencement
Specified date
Specified date: 30 December 2005: see reg 1(1).

Extent
These Regulations apply to England only: see reg 1(2).

General

[1105]

Regulation 2 defines certain terminology used in the regulations. Where they refer to 'the Act' this means the Children Act 1989 (CA 1989), as it does throughout this commentary on the Regulations. Where definitions refer to other Acts they are identified in the definition.

[1106]

Part 2
Special Guardianship Support Services

General

[1107]

Regulations 3–20 form the major part of the Regulations and make detailed provision with regard to the support services which each local authority must make arrangements to provide to meet the needs of people affected by special guardianship, as required by CA 1989, s 14F, see para [768]. Such services should not be seen in isolation from mainstream services. In planning the provision of SGSS, the local authority should take into account the similar services already being delivered in their area, such as adoption support services, see the Guidance, paras 25 and 26 and para [770]. Chapter 1 deals with the provision of services and Chapter 2 with financial support which may only be paid in the circumstances specified in reg 6. It may include a remuneration element where it is paid to a former local authority foster parent under reg 7. Regulations 8–10 provide for payment of financial support, including conditions that may be imposed. Chapter 3 deals with SGSS needs assessments, plans for provision of services, notifications of proposals and decisions in relation to the provision of services. Chapter 4 provides for reviews of SGSS and Chapter 5 for urgent cases and service of notices.

[1108]

Chapter 1
Provision of Services

3 Prescribed services

(1) For the purposes of section 14F(1)(b) of the Act the following services are prescribed as special guardianship support services (in addition to counselling, advice and information)—

(a) financial support payable under Chapter 2;
(b) services to enable groups of—

    (i) relevant children;
    (ii) special guardians;
    (iii) prospective special guardians; and
    (iv) parents of relevant children,

    to discuss matters relating to special guardianship;

(c) assistance, including mediation services, in relation to arrangements for contact between a relevant child and—

    (i) his parent or a relative of his; or
    (ii) any other person with whom such a child has a relationship which appears to the local authority to be beneficial to the welfare of the child having regard to the factors specified in section 1(3) of the Act;

(d) services in relation to the therapeutic needs of a relevant child;
(e) assistance for the purpose of ensuring the continuance of the relationship between a relevant child and a special guardian or prospective special guardian, including—

    (i) training for that person to meet any special needs of that child;
    (ii) subject to paragraph (3), respite care;
    (iii) mediation in relation to matters relating to special guardianship orders.

(2) The services prescribed in paragraph (1)(b) to (e) may include giving assistance in cash.
(3) For the purposes of paragraph (1)(e)(ii) respite care that consists of the provision of accommodation must be accommodation provided by or on behalf of a local authority under section 23 of the Act (accommodation of looked after children) or by a voluntary organisation under section 59 of the Act.

NOTES

Initial Commencement

Specified date

Specified date: 30 December 2005: see reg 1(1).

Extent

These Regulations apply to England only: see reg 1(2).

General

[1109]

SGSS are defined by CA 1989, s 14F(1) as counselling, advice and information and other services prescribed by regulations, in relation to special guardianship. Regulation 3 prescribes, in accordance with CA 1989, s 14F(1)(b), the additional SGSS. As well as financial support (see reg 3(1)(a)), a range of services and assistance (including mediation) are prescribed in regs 3(1)(b)–(e), which may include giving assistance in cash in accordance with reg 3(2). When cash is provided in this way the Guidance indicates that 'it should not be means tested as it is being provided as part of a service rather than as financial support', see para 27.

Regulation 3(3) requires that, if respite care provided in accordance with reg 3(1)(e)(ii) consists of the provision of accommodation, this must be accommodation provided by or on behalf of a local authority under CA 1989, s 23 or by a voluntary organisation under CA 1989, s 59. Hence, arrangements made by a local authority for respite care must involve the child being looked after for the duration of the period of respite care and appropriate safeguards must be in place during the respite care. Any foster parent providing respite care must have been approved under the Fostering Services Regulations 2002 (SI 2002/57), and see the Guidance, para 28.

[1110]

4 Arrangements for securing provision of services

(1) The following are prescribed for the purposes of section 14F(9)(b) of the Act (persons who may provide special guardianship support services)—

(a)   a registered adoption society;
(b)   a registered adoption support agency;
(c)   a registered fostering agency;
(d)   a Local Health Board or Primary Care Trust;
(e)   a local education authority.

(2)   In paragraph (1)—

(a)   'registered adoption society' has the same meaning as in the Adoption and Children Act 2002;

(b)   'adoption support agency' has the same meaning as in the Adoption and Children Act 2002 and 'fostering agency' has the same meaning as in the Care Standards Act 2000 and 'registered' in relation to any such agency means that a person is registered in respect of it under Part 2 of the Care Standards Act 2000.

NOTES

Initial Commencement

Specified date

Specified date: 30 December 2005: see reg 1(1).

Extent

These Regulations apply to England only: see reg 1(2).

General

[1111]

CA 1989, s 14F(9) enables the local authority to arrange for SGSS, or part thereof, to be provided by (a) another local authority or (b) others prescribed in regulations on the authority's behalf, see para [770]. Regulation 4 identifies those who are prescribed for the purposes of CA 1989, s 14F(9)(b).

[1112]

---

5 Services for persons outside the area

(1)   Section 14F of the Act (special guardianship support services) applies to a local authority in respect of the following persons who are outside the authority's area—

(a)   a relevant child who is looked after by the local authority or was looked after by the local authority immediately before the making of a special guardianship order;

(b)   a special guardian or prospective special guardian of such a child;

(c)   a child of a special guardian or prospective special guardian mentioned in sub-paragraph (b).

(2)   But section 14F ceases to apply at the end of the period of three years from the date of the special guardianship order except in a case where the local authority are providing financial support under Chapter 2 and the decision to provide that support was made before the making of the order.

(3)   Nothing in this regulation prevents a local authority from providing special guardianship support services to persons outside their area where they consider it appropriate to do so.

NOTES

Initial Commencement

Specified date

Specified date: 30 December 2005: see reg 1(1).

Extent

These Regulations apply to England only: see reg 1(2).

General

[1113]

'The local authority where the special guardian lives is responsible for undertaking an assessment of need and provision of any special guardianship support services in response to that assessment. The only exception to this is where a child was looked after before the special guardianship order was made' the Guidance, para 31. CA 1989, s 14F(8)(g) enables regulations to provide for the circumstances in which s 14F may apply to a local authority in respect of persons outside their area. Regulation 5 makes such provision regarding a relevant child (as defined in reg 2(1)) who is looked after by the local authority or was looked after immediately before the SGO was made; an actual or prospective special guardian of such a child; and a child of such a special guardian or prospective special guardian. It distinguishes between the first three years of the order and thereafter, as discussed in the context of s 14F(8), see para [776] and the *Guidance*, paras 32 and 33.

Regulation 5(3) enables the local authority to provide SGSS to people outside their area in other circumstances where they consider it appropriate. The example given in the *Guidance*, para 36 is 'transitional arrangements by the originating authority where a family move to allow time for the new authority to review the family's existing plan without a break in service provision'.

[1114]

Chapter 2
Provision of Financial Support

General

[1115]

The *Guidance*, para 37 states that: 'Financial issues should not be the sole reason for a special guardianship arrangement failing to survive. The central principle is that financial support should be payable in accordance with the Regulations to help secure a suitable special guardianship arrangement where such an arrangement cannot be readily made because of a financial obstacle.' .

[1116]

---

6   Circumstances in which financial support is payable

(1)   Financial support is payable under this Chapter to a special guardian or prospective special guardian—

(a)   to facilitate arrangements for a person to become the special guardian of a child where the local authority consider such arrangements to be beneficial to the child's welfare; or

(b)   to support the continuation of such arrangements after a special guardianship order is made.

(2)   Such support is payable only in the following circumstances—

(a)   where the local authority consider that it is necessary to ensure that the special guardian or prospective special guardian can look after the child;

(b)   where the local authority consider that the child needs special care which requires a greater expenditure of resources than would otherwise be the case because of his illness, disability, emotional or behavioural difficulties or the consequences of his past abuse or neglect;

(c)   where the local authority consider that it is appropriate to contribute to any legal costs, including court fees, of a special guardian or prospective special guardian, as the case may be, associated with—

   (i)   the making of a special guardianship order or any application to vary or discharge such an order;

   (ii)   an application for an order under section 8 of the Act;

   (iii) an order for financial provision to be made to or for the benefit of the child; or

(d)   where the local authority consider that it is appropriate to contribute to the expenditure necessary for the purposes of accommodating and maintaining the child, including the provision of furniture and domestic equipment, alterations to and adaptations of the home, provision of means of transport and provision of clothing, toys and other items necessary for the purpose of looking after the child.

NOTES

Initial Commencement

Specified date
Specified date: 30 December 2005: see reg 1(1).

Extent
These Regulations apply to England only: see reg 1(2).

Regulation 6(1)

[1117]

This provides that financial support is payable under Chapter 2 to a special guardian or prospective special guardian (as defined in reg 2(1)) to facilitate arrangements for a person to become the child's special guardian, where this is considered by the local authority to be beneficial to the child's welfare, and to support the continuation of these arrangements after the SGO has been made.

Regulation 6(2)

[1118]

This sets out the four circumstances in which financial support may be paid to a special guardian or prospective special guardian. These are where the authority consider that:

(1)   It is necessary to ensure that that person can look after the child, see reg 6(2)(a).

(2)   The child needs special care which requires greater expenditure than would otherwise be the case because of the child's illness, disability, emotional or behavioural difficulties or the consequences of past abuse or neglect, see reg 6(2)(b). Payment of financial support under reg 6(2) (b) 'is intended where the child's condition is serious and long-term. For example, where a child needs a special diet or where items such as shoes, clothing or bedding need to be replaced at a higher rate than would normally be the case with a child of similar age who was unaffected by the particular condition', the Guidance, para 39.

(3)   It is appropriate to contribute to any legal costs, including court fees, of a special guardian or prospective special guardian associated with–

    (i)   the making of a SGO (under CA 1989, s 14A) or any application under s 14D to vary or discharge a SGO;

    (ii)   an application for an order under CA 1989, s 8 (a contact order, a prohibited steps order, a residence order or a specific issue order);

    (iii) an order for financial provision to be made to or for the benefit of the child, see reg 6(2)(c). Payment of financial support under reg 6(2)(c) is so that where the local authority consider it appropriate, they may contribute to initial legal costs and any future legal costs associated with the sgo, in order to continue to support the existence of the order, see the Guidance, paragraph 40.

(4)   It is appropriate to make a contribution to the expenditure necessary for the purpose of accommodating and maintaining the child, including the provision identified in regulation 6(2)(d).

Regulation 13 prescribes the matters that the local authority must take into account in determining the amount of financial support.

Regulation 10 prescribes the conditions to be met before financial support is payable.

[1119]

> ### 7   Remuneration for former foster parents
>
> (1)   Financial support under this Chapter may include an element of remuneration but only where the decision to include it is taken before the special guardianship order is made and the local authority consider it to be necessary in order to facilitate arrangements for a person to become a special guardian in a case where—
>
> (a)   the special guardian or prospective special guardian has been a local authority foster parent in respect of the child; and

(b)   an element of remuneration was included in the payments made by the local authority to that person in relation to his fostering the child.

(2)   But that element of remuneration ceases to be payable after the expiry of the period of two years from the making of the special guardianship order unless the local authority consider its continuation to be necessary having regard to the exceptional needs of the child or any other exceptional circumstances.

NOTES

Initial Commencement

Specified date

Specified date: 30 December 2005: see reg 1(1).

Extent

These Regulations apply to England only: see reg 1(2).

General

[1120]

'Financial support cannot normally include the payment of remuneration to the special guardian or prospective special guardian for care of the child' the *Guidance*, para 42. Regulation 7(1) provides, however, that where the special guardian or prospective special guardian has been a local authority foster parent of the child and they received an element of remuneration in the financial support paid to them as the child's foster parent; the local authority may continue to pay an element of remuneration provided that the decision to do so is taken *before* the SGO is made and the authority consider it necessary to help the person become the child's special guardian. Such remuneration is only payable for two years from the date of the SGO unless, in accordance with reg 7(2), the authority considers it should continue for longer having regard to either the child's exceptional needs or other exceptional circumstances. 'The purpose of the two-year transitional provision is to enable local authorities to maintain payments to foster carers who become special guardians, at the same rate as they received when they were fostering the child. This should give the family time to adjust to their new circumstances.' (Guidance, para 43.)

[1121]

8   Payment of financial support

Financial support under this Chapter may be paid—

(a)   periodically, if it is provided to meet a need which is likely to give rise to recurring expenditure; or

(b)   in any other case by a single payment or, if the local authority and the special guardian or prospective special guardian agree, by instalments.

NOTES

Initial Commencement

Specified date

Specified date: 30 December 2005: see reg 1(1).

Extent

These Regulations apply to England only: see reg 1(2).

General

[1122]

This provides that financial support may be paid as a regular periodical payment if it is to meet a recurring financial need; otherwise it may be paid as a single payment, or, if the local authority and special guardians or prospective special guardians agree, in instalments.

Financial support which is payable periodically is not payable until the special guardian or prospective special guardian has agreed to the conditions in reg 10(1). Any financial support may also be subject to other conditions in accordance with CA 1989, s 14F(8)(e)(f) and reg 10(2)–(4).

[1123]

9 Cessation of financial support

Financial support ceases to be payable to a special guardian or prospective special guardian if—

(a) the child ceases to have a home with him;
(b) the child ceases full-time education or training and commences employment;
(c) the child qualifies for income support or jobseeker's allowance in his own right; or
(d) the child attains the age of 18 unless he continues in full-time education or training, when it may continue until the end of the course or training he is then undertaking.

NOTES
Initial Commencement
Specified date
Specified date: 30 December 2005: see reg 1(1).

Extent
These Regulations apply to England only: see reg 1(2).

General

[1124]

This identifies the four circumstances in which financial support ceases to be payable to a special guardian or prospective special guardian, based upon the child ceasing to have a home with him; ceasing full-time education or training and commencing work; qualifying in his own right for income support or jobseeker's allowance; or attaining majority unless he continues in full-time education or training, when it may continue until the end of the course or training.

It is submitted that the child only ceases to have a home with his guardian where his departure is considered to be permanent. It does not apply to periods of temporary absence from the special guardian's home, for example, in connection with education, training, respite care or hospitalisation.

There is no specific provision for cessation of financial support if the SGO ceases to have effect or is revoked, as there is in the Special Guardianship (Wales) Regulations 2005 (SI 2005/1513 (W117)), reg 12(10)(a).

[1125]

10 Conditions

(1) Where financial support is to be paid periodically it is not payable until the special guardian or prospective special guardian agrees to the following conditions—

(a) that he will inform the local authority immediately if—

    (i) he changes his address;
    (ii) the child dies;
    (iii) any of the changes mentioned in regulation 9 (cessation of financial support) occurs; or

PART C – SIs

> (iv)   there is a change in his financial circumstances or the financial needs or resources of the child which may affect the amount of financial support payable to him,
>
> and, where the information is given orally, to confirm it in writing within seven days;
>
> (b)   that he will complete and supply the local authority with an annual statement as to the following matters—
>
> > (i)   his financial circumstances;
> > (ii)   the financial needs and resources of the child;
> > (iii)   his address and whether the child still has a home with him.
>
> (2) The local authority may provide financial support subject to any other conditions they consider appropriate, including the timescale within which, and purposes for which, any payment of financial support should be utilised.
>
> (3) Subject to paragraph (4), where any condition imposed in accordance with this regulation is not complied with, the local authority may—
>
> (a)   suspend or terminate payment of financial support; and
> (b)   seek to recover all or part of the financial support they have paid.
>
> (4) Where the condition not complied with is a failure to provide an annual statement in accordance with an agreement referred to in paragraph (1), the local authority shall not take any steps under paragraph (3) until—
>
> (a)   they have sent to the person who entered into the agreement a written reminder of the need to provide an annual statement; and
> (b)   28 days have expired since the date on which that reminder was sent.
>
> **NOTES**
> **Initial Commencement**
> *Specified date*
> Specified date: 30 December 2005: see reg 1(1).
>
> **Extent**
> These Regulations apply to England only: see reg 1(2).

General

[1126]

Regulation 10 provides that, in accordance with CA 1989, s 14F(8)(e), *periodic* financial support is not payable until the special guardian or prospective special guardian agrees to the conditions listed in reg 10(1), which were discussed in the context of s 14F(8) (see para [775]). 'The local authority should be prepared to provide advice and assistance on completing the forms, on request where necessary' (Guidance, para 47).

Regulation 10(2) further provides that the local authority may set any other conditions they consider appropriate, including the timescale within which, and purposes for which, *any* payment of financial support should be used as also discussed in the context of s 14F(8).

[1127]

> ## Chapter 3
> ## Assessment and Plans
>
> ### 11 Request for assessment
>
> (1) The following persons are prescribed for the purposes of section 14F(3) of the Act (persons at whose request an assessment must be carried out)—

(a) a relevant child who is looked after by the local authority or was looked after by the local authority immediately before the making of a special guardianship order;

(b) a special guardian or prospective special guardian of such a child;

(c) a parent of such a child.

(2) Paragraph (3) applies if the local authority receive a written request from or, in the case of a child, on behalf of any of the following persons (not being a person falling within paragraph (1)) for an assessment of his needs for special guardianship support services—

(a) a person mentioned in section 14F(3)(a) to (c) of the Act;

(b) a child of a special guardian;

(c) any person whom the local authority consider to have a significant and ongoing relationship with a relevant child.

(3) The local authority must, if they are minded not to carry out an assessment, give the person notice of the proposed decision (including the reasons for it) and must allow him a reasonable opportunity to make representations in relation to that decision.

(4) Where the request of a person for an assessment relates to a particular special guardianship support service, or it appears to the local authority that a person's needs for special guardianship support services may be adequately assessed by reference to a particular special guardianship support service, the local authority may carry out the assessment by reference to that service only.

NOTES

Initial Commencement

Specified date
Specified date: 30 December 2005: see reg 1(1).

Extent
These Regulations apply to England only: see reg 1(2).

General

[1128]

In accordance with s 14F(3) of the Act, reg 11(1) identifies those people at whose request an assessment for SGSS is mandatory. It focuses upon current or former looked after children, their parents, special guardians and prospective special guardians as mentioned in the discussion of s 14F(3), see para [772]. Regulation 11(2) and (3), as also mentioned there, prescribe those who *may* seek an assessment of their need for SGSS in accordance with s 14F(3)(d), and the notice the local authority must give if they are minded not to do so. An assessment may be by reference to a particular service in accordance with reg 11(4).

[1129]

12 Procedure for assessment

(1) Where the local authority carry out an assessment of a person's needs for special guardianship support services they must have regard to such of the following considerations as are relevant to the assessment—

(a) the developmental needs of the child;

(b) the parenting capacity of the special guardian or prospective special guardian, as the case may be;

(c) the family and environmental factors that have shaped the life of the child;

(d) what the life of the child might be like with the person falling within sub-paragraph (b);

(e) any previous assessments undertaken in relation to the child or a person falling within sub-paragraph (b);

(f) the needs of a person falling within sub-paragraph (b) and of that person's family;

> (g)   where it appears to the local authority that there is a pre-existing relationship between a person falling within sub-paragraph (b) and the parent of the child, the likely impact of the special guardianship order on the relationships between that person, that child and that parent.
>
> (2)   The local authority must, where they consider it appropriate to do so—
>
> (a)   interview the person whose needs for special guardianship support services are being assessed;
>
> (b)   where the person falling within sub-paragraph (a) is a child, interview—
>
> > (i)   any special guardian or prospective special guardian, as the case may be, of the child; or
> >
> > (ii)   any adult the local authority consider it appropriate to interview.
>
> (3)   Where it appears to the local authority that the person may have a need for services from a Local Health Board, Primary Care Trust or local education authority, they must, as part of the assessment, consult that Local Health Board, Primary Care Trust or local education authority.
>
> (4)   After undertaking an assessment, the local authority must prepare a written report of the assessment.
>
> **NOTES**
>
> **Initial Commencement**
>
> *Specified date*
>
> Specified date: 30 December 2005: see reg 1(1).
>
> **Extent**
>
> These Regulations apply to England only: see reg 1(2).

General

[1130]

The nature and scope of, and procedure for, assessment of a person's needs for SGSS are prescribed in reg 12, subject to reg 19 in urgent cases.

Regulation 12(1) lists the considerations to which the local authority are to have regard when carrying out an assessment in accordance with s 14F(8)(a) and (d). They reflect those which are considered in assessments carried out under the *Framework for the Assessment of Children in Need and their Families* (Department of Health 2000), whilst 'recognising that the context is different from that for birth families'. Professionals and other staff involved in undertaking assessments for special guardianship support services will need to be familiar with the Assessment Framework, see the Guidance, paras 57 and 58 and commentary on s 14F(3) at para [773].

Regulation 12(2) requires that the local authority, where *they* consider it appropriate, interview the person whose needs are being assessed and where that person is a child interview any special guardian or prospective special guardian or any other adult they consider it appropriate to interview. The Guidance, para 61 indicates that there should be an interview 'unless the assessment relates only to information and advice or unless it is not appropriate to interview a child. In this case the child's actual or prospective special guardian may be interviewed.'

Regulation 12(3) requires that the local authority consult the relevant LHB, PCT or LEA during the course of the assessment, if it appears to the local authority that a person may have a need for services from the relevant body.

After an assessment the local authority must prepare a written report in accordance with reg 12(4). It must also, in accordance with regs 15 and 20, supply, in writing, the information specified in reg 15(3), and give written notice of the right to make representations in accordance with reg 15(1), to the person assessed.

[1131]

---

13 Assessment of need for financial support

(1)   This regulation applies where the local authority carry out an assessment of a person's need for financial support.

(2)   In determining the amount of financial support, the local authority must take account of any other grant, benefit, allowance or resource which is available to the person in respect of his needs as a result of becoming a special guardian of the child.

(3)   Subject to paragraphs (4) and (5) the local authority must also take account of the following considerations—

(a)   the person's financial resources, including any tax credit or benefit, which would be available to him if the child lived with him;

(b)   the amount required by the person in respect of his reasonable outgoings and commitments (excluding outgoings in respect of the child);

(c)   the financial needs and resources of the child.

(4)   The local authority must disregard the considerations in paragraph (3) where they are considering providing financial support in respect of legal costs, including court fees, in a case where a special guardianship order is applied for in respect of a child who is looked after by the local authority and the authority support the making of the order or an application is made to vary or discharge a special guardianship order in respect of such a child.

(5)   The local authority may disregard any of the considerations in paragraph (3)—

(a)   where they are considering providing financial support in respect of—

(i)   initial costs of accommodating a child who has been looked after by the local authority;

(ii)   recurring costs in respect of travel for the purpose of visits between the child and a related person; or

(iii)   any special care referred to in regulation 6(2)(b) in relation to a child who has been looked after by the local authority; or

(b)   where they are considering including an element of remuneration under regulation 7.

(6)   In paragraph (5)(a)(ii) 'related person' means a relative of the child or any other person with whom the child has a relationship which appears to the local authority to be beneficial to the welfare of the child having regard to the factors specified in section 1(3) of the Act.

NOTES

Initial Commencement

Specified date

Specified date: 30 December 2005: see reg 1(1).

Extent

These Regulations apply to England only: see reg 1(2).

General

[1132]

A major form of SGSS is financial support payable under s 14F(2) and regs 6–10. Regulation 13 prescribes the matters that the local authority, when carrying out a financial needs assessment, must take into account in determining the amount of financial support, subject to reg 19 in urgent cases.

The Guidance stresses that:

'It is important to ensure that special guardians are helped to access benefits to which they are entitled. Local authorities should therefore endeavour to ensure that the special guardian or prospective special guardian is aware of, and taking advantage of, all benefits and tax credits available to them. Financial support paid under these Regulations cannot duplicate any other payment available to the special guardian or prospective special guardian' (para 63).

To that end reg 13(2) provides that in determining the amount of any financial support, the local authority must take account of any other grant, benefit, allowance or resource which is available to the person in respect of his needs as a result of becoming the child's special guardian.

Subject to the mandatory disregard provision in reg 13(4), and the discretionary disregard provision in reg 13(5), reg 13(3) requires that in determining the amount of financial support the local authority must also consider:

(a)   The person's financial resources, including any tax credit or benefit, which would be available to him if the child lived with him.

The Guidance, para 64, indicates that this 'is consistent with the fact that financial support for special guardians is disregarded for the purpose of calculating income related benefits and tax credits'. It also indicates that 'financial resources' 'should include significant income from any investments, but not their home'.

(b)   The amount required by the person in respect of his reasonable outgoings and commitments (excluding outgoings in respect of the child).

Examples given of such reasonable outgoings are housing and transport costs, and daily living expenses.

(c)   The financial needs and resources of the child.

The Guidance, paras 65 and 66, further states that:

'In determining the amount of any ongoing financial support, the local authority should have regard to the amount of fostering allowance which would have been payable if the child were fostered. The local authority's core allowance plus any enhancement that would be payable in respect of the particular child, will make up the maximum payment the local authority could consider paying the family. Any means test carried out as appropriate to the circumstances would use this maximum payment as a basis.

There is a suggested means test on the Department for Education and Skills website (www.dfes.gov.uk/adoption), which local authorities may wish to use.'

The mandatory disregard provision in regulation 13(4) provides the only circumstance in which the local authority *must* disregard the considerations in regulation 13(3). This is when they are considering providing financial support in respect of legal costs, including court fees, where a SGO is applied for under the CA 1989, s 14A in respect of a child who is looked after by the local authority, and the authority support the making of that order, or an application is made under the CA 1989, s 14D to vary or discharge a SGO in respect of such a child.

'Local authorities are not expected to meet the legal costs of a special guardianship order where they oppose an application in respect of a child they previously looked after or in a non-looked after case. Local authorities may wish to advise prospective special guardians in these circumstances that they may be able to obtain help with legal costs from the Legal Services Commission (LSC), although this will be subject to a means and merits test laid down by the Funding Code. For more details see *A Practical Guide to Community Legal Service Funding* by the LSC available from the LSC Leafletline on 0845 3000 343, email LSCLeaflets@ecgroup.uk.com or fax 020 8867 3225.' (Guidance, para 70)

The discretionary disregard provision in reg 13(5) provides for four circumstances in which the local authority *may* disregard the considerations in reg 13(3).

First, where they are considering providing financial support in respect of the initial costs of accommodating a child who has been looked after by the local authority. As the Guidance explains in para 68, where a payment is of the nature of a 'settling-in grant', it is not expected that this payment would be means tested, but local authorities might, for example, want to means test any contribution to an adaptation to the home.

Second, where they are considering providing financial support in respect of recurring costs in respect of travel for the purpose of visits between the child and a related person (as defined in reg 13(6)), 'so that, for example, where the local authority wants to underline the value of and facilitate contact for the child with a sibling, they can achieve this by not means testing payments to support this' (Guidance, para 68).

Third, where they are considering providing financial support in respect of any special care referred to in reg 6(2)(b) in relation to a child who has been looked after by the authority, ie, care which requires a greater expenditure of resources than would otherwise be the case because of his illness, disability, emotional or behavioural difficulties, or the consequences of his past abuse or neglect. This will allow local authorities to provide a financial package for a particular child to facilitate the making of a SGO (Guidance, para 68).

Fourth, where, in accordance with reg 13(5)(b), they are considering including an element of remuneration under reg 7 in financial support payments to former foster parents. This is 'so that local authorities can maintain the amount paid to a foster carer who goes on to become a special guardian for the transitional period' (Guidance, para 68).

[1133]

14 Plan

(1) This regulation applies in relation to the requirement in section 14F(6) of the Act for the local authority to prepare a plan in accordance with which special guardianship support services are to be provided.

(2) The local authority must prepare a plan if—

(a) they propose to provide special guardianship support services to a person on more than one occasion; and

(b) the services are not limited to the provision of advice or information.

(3) Where it appears to the local authority that the person may have a need for services from a Local Health Board, Primary Care Trust or a local education authority, they must consult that Local Health Board, Primary Care Trust or local education authority before preparing the plan.

(4) The local authority must nominate a person to monitor the provision of the services in accordance with the plan.

NOTES

Initial Commencement

Specified date

Specified date: 30 December 2005: see reg 1(1).

Extent

These Regulations apply to England only: see reg 1(2).

General

[1134]

If the outcome of an assessment is that an authority decide in favour of providing a person with special guardianship support services on more than one occasion, then in accordance with ss 14F(6) and 14F(8)(b)–(d) and reg 14 (if the services are not limited to the provision of advice or information), and subject to reg 19 in urgent cases, they must prepare and keep under review a special guardianship support services plan as discussed in the commentary on s 14F(6)–(8), see para [775].

'The result of this process of preparation and consultation should be that social workers, other professionals and the recipient of the services (or the appropriate adult) will be clear what the support services plan is. The plan should be set out in writing in a way that everybody affected can understand' (Guidance, para 72).

[1135]

---

15 Notice of proposal as to special guardianship support services

(1) Before making any decision under section 14F(5) of the Act as to a person's needs for special guardianship support services, the local authority must allow the person an opportunity to make representations in accordance with this regulation.
(2) The local authority must first give the person notice of the proposed decision and the time allowed for making representations.
(3) The notice must contain the following information—

(a) a statement as to the person's needs for special guardianship support services;
(b) where the assessment relates to his need for financial support, the basis upon which financial support is determined;
(c) whether the local authority propose to provide him with special guardianship support services;
(d) the services (if any) that are proposed to be provided to him;
(e) if financial support is to be paid to him, the proposed amount that would be payable; and
(f) any proposed conditions under regulation 10(2).

(4) In a case where the local authority propose to provide special guardianship support services and are required to prepare a plan under section 14F(6) of the Act, the notice must be accompanied by a draft of that plan.
(5) The local authority shall not make a decision until—

(a) the person has made representations to the local authority or notified the local authority that he is satisfied with the proposed decision and, where applicable, the draft plan; or
(b) the period of time for making representations has expired.

NOTES
Initial Commencement
Specified date
Specified date: 30 December 2005: see reg 1(1).

Extent
These Regulations apply to England only: see reg 1(2).

General

[1136]

The CA 1989, s 14F(5) provides that where, as a result of an assessment, a local authority decide that a person has needs for SGSS, they must then decide whether to provide him with such services. Before the authority make a decision under s 14F(5) as to a person's needs for services, regulation 15(1) requires that they allow him the opportunity to make representations. The regulations do not specify a period of time to be allowed for representations but the Guidance suggests that local authorities should allow a period of 28 days from the time the proposed decision is sent to the applicants (see para 76).

Regulation 15(2) requires that they give notice (which must comply with reg 20) of the proposed decision and the time allowed for making representations. The notice must contain the information listed in reg 15(3). Where the authority propose to provide SGSS and is required to prepare a plan (under s 14F(6) and reg 14), the notice must be accompanied by a draft of that plan in accordance with reg 15(4).

When providing the person with the outcome of the written assessment, the local authority should refer the person to sources of independent advice and advocacy (see the Guidance, para 75). The Guidance, para 77, further indicates that:

'After considering any representations received, the local authority must then decide whether to provide any services to the person who has been assessed, taking into account the individual circumstances of the case and the resources that are available locally.'

The local authority cannot make a decision until, in accordance with reg 15(5), the person has made representations or has notified the authority that he is satisfied with the proposed decision and, where applicable, the draft plan; or the period of time for making representations has expired.

[1137]

16 Notification of decision as to special guardianship support services

(1)   After making their decision under section 14F(5) of the Act as to whether to provide special guardianship support services to a person, the local authority must give the person notice of that decision, including the reasons for it.
(2)   Where the local authority are required to prepare a plan under section 14F(6) of the Act, the notice must include details of that plan and the person nominated under regulation 14(4).
(3)   If the local authority decide that financial support is to be provided, the notice given under paragraph (1) must include the following information—

(a)   the method of the determination of the amount of financial support;
(b)   where financial support is to be paid in instalments or periodically—

   (i)   the amount of financial support;
   (ii)   the frequency with which the payment will be made;
   (iii) the period for which financial support is to be paid;
   (iv)   when payment will commence;

(c)   where financial support is to be paid as a single payment, when the payment is to be made;
(d)   where financial support is to be paid subject to any conditions imposed in accordance with regulation 10(2), those conditions, the date (if any) by which the conditions are to be met and the consequences of failing to meet the conditions;
(e)   the arrangements and procedure for review, variation and termination of financial support;
(f)   the responsibilities of—

   (i)   the local authority under regulations 17 and 18 (reviews); and
   (ii)   the special guardian or prospective special guardian pursuant to any agreement mentioned in regulation 10.

NOTES
Initial Commencement
Specified date
Specified date: 30 December 2005: see reg 1(1).

Extent
These Regulations apply to England only: see reg 1(2).

General

[1138]

Having made their decision under s 14F(5) whether or not to provide any services, the local authority are required by reg 16(1) to give written notice (see reg 20) of that decision, including the reasons for it.

Where the local authority are required to prepare a plan under s 14F(6), reg 16(2) requires that the notice must include details of that plan and the name of the person nominated under reg 14(4) to monitor the provision of services in accordance with the plan.

If the local authority decide that financial support is to be provided, the reg 16(1) notice must include the information listed in reg 16(3).

> 'Where service providers other than social services have been involved in the assessment of support needs, the local authority should try wherever possible to ensure that decisions made by those service providers follow the same timetable as decisions made under this regulation. These should then be covered in a single notification and plan sent out by the local authority which encapsulates decisions for the whole service package wherever possible.' (Guidance, para 81)

[1139]

> ### Chapter 4
> ### Reviews

General

[1140]

'Regular reviews enable the local authority and the service user to review the effectiveness of any services provided and consider whether it is appropriate to continue that service or change the provision in some way.' (Guidance, para 82)

To that end reg 17 provides a review procedure where the local authority provide SGSS other than periodic financial support (see reg 17(1)) and reg 18 so provides where the authority provide such financial support (see reg 18(1)).

[1141]

> **17   Reviews: general procedure**
>
> (1)   This regulation applies where the local authority provide special guardianship support services for a person other than financial support payable periodically.
> (2)   The local authority must review the provision of such services—
>
> (a)   if any change in the person's circumstances which may affect the provision of special guardianship support services comes to their notice;
> (b)   at such stage in the implementation of the plan as they consider appropriate; and
> (c)   in any event, at least annually.
>
> (3)   Regulations 12 and 13 apply in relation to a review under this regulation as they apply in relation to an assessment under Chapter 3 of this Part.
> (4)   If the local authority propose to vary or terminate the provision of special guardianship support services to any person, before making any decision as a result of the review they must give the person an opportunity to make representations and for that purpose they must give him notice of the proposed decision and the time allowed for making representations.

(5)   The notice must contain the information mentioned in regulation 15(3) and, if the local authority propose to revise the plan, a draft of the revised plan.

(6)   The local authority must, having regard to the review and after considering any representations received within the period specified in the notice—

(a)   decide whether to vary or terminate the provision of special guardianship support services for the person; and

(b)   where appropriate, revise the plan.

(7)   The local authority must give the person notice of their decision (including the reasons for it) and, if applicable, details of the revised plan.

NOTES

Initial Commencement

Specified date

Specified date: 30 December 2005: see reg 1(1).

Extent

These Regulations apply to England only: see reg 1(2).

General

[1142]

Regulation 17(2) requires that where the local authority provides services other than periodic financial support, they must review the provision of such services if they become aware of any change in the person's circumstances which may affect the provision of services; at such stage in the implementation of the plan as they consider appropriate and in any event, at least annually.

The procedure out in regs 12 and 13 must be followed in reviews as for a first assessment (see reg 17(3)). Regulation 17(4) requires that if the local authority propose to vary or terminate the provision of services, before making any decision as a result of the review, they must give the affected person an opportunity to make representations and for that purpose they must give him notice of the proposed decision and the time allowed for making representations. The notice must contain the same information as the notification of the outcome of a first assessment, following the requirements in reg 15(3), and if the local authority propose to revise the plan, a draft of the revised plan in accordance with reg 17(5). The local authority must then, in accordance with reg 17(6), decide whether to vary or terminate the provision of SGSS and where appropriate, revise the plan, having regard to the review and after considering any representations received within the period specified in the notice. The local authority must give the person written notice of their decision (including the reasons for it) and, if applicable, details of the revised plan, see regs 17(7) and 20(1).

The Guidance, para 87, indicates that:

'The format and content of the review will vary depending on the circumstances of the case. Notification of changes of circumstances and any review of the provision of support services need not always necessitate direct contact between the local authority and the special guardian. Where the change of circumstances is relatively minor the review might be limited to an exchange of correspondence. In particular, the annual review of financial support might be achieved by exchange of correspondence between the local authority and the special guardian. Where the change of circumstances is relevant only to one service the review may be carried out with reference only to that service. However, where the change of circumstances is substantial, for example, a serious change in the behaviour of the child, it will normally be appropriate to conduct a new assessment of needs.'

[1143]

18 Review of financial support payable periodically

(1)   This regulation applies where the local authority provide financial support for a person payable periodically.

(2)   The local authority must review the financial support—

(a)   on receipt of the annual statement mentioned in regulation 10;

(b)   if any relevant change of circumstances or any breach of a condition mentioned in regulation 10 comes to their notice; and

(c)   at any stage in the implementation of the plan that they consider appropriate.

(3)   In paragraph (2) a relevant change of circumstances is any of the changes that the person has agreed to notify under regulation 10.

(4)   Regulations 12 and 13 apply in relation to a review under this regulation as they apply in relation to an assessment under Chapter 3 of this Part.

(5)   If the local authority propose, as a result of the review, to reduce or terminate financial support or revise the plan, before making that decision, the local authority must give the person an opportunity to make representations and for that purpose they must give the person notice of the proposed decision and the time allowed for making representations.

(6)   But paragraph (5) does not prevent the local authority from suspending payment of financial support pending that decision.

(7)   The notice must contain the information mentioned in regulation 15(3) and, if applicable, a draft of the revised plan.

(8)   The local authority must, having regard to the review, and after considering any representations received within the period specified in the notice—

(a)   decide whether to vary or terminate payment of the financial support or whether to seek to recover all or part of any financial support that has been paid; and

(b)   where appropriate, revise the plan.

(9)   The local authority must give the person notice of their decision, including the reasons for it, and, if applicable, the revised plan.

NOTES

Initial Commencement

Specified date

Specified date: 30 December 2005: see reg 1(1).

Extent

These Regulations apply to England only: see reg 1(2).

General

[1144]

Regulation 18 mirrors reg 17, with adaptations appropriate to the provision of financial support. Thus, regul 18(2) and (3) require that where the local authority provides financial support payable periodically it must review the financial support on receipt of the annual statement from the special guardian required under reg 10; if they become aware of any relevant change of circumstances that the special guardian agreed to notify in accordance with reg 10, or any breach of a condition made under reg 10 comes to the local authority's notice; and at any other stage in the implementation of the plan that the authority consider appropriate.

The procedure set out in regs 12 and 13 must again be followed in reviews as for a first assessment for financial support, see reg 18(4). Regulation 18(5) requires that if the local authority propose, as a result of the review, to reduce or terminate financial support or revise the plan, before making any decision as a result they must give the affected person an opportunity to make representations and for that purpose they must give him notice of the proposed decision and the time allowed for making representations, but reg 18(6) allows the local authority to suspend financial support pending that decision, if they think it appropriate.

The notice must contain the same information as the notification of the outcome of the first assessment, following the requirements in reg 15(3), and if the local authority propose to revise the plan, a draft of the revised plan in accordance with reg 18(7).

The local authority must then, in accordance with reg 18(8), decide whether to vary or terminate payment of the financial support, or whether to seek to recover all or part of any financial support that has been paid; and where appropriate, revise the plan, having regard to the review and after considering any representations received within the period specified in the notice. The local authority must give the person notice of their decision (including the reasons for it) and, if applicable, details of the revised plan (see reg 18(9)).

[1145]

Chapter 5
Urgent Cases and Notices

19 Urgent cases

Where any requirement applicable to the local authority in this Part in relation to carrying out an assessment, preparing a plan or giving notice would delay the provision of a service in a case of urgency, that requirement does not apply.

NOTES
Initial Commencement
Specified date
Specified date: 30 December 2005: see reg 1(1).

Extent
These Regulations apply to England only: see reg 1(2).

General

[1146]

The Guidance, para 93, recognises that it is important that the assessment process and follow up does not unnecessarily delay provision where a person has an urgent need for a service. Hence reg 19 provides that where *any* requirement placed on a local authority under Pt 2 of the regulations regarding an assessment (see regs 11–13, 17 and 18), preparing a plan (see regs 14, 17 and 18) or giving notice (see regs 15–18) would delay provision in a case of urgency, that requirement does not apply.

The local authority will need to review the provision as soon as possible after support has been provided, in accordance with the standard procedures set out in the regulations.

[1147]

20 Notices

(1) Any notice required to be given under this Part must be given in writing.
(2) If the person to whom notice is to be given is a child and—

(a) it appears to the local authority that the child is not of sufficient age and understanding for it to be appropriate to give him such notice; or
(b) in all the circumstances it is not appropriate to give him such notice,

the notice must be given to his special guardian or prospective special guardian (where applicable) or otherwise to the adult the local authority consider most appropriate.

NOTES

Initial Commencement

Specified date

Specified date: 30 December 2005: see reg 1(1).

Extent

These Regulations apply to England only: see reg 1(2).

General

[1148]

Any notice required to be given under Pt 2 of the regulations must, in accordance with reg 20(1), be given in writing.

Regulation 20(2) prescribes the arrangements for the giving of notice to a child. Where either, it appears to the local authority that the child is not of sufficient age and understanding for it to be appropriate to give him the required notice, or in all the circumstances it is not appropriate to give him such notice, the notice must be given to the child's actual, or prospective, special guardian, or otherwise to the adult that the local authority consider most appropriate.

[1149]

Part 3
Miscellaneous Provisions in Relation to Special Guardianship

General

[1150]

Regulation 21 and the Schedule prescribe the matters to be included in a report to the court under CA 1989, s 14A(8)(b). Regulation 22 specifies, for the purposes of the leaving care provisions in CA 1989, ss 24A and 24B, the relevant authority in relation to a child in respect of whom a SGO is in force and who was immediately before the making of the order looked after by a local authority.

[1151]

21 Court report

The matters specified in the Schedule are the matters prescribed for the purposes of section 14A(8)(b) of the Act (matters to be dealt with in report for the court).

NOTES

Initial Commencement

Specified date

Specified date: 30 December 2005: see reg 1(1).

Extent

These Regulations apply to England only: see reg 1(2).

General

[1152]

CA 1989, s 14A(8) requires that on receipt of a notice of an intended application for a SGO, as required by s 14A(7), the local authority must investigate the matter and prepare a report for the court dealing with (a) the suitability of the applicant to be a special guardian; (b) such matters as are prescribed and (c) any other matter which the local authority consider to be relevant (see para **[717]**). As reg 21 makes clear, the prescribed matters for the purposes of s 14(8)(b) are dealt with in the Schedule to the Regulations.

Where a court considers that a SGO should be made in the absence of an application, in accordance with the CA 1989, s 14A(6)(b), the relevant local authority's investigative and reporting functions remain (see para **[717]**). Although the Guidance, para 100, states that the 'making of a special guardianship order should not be unnecessarily delayed by the absence of the report for the court', in all cases s 14A(11) prohibits the court from making a SGO, unless it has received a report dealing with the matters in s 14A(8). The court has an independent power in s 14A(9) to ask a local authority to conduct a s 14A(8) investigation and prepare such a report. The information required for the local authority report is that in the Schedule to the Regulations whether there is an application or the court has asked the local authority to prepare a report.

CA 1989, s 14A(7) specifies which local authority is required to prepare the report for the court, see para **[716]**. During the local authority's investigation and preparation of their report, it may become necessary for another local authority to supply information, for example, where the local authority is preparing a report in respect of a child it is looking after and the prospective special guardian lives in the area of another local authority. Local authorities, wherever located, should co-operate fully, where necessary, in the investigation and preparation of the report for the court (see the Guidance, para 102). The Guidance also indicates (at para 103) that:

> 'Where the local authority has received notice from an applicant or a request from the court, it should send written information about the steps it proposes to undertake in preparing the report to the prospective special guardian and the parents of the child in question. This should include information about special guardianship support services and how to request an assessment of needs. Local authorities should also consider offering the child, the prospective special guardian or the child's parents an assessment of support needs during its investigation, if this appears to be appropriate.'

The Schedule extensively prescribes the matters to be dealt with in the report as discussed in the context of s 14A(8), see para **[717]**. These cover information about:

(i) the child who is the subject of the application or a child in respect of whom the court has required a report (see para 1(a)–(p));

(ii) the child's family (see para 2(a)–(k));

(iii) the wishes and feelings of the child and others (see para 3(a)–(c));

(iv) the prospective special guardian/s (see para 4(a)–(z) and (aa)–(bb));

(v) the local authority that compiled the report (see para 5(a)–(e)); plus

(vi) a summary prepared by the relevant medical professional (see 1(l), 4(k) and 6);

(vii) the implications of the making of a SGO for those listed in para 7;

(viii) the relative merits of special guardianship and other orders under the CA 1989 and the ACA 2002 with an assessment of whether the child's long term interests would be best met by a SGO (see para 8);

(ix)   recommendations as to (a) whether or not the SGO should be made and, if not, any alternative proposal and (b) contact arrangements between the child, his relatives and others (see paras 9 and 10).

The Guidance stresses the importance of accurately ascertaining and reporting on the child's wishes and feelings (see para 104). It also indicates (at para 106) that:

'Local authorities are expected to ensure that the social worker who conducts the investigation and prepares the report to the court is suitably qualified and experienced. In conducting the investigation, the person preparing the report should analyse and consider the information they ascertain from and about the prospective special guardian. The approach should be objective and inquiring. Information should be evaluated, and its accuracy and consistency checked. The safety of the child is of paramount concern and it is vital that the background of the prospective special guardian is checked rigorously. The special guardian (with an appropriate support package) should be considered able to meet the child's needs at the time of the making of the order and in the future.'

[1153]

22   Relevant authority for the purposes of section 24(5)(za) of the Act

For the purposes of section 24(5)(za) of the Act (persons qualifying for advice and assistance) the relevant authority shall be the local authority which last looked after the person.

NOTES
Initial Commencement
Specified date
Specified date: 30 December 2005: see reg 1(1).

Extent
These Regulations apply to England only: see reg 1(2).

General

[1154]

Miscellaneous reg 22 does not relate directly to the CA 1989, ss 14A–14F special guardianship provisions, but to a consequential amendment to the Act as a result of the introduction of special guardianship. The amendment relates to certain leaving care provisions in the CA 1989, P III as amended, in respect of children who were looked after by a local authority immediately before the making of a SGO.

The CA 1989, s 24(1) identifies persons qualifying for advice and assistance. In the context of special guardianship, s 24(1A) (as substituted by the ACA 2002, Sch 3, para 60(a)), provides that to qualify for advice and assistance, the child must (a) have reached the age of 16, but not the age of 21; (b) if aged less than 18, is the subject of a SGO or if he has reached the age of 18 was the subject of a SGO when he reached that age; and (c) was looked after by a local authority immediately before the making of the order.

The CA 1989, ss 24A and 24B, impose certain obligations regarding the provision of advice and assistance upon the 'relevant authority'. In the case of a person to whom s 24(1A) applies, the relevant authority is, by virtue of s 24(5)(za)(as inserted by ACA 2002, Sch 3, para 60(c)), determined in accordance with regulations. Regulation 22 is the relevant regulation and it provides that the 'relevant authority' shall be the local authority which last looked after the person. As the Guidance indicates, depending on the service required, it may be more appropriate for the young person to seek support locally where he is now resident, and gives the example of health care, see paragraph 97.

[1155]–[1200]

SCHEDULE
Matters to be dealt with in Report for the Court

Regulation 21

The following matters are prescribed for the purposes of section 14A(8)(b) of the Act.

1   In respect of the child—

(a)   name, sex, date and place of birth and address including local authority area;
(b)   a photograph and physical description;
(c)   nationality (and immigration status where appropriate);
(d)   racial origin and cultural and linguistic background;
(e)   religious persuasion (including details of baptism, confirmation or equivalent ceremonies);
(f)   details of any siblings including their dates of birth;
(g)   the extent of the child's contact with his relatives and any other person the local authority consider relevant;
(h)   whether the child is or has been looked after by a local authority or is or has been provided with accommodation by a voluntary organisation and details (including dates) of placements by the authority or organisation;
(i)   whether the prospective special guardian is a local authority foster parent of the child;
(j)   a description of the child's personality, his social development and his emotional and behavioural development and any related needs;
(k)   details of the child's interests, likes and dislikes;
(l)   a health history and a description of the state of the child's health which shall include any treatment the child is receiving;
(m)   names, addresses and types of nurseries or schools attended with dates;
(n)   the child's educational attainments;
(o)   whether the child is subject to a statement of special educational needs under the Education Act 1996; and
(p)   details of any order made by a court with respect to the child under the Act including—

(i)   the name of the court;
(ii)   the order made; and
(iii)   the date on which the order was made.

2   In respect of the child's family—

(a)   name, date and place of birth and address (and the date on which their last address was confirmed) including local authority area of each parent of the child and his siblings under the age of 18;
(b)   a photograph, if available, and physical description of each parent;
(c)   nationality (and immigration status where appropriate) of each parent;
(d)   racial origin and cultural and linguistic background of each parent;
(e)   whether the child's parents were married to each other at the time of the child's birth or have subsequently married and whether they are divorced or separated;
(f)   where the child's parents have been previously married or formed a civil partnership, the date of the marriage or civil partnership;
(g)   where the child's parents are not married, whether the father has parental responsibility and, if so, how it was acquired;
(h)   if the identity or whereabouts of the father are not known, the information about him that has been ascertained and from whom, and the steps that have been taken to establish paternity;
(i)   the past and present relationship of the child's parents;
(j)   where available, the following information in respect of each parent—

	(i)	health history, including details of any serious physical or mental illness, any hereditary disease or disorder or disability;
	(ii)	religious persuasion;
	(iii)	educational history;
	(iv)	employment history;
	(v)	personality and interests;

(k) in respect of the child's siblings under the age of 18—

    (i) the person with whom the sibling is living;

    (ii) whether the sibling is looked after by a local authority or provided with accommodation by a voluntary organisation; and

    (iii) details of any court order made with respect to the sibling under the Act, including the name of the court, the order made and the date on which the order was made.

3 In respect of the wishes and feelings of the child and others—

(a) an assessment of the child's wishes and feelings (considered in light of his age and understanding) regarding—

    (i) special guardianship;

    (ii) his religious and cultural upbringing; and

    (iii) contact with his relatives and any other person the local authority consider relevant,

and the date on which the child's wishes and feelings were last ascertained.

(b) the wishes and feelings of each parent regarding—

    (i) special guardianship;

    (ii) the child's religious and cultural upbringing; and

    (iii) contact with the child,

and the date on which the wishes and feelings of each parent were last ascertained; and

(c) the wishes and feelings of any of the child's relatives, or any other person the local authority consider relevant regarding the child and the dates on which those wishes and feelings were last ascertained.

4 In respect of the prospective special guardian or, where two or more persons are jointly prospective special guardians, each of them—

(a) name, date and place of birth and address including local authority area;

(b) a photograph and physical description;

(c) nationality (and immigration status where appropriate);

(d) racial origin and cultural and linguistic background;

(e) if the prospective special guardian is—

    (i) married, the date and place of marriage;

    (ii) has formed a civil partnership, the date and place of registration of the civil partnership; or

    (iii) has a partner, details of that relationship;

(f) details of any previous marriage, civil partnership, or relationship;

(g) where the prospective special guardians wish to apply jointly, the nature of their relationship and an assessment of the stability of that relationship;

(h) if the prospective special guardian is a member of a couple and is applying alone for a special guardianship order, the reasons for this;

(i) whether the prospective special guardian is a relative of the child;

(j) prospective special guardian's relationship with the child;

(k) a health history of the prospective special guardian including details of any serious physical or mental illness, any hereditary disease or disorder or disability;

(l) a description of how the prospective special guardian relates to adults and children;

(m) previous experience of caring for children;

(n)   parenting capacity, to include an assessment of the prospective special guardian's ability and suitability to bring up the child;

(o)   where there have been any past assessments as a prospective adopter, foster parent or special guardian, relevant details as appropriate;

(p)   details of income and expenditure;

(q)   information about the prospective special guardian's home and the neighbourhood in which he lives;

(r)   details of other members of the household and details of any children of the prospective special guardian even if not resident in the household;

(s)   details of the parents and any siblings of the prospective special guardian, with their ages or ages at death;

(t)   the following information—

    (i)   religious persuasion;
    (ii)   educational history;
    (iii)   employment history; and
    (iv)   personality and interests;

(u)   details of any previous family court proceedings in which the prospective special guardian has been involved (which have not been referred to elsewhere in this report);

(v)   a report of each of the interviews with the three persons nominated by the prospective special guardian to provide personal references for him;

(w)   whether the prospective special guardian is willing to follow any wishes of the child or his parents in respect of the child's religious and cultural upbringing;

(x)   the views of other members of the prospective special guardian's household and wider family in relation to the proposed special guardianship order;

(y)   an assessment of the child's current and future relationship with the family of the prospective special guardian;

(z)   reasons for applying for a special guardianship order and extent of understanding of the nature and effect of special guardianship and whether the prospective special guardian has discussed special guardianship with the child;

    (aa)   any hopes and expectations the prospective special guardian has for the child's future; and

    (bb)   the prospective special guardian's wishes and feelings in relation to contact between the child and his relatives or any other person the local authority considers relevant.

5   In respect of the local authority which completed the report—

(a)   name and address;

(b)   details of any past involvement of the local authority with the prospective special guardian, including any past preparation for that person to be a local authority foster parent or adoptive parent or special guardian;

(c)   where section 14A(7)(a) of the Act applies and the prospective special guardian lives in the area of another local authority, details of the local authority's enquiries of that other local authority about the prospective special guardian;

(d)   a summary of any special guardianship support services provided by the authority for the prospective special guardian, the child or the child's parent and the period for which those services are to be provided; and

(e)   where the local authority has decided not to provide special guardianship support services, the reasons why.

6   A summary prepared by the medical professional who provided the information referred to in paragraphs 1(l) and 4(k).

7   The implications of the making of a special guardianship order for—

(a)   the child;
(b)   the child's parent;
(c)   the prospective special guardian and his family; and
(d)   any other person the local authority considers relevant.

PART C – SIs

8   The relative merits of special guardianship and other orders which may be made under the Act or the Adoption and Children Act 2002 with an assessment of whether the child's long term interests would be best met by a special guardianship order.

9   A recommendation as to whether or not the special guardianship order sought should be made in respect of the child and, if not, any alternative proposal in respect of the child.

10   A recommendation as to what arrangements there should be for contact between the child and his relatives or any person the local authority consider relevant.

NOTES

Initial Commencement

Specified date

Specified date: 30 December 2005: see reg 1(1).

Extent

These Regulations apply to England only: see reg 1(2).

Special Guardianship (Wales) Regulations 2005

(SI 2005/1513)

Made	*7 June 2005*
Coming into force	*20 December 2005*

The National Assembly for Wales, in exercise of the powers conferred upon it by sections 14A(8)(b), 14F, 24(5)(za), 26(3C) and 104 of the Children Act 1989 hereby makes the following Regulations:

General

[1201]

The Special Guardianship (Wales) Regulations 2005 (SI 2005/1513) (the regulations) supplement the CA 1989, ss 14A–14G as inserted by the ACA 2002, s 115(1) regarding special guardianship orders in relation to Wales. Part 2 and the Schedule prescribe the matters to be included in a report to the court under s 14A(8) (reg 2 and Schedule). Part 3 forms the bulk of the regulations and makes detailed provision regarding special guardianship support services ('*gwasanaethau cymorth gwarcheidiaeth arbennig*' hereafter SGSS) (see regs 3–12). Part 4 specifies, for the purposes of the CA 1989, ss 24A and 24B, the relevant authority in relation to a child in respect of whom a special guardianship order (hereafter SGO) is in force and who was immediately before the making of the order looked after by a local authority (reg 13). It also makes provision in connection with representations (including complaints) about SGSS (reg 14).

Guidance to Support The Special Guardianship (Wales) Regulations 2005 (Canllawiau I Gefnogi Rheoliadau Gwarcheidiaeth Arbennig (Cymru) 2005 hereafter 'the Guidance') has been issued by the Welsh Assembly Government/ Llywodraeth Cynulliad Cymru (see *National Assembly for Wales Circular/Cylchlythyr Cynulliad Cenedlaethol Cymru*, NAFWC 26/2006). The Guidance does not have statutory force 'but should be complied with unless local circumstances indicate exceptional reasons which justify a variation', see para 2. Appropriate reference is made to the Guidance throughout the commentary on the regulations.

'Local authorities will need to review their existing policies and practice in the light of the Regulations and this guidance and give the same priority to these responsibilities as to other statutory duties' (see the Guidance, para 3).

[1202]

Part 1
General

1 Title, commencement, application and interpretation

(1) The title of these Regulations is the Special Guardianship (Wales) Regulations 2005 and they come into force on 30 December 2005.
(2) These Regulations apply in relation to Wales.
(3) In these Regulations—

'the Act' ('*y Ddeddf*') means the Children Act 1989;
'adoption support agencies' ('*asiantaethau cymorth mabwysiadu*') has the same meaning as in the Care Standards Act 2000;
'couple' ('*cwpl*') has the same meaning as in section 144 of the Adoption and Children Act 2002;
'independent fostering agencies' ('*asiantaethau maethu annibynnol*') has the same meaning as in regulation 2(1) of the Fostering Services (Wales) Regulations 2003;

'local education authority' ('*awdurdod addysg lleol*') has the same meaning as in the Education Act 1996;

'prospective special guardian' ('*darpar warcheidwad arbennig*') means a person—

(a) who has given notice to a local authority under section 14A(7) of the Act of an intention to apply for an SGO in accordance with section 14A(3) of the Act; or

(b) in respect of whom a court has requested a local authority to conduct an investigation and prepare a report pursuant to section 14A(9) of the Act;

'related person' ('*person perthynol*') means, in relation to a relevant child—

(a) a relative of the child within the meaning of section 105 of the Act; and

(b) any other person with whom the child has a relationship which appears to the local authority to be beneficial to the child's welfare;

'relevant child' ('*plentyn perthnasol*') means a child in respect of whom—

(a) an SGO is in force (referred to in these regulations as 'a child subject to an SGO');

(b) a person has given notice to a local authority under section 14A(7) of the Act of an intention to apply for an SGO in accordance with section 14A(3) of the Act (referred to in these regulations as 'a child in respect of whom an SGO is sought'); or

(c) a court has asked a local authority to conduct an investigation and prepare a report pursuant to section 14A(9) of the Act (referred to in these regulations as 'a child in respect of whom the court has required a report'),

and references to 'relevant children' shall be construed accordingly;

'SGO' ('*GGA*') means a special guardianship order;

'special guardian' ('*gwarcheidwad arbennig*') means a person appointed to be a special guardian under an SGO made pursuant to section 14A of the Act;

'special guardianship support services' ('*gwasanaethau cymorth gwarcheidiaeth arbennig*') means those services falling within regulation 3(1) and section 14F(1)(a) of the Act; and

'voluntary adoption agencies' ('*asiantaethau mabwysiadu gwirfoddol*') has the same meaning as in section 4 of the Care Standards Act 2000.

(4) In these Regulations, a reference—

(a) to the Schedule is to the Schedule to these Regulations;

(b) to a numbered regulation is to the regulation in these Regulations bearing that number;

(c) in a regulation to a numbered paragraph is to the paragraph in that regulation bearing that number.

NOTES

Initial Commencement

Specified date

Specified date: 30 December 2005: see para (1) above.

General

[1203]

The regulations apply in relation to Wales only (regulation 1(2)). For the English regulations see the Special Guardianship Regulations 2005 (SI 2005/1109) (para [1101]).

Regulation 1(3) defines certain terminology used in the regulations. Where they refer to 'the Act' ('y Ddeddf') this means the Children Act 1989 (CA 1989), as it does throughout this commentary on the regulations. Where definitions refer to other Acts they are identified in the definition.

[1204]

Part 2
Special Guardianship Orders—Reports

2 Reports

The matters specified in the Schedule are prescribed for the purposes of section 14A(8)(b) of the Act.

NOTES
Initial Commencement
Specified date
Specified date: 30 December 2005: see reg 1(1).

General

[1205]

CA 1989, s 14A(8) requires that on receipt of a notice of an intended application for a SGO, as required by CA 1989, s 14A(7), the local authority must investigate the matter and prepare a report for the court dealing with:

(a)   the suitability of the applicant to be a special guardian;

(b)   such matters as are prescribed; and

(c)   any other matter which the local authority consider to be relevant (see para [717]).

As reg 2 makes clear, the prescribed matters for the purposes of CA 1989, s 14(8)(b) are dealt with in the Schedule to the regulations.

Where a court considers that a SGO should be made in the absence of an application, in accordance with the CA 1989, s 14A(6)(b), the relevant local authority's investigative and reporting functions remain (see para [717]). In all cases, CA 1989, s 14A(11) prohibits the court from making a SGO, unless it has received a report dealing with the matters in s 14A(8). The court has an independent power in CA 1989, s 14A(9) to ask a local authority to conduct a s 14A(8) investigation and prepare such a report. The information required for the local authority report is that in the Schedule to the regulations, whether there is an application or the court has asked the local authority to prepare a report.

The CA 1989, s 14A(7) specifies which local authority is required to prepare the report for the court (see para [716]). During the local authority's investigation and preparation of their report, it may become necessary for another local authority to supply information, for example, where the local authority is preparing a report in respect of a child it is looking after and the prospective special guardian lives in the area of another local authority. Local authorities, wherever located, should co-operate fully, where necessary, in the investigation and preparation of the report for the court. The local authority may also need to contact the local health services, (see the Guidance para 37). The Guidance (para 38), also indicates that:

'Where the local authority has received notice from an applicant or a request from the court, it should send written information about the steps it proposes to undertake in preparing the report to the prospective special guardian and the parents of the child in question. This should include information about special guardianship support services and how to request an assessment of needs. Local authorities should also consider offering the child, the prospective special guardian or the child's parents an assessment of support needs during its investigation if this appears to be appropriate.'

The Schedule extensively prescribes the matters to be dealt with in the report. These cover information about: (i) the child who is the subject of the application, or a child in respect of whom the court has required a report (see para 2(a)–(j)); (ii) the child's family (see para 3(a)–(k)); (iii) the prospective special guardian/s (see para 4(a)–(j)); (iv) the local authority that compiled the report (see para 5(a)–(g)); and (v) the conclusions and recommendations reached in the report (see para 6(a)–(c)).

The Guidance (para 40), also indicates that:

> 'Local authorities are expected to ensure that the social worker who conducts the investigation and prepares the report to the court is suitably qualified and experienced. In conducting the investigation, the person preparing the report should analyse and consider the information they ascertain from and about the prospective special guardian. The approach should be objective and inquiring. Information should be evaluated and its accuracy and consistency checked. The safety of the child is most important and it is vital that the background of prospective special guardians is checked thoroughly.'

[1206]

Part 3
Special Guardianship Support Services

General

[1207]

Regulations 3–12 form the major part of the regulations and make detailed provision with regard to the support services which each local authority must make arrangements to provide to meet the needs of people affected by special guardianship, as required by the CA 1989, s 14F (see para [769]). Regulation 3 deals with the provision of services and regs 4 and 7 specifically with financial support. Regulations 5, 6 and 8 provide for needs assessments, procedure and notification of assessment. Regulation 9 deals with decisions in relation to SGSS, reg 10 with notices, reg 11 with SGSS plans, and reg 12 with reviews and cessation of SGSS provision.

These regulations placed new duties on local authorities to carry out assessments of needs for sgss and thereafter to decide whether to provide any services. The Guidance emphasises (at para 26) that:

> 'Special guardianship support services should not be seen in isolation from mainstream services. There are very few services that are only applicable to special guardianship. While such services are important it is vital to ensure that special guardians and the respective child are assisted in accessing mainstream services. They may also need to be helped to negotiate their way through the benefits system and the statementing process. There are many other services that are typically provided to children and families in need from which special guardians and the child may also derive great benefit if an assessment indicates that they have needs which may effectively be met by such support.'

Mainstream services are provided to children, young people, and families with particular needs through a variety of routes for example health services, including child and adolescent mental health services (CAMHS); local education authorities, particularly to meet special educational needs; the benefits and tax credits system; housing services and family centres. 'It is important that service providers are aware of the particular and additional dimension special guardianship brings to the lives of special guardians and the respective child' (Guidance, para 27).

In planning the provision of SGSS, the local authority should take into account the similar services already being delivered in their area, particularly adoption support services. The ACA 2002, s 3(4)(b) provides that a local authority may arrange for the adoption support services that it has a duty to establish and maintain under s 3, to be provided by others. This includes the arrangements that authorities are required to make for the provision of SGSS (see the Guidance, para 25). The Guidance (para 28), further states that:

'Local authorities have the same obligations to assess and provide support services for special guardianship orders as for adoptions. However, special guardianship is a new option for permanency and the level and type of support services that may be required are currently unknown. There may be a natural cross over of services between special guardianship and adoption.'

At the very least, the local authority will need to provide advice, information (including leaflets) and counselling. The following are also included, inter alia, in para 29 as being useful: training; named local authority contacts/advocates; help lines; and mediation services. Depending on demand, support groups or networks could be established. Other support may be that provided as a matter of course, and as appropriate, to any child by statutory agencies or voluntary agencies. Other examples include; Cymorth; Sure Start; financial support; voluntary sector parenting support; and organisations funded by The Children and Families Organisation Grant.

'It is important when Local Authorities are planning the provision of services within the authority, that the potential needs of children subject to a special guardianship order and their families, for such services are not overlooked. Local authorities will need to consider what they have to provide, what they can provide and how they allocate provision of services.' (Guidance, para 30)

[1208]

3 Provision of special guardianship support services

(1) For the purposes of section 14F(1)(b) of the Act, the following services are prescribed in relation to special guardianship—

(a) the provision of financial support under regulation 4;
(b) services to enable groups of relevant children, special guardians, prospective special guardians and parents of relevant children (or groups consisting of any combination of those individuals) to discuss matters relating to special guardianship;
(c) assistance for relevant children, their parents and related persons in relation to arrangements made for contact between such children and any of the following—

   (i) their parents;
   (ii) their former guardians or special guardians;
   (iii) related persons;

(d) services provided in relation to the therapeutic needs of a relevant child;
(e) assistance for the purpose of ensuring the continuance of the relationship between a relevant child and a special guardian or prospective special guardian, including—

   (i) training for that person to meet any special needs of the child; and
   (ii) respite care;

(f)   where the relationship between a child and his or her special guardian is in danger of breaking down, assistance whose aim is to prevent that occurring, including—

    (i)   mediation; and
    (ii) organising and holding meetings between such persons as appear to the authority to be appropriate in order to address the difficulties faced by the relationship between the child and his or her special guardian.

(2)   The fact that a person is outside a local authority's area does not prevent the provision of special guardianship support services to him or her in accordance with these Regulations.

(3)   The following are prescribed for the purposes of section 14F(9)(b) of the Act—

(a)   adoption support agencies;
(b)   Local Health Boards, NHS Trusts and Primary Care Trusts;
(c)   local education authorities;
(d)   voluntary adoption agencies; and
(e)   independent fostering agencies.

NOTES
Initial Commencement
Specified date
Specified date: 30 December 2005: see reg 1(1).

General

[1209]

SGSS are defined by the CA 1989, s 14F(1) as counselling, advice and information and other services prescribed by regulations, in relation to special guardianship. Regulation 3 prescribes, in accordance with CA 1989, s 14F(1)(b), the additional SGSS. As well as financial support under reg 4 (see reg 3(1)(a)), a range of services and assistance (including mediation) are prescribed in regs 3(1)(b)–(f).

The Guidance (para 42), provides that:

> 'Local authorities are required to make arrangements for all of these services to be available, regardless of whether they have decided to provide any service to any person.'

Under the CA 1989, s 14F(1) local authorities are responsible for making arrangements for the provision of SGSS. That does not mean, however, that the local authority are required to provide a service themselves. For example, a child with communication problems may require the help of an NHS Trust or Local Health Board speech therapist and additional classroom support at school rather than any specialist social services. As for any other child, these services would be provided by the responsible health or education agency (see the Guidance, para 45). CA 1989, s 14F(9) enables the local authority to arrange for SGSS, or part thereof, to be provided by (a) another local authority or (b) others prescribed in regulations on the authority's behalf (see para [770]). Regulation 3(3) identifies those who are prescribed for the purposes of CA 1989, s 14F(9)(b).

The fact that a person is outside a local authority's area does not prevent the provision of SGSS (see reg 3(2))

[1210]

4   Circumstances in which financial support can be paid

(1)   Financial support can only be paid to a special guardian or prospective special guardian in the following cases, namely where—

(a)   a child subject to an SGO lives with his or her special guardian and the local authority consider that financial support is necessary to ensure that the guardian can continue to look after the child;

(b)   a child in respect of whom an SGO is sought or a child in respect of whom the court has required a report lives with a prospective special guardian and the local authority consider that—

    (i)   it would be beneficial for the child for an SGO to be made; and

    (ii)   financial support is necessary to ensure that the prospective special guardian can continue to look after the child pending the court's decision on whether to make an SGO;

(c)   the local authority consider that—

    (i)   the making of an SGO, or of an order for financial provision to be made to or for the benefit of a child, would be beneficial for a relevant child; and

    (ii)   it is appropriate to contribute to or meet any legal costs, including court fees, of a prospective special guardian or special guardian associated with seeking an SGO or an order for financial provision; or

(d)   a relevant child lives with his or her prospective special guardian or special guardian and the local authority consider that the child needs special care which requires a greater expenditure of resources than would otherwise be the case due to the child's illness, disability, emotional or behavioural difficulties or the consequences of past abuse or neglect.

(2) Financial support must not be paid under this regulation unless the local authority has required the special guardian or prospective special guardian ('the guardian') to undertake to—

(a)   inform them forthwith if—

    (i)   the guardian changes his or her address;

    (ii)   the relevant child no longer has his or her home with the guardian;

    (iii)   the child dies; or

    (iv)   the guardian's financial circumstances, or the relevant child's financial needs or resources, change;

either orally or in writing, provided that where the information is provided orally it must be confirmed in writing within 7 days; and

(b)   provide the authority with an annual statement (starting from a date to be specified by the authority) of his or her financial circumstances and the relevant child's financial needs and resources.

NOTES

Initial Commencement

Specified date

Specified date: 30 December 2005: see reg 1(1).

General

[1211]

The Guidance (para 67), states that:

'Financial barriers should not be the sole reason for a special guardianship arrangement failing to survive, or to go ahead where this would be in the best interests of the child. The central principle therefore remains that financial support may be payable to help secure a suitable special guardianship arrangement where such an arrangement cannot be readily made because of a financial obstacle. The local authority should:

– Ensure that the prospective special guardian or special guardian and their family are aware of, and taking advantage of, all benefits and tax credits available to them;

– Consider the impact of special guardianship on the prospective special guardian or special guardian's family, and whether any lump sum payments are required to secure the success of the arrangement, eg settling in costs, home adaptations/ extension, costs of a course of therapeutic treatment, etc;

– Consider the residual ongoing impact of special guardianship that might necessitate regular payments;

– Consider any special circumstances that apply to the child and (prospective) special guardian, eg where foster carers wish to become a special guardian to a child for whom they are currently caring'.

Regulation 4(1) prescribes the four circumstances in which financial support is payable to a special guardian or prospective special guardian (as defined in reg 1(3)). These are where the local authority consider that:

(1) financial support is necessary to ensure that a special guardian can continue to look after a child subject to a SGO who is living with him (see reg 4(1)(a));

(2) in the case of a child subject to a special guardianship application (or a child in respect of whom the court has required a report under CA 1989, s 14A(9)), and who lives with a prospective guardian, a SGO would be for the child's benefit and financial support is necessary to ensure that the prospective special guardian can continue to look after the child pending the court's decision whether to make a SGO (see reg 4(1)(b) and the Guidance, para 73);

(3) it is appropriate either to contribute to, or meet, any legal costs, including court fees, of a special guardian or prospective special guardian, associated with seeking an SGO or order for financial provision to be made to or for the benefit of the child, where the making of either order would be for the child's benefit, see reg 4(1)(c);

(4) a relevant child (as defined in reg 1(3)) who lives with a prospective special guardian or special guardian needs special care which requires greater expenditure than would otherwise be the case because of the child's illness, disability, emotional or behavioural difficulties or the consequences of past abuse or neglect (see reg 4(1)(d)).

Paragraph 50 of the Guidance indicates that the regulations are intended to give agencies greater flexibility to respond to the individual needs of a child and their circumstances and then goes on to provide a broad interpretation of reg 4(1).

Regulation 4(2) provides that, in accordance with CA 1989, s 14F(8)(e), financial support is not payable under reg 4 unless the local authority has required the special guardian, or prospective special guardian, to undertake:

(a) immediately to inform the local authority if:

(i) he changes his address,

(ii) the child's home is no longer with him,

(iii) the child dies, or

(iv) there is a change in his financial circumstances or the child's financial needs or resources (see Guidance, para 79), and where the information is given orally, that he will confirm it in writing within seven days; and

(b) that he will provide the authority with an annual statement of his financial circumstances and the financial needs and resources of the child.

This should include details such as the special guardian's address and whether the child still has its home with the special guardian, in accordance with the Guidance, para.

If the guardian fails to provide an annual statement of circumstances as required by reg 4(2)(b), the local authority may review, suspend or cease payment or seek to recover all or part of it, provided that they have sent a written reminder and 28 days have expired (see reg 12(6)–(7)). They may lift any suspension when the statement of financial circumstances is received in accordance with reg 12(8).

The provision of financial support must be reviewed if any relevant change of circumstances, including a change of address, comes to the notice of the local authority and upon receipt of the annual statement required by reg 4(2)(b) (see reg 12(2)).

Paragraph 54 of the Guidance indicates that 'Payment of financial support is intended where the child's condition is serious and long-term. For example, where a child needs a special diet or where items such as shoes, clothing or bedding need to be replaced at a higher rate than would normally be the case with a child of similar age who is not affected by the particular condition'.

Regulation 7 prescribes the matters that the local authority must take into account in determining the amount of any financial support and the limited circumstances in which it can include an element of remuneration.

Regulation 12(9) and (10) prescribe for cessation of payment of financial support.

[1212]

5 Assessment of needs for special guardianship support services

(1) Subject to paragraph (2), a local authority must, on request, carry out an assessment of the following persons' needs for special guardianship support services, namely—

(a) a person falling within section 14F(3)(a) to (c) of the Act;
(b) a child of a special guardian;
(c) a child in respect of whom an SGO is sought or a child in respect of whom the court has required a report;
(d) a child (other than one falling within (a) to (c) above) who is named in a report produced under section 14A(8) of the Act;
(e) a prospective special guardian; and
(f) a related person provided that before the request for an assessment was made arrangements were in place for contact between the person and the relevant child,

and, accordingly, the persons in sub-paragraphs (b) to (f) are hereby prescribed for the purposes of section 14F(3)(d) of the Act.

(2) Paragraph (1) does not apply unless—

(a) the person who has requested an assessment falls within any of sub-paragraphs (a) to (e) of paragraph (1) and he or she either—

(i) lives in the area of the local authority;
(ii) intends to live in that area;
(iii) is a child looked after by that authority; or
(iv) is a person in respect of whom the court asked the local authority to prepare a report under section 14A(9), or a child to whom such a report relates or would relate; or

(b) where the person falls within sub-paragraph (f) of paragraph (1), the relevant child lives or intends to live in the authority's area or is looked after by the authority.

PART C – SIs

(3)   An assessment of a person's needs for special guardianship support services may be carried out by reference only to a particular special guardianship support service where—

(a)   the person whose needs are being assessed has requested a particular special guardianship support service; or

(b)   it appears to the authority that the person's needs for special guardianship support services may be adequately assessed by reference only to a particular special guardianship support service.

NOTES

Initial Commencement

Specified date

Specified date: 30 December 2005: see reg 1(1).

General

[1213]

In accordance with CA 1989, s 14F(3), reg 5(1) and (2) identify those people at whose request an assessment for SGSS is mandatory. An assessment may be by reference to a particular service in accordance with reg 5(3).

Local authorities have a residual discretion under CA 1989, s 14F(4), at the request of any other person, to assess his needs for SGSS. If they do so, they should follow the same procedure (see reg 6) as they would for those entitled to an assessment.

[1214]

6   Assessment procedure

(1)   In carrying out an assessment of a person's needs for special guardianship support services, a local authority must—

(a)   have regard to the following considerations, namely—

(i)   the needs of the person being assessed and how these might be met;

(ii)   the needs of the relevant child and the family members of any special guardian or prospective special guardian, in so far as they have not been addressed under head (i) above, and how these might be met;

(iii)   the circumstances that led up to the making of an SGO in respect of a child subject to an SGO;

(iv)   any special needs of a child subject to an SGO arising from the fact that—

(aa)   the child has been looked after by a local authority;

(bb)   the child has been habitually resident outside the British Islands; or

(cc)   the special guardian is a relative of the child; and

(v)   where the assessment relates to financial support, the requirements of regulation 7.

(b)   interview the person whose needs are being assessed and, where that person is a child subject to an SGO, the special guardian; and

(c)   where it appears to the authority that there may be a need for the provision of services for the person whose needs are being assessed by a Local Health Board, NHS Trust, Primary Care Trust or local education authority, consult that Board, Trust or authority.

(2)   A local authority must ensure that an assessment of a person's needs for special guardianship support services—

(a)   is carried out by, or under the supervision of, an individual who has suitable qualifications, experience and skills for that purpose; and

(b)   results in a written report of the assessment.

NOTES
Initial Commencement
Specified date
Specified date: 30 December 2005: see reg 1(1).

General

[1215]

The nature and scope of, and procedure for, assessment of a person's needs for SGSS are prescribed in reg 6.

Regulation 6(1)(a) lists the considerations to which the local authority are to have regard when carrying out an assessment in accordance with the CA 1989, s 14F(8)(a) and (d). It focuses upon the needs of the person being assessed, the relevant child (as defined in reg 1(3)), the family members of any special guardian or prospective special guardian; the circumstances that led up to the making of a SGO; any special needs of the child subject to the order arising from any fact identified in reg 6(a)(iv) and where the assessment relates to financial support the requirements of reg 7.

Regulation 6(1)(b) requires that the local authority must interview the person whose needs are being assessed and where that person is a child subject to a SGO, the special guardian.

Regulation 6(1)(c) requires that the local authority consults the relevant Local Health Board, NHS Trust, Primary Care Trust or local education authority (as defined in the Education Act 1996, see reg 1(3)) if it appears to the local authority that a person may have a need for services from the relevant body.

The local authority must, in accordance with reg 6(2)(a), ensure that the assessment is carried out by, or under the supervision of a suitably qualified and experienced individual. 'The assessment needs to be co-ordinated to ensure that all relevant agencies and individuals are included and a suitable professional carries out the process' (see the Guidance para 58). In accordance with the Guidance (paras 60–64), the *Framework for the Assessment of Children in Need and their Families* should be followed:

'60.   This takes into account the child's developmental needs, the parenting capacity of the special guardians and consideration of the family and environmental factors that together help to explain the child's life so far and what life might be like with the new family. Taking this approach means that past assessments for the child who has previously been a child in need or looked after by a local authority, can inform the assessment of special guardianship support needs.

61.   The families seeking help from local authorities will have differing levels of need. Advice, practical services or short-term interventions will help many. A smaller proportion will have problems of a more difficult or serious nature that they require more detailed assessment, involving contributions from other agencies and leading to appropriate plans and interventions. In their assessment of whether the child has special guardianship support needs, and in considering how to respond to those needs, a local authority also has to take into account the needs of the special guardians and other children in the family. The general circumstances of the parents and relatives of the child will also be relevant. Providing services that meet the needs of the special guardians may be the most effective means of benefiting the child. The assessment process is expected to be flexible one and should not delay the appropriate services being provided.

62.   In many cases, families are likely to be clear about their problems but may not be

sure where to turn or how to obtain services. With advice and information, they will be able to take appropriate action. Providing this advice and information may be all that is required of a local authority in a majority of cases.

63.   Where there is a question about whether the child has special guardianship support needs and therefore whether special guardianship support services are necessary, an assessment is required. The processes set out in the Assessment Framework for an initial assessment and, where appropriate a core assessment, should be followed. For some families, the process of assessment is likely to be very helpful and therapeutic in itself. Being able to look at problems in a constructive manner with a professional who is willing to listen and who helps family members to reflect on what is happening, may be enough to help them find their own solutions. During the assessment process it may emerge that families will be best helped by agencies other than social services. Armed with this information, families may wish to refer themselves to a particular agency direct; others may wish to have help in gaining access to other agencies or services.

64.   The initial and core assessment recording forms and the child's plan and review (The Exemplar Records for the Integrated Children's System) have been designed to assist in the analysis of the child and family's circumstances and in the development and reviewing of a plan of action.'

After carrying out an assessment under reg 6, the local authority must prepare a written report in accordance with reg 6(2)(b). It must also, in accordance with regs 8 and 10, supply, in writing, the information specified in reg 8(2), and give written notice of the right to make representations in accordance with reg 8(3), to the person assessed. Thereafter the local authority must decide whether to provide any SGSS, including financial support, in accordance with reg 9. The amount of any financial support is determined in accordance with reg 7.

[1216]

---

7 Financial support—amount

(1) In determining the amount of any financial support, the local authority must take account of—

(a)   the financial resources available to the special guardian or the prospective special guardian as the case may be;

(b)   the amount required by the person just mentioned in respect of his or her reasonable outgoings and commitments (excluding outgoings in respect of the relevant child);

(c)   the needs and resources of the relevant child;

(d)   necessary expenditure on legal costs (to include court fees) in respect of proceedings relating to an SGO or an application for financial provision to be made in relation to, or for the benefit of, the relevant child;

(e)   necessary expenditure in order to facilitate the relevant child having his or her home with a person falling within sub-paragraph (a) above, including any initial expenditure necessary for the purposes of accommodating the child, to include any necessary provision of furniture and domestic equipment, alterations to and adaptations of the home, provision of means of transport and of clothing, toys and other items necessary for the purposes of looking after the child;

(f)   necessary expenditure of the person falling within sub-paragraph (a) above associated with any special educational needs or special behavioural difficulties of the relevant child, including—

(i)   the costs of equipment required for the purposes of meeting any special educational needs of the child;

> (ii) the costs of rectifying any damage in the home in which the child lives, where such costs arise out of the special behavioural difficulties of the child;
>
> (iii) the costs of placing the child in a boarding school, where that placement is necessary to meet the special educational needs of the child; and
>
> (iv) any other costs of meeting any special needs of the child; and
>
> (g) expenditure on travel for the purposes of visits between a relevant child and his or her parent or related persons.
>
> (2) Financial support must not be paid to meet any needs in so far as those needs can reasonably be expected to be met by virtue of the payment of any benefit (including tax credit) or allowance.
>
> (3) Unless paragraph (4) applies, financial support must not include any element of remuneration for the care of a relevant child.
>
> (4) This paragraph applies where—
>
> (a) as a prospective special guardian, a person was also the foster parent of a relevant child;
>
> (b) the local authority consider that any fostering allowance paid to that person for fostering that child will cease upon the making of an SGO; and
>
> (c) before an SGO is made, the local authority decide to pay financial support and determine that it is to be paid periodically.
>
> **NOTES**
>
> **Initial Commencement**
>
> *Specified date*
>
> Specified date: 30 December 2005: see reg 1(1).

General

[1217]

This key regulation regarding financial support prescribes the matters which the local authority must take into account in determining the amount of any financial support and the limited circumstances in which it can include an element of remuneration for the care of a child. It is to be read with the other regulations relating to financial support (see regs 4, 8, 9 and 12).

'The term "financial support" is intended to apply to:

- A single lump sum payment to meet a specific assessed need;

- A series of lump sum payments to meet a specific assessed need;

- A periodic or regular payment payable at intervals to be determined by the local authority to meet a specific assessed ongoing need.' (Guidance, para 70)

See also reg 9(7)(8) and (9) for the circumstances in which financial support may be paid other than as a single payment.

Regulation 7(1) prescribes the factors which the local authority must take into account to determine the amount of any financial support, namely;

- The financial resources and reasonable outgoings and commitments (excluding outgoings in respect of the child) of the special guardian or prospective special guardian ('the guardian').

  Reasonable outgoings will include housing and transport costs, and daily living expenses.

- The financial needs and resources of the child.

- Expenditure on travel for the purposes of visits between a relevant child (as defined in reg 1(3)) and his parent or related persons (as defined in reg 1(3)) in accordance with reg 7(1)(g);

- Necessary expenditure identified in reg 7(1)(d)–(f) on:

  (i) legal costs, including court fees relating to the SGO, or an application for financial provision for the relevant child;

  (ii) the costs involved in facilitating the child to have his home with the guardian including the matters listed in reg 7(1)(e);

  (iii) the costs associated with any special educational or behavioural needs of the child, including the matters identified in regulation 7(1)(f).

The Guidance states (in paras 74–76) that:

'Regulation 7(1)(f) applies where the child is identified as having an illness, disability, emotional or behavioural difficulties or suffering from the continuing consequences of past abuse or neglect, and, as a result of the condition, the child requires a special degree of care that necessitates extra expenditure.

In cases to which regulation 7(1)(f) applies, the role of medical and other professionals will usually be of special value in evaluating the degree of the child's condition and in providing advice to the local authority who will in turn notify the special guardian. The local authority would be expected to seek specialist medical advice where appropriate.

Payment of financial support under regulation 7(1)(f) is intended to be made where the child's condition is serious and long-term. For example, where the child needs a special diet or where items such as shoes, clothing or bedding need to be replaced at a higher rate than would normally be the case with a child of similar age who was not affected by the particular condition. Specialist assistance may be needed to help with, for example, regular attendance at a nursery, possibly with special ancillary assistance, or visits to a clinic or consultations with a paediatrician, that may result in unexpected expenses for the special guardian.'

The Guidance emphasises (para 71) that: 'It is important to ensure that families involved in special guardianship arrangements are helped to access benefits to which they are entitled. Local authorities should ensure that the special guardian is aware of, and taking advantage of, all benefits and tax credits available to them'. To that end, reg 7(2) provides that financial support is not payable to meet any needs which can reasonably be expected to be met through the benefits and tax credits system.

By virtue of reg 7(3), financial support must not, as a general principle, include the payment of remuneration for the care of the child. This 'reward element' is the professional foster care fees that may be payable to foster parents as part of a fostering allowance in recognition of the service that the foster parent provides to a local authority in caring for a child who is the responsibility of the authority (see the Guidance, para 78). Regulation 7(4) permits financial support to be paid above the usual level, however, to a prospective special guardian who was the foster parent of a relevant child (as defined in reg 1(3)), where the local authority consider that any fostering allowance paid to him will cease upon the making of a SGO, and before an order is made they decide to pay financial support periodically. The regulations do not specify any time limit on the duration of such payment, whereas the English regulation provides that additional payments cease after two years unless the local authority considers that the payments are necessary having regard to the child's exceptional needs or other of exceptional circumstances, see the Special Guardianship Regulations 2005 (SI 2005/1109), reg 7(2) (para [1119]).

[1218]

8 Notification of assessment

(1) After carrying out an assessment under regulation 6 the local authority must, in accordance with regulation 10—

(a)   supply the information specified in paragraph (2); and
(b)   give notice of the right to make representations under paragraph (3).

(2) The information specified is—

(a)   the authority's provisional view as to the person's needs for special guardianship support services;
(b)   whether the local authority proposes to provide special guardianship support services to the person;
(c)   details of the services, if any, which it is proposed to provide to the person; and
(d)   where the assessment relates to the person's need for financial support—

    (i)   the basis on which that financial support is determined;
    (ii)   the proposed amount which would be payable; and
    (iii)   any conditions which the local authority proposes to impose on the provision of that financial support in accordance with regulation 9(10).

(3) The person notified in accordance with paragraph (1) shall have the right to make representations to the local authority concerning the proposal in paragraph (2)(b) within a period specified by the local authority in that notice.

(4) The local authority shall not make a decision under regulation 9 until—

(a)   the person referred to in paragraph (3) has—

    (i)   made representations to the local authority; or
    (ii)   notified the local authority that he or she is satisfied with the proposed decision; or

(b)   the period specified for making representations has expired.

NOTES

Initial Commencement

Specified date
Specified date: 30 December 2005: see reg 1(1).

General

[1219]

As mentioned in the context of reg 6, after carrying out an assessment of needs for SGSS under that regulation, the local authority must, in accordance with regs 8(1) and 10, give the information specified in reg 8(2), in writing, to the person assessed (see reg 8(1)(a)). They must also give him written notice of the right to make representations under reg 8(3) regarding whether or not the authority proposes to provide him with SGSS (see reg 8(1)(b)).

Regulation 8(3) does not specify a period of time to be allowed for making representations, but the Guidance suggests that local authorities should allow a period of 28 days (see para 82). It is submitted this period runs from the time the proposed decision is sent to the person assessed.

The local authority must not make a decision under reg 9 as to the provision of SGSS until representations have been made, or the person assessed has notified the authority that he is satisfied with the proposed decision or the time period has expired. Hence, a decision may be made within the 28-day period if the person tells the local authority that they are satisfied with the proposal, or makes representations in writing before the end of the period. This is to ensure that there is no delay in the provision of services (see the Guidance, para 83).

[1220]

9 Decision as to special guardianship support services

(1) The local authority must, having regard to the assessment, and after considering any representations received during the period specified under regulation 8—

(a)   consider whether the assessed person has needs for special guardianship support services; and

(b)   decide whether any such services are to be provided to the person.

(2) The local authority must give notice of the decision under paragraph (1), and of the reasons for that decision, in accordance with regulation 10.

(3) Where the assessment relates only to the provision of information, the requirement in paragraph (2) to give notice does not apply where the local authority do not consider it appropriate to give such notice.

(4) Paragraphs (5) to (10) apply where the local authority decide that financial support is to be paid.

(5) The local authority must determine and notify in accordance with regulation 10—

(a)   in accordance with regulation 7, the amount that is to be payable;

(b)   the conditions, if any, which are to be imposed in accordance with paragraph (10) on the provision or use of that financial support;

(c)   the date, if any, by which any conditions are to be met;

(d)   the consequences of not meeting any conditions;

(e)   where the financial support is to be paid as a single payment, the date on which the payment is to be made;

(f)   where the financial support is to be paid in instalments or periodically—

(i)   the frequency with which payment will be made;

(ii)   the date of the first payment, and

(iii)   the date, if any, on which payment will cease.

(6) The notification under paragraph (2) must also include information as to—

(a)   the method of determination of the amount of the financial support;

(b)   the arrangements for the review, variation or termination of the financial support; and

(c)   the responsibilities of the local authority under regulation 12 and of the person receiving support pursuant to regulation 4(2) and paragraph (10).

(7) Subject to paragraphs (8) and (9), financial support must be paid as a single payment.

(8) The person to whom the financial support is to be paid and the local authority may agree that the support shall be paid—

(a)   in instalments; or

(b)   periodically,

on and until such dates as the local authority may specify.

(9) Where the local authority decide that the financial support is to meet any needs which are likely to give rise to recurring expenditure, they may determine that that financial support shall be paid—

(a)   in instalments; or

(b)   periodically,

on and until such dates as the local authority may specify.

(10) The local authority may impose such conditions as they consider appropriate upon the payment of financial support, which may include conditions as to—

(a)   the timescale within which and the purpose for which the payment should be utilised; and

(b) compliance with the matters referred to in regulation 4(2).

NOTES
Initial Commencement
Specified date
Specified date: 30 December 2005: see reg 1(1).

General .

[1221]

As the Guidance (para 25) states:

'Local authorities must act reasonably in deciding whether to provide special guardianship support services following an assessment. However, the requirement to make a decision presumes that an assessment of need for a particular service does not automatically result in the provision of that service. In making this decision, local authorities will be expected to take into account the circumstances of each individual case and the resources that are available locally.'

After considering any representations made in accordance with reg 8(3) and having regard to the assessment of needs made under reg 6, the local authority must, in accordance with reg 9(1), consider whether the assessed person has need for SGSS and decide whether or not to provide him with any SGSS. They must then give him written notice of their decision, including the reasons for it, in accordance with regs 9(2) and 10, save where the assessment of needs is related only to the provision of information and the authority do not consider it appropriate to give such notice (see reg 9(3)).

Where a local authority decide to provide financial support they must give written notice in accordance with regs 9(5), (10) and 10 of:

(a)   the amount payable;

(b)   the conditions, if any, that are to be imposed on the timescale within which, and purpose for which, it should be used and compliance with the matters in regulation 4(2);

(c)   the date, if any, by which any conditions must be met;

(d)   the consequences of not meeting any conditions;

(e)   where financial support is to be paid as a single payment, the date on which the payment is to be made; and

(f)   where the financial support is to be paid in instalments or periodically:

   —   the frequency of the payment, the date of the first payment, and the date, if any, on which the payment will cease.

Where any condition imposed by reg 9(10) is not complied with the local authority may review, suspend or cease payment of financial support and seek to recover all or part of support paid (see further reg 12(6)–(8)). The reg 9(2) notice must also include the information specified in reg 9(6).

As a general principle, financial support shall be made as a single payment in accordance with reg 9(7). There are two exceptions. First, where the recipient and the local authority agree that it will be paid in instalments or periodically, on and until such dates as the authority may specify in accordance with reg 9(8). Second, where the authority decide that financial support is to meet any needs that are likely to require repeated expenditure, they may in accordance with reg 9(9) make payments in instalments or periodically on and until such dates as the authority may specify. 'This may be important where the child has special needs that can be met in whole or in part by financial support.' (See the Guidance, para 88.)

[1222]

10 Notices

(1) Any information required to be supplied, or notice required to be given, under regulations 8, 9 and 12, must be given in writing and—

(a) where the person whose needs for special guardianship support services have been assessed is an adult, to that person;

(b) where the person whose needs for special guardianship support services have been assessed is a child and paragraph (2) applies—

    (i) to the child; and

    (ii) except where it appears inappropriate to the local authority to do so, to—

        (aa) the special guardian or prospective special guardian; or

        (bb) where the child does not have a special guardian or prospective special guardian, to the adult the local authority consider most appropriate;

(c) where the person whose needs for special guardianship support services have been assessed is a child and paragraph (2) does not apply, to the person, if any, to whom sub-paragraph (b)(ii) above applies.

(2) This paragraph applies where—

(a) it appears to the local authority that the child is of sufficient age and understanding for it to be appropriate to give him or her such notice; and

(b) it does not appear to the local authority to be inappropriate to give him or her such notice.

NOTES

Initial Commencement

Specified date

Specified date: 30 December 2005: see reg 1(1).

General

[1223]

Regulation 10 provides that any notice required under regs 8, 9 and 12 must be given in writing (see reg 10(1)). Where the person assessed for SGSS is an adult notice, notice must be given to him (see reg 10(1)(a)).

Regulation 10(1)(b)(c) and (2) make special provision where the person assessed is a child. A child who appears to the local authority to be of sufficient age and understanding to be given notice, must also be given notice, provided that it does not appear to the local authority to be inappropriate to do so, for example, because it would be potentially harmful to the welfare of the child (see reg 10(1)(b)(i) and (2) and the Guidance, para 90). Notice must also be given to the special guardian or prospective special guardian (or in the absence of special guardian or prospective special guardian the adult the authority consider most appropriate) unless it appears to the local authority to be inappropriate to do so (see reg 10(1)(b)(ii)).

[1224]

11 Special guardianship support services plan

(1) The circumstances prescribed for the purposes of section 14F(6)(b) of the Act are that the local authority decide to provide special guardianship support services to a person on more than a single occasion.

(2) If the local authority considers it appropriate, for the purposes of preparing the plan, they must consult—

(a) any person falling within regulation 10(1); and

(b) where the person to whom the plan relates lives in another local authority area, that local authority,

and such consultation must include discussion as to when the plan should be reviewed.

(3) Where it appears to the local authority that there may be a need for the provision of services to the person to whom the plan will relate by a Local Health Board, NHS Trust, Primary Care Trust or local education authority, the local authority must consult that Board, Trust or authority, for the purposes of preparing the plan.

(4) The local authority must provide a copy of the plan—

(a) in accordance with regulation 10;

(b) where paragraph 3 applies, to the Local Health Board, Trust or authority; and

(c) unless the authority considers it unnecessary, where the person to whom the plan relates lives in another local authority area, to that local authority.

NOTES

Initial Commencement

Specified date

Specified date: 30 December 2005: see reg 1(1).

General

[1225]

If the outcome of an assessment is that the authority decide in favour of providing a person with special guardianship support services on more than one occasion (see reg 11(1)), then in accordance with CA 1989, s 14F(6) they must prepare and keep under review a special guardianship support services plan. Where services are being provided on a single occasion, the notice provided should include all the necessary information. Otherwise, the services should be provided in accordance with that plan and reg 11.

Where it appears to the local authority that the person may need services from a Local Health Board, NHS Trust, Primary Care Trust or local education authority (as defined in the Education Act 1996, see reg 1(3)) they must consult with the Board, Trust or authority before preparing the plan in accordance with reg 11(3) and in due course supply a copy of the plan (see reg 11(4)).

The Guidance indicates (at para 92) that: 'The preparation of a support services plan is essential to ensure the coordination of the provision of those services. The requirement for local authorities to prepare a support services plan is intended to help promote certainty for special guardians. It will also make clear where responsibilities for provision lie to help manage the provision of services that have been agreed.'

Regulation 11(2) specifies those who should be consulted in the preparation of the plan. The local authority should, if they consider it appropriate, consult the intended recipient. The Guidance states that an adult recipient should always be consulted (see para 95). If the recipient is a child the consultation procedure is the same as that for the giving of notice under reg 10(1). 'The general assumption is that a child who is of sufficient age and understanding will always be consulted, unless the circumstances of the case mean that it would be inappropriate to do so, for example, because it would be potentially harmful to the welfare of the child. Similarly, where the recipient is a child, the assumption is that the special guardian or appropriate adult will always be consulted unless the circumstances of the case mean that it would be inappropriate to do so.' (Guidance, para 96)

Where the person to whom the plan relates lives in the area of another local authority, that local authority should also be consulted in accordance with reg 11(2)(b), if this appears appropriate.

Consultation must include discussion of when the plan should be reviewed. 'The agreed review process should not be too burdensome or intrusive and should reflect whether the services are being provided on a short term or ongoing basis. If the services are to meet a need that is likely to last until the child is 18, for example, it may be necessary to review the provision of the service only occasionally. Where the services are due to last a matter of weeks it may be appropriate to review the provision of those services at the end of the course. As a guide to good practice it is suggested that plans, other than those relating solely to ongoing financial support, should be reviewed at least every 6 months' (Guidance, para 101). Specific provision for the review of SGSS is prescribed by reg 12.

'The result of this process of preparation and consultation should be that social workers, other professionals and the recipient of the services (or the appropriate adult) will be clear what the support services plan is. The plan should be set out in writing in a way that everybody affected can understand' (Guidance, para 98).

The plan should set out clearly: its objectives plan; the key services to be provided; the timescales for achieving the plan; the individual worker who will be responsible for co-ordinating and monitoring the delivery of the services in the plan; the respective roles of others responsible for implementing the plan; the criteria that will be used to evaluate the success of the plan; and the procedures for the review of the plan, so as to provide a clear picture for all those involved in the provision of the services and the person to receive the services, what should be provided, when, by whom and how the success of the services will be measured and reviewed (see the Guidance, paras 99 and 100).

The local authority must send a copy of the plan to the recipient of the SGSS (or the special guardian or appropriate adult) in accordance with reg 11(4)(a) and reg 10. Where, in accordance with reg 11(3), it appears to the local authority that a Local Health Board, NHS Trust, Primary Care Trust or local education authority (as defined in the Education Act 1996, see reg 1(3)) may be involved in the delivery of the plan they must provide a copy of the plan to the Board, Trust or authority in accordance with reg 11(4)(b). Where the person to whom the plan relates to lives in the area of another local authority, the local authority that prepared the plan must, unless they consider it unnecessary, provide a copy of the plan to that local authority in accordance with reg 11(4)(c).

[1226]

12 Review of the provision of special guardianship support services

(1) Where a local authority provide special guardianship support services for a person which do not include financial support, they must review the provision of such services—

(a)   if any relevant change in the person's circumstances, including a change of address, comes to their notice; and

(b)   in any event, from time to time.

(2) Where a local authority provide special guardianship support services for a person which comprise, or include, financial support they must review the provision of such services—

(a) if any relevant change in the person's circumstances, including a change of address, comes to their notice; and

(b) upon receipt of the annual statement referred to in regulation 4(2)(b).

(3) Regulations 6 to 8 apply with any necessary modifications in relation to a review under this regulation as they apply in relation to an assessment under regulation 5.

(4) The local authority must, having regard to the review and after considering any representations received within the period specified under regulation 8—

(a) decide whether to vary or terminate the provision of special guardianship support services; and

(b) review and, where appropriate, revise the plan.

(5) If the local authority decide to vary or terminate the provision of special guardianship support services, or revise the plan—

(a) they must give notice of their decision in accordance with regulation 10, and that notice must include the reasons for the decision; and

(b) paragraphs (3) to (10) of regulation 9 apply to a decision under paragraph (4) as they apply to a decision under paragraph (1) of regulation 9.

(6) Subject to paragraph (7), where any condition imposed in accordance with regulation 9(10) is not complied with, the local authority may—

(a) review, suspend, or cease payment of financial support; and

(b) seek to recover all or part of the financial support they have paid.

(7) Where the condition not complied with is the requirement to provide an annual statement in accordance with an agreement referred to in regulation 4(2), the local authority must not take any steps under paragraph (6) until—

(a) they have sent to the person who entered into the agreement a written reminder of the need to provide an annual statement; and

(b) 28 working days have expired since the date on which that notice was sent.

(8) Where, having taken the steps specified in paragraph (7), the local authority determine under paragraph (6) that payment of financial support should be suspended, they may lift that suspension upon receipt of the annual statement referred to in regulation 4(2)(b).

(9) The local authority must cease payment of financial support with effect from the date that they become aware that the circumstances in paragraph (10) apply.

(10) The circumstances are that—

(a) a special guardianship order has ceased to have effect, or has been revoked; or

(b) the child in respect of whom the special guardianship support services are provided—

(i) has ceased to have his or her home with a special guardian or prospective special guardian;

(ii) is in receipt of income support under Part VII of the Social Security Contributions and Benefits Act 1992 or of jobseeker's allowance under the Jobseekers Act 1995; or

(iii) has begun full-time paid employment.

NOTES

Initial Commencement

Specified date

Specified date: 30 December 2005: see reg 1(1).

PART C – SIs

General

[1227]

Regulation 12 is an extensive regulation which provides for the inter-related issues of review of SGSS provision (reg 12(1)–(5)); non compliance with any condition imposed by reg 9(10) (reg 12(6)–(8)) and cessation of payment of financial support (reg 12(9) and (10)).

Regulation 12(1)–(5)

Review of special guardianship support services

[1228]

'Regular review of the services would allow the local authority and the service user to review the effectiveness of the service against the criteria set out in the support services plan and consider whether it is appropriate to continue that service or alter the provision in any way' (Guidance, para 102; see also para 106). Where it is decided following the review and after considering representations, that the services to be provided should be changed, the SGSS plan prepared in accordance with reg 11 should also be reviewed and, where appropriate, revised in accordance with reg 12(4) and having regard to the review procedures set out in the plan (see para [1226]).

Regulation 12(1)–(5) provide the review procedure. Regulation 12(1)(a) and (2)(a) require that where the local authority provides services they must review the provision if they become aware of any change in the person's circumstances, including a change of address. 'The expectation is that the review should take place within four weeks of the change of circumstances coming to the attention of the local authority' (Guidance, para 107). In any event, by virtue of reg 12(1)(b) and 12(2)(b) where the services do not include financial support their provision must be reviewed from time to time and where the services comprise, or include, financial support, upon receipt of the annual statement required by reg 4(2)(b).

It is good practice for the person who conducted the original assessment to conduct the review, although the Guidance recognises that this is unlikely to be possible where services are being delivered over a period of several years (see Guidance, para 111). The procedure set out in reg 6 (assessment), 7 (amount) and 8 (notification of assessment) for a first assessment under reg 5, must be followed, with any necessary modifications, for reviews (see reg 12(3) and the Guidance, paras 111, 112).

'The format and content of the review will vary depending on the circumstances of the case. Where the change of circumstances is relevant only to one service the review may be carried out with reference only to that service. Where the change of circumstances is relatively minor the review might be limited to an exchange of correspondence. However, where the change of circumstances is substantial, such as a serious change in the behaviour of the child, it may be appropriate to conduct a new assessment of needs for special guardianship support services,' (Guidance, para 108)

The Guidance (paras 113 and 114) also states that:

'Local authorities should demonstrate flexibility in responding to changes of circumstance and at the annual review of financial support. Financial support may increase or decrease as appropriate in an individual case. For example, a change of address involving higher housing costs may arise from a move to a home that is more appropriate to the needs of the child. In other cases it may have no connection with the child's needs. Deterioration in the child's condition leading to extra expenditure for the special guardians may necessitate additional financial assistance. Conversely, a change in circumstance may result in a reduction in financial support or may result in financial support being suspended until further review. In such a case, payment may recommence if circumstances again require the need for financial support.

The local authority will need to operate with sensitivity in determining how far changes in financial circumstances or needs affect the provision of financial support. It may, for example, be inappropriate to offset the cost of living earnings increases against the financial support provided although marked increases may be taken into consideration.'

If the local authority decide to vary or terminate the service provision they must, in accordance with reg 12(5)(a), give the person written notice of their decision including the reasons for it. Regard should be paid to the advice given in paras 109 and 110 of the Guidance about review and notification:

'Notification of changes of circumstances and any review of the provision of special guardianship support services need not normally necessitate direct contact in person between the local authority and the special guardians. In particular, the annual review of financial support will generally be based on an exchange of correspondence between the local authority and the special guardian.

Visits to the special guardian's home, by agreement between the special guardian and the local authority, may be beneficial in certain circumstances, for example where a complex package of special guardianship support services is being provided. Some special guardians may welcome an opportunity for contact with the local authority. Local authorities may wish to give special guardians the option of a home visit so that the special guardian and local authority have an opportunity to discuss and evaluate recent experiences. This may be helpful before completion of the annual statement where financial support is in payment'

Regulation 9(3)–(10) apply to a decision whether to vary or terminate service provision under reg 12(4) as they do to a decision under reg 9(1) (see reg 12(5)(b)).

Regulation 12(6)–(8)

Non-compliance with any reg 9(10) condition

[1229]

Where any condition imposed by reg 9(10) is not complied with the local authority may review, suspend or cease payment of financial support and seek to recover all or part of support paid (see reg 12(6)).

Where the non-compliance is the requirement to submit an annual statement in accordance with reg 4(2)(b), the local authority may not take any such steps until, in accordance with reg 12(7), they have sent a written reminder of the requirement to provide the annual statement and allowed 28 days for the special guardian to provide it. The Guidance advises local authorities to ensure that special guardians are made aware of this provision by including it in the formal notification to special guardians about financial support and prompt them each year to provide the necessary information in advance of each annual review (see para 115).

If, in accordance with reg 12(6) and (7), the local authority suspend payment, they can reinstate it if the annual statement is received (see reg 12(8)).

Regulation 12(9) and (10)

Cessation of financial support

[1230]

Regulation 12(9) and (10) identify the four circumstances in which financial support ceases to be payable. They are when the local authority become aware that:

(1)   A SGO has ceased to have effect or has been revoked (see reg 12(10)(a)). An order ceases, for example, when the child attains the age of 18 (see CA 1989, s 91(13)), or has died (in which case he also ceases to have his home with the guardian). Revocation of a SGO is provided for by the CA 1989, s 14D (see paras [751]–[762])).

(2)   The child in respect of whom SGSS are provided has ceased to have his home with the guardian or prospective guardian (reg 12(10)(b)(i)). 'This applies where the child's departure from the special guardian's home is considered to be permanent. It does not apply to periods of temporary absence away from the special guardian's home, for example, in connection with education, respite care or hospitalisation' (Guidance, paras 52 and 116):

(3)   The child is in receipt of income support or jobseeker's allowance (reg 12(10)(b)(ii)).

(4)   The child has begun full-time paid employment (see reg 12(10)(b)(iii)).

[1231]

Part 4
Miscellaneous Provisions in Relation to Special Guardianship

13   Relevant authority for the purposes of sections 24(5)(za) of the Act

For the purposes of section 24(5)(za) of the Act (persons qualifying for advice and assistance), the relevant authority shall be the local authority which last looked after the person.

NOTES
Initial Commencement
Specified date
Specified date: 30 December 2005: see reg 1(1).

General

[1232]

Regulation 13 does not relate directly to the CA 1989, ss 14A–14F special guardianship provisions, but to a consequential amendment to the Act as a result of the introduction of special guardianship. The amendment relates to certain leaving care provisions in the CA 1989, Pt III as amended, in respect of children who were looked after by a local authority immediately before the making of a SGO.

The CA 1989, s 24(1) identifies persons qualifying for advice and assistance. In the context of special guardianship, s 24(1A) (as substituted by the ACA 2002, Sch 3, para 60(a)), provides that to qualify for advice and assistance, the child must:

(a)   have reached the age of 16, but not the age of 21;

(b)   if aged less than 18, is the subject of a SGO or if he has reached the age of 18 was the subject of a SGO when he reached that age; and

(c)   was looked after by a local authority immediately before the making of the order.

The CA 1989, ss 24A and 24B impose certain obligations regarding the provision of advice and assistance upon the 'relevant authority'. In the case of a person to whom CA 1989, s 24(1A) applies, the relevant authority is, by virtue of CA 1989, s 24(5)(za)(as inserted by ACA 2002, Sch 3, para 60(c)), determined in accordance with regulations. Regulation 13 is the relevant regulation and it provides that the 'relevant authority' shall be the local authority which last looked after the person. In accordance with the Guidance, para 21, the 'relevant local authority should make arrangements for children who meet these criteria to receive advice and assistance in the same way as for any other child who qualifies for advice and assistance under the Children Act 1989, as amended'. Depending on the service required, it may be more appropriate for the young person to seek support where he is now resident, for example of health care.

[1233]

---

14 Functions specified under section 26(3C) of the Act

The following functions under section 14F of the Act are specified for the purposes of section 26(3C) of the Act (review of cases and inquiries into representations—special guardianship support services)—

(a) financial support;
(b) support groups referred to in regulation 3(1)(b);
(c) assistance in relation to contact referred to in regulation 3(1)(c);
(d) therapeutic services referred to in regulation 3(1)(d); and
(e) assistance for the purpose of ensuring continuation of relationships referred to in regulation 3(1)(e).

NOTES
Initial Commencement
Specified date
Specified date: 30 December 2005: see reg 1(1).

General

[1234]

Regulation 14 relates to local authorities representations procedure under the CA 1989, s 26, as amended and in particular, s 26(3C) as inserted.

The CA 1989, s 14G, as enacted, required every local authority to establish a procedure for considering representations, including complaints, about the discharge of their CA 1989, s 14F SGSS functions (see para [780]). Prior to its implementation, CA 1989, s 14G was repealed (by the Health and Social Care (Community Health and Standards) Act 2003, ss 117, 196 and Sch 14, Pt 2), and s 26(3C) inserted in the CA 1989 so as to extend the s 26 procedure to any representations which are made to a local authority by:

'(a) a child with respect to whom a special guardianship order is in force,

(b) a special guardian or a parent of such a child,

(c) any other person the authority consider has a sufficient interest in the welfare of such a child to warrant his representations being considered by them, or

(d) any person who has applied for an assessment under section 14F(3) or (4),

about the discharge by the authority of such functions under section 14F as may be specified by the Secretary of State in regulations.'

Regulation 14 identifies the following, in relation to Wales, as specified functions under CA 1989, s 14F for the purposes of CA 1989, s 26(3C):

(a) the provision of financial support payable under the regulations;

(b) support group services to enable groups of relevant children (as defined in reg 1(3)), special guardians, prospective special guardians and parents of relevant children (or groups consisting of any combination of those individuals) to discuss matters relating to special guardianship;

(c) assistance for relevant children, their parents and related persons (as defined in regulation 1(3)) in relation to contact arrangements between such children and:

      (i)   their parents;

      (ii)   their former guardians or special guardians; and

      (iii) related persons;

(d)   services in relation to the therapeutic needs of a relevant child;

(e)   assistance for the purpose of ensuring the continuance of the relationship between a relevant child and a special guardian or prospective special guardian, including

      (i)   training for that person to meet any special needs of the child; and

      (ii)   respite care.

The procedure to be followed in Wales in the consideration of representations is prescribed by the Representations Procedure (Children)(Wales) Regulations 2005 (SI 2005/3365 (W 262)).

[1235]–[1300]

THE SCHEDULE
Reports—Matters Prescribed for the Purposes of Section 14A(8)(B) of the Act

Regulation 2

1   The following matters are prescribed for the purposes of section 14A(8)(b) of the Act.

2   In respect of a child in respect of whom a special guardianship order is sought or a child in respect of whom the court has required a report (referred to in this Schedule as 'the child')—

(a)   name, sex, date and place of birth and home address;
(b)   nationality and immigration status;
(c)   physical description;
(d)   developmental needs, to include physical, educational and emotional needs and a report on the child's health;
(e)   religious persuasion, racial origin and cultural and linguistic background;
(f)   details of any court proceedings relating to parental responsibility or maintenance for the child or relating to the child's residence;
(g)   the extent of the child's contact with members of his or her family;
(h)   any placement with foster parents or any other care arrangements relating to the child;
(i)   education, to include any special educational needs; and
(j)   the child's wishes and feelings about special guardianship.

3   In respect of the family of the child—

(a)   name, date, place of birth and home address of the child's parents, siblings and any other person the local authority considers to be relevant;
(b)   nationality and immigration status of the child's parents;
(c)   if the child's parent is a member of a couple, an assessment of the stability of that relationship and, if the parent is married or has entered into a civil partnership, the date and place of marriage or civil partnership;
(d)   whether the child's father has parental responsibility for the child;
(e)   whether either parent is considered by the local authority to be likely to apply for an order under the Act in respect of the child;
(f)   physical description of the parents, siblings and any other person the local authority considers to be relevant;
(g)   religious persuasion, racial origin and cultural and linguistic background of the parents;
(h)   the occupations, past and present, and educational attainment of the parents;

(i)   the care arrangements in respect of any of the child's siblings who have not attained the age of 18 years;

(j)   the views of the parents in relation to the application for a special guardianship order in respect of the child; and

(k)   the reason why any of the information prescribed above in this paragraph is not available.

4   In respect of the prospective special guardian or, where two or more persons are jointly prospective special guardians, each of them—

(a)   name, date and place of birth and home address;

(b)   nationality and immigration status;

(c)   relationship to the child;

(d)   a physical description;

(e)   if the prospective special guardian is a member of a couple, an assessment of the stability of that relationship and, if the prospective special guardian is married or has entered into a civil partnership, the date and place of marriage or civil partnership;

(f)   religious persuasion, racial origin and cultural and linguistic background of the prospective special guardian and willingness of the prospective special guardian to follow the wishes of the child or of the child's parent in relation to the religious or cultural upbringing of the child;

(g)   occupations, past and present, and educational attainment;

(h)   a report on the health of the prospective special guardian;

(i)   particulars of the prospective special guardian's home, to include details of income, comments on the living standards of the household and any wider family and environmental factors which may impact on the parenting capacity of the prospective special guardian;

(j)   previous experience of caring for children;

(k)   any past assessment as a prospective adopter, foster parent or special guardian;

(l)   reasons for applying for a special guardianship order;

(m)   parenting capacity, to include an assessment of the prospective special guardian's ability to bring the child up throughout the child's childhood;

(n)   details of three personal referees, no more than one of whom is a relative of the prospective special guardian, with a report of the referees' views in respect of the prospective special guardian; and

(o)   details of the proposed living arrangements for the child, if these are intended to change after a special guardianship order is made.

5   In respect of the local authority which compiled the report—

(a)   name and address;

(b)   details as to whether any of the information referred to in paragraphs 2 to 4 was initially obtained by the local authority otherwise than for the purposes of preparing the report and, if so, the purpose for which, and the date upon which, it was obtained;

(c)   details of steps taken to verify the identity of the prospective special guardian;

(d)   details of any past involvement of the local authority with the prospective special guardian, including any past preparation for that person to be a foster parent or adoptive parent;

(e)   details of any assessment which the local authority has undertaken in respect of special guardianship support services for the prospective special guardian, the child or the child's parent;

(f)   where section 14A(7)(a) of the Act applies and the prospective special guardian lives in the area of another local authority, details of the local authority's enquiries of that other local authority about the prospective special guardian; and

(g)   details of the local authority's opinions as to whether the prospective special guardian would or would not be a suitable special guardian for the child.

6   In respect of the conclusions reached in the report—

(a)   a summary prepared by the medical professional who provided the information referred to in paragraphs 2(d) and 4(h) above on the health of the child and of the prospective special guardian;

(b)   details of the opinion of the person making the report on—

(i)   the implications of the making of a special guardianship order for the child;

(ii)   how any special health needs of the child may be met;

(iii) whether the making of a special guardianship order would be in the best long-term interests of the child;

(iv)   how any emotional, behavioural and educational needs of the child may be met;

(v)   the effect on the child's parents of the making of a special guardianship order; and

(vi)   if appropriate, the merits of the making of a placement order or an adoption order under the Adoption and Children Act 2002 or a residence order under section 8 of the Act in respect of the child; and

(c)   details of the conclusions and recommendations of the person making the report on the issue of whether a special guardianship order should be made in respect of the child.

NOTES

Initial Commencement

Specified date

Specified date: 30 December 2005: see reg 1(1).

Part D   Appendix

Adoption (Intercountry Aspects) Act 1999

1999 CHAPTER 18

An Act to make provision for giving effect to the Convention on Protection of Children and Co-operation in respect of Inter-country Adoption, concluded at the Hague on 29th May 1993; to make further provision in relation to adoptions with an international element; and for connected purposes.

[27th July 1999]

BE IT ENACTED by the Queen's most Excellent Majesty, by and with the advice and consent of the Lords Spiritual and Temporal, and Commons, in this present Parliament assembled, and by the authority of the same, as follows:

[1301]–[1350]

Implementation of Convention

1 Regulations giving effect to Convention

(1) Subject to the provisions of this Act, regulations made by the Secretary of State may make provision for giving effect to the Convention on Protection of Children and Co-operation in respect of Intercountry Adoption, concluded at the Hague on 29th May 1993 ('the Convention').

(2) The text of the Convention (so far as material) is set out in Schedule 1 to this Act.

(3) Regulations under this section may—

(a) apply, with or without modifications, any provision of the enactments relating to adoption;

(b) provide that any person who contravenes or fails to comply with any provision of the regulations is to be guilty of an offence and liable on summary conviction to imprisonment for a term not exceeding three months, or a fine not exceeding level 5 on the standard scale, or both;

(c) make different provision for different purposes or areas; and

(d) make such incidental, supplementary, consequential or transitional provision as appears to the Secretary of State to be expedient.

(4) Regulations under this section shall be made by statutory instrument which shall be subject to annulment in pursuance of a resolution of either House of Parliament.

(5) Subject to subsection (6), any power to make subordinate legislation under or for the purposes of the enactments relating to adoption includes power to do so with a view to giving effect to the provisions of the Convention.

(6) Subsection (5) does not apply in relation to any power which is exercisable by the National Assembly for Wales.

NOTES

Initial Commencement

To be appointed

To be appointed: see s 18(3).

Appointment

Appointment (in relation to Scotland): 14 January 2003: see SSI 2002/562, art 2(a); appointment (in relation to England and Wales): 23 January 2003: see SI 2003/189, art 2(1)(a).

Subordinate Legislation

UK

Adoptions with a Foreign Element Regulations 2005, SI 2005/392 (made under sub-ss (1), (3), (5)); Adoption and Children (Miscellaneous Amendments) Regulations 2005, SI 2005/3482.

Scotland

Intercountry Adoption (Hague Convention) (Scotland) Regulations 2003, SSI 2003/19 (made under sub-ss (1)–(3), (5)).

2 Central Authorities and accredited bodies

(1) The functions under the Convention of the Central Authority are to be discharged—

(a) separately in relation to England and Scotland by the Secretary of State; and

(b) in relation to Wales by the National Assembly for Wales.

(2) *A communication may be sent to the Central Authority in relation to any part of Great Britain by sending it (for forwarding if necessary) to the Central Authority in relation to England.*

[(2A) [A registered adoption society] is an accredited body for the purposes of the Convention if, in accordance with the conditions of the registration, the [society] may provide facilities in respect of Convention adoptions and adoptions effected by Convention adoption orders.]

[(2B) A registered adoption service is an accredited body for the purposes of the Convention if, in accordance with the conditions of its registration, the service may provide facilities in respect of Convention adoptions and adoptions effected by Convention adoption orders.] NB red text

(3) An approved adoption society is an accredited body for the purposes of the Convention if the approval extends to the provision of facilities in respect of Convention adoptions and adoptions effected by Convention adoption orders.

(4) The functions under Article 9(a) to (c) of the Convention are to be discharged by local authorities and accredited bodies on behalf of the Central Authority.

[(5) In this section, 'registered adoption society' has the same meaning as in section 2 of the Adoption and Children Act 2002 (basic definitions); and expressions used in this section in its application to England and Wales which are also used in that Act have the same meanings as in that Act.]

[(6) In this section in its application to Scotland, 'registered adoption service' means an adoption service provided as mentioned in section 2(11)(b) of the Regulation of Care (Scotland) Act 2001 (asp 8) and registered under Part 1 of that Act; and 'registration' shall be construed accordingly.]

NOTES

Initial Commencement

To be appointed

To be appointed: see s 18(3).

Appointment

Sub-ss (1), (2), (4): appointment (in relation to England and Wales): 1 June 2003: see SI 2003/189, art 2(2)(a); sub-ss (1), (2), (4): appointment (in relation to Scotland): 1 June 2003: see SSI 2003/121, art 2(a); sub-s (3): appointment (in relation to Scotland): 1 June 2003: see SSI 2003/121, art 2(a).

Amendment

Sub-s (2): repealed, in relation to Scotland, by the Regulation of Care (Scotland) Act 2001, s 79, Sch 3, para 22(a); date in force: to be appointed: see the Regulation of Care (Scotland) Act 2001, s 81(2); sub-s (2A): inserted by the Care Standards Act 2000, s 116, Sch 4, para 27(a); date in force (in relation to Wales): 30 April 2003: see SI 2003/501, art 2(3)(a); date in force (in relation to England): 1 June 2003: see SI 2003/365, art 3(6)(a); for transitional provisions see arts 2, 3(1), Schedule thereto; sub-s (2A): words 'A registered adoption society' in square brackets substituted by the Adoption and Children Act 2002, s 139(1), Sch 3, paras 96, 97(a); date in force: 30 December 2005: see SI 2005/2213, art 2(o); sub-s (2A): word 'society' in square brackets substituted by the Adoption and Children Act 2002, s 139(1), Sch 3, paras 96, 97(b); date in force: 30 December 2005: see SI 2005/2213, art 2(o); sub-s (2B): inserted, in relation to Scotland, by the Regulation of Care (Scotland) Act 2001, s 79, Sch 3, para 22(b); date in force: 1 April 2004: see SSI 2004/100, art 2(d), (e) sub-s (5): substituted by the Adoption and Children Act 2002, s 139(1), Sch 3, paras 96, 98; date in force: 30 December 2005: see SI 2005/2213, art 2(o); sub-s (6): substituted by the Regulation of Care (Scotland) Act 2001, s 79, Sch 3, para 22(c); date in force: 1 April 2004: see SSI 2004/100, art 2(d), (e); for transitional provisions see art 4 thereof (as amended by SSI 2004/377, art 2).

Convention adoptions

3 ...

...

NOTES
Amendment
Repealed by the Adoption and Children Act 2002, s 139(1), Sch 3, para 95; date in force: 30 December 2005: see SI 2005/2213, art 2(o).

4 Effect of Convention adoptions in England and Wales

(1) In subsection (1) of section 38 of the 1976 Act (meaning of 'adoption' for purposes of provisions relating to status of adopted children), after paragraph (c) there shall be inserted—

'(cc) which is a Convention adoption;'.

(2) In subsection (2) of section 39 of that Act (status conferred by adoption), for 'subsection (3)' there shall be substituted 'subsections (3) and (3A)'.
(3) After subsection (3) of that section there shall be inserted—

'(3A) Where, in the case of a Convention adoption, the High Court is satisfied, on an application under this subsection—

(a) that under the law of the country in which the adoption was effected the adoption is not a full adoption;
(b) that the consents referred to in Article 4(c) and (d) of the Convention have not been given for a full adoption, or that the United Kingdom is not the receiving State (within the meaning of Article 2 of the Convention); and
(c) that it would be more favourable to the adopted child for a direction to be given under this subsection,

the Court may direct that subsection (2) shall not apply, or shall not apply to such extent as may be specified in the direction.
In this subsection "full adoption" means an adoption by virtue of which the adopted child falls to be treated in law as if he were not the child of any person other than the adopters or adopter.
(3B) The following provisions of the Family Law Act 1986—

(a) section 59 (provisions relating to the Attorney General); and
(b) section 60 (supplementary provision as to declarations), shall apply in relation to, and to an application for, a direction under subsection (3A) as they apply in relation to, and to an application for, a declaration under Part III of that Act.'

NOTES
Initial Commencement
To be appointed
To be appointed: see s 18(3).

Appointment
Appointment: 1 June 2003: see SI 2003/189, art 2(2)(c).

5 Effect of Convention adoptions in Scotland

(1) In subsection (1) of section 38 of the 1978 Act (meaning of 'adoption order' for purposes of provisions relating to status of adopted children), after paragraph (c) there shall be inserted—

'(cc) a Convention adoption;'.

(2) In subsection (1) of section 39 of that Act (status conferred by adoption), in sub-paragraph (ii) of each of paragraphs (a), (b) and (c), at the beginning there shall be inserted 'subject to subsection (2A)'.
(3) After subsection (2) of that section there shall be inserted—

'(2A) Where, in the case of a child adopted under a Convention adoption, the Court of Session is satisfied, on an application under this subsection—

(a) that d be more favourable to the child for a direction to be given under this subsection, the Court may direct that sub-paragraph (ii) of, as the case may be, paragraph (a), (b) or (c) of subsection (1) shall not apply, or shall not apply to such extent as may be specified in the direction: and in this subsection "full adoption" means an adoption by virtue of which the child falls to be treated in law as if he were not the child of any person other than the adopters or adopter.'

NOTES

Initial Commencement

To be appointed

To be appointed: see s 18(3).

Appointment

Appointment: 1 June 2003: see SSI 2003/121, art 2(c).

6 ...

...

NOTES

Amendment

Repealed by the Adoption and Children Act 2002, s 139(1), Sch 3, para 95; date in force: 30 December 2005: see SI 2005/2213, art 2(o).

7 Acquisition of British citizenship by Convention adoptions

(1) For subsection (5) of section 1 of the British Nationality Act 1981 (acquisition by birth or adoption) there shall be substituted—

'(5) Where—

(a) any court in the United Kingdom makes an order authorising the adoption of a minor who is not a British citizen; or

(b) a minor who is not a British citizen is adopted under a Convention adoption,

that minor shall, if the requirements of subsection (5A) are met, be a British citizen as from the date on which the order is made or the Convention adoption is effected, as the case may be.

(5A) Those requirements are that on the date on which the order is made or the Convention adoption is effected (as the case may be)—

(a) the adopter or, in the case of a joint adoption, one of the adopters is a British citizen; and

(b) in a case within subsection (5)(b), the adopter or, in the case of a joint adoption, both of the adopters are habitually resident in the United Kingdom.'

(2) In subsection (6) of that section, after 'order' there shall be inserted 'or a Convention adoption'.

(3) ...

NOTES

Initial Commencement

To be appointed

To be appointed: see s 18(3).

Appointment

Appointment: 1 June 2003: see SI 2003/362, art 2(a).

Amendment

Sub-s (3): repealed by the Adoption and Children Act 2002, s 139(3), Sch 5; date in force: 30 December 2005: see SI 2005/2897, art 2(b).

8 ...

...

NOTES

Amendment

Repealed by the Adoption and Children Act 2002, s 139(1), Sch 3, para 95; date in force: 30 December 2005: see SI 2005/2213, art 2(o).

...

NOTES

Amendment

Repealed by virtue of the Adoption and Children Act 2002, s 139(1), Sch 3, para 95; date in force: 30 December 2005: see SI 2005/2213, art 2(o).

9 ...

...

NOTES

Amendment

Repealed by the Adoption and Children Act 2002, s 139(1), Sch 3, para 95; date in force: 30 December 2005: see SI 2005/2213, art 2(o).

10 ...

...

NOTES

Amendment

Repealed by the Care Standards Act 2000, s 117(2), Sch 6; date in force (in relation to Wales): 30 April 2003: see SI 2003/501, art 2(3)(b);date in force (in relation to England): 1 June 2003: see SI 2003/365, art 3(6)(b).

11 ...

...

NOTES

Amendment

Repealed by the Adoption and Children Act 2002, s 139(1), Sch 3, para 95; date in force: 30 December 2005: see SI 2005/2213, art 2(o).

12 ...

...

NOTES

Amendment

Repealed by the Adoption and Children Act 2002, s 139(1), Sch 3, para 95; date in force: 30 December 2005: see SI 2005/2213, art 2(o).

13 ...

...

NOTES

Amendment

Repealed by the Adoption and Children Act 2002, s 139(1), Sch 3, para 95 date in force: 30 December 2005: see SI 2005/2213, art 2(o).

Miscellaneous and supplemental

14 Restriction on bringing children into the United Kingdom for adoption

The following provision shall be inserted after section 56 of the 1976 Act as section 56A and after section 50 of the 1978 Act as section 50A—

> **'Restriction on bringing children into the United Kingdom for adoption**
> (1) A person habitually resident in the British Islands who at any time brings into the United Kingdom for the purpose of adoption a child who

PART D – Appendix

is habitually resident outside those Islands shall be guilty of an offence unless such requirements as may be prescribed by regulations made by the Secretary of State are satisfied either—

(a)   *before that time; or*

(b)   *within such period beginning with that time as may be so prescribed.*

(2)   *Subsection (1) does not apply where the child is brought into the United Kingdom for the purpose of adoption by a parent, guardian or relative.*

(3)   *A person guilty of an offence under this section is liable on summary conviction to imprisonment for a term not exceeding three months, or a fine not exceeding level 5 on the standard scale, or both.*

(4)   *Proceedings for an offence under this section may be brought within a period of six months from the date on which evidence sufficient in the opinion of the prosecutor to warrant the proceedings came to his knowledge; but no such proceedings shall be brought by virtue of this subsection more than three years after the commission of the offence.'*

NOTES

Initial Commencement

To be appointed

To be appointed: see s 18(3).

Appointment

Appointment (for certain purposes): 30 April 2001: see SI 2001/1279, art 2; appointment (for remaining purposes): 2 July 2001: see SSI 2001/235, art 2.

Amendment

Repealed by the Adoption and Children Act 2002, s 139(1), (3), Sch 3, para 100, Sch 5; date in force: to be appointed: see the Adoption and Children Act 2002, s 148(1), (2).

15   Amendments and repeals

(1)   The enactments mentioned in Schedule 2 to this Act shall have effect subject to the amendments specified in that Schedule, being minor amendments and amendments consequential on the provisions of this Act.

(2)   The enactments mentioned in Schedule 3 to this Act are repealed to the extent specified in that Schedule.

NOTES

Initial Commencement

To be appointed

To be appointed: see s 18(3).

Appointment

Sub-s (1): appointment (in relation to England and Wales for certain purposes): 1 June 2003: see SI 2003/189, art 2(2)(h); sub-s (1): appointment (in relation to England and Wales for remaining purposes): 1 June 2003: see SI 2003/362, art 2(b); sub-s (1): appointment (in relation to Scotland for certain purposes): 1 June 2003: see SI 2003/362, art 2(b); sub-s (1): appointment (in relation to Scotland for remaining purposes): 1 June 2003: see SSI 2003/121, art 2(g); sub-s (2): appointment (in relation to England and Wales): 1 June 2003: see SI 2003/189, art 2(2)(i); sub-s (2): appointment (in relation to Scotland): 1 June 2003: see SSI 2003/121, art 2(g).

16   Devolution

(1)   Any function of the Secretary of State under section 1 or 18(3)... is exercisable only after consultation with the National Assembly for Wales.

(2)   For the purposes of the Scotland Act 1998, any provision of this Act which extends to Scotland is to be taken to be a pre-commencement enactment within the meaning of that Act.

NOTES

Initial Commencement

To be appointed

To be appointed: see s 18(3).

Appointment

Sub-s (1): appointment: 23 January 2003: see SI 2003/189, art 2(1)(a); sub-s (2): appointment: 16 October 2000: see SI 2000/2821, art 2.

Amendment
Sub-s (1): words omitted repealed by the Adoption and Children Act 2002, s 139(1), (3), Sch 3, para 101, Sch 5; date in force: 30 December 2005: see SI 2005/2213, art 2(o).

17 Savings for adoptions etc under 1965 Convention

(1) In relation to—

(a) a 1965 Convention adoption order or an application for such an order; or
(b) a 1965 Convention adoption,

the 1976 and 1978 Acts shall have effect without the amendments made by sections 3 to 6 and 8 and Schedule 2 to this Act and the associated repeals made by Schedule 3 to this Act.

(2) In subsection (1) in its application to the 1976 or 1978 Act—

'1965 Convention adoption order' has the meaning which 'Convention adoption order' has in that Act as it has effect without the amendments and repeals mentioned in that subsection;
'1965 Convention adoption' has the meaning which 'regulated adoption' has in that Act as it so has effect.

NOTES
Initial Commencement
To be appointed
To be appointed: see s 18(3).

Appointment
Appointment (in relation to England and Wales): 1 June 2003: see SI 2003/189, art 2(2)(g); appointment (in relation to Scotland): 1 June 2003: see SSI 2003/121, art 2(k).

18 Short title, interpretation, commencement and extent

(1) This Act may be cited as the Adoption (Intercountry Aspects) Act 1999.
(2) In this Act—

'the 1976 Act' means the Adoption Act 1976;
'the 1978 Act' means the Adoption (Scotland) Act 1978;
'the Convention' means the Convention on Protection of Children and Co-operation in respect of Intercountry Adoption, concluded at the Hague on 29th May 1993.

(3) This Act, except this section, shall come into force on such day as the Secretary of State may by order made by statutory instrument appoint and different days may be appointed for different purposes.
(4) Subject to subsection (5), this Act extends to Great Britain only.
(5) Any amendment of an enactment which extends to any other part of the British Islands or any colony also extends to that part or colony.

NOTES
Initial Commencement
Royal Assent
Royal Assent: 27 July 1999: (no specific commencement provision).

Subordinate Legislation
UK
Adoption (Intercountry Aspects) Act 1999 (Commencement No 1) Order 2000, SI 2000/52 (made under sub-s (3)); Adoption (Intercountry Aspects) Act 1999 (Commencement No 3) Order 2000, SI 2000/2821 (made under sub-s (3)); Adoption (Intercountry Aspects) Act 1999 (Commencement No 5) Order 2001, SI 2001/1279 (made under sub-s (3)); Adoption (Intercountry Aspects) Act 1999 (Commencement No 8) Order 2003, SI 2003/189 (made under sub-s (3)); Adoption (Intercountry Aspects) Act 1999 (Commencement No 9) Order 2003, SI 2003/362 (made under sub-s (3)).

Scotland
Adoption (Intercountry Aspects) Act 1999 (Commencement No 2) (Scotland) Order 2000, SSI 2000/223 (made under sub-s (3)); Adoption (Intercountry Aspects) Act 1999 (Commencement No 4) (Scotland) Order 2000, SSI 2000/390 (made under sub-s (3)); Adoption (Intercountry Aspects) Act 1999 (Commencement No 6) Order 2001, SSI 2001/235 (made under sub-s (3)); Adoption (Intercountry Aspects) Act 1999 (Commencement No 7) (Scotland) Order 2002,

PART D – Appendix

539

SSI 2002/562 (made under sub-s (3)); Adoption (Intercountry Aspects) Act 1999 (Commencement No 10) (Scotland) Order 2003, SSI 2003/121 (made under sub-s (3)).

SCHEDULE 1
Convention on Protection of Children and Co-operation in Respect of Intercountry Adoption

Section 1

The States signatory to the present Convention.

Recognizing that the child, for the full and harmonious development of his or her personality, should grow up in a family environment, in an atmosphere of happiness, love and understanding,

Recalling that each State should take, as a matter of priority, appropriate measures to enable the child to remain in the care of his or her family of origin,

Recognizing that intercountry adoption may offer the advantage of a permanent family to a child for whom a suitable family cannot be found in his or her State of origin,

Convinced of the necessity to take measures to ensure that intercountry adoptions are made in the best interests of the child and with respect for his or her fundamental rights, and to prevent the abduction, the sale of, or traffic in children,

Desiring to establish common provisions to this effect, taking into account the principles set forth in international instruments, in particular the United Nations Convention on the Rights of the Child, of 20 November 1989, and the United Nations Declaration on Social and Legal Principles relating to the Protection and Welfare of Children, with Special Reference to Foster Placement and Adoption Nationally and Internationally (General Assembly Resolution 41/85, of 3 December 1986),

Have agreed upon the following provisions—

Chapter I
Scope of the Convention

Article 1

The objects of the present Convention are—

(a)   to establish safeguards to ensure that intercountry adoptions take place in the best interests of the child and with respect for his or her fundamental rights as recognised in international law;

(b)   to establish a system of co-operation amongst Contracting States to ensure that those safeguards are respected and thereby prevent the abduction, the sale of, or traffic in children;

(c)   to secure the recognition in Contracting States of adoptions made in accordance with the Convention.

Article 2

1   The Convention shall apply where a child habitually resident in one Contracting State ('the State of origin') has been, is being, or is to be moved to another Contracting State ('the receiving State') either after his or her adoption in the State of origin by spouses or a person habitually resident in the receiving State, or for the purposes of such an adoption in the receiving State or in the State of origin.

2   The Convention covers only adoptions which create a permanent parent-child relationship.

Article 3

The Convention ceases to apply if the agreements mentioned in Article 17, sub-paragraph (c), have not been given before the child attains the age of eighteen years.

Chapter II
Requirements for Intercountry Adoptions

Article 4

An adoption within the scope of the Convention shall take place only if the competent authorities of the State of origin—

(a)   have established that the child is adoptable;

(b)   have determined, after possibilities for placement of the child within the State of origin have been given due consideration, that an intercountry adoption is in the child's best interests;

(c)   have ensured that—

    (i)   the persons, institutions and authorities whose consent is necessary for adoption, have been counselled as may be necessary and duly informed of the effects of their consent, in particular whether or not an adoption will result in the termination of the legal relationship between the child and his or her family of origin,

    (ii)   such persons, institutions and authorities have given their consent freely, in the required legal form, and expressed or evidenced in writing,

    (iii)   the consents have not been induced by payment or compensation of any kind and have not been withdrawn, and

    (iv)   the consent of the mother, where required, has been given only after the birth of the child; and

(d)   have ensured, having regard to the age and degree of maturity of the child, that—

    (i)   he or she has been counselled and duly informed of the effects of the adoption and of his or her consent to the adoption, where such consent is required,

    (ii)   consideration has been given to the child's wishes and opinions,

    (iii)   the child's consent to the adoption, where such consent is required, has been given freely, in the required legal form, and expressed or evidenced in writing, and

    (iv)   such consent has not been induced by payment or compensation of any kind.

Article 5

An adoption within the scope of the Convention shall take place only if the competent authorities of the receiving State—

(a)   have determined that the prospective adoptive parents are eligible and suited to adopt;

(b)   have ensured that the prospective adoptive parents have been counselled as may be necessary; and

(c)   have determined that the child is or will be authorised to enter and reside permanently in that State.

PART D – Appendix

Chapter III
Central Authorities and Accredited Bodies

Article 6

1   A Contracting State shall designate a Central Authority to discharge the duties which are imposed by the Convention upon such authorities.

2   Federal States, States with more than one system of law or States having autonomous territorial units shall be free to appoint more than one Central Authority and to specify the territorial or personal extent of their functions. Where a State has appointed more than one Central Authority, it shall designate the Central Authority to which any communication may be addressed for transmission to the appropriate Central Authority within that State.

Article 7

1   Central Authorities shall co-operate with each other and promote co-operation amongst the competent authorities in their States to protect children and to achieve the other objects of the Convention.

2   They shall take directly all appropriate measures to—

(a)   provide information as to the laws of their States concerning adoption and other general information, such as statistics and standard forms;
(b)   keep one another informed about the operation of the Convention and, as far as possible, eliminate any obstacles to its application.

Article 8

Central Authorities shall take, directly or through public authorities, all appropriate measures to prevent improper financial or other gain in connection with an adoption and to deter all practices contrary to the objects of the Convention.

Article 9

Central Authorities shall take, directly or through public authorities or other bodies duly accredited in their State, all appropriate measures, in particular to—

(a)   collect, preserve and exchange information about the situation of the child and the prospective adoptive parents, so far as is necessary to complete the adoption;
(b)   facilitate, follow and expedite proceedings with a view to obtaining the adoption;
(c)   promote the development of adoption counselling and post-adoption services in their States;
(d)   provide each other with general evaluation reports about experience with intercountry adoption;
(e)   reply, in so far as is permitted by the law of their State, to justified requests from other Central Authorities or public authorities for information about a particular adoption situation.

Article 10

Accreditation shall only be granted to and maintained by bodies demonstrating their competence to carry out properly the tasks with which they may be entrusted.

Article 11

An accredited body shall—

(a) pursue only non-profit objectives according to such conditions and within such limits as may be established by the competent authorities of the State of accreditation;

(b) be directed and staffed by persons qualified by their ethical standards and by training or experience to work in the field of intercountry adoption; and

(c) be subject to supervision by competent authorities of that State as to its composition, operation and financial situation.

Article 12

A body accredited in one Contracting State may act in another Contracting State only if the competent authorities of both States have authorised it to do so.

Article 13

The designation of the Central Authorities and, where appropriate, the extent of their functions, as well as the names and addresses of the accredited bodies shall be communicated by each Contracting State to the Permanent Bureau of the Hague Conference on Private International Law.

Chapter IV
Procedural Requirements in Intercountry Adoption

Article 14

Persons habitually resident in a Contracting State, who wish to adopt a child habitually resident in another Contracting State, shall apply to the Central Authority in the State of their habitual residence.

Article 15

1 If the Central Authority of the receiving State is satisfied that the applicants are eligible and suited to adopt, it shall prepare a report including information about their identity, eligibility and suitability to adopt, background, family and medical history, social environment, reasons for adoption, ability to undertake an intercountry adoption, as well as the characteristics of the children for whom they would be qualified to care.

2 It shall transmit the report to the Central Authority of the State of origin.

Article 16

1 If the Central Authority of the State of origin is satisfied that the child is adoptable, it shall—

(a) prepare a report including information about his or her identity, adoptability, background, social environment, family history, medical history including that of the child's family, and any special needs of the child;

(b) give due consideration to the child's upbringing and to his or her ethnic, religious and cultural background;

(c) ensure that consents have been obtained in accordance with Article 4; and

(d) determine, on the basis in particular of the reports relating to the child and the prospective adoptive parents, whether the envisaged placement is in the best interests of the child.

2 It shall transmit to the Central Authority of the receiving State its report on the child, proof that the necessary consents have been obtained and the reasons for its determination on the placement, taking care not to reveal the identity of the mother and the father if, in the State of origin, these identities may not be disclosed.

PART D – Appendix

Article 17

Any decision in the State of origin that a child should be entrusted to prospective adoptive parents may only be made if—

(a)   the Central Authority of that State has ensured that the prospective adoptive parents agree;

(b)   the Central Authority of the receiving State has approved such decision, where such approval is required by the law of that State or by the Central Authority of the State of origin;

(c)   the Central Authorities of both States have agreed that the adoption may proceed; and

(d)   it has been determined, in accordance with Article 5, that the prospective adoptive parents are eligible and suited to adopt and that the child is or will be authorised to enter and reside permanently in the receiving State.

Article 18

The Central Authorities of both States shall take all necessary steps to obtain permission for the child to leave the State of origin and to enter and reside permanently in the receiving State.

Article 19

1   The transfer of the child to the receiving State may only be carried out if the requirements of Article 17 have been satisfied.

2   The Central Authorities of both States shall ensure that this transfer takes place in secure and appropriate circumstances and, if possible, in the company of the adoptive or prospective adoptive parents.

3   If the transfer of the child does not take place, the reports referred to in Articles 15 and 16 are to be sent back to the authorities who forwarded them.

Article 20

The Central Authorities shall keep each other informed about the adoption process and the measures taken to complete it, as well as about the progress of the placement if a probationary period is required.

Article 21

1   Where the adoption is to take place after the transfer of the child to the receiving State and it appears to the Central Authority of that State that the continued placement of the child with the prospective adoptive parents is not in the child's best interests, such Central Authority shall take the measures necessary to protect the child, in particular—

(a)   to cause the child to be withdrawn from the prospective adoptive parents and to arrange temporary care;

(b)   in consultation with the Central Authority of the State of origin, to arrange without delay a new placement of the child with a view to adoption or, if this is not appropriate, to arrange alternative long-term care; an adoption shall not take place until the Central Authority of the State of origin has been duly informed concerning the new prospective adoptive parents;

(c)   as a last resort, to arrange the return of the child, if his or her interests so require.

2   Having regard in particular to the age and degree of maturity of the child, he or she shall be consulted and, where appropriate, his or her consent obtained in relation to measures to be taken under this Article.

Article 22

1 The functions of a Central Authority under this Chapter may be performed by public authorities or by bodies accredited under Chapter III, to the extent permitted by the law of its State.

2 Any Contracting State may declare to the depositary of the Convention that the functions of the Central Authority under Articles 15 to 21 may be performed in that State, to the extent permitted by the law and subject to the supervision of the competent authorities of that State, also by bodies or persons who—

(a) meet the requirements of integrity, professional competence, experience and accountability of that State; and
(b) are qualified by their ethical standards and by training or experience to work in the field of intercountry adoption.

3 A Contracting State which makes the declaration provided for in paragraph 2 shall keep the Permanent Bureau of the Hague Conference on Private International Law informed of the names and addresses of these bodies and persons.

4 Any Contracting State may declare to the depositary of the Convention that adoptions of children habitually resident in its territory may only take place if the functions of the Central Authorities are performed in accordance with paragraph 1.

5 Notwithstanding any declaration made under paragraph 2, the reports provided for in Articles 15 and 16 shall, in every case, be prepared under the responsibility of the Central Authority or other authorities or bodies in accordance with paragraph 1.

Chapter V
Recognition and Effects of the Adoption

Article 23

1 An adoption certified by the competent authority of the State of the adoption as having been made in accordance with the Convention shall be recognised by operation of law in the other Contracting States. The certificate shall specify when and by whom the agreements under Article 17, sub-paragraph c, were given.

2 Each Contracting State shall, at the time of signature, ratification, acceptance, approval or accession, notify the depositary of the Convention of the identity and the functions of the authority or the authorities which, in that State, are competent to make the certification. It shall also notify the depositary of any modification in the designation of these authorities.

Article 24

The recognition of an adoption may be refused in a contracting State only if the adoption is manifestly contrary to its public policy, taking into account the best interests of the child.

Article 25

Any Contracting State may declare to the depositary of the convention that it will not be bound under this Convention to recognise adoptions made in accordance with an agreement concluded by application of Article 39, paragraph 2.

Article 26

1 The recognition of an adoption includes recognition of—

PART D – Appendix

(a)   the legal parent-child relationship between the child and his or her adoptive parents;
(b)   parental responsibility of the adoptive parents for the child;
(c)   the termination of a pre-existing legal relationship between the child and his or her mother and father, if the adoption has this effect in the Contracting State where it was made.

2   In the case of an adoption having the effect of terminating a pre-existing legal parent-child relationship, the child shall enjoy in the receiving State, and in any other Contracting State where the adoption is recognised, rights equivalent to those resulting from adoptions having this effect in each such State.

3   The preceding paragraphs shall not prejudice the application of any provision more favourable for the child, in force in the Contracting State which recognises the adoption.

Article 27

1   Where an adoption granted in the State of origin does not have the effect of terminating a pre-existing legal parent-child relationship, it may, in the receiving State which recognises the adoption under the Convention, be converted into an adoption having such an effect—

(a)   if the law of the receiving State so permits; and
(b)   if the consents referred to in Article 4, sub-paragraphs c and d, have been or are given for the purpose of such an adoption.

2   Article 23 applies to the decision converting the adoption.

Chapter VI
General Provisions

Article 28

The Convention does not affect any law of a State of origin which requires that the adoption of a child habitually resident within that State take place in that State or which prohibits the child's placement in, or transfer to, the receiving State prior to adoption.

Article 29

There shall be no contact between the prospective adoptive parents and the child's parents or any other person who has care of the child until the requirements of Article 4, sub-paragraphs a to c, and Article 5, sub-paragraph a, have been met, unless the adoption takes place within a family or unless the contact is in compliance with the conditions established by the competent authority of the State of origin.

Article 30

1   The competent authorities of a Contracting State shall ensure that information held by them concerning the child's origin, in particular information concerning the identity of his or her parents, as well as the medical history, is preserved.

2   They shall ensure that the child or his or her representative has access to such information, under appropriate guidance, in so far as is permitted by the law of that State.

Article 31

Without prejudice to Article 30, personal data gathered or transmitted under the Convention, especially data referred to in Articles 15 and 16, shall be used only for the purposes for which they were gathered or transmitted.

Article 32

1 No one shall derive improper financial or other gain from an activity related to an intercountry adoption.

2 Only costs and expenses, including reasonable professional fees of persons involved in the adoption, may be charged or paid.

3 The directors, administrators and employees of bodies involved in an adoption shall not receive remuneration which is unreasonably high in relation to services rendered.

Article 33

A competent authority which finds that any provision of the Convention has not been respected or that there is a serious risk that it may not be respected, shall immediately inform the Central Authority of its State. This Central Authority shall be responsible for ensuring that appropriate measures are taken.

Article 34

If the competent authority of the State of destination of a document so requests, a translation certified as being in conformity with the original must be furnished. Unless otherwise provided, the costs of such translation are to be borne by the prospective adoptive parents.

Article 35

The competent authorities of the contracting States shall act expeditiously in the process of adoption.

Article 36

In relation to a State which has two or more systems of law with regard to adoption applicable in different territorial units—

(a)   any reference to habitual residence in that State shall be construed as referring to habitual residence in a territorial unit of that State;

(b)   any reference to the law of that State shall be construed as referring to the law in force in the relevant territorial unit;

(c)   any reference to the competent authorities or to the public authorities of that State shall be construed as referring to those authorised to act in the relevant territorial unit;

(d)   any reference to the accredited bodies of that State shall be construed as referring to bodies accredited in the relevant territorial unit.

Article 37

In relation to a State which with regard to adoption has two or more systems of law applicable to different categories of persons, any reference to the law of that State shall be construed as referring to the legal system specified by the law of that State.

Article 38

A State within which different territorial units have their own rules of law in respect of adoption shall not be bound to apply the Convention where a State with a unified system of law would not be bound to do so.

Article 39

1 The convention does not affect any international instrument to which Contracting States are Parties and which contains provisions on matters governed by the Convention, unless a contrary declaration is made by the States parties to such instrument.

2 Any Contracting State may enter into agreements with one or more other Contracting States, with a view to improving the application of the Convention in their mutual relations. These agreements may derogate only from the provisions of Articles 14 to 16 and 18 to 21. The States which have concluded such an agreement shall transmit a copy to the depositary of the Convention.

Article 40

No reservation to the Convention shall be permitted.

Article 41

The Convention shall apply in every case where an application pursuant to Article 14 has been received after the Convention has entered into force in the receiving State and the State of origin.

Article 42

The Secretary General of the Hague Conference on Private International Law shall at regular intervals convene a Special Commission in order to review the practical operation of the Convention.

NOTES

Initial Commencement

To be appointed
To be appointed: see s 18(3).

Appointment
Appointment (in relation to Scotland): 14 January 2003: by virtue of SSI 2002/562, art 2(a); appointment (in relation to England and Wales): 23 January 2003: see SI 2003/189, art 2(1)(a).

SCHEDULE 2
Minor and Consequential Amendments

Section 15(1)

Local Authority and Social Services Act 1970 (c 42)

1 In Schedule 1 to the Local Authority and Social Services Act 1970 (enactments conferring functions assigned to social services committee), at the end there shall be inserted—

'Adoption (Intercountry Aspects) Act 1999
(c 18)

Section 2(4)	Functions under Article 9(a) to (c) of the Convention on Protection of Children and Co-operation in respect of Intercountry Adoption, concluded at the Hague on 29th May 1993.'

Immigration Act 1971 (c 77)

2 In subsection (1) of section 33 of the Immigration Act 1971 (interpretation)—

(a)　after the definition of 'certificate of entitlement' there shall be inserted—

'"Convention adoption" has the same meaning as in the Adoption Act 1976 and the Adoption (Scotland) Act 1978;'; and

(b)　in the definition of 'legally adopted', after 'Islands' there shall be inserted ', under a Convention adoption'.

...

3　...

Adoption (*Scotland*) Act 1978 (*c 28*)

4　(1)　In subsection (2) of section 14 of the 1978 Act (adoption by married couple), in paragraph (b), for 'section 17 is' there shall be substituted 'the requirements of regulations under section 17 are'.

(2)　In subsection (2) of section 15 of that Act (adoption by one person), in paragraph (b), for 'section 17 is' there shall be substituted 'the requirements of regulations under section 17 are'.

(3)　In section 16 of that Act (parental agreement), subsection (3) shall cease to have effect.

(4)　In section 46 of that Act (revocation of adoptions on legitimation), subsection (2) shall cease to have effect.

(5)　In section 56 of that Act (courts)—

(a)　in subsection (2), for 'subsections (4) and (5)' there shall substituted 'subsection (5)'; and

(b)　subsection (4) shall cease to have effect.

(6)　In subsection (6) of section 60 of that Act (orders, rules and regulations), after 'paragraph 1(1)' there shall be inserted 'or 3'.

(7)　Section 63 of that Act (nationality) shall cease to have effect.

(8)　In subsection (2) of section 65 of that Act (interpretation), for 'Great Britain' there shall be substituted 'the British Islands'.

Family Law Act 1986 (*c 55*)

5　In subsection (1) of section 57 of the Family Law Act 1986 (declarations as to adoptions effected overseas), for paragraph (a) there shall be substituted—

'(a)　a Convention adoption as defined by subsection (1) of section 72 of the Adoption Act 1976 or an overseas adoption as defined by subsection (2) of that section, or'.

NOTES

Initial Commencement

To be appointed

To be appointed: see s 18(3).

Appointment

Paras 1, 3, 5: appointment: 1 June 2003: see SI 2003/189, art 2(2)(h); para 2: appointment: 1 June 2003: see SI 2003/362, art 2(b); para 4: appointment: 1 June 2003: see SSI 2003/121, art 2(g), (i).

Amendment

Para 3: repealed by the Adoption and Children Act 2002, s 139(3), Sch 5; date in force: 30 December 2005: see SI 2005/2897, art 2(b).

SCHEDULE 3
Repeals

Section 15(2)

Chapter	Short title	Extent of repeal

1976 c 36	Adoption Act 1976.	Section 16(3).
		Section 52(3).
		In section 53(5), the words 'and section 52(3)'.
		In section 54, in subsections (1) and (2), the words '52(3) or', and in subsection (4), the definitions of 'notified provision' and 'relevant time'.
		In section 61(1), the words '(other than an order to which section 17(6) applies)'.
		Section 70.
		In section 72(1), the definitions of 'regulated adoption' and 'specified order'.
		In Schedule 1, paragraph 1(2).
1978 c 28	Adoption (Scotland) Act 1978.	Section 16(3).
		Section 46(2).
		In section 47(5), the words 'and section 46(2)'.
		In section 48, in subsections (1) and (2), the words '46(2) or', and in subsection (4), the definitions of 'notified provision' and 'relevant time'.
		In section 55(1), the words '(other than an order to which section 17(6) applies)'.
		Section 56(4).
		Section 63.
		In section 65(1), the definitions of 'regulated adoption' and 'specified order'.
		In Schedule 1, paragraph 1(2).

NOTES
Initial Commencement
To be appointed
To be appointed: see s 18(3).

Appointment
Appointment (in relation to England and Wales): 1 June 2003: see SI 2003/189, art 2(2)(i): appointment (in relation to Scotland): 1 June 2003: see SSI 2003/121, art 2(g), (j).

Adoption (Designation of Overseas Adoptions) Order 1973

(SI 1973/19)

Made – 1st January 1973

Authority: Adoption Act 1976, s 72(2)

NOTES
Continuation
Authority: changed as a result of the consolidation of certain enactments relating to adoption in the Adoption Act 1976.

[1351]–[1400]

1

This Order may be cited as the Adoption (Designation of Overseas Adoptions) Order 1973 and shall come into operation on 1st February 1973.

2

The Interpretation Act 1889 shall apply to the interpretation of this Order as it applies to the interpretation of an Act of Parliament.

3

(1)   An adoption of an infant is hereby specified as an overseas adoption if it is an adoption effected in a place in relation to which this Article applies and under the law in force in that place.

(2)   [Subject to paragraph (2A) of this Article,] as respects any adoption effected before the date on which this Order comes into operation, this Article applies in relation to any place which, at that date, forms part of a country or territory described in Part I or II of the Schedule to this Order and as respects any adoption effected on or after that date, this Article applies in relation to any place which, at the time the adoption is effected, forms part of a country or territory which at that time is a country or territory described in Part I or II of the Schedule to this Order.

[(2A)   This Article also applies, as respects any adoption effected on or after 5th April 1993, in relation to any place which, at the time the adoption is effected, forms part of the People's Republic of China.]

(3)   In this Article the expression—

'infant' means a person who at the time when the application for adoption was made had not attained the age of 18 years and had not been married;
'law' does not include customary or common law.

NOTES
Amendment
Para (2): words in square brackets inserted by SI 1993/690, art 2(a); para (2A): inserted by SI 1993/690, art 2(b).

4

(1)   Evidence that an overseas adoption has been effected may be given by the production of a document purporting to be—

(a)   a certified copy of an entry made, in accordance with the law of the country or territory concerned, in a public register relating to the recording of adoptions and showing that the adoption has been effected; or

(b)   a certificate that the adoption has been effected, signed or purporting to be signed by a person authorised by the law of the country or territory concerned to sign such a certificate, or a certified copy of such certificate.

(2)   Where a document produced by virtue of paragraph (1) of this Article is not in English, the Registrar General or the Registrar General of Births, Deaths and

Marriages for Scotland, as the case may be, may require the production of an English translation of the document before satisfying himself of the matters specified in section 8 of the Adoption Act 1968.

(3)   Nothing in this Article shall be construed as precluding proof, in accordance with the Evidence (Foreign, Dominion and Colonial Documents) Act 1933, or the Oaths and Evidence (Overseas Authorities and Countries) Act 1963, or otherwise, than an overseas adoption has been effected.

SCHEDULE

Part I
Commonwealth Countries and United Kingdom [British Overseas Territories]

NOTES

Amendment

Part heading: words 'British Overseas Territories' in square brackets substituted by virtue of the British Overseas Territories Act 2002, s 2(3).

Date in force: this amendment came into force on 26 February 2002 (date of Royal Assent of the British Overseas Territories Act 2002) in the absence of any specific commencement provision.

Australia
Bahamas
Barbados
Bermuda
Botswana
British Honduras
British Virgin Islands
Canada
Cayman Islands
The Republic of Cyprus
Dominica
Fiji
Ghana
Gibraltar
Guyana
Hong Kong
Jamaica
Kenya
Lesotho
Malawi
Malaysia
Malta
Mauritius
Montserrat
New Zealand
Nigeria
Pitcairn
St Christopher, Nevis and Anguilla
St Vincent
Seychelles
Singapore
Southern Rhodesia
Sri Lanka
Swaziland
Tanzania
Tonga
Trinidad and Tobago
Uganda
Zambia

Part II
Other Countries and Territories

Austria
Belgium
Denmark (including Greenland and the Faroes)
Finland
France (including Reunion, Martinique, Guadeloupe and French Guyana)
The Federal Republic of Germany and Land Berlin (West Berlin)
Greece
Iceland
The Republic of Ireland
Israel
Italy
Luxembourg
The Netherlands (including Surinam and the Antilles)
Norway
Portugal (including the Azores and Madeira)
South Africa and South West Africa
Spain (including the Balearics and the Canary Islands)
Sweden
Switzerland
Turkey
The United States of America
Yugoslavia

Family Procedure (Adoption) Rules 2005

(SI 2005/2795)

Made	*10th October 2005*
Laid before Parliament	*12th October 2005*
Coming into force	*30th December 2005*

The Family Procedure Rule Committee makes the following Rules in exercise of the powers conferred by sections 75 and 76 of the Courts Act 2003, sections 52(7) and (8), 60(4), 90(1), 102, 109(2) and 141(1) and (3) of, and paragraphs 1(4), 4(4) and 6(2) of Schedule 1 to, the Adoption and Children Act 2002 and section 54(1) of the Access to Justice Act 1999.

In accordance with section 79 of the Courts Act 2003 the Committee has consulted with persons it considered appropriate.

These Rules may be cited as the Family Procedure (Adoption) Rules 2005.

[1401]–[1450]

Part 1
Overriding Objective

1 The overriding objective

(1)   These Rules are a new procedural code with the overriding objective of enabling the court to deal with cases justly, having regard to the welfare issues involved.

(2)   Dealing with a case justly includes, so far as is practicable—

(a)   ensuring that it is dealt with expeditiously and fairly;

(b)   dealing with the case in ways which are proportionate to the nature, importance and complexity of the issues;

(c)   ensuring that the parties are on an equal footing;

(d)   saving expense; and

(e)   allotting to it an appropriate share of the court's resources, while taking into account the need to allot resources to other cases.

NOTES
Initial Commencement
Specified date
Specified date: 30 December 2005: see Prelims.

2 Application by the court of the overriding objective

The court must seek to give effect to the overriding objective when it—

(a)   exercises any power given to it by these Rules; or

(b)   interprets any rule.

NOTES
Initial Commencement
Specified date
Specified date: 30 December 2005: see Prelims.

3 Duty of the parties

The parties are required to help the court to further the overriding objective.

NOTES
Initial Commencement
Specified date
Specified date: 30 December 2005: see Prelims.

4 Court's duty to manage cases

(1) The court must further the overriding objective by actively managing cases.

(2) Active case management includes—

(a) encouraging the parties to co-operate with each other in the conduct of the proceedings;

(b) identifying at an early stage—

(i) the issues; and

(ii) who should be a party to the proceedings;

(c) deciding promptly—

(i) which issues need full investigation and hearing and which do not; and

(ii) the procedure to be followed in the case;

(d) deciding the order in which issues are to be resolved;

(e) encouraging the parties to use an alternative dispute resolution procedure if the court considers that appropriate and facilitating the use of such procedure;

(f) helping the parties to settle the whole or part of the case;

(g) fixing timetables or otherwise controlling the progress of the case;

(h) considering whether the likely benefits of taking a particular step justify the cost of taking it;

(i) dealing with as many aspects of the case as it can on the same occasion;

(j) dealing with the case without the parties needing to attend at court;

(k) making use of technology; and

(l) giving directions to ensure that the case proceeds quickly and efficiently.

NOTES

Initial Commencement

Specified date

Specified date: 30 December 2005: see Prelims.

Part 2
Interpretation and Application of Other Rules

5 Extent and application of other rules

(1) Unless the context otherwise requires, these Rules apply to proceedings in—

(a) the High Court;

(b) a county court; and

(c) a magistrates' court.

(2) Rule 35.15 of the CPR shall apply in detailed assessment proceedings in the High Court and a county court.

(3) Subject to paragraph (4), Parts 43, 44 (except rules 44.3(2) and (3) and 44.9 to 44.12A), 47 and 48 and rule 45.6 of the CPR apply to costs in proceedings, with the following modifications—

(a) in rule 43.2(1)(c)(ii), 'district judge' includes a district judge of the principal registry of the Family Division;

(b) after rule 43.2(1)(d)(iv), insert—

'or

(v) a magistrates' court.'; and

(c) in rule 48.7(1) after 'section 51(6) of the Supreme Court Act 1981' insert 'or section 145A of the Magistrates' Courts Act 1980'.

(4) Part 47 of the CPR does not apply to proceedings in a magistrates' court.

(5) Parts 50 and 70 to 74 of, and Schedules 1 and 2 to, the CPR apply, as far as they are relevant, to the enforcement of orders made in proceedings in the High Court and county courts with necessary modifications.

NOTES
Initial Commencement
Specified date
Specified date: 30 December 2005: see Prelims.

6 Interpretation

(1)   In these Rules—

'the Act' means Part 1 of the Adoption and Children Act 2002;
'the 1989 Act' means the Children Act 1989;
'adoption proceedings' means proceedings for the making of an adoption order under the Act;
'application notice' means a document in which the applicant states his intention to seek a court order in accordance with the procedure in Part 9;
'business day' means any day other than—

(a)   a Saturday, Sunday, Christmas Day or Good Friday; or
(b)   a bank holiday under the Banking and Financial Dealings Act 1971, in England and Wales;

'Central Authority' means, in relation to England, the Secretary of State for Education and Skills, and in relation to Wales, the National Assembly for Wales;
'child'—

(a)   means, subject to paragraph (b), a person under the age of 18 years who is the subject of the proceedings; and
(b)   in adoption proceedings, also includes a person who has attained the age of 18 years before the proceedings are concluded;

'children and family reporter' means an officer of the Service or a Welsh family proceedings officer who prepares a report on matters relating to the welfare of the child;
'children's guardian' means an officer of the Service or a Welsh family proceedings officer appointed to act on behalf of a child who is a party to the proceedings with the duty of safeguarding the interests of the child;
'civil restraint order' means an order restraining a party—

(a)   from making any further applications in current proceedings (a limited civil restraint order);
(b)   from making certain applications in specified courts (an extended civil restraint order); or
(c)   from making any application in specified courts (a general civil restraint order);

'court officer' means, in the High Court and a county court, a member of court staff, and in a magistrates' court, the designated officer;
'CPR' means the Civil Procedure Rules 1998;
'detailed assessment proceedings' means the procedure by which the amount of costs is decided in accordance with Part 47 of the CPR;
'filing', in relation to a document, means delivering it, by post or otherwise, to the court office;
'jurisdiction' means, unless the context requires otherwise, England and Wales and any part of the territorial waters of the United Kingdom adjoining England and Wales;
'legal representative' means a barrister or a solicitor, solicitor's employee or other authorised litigator (as defined in section 119 of the Courts and Legal Services Act 1990) who has been instructed to act for a party in relation to an application;
'litigation friend' has the meaning given by section 1 of Part 7;
'non-subject child' means a person under the age of 18 years who is a party to the proceedings but is not the subject of the proceedings;
'officer of the Service' has the meaning given by section 11(3) of the Criminal Justice and Court Services Act 2000;
'patient' means a party to proceedings who, by reason of mental disorder within the meaning of the Mental Health Act 1983, is incapable of managing and administering his property and affairs;
'placement proceedings' means proceedings for the making, varying or revoking of a placement order under the Act;

'proceedings' means, unless the context otherwise requires, proceedings brought under the Act (whether at first instance or appeal) or proceedings for the purpose of enforcing an order made in any proceedings under that Act, as the case may be;

'provision for contact' means a contact order under section 8 or 34 of the 1989 Act or a contact order under section 26;

'reporting officer' means an officer of the Service or a Welsh family proceedings officer appointed to witness the documents which signify a parent or guardian's consent to the placing of the child for adoption or to the making of an adoption order or a section 84 order;

'section 84 order' means an order made by the High Court under section 84 giving parental responsibility prior to adoption abroad;

'section 88 direction' means a direction given by the High Court under section 88 that section 67(3) (status conferred by adoption) does not apply or does not apply to any extent specified in the direction;

'section 89 order' means an order made by the High Court under section 89—

    (a)   annulling a Convention adoption or Convention adoption order;

    (b)   providing for an overseas adoption or determination under section 91 to cease to be valid; or

    (c)   deciding the extent, if any, to which a determination under section 91 has been affected by a subsequent determination under that section;

'the Service Regulation' means Council Regulation (EC) No 1348/2000 of 29 May 2000 on the service in the Member States of judicial and extrajudicial documents in civil or commercial matters;

'Welsh family proceedings officer' has the meaning given by section 35(4) of the Children Act 2004.

(2)   A section or Schedule referred to by number alone means the section or Schedule so numbered in the Adoption and Children Act 2002.

(3)   Any provision in these Rules—

(a)   requiring or permitting directions to be given by the court is to be taken as including provision for such directions to be varied or revoked; and

(b)   requiring or permitting a date to be set is to be taken as including provision for that date to be set aside.

NOTES

Initial Commencement

Specified date

Specified date: 30 December 2005: see Prelims.

7   Power to perform functions of the court

(1)   Where these Rules or a practice direction provide for the court to perform any act then, except where any rule or practice direction, any other enactment, or the Family Proceedings (Allocation to Judiciary) Directions, provides otherwise, that act may be performed—

(a)   in relation to proceedings in the High Court or in a district registry, by any judge or district judge of that Court including a district judge of the principal registry of the Family Division;

(b)   in relation to proceedings in a county court, by any judge or district judge including a district judge of the principal registry of the Family Division when the principal registry of the Family Division is treated as if it were a county court; and

(c)   in relation to proceedings in a magistrates' court—

    (i)   by any family proceedings court constituted in accordance with sections 66 and 67 of the Magistrates' Courts Act 1980; or

    (ii)   by a single justice of the peace who is a member of the family panel—

        (aa)   where an application without notice is made under section 41(2) (recovery orders); and

        (bb)   in accordance with the relevant practice direction.

(The Justices' Clerks Rules 2005 make provision for a justices' clerk or assistant clerk to carry out certain functions of a single justice of the peace.)

(2)   A deputy High Court judge and a district judge, including a district judge of the principal registry of the Family Division, may not try a claim for a declaration of incompatibility in accordance with section 4 of the Human Rights Act 1998.

NOTES

Initial Commencement

Specified date

Specified date: 30 December 2005: see Prelims.

8   Court's discretion as to where it deals with cases

The court may deal with a case at any place that it considers appropriate.

NOTES

Initial Commencement

Specified date

Specified date: 30 December 2005: see Prelims.

9   Court documents

(1)   A court officer must seal, or otherwise authenticate with the stamp of the court, the following documents on issue—

(a)   the application form;

(b)   the order; and

(c)   any other document which a rule or practice direction requires it to seal or stamp.

(2)   The court officer may place the seal or the stamp on the document—

(a)   by hand; or

(b)   by printing a facsimile of the seal on the document whether electronically or otherwise.

(3)   A document purporting to bear the court's seal or stamp will be admissible in evidence without further proof.

(4)   The relevant practice direction contains provisions about court documents.

NOTES

Initial Commencement

Specified date

Specified date: 30 December 2005: see Prelims.

10   Computation of time

(1)   This rule shows how to calculate any period of time for doing any act which is specified—

(a)   by these Rules;

(b)   by a practice direction; or

(c)   by a direction or order of the court.

(2)   A period of time expressed as a number of days must be computed as clear days.

(3)   In this rule 'clear days' means that in computing the numbers of days—

(a)   the day on which the period begins; and

(b)   if the end of the period is defined by reference to an event, the day on which that event occurs

are not included.

(4)   Where the specified period is 7 days or less and would include a day which is not a business day, that day does not count.

(5)   When the period specified—

(a)   by these Rules or a practice direction; or

(b)   by any direction or order of the court,

for doing any act at the court office ends on a day on which the office is closed, that act will be in time if done on the next day on which the court office is open.

PART D – Appendix

NOTES
Initial Commencement
Specified date
Specified date: 30 December 2005: see Prelims.

11 Dates for compliance to be calendar dates and to include time of day

(1) Where the court makes an order or gives a direction which imposes a time limit for doing any act, the last date for compliance must, wherever practicable—

(a) be expressed as a calendar date; and
(b) include the time of day by which the act must be done.

(2) Where the date by which an act must be done is inserted in any document, the date must, wherever practicable, be expressed as a calendar date.
(3) Where 'month' occurs in any order, direction or other document, it means a calendar month.

NOTES
Initial Commencement
Specified date
Specified date: 30 December 2005: see Prelims.

Part 3
General Case Management Powers

12 The court's general powers of management

(1) The list of powers in this rule is in addition to any powers given to the court by any other rule or practice direction or by any other enactment or any powers it may otherwise have.
(2) Except where these Rules provide otherwise, the court may—

(a) extend or shorten the time for compliance with any rule, practice direction or court direction (even if an application for extension is made after the time for compliance has expired);
(b) adjourn or bring forward a hearing;
(c) require a party or a party's legal representative to attend the court;
(d) hold a hearing and receive evidence by telephone or by using any other method of direct oral communication;
(e) direct that part of any proceedings be dealt with as separate proceedings;
(f) stay the whole or part of any proceedings or judgment either generally or until a specified date or event;
(g) consolidate proceedings;
(h) hear two or more applications on the same occasion;
(i) direct a separate hearing of any issue;
(j) decide the order in which issues are to be heard;
(k) exclude an issue from consideration;
(l) dismiss or give judgment on an application after a decision on a preliminary issue;
(m) direct any party to file and serve an estimate of costs; and
(n) take any other step or give any other direction for the purpose of managing the case and furthering the overriding objective.

(3) The court may not extend the period within which a section 89 order must be made.
(4) Paragraph (2)(f) does not apply to proceedings in a magistrates' court.

NOTES
Initial Commencement
Specified date
Specified date: 30 December 2005: see Prelims.

13 Exercise of powers of court's own initiative

(1) Except where an enactment provides otherwise, the court may exercise the powers in rule 12 on an application or of its own initiative.
(Part 9 sets out the procedure for making an application.)
(2) Where the court proposes to exercise its powers of its own initiative—

(a) it may give any person likely to be affected an opportunity to make representations; and
(b) where it does so it must specify the time by and the manner in which the representations must be made.

(3) Where the court proposes to hold a hearing to decide whether to exercise its powers of its own initiative it must give each party likely to be affected at least 3 days' notice of the hearing.
(4) The court may exercise its powers of its own initiative, without hearing the parties or giving them an opportunity to make representations.
(5) Where the court has exercised its powers under paragraph (4)—

(a) a party affected by the direction may apply to have it set aside or varied; and
(b) the direction must contain a statement of the right to make such an application.

(6) An application under paragraph (5)(a) must be made—

(a) within such period as may be specified by the court; or
(b) if the court does not specify a period, within 7 days beginning with the date on which the order was served on the party making the application.

(7) If the High Court or a county court of its own initiative dismisses an application (including an application for permission to appeal) and it considers that the application is totally without merit—

(a) the court's order must record that fact; and
(b) the court must at the same time consider whether it is appropriate to make a civil restraint order.

NOTES
Initial Commencement
Specified date
Specified date: 30 December 2005: see Prelims.

14 Court officer's power to refer to the court

Where these Rules require a step to be taken by a court officer—

(a) the court officer may consult the court before taking that step;
(b) the step may be taken by the court instead of the court officer.

NOTES
Initial Commencement
Specified date
Specified date: 30 December 2005: see Prelims.

15 General power of the court to rectify matters where there has been an error of procedure

Where there has been an error of procedure such as a failure to comply with a rule or practice direction—

(a) the error does not invalidate any step taken in the proceedings unless the court so orders; and
(b) the court may make an order to remedy the error.

NOTES
Initial Commencement
Specified date
Specified date: 30 December 2005: see Prelims.

PART D – Appendix

16   Power of the court to make civil restraint orders

The relevant practice direction sets out—

(a)   the circumstances in which the High Court or a county court has the power to make a civil restraint order against a party to proceedings;

(b)   the procedure where a party applies for a civil restraint order against another party; and

(c)   the consequences of the court making a civil restraint order.

NOTES

Initial Commencement

Specified date

Specified date: 30 December 2005: see Prelims.

Part 4
How to Start Proceedings

17   Forms

Subject to rule 28(2) and (3), the forms set out in the relevant practice direction or forms to the like effect must be used in the cases to which they apply.

NOTES

Initial Commencement

Specified date

Specified date: 30 December 2005: see Prelims.

18   Documents to be attached to the application form

The application form must have attached to it any documents referred to in the application form.

NOTES

Initial Commencement

Specified date

Specified date: 30 December 2005: see Prelims.

19   How to start proceedings

(1)   Proceedings are started when a court officer issues an application at the request of the applicant.

(2)   An application is issued on the date entered in the application form by the court officer.

(Restrictions on where proceedings may be started are set out in the Children (Allocation of Proceedings) Order 1991.)

NOTES

Initial Commencement

Specified date

Specified date: 30 December 2005: see Prelims.

20   Application for a serial number

(1)   This rule applies to any application in proceedings by a person who intends to adopt the child.

(2)   If the applicant wishes his identity to be kept confidential in the proceedings, he may, before those proceedings have started, request a court officer to assign a serial number to him to identify him in connection with the proceedings, and a number will be assigned to him.

(3)   The court may at any time direct that a serial number identifying the applicant in the proceedings referred to in paragraph (2) must be removed.

(4)   If a serial number has been assigned to a person under paragraph (2)—

(a)   the court officer will ensure that any application form or application notice sent in accordance with these Rules does not contain information which discloses, or is likely to disclose, the identity of that person to any other party to that application who is not already aware of that person's identity; and

(b)   the proceedings on the application will be conducted with a view to securing that the applicant is not seen by or made known to any party who is not already aware of his identity except with his consent.

NOTES

Initial Commencement

Specified date

Specified date: 30 December 2005: see Prelims.

21 Personal details

(1)   Unless the court directs otherwise, a party is not required to reveal—

(a)   the address or telephone number of their private residence;
(b)   the address of the child;
(c)   the name of a person with whom the child is living, if that person is not the applicant; or
(d)   in relation to an application under section 28(2) (application for permission to change the child's surname), the proposed new surname of the child.

(2)   Where a party does not wish to reveal any of the particulars in paragraph (1), he must give notice of those particulars to the court and the particulars will not be revealed to any person unless the court directs otherwise.

(3)   Where a party changes his home address during the course of proceedings, he must give notice of the change to the court.

NOTES

Initial Commencement

Specified date

Specified date: 30 December 2005: see Prelims.

Part 5
Procedure for Applications in Adoption, Placement and Related Proceedings

22 Application of this Part

The rules in this Part apply to the following proceedings—

(a)   adoption proceedings;
(b)   placement proceedings; or
(c)   proceedings for—

    (i)   the making of a contact order under section 26;
    (ii)   the variation or revocation of a contact order under section 27;
    (iii) an order giving permission to change a child's surname or remove a child from the United Kingdom under section 28(2) and (3);
    (iv) a section 84 order;
    (v)   a section 88 direction;
    (vi) a section 89 order; or
    (vii) any other order that may be referred to in a practice direction.

(Parts 9 and 10 set out the procedure for making an application in proceedings not dealt with in this Part.)

NOTES

Initial Commencement

Specified date

Specified date: 30 December 2005: see Prelims.

PART D – Appendix

23   Who the parties are

(1)   In relation to the proceedings set out in column 1 of each of the following tables, column 2 of Table 1 sets out who the application may be made by and column 2 of Table 2 sets out who the respondents to those proceedings will be.

Table 1

Proceedings for	Applicants
An adoption order (section 46) A section 84 order	The prospective adopters (section 50 and 51). The prospective adopters asking for parental responsibility prior to adoption abroad.
A placement order (section 21) An order varying a placement order (section 23)	A local authority (section 22). The joint application of the local authority authorised by the placement order to place the child for adoption and the local authority which is to be substituted for that authority (section 23).
An order revoking a placement order (section 24)	The child; the local authority authorised to place the child for adoption; or where the child is not placed for adoption by the authority, any other person who has the permission of the court to apply (section 24).
A contact order (section 26)	The child; the adoption agency; any parent, guardian or relative; any person in whose favour there was provision for contact under the 1989 Act which ceased to have effect on an adoption agency being authorised to place a child for adoption, or placing a child for adoption who is less than six weeks old (section 26(1)); a person in whose favour there was a residence order in force immediately before the adoption agency was authorised to place the child for adoption or placed the child for adoption at a time when he was less than six weeks old; a person who by virtue of an order made in the exercise of the High Court's inherent jurisdiction with respect to children had care of the child immediately before that time; or any person who has the permission of the court to make the application (section 26).
An order varying or revoking a contact order (section 27)	The child; the adoption agency; or any person named in the contact order (section 27(1)).
An order permitting the child's name to be changed or the removal of the child from the United Kingdom (section 28(2) and (3))	Any person including the adoption agency or the local authority authorised to place, or which has placed, the child for adoption (section 28(2)).

A section 88 direction	The adopted child;
	the adopters;
	any parent; or
	any other person.
A section 89 order	The adopters;
	the adopted person;
	any parent;
	the relevant Central Authority;
	the adoption agency;
	the local authority to whom notice under section 44 (notice of intention to adopt or apply for a section 84 order) has been given;
	the Secretary of State for the Home Department; or
	any other person.

Table 2

Proceedings for	Respondents
An adoption order (section 46) or a section 84 order	Each parent who has parental responsibility for the child or guardian of the child unless he has given notice under section 20(4)(a) (statement of wish not to be informed of any application for an adoption order) which has effect;
	any person in whose favour there is provision for contact;
	any adoption agency having parental responsibility for the child under section 25;
	any adoption agency which has taken part at any stage in the arrangements for adoption of the child;
	any local authority to whom notice under section 44 (notice of intention to adopt or apply for a section 84 order) has been given;
	any local authority or voluntary organisation which has parental responsibility for, is looking after, or is caring for, the child; and

	the child where—
	permission has been granted to a parent or guardian to oppose the making of the adoption order (section 47(3) or 47(5));
	he opposes the making of an adoption order;
	a children and family reporter recommends that it is in the best interests of the child to be a party to the proceedings and that recommendation is accepted by the court;
	he is already an adopted child;
	any party to the proceedings or the child is opposed to the arrangements for allowing any person contact with the child, or a person not being allowed contact with the child after the making of the adoption order;
	the application is for a Convention adoption order or a section 84 order;
	he has been brought into the United Kingdom in the circumstances where section 83(1) applies (restriction on bringing children in);
	the application is for an adoption order other than a Convention adoption order and the prospective adopters intend the child to live in a country or territory outside the British Islands after the making of the adoption order; or
	—the prospective adopters are relatives of the child.
A placement order (section 21)	Each parent who has parental responsibility for the child or guardian of the child;
	any person in whose favour an order under the 1989 Act is in force in relation to the child;
	any adoption agency or voluntary organisation which has parental responsibility for, is looking after, or is caring for, the child;
	the child; and
	the parties or any persons who are or have been parties to proceedings for a care order in respect of the child where those proceedings have led to the application for the placement order.
An order varying a placement order (section 23)	The parties to the proceedings leading to the placement order which it is sought to have varied except the child who was the subject of those proceedings; and
	any person in whose favour there is provision for contact.
An order revoking a placement order (section 24)	The parties to the proceedings leading to the placement order which it is sought to have revoked; and
	any person in whose favour there is provision for contact.

A contact order (section 26)	The adoption agency authorised to place the child for adoption or which has placed the child for adoption;
	the person with whom the child lives or is to live;
	each parent with parental responsibility for the child or guardian of the child; and
	the child where—
	the adoption agency authorised to place the child for adoption or which has placed the child for adoption or a parent with parental responsibility for the child opposes the making of the contact order under section 26;
	he opposes the making of the contact order under section 26;
	existing provision for contact is to be revoked;
	relatives of the child do not agree to the arrangements for allowing any person contact with the child, or a person not being allowed contact with the child; or
	he is suffering or is at risk of suffering harm within the meaning of the 1989 Act.
An order varying or revoking a contact order (section 27)	The parties to the proceedings leading to the contact order which it is sought to have varied or revoked; and
	any person named in the contact order.
An order permitting the child's name to be changed or the removal of the child from the United Kingdom (section 28(2) and (3))	The parties to proceedings leading to any placement order;
	the adoption agency authorised to place the child for adoption or which has placed the child for adoption;
	any prospective adopters with whom the child is living; and
	each parent with parental responsibility for the child or guardian of the child.
A section 88 direction	The adopters;
	the parents;
	the adoption agency;
	the local authority to whom notice under section 44 (notice of intention to apply for a section 84 order) has been given; and
	the Attorney-General.
A section 89 order	The adopters;
	the parents;
	the adoption agency; and
	the local authority to whom notice under section 44 (notice of intention to adopt or apply for a section 84 order) has been given.

(2)   The court may at any time direct that a child, who is not already a respondent to proceedings, be made a respondent to proceedings where—

(a)   the child—

    (i)   wishes to make an application; or

    (ii)   has evidence to give to the court or a legal submission to make which has not been given or made by any other party; or

(b)   there are other special circumstances.

(3)   The court may at any time direct that—

(a)   any other person or body be made a respondent to proceedings; or

(b)   a respondent be removed.

(4)   If the court makes a direction for the addition or removal of a party, it may give consequential directions about—

(a)   serving a copy of the application form on any new respondent;

(b)   serving relevant documents on the new party; and

(c)   the management of the proceedings.

NOTES

Initial Commencement

Specified date

Specified date: 30 December 2005: see Prelims.

24   What the court or a court officer will do when the application has been issued

(1)   As soon as practicable after the application has been issued in proceedings—

(a)   the court will—

(i)   if section 48(1) (restrictions on making adoption orders) applies, consider whether it is proper to hear the application;

(ii)   subject to paragraph (4), set a date for the first directions hearing;

(iii)   appoint a children's guardian in accordance with rule 59;

(iv)   appoint a reporting officer in accordance with rule 69;

(v)   consider whether a report relating to the welfare of the child is required, and if so, request such a report in accordance with rule 73;

(vi)   set a date for the hearing of the application; and

(vii)   do anything else that may be set out in a practice direction; and

(b)   a court officer will—

(i)   subject to receiving confirmation in accordance with para-graph (2)(b)(ii), give notice of any directions hearing set by the court to the parties and to any children's guardian, reporting officer or children and family reporter;

(ii)   serve a copy of the application form (but, subject to sub-paragraphs (iii) and (iv), not the documents attached to it) on the persons referred to in the relevant practice direction;

(iii)   send a copy of the certified copy of the entry in the register of live-births or Adopted Children Register and any health report attached to an application for an adoption order to—

(aa)   any children's guardian, reporting officer or children and family reporter; and

(bb)   the local authority to whom notice under section 44 (notice of intention to adopt or apply for a section 84 order) has been given;

(iv)   if notice under rule 27 has been given (request to dispense with consent of parent or guardian), in accordance with that rule inform the parent or guardian of the request and send a copy of the statement of facts to—

(aa)   the parent or guardian;

(bb)   any children's guardian, reporting officer or children and family reporter;

(cc)   any local authority to whom notice under section 44 (notice of intention to adopt or apply for a section 84 order) has been given; and

(dd)   any adoption agency which has placed the child for adoption; and

(v)   do anything else that may be set out in a practice direction.

(2)   In addition to the matters referred to in paragraph (1), as soon as practicable after an application for an adoption order or a section 84 order has been issued the court or the court officer will—

(a)   where the child is not placed for adoption by an adoption agency—

    (i)   ask either the Service or the Assembly to file any relevant form of consent to an adoption order or a section 84 order; and

    (ii)   ask the local authority to prepare a report on the suitability of the prospective adopters if one has not already been prepared; and

(b)   where the child is placed for adoption by an adoption agency, ask the adoption agency to—

    (i)   file any relevant form of consent to—

        (aa)   the child being placed for adoption;

        (bb)   an adoption order;

        (cc)   a future adoption order under section 20; or

        (dd)   a section 84 order;

    (ii)   confirm whether a statement has been made under section 20(4)(a) (statement of wish not to be informed of any application for an adoption order) and if so, to file that statement;

    (iii)   file any statement made under section 20(4)(b) (withdrawal of wish not to be informed of any application for an adoption order) as soon as it is received by the adoption agency; and

    (iv)   prepare a report on the suitability of the prospective adopters if one has not already been prepared.

(3)   In addition to the matters referred to in paragraph (1), as soon as practicable after an application for a placement order has been issued—

(a)   the court will consider whether a report giving the local authority's reasons for placing the child for adoption is required, and if so, will direct the local authority to prepare such a report; and

(b)   the court or the court officer will ask either the Service or the Assembly to file any form of consent to the child being placed for adoption.

(4)   Where it considers it appropriate the court may, instead of setting a date for a first directions hearing, give the directions provided for by rule 26.

NOTES

Initial Commencement

Specified date

Specified date: 30 December 2005: see Prelims.

25   Date for first directions hearing

Unless the court directs otherwise, the first directions hearing must be within 4 weeks beginning with the date on which the application is issued.

NOTES

Initial Commencement

Specified date

Specified date: 30 December 2005: see Prelims.

26   The first directions hearing

(1)   At the first directions hearing in the proceedings the court will—

(a)   fix a timetable for the filing of—

    (i)   any report relating to the suitability of the applicants to adopt a child;

    (ii)   any report from the local authority;

    (iii)   any report from a children's guardian, reporting officer or children and family reporter;

    (iv)   if a statement of facts has been filed, any amended statement of facts;

    (v)   any other evidence, and

PART D – Appendix

give directions relating to the reports and other evidence;

(b) consider whether an alternative dispute resolution procedure is appropriate and, if so, give directions relating to the use of such procedure;

(c) consider whether the child or any other person should be a party to the proceedings and, if so, give directions in accordance with rule 23(2) or (3) joining that child or person as a party;

(d) give directions relating to the appointment of a litigation friend for any patient or non-subject child unless a litigation friend has already been appointed;

(e) consider whether the case needs to be transferred to another court and, if so, give directions to transfer the proceedings to another court in accordance with any order made by the Lord Chancellor under Part I of Schedule 11 to the 1989 Act;

(f) give directions about—

    (i) tracing parents or any other person the court considers to be relevant to the proceedings;

    (ii) service of documents;

    (iii) subject to paragraph (2), disclosure as soon as possible of information and evidence to the parties; and

    (iv) the final hearing; and

(2) Rule 77(2) applies to any direction given under paragraph (1)(f)(iii) as it applies to a direction given under rule 77(1).

(3) In addition to the matters referred to in paragraph (1), the court will give any of the directions listed in the relevant practice direction in proceedings for—

(a) a Convention adoption order;

(b) a section 84 order;

(c) a section 88 direction;

(d) a section 89 order; or

(e) an adoption order where section 83(1) applies (restriction on bringing children in).

(4) The parties or their legal representatives must attend the first directions hearing unless the court directs otherwise.

(5) Directions may also be given at any stage in the proceedings—

(a) of the court's own initiative; or

(b) on the application of a party or any children's guardian or, where the direction concerns a report by a reporting officer or children and family reporter, the reporting officer or children and family reporter.

(6) For the purposes of giving directions or for such purposes as the court directs—

(a) the court may set a date for a further directions hearing or other hearing; and

(b) the court officer will give notice of any date so fixed to the parties and to any children's guardian, reporting officer or children and family reporter.

(7) After the first directions hearing the court will monitor compliance with the court's timetable and directions by the parties.

NOTES

Initial Commencement

Specified date

Specified date: 30 December 2005: see Prelims.

27 Requesting the court to dispense with the consent of any parent or guardian

(1) The following paragraphs apply where the applicant wants to ask the court to dispense with the consent of any parent or guardian of a child to—

(a) the child being placed for adoption;

(b) the making of an adoption order except a Convention adoption order; or

(c) the making of a section 84 order.

(2) The applicant requesting the court to dispense with the consent must—

(a) give notice of the request in the application form or at any later stage by filing a written request setting out the reasons for the request; and

(b) file a statement of facts setting out a summary of the history of the case and any other facts to satisfy the court that—

   (i) the parent or guardian cannot be found or is incapable of giving consent; or

   (ii) the welfare of the child requires the consent to be dispensed with.

(3) If a serial number has been assigned to the applicant under rule 20, the statement of facts supplied under paragraph (2)(b) must be framed so that it does not disclose the identity of the applicant.

(4) On receipt of the notice of the request—

(a) a court officer will—

   (i) inform the parent or guardian of the request; and

   (ii) send a copy of the statement of facts filed in accordance with paragraph (2)(b) to—

      (aa) the parent or guardian;

      (bb) any children's guardian, reporting officer or children and family reporter;

      (cc) any local authority to whom notice under section 44 (notice of intention to adopt or apply for a section 84 order) has been given; and

      (dd) any adoption agency which has placed the child for adoption; and

(b) if the applicant considers that the parent or guardian is incapable of giving consent, the court will consider whether to—

   (i) appoint a litigation friend for the parent or guardian under rule 55(1); or

   (ii) give directions for an application to be made under rule 55(3),

   unless a litigation friend is already appointed for that parent or guardian.

NOTES

Initial Commencement

Specified date

Specified date: 30 December 2005: see Prelims.

28 Consent

(1) Consent of any parent or guardian of a child—

(a) under section 19, to the child being placed for adoption; and

(b) under section 20, to the making of a future adoption order

must be given in the form required by the relevant practice direction or a form to the like effect.

(2) Subject to paragraph (3), consent—

(a) to the making of an adoption order; or

(b) to the making of a section 84 order,

may be given in the form required by the relevant practice direction or a form to the like effect.

(3) Any consent to a Convention adoption order must be in a form which complies with the internal law relating to adoption of the Convention country of which the child is habitually resident.

(4) Any form of consent executed in Scotland must be witnessed by a Justice of the Peace or a Sheriff.

(5) Any form of consent executed in Northern Ireland must be witnessed by a Justice of the Peace.

(6) Any form of consent executed outside the United Kingdom must be witnessed by—

(a)   any person for the time being authorised by law in the place where the document is executed to administer an oath for any judicial or other legal purpose;

(b)   a British Consular officer;

(c)   a notary public; or

(d)   if the person executing the document is serving in any of the regular armed forces of the Crown, an officer holding a commission in any of those forces.

NOTES

Initial Commencement

Specified date

Specified date: 30 December 2005: see Prelims.

29 Reports by the adoption agency or local authority

(1)   The adoption agency or local authority must file the report on the suitability of the applicant to adopt a child within the timetable fixed by the court.

(2)   A local authority that is directed to prepare a report on the placement of the child for adoption must file that report within the timetable fixed by the court.

(3)   The reports must cover the matters specified in the relevant practice direction.

(4)   The court may at any stage request a further report or ask the adoption agency or local authority to assist the court in any other manner.

(5)   A court officer will send a copy of any report referred to in this rule to any children's guardian, reporting officer or children and family reporter.

(6)   Any report to the court under this rule will be confidential.

NOTES

Initial Commencement

Specified date

Specified date: 30 December 2005: see Prelims.

30 Health reports

(1)   Reports by a registered medical practitioner ('health reports') made not more than three months earlier on the health of the child and of each applicant must be attached to an application for an adoption order or a section 84 order except where—

(a)   the child was placed for adoption with the applicant by an adoption agency;

(b)   the applicant or one of the applicants is a parent of the child; or

(c)   the applicant is the partner of a parent of the child.

(2)   Health reports must contain the matters set out in the relevant practice direction.

(3)   Any health report will be confidential.

NOTES

Initial Commencement

Specified date

Specified date: 30 December 2005: see Prelims.

31 Notice of final hearing

A court officer will give notice to the parties, any children's guardian, reporting officer or children and family reporter and to any other person that may be referred to in a practice direction—

(a)   of the date and place where the application will be heard; and

(b)   of the fact that, unless the person wishes or the court requires, the person need not attend.

NOTES

Initial Commencement

Specified date

Specified date: 30 December 2005: see Prelims.

32 The final hearing

(1) Any person who has been given notice in accordance with rule 31 may attend the final hearing and, subject to paragraph (2), be heard on the question of whether an order should be made.

(2) A person whose application for the permission of the court to oppose the making of an adoption order under section 47(3) or (5) has been refused is not entitled to be heard on the question of whether an order should be made.

(3) Any member or employee of a party which is a local authority, adoption agency or other body may address the court at the final hearing if he is authorised to do so.

(4) The court may direct that any person must attend a final hearing.

(5) Paragraphs (6) and (7) apply to—

(a)   an adoption order;
(b)   a section 84 order; or
(c)   a section 89 order.

(6) Subject to paragraphs (7) and (8), the court cannot make an order unless the applicant and the child personally attend the final hearing.

(7) The court may direct that the applicant or the child need not attend the final hearing.

(8) In a case of adoption by a couple under section 50 the court may make an adoption order after personal attendance of one only of the applicants if there are special circumstances.

(9) The court cannot make a placement order unless a legal representative of the applicant attends the final hearing.

NOTES

Initial Commencement

Specified date

Specified date: 30 December 2005: see Prelims.

33 Proof of identity of the child

(1) Unless the contrary is shown, the child referred to in the application will be deemed to be the child referred to in the form of consent—

(a)   to the child being placed for adoption;
(b)   to the making of an adoption order; or
(c)   to the making of a section 84 order

where the conditions in paragraph (2) apply.

(2) The conditions are—

(a)   the application identifies the child by reference to a full certified copy of an entry in the registers of live-births;
(b)   the form of consent identifies the child by reference to a full certified copy of an entry in the registers of live-births attached to the form; and
(c)   the copy of the entry in the registers of live-births referred to in sub-paragraph (a) is the same or relates to the same entry in the registers of live-births as the copy of the entry in the registers of live-births attached to the form of consent.

(3) Where the child is already an adopted child paragraph (2) will have effect as if for the references to the registers of live-births there were substituted references to the Adopted Children Register.

(4) Subject to paragraph (7), where the precise date of the child's birth is not proved to the satisfaction of the court, the court will determine the probable date of birth.

(5) The probable date of the child's birth may be specified in the placement order, adoption order or section 84 order as the date of his birth.

(6) Subject to paragraph (7), where the child's place of birth cannot be proved to the satisfaction of the court—

(a)   he may be treated as having been born in the registration district of the court where it is probable that the child may have been born in—

(i)   the United Kingdom;
(ii)   the Channel Islands; or

(iii)   the Isle of Man; or

(b)   in any other case, the particulars of the country of birth may be omitted from the placement order, adoption order or section 84 order.

(7)   A placement order identifying the probable date and place of birth of the child will be sufficient proof of the date and place of birth of the child in adoption proceedings and proceedings for a section 84 order.

NOTES
Initial Commencement
Specified date
Specified date: 30 December 2005: see Prelims.

Part 6
Service

Section 1
General Rules about Service

34   Scope of this Part

The rules in this Part apply to the service of documents, including a document that is required to be given or sent by these Rules or any practice direction, except where—

(a)   any other enactment, a rule in another Part or a practice direction makes a different provision; or
(b)   the court directs otherwise.

NOTES
Initial Commencement
Specified date
Specified date: 30 December 2005: see Prelims.

35   Methods of service

(1)   Subject to paragraph (2), a document may be served—

(a)   where it is not known whether a solicitor is acting on behalf of a party—

(i)   by delivering it to the party personally; or
(ii)   by delivering it at, or by sending it by first class post to, the party's residence or last known residence; or

(b)   where a solicitor is known to be acting on behalf of a party—

(i)   by delivering the document at, or sending it by first class post to, the solicitor's address for service; or
(ii)   through a document exchange in accordance with the relevant practice direction.

(2)   A notice of hearing must be served in accordance with paragraph (1)(a)(i) or (ii) irrespective of whether a solicitor is acting on behalf of a party.
(3)   Where it appears to the court that there is a good reason to authorise service by a method not permitted by paragraph (1), the court may direct that service is effected by an alternative method.
(4)   A direction that service is effected by an alternative method must specify—

(a)   the method of service; and
(b)   the date when the document will be deemed to be served.

NOTES
Initial Commencement
Specified date
Specified date: 30 December 2005: see Prelims.

36   Who is to serve

(1)   A document which has been issued or prepared by a court officer will be served by the court officer except where—

(a)   a practice direction provides otherwise; or
(b)   the court directs otherwise.

(2)   Where a court officer is to serve a document, it is for the court to decide which of the methods of service specified in rule 35(1) is to be used.

NOTES
Initial Commencement
Specified date
Specified date: 30 December 2005: see Prelims.

37   Service of documents on children and patients

(1)   The following table shows the person on whom a document must be served if it is a document which would otherwise be served on a child, non-subject child or patient—

Nature of party	Type of document	Person to be served
Child who is not also a patient	Any document	The solicitor acting for the child; where there is no such solicitor, the children's guardian or the children and family reporter.
Non-subject child who is not also a patient	Application form	One of the non-subject child's parents or guardians; if there is no parent or guardian, the person with whom the non-subject child resides or in whose care the non-subject child is.
Patient	Application form	The person authorised under Part VII of the Mental Health Act 1983 to conduct the proceedings in the name of the patient or on his behalf; if there is no person so authorised, the person with whom the patient resides or in whose care the patient is.
Non-subject child or patient	Application for an order appointing a litigation friend, where the non-subject child or patient has no litigation friend	See rule 57.

Nature of party	Type of document	Person to be served
	Any other document	The litigation friend who is conducting proceedings on behalf of the non-subject child or patient.

(2)   Where a child is directed by the court to serve a document, service is to be effected by—

(a)   the solicitor acting for the child;
(b)   where there is no such solicitor, the children's guardian;
(c)   where there is neither a solicitor or children's guardian, the litigation friend; or
(d)   where there is neither a solicitor, children's guardian, or litigation friend, a court officer.

(3)   Where a non-subject child or patient is directed by the court to serve a document, service is to be effected by—

(a)   the solicitor acting for the non-subject child or patient; or
(b)   where there is no such solicitor, the litigation friend.

(4)   The court may give directions permitting a document to be served on the child, non-subject child or patient, or on some other person other than the person specified in the table in this rule.

(5)   The court may direct that, although a document has been served on someone other than the person specified in the table, the document is to be treated as if it had been properly served.

(6)   This rule does not apply where a non-subject child is conducting proceedings without a litigation friend in accordance with rule 51.

NOTES

Initial Commencement

Specified date
Specified date: 30 December 2005: see Prelims.

38   Deemed service

(1)   Unless the contrary is proved, a document which is served in accordance with these Rules or any relevant practice direction will be deemed to be served on the day shown in the following table—

Method of service	Deemed day of service
First class post	The second day after it was posted.
Document exchange	The second day after it was left at the document exchange.
Delivering the document to address	The day after the document was delivered to that address.

(2)   If a document is served personally—

(a)   after 5 pm on a business day; or
(b)   at any time on a day which is not a business day

it will be treated as being served on the next business day.

NOTES
Initial Commencement
Specified date
Specified date: 30 December 2005: see Prelims.

39 Power of court to dispense with service

Where a rule or practice direction requires a document to be served, the court may direct that the requirement is dispensed with.

NOTES

Initial Commencement

Specified date

Specified date: 30 December 2005: see Prelims.

40 Certificate of service

(1)   Where a rule, practice direction or court order requires a certificate of service, the certificate must state the details set out in the following table—

Method of service	Details to be certified
Post	Date of posting.
Personal	Date of personal service.
Document exchange	Date of delivery to the document exchange.
Delivery of document to address	Date when the document was delivered to the address.
Alternative method permitted by the court	As required by the court.

(2)   Where an application form is to be served by the applicant he must file a certificate of service within 7 days beginning with the date on which the application form was served.

NOTES

Initial Commencement

Specified date

Specified date: 30 December 2005: see Prelims.

41 Notice of non-service

Where a person fails to serve any document under these Rules or as directed by the court he must file a certificate of non-service stating the reason why service has not been effected.

NOTES

Initial Commencement

Specified date

Specified date: 30 December 2005: see Prelims.

Section 2
Service Out of the Jurisdiction

42 Scope and definitions

(1)   This Section contains rules about—

(a)   service out of the jurisdiction; and

(b)   the procedure for serving out of the jurisdiction.

(Rule 6 defines 'jurisdiction'.)

(2)   In this Section—

'application form' includes application notice; and

'the Hague Convention' means the Convention on the service abroad of judicial and extra-judicial documents in civil or commercial matters signed at the Hague on November 15, 1965.

NOTES

Initial Commencement

Specified date
Specified date: 30 December 2005: see Prelims.

43 Service of documents

(1) Any document to be served for the purposes of these Rules may be served out of the jurisdiction without the permission of the court.
(2) Subject to paragraph (4) or (5), any document served out of the jurisdiction in a country in which English is not the official language must be accompanied by a translation of the document—

(a)   in the official language of the country in which the document is to be served; or
(b)   if there is more than one official language of the country, in any one of those languages which is appropriate to the place in that country in which the document is to be served.

(3) Every translation filed under this rule must be signed by the translator to certify that the translation is accurate.
(4) Any document served out of the jurisdiction in a country in which English is not the official language need not be accompanied by a translation of the document where—

(a)   the person on whom the document is to be served is able to read and understand English; and
(b)   service of the document is to be effected directly on that person.

(5) Paragraphs (2) and (3) do not apply where service is to be effected in accordance with the Service Regulation.

NOTES

Initial Commencement

Specified date
Specified date: 30 December 2005: see Prelims.

44 Method of service—general provisions

(1) Where an application form is to be served out of the jurisdiction, it may be served by any method—

(a)   permitted by the law of the country in which it is to be served; or
(b)   provided for by—

(i)   rule 45 (service through foreign governments, judicial authorities and British Consular authorities); or
(ii)   rule 47 (service in accordance with the Service Regulation).

(2) Nothing in this rule or in any court order will authorise or require any person to do anything in the country where the application form is to be served which is against the law of that country.

NOTES

Initial Commencement

Specified date
Specified date: 30 December 2005: see Prelims.

45 Service through foreign governments, judicial authorities and British Consular authorities

(1) Where an application form is to be served on a respondent in any country which is a party to the Hague Convention, the application form may be served—

(a)   through the authority designated under the Hague Convention in respect of that country; or

(b)   if the law of that country permits—

    (i)   through the judicial authorities of that country; or

    (ii)   through a British Consular authority in that country.

(2)   Where an application form is to be served on a respondent in any country which is not a party to the Hague Convention, the application form may be served, if the law of that country so permits—

(a)   through the government of that country, where that government is willing to serve it; or

(b)   through a British Consular authority in that country.

(3)   Paragraph (2) does not apply where the application form is to be served in—

(a)   Scotland, Northern Ireland, the Isle of Man or the Channel Islands;

(b)   any Commonwealth State; or

(c)   any United Kingdom Overseas Territory listed in the relevant practice direction.

(4)   This rule does not apply where service is to be effected in accordance with the Service Regulation.

NOTES

Initial Commencement

Specified date

Specified date: 30 December 2005: see Prelims.

46   Procedure where service is to be through foreign governments, judicial authorities and British Consular authorities

(1)   This rule applies where the applicant wishes to serve the application form through—

(a)   the judicial authorities of the country where the application form is to be served;

(b)   a British Consular authority in that country;

(c)   the authority designated under the Hague Convention in respect of that country; or

(d)   the government of that country.

(2)   Where this rule applies, the applicant must file—

(a)   a request for service of the application form by the method in paragraph (1) that he has chosen;

(b)   a copy of the application form;

(c)   any translation required under rule 43; and

(d)   any other documents, copies of documents or translations required by the relevant practice direction.

(3)   When the applicant files the documents specified in paragraph (2), a court officer will—

(a)   seal, or otherwise authenticate with the stamp of the court, the copy of the application form; and

(b)   forward the documents to the Senior Master of the Queen's Bench Division.

(4)   The Senior Master will send documents forwarded under this rule—

(a)   where the application form is being served through the authority designated under the Hague Convention, to that authority; or

(b)   in any other case, to the Foreign and Commonwealth Office with a request that it arranges for the application to be served by the method indicated in the request for service filed under paragraph (2) or, where that request indicates alternative methods, by the most convenient method.

(5)   An official certificate will be evidence of the facts stated in the certificate if it—

PART D – Appendix

(a) states that the application form has been served in accordance with this rule either personally, or in accordance with the law of the country in which service was effected;

(b) specifies the date on which the application form was served; and

(c) is made by—

(i) a British Consular authority in the country where the application form was served;

(ii) the government or judicial authorities in that country; or

(iii) any other authority designated in respect of that country under the Hague Convention.

(6) A document purporting to be an official certificate under paragraph (5) will be treated as such a certificate, unless it is proved not to be.

(7) This rule does not apply where service is to be effected in accordance with the Service Regulation.

NOTES

Initial Commencement

Specified date

Specified date: 30 December 2005: see Prelims.

47   Service in accordance with the Service Regulation

(1) This rule applies where an application form is to be served in accordance with the Service Regulation.

(2) The applicant must file the application form and any translations or other documents required by the Service Regulation.

(3) When the applicant files the documents referred to in paragraph (2), a court officer will—

(a) seal, or otherwise authenticate with the stamp of the court, the copy of the application form; and

(b) forward the documents to the Senior Master of the Queen's Bench Division.

(The Service Regulation is annexed to the relevant practice direction.)

NOTES

Initial Commencement

Specified date

Specified date: 30 December 2005: see Prelims.

48   Undertaking to be responsible for expenses of the Foreign and Commonwealth Office

Every request for service filed under rule 46 (service through foreign governments, judicial authorities etc) must contain an undertaking by the person making the request—

(a) to be responsible for all expenses incurred by the Foreign and Commonwealth Office or foreign judicial authority; and

(b) to pay those expenses to the Foreign and Commonwealth Office or foreign judicial authority on being informed of the amount.

NOTES

Initial Commencement

Specified date

Specified date: 30 December 2005: see Prelims.

Part 7
Litigation Friend, Children's Guardian, Reporting Officer and Children and Family Reporter

Section 1
Litigation Friend

49   Application of this Section

(1) This Section—

(a)   contains special provisions which apply in proceedings involving non-subject children and patients; and

(b)   sets out how a person becomes a litigation friend.

(2)   The provisions of this Section also apply to a child who does not have a children's guardian, in which case, any reference to a 'non-subject child' in these Rules is to be taken as including a child.

NOTES

Initial Commencement

Specified date

Specified date: 30 December 2005: see Prelims.

50   Requirement for litigation friend in proceedings

(1)   Subject to rule 51, a non-subject child must have a litigation friend to conduct proceedings on his behalf.

(2)   A patient must have a litigation friend to conduct proceedings on his behalf.

NOTES

Initial Commencement

Specified date

Specified date: 30 December 2005: see Prelims.

51   Circumstances in which the non-subject child does not need a litigation friend

(1)   A non-subject child may conduct proceedings without a litigation friend—

(a)   where he has obtained the court's permission to do so; or

(b)   where a solicitor—

(i)   considers that the non-subject child is able, having regard to his understanding, to give instructions in relation to the proceedings; and

(ii)   has accepted instructions from that child to act for him in the proceedings and, if the proceedings have begun, he is already acting.

(2)   An application for permission under paragraph (1)(a) may be made by the non-subject child without notice.

(3)   Where a non-subject child has a litigation friend in proceedings and he wishes to conduct the remaining stages of the proceedings without a litigation friend, the non-subject child may apply to the court, on notice to the litigation friend, for permission for that purpose and for the removal of the litigation friend.

(4)   Where the court is considering whether to—

(a)   grant permission under paragraph (1)(a); or

(b)   grant permission under paragraph (3) and remove a litigation friend

it will grant the permission sought and, as the case may be, remove the litigation friend if it considers that the non-subject child concerned has sufficient understanding to conduct the proceedings concerned or proposed without a litigation friend.

(5)   In exercising its powers under paragraph (4) the court may require the litigation friend to take such part in the proceedings as the court directs.

(6)   The court may revoke any permission granted under paragraph (1)(a) where it considers that the non-subject child does not have sufficient understanding to participate as a party in the proceedings concerned without a litigation friend.

(7)   Where a solicitor is acting for a non-subject child in proceedings without a litigation friend by virtue of paragraph (1)(b) and either of the conditions specified in paragraph (1)(b)(i) or (ii) cease to be fulfilled, he must inform the court immediately.

(8)   Where—

(a)   the court revokes any permission under paragraph (6); or

(b)   either of the conditions specified in paragraph (1)(b)(i) or (ii) is no longer fulfilled

the court may, if it considers it necessary in order to protect the interests of the non-subject child concerned, appoint a person to be that child's litigation friend.

PART D – Appendix

NOTES

Initial Commencement

Specified date

Specified date: 30 December 2005: see Prelims.

52 Stage of proceedings at which a litigation friend becomes necessary

(1) This rule does not apply where a non-subject child is conducting proceedings without a litigation friend in accordance with rule 51.

(2) A person may not without the permission of the court take any step in proceedings except—

(a) filing an application form; or
(b) applying for the appointment of a litigation friend under rule 55

until the non-subject child or patient has a litigation friend.

(3) If a party becomes a patient during proceedings, no party may take any step in proceedings without the permission of the court until the patient has a litigation friend.

NOTES

Initial Commencement

Specified date

Specified date: 30 December 2005: see Prelims.

53 Who may be a litigation friend for a patient without a court order

(1) This rule does not apply if the court has appointed a person to be a litigation friend.

(2) A person authorised under Part VII of the Mental Health Act 1983 to conduct legal proceedings in the name of a patient or on his behalf is entitled to be the litigation friend of the patient in any proceedings to which his authority extends.

(3) If nobody has been appointed by the court or, in the case of a patient, authorised under Part VII of the Mental Health Act 1983, a person may act as a litigation friend if he—

(a) can fairly and competently conduct proceedings on behalf of the non-subject child or patient;
(b) has no interest adverse to that of the non-subject child or patient; and
(c) subject to paragraph (4), undertakes to pay any costs which the non-subject child or patient may be ordered to pay in relation to the proceedings, subject to any right he may have to be repaid from the assets of the non-subject child or patient.

(4) Paragraph (3)(c) does not apply to the Official Solicitor, an officer of the Service or a Welsh family proceedings officer.

NOTES

Initial Commencement

Specified date

Specified date: 30 December 2005: see Prelims.

54 How a person becomes a litigation friend without a court order

(1) If the court has not appointed a litigation friend, a person who wishes to act as a litigation friend must follow the procedure set out in this rule.

(2) A person authorised under Part VII of the Mental Health Act 1983 must file an official copy of the order or other document which constitutes his authorisation to act.

(3) Any other person must file a certificate of suitability stating that he satisfies the conditions specified in rule 53(3).

(4) A person who is to act as a litigation friend must file—

(a) the authorisation; or
(b) the certificate of suitability

at the time when he first takes a step in the proceedings on behalf of the non-subject child or patient.

(5) A court officer will send the certificate of suitability to every person on whom, in accordance with rule 37(1) (service on parent, guardian etc), the application form should be served.

(6) This rule does not apply to the Official Solicitor, an officer of the Service or a Welsh family proceedings officer.

NOTES

Initial Commencement

Specified date

Specified date: 30 December 2005: see Prelims.

55 How a person becomes a litigation friend by court order

(1) The court may make an order appointing—

(a)   the Official Solicitor;

(b)   in the case of a non-subject child, an officer of the Service or a Welsh family proceedings officer (if he consents); or

(c)   some other person (if he consents)

as a litigation friend.

(2) An order appointing a litigation friend may be made by the court of its own initiative or on the application of—

(a)   a person who wishes to be a litigation friend; or

(b)   a party to the proceedings.

(3) The court may at any time direct that a party make an application for an order under paragraph (2).

(4) An application for an order appointing a litigation friend must be supported by evidence.

(5) Unless the court directs otherwise, a person appointed under this rule to be a litigation friend for a non-subject child or patient will be treated as a party for the purpose of any provision in these Rules requiring a document to be served on, or sent to, or notice to be given to, a party to the proceedings.

(6) Subject to rule 53(4), the court may not appoint a litigation friend under this rule unless it is satisfied that the person to be appointed complies with the conditions specified in rule 53(3).

NOTES

Initial Commencement

Specified date

Specified date: 30 December 2005: see Prelims.

56 Court's power to change litigation friend and to prevent person acting as litigation friend

(1) The court may—

(a)   direct that a person may not act as a litigation friend;

(b)   terminate a litigation friend's appointment; or

(c)   appoint a new litigation friend in substitution for an existing one.

(2) An application for an order under paragraph (1) must be supported by evidence.

(3) Subject to rule 53(4), the court may not appoint a litigation friend under this rule unless it is satisfied that the person to be appointed complies with the conditions specified in rule 53(3).

NOTES

Initial Commencement

Specified date

Specified date: 30 December 2005: see Prelims.

PART D – Appendix

57 Appointment of litigation friend by court order—supplementary

(1)   A copy of the application for an order under rule 55 or 56 must be sent by a court officer to every person on whom, in accordance with rule 37(1) (service on parent, guardian etc), the application form should be served.

(2)   Where an application for an order under rule 55 is in respect of a patient, the court officer must also send a copy of the application to the patient unless the court directs otherwise.

(3)   A copy of an application for an order under rule 56 must also be sent to—

(a)   the person who is the litigation friend, or who is purporting to act as the litigation friend, when the application is made; and

(b)   the person who it is proposed should be the litigation friend, if he is not the applicant.

NOTES

Initial Commencement

Specified date

Specified date: 30 December 2005: see Prelims.

58 Procedure where appointment of litigation friend comes to an end

(1)   When a non-subject child who is not a patient reaches the age of 18, a litigation friend's appointment comes to an end.

(2)   When a party ceases to be a patient, the litigation friend's appointment continues until it is brought to an end by a court order.

(3)   An application for an order under paragraph (2) may be made by—

(a)   the former patient;

(b)   the litigation friend; or

(c)   a party.

(4)   A court officer will send a notice to the other parties stating that the appointment of the non-subject child or patient's litigation friend to act has ended.

NOTES

Initial Commencement

Specified date

Specified date: 30 December 2005: see Prelims.

Section 2
Children's Guardian

59 Appointment of children's guardian

(1)   In proceedings to which Part 5 applies, the court will appoint a children's guardian where the child is a party to the proceedings unless it is satisfied that it is not necessary to do so to safeguard the interests of the child.

(2)   At any stage in proceedings where the child is a party to the proceedings—

(a)   a party may apply, without notice to the other parties unless the court directs otherwise, for the appointment of a children's guardian; or

(b)   the court may of its own initiative appoint a children's guardian.

(3)   The court will grant an application under paragraph (2)(a) unless it considers that such an appointment is not necessary to safeguard the interests of the child.

(4)   When appointing a children's guardian the court will consider the appointment of anyone who has previously acted as a children's guardian of the same child.

NOTES

Initial Commencement

Specified date

Specified date: 30 December 2005: see Prelims.

60 What the court or a court officer will do once the court has made a decision about appointing a children's guardian

(1) Where the court refuses an application under rule 59(2)(a) it will give reasons for the refusal and the court or a court officer will—

(a) record the refusal and the reasons for it; and

(b) as soon as practicable, notify the parties and either the Service or the Assembly of a decision not to appoint a children's guardian.

(2) Where the court appoints a children's guardian under rule 59 a court officer will record the appointment and, as soon as practicable, will—

(a) inform the parties and either the Service or the Assembly; and

(b) unless it has already been sent, send the children's guardian a copy of the application and copies of any document filed with the court in the proceedings.

(3) A court officer also has a continuing duty to send the children's guardian a copy of any other document filed with the court during the course of the proceedings.

NOTES

Initial Commencement

Specified date

Specified date: 30 December 2005: see Prelims.

61 Termination of the appointment of the children's guardian

(1) The appointment of a children's guardian under rule 59 continues for such time as is specified in the appointment or until terminated by the court.

(2) When terminating an appointment in accordance with paragraph (1), the court will give reasons for doing so, a note of which will be taken by the court or a court officer.

NOTES

Initial Commencement

Specified date

Specified date: 30 December 2005: see Prelims.

62 Powers and duties of the children's guardian

(1) The children's guardian is to act on behalf of the child upon the hearing of any application in proceedings to which Part 5 applies with the duty of safeguarding the interests of the child.

(2) The children's guardian must also provide the court with such other assistance as it may require.

NOTES

Initial Commencement

Specified date

Specified date: 30 December 2005: see Prelims.

63 How the children's guardian exercises his duties—investigations and appointment of solicitor

(1) The children's guardian must make such investigations as are necessary for him to carry out his duties and must, in particular—

(a) contact or seek to interview such persons as he thinks appropriate or as the court directs; and

(b) obtain such professional assistance as is available to him which he thinks appropriate or which the court directs him to obtain.

(2) The children's guardian must—

(a) appoint a solicitor for the child unless a solicitor has already been appointed;

(b) give such advice to the child as is appropriate having regard to his understanding; and

(c)   where appropriate instruct the solicitor representing the child on all matters relevant to the interests of the child, including possibilities for appeal, arising in the course of proceedings.

(3)   Where the children's guardian is authorised in the terms mentioned by and in accordance with section 15(1) of the Criminal Justice and Court Services Act 2000 or section 37(1) of the Children Act 2004 (right of officer of the Service or Welsh family proceedings officer to conduct litigation or exercise a right of audience), paragraph (2)(a) will not apply if he intends to have conduct of the proceedings on behalf of the child unless—

(a)   the child wishes to instruct a solicitor direct; and
(b)   the children's guardian or the court considers that he is of sufficient understanding to do so.

NOTES
Initial Commencement
Specified date
Specified date: 30 December 2005: see Prelims.

64   Where the child instructs a solicitor or conducts proceedings on his own behalf

(1)   Where it appears to the children's guardian that the child—

(a)   is instructing his solicitor direct; or
(b)   intends to conduct and is capable of conducting the proceedings on his own behalf

he must inform the court of that fact.

(2)   Where paragraph (1) applies, the children's guardian—

(a)   must perform the duties set out in rules 62, 63, 65 to 67 and this rule, other than those duties in rule 63(2)(a) and (c), and such other duties as the court may direct;
(b)   must take such part in the proceedings as the court may direct; and
(c)   may, with the permission of the court, have legal representation in the conduct of those duties.

NOTES
Initial Commencement
Specified date
Specified date: 30 December 2005: see Prelims.

65   How the children's guardian exercises his duties—attendance at court, advice to the court and reports

(1)   The children's guardian or the solicitor appointed under section 41(3) of the 1989 Act or in accordance with rule 63(2)(a) must attend all directions hearings unless the court directs otherwise.

(2)   The children's guardian must advise the court on the following matters—

(a)   whether the child is of sufficient understanding for any purpose including the child's refusal to submit to a medical or psychiatric examination or other assessment that the court has the power to require, direct or order;
(b)   the wishes of the child in respect of any matter relevant to the proceedings including his attendance at court;
(c)   the appropriate forum for the proceedings;
(d)   the appropriate timing of the proceedings or any part of them;
(e)   the options available to it in respect of the child and the suitability of each such option including what order should be made in determining the application; and
(f)   any other matter on which the court seeks his advice or on which he considers that the court should be informed.

(3)   The advice given under paragraph (2) may, subject to any direction of the court, be given orally or in writing.

(4)   The children's guardian must—

(a)   unless the court directs otherwise, file a written report advising on the interests of the child in accordance with the timetable set by the court; and

(b)   where practicable, notify any person the joining of whom as a party to those proceedings would be likely, in his opinion, to safeguard the interests of the child, of the court's power to join that person as a party under rule 23 and must inform the court—

(i)   of any notification;

(ii)   of anyone whom he attempted to notify under this paragraph but was unable to contact; and

(iii)   of anyone whom he believes may wish to be joined to the proceedings.

(5)   Any report to the court under this rule will be confidential.

(Part 9 sets out the procedure for making an application to be joined as a party in proceedings.)

NOTES

Initial Commencement

Specified date

Specified date: 30 December 2005: see Prelims.

66   How the children's guardian exercises his duties—service of documents and inspection of records

(1)   The children's guardian must—

(a)   serve documents on behalf of the child in accordance with rule 37(2)(b); and

(b)   accept service of documents on behalf of the child in accordance with the table in rule 37(1),

and, where the child has not himself been served and has sufficient understanding, advise the child of the contents of any document so served.

(2)   Where the children's guardian inspects records of the kinds referred to in—

(a)   section 42 of the 1989 Act (right to have access to local authority records); or

(b)   section 103 (right to have access to adoption agency records)

he must bring all records and documents which may, in his opinion, assist in the proper determination of the proceedings to the attention of—

(i)   the court; and

(ii)   unless the court directs otherwise, the other parties to the proceedings.

NOTES

Initial Commencement

Specified date

Specified date: 30 December 2005: see Prelims.

67   How the children's guardian exercises his duties—communication of a court's decision to the child

The children's guardian must ensure that, in relation to a decision made by the court in the proceedings—

(a)   if he considers it appropriate to the age and understanding of the child, the child is notified of that decision; and

(b)   if the child is notified of the decision, it is explained to the child in a manner appropriate to his age and understanding.

NOTES

Initial Commencement

Specified date

Specified date: 30 December 2005: see Prelims.

PART D – Appendix

68 Solicitor for child

(1) A solicitor appointed under section 41(3) of the 1989 Act or in accordance with rule 63(2)(a) must represent the child—

(a) in accordance with instructions received from the children's guardian unless the solicitor considers, having taken into account the views of the children's guardian and any direction of the court under rule 64(2)—

    (i) that the child wishes to give instructions which conflict with those of the children's guardian; and

    (ii) that he is able, having regard to his understanding, to give such instructions on his own behalf,

in which case the solicitor must conduct the proceedings in accordance with instructions received from the child;

(b) where no children's guardian has been appointed and the condition in section 41(4)(b) of the 1989 Act is satisfied, in accordance with instructions received from the child; or

(c) in default of instructions under sub-paragraph (a) or (b), in furtherance of the best interests of the child.

(2) A solicitor appointed under section 41(3) of the 1989 Act or in accordance with rule 63(2)(a) must—

(a) serve documents on behalf of the child in accordance with rule 37(2)(a); and

(b) accept service of documents on behalf of the child in accordance with the table in rule 37(1),

and, where the child has not himself been served and has sufficient understanding, advise the child of the contents of any document so served.

(3) Where the child wishes an appointment of a solicitor under section 41(3) of the 1989 Act or in accordance with rule 63(2)(a) to be terminated—

(a) he may apply to the court for an order terminating the appointment; and

(b) the solicitor and the children's guardian will be given an opportunity to make representations.

(4) Where the children's guardian wishes an appointment of a solicitor under section 41(3) of the 1989 Act or in accordance with rule 63(2)(a) to be terminated—

(a) he may apply to the court for an order terminating the appointment; and

(b) the solicitor and, if he is of sufficient understanding, the child, will be given an opportunity to make representations.

(5) When terminating an appointment in accordance with paragraph (3) or (4), the court will give its reasons for so doing, a note of which will be taken by the court or a court officer.

(6) The court or a court officer will record the appointment under section 41(3) of the 1989 Act or in accordance with rule 63(2)(a) or the refusal to make the appointment.

NOTES

Initial Commencement

Specified date

Specified date: 30 December 2005: see Prelims.

Section 3
Reporting Officer

69 When the court appoints a reporting officer

In proceedings to which Part 5 applies, the court will appoint a reporting officer where—

(a) it appears that a parent or guardian of the child is willing to consent to the placing of the child for adoption, to the making of an adoption order or to a section 84 order; and

(b) that parent or guardian is in England or Wales.

NOTES

Initial Commencement

Specified date

Specified date: 30 December 2005: see Prelims.

70 Appointment of the same reporting officer in respect of two or more parents or guardians

The same person may be appointed as the reporting officer for two or more parents or guardians of the child.

NOTES

Initial Commencement

Specified date

Specified date: 30 December 2005: see Prelims.

71 The duties of the reporting officer

The reporting officer must witness the signature by a parent or guardian on the document in which consent is given to—

(a) the placing of the child for adoption;

(b) the making of an adoption order; or

(c) the making of a section 84 order.

NOTES

Initial Commencement

Specified date

Specified date: 30 December 2005: see Prelims.

72 How the reporting officer exercises his duties

(1) The reporting officer must—

(a) ensure so far as reasonably practicable that the parent or guardian is—

(i) giving consent unconditionally; and

(ii) with full understanding of what is involved;

(b) investigate all the circumstances relevant to a parent's or guardian's consent to the placing of the child for adoption or to the making of an adoption order or a section 84 order; and

(c) on completing his investigations the reporting officer must—

(i) make a report in writing to the court in accordance with the timetable set by the court, drawing attention to any matters which, in his opinion, may be of assistance to the court in considering the application; or

(ii) make an interim report to the court if a parent or guardian of the child is unwilling to consent to the placing of the child for adoption or to the making of an adoption order or section 84 order.

(2) On receipt of an interim report under paragraph (1)(c)(ii) a court officer must inform the applicant that a parent or guardian of the child is unwilling to consent to the placing of the child for adoption or to the making of an adoption order or section 84 order.

(3) The reporting officer may at any time before the final hearing make an interim report to the court if he considers necessary and ask the court for directions.

(4) The reporting officer must attend all directions hearings unless the court directs otherwise.

(5) Any report to the court under this rule will be confidential.

PART D – Appendix

589

NOTES
Initial Commencement
Specified date
Specified date: 30 December 2005: see Prelims.

Section 4
Children and Family Reporter

73 Request by court for a welfare report in respect of the child

(1) In proceedings to which Part 5 applies, where the court is considering an application for an order in proceedings the court may ask a children and family reporter to prepare a report on matters relating to the welfare of the child.
(2) It is the duty of a children and family reporter to—

(a) comply with any request for a report under this rule; and
(b) provide the court with such other assistance as it may require.

(3) Any report to the court under this rule will be confidential.

NOTES
Initial Commencement
Specified date
Specified date: 30 December 2005: see Prelims.

74 How the children and family reporter exercises his powers and duties

(1) The children and family reporter must make such investigations as may be necessary for him to perform his powers and duties and must, in particular—

(a) contact or seek to interview such persons as he thinks appropriate or as the court directs; and
(b) obtain such professional assistance as is available to him which he thinks appropriate or which the court directs him to obtain.

(2) The children and family reporter must—

(a) notify the child of such contents of his report (if any) as he considers appropriate to the age and understanding of the child, including any reference to the child's own views on the application and his recommendation; and
(b) if he does notify the child of any contents of his report, explain them to the child in a manner appropriate to his age and understanding.

(3) The children and family reporter must—

(a) attend all directions hearings unless the court directs otherwise;
(b) advise the court of the child's wishes and feelings;
(c) advise the court if he considers that the joining of a person as a party to the proceedings would be likely to safeguard the interests of the child;
(d) consider whether it is in the best interests of the child for the child to be made a party to the proceedings, and if so, notify the court of his opinion together with the reasons for that opinion; and
(e) where the court has directed that a written report be made, file the report in accordance with the timetable set by the court.

NOTES
Initial Commencement
Specified date
Specified date: 30 December 2005: see Prelims.

Section 5
Who can Act as Children's Guardian, Reporting Officer and Children and Family Reporter

75 Persons who may not be appointed as children's guardian, reporting officer or children and family reporter

(1)   In adoption proceedings or proceedings for a section 84 order or a section 89 order, a person may not be appointed as a children's guardian, reporting officer or children and family reporter if he—

(a)   is a member, officer or servant of a local authority which is a party to the proceedings;

(b)   is, or has been, a member, officer or servant of a local authority or voluntary organisation who has been directly concerned in that capacity in arrangements relating to the care, accommodation or welfare of the child during the five years prior to the commencement of the proceedings; or

(c)   is a serving probation officer who has, in that capacity, been previously concerned with the child or his family.

(2)   In placement proceedings, a person described in paragraph (1)(b) or (c) may not be appointed as a children's guardian, reporting officer or children and family reporter.

NOTES

Initial Commencement

Specified date

Specified date: 30 December 2005: see Prelims.

76 Appointment of the same person as children's guardian, reporting officer and children and family reporter

The same person may be appointed to act as one or more of the following—

(a)   the children's guardian;
(b)   the reporting officer; and
(c)   the children and family reporter.

NOTES

Initial Commencement

Specified date

Specified date: 30 December 2005: see Prelims.

Part 8
Documents and Disclosure of Documents and Information

77 Confidential reports to the court and disclosure to the parties

(1)   The court will consider whether to give a direction that a confidential report be disclosed to each party to the proceedings.

(2)   Before giving such a direction the court will consider whether any information should be deleted including information which—

(a)   discloses, or is likely to disclose, the identity of a person who has been assigned a serial number under rule 20(2); or

(b)   discloses the particulars referred to in rule 21(1) where a party has given notice under rule 21(2) (disclosure of personal details).

(3)   The court may direct that the report will not be disclosed to a party.

NOTES

Initial Commencement

Specified date

Specified date: 30 December 2005: see Prelims.

PART D – Appendix

78 Communication of information relating to proceedings

(1) For the purposes of the law relating to contempt of court, information (whether or not it is recorded in any form) relating to proceedings held in private may be communicated—

(a) where the court gives permission;

(b) unless the court directs otherwise, in accordance with the relevant practice direction; or

(c) where the communication is to—

    (i) a party;
    (ii) the legal representative of a party;
    (iii) a professional legal adviser;
    (iv) an officer of the Service or a Welsh family proceedings officer;
    (v) a welfare officer;
    (vi) the Legal Services Commission;
    (vii) an expert whose instruction by a party has been authorised by the court; or
    (viii) a professional acting in furtherance of the protection of children.

(2) In this rule—

'professional acting in furtherance of the protection of children' includes—

(a) an officer of a local authority exercising child protection functions;

(b) a police officer who is—

    (i) exercising powers under section 46 of the 1989 Act; or
    (ii) serving in a child protection unit or a paedophile unit of a police force;

(c) any professional person attending a child protection conference or review in relation to a child who is the subject of the proceedings to which the information relates; or

(d) an officer of the National Society for the Prevention of Cruelty to Children;

'professional legal adviser' means a barrister or a solicitor, solicitor's employee or other authorised litigator (as defined in section 119 of the Courts and Legal Services Act 1990) who is providing advice to a party but is not instructed to represent that party in the proceedings;

'welfare officer' means a person who has been asked to prepare a report under section 7(1)(b) of the 1989 Act.

NOTES

Initial Commencement

Specified date

Specified date: 30 December 2005: see Prelims.

79 Orders for disclosure against a person not a party

(1) This rule applies where an application is made to the court under any Act for disclosure by a person who is not a party to the proceedings.

(2) The application must be supported by evidence.

(3) The court may make an order under this rule only where—

(a) the documents of which disclosure is sought are likely to support the case of the applicant or adversely affect the case of one of the other parties to the proceedings; and

(b) disclosure is necessary in order to dispose fairly of the application or to save costs.

(4) An order under this rule must—

(a) specify the documents or the classes of documents which the respondent must disclose; and

(b) require the respondent, when making disclosure, to specify any of those documents—

>   (i)   which are no longer in his control; or
>   (ii)   in respect of which he claims a right or duty to withhold inspection.

(5)   Such an order may—

(a)   require the respondent to indicate what has happened to any documents which are no longer in his control; and
(b)   specify the time and place for disclosure and inspection.

(6)   This rule does not apply to proceedings in a magistrates' court.

NOTES
Initial Commencement
Specified date
Specified date: 30 December 2005: see Prelims.

80   Rules not to limit other powers of the court to order disclosure

(1)   Rule 79 does not limit any other power which the court may have to order—

(a)   disclosure before proceedings have started; and
(b)   disclosure against a person who is not a party to proceedings.

(2)   This rule does not apply to proceedings in a magistrates' court.

NOTES
Initial Commencement
Specified date
Specified date: 30 December 2005: see Prelims.

81   Claim to withhold inspection or disclosure of a document

(1)   A person may apply, without notice, for an order permitting him to withhold disclosure of a document on the ground that disclosure would damage the public interest.
(2)   Unless the court orders otherwise, an order of the court under paragraph (1)—

(a)   must not be served on any other person; and
(b)   must not be open to inspection by any person.

(3)   A person who wishes to claim that he has a right or a duty to withhold inspection of a document, or part of a document, must state in writing—

(a)   that he has such a right or duty; and
(b)   the grounds on which he claims that right or duty.

(4)   The statement referred to in paragraph (3) must be made to the person wishing to inspect the document.
(5)   A party may apply to the court to decide whether a claim made under paragraph (3) should be upheld.
(6)   For the purpose of deciding an application under paragraph (1) (application to withhold disclosure) or paragraph (3) (claim to withhold inspection) the court may—

(a)   require the person seeking to withhold disclosure or inspection of a document to produce that document to the court; and
(b)   invite any person, whether or not a party, to make representations.

(7)   An application under paragraph (1) or (5) must be supported by evidence.
(8)   This rule does not affect any rule of law which permits or requires a document to be withheld from disclosure or inspection on the ground that its disclosure or inspection would damage the public interest.
(9)   This rule does not apply to proceedings in a magistrates' court.

NOTES
Initial Commencement
Specified date
Specified date: 30 December 2005: see Prelims.

PART D – Appendix

82 Custody of documents

All documents relating to proceedings under the Act must, while they are in the custody of the court, be kept in a place of special security.

NOTES
Initial Commencement
Specified date
Specified date: 30 December 2005: see Prelims.

83 Inspection and copies of documents

Subject to the provisions of these Rules, any practice direction or any direction given by the court—

(a)　no document or order held by the court in proceedings under the Act will be open to inspection by any person; and

(b)　no copy of any such document or order, or of an extract from any such document or order, will be taken by or given to any person.

NOTES
Initial Commencement
Specified date
Specified date: 30 December 2005: see Prelims.

84 Disclosing information to an adopted adult

(1)　The adopted person has the right, at his request, to receive from the court which made the adoption order a copy of the following—

(a)　the application form for an adoption order (but not the documents attached to that form);

(b)　the adoption order and any other orders relating to the adoption proceedings;

(c)　orders allowing any person contact with the child after the adoption order was made; and

(d)　any other document or order referred to in the relevant practice direction.

(2)　The court will remove any protected information from any copy of a document or order referred to in paragraph (1) before the copies are given to the adopted person.

(3)　This rule does not apply to an adopted person under the age of 18 years.

(4)　In this rule 'protected information' means information which would be protected information under section 57(3) if the adoption agency gave the information and not the court.

NOTES
Initial Commencement
Specified date
Specified date: 30 December 2005: see Prelims.

85 Translation of documents

(1)　Where a translation of any document is required for the purposes of proceedings for a Convention adoption order the translation must—

(a)　unless the court directs otherwise, be provided by the applicant; and

(b)　be signed by the translator to certify that the translation is accurate.

(2)　This rule does not apply where the document is to be served in accordance with the Service Regulation.

NOTES
Initial Commencement
Specified date
Specified date: 30 December 2005: see Prelims.

Part 9
Procedure for Other Applications in Proceedings

86   Types of application for which Part 9 procedure may be followed

(1)   The Part 9 procedure is the procedure set out in this Part.
(2)   An applicant may use the Part 9 procedure if the application is made—

(a)   in the course of existing proceedings;
(b)   to commence proceedings other than those to which Part 5 applies; or
(c)   in connection with proceedings which have been concluded.

(Rule 22 lists the proceedings to which Part 5 applies.)
(3)   Paragraph (2) does not apply—

(a)   to applications made in accordance with—

(i)   section 60(3) (order to prevent disclosure of information to an adopted person);
(ii)   section 79(4) (order for Registrar General to give any information referred to in section 79(3));
(iii)   rule 27 (request to dispense with consent);
(iv)   rule 59(2) (appointment of children's guardian);
(v)   rule 84 (disclosure of information to adopted adult);
(vi)   rule 106 (withdrawal of application); or
(vii)   rule 107 (recovery orders); or

(b)   if a practice direction provides that the Part 9 procedure may not be used in relation to the type of application in question.

(4)   The following persons are to be respondents to an application under this Part—

(a)   where there are existing proceedings or the proceedings have concluded, the parties to those proceedings;
(b)   where there are no existing proceedings—

(i)   if notice has been given under section 44 (notice of intention to adopt or apply for a section 84 order), the local authority to whom notice has been given; and
(ii)   if an application is made in accordance with—

(aa)   section 26(3)(f) (permission to apply for contact order); or
(bb)   section 42(6) (permission to apply for adoption order),

any person who, in accordance with rule 23, will be a party to the proceedings brought if permission is granted; and

(c)   any other person as the court may direct.

NOTES
Initial Commencement
Specified date
Specified date: 30 December 2005: see Prelims.

87   Application notice to be filed

(1)   Subject to paragraph (2), the applicant must file an application notice.
(2)   An applicant may make an application without filing an application notice if—

(a)   this is permitted by a rule or practice direction; or
(b)   the court dispenses with the requirement for an application notice.

NOTES
Initial Commencement
Specified date
Specified date: 30 December 2005: see Prelims.

PART D – Appendix

88 Notice of an application

(1) Subject to paragraph (2), a copy of the application notice will be served on each respondent.

(2) An application may be made without serving a copy of the application notice if this is permitted by—

(a) a rule;
(b) a practice direction; or
(c) the court.

(Rule 91 deals with service of a copy of the application notice.)

NOTES
Initial Commencement
Specified date
Specified date: 30 December 2005: see Prelims.

89 Time when an application is made

Where an application must be made within a specified time, it is so made if the court receives the application notice within that time.

NOTES
Initial Commencement
Specified date
Specified date: 30 December 2005: see Prelims.

90 What an application notice must include

(1) An application notice must state—

(a) what order the applicant is seeking; and
(b) briefly, why the applicant is seeking the order.

(2) The applicant may rely on the matters set out in his application notice as evidence if the application is verified by a statement of truth.

NOTES
Initial Commencement
Specified date
Specified date: 30 December 2005: see Prelims.

91 Service of a copy of an application notice

(1) A court officer will serve a copy of the application notice—

(a) as soon as practicable after it is filed; and
(b) in any event at least 7 days before the court is to deal with the application.

(2) The applicant must, when he files the application notice, file a copy of any written evidence in support.

(3) When a copy of an application notice is served by a court officer it will be accompanied by—

(a) a notice of the date and place where the application will be heard;
(b) a copy of any witness statement in support; and
(c) a copy of any draft order which the applicant has attached to his application.

(4) If—

(a) an application notice is served; but
(b) the period of notice is shorter than the period required by these Rules or a practice direction,

the court may direct that, in the circumstances of the case, sufficient notice has been given and hear the application.

(5) This rule does not require written evidence—

(a) to be filed if it has already been filed; or
(b) to be served on a party on whom it has already been served.

NOTES
Initial Commencement
Specified date
Specified date: 30 December 2005: see Prelims.

92 Applications which may be dealt with without a hearing

The court may deal with an application without a hearing if—

(a)   the parties agree as to the terms of the order sought;

(b)   the parties agree that the court should dispose of the application without a hearing; or

(c)   the court does not consider that a hearing would be appropriate.

NOTES
Initial Commencement
Specified date
Specified date: 30 December 2005: see Prelims.

93 Service of application where application made without notice

(1)   This rule applies where the court has disposed of an application which it permitted to be made without service of a copy of the application notice.

(2)   Where the court makes an order, whether granting or dismissing the application, a copy of the application notice and any evidence in support will, unless the court directs otherwise, be served with the order on all the parties in the proceedings.

(3)   The order must contain a statement of the right to make an application to set aside or vary the order under rule 94.

NOTES
Initial Commencement
Specified date
Specified date: 30 December 2005: see Prelims.

94 Application to set aside or vary order made without notice

(1)   A person who was not served with a copy of the application notice before an order was made under rule 93 may apply to have the order set aside or varied.

(2)   An application under this rule must be made within 7 days beginning with the date on which the order was served on the person making the application.

NOTES
Initial Commencement
Specified date
Specified date: 30 December 2005: see Prelims.

95 Power of the court to proceed in the absence of a party

(1)   Where the applicant or any respondent fails to attend the hearing of an application, the court may proceed in his absence.

(2)   Where—

(a)   the applicant or any respondent fails to attend the hearing of an application; and

(b)   the court makes an order at the hearing,

the court may, on application or of its own initiative, re-list the application.

NOTES
Initial Commencement
Specified date
Specified date: 30 December 2005: see Prelims.

96 Dismissal of totally without merit applications

If the High Court or a county court dismisses an application (including an application for permission to appeal) and it considers that the application is totally without merit—

(a)   the court's order must record that fact; and
(b)   the court must at the same time consider whether it is appropriate to make a civil restraint order.

NOTES
Initial Commencement
Specified date
Specified date: 30 December 2005: see Prelims.

Part 10
Alternative Procedure for Applications

97   Types of application for which Part 10 procedure may be followed

(1)   The Part 10 procedure is the procedure set out in this Part.
(2)   An applicant may use the Part 10 procedure where the procedure set out in Part 9 does not apply and—

(a)   there is no form prescribed by a rule or practice direction in which to make the application;
(b)   he seeks the court's decision on a question which is unlikely to involve a substantial dispute of fact; or
(c)   paragraph (5) applies.

(3)   The court may at any stage direct that the application is to continue as if the applicant had not used the Part 10 procedure and, if it does so, the court may give any directions it considers appropriate.
(4)   Paragraph (2) does not apply—

(a)   to applications made in accordance with—

(i)   rule 27 (request to dispense with consent);
(ii)   rule 59(2) (appointment of children's guardian);
(iii)   rule 84 (disclosure of information to adopted adult);
(iv)   rule 106 (withdrawal of application); or
(v)   rule 107 (recovery orders); or

(b)   if a practice direction provides that the Part 10 procedure may not be used in relation to the type of application in question.

(5)   A rule or practice direction may, in relation to a specified type of proceedings—

(a)   require or permit the use of the Part 10 procedure; and
(b)   disapply or modify any of the rules set out in this Part as they apply to those proceedings.

NOTES
Initial Commencement
Specified date
Specified date: 30 December 2005: see Prelims.

98   Contents of the application

(1)   In this Part 'application' means an application made under this Part.
(2)   Where the applicant uses the Part 10 procedure the application must state—

(a)   that this Part applies;
(b)

(i)   the question which the applicant wants the court to decide; or
(ii)   the order which the applicant is seeking and the legal basis of the application for that order;

(c)   if the application is being made under an enactment, what that enactment is;
(d)   if the applicant is applying in a representative capacity, what that capacity is; and

(e)   if the respondent appears or is to appear in a representative capacity, what that capacity is.

(3)   A court officer will serve a copy of the application on the respondent.

NOTES
Initial Commencement
Specified date
Specified date: 30 December 2005: see Prelims.

99   Issue of application without naming respondents

(1)   A practice direction may set out circumstances in which an application may be issued under this Part without naming a respondent.
(2)   The practice direction may set out those cases in which an application for permission must be made before the application is issued.
(3)   The application for permission—

(a)   need not be served on any other person; and
(b)   must be accompanied by a copy of the application that the applicant proposes to issue.

(4)   Where the court gives permission it will give directions about the future management of the application.

NOTES
Initial Commencement
Specified date
Specified date: 30 December 2005: see Prelims.

100   Acknowledgement of service

(1)   Subject to paragraph (2), each respondent must file an acknowledgement of service within 14 days beginning with the date on which the application is served.
(2)   If the application is to be served out of the jurisdiction the respondent must file an acknowledgement of service within the period set out in the practice direction supplementing Part 6, section 2.
(3)   A court officer will serve the acknowledgement of service on the applicant and any other party.
(4)   The acknowledgement of service must—

(a)   state whether the respondent contests the application;
(b)   state, if the respondent seeks a different order from that set out in the application, what that order is; and
(c)   be signed by the respondent or his legal representative.

NOTES
Initial Commencement
Specified date
Specified date: 30 December 2005: see Prelims.

101   Consequence of not filing an acknowledgement of service

(1)   This rule applies where—

(a)   the respondent has failed to file an acknowledgement of service; and
(b)   the time period for doing so has expired.

(2)   The respondent must attend the hearing of the application but may not take part in the hearing unless the court gives permission.

NOTES
Initial Commencement
Specified date
Specified date: 30 December 2005: see Prelims.

PART D – Appendix

102 Filing and serving written evidence

(1) The applicant must file written evidence on which he intends to rely when he files his application.

(2) A court officer will serve the applicant's evidence on the respondent with the application.

(3) A respondent who wishes to rely on written evidence must file it when he files his acknowledgement of service.

(4) A court officer will serve the respondent's evidence, if any, on the other parties with the acknowledgement of service.

(5) The applicant may, within 14 days beginning with the date on which a respondent's evidence was served on him, file further written evidence in reply.

(6) If he does so, a court officer will serve a copy of that evidence on the other parties.

(7) The applicant may rely on the matters set out in his application as evidence under this rule if the application is verified by a statement of truth.

NOTES

Initial Commencement

Specified date

Specified date: 30 December 2005: see Prelims.

103 Evidence—general

(1) No written evidence may be relied on at the hearing of the application unless—

(a) it has been served in accordance with rule 102; or

(b) the court gives permission.

(2) The court may require or permit a party to give oral evidence at the hearing.

(3) The court may give directions requiring the attendance for cross-examination of a witness who has given written evidence.

NOTES

Initial Commencement

Specified date

Specified date: 30 December 2005: see Prelims.

104 Procedure where respondent objects to use of the Part 10 procedure

(1) Where a respondent contends that the Part 10 procedure should not be used because—

(a) there is a substantial dispute of fact; and

(b) the use of the Part 10 procedure is not required or permitted by a rule or practice direction,

he must state his reasons when he files his acknowledgement of service.

(2) When the court receives the acknowledgement of service and any written evidence it will give directions as to the future management of the case.

NOTES

Initial Commencement

Specified date

Specified date: 30 December 2005: see Prelims.

105 Applications under section 60(3) and 79(4) or rule 108

(1) The Part 10 procedure must be used in an application made in accordance with—

(a) section 60(3) (order to prevent disclosure of information to an adopted person);

(b) section 79(4) (order for Registrar General to give any information referred to in section 79(3)); and

(c) rule 108 (directions of High Court regarding fathers without parental responsibility).

(2)   The respondent to an application made in accordance with paragraph (1)(b) is the Registrar General.

NOTES

Initial Commencement

Specified date

Specified date: 30 December 2005: see Prelims.

Part 11
Miscellaneous

106   Withdrawal of application

(1)   An application may be withdrawn with the permission of the court.

(2)   Subject to paragraph (3), a person seeking permission to withdraw an application must file a written request for permission setting out the reasons for the request.

(3)   The request under paragraph (2) may be made orally to the court if the parties and any children's guardian, reporting officer or children and family reporter are present.

(4)   A court officer will notify the other parties and any children's guardian, reporting officer or children and family reporter of a written request.

(5)   The court may deal with a written request under paragraph (2) without a hearing if the other parties and any children's guardian, reporting officer or children and family reporter have had an opportunity to make written representations to the court about the request.

NOTES

Initial Commencement

Specified date

Specified date: 30 December 2005: see Prelims.

107   Application for recovery orders

(1)   An application for any of the orders referred to in section 41(2) (recovery orders) may—

(a)   in the High Court or a county court, be made without notice in which case the applicant must file the application—

   (i)   where the application is made by telephone, the next business day after the making of the application; or

   (ii)   in any other case, at the time when the application is made; and

(b)   in a magistrates' court, be made, with the permission of the court, without notice in which case the applicant must file the application at the time when the application is made or as directed by the court.

(2)   Where the court refuses to make an order on an application without notice it may direct that the application is made on notice in which case the application will proceed in accordance with Part 5.

(3)   The respondents to an application under this rule are—

(a)   in a case where—

   (i)   placement proceedings;

   (ii)   adoption proceedings; or

   (iii)   proceedings for a section 84 order

   are pending, all parties to those proceedings;

(b)   any adoption agency authorised to place the child for adoption or which has placed the child for adoption;

(c)   any local authority to whom notice under section 44 (notice of intention to adopt or apply for a section 84 order) has been given;

(d)   any person having parental responsibility for the child;

(e)   any person in whose favour there is provision for contact;

(f)   any person who was caring for the child immediately prior to the making of the application; and

(g)   any person whom the applicant alleges to have effected or to have been or to be responsible for taking or keeping the child.

NOTES
Initial Commencement
Specified date
Specified date: 30 December 2005: see Prelims.

108   Inherent jurisdiction and fathers without parental responsibility

Where no proceedings have started an adoption agency or local authority may ask the High Court for directions on the need to give a father without parental responsibility notice of the intention to place a child for adoption.

NOTES
Initial Commencement
Specified date
Specified date: 30 December 2005: see Prelims.

109   Timing of applications for section 89 order

An application for a section 89 order must be made within 2 years beginning with the date on which—

(a)   the Convention adoption or Convention adoption order; or
(b)   the overseas adoption or determination under section 91

to which it relates was made.

NOTES
Initial Commencement
Specified date
Specified date: 30 December 2005: see Prelims.

110 Costs

The court may at any time make such order as to costs as it thinks just including an order relating to the payment of expenses incurred by any officer of the Service or a Welsh family proceedings officer.
(Rule 5(3) provides that Parts 43, 44 (except rules 44.3(2) and (3) and 44.9 to 44.12A), 47 and 48 and rule 45.6 of the CPR apply to costs in proceedings.)

NOTES
Initial Commencement
Specified date
Specified date: 30 December 2005: see Prelims.

111 Orders

(1)   An order takes effect from the date when it is made, or such later date as the court may specify.
(2)   In proceedings in Wales a party may request that an order be drawn up in Welsh as well as English.

NOTES
Initial Commencement
Specified date
Specified date: 30 December 2005: see Prelims.

112 Copies of orders

(1)   Within 7 days beginning with the date on which the final order was made in proceedings or such shorter time as the court may direct a court officer will send—

(a)   a copy of the order to the applicant;

(b) a copy, which is sealed, authenticated with the stamp of the court or certified as a true copy, of—

    (i) an adoption order;
    (ii) a section 89 order; or
    (iii) an order quashing or revoking an adoption order or allowing an appeal against an adoption order

    to the Registrar General;

(c) a copy of a Convention adoption order to the relevant Central Authority;
(d) a copy of a section 89 order relating to a Convention adoption order or a Convention adoption to the—

    (i) relevant Central Authority;
    (ii) adopters;
    (iii) adoption agency; and
    (iv) local authority;

(e) unless the court directs otherwise, a copy of a contact order or a variation or revocation of a contact order to the—

    (i) person with whom the child is living;
    (ii) adoption agency; and
    (iii) local authority; and

(f) a notice of the making or refusal of—

    (i) the final order; or
    (ii) an order quashing or revoking an adoption order or allowing an appeal against an order in proceedings

    to every respondent and, with the permission of the court, any other person.

(2) The court officer will also send notice of the making of an adoption order or a section 84 order to—

(a) any court in Great Britain which appears to him to have made any such order as is referred to in section 46(2) (order relating to parental responsibility for, and maintenance of, the child); and
(b) the principal registry of the Family Division, if it appears to him that a parental responsibility agreement has been recorded at the principal registry.

(3) A copy of any final order may be sent to any other person with the permission of the court.
(4) The court officer will send a copy of any order made during the course of the proceedings to all the parties to those proceedings unless the court directs otherwise.
(5) If an order has been drawn up in Welsh as well as English in accordance with rule 111(2) any reference in this rule to sending an order is to be taken as a reference to sending both the Welsh and English orders.

NOTES
Initial Commencement
Specified date
Specified date: 30 December 2005: see Prelims.

113 Amendment and revocation of orders

(1) Subject to paragraph (2), an application under—

(a) section 55 (revocation of adoptions on legitimation); or
(b) paragraph 4 of Schedule 1 (amendment of adoption order and revocation of direction)

may be made without serving a copy of the application notice.

(2) The court may direct that an application notice be served on such persons as it thinks fit.
(3) Where the court makes an order granting the application, a court officer will send the Registrar General a notice—

PART D – Appendix

(a)   specifying the amendments; or

(b)   informing him of the revocation,

giving sufficient particulars of the order to enable the Registrar General to identify the case.

(4)   The court may at any time correct an accidental slip or omission in an order.

(5)   A party may apply for a correction under paragraph (4) without notice to the other parties.

NOTES

Initial Commencement

Specified date

Specified date: 30 December 2005: see Prelims.

114   Keeping of registers

(1)   A magistrates' court officer will keep a register in which there will be entered a minute or memorandum of every adjudication of the court in proceedings to which these Rules apply.

(2)   The register may be stored in electronic form on the court computer system and entries in the register will include, where relevant, the following particulars—

(a)   the name and address of the applicant;

(b)   the name of the child including, in adoption proceedings, the name of the child prior to, and after, adoption;

(c)   the age and sex of the child;

(d)   the nature of the application; and

(e)   the minute of adjudication.

(3)   The part of the register relating to adoption proceedings will be kept separately to any other part of the register and will—

(a)   not contain particulars of any other proceedings; and

(b)   be kept by the court in a place of special security.

NOTES

Initial Commencement

Specified date

Specified date: 30 December 2005: see Prelims.

Part 12
Disputing the Court's Jurisdiction

115   Procedure for disputing the court's jurisdiction

(1)   A respondent who wishes to—

(a)   dispute the court's jurisdiction to hear the application; or

(b)   argue that the court should not exercise its jurisdiction

may apply to the court for an order declaring that it has no such jurisdiction or should not exercise any jurisdiction which it may have.

(2)   An application under this rule must—

(a)   be made within 14 days beginning with the date on which the notice of the directions hearing is sent to the parties; and

(b)   be supported by evidence.

(3)   If the respondent does not make an application within the period specified in paragraph (2) he is to be treated as having accepted that the court has jurisdiction to hear the application.

(4)   An order containing a declaration that the court has no jurisdiction or will not exercise its jurisdiction may also make further provision including—

(a)   setting aside the application form;

(b)   discharging any order made before the application was commenced or, where applicable, before the application form was served; and

(c)   staying the proceedings.

(5)   If a respondent makes an application under this rule, he must file his written evidence in support with the application notice, but he need not before the hearing of the application file any other written evidence.

(6)   Paragraph (4) does not apply to proceedings in a magistrates' court.

NOTES

Initial Commencement

Specified date

Specified date: 30 December 2005: see Prelims.

Part 13
Human Rights

116   Human Rights Act 1998

(1)   A party who seeks to rely on any provision of or right arising under the Human Rights Act 1998 or seeks a remedy available under that Act must inform the court in his application or otherwise in writing specifying—

(a)   the Convention right which it is alleged has been infringed and details of the alleged infringement; and

(b)   the relief sought and whether this includes a declaration of incompatibility.

(2)   The High Court may not make a declaration of incompatibility unless 21 days' notice, or such other period of notice as the court directs, has been given to the Crown.

(3)   Where notice has been given to the Crown, a Minister, or other person permitted by that Act, will be joined as a party on giving notice to the court.

(4)   Where a claim is made under section 7(1) of the Human Rights Act 1998 (claim that public authority acted unlawfully) in respect of a judicial act—

(a)   that claim must be set out in the application form or the appeal notice; and

(b)   notice must be given to the Crown.

(5)   Where paragraph (4) applies and the appropriate person (as defined in section 9(5) of the Human Rights Act 1998) has not applied within 21 days, or such other period as the court directs, beginning with the date on which the notice to be joined as a party was served, the court may join the appropriate person as a party.

(6)   On any application concerning a committal order, if the court ordering the release of the person concludes that his Convention rights have been infringed by the making of the order to which the application or appeal relates, the judgment or order should so state, but if the court does not do so, that failure will not prevent another court from deciding the matter.

(7)   Where by reason of a rule, practice direction or court order the Crown is permitted or required—

(a)   to make a witness statement;

(b)   to swear an affidavit;

(c)   to verify a document by a statement of truth; or

(d)   to discharge any other procedural obligation,

that function will be performed by an appropriate officer acting on behalf of the Crown, and the court may if necessary nominate an appropriate officer.

(8)   In this rule—

'Convention right' has the same meaning as in the Human Rights Act 1998; and 'declaration of incompatibility' means a declaration of incompatibility under section 4 of the Human Rights Act 1998.

(A practice direction makes provision for the notices mentioned in this rule.)

PART D – Appendix

NOTES
Initial Commencement
Specified date
Specified date: 30 December 2005: see Prelims.

Part 14
Interim Injunctions

117 Scope of this Part

The rules in this Part do not apply to proceedings in a magistrates' court.

NOTES
Initial Commencement
Specified date
Specified date: 30 December 2005: see Prelims.

118 Order for interim injunction

(1) The court may grant an interim injunction.
(2) Paragraph (1) does not limit any other power which the court may have to grant an injunction.
(3) The court may grant an interim injunction whether or not there has been an application.

NOTES
Initial Commencement
Specified date
Specified date: 30 December 2005: see Prelims.

119 Time when an order for an interim injunction may be made

(1) An order for an interim injunction may be made at any time, including—

(a) before proceedings are started; and
(b) after judgment has been given.

(Rule 19 provides that proceedings are started when the court issues an application form.)
(2) However—

(a) paragraph (1) is subject to any rule, practice direction or other enactment which provides otherwise; and
(b) the court may grant an interim injunction before an application has been made only if—

(i) the matter is urgent; or
(ii) it is otherwise desirable to do so in the interests of justice.

(3) Where the court grants an interim injunction before an application has been commenced, it may give directions requiring an application to be commenced.

NOTES
Initial Commencement
Specified date
Specified date: 30 December 2005: see Prelims.

120 How to apply for an interim injunction

(1) The court may grant an interim injunction on an application made without notice if it appears to the court that there are good reasons for not giving notice.
(2) An application for an interim injunction must be supported by evidence, unless the court orders otherwise.
(3) If the applicant makes an application without giving notice, the evidence in support of the application must state the reasons why notice has not been given.
(Rule 12 lists general case-management powers of the court.)

(Part 9 contains general rules about making an application.)

NOTES
Initial Commencement
Specified date
Specified date: 30 December 2005: see Prelims.

121 Interim injunction to cease if application is stayed

If—

(a)　the court has granted an interim injunction; and
(b)　the application is stayed other than by agreement between the parties,

the interim injunction shall be set aside unless the court orders that it should continue to have effect even though the application is stayed.

NOTES
Initial Commencement
Specified date
Specified date: 30 December 2005: see Prelims.

Part 15
Admissions and Evidence

122　Making an admission

(1)　A party may admit the truth of the whole or any part of another party's case by giving notice in writing.
(2)　The court may allow a party to amend or withdraw an admission.

NOTES
Initial Commencement
Specified date
Specified date: 30 December 2005: see Prelims.

123　Power of court to control evidence

(1)　The court may control the evidence by giving directions as to—

(a)　the issues on which it requires evidence;
(b)　the nature of the evidence which it requires to decide those issues; and
(c)　the way in which the evidence is to be placed before the court.

(2)　The court may use its power under this rule to exclude evidence that would otherwise be admissible.
(3)　The court may limit cross-examination.

NOTES
Initial Commencement
Specified date
Specified date: 30 December 2005: see Prelims.

124　Evidence of witnesses—general rule

(1)　The general rule is that any fact which needs to be proved by the evidence of witnesses is to be proved—

(a)　at final hearing, by their oral evidence; and
(b)　at any other hearing, by their evidence in writing.

(2)　This is subject—

(a)　to any provision to the contrary contained in these Rules or elsewhere; or
(b)　to any order of the court.

NOTES
Initial Commencement
Specified date
Specified date: 30 December 2005: see Prelims.

125 Evidence by video link or other means

The court may allow a witness to give evidence through a video link or by other means.

NOTES
Initial Commencement
Specified date
Specified date: 30 December 2005: see Prelims.

126 Service of witness statements for use at final hearing

(1)   A witness statement is a written statement signed by a person which contains the evidence which that person would be allowed to give orally.
(2)   The court will give directions about the service of any witness statement of the oral evidence which a party intends to rely on in relation to any issues of fact to be decided at the final hearing on the other parties.
(3)   The court may give directions as to—

(a)   the order in which witness statements are to be served; and
(b)   whether or not the witness statements are to be filed.

NOTES
Initial Commencement
Specified date
Specified date: 30 December 2005: see Prelims.

127 Use at final hearing of witness statements which have been served

(1)   If—

(a)   a party has filed a witness statement which has been served on the other parties; and
(b)   he wishes to rely at the final hearing on the evidence of the witness who made the statement,

he must call the witness to give oral evidence unless the court directs otherwise or he puts the statement in as hearsay evidence.

(2)   Where a witness is called to give oral evidence under paragraph (1), his witness statement shall stand as his evidence in chief unless the court directs otherwise.
(3)   A witness giving oral evidence at final hearing may with the permission of the court—

(a)   amplify his witness statement; and
(b)   give evidence in relation to new matters which have arisen since the witness statement was served on the other parties.

(4)   The court will give permission under paragraph (3) only if it considers that there is good reason not to confine the evidence of the witness to the contents of his witness statement.
(5)   If a party who has filed a witness statement which has been served on the other parties does not—

(a)   call the witness to give evidence at final hearing; or
(b)   put the witness statement in as hearsay evidence, any other party may put the witness statement in as hearsay evidence.

NOTES
Initial Commencement
Specified date
Specified date: 30 December 2005: see Prelims.

128   Evidence in proceedings other than at final hearing

(1)   Subject to paragraph (2), the general rule is that evidence at hearings other than the final hearing is to be by witness statement unless the court, a practice direction or any other enactment requires otherwise.

(2)   At hearings other than the final hearing, a party may, rely on the matters set out in—

(a)   his application form; or
(b)   his application notice, if it is verified by a statement of truth.

NOTES

Initial Commencement

Specified date
Specified date: 30 December 2005: see Prelims.

129   Order for cross-examination

(1)   Where, at a hearing other than the final hearing, evidence is given in writing, any party may apply to the court for permission to cross-examine the person giving the evidence.

(2)   If the court gives permission under paragraph (1) but the person in question does not attend as required by the order, his evidence may not be used unless the court gives permission.

NOTES

Initial Commencement

Specified date
Specified date: 30 December 2005: see Prelims.

130   Form of witness statement

A witness statement must comply with the requirements set out in the relevant practice direction.

NOTES

Initial Commencement

Specified date
Specified date: 30 December 2005: see Prelims.

131   Witness summaries

(1)   A party who—

(a)   is required to file a witness statement for use at final hearing; but
(b)   is unable to obtain one, may apply, without notice, for permission to file a witness summary instead.

(2)   A witness summary is a summary of—

(a)   the evidence, if known, which would otherwise be included in a witness statement; or
(b)   if the evidence is not known, the matters about which the party filing the witness summary proposes to question the witness.

(3)   Unless the court directs otherwise, a witness summary must include the name and address of the intended witness.

(4)   Unless the court directs otherwise, a witness summary must be filed within the period in which a witness statement would have had to be filed.

(5)   Where a party files a witness summary, so far as practicable, rules 126 (service of witness statements for use at final hearing), 127(3) (amplifying witness statements), and 130 (form of witness statement) shall apply to the summary.

NOTES

Initial Commencement

Specified date
Specified date: 30 December 2005: see Prelims.

PART D – Appendix

132   Cross-examination on a witness statement

Where a witness is called to give evidence at final hearing, he may be cross-examined on his witness statement whether or not the statement or any part of it was referred to during the witness's evidence in chief.

NOTES
Initial Commencement
Specified date
Specified date: 30 December 2005: see Prelims.

133   False statements

(1)   Proceedings for contempt of court may be brought against a person if he makes, or causes to be made, a false statement in a document verified by a statement of truth without an honest belief in its truth.
(2)   Proceedings under this rule may be brought only—

(a)   by the Attorney General; or
(b)   with the permission of the court.

(3)   This rule does not apply to proceedings in a magistrates' court.

NOTES
Initial Commencement
Specified date
Specified date: 30 December 2005: see Prelims.

134   Affidavit evidence

Evidence must be given by affidavit instead of or in addition to a witness statement if this is required by the court, a provision contained in any other rule, a practice direction or any other enactment.

NOTES
Initial Commencement
Specified date
Specified date: 30 December 2005: see Prelims.

135   Form of affidavit

An affidavit must comply with the requirements set out in the relevant practice direction.

NOTES
Initial Commencement
Specified date
Specified date: 30 December 2005: see Prelims.

136   Affidavit made outside the jurisdiction

A person may make an affidavit outside the jurisdiction in accordance with—

(a)   this Part; or
(b)   the law of the place where he makes the affidavit.

NOTES
Initial Commencement
Specified date
Specified date: 30 December 2005: see Prelims.

137   Notarial acts and instruments

A notarial act or instrument may be received in evidence without further proof as duly authenticated in accordance with the requirements of law unless the contrary is proved.

NOTES
Initial Commencement
Specified date
Specified date: 30 December 2005: see Prelims.

138 Use of plans, photographs and models as evidence

(1)   This rule applies to evidence (such as a plan, photograph or model) which is not—

(a)   contained in a witness statement, affidavit or expert's report; and
(b)   to be given orally at the final hearing.

(2)   This rule includes documents which may be received in evidence without further proof under section 9 of the Civil Evidence Act 1995.

(3)   Unless the court orders otherwise the evidence shall not be receivable at the final hearing unless the party intending to put it in evidence has given notice to the court in accordance with this rule and the court will give directions about service of the notice on any other party.

(4)   Where the party intends to use the evidence as evidence of any fact then, subject to paragraph (6), he must give notice not later than the latest date for filing witness statements.

(5)   He must give notice at least 21 days before the hearing at which he proposes to put in the evidence, if—

(a)   there are not to be witness statements; or
(b)   he intends to put in the evidence solely in order to disprove an allegation made in a witness statement.

(6)   Where the evidence forms part of expert evidence, he must give notice when the expert's report is filed.

(7)   Where the evidence is being produced to the court for any reason other than as part of factual or expert evidence, he must give notice at least 21 days before the hearing at which he proposes to put in the evidence.

(8)   Where a party has given notice that he intends to put in the evidence, the court may direct that every other party be given an opportunity to inspect it and to agree to its admission without further proof.

NOTES
Initial Commencement
Specified date
Specified date: 30 December 2005: see Prelims.

139 Evidence of finding on question of foreign law

(1)   This rule sets out the procedure which must be followed by a party who intends to put in evidence a finding on a question of foreign law by virtue of section 4(2) of the Civil Evidence Act 1972.

(2)   He must give the court notice of his intention—

(a)   if there are to be witness statements, not later than the latest date for filing them; or
(b)   otherwise, not less than 21 days before the hearing at which he proposes to put the finding in evidence

and the court will give directions about service of the notice on any other party.

(3)   The notice must—

(a)   specify the question on which the finding was made; and
(b)   enclose a copy of a document where it is reported or recorded.

NOTES
Initial Commencement
Specified date
Specified date: 30 December 2005: see Prelims.

PART D – Appendix

Part 16
Witnesses, Depositions and Evidence for Foreign Courts

Section 1
Witnesses and Depositions

140   Scope of this Section

(1)   This Section of this Part provides—

(a)   for the circumstances in which a person may be required to attend court to give evidence or to produce a document; and
(b)   for a party to obtain evidence before a hearing to be used at the hearing.

(2)   This Section, except for rule 149(2) to (4), does not apply to proceedings in a magistrates' court.
(Section 97 of the Magistrates' Courts Act 1980 sets out the procedure for obtaining a witness summons in proceedings in a magistrates' court.)

NOTES
Initial Commencement
Specified date
Specified date: 30 December 2005: see Prelims.

141   Witness summonses

(1)   A witness summons is a document issued by the court requiring a witness to—

(a)   attend court to give evidence; or
(b)   produce documents to the court.

(2)   A witness summons must be in the relevant form.
(3)   There must be a separate witness summons for each witness.
(4)   A witness summons may require a witness to produce documents to the court either—

(a)   on the date fixed for a hearing; or
(b)   on such date as the court may direct.

(5)   The only documents that a summons under this rule can require a person to produce before a hearing are documents which that person could be required to produce at the hearing.

NOTES
Initial Commencement
Specified date
Specified date: 30 December 2005: see Prelims.

142   Issue of a witness summons

(1)   A witness summons is issued on the date entered on the summons by the court.
(2)   A party must obtain permission from the court where he wishes to—

(a)   have a summons issued less than 7 days before the date of the final hearing;
(b)   have a summons issued for a witness to attend court to give evidence or to produce documents on any date except the date fixed for the final hearing; or
(c)   have a summons issued for a witness to attend court to give evidence or to produce documents at any hearing except the final hearing.

(3)   A witness summons must be issued by—

(a)   the court where the case is proceeding; or
(b)   the court where the hearing in question will be held.

(4)   The court may set aside or vary a witness summons issued under this rule.

NOTES
Initial Commencement
Specified date
Specified date: 30 December 2005: see Prelims.

143 Time for serving a witness summons

(1)   The general rule is that a witness summons is binding if it is served at least 7 days before the date on which the witness is required to attend before the court or tribunal.

(2)   The court may direct that a witness summons shall be binding although it will be served less than 7 days before the date on which the witness is required to attend before the court or tribunal.

(3)   A witness summons which is—

(a)   served in accordance with this rule; and

(b)   requires the witness to attend court to give evidence,

is binding until the conclusion of the hearing at which the attendance of the witness is required.

NOTES
Initial Commencement
Specified date
Specified date: 30 December 2005: see Prelims.

144 Who is to serve a witness summons

(1)   Unless the court directs otherwise, a witness summons is to be served by the court.

(2)   Where the court is to serve the witness summons, the party on whose behalf it is issued must deposit, in the court office, the money to be paid or offered to the witness under rule 145.

NOTES
Initial Commencement
Specified date
Specified date: 30 December 2005: see Prelims.

145 Right of witness to travelling expenses and compensation for loss of time

At the time of service of a witness summons the witness must be offered or paid—

(a)   a sum reasonably sufficient to cover his expenses in travelling to and from the court; and

(b)   such sum by way of compensation for loss of time as may be specified in the relevant practice direction.

NOTES
Initial Commencement
Specified date
Specified date: 30 December 2005: see Prelims.

146 Evidence by deposition

(1)   A party may apply for an order for a person to be examined before the hearing takes place.

(2)   A person from whom evidence is to be obtained following an order under this rule is referred to as a 'deponent' and the evidence is referred to as a 'deposition'.

(3)   An order under this rule shall be for a deponent to be examined on oath before—

(a)   a judge or district judge, including a district judge of the principal registry of the Family Division;

(b)   an examiner of the court; or

(c)   such other person as the court appoints.

PART D – Appendix

(4) The order may require the production of any document which the court considers is necessary for the purposes of the examination.

(5) The order must state the date, time and place of the examination.

(6) At the time of service of the order the deponent must be offered or paid—

(a) a sum reasonably sufficient to cover his expenses in travelling to and from the place of examination; and

(b) such sum by way of compensation for loss of time as may be specified in the relevant practice direction.

(7) Where the court makes an order for a deposition to be taken, it may also order the party who obtained the order to file a witness statement or witness summary in relation to the evidence to be given by the person to be examined.

(Part 15 contains the general rules about witness statements and witness summaries.)

NOTES

Initial Commencement

Specified date

Specified date: 30 December 2005: see Prelims.

147 Conduct of examination

(1) Subject to any directions contained in the order for examination, the examination must be conducted in the same way as if the witness were giving evidence at a final hearing.

(2) If all the parties are present, the examiner may conduct the examination of a person not named in the order for examination if all the parties and the person to be examined consent.

(3) The examiner will conduct the examination in private unless he considers it is not appropriate to do so.

(4) The examiner must ensure that the evidence given by the witness is recorded in full.

(5) The examiner must send a copy of the deposition—

(a) to the person who obtained the order for the examination of the witness; and

(b) to the court where the case is proceeding.

(6) The court will make directions as to the service of a copy of the deposition on the other parties.

NOTES

Initial Commencement

Specified date

Specified date: 30 December 2005: see Prelims.

148 Enforcing attendance of witness

(1) If a person served with an order to attend before an examiner—

(a) fails to attend; or

(b) refuses to be sworn for the purpose of the examination or to answer any lawful question or produce any document at the examination,

a certificate of his failure or refusal, signed by the examiner, must be filed by the party requiring the deposition.

(2) On the certificate being filed, the party requiring the deposition may apply to the court for an order requiring that person to attend or to be sworn or to answer any question or produce any document, as the case may be.

(3) An application for an order under this rule may be made without notice.

(4) The court may order the person against whom an order is made under this rule to pay any costs resulting from his failure or refusal.

NOTES

Initial Commencement

Specified date

Specified date: 30 December 2005: see Prelims.

149   Use of deposition at a hearing

(1)   A deposition ordered under rule 146 may be given in evidence at a hearing unless the court orders otherwise.

(2)   A party intending to put in evidence a deposition at a hearing must file notice of his intention to do so on the court and the court will make directions about serving the notice on every other party.

(3)   He must file the notice at least 21 days before the day fixed for the hearing.

(4)   The court may require a deponent to attend the hearing and give evidence orally.

NOTES

Initial Commencement

Specified date

Specified date: 30 December 2005: see Prelims.

150   Where a person to be examined is out of the jurisdiction—letter of request

(1)   This rule applies where a party wishes to take a deposition from a person who is—

(a)   out of the jurisdiction; and

(b)   not in a Regulation State within the meaning of Section 2 of this Part.

(2)   The High Court may order the issue of a letter of request to the judicial authorities of the country in which the proposed deponent is.

(3)   A letter of request is a request to a judicial authority to take the evidence of that person, or arrange for it to be taken.

(4)   The High Court may make an order under this rule in relation to county court proceedings.

(5)   If the government of a country allows a person appointed by the High Court to examine a person in that country, the High Court may make an order appointing a special examiner for that purpose.

(6)   A person may be examined under this rule on oath or affirmation or in accordance with any procedure permitted in the country in which the examination is to take place.

(7)   If the High Court makes an order for the issue of a letter of request, the party who sought the order must file—

(a)   the following documents and, subject to paragraph (8), a translation of them,—

  (i)   a draft letter of request;

  (ii)   a statement of the issues relevant to the proceedings; and

  (iii)   a list of questions or the subject matter of questions to be put to the person to be examined; and

(b)   an undertaking to be responsible for the Secretary of State's expenses.

(8)   There is no need to file a translation if—

(a)   English is one of the official languages of the country where the examination is to take place; or

(b)   a practice direction has specified that country as a country where no translation is necessary.

NOTES

Initial Commencement

Specified date

Specified date: 30 December 2005: see Prelims.

151   Fees and expenses of examiner of the court

(1)   An examiner of the court may charge a fee for the examination.

(2)   He need not send the deposition to the court unless the fee is paid.

(3)   The examiner's fees and expenses must be paid by the party who obtained the order for examination.

(4) If the fees and expenses due to an examiner are not paid within a reasonable time, he may report that fact to the court.

(5) The court may order the party who obtained the order for examination to deposit in the court office a specified sum in respect of the examiner's fees and, where it does so, the examiner will not be asked to act until the sum has been deposited.

(6) An order under this rule does not affect any decision as to the party who is ultimately to bear the costs of the examination.

NOTES
Initial Commencement
Specified date
Specified date: 30 December 2005: see Prelims.

Section 2
Taking of Evidence—Member States of the European Union

152 Interpretation

In this Section—

'designated court' has the meaning given in the relevant practice direction;
'Regulation State' has the same meaning as 'Member State' in the Taking of Evidence Regulation, that is all Member States except Denmark;
'the Taking of Evidence Regulation' means Council Regulation (EC) No 1206/2001 of 28 May 2001 on co-operation between the courts of the Member States in the taking of evidence in civil and commercial matters.

NOTES
Initial Commencement
Specified date
Specified date: 30 December 2005: see Prelims.

153 Where a person to be examined is in another Regulation State

(1) This rule applies where a party wishes to take a deposition from a person who is in another Regulation State—

(a) outside the jurisdiction; and
(b) in a Regulation State.

(2) The court may order the issue of a request to a designated court ('the requested court') in the Regulation State in which the proposed deponent is.

(3) If the court makes an order for the issue of a request, the party who sought the order must file—

(a) a draft Form A as set out in the annex to the Taking of Evidence Regulation (request for the taking of evidence);
(b) subject to paragraph (4), a translation of the form;
(c) an undertaking to be responsible for costs sought by the requested court in relation to—

(i) fees paid to experts and interpreters; and
(ii) where requested by that party, the use of special procedures or communications technology; and

(d) an undertaking to be responsible for the court's expenses.

(4) There is no need to file a translation if—

(a) English is one of the official languages of the Regulation State where the examination is to take place; or
(b) the Regulation State has indicated, in accordance with the Taking of Evidence Regulation, that English is a language which it will accept.

(5)   Where article 17 of the Taking of Evidence Regulation (direct taking of evidence by the requested court) allows evidence to be taken directly in another Regulation State, the court may make an order for the submission of a request in accordance with that article.

(6)   If the court makes an order for the submission of a request under paragraph (5), the party who sought the order must file—

(a)   a draft Form I as set out in the annex to the Taking of Evidence Regulation (request for direct taking of evidence);
(b)   subject to paragraph (4), a translation of the form; and
(c)   an undertaking to be responsible for the court's expenses.

NOTES
Initial Commencement
Specified date
Specified date: 30 December 2005: see Prelims.

Part 17
Experts

154   Duty to restrict expert evidence

Expert evidence shall be restricted to that which is reasonably required to resolve the proceedings.

NOTES
Initial Commencement
Specified date
Specified date: 30 December 2005: see Prelims.

155   Interpretation

A reference to an 'expert' in this Part—

(a)   is a reference to an expert who has been instructed to give or prepare evidence for the purpose of court proceedings; and
(b)   does not include—

(i)   a person who is within a prescribed description for the purposes of section 94(1) of the Act (persons who may prepare a report for any person about the suitability of a child for adoption or of a person to adopt a child or about the adoption, or placement for adoption, of a child); or
(ii)   an officer of the Service or a Welsh family proceedings officer when acting in that capacity.

(Regulation 3 of the Restriction on the Preparation of Adoption Reports Regulations 2005 (SI 2005/1711) sets out which persons are within a prescribed description for the purposes of section 94(1) of the Act.)

NOTES
Initial Commencement
Specified date
Specified date: 30 December 2005: see Prelims.

156   Experts—overriding duty to the court

(1)   It is the duty of an expert to help the court on the matters within his expertise.
(2)   This duty overrides any obligation to the person from whom he has received instructions or by whom he is paid.

NOTES
Initial Commencement
Specified date
Specified date: 30 December 2005: see Prelims.

PART D – Appendix

157 Court's power to restrict expert evidence

(1) No party may call an expert or put in evidence an expert's report without the court's permission.

(2) When a party applies for permission under this rule he must identify—

(a) the field in which he wishes to rely on expert evidence; and

(b) where practicable the expert in that field on whose evidence he wishes to rely.

(3) If permission is granted under this rule it shall be in relation only to the expert named or the field identified under paragraph (2).

(4) The court may limit the amount of the expert's fees and expenses that the party who wishes to rely on the expert may recover from any other party.

NOTES

Initial Commencement

Specified date

Specified date: 30 December 2005: see Prelims.

158 General requirement for expert evidence to be given in a written report

Expert evidence is to be given in a written report unless the court directs otherwise.

NOTES

Initial Commencement

Specified date

Specified date: 30 December 2005: see Prelims.

159 Written questions to experts

(1) A party may put to—

(a) an expert instructed by another party; or

(b) a single joint expert appointed under rule 160,

written questions about his report.

(2) Written questions under paragraph (1)—

(a) may be put once only;

(b) must be put within 5 days beginning with the date on which the expert's report was served; and

(c) must be for the purpose only of clarification of the report,

unless in any case—

(i) the court gives permission;

(ii) the other party agrees; or

(iii) any practice direction provides otherwise.

(3) An expert's answers to questions put in accordance with paragraph (1) shall be treated as part of the expert's report.

(4) Where—

(a) a party has put a written question to an expert instructed by another party in accordance with this rule; and

(b) the expert does not answer that question,

the court may make one or both of the following orders in relation to the party who instructed the expert—

(i) that the party may not rely on the evidence of that expert; or

(ii) that the party may not recover the fees and expenses of that expert from any other party.

NOTES

Initial Commencement

Specified date

Specified date: 30 December 2005: see Prelims.

160 Court's power to direct that evidence is to be given by a single joint expert

(1)   Where two or more parties wish to submit expert evidence on a particular issue, the court may direct that the evidence on that issue is to given by one expert only.
(2)   The parties wishing to submit the expert evidence are called 'the instructing parties'.
(3)   Where the instructing parties cannot agree who should be the expert, the court may—

(a)   select the expert from a list prepared or identified by the instructing parties; or
(b)   direct that the expert be selected in such other manner as the court may direct.

NOTES
Initial Commencement
Specified date
Specified date: 30 December 2005: see Prelims.

161 Instructions to a single joint expert

(1)   Where the court gives a direction under rule 160 for a single joint expert to be used, each instructing party may give instructions to the expert.
(2)   When an instructing party gives instructions to the expert he must, at the same time, send a copy of the instructions to the other instructing parties.
(3)   The court may give directions about—

(a)   the payment of the expert's fees and expenses; and
(b)   any inspection, examination or experiments which the expert wishes to carry out.

(4)   The court may, before an expert is instructed, limit the amount that can be paid by way of fees and expenses to the expert.
(5)   Unless the court otherwise directs, the instructing parties are jointly and severally liable for the payment of the expert's fees and expenses.

NOTES
Initial Commencement
Specified date
Specified date: 30 December 2005: see Prelims.

162 Power of court to direct a party to provide information

(1)   Where a party has access to information which is not reasonably available to the other party, the court may direct the party who has access to the information to prepare and file a document recording the information.
(2)   A court officer will send a copy of that document to the other party.

NOTES
Initial Commencement
Specified date
Specified date: 30 December 2005: see Prelims.

163 Contents of report

(1)   An expert's report must comply with the requirements set out in the relevant practice direction.
(2)   At the end of an expert's report there must be a statement that—

(a)   the expert understands his duty to the court; and
(b)   he has complied with that duty.

(3)   The expert's report must state the substance of all material instructions, whether written or oral, on the basis of which the report was written.
(4)   The instructions referred to in paragraph (3) shall not be privileged against disclosure.

PART D – Appendix

NOTES
Initial Commencement
Specified date
Specified date: 30 December 2005: see Prelims.

164 Use by one party of expert's report disclosed by another

Where a party has disclosed an expert's report, any party may use that expert's report as evidence at the final hearing.

NOTES
Initial Commencement
Specified date
Specified date: 30 December 2005: see Prelims.

165 Discussions between experts

(1) The court may, at any stage, direct a discussion between experts for the purpose of requiring the experts to—

(a) identify and discuss the expert issues in the proceedings; and
(b) where possible, reach an agreed opinion on those issues.

(2) The court may specify the issues which the experts must discuss.
(3) The court may direct that following a discussion between the experts they must prepare a statement for the court showing—

(a) those issues on which they agree; and
(b) those issues on which they disagree and a summary of their reasons for disagreeing.

NOTES
Initial Commencement
Specified date
Specified date: 30 December 2005: see Prelims.

166 Consequence of failure to disclose expert's report

A party who fails to disclose an expert's report may not use the report at the final hearing or call the expert to give evidence orally unless the court gives permission.

NOTES
Initial Commencement
Specified date
Specified date: 30 December 2005: see Prelims.

167 Expert's right to ask court for directions

(1) An expert may file a written request for directions to assist him in carrying out his function as an expert.
(2) An expert must, unless the court directs otherwise, provide a copy of any proposed request for directions under paragraph (1)—

(a) to the party instructing him, at least 7 days before he files the request; and
(b) to all other parties, at least 4 days before he files it.

(3) The court, when it gives directions, may also direct that a party be served with a copy of the directions.

NOTES
Initial Commencement
Specified date
Specified date: 30 December 2005: see Prelims.

Part 18
Change of Solicitor

168   Change of solicitor—duty to give notice

(1)   This rule applies where—

(a)   a party for whom a solicitor is acting wants to change his solicitor;
(b)   a party, after having conducted the application in person, appoints a solicitor to act on his behalf (except where the solicitor is appointed only to act as an advocate for a hearing); or
(c)   a party, after having conducted the application by a solicitor, intends to act in person.

(2)   Where this rule applies, the party or his solicitor (where one is acting) must—

(a)   file notice of the change; and
(b)   where paragraph (1)(a) or (c) applies, serve notice of the change on the former solicitor.

(3)   The court will give directions about serving notice of the change on every other party.
(4)   The notice filed at court must state that notice has been served as required by paragraph (2)(b).
(5)   Subject to paragraph (6), where a party has changed his solicitor or intends to act in person, the former solicitor will be considered to be the party's solicitor unless and until—

(a)   notice is filed and served in accordance with paragraphs (2) and (3); or
(b)   the court makes an order under rule 169 and the order is served as required by paragraph (3) of that rule.

(6)   Where the certificate of a LSC funded client or an assisted person is revoked or discharged—

(a)   the solicitor who acted for that person will cease to be the solicitor acting in the case as soon as his retainer is determined under regulation 4 of the Community Legal Service (Costs) Regulations 2000; and
(b)   if that person wishes to continue where he appoints a solicitor to act on his behalf, paragraph (2) will apply as if he had previously conducted the application in person;

(7)   In this rule—

'assisted person' means an assisted person within the statutory provisions relating to legal aid;
'certificate' means a certificate issued under the Funding Code (approved under section 9 of the Access to Justice Act 1999);
'LSC funded client' means an individual who receives services funded by the Legal Services Commission as part of the Community Legal Service within the meaning of Part I of the Access to Justice Act 1999.

NOTES
Initial Commencement
Specified date
Specified date: 30 December 2005: see Prelims.

169   Order that a solicitor has ceased to act

(1)   A solicitor may apply for an order declaring that he has ceased to be the solicitor acting for a party.
(2)   Where an application is made under this rule—

(a)   notice of the application must be given to the party for whom the solicitor is acting, unless the court directs otherwise; and
(b)   the application must be supported by evidence.

(3)   Where the court makes an order that a solicitor has ceased to act—

(a)	the court will give directions about serving the order on every party to the proceedings; and
(b)	if it is served by a party or the solicitor, the party or the solicitor (as the case may be) must file a certificate of service.

NOTES

Initial Commencement

Specified date

Specified date: 30 December 2005: see Prelims.

170 Removal of solicitor who has ceased to act on application of another party

(1) Where—

(a) a solicitor who has acted for a party—

    (i) has died;
    (ii) has become bankrupt;
    (iii) has ceased to practice; or
    (iv) cannot be found; and

(b) the party has not given notice of a change of solicitor or notice of intention to act in person as required by rule 168(2),

any other party may apply for an order declaring that the solicitor has ceased to be the solicitor acting for the other party in the case.

(2) Where an application is made under this rule, notice of the application must be given to the party to whose solicitor the application relates unless the court directs otherwise.

(3) Where the court makes an order made under this rule—

(a) the court will give directions about serving the order on every party to the proceedings; and

(b) where it is served by a party, that party must file a certificate of service.

NOTES

Initial Commencement

Specified date

Specified date: 30 December 2005: see Prelims.

Part 19
Appeals

171 Scope and interpretation

(1) The rules in this Part apply to appeals to—

(a) the High Court; and
(b) a county court.

(2) This Part does not apply to an appeal in detailed assessment proceedings against a decision of an authorised court officer
(Rules 47.20 to 47.23 of the CPR deal with appeals against a decision of an authorised court officer in detailed assessment proceedings.)

(3) In this Part—

'appeal' includes an appeal by way of case stated;
'appeal court' means the court to which an appeal is made;
'appeal notice' means an appellant's or respondent's notice;
'appellant' means a person who brings or seeks to bring an appeal;
'lower court' means the court from whose decision an appeal is brought;
'respondent' means—

    (a) a person other than the appellant who was a party to the proceedings in the lower court and who is affected by the appeal; and

(b)   a person who is permitted by the appeal court to be a party to the appeal.

(4)   This Part is subject to any rule, enactment or practice direction which sets out special provisions with regard to any particular category of appeal.

NOTES

Initial Commencement

Specified date

Specified date: 30 December 2005: see Prelims.

172 Parties to comply with the practice direction

All parties to an appeal must comply with the relevant practice direction.

NOTES

Initial Commencement

Specified date

Specified date: 30 December 2005: see Prelims.

173 Permission

(1)   An appellant or respondent requires permission to appeal—

(a)   against a decision in assessment proceedings relating to costs in proceedings where the decision appealed against was made by a district judge or a costs judge; or

(b)   as provided by the relevant practice direction.

(2)   An application for permission to appeal may be made—

(a)   to the lower court, if that court is a county court or the High Court, at the hearing at which the decision to be appealed was made; or

(b)   to the appeal court in an appeal notice.

(Rule 174 sets out the time limits for filing an appellant's notice at the appeal court. Rule 175 sets out the time limits for filing a respondent's notice at the appeal court. Any application for permission to appeal to the appeal court must be made in the appeal notice (see rules 174(1) and 175(3).)

(3)   Where the lower court refuses an application for permission to appeal, a further application for permission to appeal may be made to the appeal court.

(4)   Where the appeal court, without a hearing, refuses permission to appeal, the person seeking permission may request the decision to be reconsidered at a hearing.

(5)   A request under paragraph (4) must be filed within 7 days beginning with the date on which the notice that permission has been refused was served.

(6)   Permission to appeal will only be given where—

(a)   the court considers that the appeal would have a real prospect of success; or

(b)   there is some other compelling reason why the appeal should be heard.

(7)   An order giving permission may—

(a)   limit the issues to be heard; and

(b)   be made subject to conditions.

(8)   In this rule 'costs judge' means a taxing master of the Supreme Court.

NOTES

Initial Commencement

Specified date

Specified date: 30 December 2005: see Prelims.

174 Appellant's notice

(1)   Where the appellant seeks permission from the appeal court it must be requested in the appellant's notice.

(2)   The appellant must file the appellant's notice at the appeal court within—

(a) such period as may be directed by the lower court, if that court is a county court or the High Court; or

(b)

    (i) where the lower court makes no such direction; or

    (ii) the lower court is a magistrates' court,

14 days beginning with the date on which the decision of the lower court that the appellant wishes to appeal was made.

(3) Unless the appeal court directs otherwise, an appeal notice must be served on the persons referred to in paragraph (4)—

(a) as soon as practicable; and

(b) in any event not later than 7 days,

after it is filed.

(4) The persons referred to in paragraph (3) are—

(a) each respondent;

(b) any children's guardian, reporting officer or children and family reporter; and

(c) where the appeal is from a magistrates' court, the court officer.

(5) Unless the appeal court directs otherwise, a court officer will serve the appeal notice.

NOTES

Initial Commencement

Specified date

Specified date: 30 December 2005: see Prelims.

175 Respondent's notice

(1) A respondent may file a respondent's notice.

(2) A respondent who—

(a) is seeking permission to appeal from the appeal court; or

(b) wishes to ask the appeal court to uphold the order of the lower court for reasons different from or additional to those given by the lower court,

must file a respondent's notice.

(3) Where the respondent seeks permission from the appeal court it must be requested in the respondent's notice.

(4) A respondent's notice must be filed within—

(a) such period as may be directed by the lower court, if that court is a county court or the High Court; or

(b)

    (i) where the lower court makes no such direction; or

    (ii) the lower court is a magistrates' court,

14 days beginning with the date referred to in paragraph (5).

(5) The date referred to in paragraph (4) is—

(a) the date on which the respondent is served with the appellant's notice where—

    (i) permission to appeal was given by the lower court; or

    (ii) permission to appeal is not required;

(b) the date on which the respondent is served with notification that the appeal court has given the appellant permission to appeal; or

(c) the date on which the respondent is served with notification that the application for permission to appeal and the appeal itself are to be heard together.

(6) Unless the appeal court directs otherwise, a respondent's notice must be served on the appellant and any other respondent—

(a) as soon as practicable; and

(b) in any event not later than 7 days,

after it is filed.

(7)   Unless the appeal court directs otherwise, a court officer will serve a respondent's notice.

NOTES
Initial Commencement
Specified date
Specified date: 30 December 2005: see Prelims.

176   Variation of time

(1)   An application to vary the time limit for filing an appeal notice must be made to the appeal court.
(2)   The parties may not agree to extend any date or time limit set by—

(a)   these Rules;
(b)   the relevant practice direction; or
(c)   an order of the appeal court or the lower court.

(Rule 12(2)(a) provides that the court may extend or shorten the time for compliance with any rule, practice direction or court order (even if an application for extension is made after the time for compliance has expired).)
(Rule 12(2)(b) provides that the court may adjourn or bring forward a hearing.)

NOTES
Initial Commencement
Specified date
Specified date: 30 December 2005: see Prelims.

177   Stay

Unless the appeal court or the lower court, other than a magistrates' court, orders otherwise an appeal shall not operate as a stay of any order or decision of the lower court.

NOTES
Initial Commencement
Specified date
Specified date: 30 December 2005: see Prelims.

178   Amendment of appeal notice

An appeal notice may not be amended without the permission of the appeal court.

NOTES
Initial Commencement
Specified date
Specified date: 30 December 2005: see Prelims.

179   Striking out appeal notices and setting aside or imposing conditions on permission to appeal

(1)   The appeal court may—

(a)   strike out the whole or part of an appeal notice;
(b)   set aside permission to appeal in whole or in part; or
(c)   impose or vary conditions upon which an appeal may be brought.

(2)   The court will only exercise its powers under paragraph (1) where there is a compelling reason for doing so.
(3)   Where a party was present at the hearing at which permission was given he may not subsequently apply for an order that the court exercise its powers under paragraphs (1)(b) or (c).

NOTES
Initial Commencement
Specified date
Specified date: 30 December 2005: see Prelims.

PART D – Appendix

180 Appeal court's powers

(1) In relation to an appeal the appeal court has all the powers of the lower court. (Rule 171(4) provides that this Part is subject to any enactment that sets out special provisions with regard to any particular category of appeal.)

(2) The appeal court has power to—

(a) affirm, set aside or vary any order or judgment made or given by the lower court;

(b) refer any application or issue for determination by the lower court;

(c) order a new hearing;

(d) make orders for the payment of interest; and

(e) make a costs order.

(3) The appeal court may exercise its powers in relation to the whole or part of an order of the lower court.

(Rule 12 contains general rules about the court's case management powers.)

(4) If the appeal court—

(a) refuses an application for permission to appeal;

(b) strikes out an appellant's notice; or

(c) dismisses an appeal,

and it considers that the application, the appellant's notice or the appeal is totally without merit, the provisions of paragraph (5) must be complied with.

(5) Where paragraph (4) applies—

(a) the court's order must record the fact that it considers the application, the appellant's notice or the appeal to be totally without merit; and

(b) the court must at the same time consider whether it is appropriate to make a civil restraint order.

NOTES

Initial Commencement

Specified date

Specified date: 30 December 2005: see Prelims.

181 Hearing of appeals

(1) Every appeal will be limited to a review of the decision of the lower court unless—

(a) a practice direction makes different provision for a particular category of appeal; or

(b) the court considers that in the circumstances of an individual appeal it would be in the interests of justice to hold a re-hearing.

(2) Unless it orders otherwise, the appeal court will not receive—

(a) oral evidence; or

(b) evidence which was not before the lower court.

(3) The appeal court will allow an appeal where the decision of the lower court was—

(a) wrong; or

(b) unjust because of a serious procedural or other irregularity in the proceedings in the lower court.

(4) The appeal court may draw any inference of fact which it considers justified on the evidence.

(5) At the hearing of the appeal a party may not rely on a matter not contained in his appeal notice unless the appeal court gives permission.

NOTES

Initial Commencement

Specified date

Specified date: 30 December 2005: see Prelims.

182 Assignment of appeals to the Court of Appeal

(1)   Where the court from or to which an appeal is made or from which permission to appeal is sought ('the relevant court') considers that—

(a)   an appeal which is to be heard by a county court or the High Court would raise an important point of principle or practice; or
(b)   there is some other compelling reason for the Court of Appeal to hear it,

the relevant court may order the appeal to be transferred to the Court of Appeal.

(2)   This rule does not apply to proceedings in a magistrates' court.

NOTES

Initial Commencement

Specified date
Specified date: 30 December 2005: see Prelims.

183 Reopening of final appeals

(1)   The High Court will not reopen a final determination of any appeal unless—

(a)   it is necessary to do so in order to avoid real injustice;
(b)   the circumstances are exceptional and make it appropriate to reopen the appeal; and
(c)   there is no alternative effective remedy.

(2)   In paragraphs (1), (3), (4) and (6), 'appeal' includes an application for permission to appeal.
(3)   This rule does not apply to appeals to a county court.
(4)   Permission is needed to make an application under this rule to reopen a final determination of an appeal.
(5)   There is no right to an oral hearing of an application for permission unless, exceptionally, the judge so directs.
(6)   The judge will not grant permission without directing the application to be served on the other party to the original appeal and giving him an opportunity to make representations.
(7)   There is no right of appeal or review from the decision of the judge on the application for permission, which is final.
(8)   The procedure for making an application for permission is set out in the practice direction.

NOTES

Initial Commencement

Specified date
Specified date: 30 December 2005: see Prelims.

Index

G

H